# Cisco IOS Solutions for Network Protocols, Volume II: IPX, AppleTalk, and More

**Cisco Systems, Inc.**

MACMILLAN
TECHNICAL
PUBLISHING
U·S·A

Macmillan Technical Publishing
201 West 103rd Street
Indianapolis, IN 46290 USA

**Cisco IOS Solutions for Network Protocols, Volume II: IPX, AppleTalk, and More**

Cisco Systems, Inc.

Copyright© 1998 Cisco Systems, Inc.

Cisco Press logo is a trademark of Cisco Systems, Inc.

Published by:

Macmillan Technical Publishing

201 West 103rd Street

Indianapolis, IN 46290 USA

Printed in the United States of America   2 3 4 5 6 7 8 9 0

Library of Congress Cataloging-in-Publication Number 98-84216

ISBN: 1-57870-050-7

**Warning and Disclaimer**

| | |
|---|---|
| Associate Publisher | Jim LeValley |
| Executive Editor | Julie Fairweather |
| Cisco Systems Program Manager | H. Kim Lew |
| Managing Editor | Caroline Roop |
| Acquisitions Editor | Tracy Hughes |
| Copy Editors | Jill Bond |
| | Michael Hughes |
| Team Coordinator | Amy Lewis |
| Book Designer | Louisa Klucznik |
| Cover Designer | Jean Bisesi |
| Production Team | Deb Kincaid |
| | Nicole Ritch |
| | Lisa Stumpf |
| Indexer | Kevin Fulcher |

# Trademark
# Acknowledgments

# Acknowledgments

The Cisco IOS Reference Library is a result of collaborative efforts of many Cisco technical writers and editors over the years. This bookset represents the continuing development and integration of user documentation for the ever-increasing set of Cisco IOS networking features and functionality.

The current team of Cisco IOS technical writers and editors includes Katherine Anderson, Jennifer Bridges, Joelle Chapman, Christy Choate, Meredith Fisher, Tina Fox, Marie Godfrey, Dianna Johansen, Sheryl Kelly, Yvonne Kucher, Doug MacBeth, Lavanya Mandavilli, Mary Mangone, Spank McCoy, Greg McMillan, Madhu Mitra, Oralee Murillo, Vicki Payne, Jane Phillips, George Powers, Teresa Oliver Schuetz, Wink Schuetz, Karen Shell, Grace Tai, and Bethann Watson.

This writing team wants to acknowledge the many engineering, customer support, and marketing subject-matter experts for their participation in reviewing draft documents and, in many cases, providing source material from which this bookset is developed.

# Contents at a Glance

# Table of Contents

# About the Cisco IOS Reference Library

The Cisco IOS Reference Library books are Cisco documentation that describes the tasks and commands necessary to configure and maintain your Cisco IOS network.

The Cisco IOS software bookset is intended primarily for users who configure and maintain access servers and routers, but are not necessarily familiar with the tasks, the relationships between tasks, or the commands necessary to perform particular tasks.

## CISCO IOS REFERENCE LIBRARY ORGANIZATION

The Cisco IOS Reference library consists of eight books. Each book contains technology-specific configuration chapters with corresponding command-reference chapters. Each configuration chapter describes Cisco's implementation of protocols and technologies, related configuration tasks, and contains comprehensive configuration examples. Each command-reference chapter complements the organization of its corresponding configuration chapter and provides complete command syntax information.

## OTHER BOOKS AVAILABLE IN THE CISCO IOS REFERENCE LIBRARY

- *Cisco IOS Configuration Fundamentals.* 1-57870-044-2; December 1997

  This comprehensive guide details Cisco IOS software configuration basics. Cisco IOS Configuration Fundamentals offers thorough coverage of router and access server configuration and maintenance techniques. In addition to hands-on implementation and task instruction, this book also presents the complete syntax for router and access server commands, and individual examples for each command. Learn to configure interfaces in addition to system management, file loading, AutoInstall, and set up functions.

- *Cisco IOS Dial Solutions.* 1-57870-055-8; March 1998

This book provides readers with real-world solutions and how to implement those solutions on a network. Customers interested in implementing dial solutions across their network environment include those who operate from remote sites and dial in to a central office, Internet Service Providers (ISPs), ISP customers at home offices, and enterprise WAN system administrators implementing dial-on-demand routing (DDR).

- *Cisco IOS Wide Area Networking Solutions.* 1-57870-054-x; March 1998

  This book offers thorough, comprehensive coverage of internetworking technologies, particularly ATM, Frame Relay, SMDS, LAPB, and X.25, teaching the reader how to configure the technologies in a LAN/WAN environment.

- *Cisco IOS Switching Services.* 1-57870-053-1; March 1998

  This book is a comprehensive guide detailing available Cisco IOS switching alternatives. Cisco's switching services range from fast switching and Netflow switching to LAN Emulation.

- *Cisco IOS Solutions for Network Protocols, Vol. I: IP.* 1-57870-049-3; April 1998

  This book is a comprehensive guide detailing available IP and IP routing alternatives. It describes how to implement IP addressing and IP services and how to configure support for a wide range of IP routing protocols including BGP for ISP networks and basic and advanced IP Multicast functionality.

- *Cisco IOS Bridging and IBM Network Solutions.* 1-57870-051-5; April 1998

  This book describes Cisco's support for networks in IBM and bridging environments. Support includes transparent and source-route transparent bridging, source-route bridging (SRB), remote source-route bridging (RSRB), data link switching plus (DLS+), serial tunnel and block serial tunnel, SDLC and LLC2 parameter, IBM network media translation, downstream physical unit and SNA service point, SNA Frame Relay access support, Advanced Peer-to-Peer Networking, and native client interface architecture (NCIA).

- *Cisco IOS Network Security.* 1-57870-057-4; May 1998

  This book documents security configuration from a remote site and for a central enterprise or service provider network. It describes AAA, Radius, TACACS+, and Kerberos network security features. It also explains how to encrypt data across enterprise networks. The book includes many illustrations that show configurations and functionality, along with a discussion of network security policy choices and some decision-making guidelines.

## BOOK CONVENTIONS

Software and hardware documentation uses the following conventions:

- The caret character (^) represents the Control key.

  For example, the key combinations ^D and Ctrl-D are equivalent: Both mean hold down the Control key while you press the D key. Keys are indicated in capital letters but are not case sensitive.

- A string is defined as a nonquoted set of characters.

  For example, when setting an SNMP community string to *public*, do not use quotation marks around the string; otherwise, the string will include the quotation marks.

Command descriptions use these conventions:

- Vertical bars ( | ) separate alternative, mutually exclusive, elements.
- Square brackets ([ ]) indicate optional elements.
- Braces ({ }) indicate a required choice.
- Braces within square brackets ([{ }]) indicate a required choice within an optional element.
- **Boldface** indicates commands and keywords that are entered literally as shown.
- *Italics* indicate arguments for which you supply values; in contexts that do not allow italics, arguments are enclosed in angle brackets (< >).

Examples use these conventions:

- Examples that contain system prompts denote interactive sessions, indicating that the user enters commands at the prompt. The system prompt indicates the current command mode. For example, the prompt `Router(config)#` indicates global configuration mode.
- Terminal sessions and information the system displays are in `screen` font.
- Information you enter is in `boldface screen` font.
- Nonprinting characters, such as passwords, are in angle brackets (< >).
- Default responses to system prompts are in square brackets ([ ]).
- Exclamation points (!) at the beginning of a line indicate a comment line. They are also displayed by the Cisco IOS software for certain processes.

---

**CAUTION**

Means *reader be careful*. In this situation, you might do something that could result in equipment damage or loss of data.

---

**NOTES**

Means *reader take note*. Notes contain helpful suggestions or references to materials not contained in this manual.

---

**TIMESAVER**

Means *the described action saves time*. You can save time by performing the action described in the paragraph.

Within the Cisco IOS Reference Library, the term *router* is used to refer to both access servers and routers. When a feature is supported on the access server only, the term *access server* is used. When a feature is supported on one or more specific router platforms (such as the Cisco 4500), but not on other platforms (such as the Cisco 2500), the text specifies the supported platforms.

Within examples, routers and access servers are alternately shown. These products are used only for example purposes; an example that shows one product does not indicate that the other product is not supported.

# CHAPTER 1

# AppleTalk and Novell IPX Overview

The Cisco IOS software supports a variety of routing protocols. This book discusses the following network protocols:

- AppleTalk
- Novell IPX
- Apollo Domain
- Banyan VINES
- DECnet
- ISO CLNS
- XNS

This overview chapter provides a high-level description of AppleTalk and Novell IPX. For configuration information, refer to the appropriate chapter in this publication.

## APPLETALK

This section provides background on AppleTalk and briefly describes Cisco's implementation of AppleTalk.

### Background on AppleTalk

AppleTalk is a LAN system designed and developed by Apple Computer, Inc. It can run over Ethernet, Token Ring, and Fiber Distributed Data Interface (FDDI) networks as well as over Apple's proprietary twisted-pair media access system (LocalTalk). AppleTalk specifies a protocol stack comprising several protocols that direct the flow of traffic over the network.

Apple Computer uses the name *AppleTalk* to refer to the Apple network protocol architecture. Apple Computer refers to the actual transmission media used in an AppleTalk network as

5

LocalTalk, TokenTalk (AppleTalk over Token Ring), EtherTalk (AppleTalk over Ethernet), and FDDITalk (AppleTalk over FDDI).

## Cisco's Implementation of AppleTalk

Cisco IOS software supports AppleTalk Phase 1 and AppleTalk Phase 2. For AppleTalk Phase 2, Cisco devices support both *extended* and *nonextended* networks.

A Cisco router or access server may receive equivalent routes advertised by neighboring routers, with one router giving an AppleTalk Phase 1 form of the route (for example, 101) and another giving an AppleTalk Phase 2 form of the route (for example, 101-101). When neighboring routers advertise equivalent overlapping routes to a router, the router always uses the AppleTalk Phase 2 form of the route and discards the AppleTalk Phase 1 route.

### Supported Media

Cisco's implementation of AppleTalk routes packets over Ethernet, Token Ring, and FDDI LANs, as well as over X.25, High-Level Data Link Control (HDLC), Frame Relay, and Switched Multimegabit Data Service (SMDS) WANs.

### Standard AppleTalk Services

The Cisco implementation of AppleTalk supports the following standard AppleTalk protocols:

- AppleTalk Address Resolution Protocol (AARP)
- AppleTalk Port Group
- Datagram Delivery Protocol (DDP)
- Routing Table Maintenance Protocol (RTMP)
- Name Binding Protocol (NBP)
- Zone Information Protocol (ZIP)
- AppleTalk Echo Protocol (AEP)
- AppleTalk Transaction Protocol (ATP)

AARP, DDP, and RTMP provide end-to-end connectivity between internetworked nodes. AARP maps AppleTalk node addresses to the addresses of the underlying data link, thus making it possible for AppleTalk to run on several data links. DDP provides socket-to-socket delivery of packets. RTMP establishes and maintains routing tables.

NBP and ZIP maintain node name and zone information. NBP maps network names to AppleTalk addresses. ZIP tracks which networks are in which zones.

AEP is an echo (or **ping**-type) protocol. It generates packets that test the reachability of network nodes.

ATP is a reliable transport protocol that provides data acknowledgment and retransmission for transaction-based applications, such as file services provided by the AppleTalk Filing Protocol (AFP) and print services provided by the Printer Access Protocol (PAP).

Cisco software provides support for the AppleTalk Management Information Base (MIB) variables, as described in RFC 1243.

## Enhancements to Standard AppleTalk Services

The Cisco AppleTalk implementation includes the following enhancements to standard AppleTalk support:

- Support for AppleTalk Enhanced Internet Gateway Protocol (Enhanced IGRP). AppleTalk Enhanced IGRP provides the following features:

  o Automatic redistribution. By default, AppleTalk Routing Table Maintenance Protocol (RTMP) routes are automatically redistributed into Enhanced IGRP, and AppleTalk Enhanced IGRP routes are automatically redistributed into RTMP. If desired, you can turn off redistribution. You can also completely turn off AppleTalk Enhanced IGRP and AppleTalk RTMP on the device or on individual interfaces.

  o Configuration of routing protocols on individual interfaces. You can configure interfaces that are configured for AppleTalk to use either RTMP, Enhanced IGRP, or both routing protocols. If two neighboring routers are configured to use both RTMP and Enhanced IGRP, the Enhanced IGRP routing information supersedes the RTMP information. However, both routers continue to send RTMP routing updates. This feature allows you to control the excessive bandwidth usage of RTMP on WAN links. Because a WAN link is a point-to-point link (that is, there are no other devices on the link), there is no need to run RTMP to perform end-node router discovery. Using Enhanced IGRP on WAN links allows you to save bandwidth and, in the case of Packet-Switched Data Networks (PSDN), traffic charges.

- Support for EtherTalk 1.2 and EtherTalk 2.0 without the need for translation or transition routers.

- Support for Ethernet-emulated LANs.

- Support for VLANs.

- Support for WAN protocols, including SMDS, Frame Relay, X.25, and HDLC.

- Configurable protocol constants (including the control of the aging of entries in the routing table and control of the AARP interval and number of retransmissions).

- No software limits on the number of zones or routes. However, per AppleTalk specification, you can only have a maximum of 255 zones per segment.

- MacTCP support via a MacIP server.

- Support of IPTalk, which provides Internet Protocol (IP) encapsulation of AppleTalk, IPTalk, and the Columbia AppleTalk Package (CAP).

- Access control for filtering network traffic by network number, ZIP filtering, by NBP entity names, filtering routing table updates, and filtering GetZoneList (GZL) responses.
- Integrated node name support to simplify AppleTalk network management.
- Interactive access to AEP and NBP provided by the **test appletalk** command.
- Configured (seed) and discovered interface configuration.
- Support for the AppleTalk Responder, which is used by network monitoring packages such as *Inter•Poll*.
- SNMP over AppleTalk.
- Encapsulation (tunneling) of AppleTalk RTMP packets over an IP backbone.
- Support for AppleTalk static routes.
- SMRP over AppleTalk.

### Security

AppleTalk, like many network protocols, makes no provisions for network security. The design of the AppleTalk protocol architecture requires that security measures be implemented at higher application levels. Cisco supports AppleTalk distribution lists, allowing control of routing updates on a per-interface basis. This security feature is similar to those that Cisco provides for other protocols.

Note that Cisco's implementation of AppleTalk does not forward packets with local source and destination network addresses. This behavior does not conform with the definition of AppleTalk in Apple Computer's *Inside AppleTalk* publication. However, this behavior is designed to prevent any possible corruption of the AARP table in any AppleTalk node that is performing address gleaning through Media Access Control (MAC).

## NOVELL IPX

This section offers background information and briefly describes Cisco's implementation of Novell IPX.

### Background on Novell IPX

Novell Internet Packet Exchange (IPX) is derived from the Xerox Network Systems (XNS) Internet Datagram Protocol (IDP). IPX and XNS have the following differences:

- IPX and XNS do not always use the same Ethernet encapsulation format.
- IPX uses Novell's proprietary Service Advertising Protocol (SAP) to advertise special network services. File servers and print servers are examples of services that typically are advertised.
- IPX uses delay (measured in ticks), while XNS uses hop count as the primary metric in determining the best path to a destination.

## Cisco's Implementation of Novell's IPX

Cisco's implementation of Novell's IPX protocol is certified to provide full IPX routing functionality.

### IPX MIB Support

Cisco supports the IPX MIB (currently, read-only access is supported). The IPX Accounting group represents one of the local Cisco-specific IPX variables we support. This group provides access to the active database that is created and maintained if IPX accounting is enabled on a router or access server.

### IPX Enhanced IGRP Support

Cisco IOS software also supports IPX Enhanced IGRP, which provides the following features:

- Automatic redistribution—IPX RIP routes are automatically redistributed into Enhanced IGRP, and Enhanced IGRP routes are automatically redistributed into Routing Information Protocol (RIP). If desired, you can turn off redistribution. You also can completely turn off Enhanced IGRP and IPX RIP on the device or on individual interfaces.

- Increased network width—With IPX RIP, the largest possible width of your network is 15 hops. When Enhanced IGRP is enabled, the largest possible width is 224 hops. Because the Enhanced IGRP metric is large enough to support thousands of hops, the only barrier to expanding the network is the transport layer hop counter. Cisco works around this problem by incrementing the transport control field only when an IPX packet has traversed 15 routers and the next hop to the destination has been learned via Enhanced IGRP. When a RIP route is being used as the next hop to the destination, the transport control field is incremented as usual.

- Incremental SAP updates—Complete SAP updates are sent periodically on each interface until an Enhanced IGRP neighbor is found, and thereafter only when changes are made to the SAP table. This procedure works by taking advantage of Enhanced IGRP's reliable transport mechanism, which means that an Enhanced IGRP peer must be present for incremental SAPs to be sent. If no peer exists on a particular interface, periodic SAPs are sent on that interface until a peer is found. This functionality is automatic on serial interfaces and can be configured on LAN media.

### LANE Support

Cisco IOS software also supports routing IPX between Ethernet-emulated LANs and Token Ring-emulated LANs.

### VLAN Support

Cisco IOS software supports routing IPX between VLANs. Users with Novell NetWare environments can configure any one of the four IPX Ethernet encapsulations to be routed using the Inter-Switch Link (ISL) encapsulation across VLAN boundaries.

# CHAPTER 2

# Configuring AppleTalk

This chapter describes how to configure AppleTalk and provides configuration examples. For a complete description of the AppleTalk commands mentioned in this chapter, see Chapter 3, "AppleTalk Commands."

## APPLETALK PHASES

The AppleTalk network architecture has the following two phases:

- AppleTalk Phase 1
- AppleTalk Phase 2

### AppleTalk Phase 1

*AppleTalk Phase 1* is the initial implementation of AppleTalk and is designed for logical workgroups. AppleTalk Phase 1 supports a single physical network that can have one network number and be in one zone. This network can have up to 254 devices, which can consist of 127 end nodes and 127 servers.

### AppleTalk Phase 2

*AppleTalk Phase 2* is an enhancement to AppleTalk Phase 1. It is designed for larger networks and has improved routing capabilities. It supports multiple logical networks on a single physical network and multiple logical networks in a given zone. This means that one cable segment can have multiple network numbers. Each logical network in Phase 2 can support up to 253 devices, with no restrictions on the type of devices (end nodes or servers). Also, in AppleTalk Phase 2, a network can be in more than one zone.

## Types of AppleTalk Networks

AppleTalk Phase 2 distinguishes between two types of networks based on their media-level encapsulation and cable addressing methods. The two types of networks are as follows:

- Nonextended
- Extended

## Comparison of Nonextended and Extended Networks

Table 2–1 compares the attributes of nonextended and extended networks.

**Table 2–1**   *Comparison of Nonextended and Extended Networks*

| Attribute | Nonextended | Extended |
|---|---|---|
| Media-level encapsulation method | Encapsulation of the 3-byte LocalTalk packet in an Ethernet frame. | ISO-type encapsulations only (that is, no encapsulation of the 3-byte LocalTalk packets) |
| Physical media that supports media-level encapsulation methods | LocalTalk | All physical media except LocalTalk |
| Node addressing method | Each node number is unique | Each *network.node* combination is unique |
| Cable addressing method | A single number per cable | A number range corresponding to one or more logical networks |

## Relationship Between AppleTalk Phases and Network Types

Nonextended networks were the sole network type defined in AppleTalk Phase 1. You can consider AppleTalk Phase 1 networks to be nonextended networks.

You can consider AppleTalk Phase 2 networks to be extended networks.

## Comparison of AppleTalk Phases

Table 2–2 compares the capabilities of AppleTalk Phase 1 and Phase 2.

**Table 2–2**  *AppleTalk Phase 1 and Phase 2*

| Capability | AppleTalk Phase 1 | AppleTalk Phase 2 |
|---|---|---|
| **Networks, nodes, and zones** | | |
| Number of logical networks (cable segments) | 1 | 65279* |
| Maximum number of devices | 254† | 253‡ |
| Maximum number of end nodes | 127 | Does not apply** |
| Maximum number of servers | 127 | Does not apply |
| Number of zones in which a network can be | 1†† | 1 (nonextended) 255 (extended) |
| **Media-level encapsulation** | | |
| Nonextended network | Does not apply | Yes |
| Extended network | Does not apply | Yes |
| Cable addressing | Does not apply; uses network numbers | Single network number (nonextended) Cable range of 1 or more (extended) |

\* The 65279 value is per AppleTalk specifications.
† The node addresses 0 and 255 are reserved.
‡ The node addresses 0, 254, and 255 are reserved.
** There is no restriction on the types of devices. There can be a total of 253 end nodes and servers.
†† In terms of zones, an AppleTalk Phase 1 network can be thought of as a nonextended AppleTalk Phase 2 network.

## Cisco-Supported AppleTalk Phases

Routers running Software Release 8.2 or later support AppleTalk Phase 1 and Phase 2.

## APPLETALK ADDRESSES

An AppleTalk *address* consists of a network number and a node number expressed in decimal in the format *network.node*.

## Network Numbers

The *network number* identifies a network, or cable segment. A *network* is a single logical cable. Although the logical cable is frequently a single physical cable, bridges and routers can interconnect several physical cables.

The network number is a 16-bit decimal number that must be unique throughout the entire AppleTalk internetwork.

### *AppleTalk Phase 1 Network Numbers*

In AppleTalk Phase 1, networks are identified by a single network number that corresponds to a physical network. In AppleTalk Phase 1, the network number 0 is reserved.

### *AppleTalk Phase 2 Network Numbers*

In AppleTalk Phase 2, networks are identified by a cable range that corresponds to one or more logical networks. In Phase 2, a single cable can have multiple network numbers.

A cable range is either one network number or a contiguous sequence of several network numbers in the format *start–end*. For example, the cable range 4096–4096 identifies a logical network that has a single network number, and the cable range 10–12 identifies a logical network that spans three network numbers.

In AppleTalk Phase 2, the network number 0 is reserved.

## Node Numbers

The *node number* identifies the node, which is any device connected to the AppleTalk network. The node number is an 8-bit decimal number that must be unique on that network.

### *AppleTalk Phase 1 Node Numbers*

In AppleTalk Phase 1, node numbers 1 through 127 are for user nodes, node numbers 128 through 254 are for servers, and node numbers 0 and 255 are reserved.

### *AppleTalk Phase 2 Node Numbers*

In AppleTalk Phase 2, you can use node numbers 1 through 253 for any nodes attached to the network. Node numbers 0, 254, and 255 are reserved.

### AppleTalk Address Example

The following is an example of an AppleTalk network address:

```
3.45
```

In this example, the network number is 3 and the node number is 45. You enter both numbers in decimal. Cisco IOS software also displays them in decimal.

## AppleTalk Zones

A *zone* is a logical group of networks. The networks in a zone can be contiguous or noncontiguous. A zone is identified by a zone name, which can be up to 32 characters long. The zone name can include standard characters and AppleTalk special characters. To include a special character, type a colon, followed by two hexadecimal characters that represent the special character in the Macintosh character set.

## AppleTalk Phase 1 Zones

An AppleTalk Phase 1 network can have only one zone.

## AppleTalk Phase 2 Zones

In AppleTalk Phase 2, an extended network can have up to 255 zones; a nonextended network can have only 1 zone.

## CONFIGURATION GUIDELINES AND COMPATIBILITY RULES

AppleTalk Phase 1 and AppleTalk Phase 2 networks are incompatible and cannot run simultaneously on the same internetwork. As a result, all routers in an internetwork must support AppleTalk Phase 2 before the network can use Phase 2 routing.

## Combining AppleTalk Phase1 and Phase 2 Routers

If your internetwork has a combination of AppleTalk Phase 1 and Phase 2 routers, you must observe the following configuration guidelines. If you do not follow these guidelines, unpredictable behavior might result. Note, however, that you do not need to upgrade all end nodes to use the features provided by Cisco's AppleTalk enhancements.

- The cable range must be one (for example, 23–23).
- Each AppleTalk network can be a member of only one zone.

## Combining Cisco Routers with Other Vendors

When using Cisco routers with implementations of AppleTalk by other vendors, follow these guidelines:

- For a Macintosh with an Ethernet card to support extended AppleTalk, the Macintosh must be running EtherTalk Version 2.0 or later. This restriction does not apply to Macintoshes with only LocalTalk interfaces.
- Shiva FastPath routers must run K-Star Version 8.0 or later and must be explicitly configured for extended AppleTalk.
- Apple's Internet Router software Version 2.0 supports a transition mode for translation between nonextended AppleTalk and extended AppleTalk on the same network. Transition mode requires the Apple upgrade utility and a special patch file from Apple.

## APPLETALK CONFIGURATION TASK LIST

To configure AppleTalk routing, complete the tasks in the following sections. At a minimum, you must enable AppleTalk routing. The remaining tasks are optional.

- Enabling AppleTalk Routing
- Controlling Access to AppleTalk Networks

- Configuring the Name Display Facility
- Setting Up Special Configurations
- Configuring AppleTalk Control Protocol for Point-to-Point Protocol
- Tuning AppleTalk Network Performance
- Configuring AppleTalk Enhanced IGRP
- Configuring AppleTalk Interenterprise Routing
- Configuring AppleTalk over WANs
- Monitoring and Maintaining the AppleTalk Network

See the "AppleTalk Configuration Examples" section near the end of this chapter for configuration examples.

## ENABLING APPLETALK ROUTING

You enable AppleTalk routing by first enabling it on the router and then configuring it on each interface.

You can also enable the Cisco IOS software to perform transition mode routing from nonextended AppleTalk to extended AppleTalk.

You can route AppleTalk on some interfaces and transparently bridge it on other interfaces simultaneously. To do this, you must enable concurrent routing and bridging.

You can also route AppleTalk traffic between routed interfaces and bridge groups or route AppleTalk traffic between bridge groups. To do this, you must enable integrated routing and bridging.

## Enable AppleTalk Routing Task List

Complete the tasks in the following sections to enable AppleTalk routing. The first two tasks are required; the rest are optional.

- Enable AppleTalk Routing
- Configure an Interface for AppleTalk
- Select an AppleTalk Routing Protocol
- Configure Transition Mode
- Enable Concurrent Routing and Bridging
- Configure Integrated Routing and Bridging

## Enable AppleTalk Routing

To enable AppleTalk routing, perform the following task in global configuration mode:

| Task | Command |
|------|---------|
| Enable AppleTalk routing. | **appletalk routing** |

The **appletalk routing** command without any keywords or arguments enables AppleTalk routing using the Routing Table Maintenance Protocol (RTMP) routing protocol. You can enable Apple-Talk routing to use AppleTalk Enhanced IGRP routing protocol instead of RTMP. For more information, refer to the "Enable AppleTalk Enhanced IGRP" section later in this chapter.

For an example of how to enable AppleTalk routing, see the "Extended AppleTalk Network Example" section near the end of this chapter.

## Configure an Interface for AppleTalk

You configure an interface for AppleTalk by assigning an AppleTalk address or cable range to the interface and then assigning one or more zone names to the interface. You can perform these tasks either manually or dynamically.

### Manually Configure an Interface

You can manually configure an interface for nonextended AppleTalk or extended AppleTalk routing.

#### Configure for Nonextended AppleTalk Routing

To manually configure an interface for nonextended AppleTalk routing, perform the following tasks in interface configuration mode:

| Task | Command |
|------|---------|
| **Step 1** Assign an AppleTalk address to the interface. | **appletalk address** *network.node* |
| **Step 2** Assign a zone name to the interface. | **appletalk zone** *zone-name* |

After you assign the address and zone names, the interface will attempt to verify them with another operational router on the connected network. If there are any discrepancies, the interface will not become operational. If there are no neighboring operational routers, the device will assume the interface's configuration is correct, and the interface will become operational.

For an example of how to configure an interface for nonextended AppleTalk routing, see the "Nonextended AppleTalk Network Example" section in this chapter.

### Configure for Extended AppleTalk Routing

To manually configure an interface for extended AppleTalk routing, perform the following tasks in interface configuration mode:

| Task | Command |
|------|---------|
| **Step 1**   Assign a cable range to an interface. | **appletalk cable-range** *cable-range* [*network.node*] |
| **Step 2**   Assign a zone name to the interface. | **appletalk zone** *zone-name* |

You can assign more than one zone name to a cable range. If you do so, the first name you assign is considered to be the default zone. You can define up to 255 zones.

For an example of how to configure an interface for extended AppleTalk routing, see the "Extended AppleTalk Network Example" section later in this chapter.

## Dynamically Configure an Interface

If a nonextended or an extended interface is connected to a network that has at least one other operational AppleTalk router, you can dynamically configure the interface using *discovery mode*. In discovery mode, an interface acquires information about the attached network from an operational router and then uses this information to configure itself.

### Benefits of Dynamically Configuring an Interface

Using discovery mode to configure interfaces saves time if the network numbers, cable ranges, or zone names change. If this happens, you must make the changes on only one seed router on each network.

Discovery mode is useful when you are changing a network configuration or when you are adding a router to an existing network.

### Restrictions of Dynamically Configuring an Interface

If there is no operational router on the attached network, you must manually configure the interface as described in the previous sections. Also, if a discovery mode interface is restarted, another operational router must be present before the interface can become operational.

Discovery mode does not run over serial lines.

---

**CAUTION**

---

Do not enable discovery mode on all routers on a network. If you do so and all the devices restart simultaneously (for example, after a power failure), the network will be inaccessible until you manually configure at least one router.

---

## Seed Router Starting Sequence

A nondiscovery-mode interface (also called a *seed router*) starts up as follows:

1. The seed router acquires its configuration from memory.
2. If the stored configuration is not completely specified when you assign an AppleTalk address to an interface on which you assign a cable range and a zone name, the interface will not start up.
3. If the stored configuration is completely specified, the interface attempts to verify the stored configuration with another router on the attached network. If any discrepancy exists, the interface will not start up.
4. If there are no neighboring operational routers, the device will assume the interface's stored configuration is correct, and the interface will become operational.

## Response to Configuration Queries

Using discovery mode does not affect an interface's capability to respond to configuration queries from other routers on the connected network after the interface becomes operational.

## Dynamically Configure a Nonextended Interface

You can activate discovery mode on a nonextended interface in one of two ways, depending on whether you know the network number of the attached network.

In the first method, you immediately place the interface into discovery mode by specifying an Apple-Talk address of 0.0. Use this method when you do not know the network number of the attached network. To use this method, perform the following task in interface configuration mode:

| Task | Command |
|------|---------|
| Place the interface into discovery mode by assigning it the AppleTalk address 0.0. | **appletalk address 0.0** |

For an example of how to configure discovery mode using this method, see the "Nonextended Network in Discovery Mode Example" section near the end of this chapter.

In the second method, you first assign an address to the interface and then explicitly enable discovery mode. Use this method when you know the network number of the attached network. Note, however, that you are not required to use this method when you know the network number. To use this method, perform the following tasks in interface configuration mode:

| Task | | Command |
|------|------|---------|
| **Step 1** | Assign an AppleTalk address to the interface. | **appletalk address** *network.node* |

| Task | Command |
|---|---|
| **Step 2** Place the interface into discovery mode. | **appletalk discovery** |

### Dynamically Configure an Extended Interface

You can activate discovery mode on an extended interface in one of two ways, depending on whether you know the cable range of the attached network.

In the first method, you immediately place the interface into discovery mode by specifying a cable range of 0–0. Use this method when you do not know the network number of the attached network. To use this method, perform the following task in interface configuration mode:

| Task | Command |
|---|---|
| Place the interface into discovery mode by assigning it the cable range 0-0. | **appletalk cable-range 0–0** |

In the second method, you first assign cable ranges and then explicitly enable discovery mode. Use this method when you know the cable range of the attached network. Note, however, that you are not required to use this method if you know the cable range. To use this method, perform the following tasks in interface configuration mode:

| Task | Command |
|---|---|
| **Step 1** Assign an AppleTalk address to the interface. | **appletalk cable-range** *cable-range* [*network.node*] |
| **Step 2** Place the interface into discovery mode. | **appletalk discovery** |

## Select an AppleTalk Routing Protocol

After you configure AppleTalk on an interface, you can select a routing protocol for the interface. You can enable the RTMP or Enhanced IGRP routing protocols on any interface. You can also enable the Apple Update-Based Routing Protocol (AURP) on a tunnel interface.

With this task, you can enable some AppleTalk interfaces to use RTMP, some to use Enhanced IGRP, and others to use AURP, as required by your network topology.

To select an AppleTalk routing protocol for an interface, perform the following task in interface configuration mode:

| Task | Command |
|---|---|
| Create an AppleTalk routing process. | **appletalk protocol** {aurp | eigrp | rtmp} |

This task is optional. If you do not select a routing protocol for an interface, Cisco IOS uses RTMP by default.

For an example of how to select an AppleTalk routing protocol using Enhanced IGRP, see the "AppleTalk Access List Examples" section near the end of this chapter.

## Configure Transition Mode

The Cisco IOS software can route packets between extended and nonextended AppleTalk networks that coexist on the same cable. This type of routing is referred to as *transition mode*.

To use transition mode, you must have two router ports connected to the same physical cable. One port is configured as a nonextended AppleTalk network, and the other port is configured as an extended AppleTalk network. Each port must have a unique network number because you are routing between two separate AppleTalk networks: the extended network and the nonextended network.

To configure transition mode, you must have two ports on the same router that are connected to the same physical cable. You configure one port as a nonextended AppleTalk network by performing the following tasks in interface configuration mode:

| Task | Command |
|------|---------|
| **Step 1** Assign an AppleTalk address to the interface. | **appletalk address** *network.node* |
| **Step 2** Assign a zone name to the interface. | **appletalk zone** *zone-name* |

You configure the second port as an extended AppleTalk network by performing the following tasks in interface configuration mode:

| Task | Command |
|------|---------|
| **Step 1** Assign an AppleTalk cable range to the interface. | **appletalk cable-range** *cable-range* [*network.node*] |
| **Step 2** Assign a zone name to the interface. | **appletalk zone** *zone-name* |

When you enter interface configuration mode, the type of interface must be the same for both ports (for example, both could be Ethernet), and the interface number must be different (for example, 0 and 1).

For an example of how to configure transition mode, see the "Transition Mode Example" section near the end of this chapter.

## Enable Concurrent Routing and Bridging

You can route AppleTalk on some interfaces and transparently bridge it on other interfaces simultaneously. To do this, you must enable concurrent routing and bridging.

To enable concurrent routing and bridging, perform the following task in global configuration mode:

| Task | Command |
|---|---|
| Enable concurrent routing and bridging. | **bridge crb** |

## Configure Integrated Routing and Bridging

Integrated routing and bridging (IRB) enables a user to route AppleTalk traffic between routed interfaces and bridge groups or route AppleTalk traffic between bridge groups. Specifically, local or unroutable traffic is bridged among the bridged interfaces in the same bridge group, while routable traffic is routed to other routed interfaces or bridge groups. Using IRB, you can do the following:

- Switch packets from a bridged interface to a routed interface
- Switch packets from a routed interface to a bridged interface
- Switch packets within the same bridge group

## CONTROLLING ACCESS TO APPLETALK NETWORKS

An *access list* is a list of AppleTalk network numbers, zones, or Name Binding Protocol (NBP) named entities that is maintained by the Cisco IOS software and used to control access to or from specific zones, networks, and NBP named entities.

## Types of Access Lists

The software supports the following two general types of AppleTalk access lists:

- AppleTalk-style access lists, which are based on AppleTalk zones or NBP named entities
- IP-style access lists, which are based on network numbers

### AppleTalk-Style Access Lists

AppleTalk-style access lists regulate the internetwork using zone names and NBP named entities.

#### Using Zone Names

Zone names and NBP named entities are good control points because they allow for network-level abstractions that users can access.

You can express zones names either explicitly or by using generalized-argument keywords. Thus, using AppleTalk zone name access lists simplifies network management and allows for greater flexibility when adding segments because reconfiguration requirements are minimal. Using AppleTalk zone name access lists allows you to manage and control whole sections of the network.

### Using NBP Named Entities

NBP named entities allow you to control access at the object level. Using NBP named entities, you can permit or deny NBP packets from a class of objects based on the **type** portion of the NBP tuple name, from a particular NBP named entity based on the **object** portion of the NBP tuple name, or from all NBP named entities within a particular area based on the **zone** portion of the NBP tuple name. You can fully or partially qualify an NBP tuple name to refine the access control by specifying one, two, or three parts of the NBP name tuple as separate access list entries tied together by the same sequence number.

### Benefits of AppleTalk-Style Access Lists

The main advantage of AppleTalk-style access lists is that they allow you to define access regardless of the existing network topology or any changes in future topologies—because they are based on zones and NBP named entities. A zone access list is effectively a dynamic list of network numbers. The user specifies a zone name, but the effect is as if the user had specified all the network numbers belonging to that zone. An NBP named entity access list provides a means of controlling access at the network entity level.

## IP-Style Access Lists

IP-style access lists control network access based on network numbers. This feature can be useful in defining access lists that control the disposition of networks that overlap, are contained by, or exactly match a specific network number range.

Additionally, you can use IP-style access lists to resolve conflicting network numbers. You can use an access list to restrict the network numbers and zones that a department can advertise, thereby limiting advertisement to an authorized set of networks. AppleTalk-style access lists are typically insufficient for this purpose.

In general, however, using IP-style access lists is not recommended because the controls are not optimal; they ignore the logical mapping provided by AppleTalk zones. One problem with IP-style access lists is that when you add networks to a zone, you must reconfigure each secure router. Another problem is that, because anyone can add network segments (for example, if one group of users gets a LaserWriter and installs a Cayman GatorBox, this creates a new network segment), the potential for confusion and misconfiguration is significant.

## Combining AppleTalk-Style and IP-Style Entries

You can combine zone, network, and NBP named entity entries in a single access list. Cisco IOS software performs NBP filtering independently on only NBP packets. The software applies network filtering in conjunction with zone filtering. However, for optimal performance, access lists should not include both zones (AppleTalk-style) and numeric network (IP-style) entries.

Because the Cisco IOS software applies network filtering and zone filtering simultaneously, be sure to add the appropriate **access-list permit other-access** or access-list permit additional-zones statement to the end of the access list when using only one type of filtering. For example, suppose you want to deny only zone Z. You do not want to do any network filtering, but the software by default automatically includes an **access-list deny other-access** entry near the end of each access list. You must then create an access list that explicitly permits access of all networks. Therefore, the access list for this example would have an **access-list deny zone Z** entry to deny zone Z, an **access-list permit additional-zones** entry to permit all other zones, and an **access-list permit other-access** to explicitly permit all networks.

## Types of Filters

You can filter the following types of AppleTalk packets:

- NBP packets
- Data packets
- Routing table updates
- GetZoneList (GZL) request and reply packets
- Zone Information Protocol (ZIP) reply packets

Table 2–3 shows the Cisco IOS software filters for each packet type.

**Table 2–3** *Packet Type to Filter Mapping*

| Packet type | Filters that can be applied |
|---|---|
| NBP packets | appletalk access-group in<br>appletalk access-group out |
| Data packets | appletalk access-group in<br>appletalk access-group out |
| Routing table update | appletalk distribute-list in<br>appletalk distribute-list out<br>appletalk permit-partial-zones<br>appletalk zip-reply-filter |
| ZIP reply packets | appletalk zip-reply-filter |
| GZL request and reply packets | appletalk distribute-list in<br>appletalk distribute-list out<br>appletalk getzonelist-filter<br>appletalk permit-partial-zones |

---

**NOTES**

These types of filters are completely independent of each other. This means that if, for example, you apply a data packet filter to an interface, that filter has no effect on incoming routing table updates or GZL requests that pass through that interface. The exceptions to this are that outgoing routing update filters can affect GZL updates, and ZIP reply filters can affect outgoing routing updates.

---

## Implementation Considerations

Unlike access lists in other protocols, the order of the entries in an AppleTalk access list is not important. However, keep the following constraints in mind when defining access lists:

- You must design and type access list entries properly to ensure that entries do not overlap each other. An example of an overlap is if you were to enter a **permit network** command and then enter a **deny network** command. If you do enter entries that overlap, the last one you entered overwrites and removes the previous one from the access list. In this example, this means that the "permit network" statement would be removed from the access list when you typed the "deny network" statement.

- Each access list always has a method for handling packets or routing updates that do not satisfy any of the access control statements in the access list.

  To explicitly specify how you want these packets or routing updates to be handled, use the **access-list other-access** global configuration command when defining access conditions for networks and cable ranges, use the **access-list additional-zones** global configuration command when defining access conditions for zones, and use the **access-list other-nbps** global configuration command when defining access conditions for NBP packets from named entities. If you use one of these commands, it does not matter where in the list you place it. The Cisco IOS software automatically places an **access-list deny other-access-list deny other-nbps** commands near the end of the access list when zones and NBP access conditions are denied, respectively. (With other protocols, you must type the equivalent commands last.)

  If you do not explicitly specify how to handle packets or routing updates that do not satisfy any of the access control statements in the access list, the packets or routing updates are automatically denied access and, in the case of data packets, are discarded.

## Control Access to AppleTalk Networks Task List

You perform the tasks in the following sections to control access to AppleTalk networks.

- Create Access Lists
- Create Filters

## Create Access Lists

An access list defines the conditions used to filter packets sent into or out of the interface. Each access list is identified by a number. All **access-list** commands that specify the same access list number create a single access list.

A single access list can contain any number and any combination of **access-list** commands. You can include network and cable range **access-list** commands, zone **access-list** commands, and NBP named entity **access-list** commands in the same access list.

However, you can specify only one each of the commands that specify default actions to take if none of the access conditions are matched. For example, a single access list can include only one **access-list other-access** command to handle networks and cable ranges that do not match the access conditions, only one **access-list additional-zones** command to handle zones that do not match the access conditions, and only one **access-list other-nbps** command to handle NBP packets from named entities that do not match the access conditions.

### Set Priority Queuing

You can also set priorities for the order in which outgoing packets destined for a specific network are queued, based on the access list.

---
**NOTES**
---

For priority queuing, the Cisco IOS software applies the access list to the destination network.

---

### Automatic Fast Switching

AppleTalk access lists are automatically fast switched. Access list fast switching improves the performance of AppleTalk traffic when access lists are defined on an interface.

### Create AppleTalk-Style Access Lists

Complete the tasks in the following sections to create AppleTalk-style access lists:

- Create Zone Access Lists
- Create Priority Queuing Access Lists
- Create NBP Access Lists

### Create Zone Access Lists

To create access lists that define access conditions for zones (AppleTalk-style access lists), perform one or more of the following tasks in global configuration mode:

| Task | Command |
| --- | --- |
| Define access for a zone. | **access-list** *access-list-number* {**deny** \| **permit**} **zone** *zone-name* |
| Define the default action to take for access checks that apply to zones. | **access-list** *access-list-number* {**deny** \| **permit**} **additional-zones** |

For examples of how to create access lists, see the "AppleTalk Access List Examples" and "Hiding and Sharing Resources with Access List Examples" sections near the end of this chapter.

### Create Priority Queuing Access Lists

To assign a priority in which packets destined for a specific zone are queued, based on the zone access list, perform the following task in global configuration mode:

| Task | Command |
| --- | --- |
| Define access for a single network number. | **priority-list** *list-number* **protocol** *protocol-name* {**high** \| **medium** \| **normal** \| **low**} **list** *access-list-number* |

### Create NBP Access Lists

To create access lists that define access conditions for NBP packets based on the NBP packet type, from particular NBP named entities, from classes of NBP named entities, or from NBP named entities within particular zones, perform one or both of the following tasks in global configuration mode:

| Task | Command |
| --- | --- |
| Define access for an NBP packet type, NBP named entity, type of named entity, or named entities within a specific zone. | **access-list** *access-list-number* {**deny** \| **permit**} **nbp** *sequence-number* {**BrRq** \| **FwdRq** \| **Lookup** \| **LkReply** \| **object** *string* \| **type** *string* \| **zone** *string*}\| |
| Define the default action to take for access checks that apply to NBP named entities. | **access-list** *access-list-number* {**deny** \| **permit**} **other-nbps** |

For an example of how to create NBP packet filtering access lists, see the "Defining an Access List to Filter NBP Packets Example" section near the end of this chapter.

### Create IP-Style Access Lists

To create access lists that define access conditions for networks and cable ranges (IP-style access lists), perform one or more of the following tasks in global configuration mode:

| Task | Command |
|------|---------|
| Define access for a single network number. | **access-list** *access-list-number* {**deny** \| **permit**} **network** *network* [**broadcast-deny** \| **broadcast-permit**] |
| Define access for a single cable range. | **access-list** *access-list-number* {**deny** \| **permit**} **cable-range** *cable-range* [**broadcast-deny** \| **broadcast-permit**] |
| Define access for an extended or a nonextended network that overlaps any part of the specified range. | **access-list** *access-list-number* {**deny** \| **permit**} **includes** *cable-range* [**broadcast-deny** \| **broadcast-permit**] |
| Define access for an extended or a nonextended network that is included entirely within the specified range. | **access-list** *access-list-number* {**deny** \| **permit**} **within** *cable-range* [**broadcast-deny** \| **broadcast-permit**] |
| Define the default action to take for access checks that apply to network numbers or cable ranges. | **access-list** *access-list-number* {**deny** \| **permit**} **other-access** |

### Create Filters

A filter examines specific types of packets that pass through an interface and permits or denies them, based on the conditions defined in the access lists that have been applied to that interface.

Complete the tasks in the following sections to filter different types of AppleTalk packets:

- Create NBP Packet Filters
- Create Data Packet Filters
- Create Routing Table Update Filters
- Create GetZoneList (GZL) Filters
- Enable ZIP Reply Filters
- Enable Partial Zone Filters

You can apply any number of filters on each interface. Each filter can use the same access list or different access lists. Filters can be applied to inbound and outbound interfaces.

Routing update filters, data packet filters, and ZIP reply filters use access lists that define conditions for networks, cable ranges, and zones. GZL filters use access lists that define conditions for zones only. NBP packet filters use access lists that define conditions for NBP named entities.

## Create NBP Packet Filters

To create an NBP packet filter, perform the following tasks:

**Step 1**    Create an NBP access list as described in the "Create NBP Access Lists" section earlier in this chapter.

**Step 2**    Apply an NBP filter to an interface.

To apply an NBP filter to an interface, perform the following task in interface configuration mode:

| Task | Command |
| --- | --- |
| Apply the data packet filter to the interface. | **appletalk access-group** *access-list-number* [in | out] |

---

**NOTES**

Prior to Cisco IOS Release 11.2 F, all NBP access lists were applied to inbound interfaces by default. If you are using Cisco IOS 11.2 F or later software, the default interface direction for all access lists, including NBP access lists, is outbound. In order to retain the inbound direction of access lists created with previous Cisco IOS software releases, you must specify an inbound interface for all NBP access lists using the **appletalk access-group** command.

---

## Create Data Packet Filters

A *data packet filter* checks data packets being received on an interface or sent out an interface. If the source network for the packets has access denied, these packets are discarded.

Data packet filters use access lists that define conditions for networks, cable ranges, and zones.

When you apply a data packet filter to an interface, ensure that all networks or cable ranges within a zone are governed by the same filters. For example, create a filter that works in the following way. If the router receives a packet from a network that is in a zone that contains an explicitly denied network, the router discards the packet.

To create a data packet filter, perform the following tasks:

**Step 1**    Create a network-only access list as described in the "Create Zone Access Lists" and "Create IP-Style Access Lists" sections earlier in this chapter.

**Step 2**    Apply a data packet filter to an interface.

To apply the data packet filter to an interface, perform the following task in interface configuration mode:

| Task | Command |
|------|---------|
| Apply the data packet filter to the interface. | **appletalk access-group** *access-list-number* [**in** | **out**] |

For an example of how to create data packet filters, see the "AppleTalk Access List Examples" section near the end of this chapter.

## Create Routing Table Update Filters

Routing table update filters control which updates the local routing table accepts and which routes the local router advertises in its routing updates. You create distribution lists to control the filtering of routing updates.

Filters for incoming routing updates use access lists that define conditions for networks and cable ranges only. Filters for outgoing routing updates use access lists that define conditions for networks and cable ranges and for zones.

When filtering incoming routing updates, each network number and cable range in the update is checked against the access list. If you have not applied an access list to the interface, all network numbers and cable ranges in the routing update are added to the routing table. If an access list has been applied to the interface, only network numbers and cable ranges that are not explicitly or implicitly denied are added to the routing table.

The following conditions are also applied when filtering routing updates generated by the local router:

- The network number or cable range is not a member of a zone that is explicitly or implicitly denied.
- If partial zones are permitted, at least one network number or cable range that is a member of the zone is explicitly or implicitly permitted. If partial zones are not permitted (the default), all network numbers or cable ranges that are members of the zone are explicitly or implicitly permitted.

### Create Routing Table Update Filters for Incoming Updates

To create a filter for routing table updates received on an interface, perform the following tasks:

Step 1　　Create an access list as described in the "Create IP-Style Access Lists" section of this chapter.

Step 2　　Apply a routing table update filter to an interface.

---

**NOTES**

Cisco IOS software ignores zone entries. Therefore, ensure that access lists used to filter incoming routing updates do not contain any zone entries.

---

To apply the filter to incoming routing updates on an interface, perform the following task in interface configuration mode:

| Task | Command |
|------|---------|
| Apply the routing update filter. | **appletalk distribute-list** *access-list-number* **in** |

For an example of how to create a filter for incoming routing table updates, see the "AppleTalk Access List Examples" section near the end of this chapter.

### Create Routing Table Update Filters for Outgoing Updates

To create a filter for routing table updates sent out an interface, perform the following tasks:

**Step 1**   Create an access list as described in the "Create Zone Access Lists" and "Create IP-Style Access Lists" sections of this chapter.

**Step 2**   Apply a routing table update filter to an interface.

---

**NOTES**

You can use zone entries in access lists used to filter outgoing routing updates.

---

To apply a filter to routing updates sent out on an interface, perform the following task in interface configuration mode:

| Task | Command |
|------|---------|
| Apply the routing update filter. | **appletalk distribute-list** *access-list-number* **out** |

---

**NOTES**

AppleTalk zone access lists on an Enhanced IGRP interface do not filter the distribution of Enhanced IGRP routes. When the **appletalk distribute-list out** command is applied to an Enhanced IGRP interface, any **access-list zone** commands in the specified access list are ignored.

---

## Create GetZoneList (GZL) Filters

The Macintosh Chooser uses ZIP GZL requests to compile a list of zones from which the user can select services. Any router on the same network as the Macintosh can respond to these requests with a GZL reply. You can create a GZL filter to control which zones the Cisco IOS software mentions in its GZL replies. This has the effect of controlling the list of zones that are displayed by the Chooser.

When defining GZL filters, you should ensure that all routers on the same network filter GZL replies identically. Otherwise, the Chooser will list different zones, depending on which device responded to the request. Also, inconsistent filters can result in zones appearing and disappearing every few seconds when the user remains in the Chooser. Because of these inconsistencies, you should normally apply GZL filters only when all routers in the internetwork are Cisco routers, unless the routers from other vendors have a similar feature.

When a ZIP GZL reply is generated, only zones that satisfy the following conditions are included:

- If partial zones are permitted, at least one network number or cable range that is a member of the zone is explicitly or implicitly permitted.

- If partial zones are not permitted (the default), all network numbers or cable ranges that are members of the zone are explicitly or implicitly permitted.

- The zone is explicitly or implicitly permitted.

Replies to GZL requests also are filtered by any outgoing routing update filter that has been applied to the same interface. You must apply a GZL filter only if you want additional filtering to be applied to GZL replies. This filter is rarely needed, except to eliminate zones that do not contain user services.

Using a GZL filter is not a complete replacement for anonymous network numbers. To prevent users from seeing a zone, all routers must implement the GZL filter. If any devices on the network are from other vendors, the GZL filter will not have a consistent effect.

To create a GZL filter, perform the following tasks:

**Step 1**    Create an access list as described in the "Create Zone Access Lists" section of this chapter.

**Step 2**    Apply a GZL filter to an interface.

To apply the GZL filter to an interface, perform the following task in interface configuration mode:

| Task | Command |
| --- | --- |
| Apply the GZL filter. | **appletalk getzonelist-filter** *access-list-number* |

For an example of how to create GZL filters, see the "GZL and ZIP Reply Filter Examples" section near the end of this chapter.

### Enable ZIP Reply Filters

ZIP reply filters limit the visibility of zones from routers in unprivileged regions throughout the internetwork. These filters filter the zone list for each network provided by a router to neighboring devices to remove restricted zones.

ZIP reply filters apply to downstream routers, not to end stations on networks attached to the local router. With ZIP reply filters, when downstream routers request the names of zones in a network, the local router replies with the names of visible zones only. It does not reply with the names of zones that have been hidden with a ZIP reply filter. To filter zones from end stations, use GZL filters.

ZIP reply filters determine which networks and cable ranges the Cisco IOS software sends out in routing updates. Before sending out routing updates, the software excludes the networks and cable ranges whose zones have been completely denied access by ZIP reply filters. Excluding this information ensures that routers receiving these routing updates do not send unnecessary ZIP requests.

To create a ZIP reply filter, perform the following tasks:

**Step 1**    Create an access list as described in the "Create Zone Access Lists" section of this chapter.

**Step 2**    Apply a ZIP reply filter to an interface.

To apply the ZIP reply filter to an interface, perform the following task in interface configuration mode:

| Task | Command |
|------|---------|
| Apply the ZIP reply filter. | **appletalk zip-reply-filter** *access-list-number* |

For an example of how to create GZL and ZIP reply filters, see the "GZL and ZIP Reply Filter Examples" section near the end of this chapter.

### Enable Partial Zone Filters

If access to any network in a zone is denied, access to that zone is also denied by default. However, if you enable partial zones, access to other networks in that zone is no longer denied.

The permitting of partial zones provides IP-style access control. If enabled, the access control list behavior associated with prior software releases is restored. In addition, NBP cannot ensure the consistency and uniqueness of name bindings.

If you permit partial zones, AppleTalk cannot maintain consistency for the nodes in the affected zones, and the results are undefined. With this option enabled, an inconsistency is created for the zone, and several assumptions made by some AppleTalk protocols are no longer valid.

To enable partial zone filters, perform the following task in global configuration mode:

| Task | Command |
| --- | --- |
| Permit access to networks in a zone in which access to another network in that zone is denied. | **appletalk permit-partial-zones** |

Permitting partial zones affects the outgoing routing update and GZL filters.

## CONFIGURING THE NAME DISPLAY FACILITY

The AppleTalk Name Binding Protocol (NBP) associates AppleTalk network entity names (that is, AppleTalk network-addressable services) with network addresses. NBP allows you to specify descriptive or symbolic names for entities instead of their numerical addresses. When you specify the name of an AppleTalk device, NBP translates the device's entity name into the device's network address. The name binding process includes name registration, name confirmation, name deletion, and name lookup.

Node addresses can change frequently because AppleTalk uses dynamic addresses. Therefore, NBP associates numerical node addresses with aliases that continue to reference the correct addresses if the addresses change. These node addresses do not change very frequently because each device keeps track of the last node number it was assigned. Typically, node numbers change only if a device is shut down for an extended period of time or if it is moved to another network segment.

To control the name display facility, perform one or both of the following tasks in global configuration mode:

| Task | Command |
| --- | --- |
| Specify which service types are retained in the name cache. | **appletalk lookup-type** *service-type* |
| Set the interval between service pollings by the router on its AppleTalk interfaces. | **appletalk name-lookup-interval** *seconds* |

## SETTING UP SPECIAL CONFIGURATIONS

To set up special configurations, perform the tasks in the following sections, based on desired service implementations:

- Configure AURP
- Configure Free-Trade Zones

- Configure SNMP over DDP in AppleTalk Networks
- Configure AppleTalk Tunneling
- Configure AppleTalk MacIP
- Configure IPTalk
- Configure SMRP over AppleTalk

## Configure AURP

The AppleTalk Update Routing Protocol (AURP) is a standard Apple Computer routing protocol that provides enhancements to the AppleTalk routing protocols that are compatible with AppleTalk Phase 2. The primary function of AURP is to connect two or more noncontiguous AppleTalk internetworks that are separated by a non-AppleTalk network (such as IP). In these configurations, you would want to use AURP instead of RTMP because AURP sends fewer routing packets than RTMP.

You configure AURP on a tunnel interface. Tunneling encapsulates an AppleTalk packet inside an IP packet, which is sent across the backbone to a destination router. The destination device then extracts the AppleTalk packet and, if necessary, routes it to an AppleTalk network. The encapsulated packet benefits from any features normally applied to IP packets, including fragmentation, default routes, and load balancing.

After you configure an AppleTalk domain for AppleTalk interenterprise features, you can apply the features to a tunnel interface configured for AURP by assigning the domain number to the interface.

Because route redistribution is disabled by default, you need to enable it by using the **appletalk route-redistribution** command. Route redistribution is enabled by default only when Enhanced IGRP is enabled.

To configure AURP, perform the following tasks, beginning in global configuration mode:

| Task | Command |
|------|---------|
| **Step 1** Enable route redistribution. | **appletalk route-redistribution** |
| **Step 2** Configure an interface to be used by the tunnel. | **interface** *type number* |
| **Step 3** Configure an IP address. | **ip address** *ip-address mask* |
| **Step 4** Configure tunnel interface. | **interface tunnel** *number* |
| **Step 5** Create an AURP routing process. | **appletalk protocol aurp** |
| **Step 6** Specify the interface out of which the encapsulated packets are sent. | **tunnel source** {*ip-address* | *type number*} |
| **Step 7** Specify the IP address of the router at the far end of the tunnel. | **tunnel destination** {*hostname* | *ip-address*} |
| **Step 8** Enable AURP tunneling. | **tunnel mode aurp** |

You can configure AURP on a tunnel interface to inherit AppleTalk interenterprise routing remapping, hop count reduction, and loop detection characteristics configured for a specific AppleTalk domain. To do so, these features must first be configured for the AppleTalk domain using the commands described in the tasks "Enable AppleTalk Interenterprise Routing," "Remap Network Numbers," and "Control Hop Count" within the section "Configuring AppleTalk Interenterprise Routing" later in this chapter.

To configure AURP for AppleTalk interenterprise routing features, perform the following tasks, starting in global configuration mode:

| Task | | Command |
| --- | --- | --- |
| Step 1 | Specify the tunnel interface. | **interface tunnel** *number* |
| Step 2 | Create an AURP routing process. | **appletalk protocol aurp** |
| Step 3 | Enable AURP tunneling. | **tunnel mode aurp** |
| Step 4 | Specify the interface out of which the encapsulated packets are sent. | **tunnel source** {*ip-address* | *type number*} |
| Step 5 | Specify the IP address of the router at the far end of the tunnel. | **tunnel destination** {*hostname* | *ip-address*} |
| Step 6 | Assign the number of the predefined AppleTalk domain to which the AppleTalk interenterprise features are configured to the tunnel interface configured for AURP. | **appletalk domain-group** *domain-number* |

For an example of how to configure AURP on a tunnel interface to inherit AppleTalk interenterprise routing features for a specific AppleTalk domain, see the "AppleTalk Interenterprise Routing over AURP Example" section near the end of this chapter.

By default, AURP sends routing updates every 30 seconds. To modify this interval, perform the following task in global configuration mode:

| Task | Command |
| --- | --- |
| Set the minimum interval between AURP routing updates. | **appletalk aurp update-interval** *seconds* |

To set the AURP last-heard-from timer value, perform the following task in interface configuration mode:

| Task | Command |
|------|---------|
| Set the AURP last-heard-from timer value. | **appletalk aurp tickle-time** *seconds* |

## Configure Free-Trade Zones

A free-trade zone is a part of an AppleTalk internetwork that is accessible by two other parts of the internetwork, neither of which can access the other. You might want to create a free-trade zone to allow the exchange of information between two organizations that otherwise want to keep their internetworks isolated from each other or that do not have physical connectivity with one another.

To establish a free-trade zone, perform the following task in interface configuration mode:

| Task | Command |
|------|---------|
| Establish a free-trade zone. | **appletalk free-trade-zone** |

For an example of how to configure a free-trade zone, see the "Hiding and Sharing Resources with Access List Examples" section and the "Establishing a Free-Trade Zone Example" section near the end of this chapter.

## Configure SNMP over DDP in AppleTalk Networks

The Simple Network Management Protocol (SNMP) normally uses the IP connectionless datagram service, the User Datagram Protocol (UDP), to monitor network entities. The Cisco IOS software lets you run SNMP using Datagram Delivery Protocol (DDP), the AppleTalk datagram service. Use DDP if you have SNMP consoles running on a Macintosh.

You must configure AppleTalk routing globally and on an interface basis before you configure SNMP for the router; therefore, you need to disable SNMP, as shown in the following task table.

To configure SNMP in AppleTalk networks, perform the following tasks, starting in global configuration mode:

| Task | Command |
|------|---------|
| **Step 1** Disable SNMP. | **no snmp server** |
| **Step 2** Enable AppleTalk routing. | **appletalk routing** |
| **Step 3** Enable AppleTalk event logging. | **appletalk event-logging** |
| **Step 4** Enter interface configuration mode. | **interface** *type number* |

| Task | Command |
|------|---------|
| **Step 5** Enable IP routing on the interface. | **ip address** *ip-address mask* |
| **Step 6** Enable AppleTalk routing on the interface. | **appletalk cable-range** *cable-range* [*network.node*] |
| **Step 7** Set a zone name for the AppleTalk network. | **appletalk zone** *zone-name* |
| **Step 8** Enable SNMP server operations. | **snmp-server community** *string* [**RO**] [**RW**] [*number*] |

For an example of how to configure SNMP, see the "SNMP Example" section near the end of this chapter.

## Configure AppleTalk Tunneling

When connecting two AppleTalk networks with a non-AppleTalk backbone such as IP, the relatively high bandwidth consumed by the broadcasting of Routing Table Maintenance Protocol (RTMP) data packets can severely hamper the backbone's network performance. You can solve this problem by tunneling AppleTalk through a foreign protocol, such as IP. Tunneling encapsulates an AppleTalk packet inside the foreign protocol packet, which is then sent across the backbone to a destination router. The destination router then de-encapsulates the AppleTalk packet and, if necessary, routes the packet to a normal AppleTalk network. Because the encapsulated AppleTalk packet is sent in a directed manner to a remote IP address, bandwidth usage is greatly reduced. Furthermore, the encapsulated packet benefits from any features normally enjoyed by IP packets, including default routes and load balancing.

There are two ways to tunnel AppleTalk. The first method implements Cayman tunneling as designed by Cayman Systems. This method enables routers to interoperate with Cayman GatorBoxes. The second method is a proprietary tunnel protocol known as generic routing encapsulation (GRE).

When you use Cayman tunneling, you can have Cisco routers at either end of the tunnel, or you can have a GatorBox at one end and a Cisco router at the other end. When you use GRE tunneling, you must have Cisco routers at both ends of the tunnel connection.

Multiple tunnels originating from the router are supported.

Logically, tunnels are point-to-point links. This requires that you configure a separate tunnel for each link.

To configure a Cayman tunnel, perform the following tasks in interface configuration mode:

| Task | | Command |
|------|---|---------|
| Step 1 | Configure a tunnel interface. | **interface tunnel** *number* |
| Step 2 | Specify the interface out of which the encapsulated packets are sent. | **tunnel source** {*ip-address* | *type number*} |
| Step 3 | Specify the IP address of the router at the far end of the tunnel. | **tunnel destination** {*hostname* | *ip-address*} |
| Step 4 | Enable Cayman tunneling. | **tunnel mode cayman** |

___

**CAUTION**

Do not configure a Cayman tunnel with an AppleTalk network address.

___

To configure a GRE tunnel, perform the following tasks:

| Task | | Command |
|------|---|---------|
| Step 1 | Configure a tunnel interface. | **interface tunnel** *number* |
| Step 2 | Specify the interface out of which the encapsulated packets are sent. | **tunnel source** {*ip-address* | *type number*} |
| Step 3 | Specify the IP address of the router at the far end of the tunnel. | **tunnel destination** {*hostname* | *ip-address*} |
| Step 4 | Enable GRE tunneling. | **tunnel mode gre ip** |

## Configure AppleTalk MacIP

Cisco IOS software implements MacIP, which is a protocol that allows routing of IP datagrams to IP clients using the DDP for low-level encapsulation.

### Cisco Implementation of AppleTalk MacIP

Cisco IOS software implements the MacIP address management and routing services described in the draft Internet RFC, *A Standard for the Transmission of Internet Packets over AppleTalk Networks*. Cisco's implementation of MacIP conforms to the September 1991 draft RFC, with the following exceptions:

- The software does not fragment IP datagrams that exceed the DDP maximum transmission unit (MTU) and that are bound for DDP clients of MacIP.
- The software does not route to DDP clients outside of configured MacIP client ranges.

## When to Use AppleTalk MacIP

Some situations require the use of MacIP. For example, if some of your Macintosh users use Apple-Talk Remote Access or are connected to the network using LocalTalk or PhoneNet cabling systems, then MacIP is required to provide access to IP network servers for those users.

MacIP services also can be useful when you are managing IP address allocations for a large, dynamic Macintosh population.

## Advantages of Using MacIP

The following are advantages to using MacIP when you are managing IP address allocations for a large, dynamic Macintosh population:

- Macintosh TCP/IP drivers can be configured in a completely standard way, regardless of the location of the Macintosh. Essentially, the dynamic properties of AppleTalk address management become available for IP address allocation.
- You can modify all global parameters, such as IP subnet masks, DNS services, and default routers. Macintosh IP users receive the updates by restarting their local TCP/IP drivers.
- The network administrator can monitor MacIP address allocations and packet statistics remotely by using the Telnet application to attach to the console. This allows central administration of IP allocations in remote locations. For Internet sites, it allows remote technical assistance.

## Implementation Considerations

Consider the following items when implementing MacIP on Cisco routers:

- Each packet from a Macintosh client destined for an IP host or vice versa *must* pass through the router if the client is using the device as a MacIP server. The router is not always a necessary hop, so this increases traffic through the device. There is also a slight increase in CPU use that is directly proportional to the number of packets delivered to and from active MacIP clients.
- Memory usage increases in direct proportion to the total number of active MacIP clients (about 80 bytes per client).

Also, when you configure MacIP on the Cisco IOS software, you must configure AppleTalk as follows:

- AppleTalk routing must be enabled on at least one interface.
- IP routing must be enabled on at least one interface.
- The MacIP zone name you configure must be associated with a configured or *seeded* zone name.

- The MacIP server must reside in the AppleTalk zone.

- Any IP address specified in configuring a MacIP server using an **appletalk macip** command must be associated to a specific IP interface on the router. Because the Cisco IOS software is acting as a proxy for MacIP clients, you must use an IP address to which ARP can respond.

- If you are using MacIP to allow Macintoshes to communicate with IP hosts on the same LAN segment (that is, the Macintoshes are on the router interface on which MacIP is configured) and the IP hosts have extended IP access lists, these access lists should include entries to permit IP traffic destined for these IP hosts from the MacIP addresses. If these entries are not present, packets destined for IP hosts on the local segment will be blocked (that is, they will not be forwarded).

When setting up MacIP routing, keep the following address range issues in mind:

- Static and dynamic resource statements are cumulative, and you can specify as many as necessary. However, if possible, you should specify a single all-inclusive range rather than several adjacent ranges. For example, specifying the range 131.108.121.1 to 131.108.121.10 is preferable to specifying the ranges 131.108.121.1 to 131.108.121.5 and 131.108.121.6 to 131.108.121.10.

- Overlapping resource ranges (for example, 131.108.121.1 to 131.108.121.5 and 131.108.121.5 to 131.108.121.10) are *not* allowed. If it is necessary to change a range in a running server, use the negative form of the resource address assignment command (such as **no appletalk macip dynamic** *ip-address ip-address* **zone** *server-zone*) to delete the original range, followed by the corrected range statement.

- You can add IP address allocations to a running server at any time, as long as the new address range does not overlap with one of the current ranges.

### Configure AppleTalk MacIP Task List

To configure MacIP, perform the following tasks:

**Step 1**    Establish a MacIP Server for a Zone

**Step 2**    Allocate IP Addresses for Macintosh users. You do this by specifying at least one *dynamic* or *static* resource address assignment command for each MacIP server.

### Establish a MacIP Server for a Zone

To establish a MacIP server for a specific zone, perform the following task in global configuration mode:

| Task | Command |
|------|---------|
| Establish a MacIP server for a zone. | **appletalk macip server** *ip-address* **zone** *server-zone* |

Note that the MacIP server must reside in the default AppleTalk zone.

You can configure multiple MacIP servers for a router, but you can assign only one MacIP server to a zone, and you can assign only one IP interface to a MacIP server. In general, you must be able to establish an alias between the IP address you assign with the **appletalk macip server** global configuration command and an existing IP interface. For implementation simplicity, the address you specify in this command should match an existing IP interface address.

A server is not registered by NBP until at least one MacIP resource is configured.

### Allocate IP Addresses for Macintosh users

You allocate IP Addresses for Macintosh users by specifying at least one *dynamic* or *static* resource address assignment command for each MacIP server.

### Allocate IP Addresses Using Dynamic Addresses

*Dynamic clients* are those that accept any IP address assignment within the dynamic range specified. *Dynamic addresses* are for users who do not require a fixed address but can be assigned addresses from a pool.

To allocate IP addresses for Macintosh users if you are using dynamic addresses, perform the following task in global configuration mode:

| Task | Command |
|---|---|
| Allocate an IP address to a MacIP client. | **appletalk macip dynamic** *ip-address* [*ip-address*] **zone** *server-zone* |

For an example of configuring MacIP with dynamic addresses, see the "AppleTalk Interenterprise Routing over AURP Example" section near the end of this chapter.

### Allocate IP Addresses Using Static Addresses

*Static addresses* are for users who require fixed addresses for IP DNS services and for administrators who do not want addresses to change so that they always know the IP addresses of the devices on their network.

To allocate IP addresses for Macintosh users if you are using static addresses, perform the following task in global configuration mode:

| Task | Command |
|---|---|
| Allocate an IP address to be used by a MacIP client that has reserved a static IP address. | **appletalk macip static** *ip-address* [*ip-address*] **zone** *server-zone* |

For an example of configuring MacIP with static addresses, see the "MacIP Examples" section near the end of this chapter.

In general, it is recommended that you do not use fragmented address ranges in configuring ranges for MacIP. However, if this is unavoidable, use the **appletalk macip dynamic** command to specify as many addresses or ranges as required, and use the **appletalk macip static** command to assign a specific address or address range.

## Configure IPTalk

IPTalk is a protocol for encapsulating AppleTalk packets in IP datagrams. IPTalk is used to route AppleTalk packets across non-AppleTalk backbones and to communicate with applications on hosts that cannot otherwise communicate via AppleTalk, such as the Columbia AppleTalk Package (CAP). IPTalk also allows serial connections to use IPTalk Serial Line Internet Protocol (SLIP) drivers.

If your system is a Sun or Digital Equipment Corporation ULTRIX system, it may be possible to run CAP directly in a mode that supports EtherTalk. In this case, your system would look like any other AppleTalk node and does not need any special IPTalk support. However, other UNIX systems for which EtherTalk support is not available in CAP must run CAP in a mode that depends upon IPTalk.

The installation instructions for CAP refer to Kinetics IP (KIP) gateways and to the file *atalkatab*. If you use Cisco IPTalk support, it is not necessary (nor is it desirable) to use *atalkatab*. Cisco IPTalk support assumes that you want to use the standard AppleTalk routing protocols to perform all wide-area AppleTalk routing. KIP and *atalkatab* are based on an alternative routing strategy in which AppleTalk packets are transmitted using IP routing. It is possible to use both strategies at the same time; however, the interaction between the two routing techniques is not well defined.

If your network has other vendors' routers that support *atalkatab*, you should disable *atalkatab* support on them to avoid mixing the routing strategies. The installation instructions provided with some of these products encourage you to use *atalkatab* for complex networks. However, with Cisco routers this is not necessary because Cisco's implementation of IPTalk integrates IPTalk into the standard AppleTalk network routing.

The network diagram in Figure 2–1 illustrates how you should set up IPTalk. In this configuration, you enable both standard AppleTalk (EtherTalk) and IPTalk on the Ethernet networks on Router A and Router B. These routers then use EtherTalk to communicate with the LocalTalk routers and Macintosh computers and IPTalk to communicate with the UNIX systems. On the LocalTalk routers, you also should enable both EtherTalk and IPTalk, making sure you configure IPTalk with *atalkatab* disabled. These routers then use IPTalk to communicate with the UNIX systems adjacent to them and EtherTalk to communicate with the remainder of the AppleTalk network. This config-uration strategy minimizes the number of hops between routers. If you did not enable IPTalk on the LocalTalk routers, systems on the LocalTalk router that wanted to communicate with the adjacent

UNIX system would have to go through Router A or Router B. This creates an unnecessary extra hop.

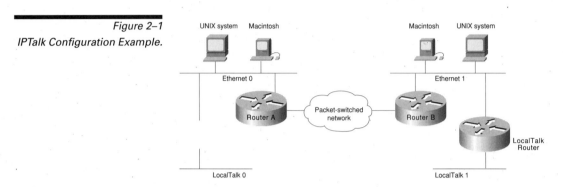

**Figure 2–1**
*IPTalk Configuration Example.*

---

**NOTES**

In the configuration in Figure 2–1, all traffic between systems on the left and right sides of the packet-switched network transit via Routers A and B using AppleTalk routing. If you were to enable *atalkatab* support on the LocalTalk routers, this would establish a hidden path between Routers A and B, unknown to the standard AppleTalk routing protocols. In a large network, this could result in traffic taking inexplicable routes.

---

To configure IPTalk on an interface, perform the following tasks:

**Step 1**    Configure IP encapsulation of AppleTalk packets.

**Step 2**    Specify the UDP port number that is the beginning of the range of UDP ports used in mapping AppleTalk well-known DDP socket numbers to UDP ports.

## Configure IP Encapsulation of AppleTalk Packets

To allow AppleTalk to communicate with UNIX hosts running older versions of CAP that do not support native AppleTalk EtherTalk encapsulations, you must configure IP encapsulation of Apple-Talk packets. (Typically, Apple Macintosh users would communicate with these servers by routing their connections through a Kinetics FastPath router running KIP software.) Newer versions of CAP provide native AppleTalk EtherTalk encapsulations, so the IPTalk encapsulation is no longer required. Cisco implementation of IPTalk assumes that AppleTalk is already being routed on the backbone because there is currently no LocalTalk hardware interface for Cisco routers.

You configure IPTalk on a tunnel interface. Tunneling encapsulates an AppleTalk packet inside an IP packet which is sent across the backbone to a destination router. The destination device then extracts the AppleTalk packet and, if necessary, routes it to an AppleTalk network. The encapsulated packet benefits from any features normally applied to IP packets, including fragmentation, default routes, and load balancing.

Cisco implementation of IPTalk does not support manually configured AppleTalk-to-IP-address mapping. The address mapping provided is the same as the Kinetics IPTalk implementation when AppleTalk-to-IP-address mapping is not enabled. This address mapping works as follows: The IP subnet mask used on the router tunnel source interface on which IPTalk is enabled is inverted (ones complement). The result is then masked against 255 (0xFF hexadecimal), and the result of this is then masked against the low-order 8 bits of the IP address to give the AppleTalk node number.

The following example configuration illustrates how the address mapping is done:

```
interface Ethernet0
ip address 172.16.1.118 255.255.255.0
appletalk address 20.129
appletalk zone Native AppleTalk
interface Tunnel0
tunnel source Ethernet0
tunnel mode iptalk
appletalk iptalk 30 UDPZone
```

First, the IP subnet mask of 255.255.255.0 is inverted to give 0.0.0.255. This value then is masked with 255 to give 255. Next, 255 is masked with the low-order 8 bits of the interface IP address (118) to yield an AppleTalk node number of 118. This means that the AppleTalk address of the Ethernet 0 interface seen in the UDPZone zone is 30.118.

─ ◀ **NOTES** ▶ ──────────────────────────────────────────────────────

If the host field of an IP subnet mask for an interface is longer than 8 bits, it will be possible to obtain conflicting AppleTalk node numbers. For instance, if the subnet mask for the preceding Ethernet 0 interface is 255.255.240.0, the host field is 12 bits wide.

───────────────────────────────────────────────────────────────────

To configure IP encapsulation of AppleTalk packets, perform the following tasks in interface configuration mode:

| Task | | Command |
|------|--|---------|
| Step 1 | Configure an interface to be used by the tunnel. | **interface** *type number* |
| Step 2 | Configure an IP address. | **ip address** *ip-address mask* |
| Step 3 | Configure tunnel interface. | **interface tunnel** *number* |
| Step 4 | Specify the interface out of which the encapsulated packets are sent. | **tunnel source** {*ip-address* \| *type number*} |
| Step 5 | Enable IPTalk tunneling. | **tunnel mode iptalk** |

For an example of configuring IPTalk, see the "IPTalk Example" section near the end of this chapter.

## Specify the UDP Port Ranges

Implementations of IPTalk prior to April 1988 mapped well-known DDP socket numbers to privileged UDP ports, starting at port number 768. In April 1988, the Network Information Center (NIC) assigned a range of UDP ports for the defined DDP well-known sockets, starting at UDP port number 200, and assigned these ports the names at-nbp, at-rtmp, at-echo, and at-zis. Release 6 and later of the CAP program dynamically decide which port mapping to use. If there are no AppleTalk service entries in the UNIX system's /etc/services file, CAP uses the older mapping, starting at UDP port number 768.

The default UDP port mapping supported by Cisco's implementation of IPTalk is 768. If there are AppleTalk service entries in the UNIX system's /etc/services file, you should specify the beginning of the UDP port mapping range.

To specify the UDP port number that is the beginning of the range of UDP ports used in mapping AppleTalk well-known DDP socket numbers to UDP ports, perform the following task in global configuration mode:

| Task | Command |
| --- | --- |
| Specify the starting UDP port number. | appletalk iptalk-baseport |

For an example of configuring IPTalk, see the "IPTalk Example" section near the end of this chapter.

## Configure SMRP over AppleTalk

The Simple Multicast Routing Protocol (SMRP) provides an internetwork-wide multicast service that supports the sending of data from a single station to multiple stations on an internetwork with minimal packet replication. SMRP is a connectionless protocol that provides best-effort delivery of multicast packets. SMRP operates independently of the network layer in use. SMRP supports routing of multicast packets to multicast groups.

Cisco's current implementation of SMRP provides multicast routing functions over AppleTalk networks. Advanced multimedia applications, such as QuickTime Conferencing (QTC), allow for two or more machines to communicate in a session. By routing AppleTalk packets to all members of a multipoint group without replicating packets on a link, SMRP presents an economical and efficient way to support this kind of communication while conserving network bandwidth.

Cisco's implementation of SMRP can be characterized by the following aspects:

- Group membership services that determine which hosts receive multicast traffic. SMRP allows a host to register dynamically for the multicast sessions in which it elects to participate.
- Dynamic multicast routing that gives Cisco routers the capability to dynamically identify the optimum path for AppleTalk multicast traffic.

- "Just-in-time" packet replication services that duplicate a packet when it reaches forks in the group's destination path. Cisco routers send only one copy of each packet over each physical network.

- Fast switching of SMRP data packets that allows higher data traffic throughput and less CPU utilization.

Figure 2–2 shows how SMRP multicasting of packets proceeds across an AppleTalk network. The source router (Router 1) sends a multicast packet only once on the local AppleTalk network.

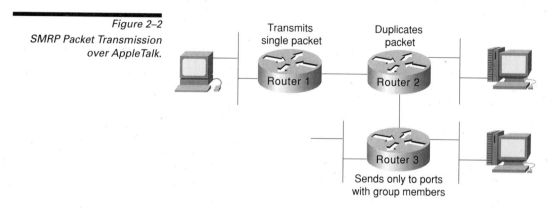

*Figure 2–2*
*SMRP Packet Transmission over AppleTalk.*

Applications produced by Apple Computer, Inc., such as QTC, support SMRP. To provide this support, Cisco Systems and Apple Computer, Inc., have entered into a partnership—becoming the first internetworking vendors to license the SMRP technology.

To enable SMRP routing over AppleTalk networks, perform the following task in global configuration mode:

| Task | Command |
|------|---------|
| Enable SMRP. | **smrp routing** |

To configure SMRP over AppleTalk for a specific interface, perform the following task in interface configuration mode:

| Task | Command |
|------|---------|
| Configure an SMRP on the interface. | **smrp protocol appletalk** [**network-range** *beginning-end*] |

NOTES

The **network-range** maps to the AppleTalk cable range by default.

Fast switching allows higher throughput by switching a packet using a cache created by previous packets. By default, fast switching is enabled on all SMRP ports. A network protocol and interface compose an SMRP port.

SMRP uses the forwarding table to forward packets for a particular SMRP group. For each group, the forwarding table lists the parent interface and address and one or more child interfaces and addresses. When data for an SMRP group arrives on the parent interface, the router forwards it to each child interface. The SMRP fast switching cache table specifies whether or not to fast switch SMRP data packets out the interfaces specified by the forwarding table.

To disable SMRP fast switching on an interface, perform the following task from interface configuration mode:

| Task | Command |
| --- | --- |
| Disable SMRP fast switching on an interface. | **no smrp mroute-cache protocol appletalk** |

## CONFIGURING APPLETALK CONTROL PROTOCOL FOR POINT-TO-POINT PROTOCOL

You can configure an asynchronous interface (including the auxiliary port on some Cisco routers) to use AppleTalk Control Protocol (ATCP) so that users can access AppleTalk zones by dialing into the router via Point-to-Point Protocol (PPP) to this interface. This is done through a negotiation protocol, as defined in RFC 1378. Users accessing the network with ATCP can run AppleTalk and IP natively on a remote Macintosh, access any available AppleTalk zones from the Chooser, use networked peripherals, and share files with other Macintosh users.

You create an internal network with the **appletalk internal-network** command. This is a virtual network and exists only for accessing an AppleTalk internetwork through the server.

To create a new AppleTalk zone, issue the **appletalk virtual-net** command and use a new zone name; this network number is then the only one associated with this zone. To add network numbers to an existing AppleTalk zone, use the existing zone name in the command; the network number is then added to the existing zone.

Routing is not supported on these interfaces.

To enable ATCP for PPP, perform the following tasks in interface configuration (asynchronous) mode:

| Task | Command |
|------|---------|
| **Step 1** Specify an asynchronous interface. | **interface async** *number* |
| **Step 2** Create an internal network on the server. | **appletalk virtual-net** *network-number zone-name* |
| **Step 3** Enable PPP encapsulation on the interface. | **encapsulation ppp** |
| **Step 4** Enable client-mode on the interface. | **appletalk client-mode** |

For an example of configuring ATCP, see the "AppleTalk Control Protocol Example" section near the end of this chapter.

## TUNING APPLETALK NETWORK PERFORMANCE

To tune AppleTalk network performance, you can perform one or more of the tasks described in the following sections:

- Control Routing Updates
- Assign Proxy Network Numbers
- Enable Round-Robin Load Sharing
- Disable Checksum Generation and Verification
- Control the AppleTalk ARP Table
- Control the Delay between ZIP Queries
- Log Significant Network Events
- Disable Fast Switching

### Control Routing Updates

The Routing Table Maintenance Protocol (RTMP) establishes and maintains the AppleTalk routing table. You can perform the tasks in the following sections to control packet routing and control routing updates:

- Disable the Processing of Routed RTMP Packets
- Enable RTMP Stub Mode
- Disable the Transmission of Routing Updates
- Prevent the Advertisement of Routes to Networks with No Associated Zones
- Set Routing Table Update Timers

### Disable the Processing of Routed RTMP Packets

By default, the Cisco IOS software performs strict RTMP checking, which discards any RTMP packets sent by routers not directly connected to the local device (that is, sent by devices that are not neighbors). This means that the local router does not accept any routed RTMP packets whose source is a remote network.

In almost all situations, you should leave RTMP checking enabled.

To disable RTMP checking and enable the processing of routed RTMP packets, perform the following task in global configuration mode:

| Task | Command |
| --- | --- |
| Disable strict checking of RTMP updates. | **no appletalk strict-rtmp-checking** |

### Enable RTMP Stub Mode

You can enable AppleTalk RTMP stub mode. This mode allows routers running Enhanced IGRP and RTMP to reduce the amount of CPU time that RTMP modules use. In this mode, RTMP modules send and receive only "stub" RTMP packets.

A stub packet is only the first tuple of an RTMP packet. The first tuple indicates the network number range assigned to that network. End nodes use stub packets to determine whether their node number is in the right network range.

To enable AppleTalk RTMP stub mode, perform the following task in interface configuration mode:

| Task | Command |
| --- | --- |
| Enable RTMP stub mode. | **appletalk rtmp-stub** |

### Disable the Transmission of Routing Updates

By default, routers receive routing updates from their neighboring devices and periodically send routing updates to their neighbors. You can configure the Cisco IOS software so that it receives routing updates but does not send any updates. You might want to do this to keep a particular router that is unreliable from sending routing updates to its neighbors.

To disable the transmission of routing updates, perform the following task in interface configuration mode:

| Task | Command |
| --- | --- |
| Disable the transmission of routing updates on an interface. | **no appletalk send-rtmps** |

### Prevent the Advertisement of Routes to Networks with No Associated Zones

NBP uses ZIP to determine which networks belong to which zones. The Cisco IOS software uses ZIP to maintain a table of the AppleTalk internetwork that maps network numbers to zone names.

By default, the software does not advertise routes to networks that have no associated zones. This prevents the occurrence of ZIP protocol storms, which can arise when corrupt routes are propagated and routers broadcast ZIP requests to determine the network-zone associations. By not advertising routes to networks that do not have associated zones, you limit any ZIP protocol storms to a single network, rather than allowing them to spread to the entire internetwork.

To allow the advertisement of routes to networks that have no associated zones, perform the following task in global configuration mode:

| Task | Command |
|---|---|
| Allow the advertisement of routes to networks that have no associated zones. | **no appletalk require-route-zones** |

The *user* zone lists can be configured to vary from interface to interface. However, this practice is discouraged because AppleTalk users expect to have the same user zone lists at any end node in the internetwork. This kind of filtering does not prevent explicit access via programmatic methods but should be considered a user optimization whereby unused zones are suppressed. Use other forms of AppleTalk access control lists to actually *secure* a zone or network.

### Set Routing Table Update Timers

Cisco IOS software sends routing table updates at regular intervals. In rare instances, you might want to change this interval, such as when a router is busy and cannot send routing updates every 10 seconds or when slower devices are incapable of processing received routing updates in a large network. If you do change the routing update interval, you must do so for *all* devices on the network.

---

**CAUTION**

Modifying the routing timers can degrade or destroy AppleTalk network connectivity. Many other AppleTalk router vendors provide no facility for modifying their routing timers, so adjusting Cisco AppleTalk timers such that routing updates do not arrive at these other routers within the normal interval might result in loss of information about the network or loss of connectivity.

To change the routing table update timers, perform the following task in global configuration mode:

| Task | Command |
| --- | --- |
| Change the routing update timers. | **appletalk timers** *update-interval valid-interval invalid-interval* |

## Assign Proxy Network Numbers

It is possible to have an AppleTalk internetwork in which some routers support only nonextended AppleTalk and others support only extended AppleTalk. You can enable interoperability between these two types of AppleTalk networks by assigning a proxy network number for each zone in which there is a device that supports only nonextended AppleTalk.

To assign proxy network numbers, perform the following task in global configuration mode:

| Task | Command |
| --- | --- |
| Assign a proxy network number for each zone in which there is a device that supports only nonextended AppleTalk. | **appletalk proxy-nbp** *network-number zone-name* |

For an example of how to configure proxy network numbers, see the "Proxy Network Number Example" section near the end of this chapter.

---

**CAUTION**

Do not also assign the proxy network number to a router or to a physical network.

---

You must assign one proxy network number for each zone. You can optionally define additional proxies with different network numbers to provide redundancy. Each proxy network number generates one or more packets for each forward request it receives but discards all other packets sent to it. Thus, defining redundant proxy network numbers increases the NBP traffic linearly.

## Enable Round-Robin Load Sharing

In order to increase throughput in the network, a router can use multiple equal-cost paths to reach a destination. By default, the router picks one best path and sends all traffic using this path. You can configure the router to remember two or more paths that have equal costs and to balance the traffic load across all of the available paths. (Note that when paths have differing costs, the Cisco IOS software chooses lower-cost routes in preference to higher-cost routes.)

The software then distributes output on a packet-by-packet basis in round-robin fashion. That is, the first packet is sent along the first path, the second packet along the second path, and so on. When the final path is reached, the next packet is sent to the first path, the next to the second path, and so on. This round-robin scheme is used regardless of whether fast switching is enabled.

Limiting the number of equal-cost paths can save memory on routers with limited memory or with very large configurations. Additionally, in networks with a large number of multiple paths and systems with limited capability to cache out-of-sequence packets, performance might suffer when traffic is split between many paths.

To set the maximum number of paths, perform the following task in global configuration mode:

| Task | Command |
|------|---------|
| Set the maximum number of equal-cost paths to a destination. | **appletalk maximum-paths** *paths* |

## Disable Checksum Generation and Verification

By default, the Cisco IOS software generates and verifies checksums for all AppleTalk packets (except routed packets). You might want to disable checksum generation and verification if you have older devices (such as LaserWriter printers) that cannot receive packets with checksums.

To disable checksum generation and verification, perform the following task in global configuration mode:

| Task | Command |
|------|---------|
| Disable the generation and verification of checksums for all AppleTalk packets. | **no appletalk checksum** |

## Control the AppleTalk ARP Table

You can perform the following tasks to control the AppleTalk ARP table:

- Set the timeout for ARP table entries
- Specify the time interval between the retransmission of ARP packets
- Specify the number of ARP retransmissions
- Disable the gleaning of ARP information from incoming packets

By default, entries in the AppleTalk ARP table are removed from the table if no update has been received in the last 4 hours. To change the ARP timeout interval, perform the following task in interface configuration mode:

| Task | Command |
| --- | --- |
| Set the timeout for ARP table entries. | **appletalk arp-timeout** *interval* |

AppleTalk ARP associates AppleTalk network addresses with media (data link) addresses. When AppleTalk must send a packet to another network node, the protocol address is passed to AppleTalk ARP, which undertakes a series of address negotiations to associate the protocol address with the media address.

If your AppleTalk network has devices that respond slowly (such as printers and overloaded file servers), you can lengthen the interval between AppleTalk ARP packets in order to allow the responses from these devices to be received. To do this, perform one or both of the following tasks in global configuration mode:

| Task | Command |
| --- | --- |
| Specify the time interval between retransmission of ARP packets. | **appletalk arp [probe | request] interval** *interval* |
| Specify the number of retransmissions that occur before abandoning address negotiations and using the selected address. | **appletalk arp [probe | request] retransmit-count** *number* |

The Cisco IOS software automatically derives ARP table entries from incoming packets. This process is referred to as *gleaning*. Gleaning speeds up the process of populating the ARP table. To disable the gleaning of ARP table entries, perform the following task in interface configuration mode:

| Task | Command |
| --- | --- |
| Disable the gleaning of ARP information from incoming packets. | **no appletalk glean-packets** |

## Control the Delay between ZIP Queries

By default, the Cisco IOS software sends ZIP queries every 10 seconds and uses the information received to update its zone table. To change the ZIP query interval, perform the following task in global configuration mode:

| Task | Command |
|------|---------|
| Set the ZIP query interval. | **appletalk zip-query-interval** *interval* |

## Log Significant Network Events

You can log information about significant network events performed on the router, including routing changes, zone creation, port status, and address. To do this, perform the following task in global configuration mode:

| Task | Command |
|------|---------|
| Log significant events. | **appletalk event-logging** |

## Disable Fast Switching

Fast switching allows higher throughput by switching a packet using a cache created by previous packets. Fast switching is enabled by default on all interfaces that support fast switching.

Packet transfer performance is generally better when fast switching is enabled. However, you may want to disable fast switching in order to save memory space on interface cards and to help avoid congestion when high-bandwidth interfaces are writing large amounts of information to low-bandwidth interfaces.

To disable AppleTalk fast switching on an interface, perform the following task in interface configuration mode:

| Task | Command |
|------|---------|
| Disable AppleTalk fast switching. | **no appletalk route-cache** |

## CONFIGURING APPLETALK ENHANCED IGRP

Enhanced IGRP is an enhanced version of the Interior Gateway Routing Protocol (IGRP) developed by Cisco Systems, Inc. Enhanced IGRP uses the same distance vector algorithm and distance information as IGRP. However, the convergence properties and the operating efficiency of Enhanced IGRP have improved significantly over IGRP.

## Benefits of Using AppleTalk Enhanced IGRP

Because Enhanced IGRP supports AppleTalk, IPX, and IP, you can use one routing protocol for multiprotocol network environments, minimizing the size of the routing tables and the amount of routing information.

## Convergence Technology

The convergence technology is based on research conducted at SRI International and employs an algorithm referred to as the Diffusing Update Algorithm (DUAL). This algorithm guarantees loop-free operation at every instant throughout a route computation and allows all routers involved in a topology change to synchronize at the same time. Devices that are not affected by topology changes are not involved in recomputations. The convergence time with DUAL rivals that of any other existing routing protocol.

## Enhanced IGRP Features

Enhanced IGRP offers the following features:

- Fast convergence—The DUAL algorithm allows routing information to converge extremely quickly.
- Partial updates—Enhanced IGRP sends incremental updates when the state of a destination changes instead of sending the entire contents of the routing table. This feature minimizes the bandwidth required for Enhanced IGRP packets.
- Neighbor discovery mechanism—This is a simple hello mechanism used to learn about neighboring routers. It is protocol independent.
- Scaling—Enhanced IGRP scales to large networks.

## Enhanced IGRP Components

Enhanced IGRP has the following four basic components:

- Neighbor Discovery/Recovery
- Reliable Transport Protocol
- DUAL Finite-State Machine
- Protocol-Dependent Modules

### Neighbor Discovery/Recovery

Neighbor discovery/recovery is the process that routers use to dynamically learn of other routers on their directly attached networks. Routers must also discover when their neighbors become unreachable or inoperative. Neighbor discovery/recovery is achieved with low overhead by periodically sending small hello packets. As long as hello packets are received, a device can determine that a neighbor is alive and functioning. After this status is determined, the neighboring routers can exchange routing information.

## Reliable Transport Protocol

The reliable transport protocol is responsible for guaranteed, ordered delivery of Enhanced IGRP packets to all neighbors. It supports intermixed transmission of multicast and unicast packets. Some Enhanced IGRP packets must be transmitted reliably and others need not be. For efficiency, reliability is provided only when necessary. For example, on a multiaccess network that has multicast capabilities (such as Ethernet), it is not necessary to send hellos reliably to all neighbors individually. Therefore, Enhanced IGRP sends a single multicast hello with an indication in the packet informing the receivers that the packet need not be acknowledged. Other types of packets (such as updates) require acknowledgment, and this is indicated in the packet. The reliable transport has a provision to send multicast packets quickly when there are unacknowledged packets pending. Doing so helps ensure that convergence time remains low in the presence of varying speed links.

## DUAL Finite-State Machine

The DUAL finite-state machine embodies the decision process for all route computations. It tracks all routes advertised by all neighbors. DUAL uses the distance information (as a routing *metric*) to select efficient, loop-free paths. DUAL selects routes to be inserted into a routing table based on feasible successors. A successor is a neighboring router used for packet forwarding that has a least-cost path to a destination that is guaranteed not to be part of a routing loop. When there are no feasible successors but there are neighbors advertising the destination, a recomputation must occur. This is the process whereby a new successor is determined. The amount of time it takes to recompute the route affects the convergence time. Recomputation is processor-intensive. It is advantageous to avoid recomputation if it is not necessary. When a topology change occurs, DUAL will test for feasible successors. If feasible successors exist, DUAL will use them in order to avoid unnecessary recomputation.

## Protocol-Dependent Modules

The protocol-dependent modules are responsible for network layer protocol-specific tasks. It is also responsible for parsing Enhanced IGRP packets and informing DUAL of the new information received. Enhanced IGRP asks DUAL to make routing decisions, but the results are stored in the AppleTalk routing table. Also, Enhanced IGRP is responsible for redistributing routes learned by other AppleTalk routing protocols.

## Cisco's Enhanced IGRP Implementation

AppleTalk Enhanced IGRP provides the following features:

- Automatic redistribution—By default, AppleTalk RTMP routes are automatically redistributed into Enhanced IGRP, and AppleTalk Enhanced IGRP routes are automatically redistributed into RTMP. If desired, you can turn off redistribution.

- Interface-specific decisions about routing protocols—You can configure AppleTalk interfaces to use either RTMP, Enhanced IGRP, or both routing protocols. If two neighboring routers are configured to use both RTMP and Enhanced IGRP, the Enhanced IGRP routing information supersedes the RTMP information. However, both devices continue to send RTMP routing updates.

  Because Enhanced IGRP supersedes RTMP, you can control the excessive bandwidth usage of RTMP on WAN links. Because a WAN link is a point-to-point link, there are no other devices on the link, and hence, there is no need to run RTMP to perform end-node router discovery. Using Enhanced IGRP on WAN links allows you to save bandwidth and, in the case of Public Switched Data Networks (PSDNs), traffic charges.

## Enhanced IGRP Configuration Task List

To configure AppleTalk Enhanced IGRP, complete the tasks in the following sections. At a minimum, you must create the AppleTalk Enhanced IGRP routing process. Configuring miscellaneous parameters is optional.

- Enable AppleTalk Enhanced IGRP
- Configure Miscellaneous Parameters

## Enable AppleTalk Enhanced IGRP

To create an AppleTalk Enhanced IGRP routing process, perform the following tasks:

| Task | Command |
|------|---------|
| **Step 1** Enable an AppleTalk Enhanced IGRP routing process in global configuration mode. | **appletalk routing eigrp** *router-number* |
| **Step 2** Enable Enhanced IGRP on an interface in interface configuration mode. | **appletalk protocol eigrp** |

For an example of how to enable AppleTalk Enhanced IGRP, see the "AppleTalk Access List Examples" section near the end of this chapter.

To associate multiple networks with an AppleTalk Enhanced IGRP routing process, you can repeat this task.

> **CAUTION**
>
> When disabling Enhanced IGRP routing with the **no appletalk routing eigrp** command, all interfaces enabled for only Enhanced IGRP (and not also RTMP) lose their AppleTalk configuration. If you want to disable Enhanced IGRP and use RTMP instead on specific interfaces, first enable RTMP on each interface using the **appletalk protocol rtmp** interface configuration command. Then, disable Enhanced IGRP routing using the **no appletalk routing eigrp** command. This process ensures that you do not lose AppleTalk configurations on interfaces for which you want to use RTMP.

## Configure Miscellaneous Parameters

To configure miscellaneous AppleTalk Enhanced IGRP parameters, perform one or more of the tasks in the following sections:

- Disable Redistribution of Routing Information
- Adjust the Interval between Hello Packets and the Hold Time
- Disable Split Horizon
- Adjust the Active State Time for Enhanced IGRP Routes
- Log Enhanced IGRP Neighbor Adjacency Changes
- Configure the Percentage of Link Bandwidth Used by Enhanced IGRP

### Disable Redistribution of Routing Information

By default, the Cisco IOS software redistributes AppleTalk RTMP routes into AppleTalk Enhanced IGRP and vice versa. Internal Enhanced IGRP routes are always preferred over external Enhanced IGRP routes. This means that if there are two Enhanced IGRP paths to a destination, the path that originated within the Enhanced IGRP autonomous system always will be preferred over the Enhanced IGRP path that originated from outside the autonomous system, regardless of the metric. Redistributed RTMP routes always are advertised in Enhanced IGRP as external.

To disable route redistribution, perform the following task in global configuration mode:

| Task | Command |
|------|---------|
| Disable redistribution of RTMP routes into Enhanced IGRP and Enhanced IGRP routes into RTMP. | **no appletalk route-redistribution** |

### Adjust the Interval between Hello Packets and the Hold Time

You can adjust the interval between hello packets and the hold time.

Routers periodically send hello packets to each other to dynamically learn of other devices on their directly attached networks. This information is used to discover who their neighbors are and to learn when their neighbors become unreachable or inoperative.

By default, hello packets are sent every 5 seconds. The exception is on low-speed, nonbroadcast, multiaccess (NBMA) media, where the default hello interval is 60 seconds. Low speed is considered to be a rate of T1 or slower, as specified with the bandwidth interface configuration command. The default hello interval remains 5 seconds for high-speed NBMA networks. Note that for the purposes of Enhanced IGRP, Frame Relay and Switched Multimegabit Data Services (SMDS) networks may or may not be considered to be NBMA. These networks are considered NBMA if the interface has not been configured to use physical multicasting; otherwise, they are considered not to be NBMA.

You can configure the hold time (in seconds) on a specified interface for the AppleTalk Enhanced IGRP routing process designated by the autonomous system number. The hold time is advertised in hello packets and indicates to neighbors the length of time they should consider the sender valid. The default hold time is 3 times the hello interval, or 15 seconds.

On very congested and large networks, the default hold time might not be sufficient time for all routers to receive hello packets from their neighbors. In this case, you may want to increase the hold time.

---

**NOTES**

Do not adjust the hold time without advising Cisco technical support.

---

To change the interval between hello packets and the hold time, perform the following task in interface configuration mode:

| Task | Command |
| --- | --- |
| Set the interval between hello packets and the hold time. | **appletalk eigrp-timers** *hello-interval hold-time* |

### Disable Split Horizon

Split horizon controls the sending of AppleTalk Enhanced IGRP update and query packets. When split horizon is enabled on an interface, these packets are not sent to destinations for which this interface is the next hop. This reduces the possibility of routing loops.

By default, split horizon is enabled on all interfaces.

Split horizon prevents route information from being advertised by a router out the interface that originated the information. This behavior usually optimizes communication among multiple routers, particularly when links are broken. However, with nonbroadcast networks (such as Frame Relay and SMDS), situations can arise for which this behavior is less than ideal. For these situations, you may want to disable split horizon.

To disable split horizon, perform the following task in interface configuration mode:

| Task | Command |
|------|---------|
| Disable split horizon. | **no appletalk eigrp-splithorizon** |

### Adjust the Active State Time for Enhanced IGRP Routes

By default, Enhanced IGRP routes remain active for one minute. When a route reaches this active state time limit of 1 minute, the Cisco IOS software logs an error and removes the route from the routing table.

You can adjust this active state time limit. To specify the length of time that Enhanced IGRP routes can remain active, perform the following task in global configuration mode:

| Task | Command |
|------|---------|
| Adjust the active state time limit. | **appletalk eigrp active-time** {*minutes* \| **disabled**} |

### Log Enhanced IGRP Neighbor Adjacency Changes

An adjacency is the next hop router. You can enable the logging of neighbor adjacency changes to monitor the stability of the routing system and to help you detect problems. By default, adjacency changes are not logged.

To enable logging of Enhanced IGRP neighbor adjacency changes, perform the following task in global configuration mode:

| Task | Command |
|------|---------|
| Enable logging of Enhanced IGRP neighbor adjacency changes. | **appletalk eigrp log-neighbor-changes** |

### Configure the Percentage of Link Bandwidth Used by Enhanced IGRP

By default, Enhanced IGRP packets consume a maximum of 50 percent of the link bandwidth, as configured with the **bandwidth** interface subcommand. If a different value is desired, use the **appletalk eigrp-bandwidth-percent** command. This command may be useful if a different level of link utilization is required, or if the configured bandwidth does not match the actual link bandwidth (it may have been configured to influence route metric calculations).

To configure the percentage of bandwidth that may be used by Enhanced IGRP on an interface, perform the following task in interface configuration mode:

| Task | Command |
|------|---------|
| Configure the percentage of bandwidth that may be used by Enhanced IGRP on an interface. | **appletalk eigrp-bandwidth-percent** *percent* |

For an example of how to configure the percentage of Enhanced IGRP bandwidth, see the "AppleTalk Enhanced IGRP Bandwidth Configuration Example" section near the end of this chapter.

## CONFIGURING APPLETALK INTERENTERPRISE ROUTING

AppleTalk interenterprise routing provides support for AppleTalk internets, or *domains*. AppleTalk interenterprise routing allows two or more AppleTalk domains to be connected through a domain router (which can also be a Cisco access server). AppleTalk interenterprise routing allows for the resolution of conflicting AppleTalk network numbers or cable ranges from different domains and hop-count reduction between domains.

### Understand AppleTalk Domains

An AppleTalk domain is a group of AppleTalk networks or cable ranges that are connected and that have the following characteristics:

- Each network number or cable range within a domain is unique within that domain.
- Each domain is separated from another domain by a domain router.
- There is no physical or virtual connection between the two AppleTalk domains other than through a domain router.

### Understand Domain Routers

The domain router uses split horizon across the entire domain, not just across an interface. This means that domain routers do not propagate routes learned from an interface in one domain back into that domain. Rather, it propagates routes only to other domains.

### AppleTalk Interenterprise Routing Features

AppleTalk interenterprise routing provides the following features:

- Network remapping—Allows you to remap remote network numbers to resolve numbering conflicts with network numbers on the local network segment.
- Hop-count reduction—Allows for the creation of larger internetworks. When you enable hop-count reduction, the hop count in a packet is set to 1 as it passes from one domain to

another. This allows you to circumvent the 15-hop limit imposed by DDP and RTMP when forwarding packets.

- Loop detection—Avoids having multiple routing table entries to the same remote network segment (domain). If the domain router detects a loop, it displays an error message on the domain router and shuts off domains. The presence of a loop implies that there is a connection between two separate domains that was not learned through any of the interfaces of the domain router.

- Fast switching—Has been implemented for networks that have been remapped or on which hop-count reduction has been configured.

## Redundant Paths between Domains

Note that only one domain router can separate two domains. That is, you cannot have two or more domain routers to create redundant paths between domains. You can, however, establish redundant paths between domains by connecting them through more than one interface on the domain router that separates them. Figure 2–3 illustrates this configuration. In this figure, one domain router separates domains A and B. Two of the router's interfaces are in domain A (Ethernet interfaces 3 and 4), and three are in domain B (Ethernet interfaces 0, 1, and 2), thus providing redundant connections between the domains. Figure 2–4 illustrates an improper configuration. This configuration would create adverse effects because domains A and B are connected by two domain routers.

*Figure 2–3*
*Allowed Configuration of Domain Router Connecting Two Domains.*

*Figure 2–4*
*Improper Configuration of Domain Routers Connecting Two Domains.*

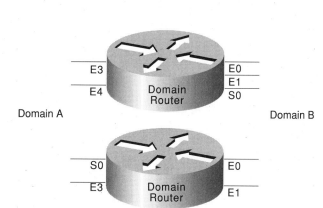

Currently, you can configure AppleTalk interenterprise routing only on routers running RTMP or Enhanced IGRP.

## AppleTalk Interenterprise Routing Task List

You configure AppleTalk interenterprise routing by completing the tasks described in the following sections. At a minimum, you must enable AppleTalk interenterprise routing. The remaining tasks are optional.

- Enable AppleTalk Interenterprise Routing
- Remap Network Numbers
- Control Hop Count

After you assign AppleTalk interenterprise routing remapping, hop-count reduction, and loop-detection features to an AppleTalk domain, you can attribute those characteristics to a tunnel interface configured for AURP by assigning the AppleTalk domain group number to the AURP tunnel interface.

## Enable AppleTalk Interenterprise Routing

To enable AppleTalk interenterprise routing, perform the following steps:

**Step 1**     Enable AppleTalk interenterprise routing on the router.

**Step 2**     Enable AppleTalk interenterprise routing on an interface.

To enable AppleTalk interenterprise routing, perform the following task in global configuration mode:

| Task | Command |
|------|---------|
| Create a domain and assign it a name and number. | **appletalk domain** *domain-number* **name** *domain-name* |

To enable AppleTalk interenterprise routing on an interface, perform the following task in interface configuration mode:

| Task | Command |
|------|---------|
| Assign a predefined domain number to an interface. | **appletalk domain-group** *domain-number* |

For an example of how to configure AppleTalk interenterprise routing, see the "AppleTalk Interenterprise Routing Example" section near the end of this chapter.

## Remap Network Numbers

When connecting two AppleTalk networks, a conflict can arise between network numbers or between cables ranges on one network and those on the other. You can avoid conflicts by remapping the remote network's network numbers or cable ranges.

Each domain can have two mapping ranges to which to remap all incoming or outgoing network numbers or cable ranges.

To remap the network numbers or cable ranges on inbound packets, perform the following task in global configuration mode:

| Task | Command |
| --- | --- |
| Remap packets inbound to the domain. | **appletalk domain** *domain-number* **remap-range in** *cable-range* |

To remap the network numbers or cable ranges on outbound packets, perform the following task in global configuration mode:

| Task | Command |
| --- | --- |
| Remap packets outbound from the domain. | **appletalk domain** *domain-number* **remap-range out** *cable-range* |

## Control Hop Count

When you join AppleTalk network segments to create domains, the distance across the combined internetworks is likely to exceed 15 hops, which is the maximum number of hops supported by RTMP. You can extend the network topology by configuring the Cisco IOS software to reduce the hop-count value of packets that traverse it.

Reducing the hop-count value allows an AppleTalk router to control the hop-count field in DDP packets so as to ensure that the packet reaches its final AppleTalk destination. Hop-count reduction allows the router to bypass the limitation of 16 hops before aging out packets. This feature is supported only on access servers and routers configured for AppleTalk Enhanced IGRP.

To enable hop-count reduction, perform the following task in global configuration mode:

| Task | Command |
| --- | --- |
| Enable hop-count reduction. | **appletalk domain** *domain-number* **hop-reduction** |

## CONFIGURING APPLETALK OVER WANS

You can configure AppleTalk over dial-on-demand routing (DDR), Frame Relay, SMDS, and X.25 networks. To do this, configure the address mappings as described in the appropriate chapters for each protocol.

### AppleTalk over DDR

To use AppleTalk over DDR, you must define AppleTalk static routes. You can configure the following two types of static routes:

- Static routes that have absolute precedence (that is, they always override any dynamically learned routes)
- Floating static routes that can be overridden by dynamically learned routes

Be careful when assigning static routes. When links associated with these static routes are lost, traffic may stop being forwarded or traffic may be forwarded to a nonexistent destination, even though an alternative path might be available.

---

**NOTES** ———————————————————————————————————————

When configuring AppleTalk over DDR, the zone name assigned to the interface must be unique. It cannot be the same as a zone name assigned to a static route. If the zone names are not unique, the sequence of AppleTalk initialization and dialer operation will cause the DDR interface to go up and down.

---

### *Configure Static Routes*

To add a static route for an extended or nonextended AppleTalk network, perform one of the following tasks in global configuration mode:

| Task | Command |
| --- | --- |
| Define a static route on an extended AppleTalk network. | **appletalk static cable-range** *cable-range* **to** *network.node* **zone** *zone-name* |
| Define a static route on a nonextended AppleTalk network. | **appletalk static network** *network-number* **to** *network.node* **zone** *zone-name* |

### *Configure Floating Static Routes*

You can use a floating static route to create a path of last resort that is used only when no dynamic routing information is available. To avoid the possibility of a routing loop occurring, floating static routes by default are not redistributed into other dynamic protocols.

To add a floating static route for an extended or nonextended AppleTalk network, perform one of the following tasks in global configuration mode:

| Task | Command |
| --- | --- |
| Define a floating static route on an extended AppleTalk network. | **appletalk static cable-range** *cable-range* **to** *network.node* **floating zone** *zone-name* |
| Define a floating static route on a nonextended AppleTalk network. | **appletalk static network** *network-number* **to** *network.node* **floating zone** *zone-name* |

For an example of how to configure AppleTalk over DDR, see the "AppleTalk over DDR Example" section near the end of this chapter.

## AppleTalk over X.25

For X.25, you can configure only a nonextended AppleTalk network. Logically, this network is the same as a LocalTalk network because both are *always* nonextended networks. All AppleTalk nodes within an X.25 network must be configured with the same AppleTalk network number. Also, the network numbers and zone names on both sides of the serial link must be the same. When mapping the AppleTalk address to the X.121 address of the router with the **x25 map** command, include the keyword **broadcast** to simulate the AppleTalk broadcast capability. This is necessary because X.25 does not support broadcasts, but AppleTalk does. The broadcast simulation is done as follows: If the broadcast flag is set, whenever a broadcast packet is sent, each X.121 address specified will receive it.

## MONITORING AND MAINTAINING THE APPLETALK NETWORK

The Cisco IOS software provides several commands that you can use to monitor and maintain an AppleTalk network. In addition, you can use network monitoring packages (such as Apple Computer's *Inter•Poll*) to verify that a router is configured and operating properly. Use the commands described in this section to monitor an AppleTalk network using both Cisco IOS software commands and network monitoring packages.

## Monitor and Maintain the AppleTalk Network Using Cisco IOS Software Commands

To monitor and maintain the AppleTalk network, perform one or more of the following tasks at the EXEC prompt:

| Task | Command |
| --- | --- |
| Enable recognition of pre-FDDITalk packets. | **appletalk pre-fdditalk** |
| Delete entries from the AppleTalk ARP (AARP) table. | **clear appletalk arp** [*network.node*] |

| Task | Command |
|---|---|
| Delete entries from the neighbor table. | **clear appletalk neighbor** [*neighbor-address* \| *all*] |
| Delete entries from the routing table. | **clear appletalk route** *network* |
| Reset AppleTalk traffic counters. | **clear appletalk traffic** |
| Clear the fast switching entries in the SMRP fast switching cache table. | **clear smrp mcache** |
| Diagnose basic AppleTalk network connectivity (user-level command). | **ping appletalk** *network.node* |
| Diagnose basic AppleTalk network connectivity (privileged command). | **ping** [**appletalk**] [*network.node*] |
| Display the AppleTalk access lists currently defined. | **show appletalk access-lists** |
| Display the routes to networks that are directly connected or that are one hop away. | **show appletalk adjacent-routes** |
| List the entries in the AppleTalk ARP table. | **show appletalk arp** |
| Display pending events in the AppleTalk AURP update-events queue. | **show appletalk aurp events** |
| Display entries in the AURP private path database. | **show appletalk aurp topology** |
| Display the contents of the AppleTalk fast switching cache. | **show appletalk cache** |
| Display domain-related information. | **show appletalk domain** [*domain-number*] |
| List the neighbors discovered by AppleTalk Enhanced IGRP. | **show appletalk eigrp neighbors** [*interface*] |
| Display information about interfaces configured for Enhanced IGRP. | **show appletalk eigrp interfaces** [*interface*] |
| Display the contents of the AppleTalk Enhanced IGRP topology table. | **show appletalk eigrp topology** [*network-number* \| **active** \| **zero-successors**] |
| Display information about the router's AppleTalk internetwork and other parameters. | **show appletalk globals** |
| Display AppleTalk-related interface settings. | **show appletalk interface** [**brief**] [*type number*] |
| Display the status of all known MacIP clients. | **show appletalk macip-clients** |

| Task | Command |
| --- | --- |
| Display the status of a device's MacIP servers. | **show appletalk macip-servers** |
| Display statistics about MacIP traffic. | **show appletalk macip-traffic** |
| Display a list of NBP services offered by nearby routers and by other devices that support NBP. | **show appletalk name-cache** |
| Display the contents of the NBP name registration table. | **show appletalk nbp** |
| Display information about the AppleTalk routers directly connected to any network to which the router is directly connected. | **show appletalk neighbors** [*neighbor-address*] |
| Display domain remapping information. | **show appletalk remap [domain** *domain-number* [{**in** \| **out**} [{**to** \| **from**} *domain-network*]]] |
| Display the contents of the AppleTalk routing table. | **show appletalk route** [*network* \| *type number*] |
| Display the process-level operations in all sockets in an interface. | **show appletalk sockets** [*socket-number*] |
| Display the defined static routes. | **show appletalk static** |
| Display the statistics about AppleTalk protocol traffic, including MacIP traffic. | **show appletalk traffic** |
| Display the contents of the zone information table. | **show appletalk zone** [*zone-name*] |
| Display the SMRP forwarding table. | **show smrp forward [appletalk** [*group-address*]] |
| Display global information about SMRP. | **show smrp globals** |
| Display the SMRP group table. | **show smrp group [appletalk** [*group-address*]] |
| Display the SMRP fast switching cache table. | **show smrp mcache** [**appletalk** [*group-address*]] |
| Display the SMRP neighbor table. | **show smrp neighbor [appletalk** [*network-address*]] |
| Display the SMRP port table. | **show smrp port [appletalk** [*type number*]] |
| Display the SMRP routing table. | **show smrp route [appletalk** [*network*] \| *type number*] |

| Task | Command |
|------|---------|
| Display all entries or specific entries in the SMRP traffic table. | **show smrp traffic** [**all** \| **group** \| **neighbor** \| **port** \| **route** \| **transaction**] |
| Enter test mode to test NBP protocols. | **test appletalk** |

## Monitor the AppleTalk Network Using Network Monitoring Packages

The Cisco IOS software supports network monitoring packages (such as Apple Computer's *Inter•Poll*), which are tools that use the AppleTalk responder and listener for verifying a router's configuration and operation. The software answers AppleTalk *responder* request packets. These request packets are received by the *listener*, which is installed on the AppleTalk interface name registration socket. The responder request packets include the bootstrap firmware version string, followed by the operating software version string. These strings are displayed in the Macintosh System version and the Macintosh printer driver version fields, respectively, and in applications such as Apple's *Inter•Poll*. The response packet contains strings similar to those displayed by the **show version** EXEC command.

The Cisco IOS software returns the following information in response to responder request packets:

- System bootstrap version (ROM version)
- Software version
- AppleTalk version (this is always 56, which is the first Apple Macintosh version that contained AppleTalk Phase 2 support)
- AppleTalk responder version (this is always 100, which indicates support of Version 1.0 responder packets)
- AppleShare status (this is reported as "not installed")

Figure 2–5 illustrates a typical output display for *Inter•Poll* that lists this information.

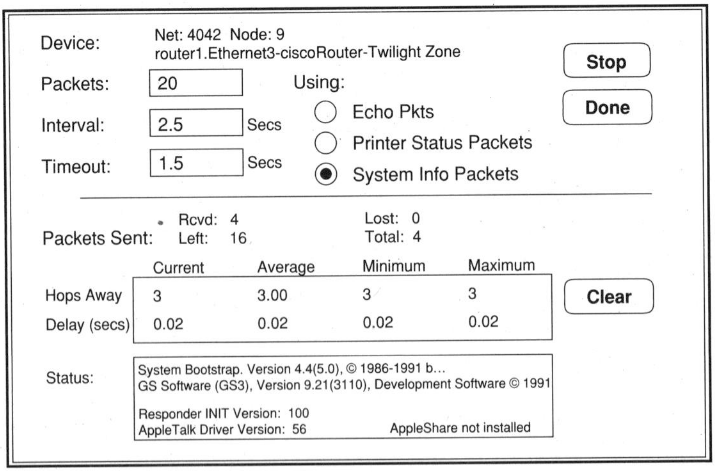

*Figure 2–5*
*Inter•Poll Output.*

## APPLETALK CONFIGURATION EXAMPLES

Use the following configuration examples in the following sections to help you configure AppleTalk routing:

- Extended AppleTalk Network Example
- Nonextended AppleTalk Network Example
- Nonextended Network in Discovery Mode Example
- AppleTalk Access List Examples
- Transition Mode Example
- AppleTalk Access List Examples
- GZL and ZIP Reply Filter Examples
- AppleTalk Interenterprise Routing over AURP Example
- SNMP Example
- MacIP Examples
- IPTalk Example
- AppleTalk Control Protocol Example
- Proxy Network Number Example
- AppleTalk Enhanced IGRP Bandwidth Configuration Example
- AppleTalk Interenterprise Routing Example
- AppleTalk over DDR Example
- AppleTalk Control Protocol for PPP Example

### Extended AppleTalk Network Example

The following example configures an extended AppleTalk network. It defines the zones Accounting and Personnel. The cable range of one allows compatibility with nonextended AppleTalk networks.

```
appletalk routing
interface ethernet 0
 appletalk cable-range 69-69 69.128
 appletalk zone Accounting
 appletalk zone Personnel
```

### Nonextended AppleTalk Network Example

The following example configures a nonextended AppleTalk network that allows routing between two Ethernet networks. Ethernet interface 0 is connected to network 1 at node 128, and Ethernet interface 1 is connected to network 2 at node 154. Network 1 is in the Twilight zone, and network 2 is in the No Parking zone. See Figure 2–6.

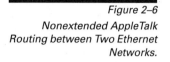
*Figure 2–6*
*Nonextended AppleTalk*
*Routing between Two Ethernet*
*Networks.*

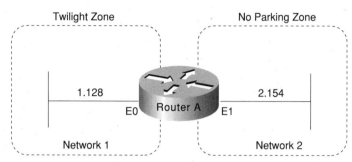

```
appletalk routing
!
interface ethernet 0
appletalk address 1.128
appletalk zone Twilight
!
interface ethernet 1
 appletalk address 2.154
 appletalk zone No Parking
```

## Nonextended Network in Discovery Mode Example

The following example configures a nonextended network in discovery mode. There are seed routers on both networks to provide the zone and network number information to the interfaces when they start. Router A supplies configuration information for Ethernet interface 1, and Router C supplies configuration information for Ethernet interface 0. See Figure 2–7.

*Figure 2–7*
*Routing in Discovery Mode.*

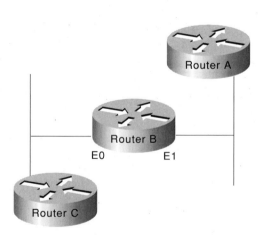

Use the following commands to configure this nonextended network in discovery mode:

```
appletalk routing
!
interface ethernet 0
 appletalk address 0.0
!
interface ethernet 1
 appletalk address 0.0
```

## AppleTalk Enhanced IGRP Example

The following example shows how to configure AppleTalk Enhanced IGRP. In this example, Ethernet interface 0 is configured for both Enhanced IGRP and RTMP routing, and serial interface 0 is configured for only AppleTalk Enhanced IGRP routing.

```
appletalk routing eigrp 1
appletalk route-redistribution
!
interface ethernet 0
 appletalk cable-range 10-10 10.51
 appletalk zone Ethernet 0
 appletalk protocol eigrp
!
interface serial 0
 appletalk cable-range 111-111 111.51
 appletalk zone Serial 0
 appletalk protocol eigrp
 no appletalk protocol rtmp
```

## Transition Mode Example

When in transition mode, the Cisco IOS software can route packets between extended and nonextended AppleTalk networks that exist on the same cable.

To configure transition mode, you must have two ports connected to the same physical cable. One port is configured as a nonextended AppleTalk network, and the other is configured as an extended AppleTalk network. Both ports must have unique network numbers because they are two separate networks. Figure 2–8 shows an example of the topology of this configuration.

*Figure 2–8*

*Transition Mode Topology and Configuration.*

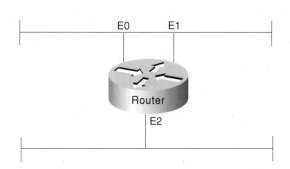

Use the following commands to configure this network. Note that networks 2-2 and 4-4 must have a cable range of one and a single zone in their zone lists. This is required to maintain compatibility with the nonextended network, network 3.

```
!This is an extended network.
interface ethernet 0
 appletalk cable-range 2-2
 appletalk zone No Parking
!
!This is a nonextended network.
interface ethernet 1
 appletalk address 3.128
 appletalk zone Twilight
!
!This is an extended network.
interface ethernet 2
 appletalk cable-range 4-4
 appletalk zone Do Not Enter
```

## AppleTalk Access List Examples

Cisco's implementation of AppleTalk provides several methods using access lists to control access to AppleTalk networks. The examples that follow illustrate these methods and show different approaches in applying access lists.

### Defining an Access List to Filter Data Packets Example

The following commands create access list 601:

```
!Permit packets to be routed from network 55.
access-list 601 permit network 55

!Permit packets to be routed from network 500.
access-list 601 permit network 500

!Permit packets to be routed from networks 900 through 950.
access-list 601 permit cable-range 900-950

!Do not permit packets to be routed from networks 970 through 990.
access-list 601 deny includes 970-990

!Do not permit packets to be routed from networks 991 through 995.
access-list 601 permit within 991-995

!Deny routing to any network and cable range not specifically enumerated.
access-list 601 deny other-access
```

To use access list 601 to filter data packets, you apply it to an interface (for example, Ethernet interface 0) using the following commands:

```
appletalk routing
interface ethernet 0
```

```
appletalk cable-range 50-50
appletalk zone No Parking
appletalk access-group 601 out
```

The following examples illustrate how Ethernet interface 0 would handle outgoing data packets:

- Packets sourced from cable range 50–50 would be permitted.

- Packets sourced from any network in the cable range 972–980 are denied because they explicitly match the **access-list deny includes 970-990** command.

### Defining an Access List to Filter Incoming Routing Table Updates Example

The following commands create access list 602. This example illustrates how packets are processed by access lists; you cannot create such a redundant access list.

```
access-list 602 permit network 55
access-list 602 permit cable 55-55
access-list 602 permit includes 55-55
access-list 602 permit within 55-55
```

To use this access list to filter routing table updates received on Ethernet interface 0, apply it to the interface using the following commands:

```
appletalk routing
interface ethernet 0
 appletalk cable-range 55-55
 appletalk zone No Parking
 appletalk distribute-list 602 in
```

The following tables illustrate the process for accepting or rejecting routing update information. If the outcome of a test is *true*, the condition passes the access list specification and the **distribute-list** command specification is then applied.

Routing updates containing network 55 would be processed as follows:

| Access List Command | Outcome of Test |
| --- | --- |
| access-list 602 permit network 55 | True |
| access-list 602 permit cable range 55-55 | False |
| access-list 602 permit includes 55-55 | True |
| access-list 602 permit within 55-55 | True |

Routing updates containing cable range 55-55 would be processed as follows:

| Access List Command | Outcome of Test |
| --- | --- |
| access-list 602 permit network 55 | False |
| access-list 602 permit cable range 55-55 | True |

| Access List Command | Outcome of Test |
|---|---|
| access-list 602 permit includes 55-55 | True |
| access-list 602 permit within 55-55 | True |

Routing updates containing cable range 55-56 would be processed as follows:

| Access List Command | Outcome of Test |
|---|---|
| access-list 602 permit network 55 | False |
| access-list 602 permit cable-range 55-56 | False |
| access-list 602 permit includes 55-56 | True |
| access-list 602 permit within 55-56 | False |

## Comparison of Alternative Segmentation Solutions

With the flexibility allowed by Cisco's access list implementation, determining the optimal method to segment an AppleTalk environment using access control lists can be unclear. The following scenario and configuration examples illustrate two solutions to a particular problem and point out the inherent advantages of using AppleTalk-style access lists.

Consider a situation in which a company wants to permit customers to have direct access to several corporate file servers. Access is to be permitted to all devices in the zones named MIS and Corporate, but access is restricted to the Engineering zone because the file servers in these zones contain sensitive information. The solution is to create the appropriate access lists to enforce these access policies.

The company's AppleTalk internetwork consists of the following networks and zones:

| Zone | Network Number or Cable Range |
|---|---|
| Engineering | 69–69<br>3<br>4160–4160<br>15 |
| MIS | 666–777 |

| Zone | Network Number or Cable Range |
|------|-------------------------------|
| Corporate | 70–70<br>55<br>51004<br>4262–4262 |
| World | 88–88<br>9<br>9000–9999 (multiple networks exist in this range) |

The router named Gatekeeper is placed between the World zone and the various company-specific zones. An arbitrary number of routers can be on either side of Gatekeeper. An Ethernet backbone exists on each side of Gatekeeper, connecting these other routers to Gatekeeper. On the router Gatekeeper, Ethernet interface 0 connects to the World backbone and Ethernet interface 1 connects to the Corporate backbone.

For the purposes of this configuration, assume Gatekeeper is the only router that needs any access list configuration. There are two solutions, depending on the level of security desired.

A minimal configuration might be as follows. In this configuration, the Engineering zone is secured, but all other zones are publicly accessible.

```
appletalk routing
access-list 603 deny zone Engineering
access-list 603 permit additional-zones
access-list 603 permit other-access

interface ethernet 0
appletalk network 3
 appletalk distribute-list 603 out
 appletalk access-group 603
```

A more comprehensive configuration might be the following, in which the Corporate and MIS zones are public and all other zones are secured:

```
appletalk routing
access-list 603 permit zone Corporate
access-list 603 permit zone MIS
access-list 603 deny additional-zones
access-list 603 permit other-access

interface ethernet 0
appletalk network 3
 appletalk distribute-list 603 out
 appletalk access 603
```

Both configurations satisfy the basic goal of isolating the Engineering servers, but the second example continues to be secure when more zones are added in the future.

### Defining an Access List to Filter NBP Packets Example

The following example adds entries to access list number 607 to allow forwarding of NBP packets from specific sources and deny forwarding of NBP packets from all other sources. The first command adds an entry that allows NBP packets from all printers of type *LaserWriter*. The second command adds an entry that allows NBP packets from all AppleTalk file servers of type *AFPServer*. The third command adds an entry that allows NBP packets from all applications called *HotShotPaint*. For example, an application might have a **zone** name of *Accounting* and an application might have a **zone** name of *engineering*, both having the object name of *HotShotPaint*. NBP packets forwarded from both applications are allowed.

The final **access-list other-nbps** command denies forwarding of NBP packets from all other sources.

```
access-list 607 permit nbp 1 type LaserWriter
access-list 607 permit nbp 2 type AFPServer
access-list 607 permit nbp 3 object HotShotPaint
access-list 607 deny other-nbps
```

To use this access list to filter inbound NBP packets on Ethernet interface 0, apply it to the interface using the following commands:

```
appletalk routing
interface ethernet 0
 appletalk cable-range 55-55
 appletalk zone No Parking
 appletalk access-group 607 in
```

The following example adds entries to access list number 608 to deny forwarding of NBP packets from two specific servers whose fully qualified NBP names are specified. It permits forwarding of NBP packets from all other sources.

```
access-list 608 deny nbp 1 object ServerA
access-list 608 deny nbp 1 type AFPServer
access-list 608 deny nbp 1 zone Bld3
access-list 608 deny nbp 2 object ServerB
access-list 608 deny nbp 2 type AFPServer
access-list 608 deny nbp 2 zone Bld3
access-list 608 permit other-nbps
access-list 608 permit other-access
```

To use this access list to filter NBP packets on Ethernet interface 0, apply it to the interface using the following commands:

```
appletalk routing
interface ethernet 0
 appletalk cable-range 55-55
 appletalk zone No Parking
 appletalk access-group 608 in
```

---

**NOTES**

Prior to Cisco IOS Release 11.2 F, all NBP access lists were applied to inbound interfaces by default. If you are using Cisco IOS 11.2 F or later software, the default interface direction for all access lists, including NBP access lists, is outbound. In order to retain the inbound direction of access lists created with previous Cisco IOS software releases, you must specify an inbound interface for all NBP access lists using the **appletalk access-group** command.

---

The following example creates an access list that denies forwarding of the following:

- All NBP Lookup Reply packets
- NBP packets from the server named *Bob's Server*
- Packets from all AppleTalk file servers of type *AFPServer*
- All NBP Lookup Reply packets that contain the specified named entities belonging to the zone *twilight*

```
access-list 600 deny nbp 1 LkReply
access-list 600 deny nbp 1 object Bob's Server
access-list 600 deny nbp 1 type AFPServer
access-list 600 deny nbp 1 zone twilight
access-list 600 permit other-nbps
```

There may be a case in which a fully qualified filter for *Bob's Server:AFPServer@twilight* will not work for an NBP Lookup Reply in response to a Lookup generated by the Chooser application. This is because the Lookup Request is transmitted as *=:AFPServer@twilight*, and the Lookup Reply from *Bob's Server* comes back as *Bob's Server:AFPServer@\**.

The following example creates an access list to filter a Lookup Reply generated by *Bob's Server* to a request by the Chooser application:

```
access-list 609 deny nbp 1 LkReply
access-list 609 deny nbp 1 object Bob's Server
access-list 609 deny nbp 1 type AFPServer
access-list 609 permit other-nbps
access-list 609 permit other-access
```

## Configuring Partial Zone Advertisement Example

Figure 2–9 illustrates a configuration in which you might want to allow partial advertisement of a particular zone.

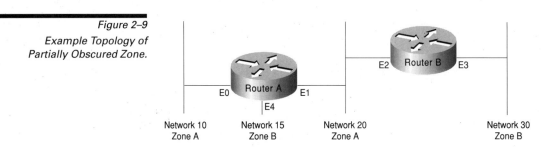

**Figure 2–9**

*Example Topology of Partially Obscured Zone.*

Assume that Router B includes a router-update filter (applied with the **appletalk distribute-list** interface configuration command) on the Ethernet interface 3 that does not accept routing table updates from network 10 or send routing table updates to that network.

```
access-list 612 deny network 10
access-list 612 permit other-access
interface ethernet 3
 appletalk distribute-list 612 out
 appletalk distribute-list 612 in
```

For Network 30, normal (default) behavior would be for Network 10 and Network 20 to be eliminated from any routing updates sent, although Network 15 would be included in routing updates (same zone as Network 30). Using the **appletalk permit-partial-zones** global configuration command has the following effects:

- If permit-partial-zones is enabled (**appletalk permit-partial-zones**), the routing updates exclude Network 10 but *include* Network 15 and Network 20.

- If permit-partial-zones is disabled (**no appletalk permit-partial-zones**), the routing updates exclude both Network 10 and Network 20 but still include Network 15. This is generally considered the preferred behavior and is the default.

Table 2–4 summarizes the associations between the networks shown in Figure 2–9. Table 2–5 details the effects of enabling and disabling partial-zone advertisement with the **appletalk permit-partial-zones** global configuration command.

**Table 2–4** *Zone and Interface Associations for Partial Zone Advertisement Example*

|  | **Network 10** | **Network 15** | **Network 20** | **Network 30** |
|---|---|---|---|---|
| Zone | A | B | A | B |
| Interfaces | Ethernet 0 | Ethernet 4 | Ethernet 1 Ethernet 2 | Ethernet 3 |

**Table 2–5** *Partial Zone Advertisement Control on Network 30*

| **Command Condition** | **Network 10** | **Network 15** | **Network 20** | **Network 30** |
|---|---|---|---|---|
| Enabled | Not Advertised on Network 30 | Advertised on Network 30 | Advertised on Network 30 | – |
| Disabled | Not Advertised on Network 30 | Advertised on Network 30 | Not Advertised on Network 30 | – |

## Hiding and Sharing Resources with Access List Examples

The following examples illustrate the use of AppleTalk access lists to manage access to certain resources.

### Establishing a Free-Trade Zone Example

The goal of the configuration shown in Figure 2–10 is to allow all users on all the networks connected to Routers A and B to be able to access the AppleShare servers AS1 and AS2 in the zone FreeAccessZone. A second requirement is to block cross access through this zone. In other words, users in the zones MIS1, MIS2, and LocalTalk (which are connected to Ethernet interface 0 on Router A) are not allowed access to any of the resources on networks connected to Ethernet interface 4 on Router B. Similarly, users in the zones Engineering, Test, and LocalTalk (which are connected to Ethernet interface 4 on Router B, interface E4) are not allowed access to any of the resources on networks connected to Ethernet interface 0 on Router A.

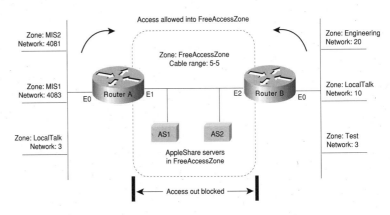

**Figure 2–10**

*Controlling Access to Common AppleTalk Network.*

**NOTES**

Although there are networks that share the same number on interfaces E0 and E4 and there are zones that have the same name, none have the same network number and zone specification (except Free-AccessZone). The two routers do *not* broadcast information about these networks through FreeAc-cessZone. The routers only broadcast the cable range 5–5. As configured, FreeAccessZone only sees itself. However, no other limitations have been placed on advertisements, so the FreeAccessZone range of 5–5 propagates out to the networks attached to E0 (Router A) and E4 (Router B); thus, re-sources in FreeAccessZone are made accessible to users on all those networks.

The following examples configure Router A and Router B for access control which is illustrated in Figure 2–10. You must configure only Ethernet interface 1 on Router A and Ethernet interface 2 on Router B to provide the desired access.

### Configuration for Router A

```
appletalk routing
!
interface ethernet 1
 appletalk cable-range 5-5
 appletalk zone FreeAccessZone
 appletalk free-trade-zone
```

### Configuration for Router B

```
appletalk routing
!
interface ethernet 2
 appletalk cable-range 5-5
 appletalk zone FreeAccessZone
 appletalk free-trade-zone
```

When configuring both routers, you do not need to define any access lists to prevent users on networks connected to Router A from accessing resources on networks connected to Router B and vice versa. The **appletalk free-trade-zone** interface configuration command implements the necessary restrictions.

### Restricting Resource Availability Example

In the preceding example, shared-resource access was granted to all users in the various AppleTalk zones connected to the two routers. At the same time, access between resources on either side of the common zone was completely denied. There might be instances in which a greater degree of control is required—possibly when resources in some zones are to be allowed access to resources in certain other zones but are denied access to other specific zones. Figure 2–11 illustrates such a situation.

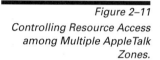

*Figure 2–11*
*Controlling Resource Access among Multiple AppleTalk Zones.*

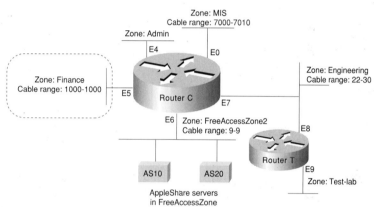

The following are the objectives of the configuration in Figure 2–11:

- Users in zones Engineering (E7) and MIS (E0) are to be allowed free access to each other.
- All users in all zones are to be allowed access to FreeAccessZone2 (E6).
- No users in any zone, with the exception of users in Finance, are to be allowed access to resources in Finance.

To meet these specifications, you define the following access lists:

```
access-list 609 permit cable 9-9
access-list 609 deny other-access
!
access-list 610 permit zone Finance
access-list 610 permit zone FreeAccessZone2
access-list 610 deny additional-zones
!
access-list 611 deny cable-range 1000-1000
```

```
access-list 611 deny cable-range 9-9
access-list 611 permit cable-range 7000-7010
access-list 611 permit cable-range 22-30
```

The effects of these access lists are as follows:

- Access list 609 is intended to be used to allow access to resources on FreeAccessZone2.

- Access list 610 is intended to be used to control access in and out of the zone Finance.

- Access list 611 is intended to be used to accommodate the requirement to allow users in zones Engineering and MIS to mutually access network resources.

### Configuration for Ethernet Interface 0

Ethernet interface 0 is associated with the MIS zone. Use the following commands to configure this interface:

```
interface ethernet 0
 appletalk cable-range 7000-7010
 appletalk zone MIS
 appletalk distribute-list 611 out
 appletalk distribute-list 611 in
```

Specifying access list 611 results in the following filtering:

- Advertisements of Finance are blocked.
- Advertisements between Engineering and MIS are allowed.

### Configuration for Ethernet Interface 5

Ethernet interface 5 is associated with the Finance zone. Use the following commands to configure this interface:

```
interface ethernet 5
 appletalk cable-range 1000-1000
 appletalk zone Finance
 appletalk distribute-list 610 out
 appletalk access-group 610
```

The effects of these access lists are as follows:

- With the **appletalk distribute-list out** interface configuration command, Finance is limited to accessing Finance and FreeAccessZone2 only.

- The **appletalk access-group** interface configuration command filters packet traffic. Thus, it blocks access to any devices in *Finance* from outside of this zone.

### Configuration for Ethernet Interface 6

Ethernet interface 6 is associated with the FreeAccessZone2 zone. Use the following commands to configure this interface:

```
interface ethernet 6
 appletalk cable 9-9
```

```
appletalk zone FreeAccessZone2
appletalk distribute-list 609 out
appletalk distribute-list 609 in
```

### Configuration for Ethernet Interface 7

Ethernet interface 7 is associated with the Engineering zone. The configuration for this interface mirrors that for Ethernet interface 0 because the users in both the MIS and Engineering zones must have access to each other's resources. Use the following commands to configure Ethernet interface 7:

```
interface ethernet 7
 appletalk cable-range 22-30
 appletalk zone Engineering
 appletalk distribute-list 611 out
 appletalk distribute-list 611 in
```

### Implicit Configuration of the Admin and Test-Lab Zones

Omitted from the configuration example in Figure 2–11 are any specific configuration commands pertaining to the zones Test-Lab (Ethernet interface 9 on Router T) and Admin (Ethernet interface 4 on Router C). No configuration is done for these zones because there are no requirements relating to them listed in the original objectives. The following access control is implicitly handled with the assignment of the stated access lists:

- Users in the Admin zone can see the Finance zone but cannot see resources in that zone. However, as for all zones, resources in FreeAccessZone2 are available, but none of the users in any of the other zones can access resources in Admin.

- In the absence of the assignment of access lists on Router T, users in Test-Lab can access the resources in the FreeAccessZone2 and Engineering zones. With the exception of Engineering, no other zones can access resources in Test-Lab.

## GZL and ZIP Reply Filter Examples

The examples in this section show how to configure GZL and ZIP reply filters, and they illustrate the differences between these two types of filters. Both examples use the configuration shown in Figure 2–12.

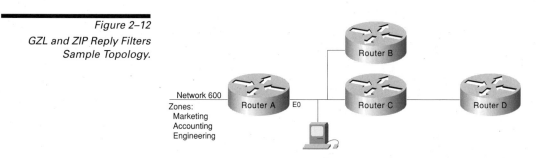

*Figure 2–12*
*GZL and ZIP Reply Filters*
*Sample Topology.*

Network 600
Zones:
Marketing
Accounting
Engineering

Both GZL and ZIP reply filters control the zones that can be seen on a network segment. GZL filters control which zones can be seen by Macintoshes on local network segments. These filters have no effect on adjacent routers. In order for GZL filters to work properly, all routers on the local segment must be configured with the same access list.

ZIP reply filters control which zones can be seen by adjacent routers and by all routers downstream from adjacent routers. You can use these filters to hide zones from all Macintoshes on all networks on adjacent routers and from all their downstream routers.

Using the configuration shown in Figure 2–12, you would use a GZL filter to prevent the Macintosh on the Ethernet 0 network segment from viewing the zones Engineering and Accounting on network 600. These zones would not be visible via the Macintosh's Chooser. To do this, you configure Router A as follows:

```
access-list 650 deny zone Engineering
access-list 650 deny zone Accounting
access-list 650 permit additional-zones
access-list 650 permit other-access
!
interface ethernet 0
 appletalk getzonelist-filter 650
```

Again using the configuration shown in Figure 2–12, you would use a ZIP reply filter to hide the Engineering and Accounting zones from Routers B and C. This filter would also hide the zones from Router D, which is downstream from Router C. The effect of this filter is that when these routers request the names of zones on network 600, the zones names Engineering and Accounting will not be returned.

```
access-list 650 deny zone Engineering
access-list 650 deny zone Accounting
access-list 650 permit additional-zones
access-list 650 permit other-access
!
interface ethernet 0
appletalk zip-reply-filter 650
```

## AppleTalk Interenterprise Routing over AURP Example

After you configure an AppleTalk domain for AppleTalk interenterprise features, you can apply the features to a tunnel interface configured for AURP by assigning the domain number to the interface.

The following example defines tunnel interface 0 and configures it for AURP. Then, it applies the features configured for domain 1 to tunnel interface 1 by assigning the AppleTalk domain group 1 to the tunnel interface.

```
appletalk domain 1 name France
appletalk domain 1 remap-range in 10000-19999
appletalk domain 1 remap-range out 200-299
!
interface Tunnel 0
 tunnel source ethernet 0
 tunnel destination 131.108.1.17
```

```
tunnel mode aurp
appletalk protocol aurp
appletalk domain-group 1
```

## SNMP Example

The following example configuration sequence illustrates proper activation of SNMP and Apple-Talk:

```
!Disable SNMP on the router.
no snmp-server
!
!Enable AppleTalk routing and event logging on the router.
appletalk routing
appletalk event-logging
!
!Configure IP and AppleTalk on Ethernet interface 0.
interface Ethernet 0
ip address 131.108.29.291 255.255.255.0
 appletalk cable-range 29-29 29.180
 appletalk zone MarketingA1
!
!Enable SNMP on the router.
snmp-server community MarketingA2 RW
snmp-server trap-authentication
snmp server host 131.108.2.160 MarketingA2
```

## MacIP Examples

The following example illustrates MacIP support for dynamically addressed MacIP clients with dynamically allocated IP addresses in the range from 131.108.0.2 to 131.108.0.10:

```
!Specify server address and zone
appletalk macip server 131.108.0.1 zone Marketing
!
!Specify dynamically addressed clients
appletalk macip dynamic 131.108.0.2 131.108.0.10 zone Marketing
!
!Assign the address and subnet mask for Ethernet interface 0
interface ethernet 0
ip address 131.108.0.2 255.255.255.0
!
!Enable AppleTalk routing
appletalk routing
!
interface ethernet 0
 appletalk cable range 69-69 69.128
 appletalk zone Marketing
```

The following example illustrates MacIP support for MacIP clients with statically allocated IP addresses:

```
!Specify the server address and zone
appletalk macip server 131.108.0.1 zone Marketing
!
!Specify statically addressed clients
appletalk macip static 131.108.0.11 131.108.0.20 zone Marketing
appletalk macip static 131.108.0.31 zone Marketing
appletalk macip static 131.108.0.41 zone Marketing
appletalk macip static 131.108.0.49 zone Marketing
!
!Assign the address and subnet mask for Ethernet interface 0
interface ethernet 0
ip address 131.108.0.1 255.255.255.0
!
!Enable AppleTalk routing
appletalk routing
!
interface ethernet 0
 appletalk cable range 69-69 69.128
 appletalk zone Marketing
```

## IPTalk Example

This section describes how to set up UNIX-based systems and Cisco IOS software to use CAP IPTalk and other IPTalk implementations.

The following procedure outlines the basic steps for setting up Cisco software and UNIX hosts for operation using IPTalk implementations.

---
**NOTES**
---

This procedure does not provide full instructions on how to install CAP on the UNIX system. However, it does address the requirements for setting up the UNIX system's configuration file that defines addresses and other network information. Generally, this is the only file that relies on the router's address and configuration information. Refer to your UNIX system and CAP software manuals for information about building the CAP software and setting up the UNIX startup scripts.

---

**Step 1**     Enable AppleTalk routing on all the routers that use IPTalk and any routers between these routers.

**Step 2**     Enable IP routing on the interfaces that communicate with the UNIX system. These interfaces must be on *the same subnet* as the UNIX system. Also, ensure that IP is enabled on the UNIX system.

**Step 3**     Allocate an AppleTalk network number for IPTalk. You need a separate AppleTalk network number for each IP subnet that is to run IPTalk.

You can have a number of UNIX machines on the same subnet. They all use the same AppleTalk network number for IPTalk. However, they must have their own individual node identifiers.

It is possible for the same router to have IPTalk enabled on several interfaces. Each interface must have a different AppleTalk network number allocated to IPTalk because each interface is using a different IP subnet.

**Step 4** Determine the CAP format of the AppleTalk network number. The CAP software is based on an older AppleTalk convention that expresses AppleTalk network numbers as two octets (decimal numbers from 0 to 255) separated by a dot. The current AppleTalk convention uses decimal numbers from 1 to 65,279. Use the following formula to convert between the two:

CAP format: $x.y$
Apple format: $d$

- To convert from AppleTalk to CAP:
  $x = d/256$ (/ represents truncating integer division)
  $y = d\%256$ (% represents the remainder of the division)

- To convert from CAP to AppleTalk: $d = x * 256 + y$

*Example*
AppleTalk format: 14087
CAP format: 55.7

**Step 5** Choose a zone name for IPTalk. No special constraints are placed on zone name choices. You can use the same zone name for several networks, and you can combine IPTalk and normal AppleTalk networks in the same zone.

**Step 6** Decide which UDP ports to use for IPTalk. The default is to use ports beginning with 768. Thus, RTMP uses port 769, NBP port 770, and so on. These are the original AppleTalk ports, and their numbers are hardcoded into older versions of CAP. The only problem with using them is that they are not officially assigned by the Internet's Network Information Center (NIC), which has assigned a set of UDP ports beginning with 200. Thus, other applications could use them, possibly causing conflicts—although this is unlikely. With CAP releases 5.0 and later, you can configure CAP to use the officially allocated ports. If you do so, RTMP will use port 201, NBP port 202, and so on. Whichever ports you use, you must configure both CAP and the router to use the same ones.

**Step 7** Enable IPTalk on each interface of the router as required. This is illustrated by the following example:

```
appletalk routing
!
interface ethernet 0
  ip address 128.6.7.22 255.255.255.0
```

```
appletalk cable 1792-1792 1792.22
appletalk zone MIS-Development
interface Tunnel0
tunnel source Ethernet0
tunnel mode iptalk
appletalk iptalk 14087 MIS-UNIX
```

In this example, AppleTalk routing is enabled on the interface in the following two ways:

- Via EtherTalk phase 2, using the cable range 1792–1792 and the zone MIS-Development

- Via IPTalk, using the network number 14087 and the zone MIS-UNIX

### NOTES

The IPTalk node identifier is chosen automatically, based on the IP address. It is normally the host number portion of the IP address. For example, with an IP address of 128.6.7.22 and a subnet mask of 255.255.255.0, the host number is 22. Thus, the IPTalk node identifier would be 22. If the IP host number is larger than 255, the low-order 8 bits are used, although fewer than 8 bits may be available, depending on the IP subnet mask. If the mask leaves fewer bits, the node number will be quietly truncated. Be sure to use a node address that is compatible with the subnet mask. In any event, you may experience problems when using IPTalk with host numbers larger than 255.

If you choose to use the official UDP ports (those beginning with 200), include the following global configuration command in your configuration:

```
appletalk iptalk-baseport 200
```

**Step 8**　Configure each UNIX host with a network number, zone name, and router.

As an example, the following are the contents of the */etc/atalk.local* file from a UNIX system with the IP address 128.6.7.26 and a network mask of 255.255.255.0:

```
# IPTalk on net 128.6.7.0:
# mynet mynode myzone
55.7  26      MIS-UNIX
# bridgenet bridgenode bridgeIP
55.7  22      128.6.7.22
```

The first noncommented line defines the address of the UNIX system, and the second noncommented line defines the address of the router. In both cases, the first column is 55.7, which is the AppleTalk network number (in CAP format) for use by IPTalk. The second column is the AppleTalk node identifier, which must be the same as the IP host number. The third column on the first line is the zone name, and on the second line it is the IP address of the router.

Note the following about the entries in the */etc/atalk.local* file:

- The AppleTalk network number in the first column in both lines must agree with the AppleTalk network number used in the **appletalk iptalk** command. However, in the */etc/atalk.local* file, the number must be in the CAP format, while in the configuration command, it must be in the Apple format.

- The host number in the second column in both lines must agree with the IP host number of the corresponding system. That is, on the first line it must be the IP host number of the UNIX machine, and on the second line it must be the IP host number for the router.

- The zone name in the third column on the first line must agree with the zone name used in the **appletalk iptalk** command.

- The IP address in the third column of the second line must be the IP address of the router.

**Step 9**  Ensure that your CAP software is using the same UDP port numbers as the router. Currently, the CAP default is the same as the router default, which is port numbers beginning with 768. If you want to use this default, you do not need to take any further action. However, if you want to use the official UDP port numbers (port numbers beginning with 200), ensure that you have included the following command in your configuration:

```
appletalk iptalk-baseport 200
```

**Step 10**  On the UNIX system, add the following lines to the */etc/services* file:

```
at-rtmp      201/udp
at-nbp       202/udp
at-3         203/udp
at-echo      204/udp
at-5         205/udp
at-zis       206/udp
at-7         207/udp
at-8         208/udp
```

If you are using Network Information Services (NIS), previously known as the *Yellow Pages*, remember to do a *make* in */var/yp* after changing */etc/services*. If you are using the default ports (those starting with 768), you do not need to modify */etc/services*.

## AppleTalk Control Protocol Example

The following example illustrates how to set up a router to accept AppleTalk client requests on interface 1. This example creates virtual network number 3 and the AppleTalk zone Twiddledee.

```
appletalk virtual-net 3 Twiddledee
interface async 1
 encapsulation ppp
 appletalk client-mode
```

## Proxy Network Number Example

Assume that your network topology looks like the one in Figure 2–13. Also assume that Router A supports only nonextended AppleTalk, that Router B supports only extended AppleTalk (not in transition mode), and that Router C supports only extended AppleTalk.

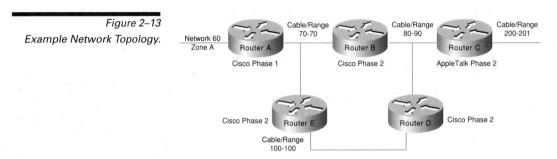

*Figure 2–13*
*Example Network Topology.*

If Router C generates a NBP hookup request for Zone A, Router B will convert this request to a forward request and send it to Router A. Because Router A supports only nonextended AppleTalk, it does not handle the forward request and ignores it. Hence, the NBP lookup from Router C fails.

To work around this problem without putting a transition router adjacent to the nonextended-only router (Router A), you could configure Router D with NBP proxy.

If you configured Router D with an NBP proxy as follows, any forward requests received for Zone A are converted into lookup requests, and, therefore, the nonextended router for Network 60 can properly respond to NBP hookup requests generated beyond Router C. The following example demonstrates the command needed to describe this configuration:

```
appletalk proxy 60 A
```

## AppleTalk Enhanced IGRP Bandwidth Configuration Example

The following example shows how to configure the bandwidth used by AppleTalk Enhanced IGRP. In this example, Enhanced IGRP process 1 is configured to use a maximum of 25 percent (or 32 kbps) of a 128 kbps circuit:

```
interface serial 0
bandwidth 128
appletalk eigrp-bandwidth-percent 1 25
```

In the following example, the bandwidth of a 56 kbps circuit has been configured to be 20 kbps for routing policy reasons. EIGRP process 1 is configured to use a maximum of 200 percent (or 40 kbps) of the circuit.

```
interface serial 1
bandwidth 20
appletalk eigrp-bandwidth-percent 1 200
```

## AppleTalk Interenterprise Routing Example

The following example configures AppleTalk interenterprise routing. It configures domain 1, which is named "France" and places Ethernet interface 2 into this domain.

```
appletalk domain 1 name France
appletalk domain 1 remap-range in 10000-19999
appletalk domain 1 remap-range out 200-299
appletalk domain 1 hop-reduction
!
interface ethernet 2
 no ip address
 no keepalive
 appletalk cable-range 300-300 300.6
 appletalk zone Europe
 appletalk protocol eigrp
 appletalk domain-group 1
```

## AppleTalk over DDR Example

The following example describes how to configure AppleTalk to run over a DDR interface, as illustrated in Figure 2–14. When configuring AppleTalk over DDR, you must specify DDR on the interface on which the static neighbor resides before you specify the static route itself. Also, the Cisco IOS software must know the network address of the static neighbor before you specify the static route. Otherwise, the software does not know to which interface the static neighbor is connected. To open an AppleTalk DDR link, there must be at least one AppleTalk access list bound to a dialer group.

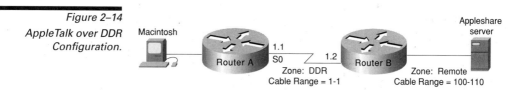

Figure 2–14
AppleTalk over DDR
Configuration.

Macintosh — Router A — 1.1 S0 — 1.2 — Router B — Appleshare server
Zone: DDR
Cable Range = 1-1
Zone: Remote
Cable Range = 100-110

To configure AppleTalk over DDR, perform the following tasks on Router A:

**Step 1**    Configure an access list and dialer group.

```
access-list 601 permit cable 100-110
dialer-list 4 list 601
```

**Step 2**    Configure the serial interface.

```
interface serial 0
 dialer in-band
 dialer string 1234
 appletalk cable 1-1 1.1
 appletalk zone DDR
 dialer-group 4
 apple distribute-list 601 in
```

**Step 3**  Create the static route.

```
appletalk static cable 100-110 to 1.2 zone Remote
```

**Step 4**  Open the Chooser on the Macintosh.

**Step 5**  Select any AppleTalk service (such as AppleShare, LaserWriter, and so on) in zone Remote. This causes Router A to dial up Router B to open a DDR link between them.

**Step 6**  Select an AppleTalk file server in the zone Remote. After some time, AppleTalk services appear in zone Remote. Select the one that you need.

**Step 7**  Close the Chooser.

**Step 8**  Open the AppleTalk session to the remote service.

**Step 9**  After the AppleTalk session is finished, close the connection to the remote service. The DDR link should go down after the DDR idle time has elapsed.

Instead of creating a static route in Step 3, you can create a floating static route. The following example adds a floating static route to cable-range 10-11 in the Eng zone, with AppleTalk address 6.5 as the next-hop router:

```
appletalk static cable-range 10-11 to 6.5 floating zone Eng
```

## AppleTalk Control Protocol for PPP Example

The following example illustrates the steps required to set up your router to accept AppleTalk client requests on interfaces 1 and 3, using the virtual network number 3 and the AppleTalk zone Twiddledee:

```
Router> enable
Router# config terminal
Router(config)# appletalk virtual-net 3 Twiddledee
Router(config)# interface async 1
Router(config-int)# encapsulation ppp
Router(config-int)# appletalk client-mode
Router(config-int)# interface async 3
Router(config-int)# encapsulation ppp
Router(config-int)# appletalk client-mode
```

# CHAPTER 3

# AppleTalk Commands

AppleTalk is a LAN system designed and developed by Apple Computer, Inc. It runs over Ethernet, Token Ring, Fiber Distributed Data Interface (FDDI) networks, and LocalTalk, Apple's proprietary twisted-pair media access system. AppleTalk specifies a protocol stack comprising several protocols that direct the flow of traffic over the network.

Apple Computer uses the name *AppleTalk* to refer to the Apple networking architecture. Apple refers to the actual transmission media used in an AppleTalk network as LocalTalk (Apple's proprietary twisted-pair transmission medium for AppleTalk), TokenTalk (AppleTalk over Token Ring), EtherTalk (AppleTalk over Ethernet), and FDDITalk (AppleTalk over FDDI).

Use the commands in this chapter to configure and monitor AppleTalk networks. For AppleTalk configuration information and examples, see Chapter 2, "Configuring AppleTalk."

## ACCESS-LIST ADDITIONAL-ZONES

To define the default action to take for access checks that apply to zones, use the **access-list additional-zones** global configuration command. To remove an access list, use the **no** form of this command.

> **access-list** *access-list-number* {**deny** | **permit**} additional-zones

| Syntax | Description |
|---|---|
| *access-list-number* | Number of the access list. This is a decimal number from 600 to 699. |
| deny | Denies access if the conditions are matched. |
| permit | Permits access if the conditions are matched. |

*Default*

No access lists are predefined.

*Command Mode*

Global configuration

*Usage Guidelines*

This command first appeared in Cisco IOS Release 10.0.

The **access-list additional-zones** command defines the action to take for access checks not explicitly defined with the **access-list zone** command. If you do not specify this command, the default action is to deny other access.

You apply access lists defined with the **access-list additional-zones** command to outgoing routing updates and GetZoneList (GZL) filters (using the **appletalk distribute-list out** and **appletalk get-zonelist-filter** commands). You cannot apply them to data-packet filters (using the **appletalk access-group** command) or to incoming routing update filters (using the **appletalk distribute-list in** command).

*Example*

The following example creates an access list based on AppleTalk zones:

```
access-list 610 deny zone Twilight
access-list 610 permit additional-zones
```

*Related Commands*

Search online to find documentation for related commands.

**access-list cable-range**
**access-list includes**
**access-list nbp**
**access-list network**
**access-list other-access**
**access-list other-nbps**
**access-list within**
**access-list zone**
**appletalk access-group**
**appletalk distribute-list in**
**appletalk distribute-list out**
**appletalk getzonelist-filter**
**appletalk permit-partial-zones**

## ACCESS-LIST CABLE-RANGE

To define an AppleTalk access list for a cable range (for extended networks only), use the **access-list cable-range** global configuration command. To remove an access list, use the **no** form of this command.

access-list *access-list-number* {deny | permit} cable-range *cable-range*
　　[broadcast-deny | broadcast-permit]
no access-list *access-list-number* [{deny | permit} cable-range *cable-range*
　　[broadcast-deny | broadcast-permit]]

| Syntax | Description |
| --- | --- |
| *access-list-number* | Number of the access list. This is a decimal number from 600 to 699. |
| deny | Denies access if the conditions are matched. |
| permit | Permits access if the conditions are matched. |
| *cable-range* | Cable range value. The argument specifies the start and end of the cable range, separated by a hyphen. These values are decimal numbers from 1 to 65279. The starting network number must be less than or equal to the ending network number. |
| broadcast-deny | (Optional) Denies access to broadcast packets if the conditions are matched. |
| broadcast-permit | (Optional) Permits access to broadcast packets if the conditions are met. |

### Default

No access lists are predefined.

### Command Mode

Global configuration

### Usage Guidelines

This command first appeared in Cisco IOS Release 10.0.

When used as a routing update filter, the **access-list cable-range** command affects matching on extended networks only. The conditions defined by this access list are used only when a cable range in a routing update exactly matches that specified in the **access-list cable-range** command. The conditions are never used to match a network number (for a nonextended network).

When used as a data-packet filter, the **access-list cable-range** command affects matching on any type of network number. The conditions defined by this access list are used only when the packet's source network lies in the range defined by the access list.

You apply access lists defined with the **access-list cable-range** command to data-packet and routing-update filters (using the **appletalk access-group, appletalk distribute-list in,** and **appletalk distribute-list out**). You cannot apply them to GZL filters (using the **appletalk getzonelist-filter** command).

To delete an access list, specify the minimum number of keywords and arguments needed to delete the proper access list. For example, to delete the entire access list, use the following command:

　　**no access-list** *access-list-number*

To delete the access list for a specific network, use the following command:

> **no access-list** *access-list-number* {**deny** | **permit**} **cable-range** *cable-range*

Priority queuing for AppleTalk operates on the destination network number, not the source network number.

### Example

The following access list forwards all packets except those from cable range 10 to 20:

```
access-list 600 deny cable-range 10-20
access-list 600 permit other-access
```

### Related Commands

Search online to find documentation for related commands.

**access-list additional-zones**
**access-list includes**
**access-list nbp**
**access-list network**
**access-list other-access**
**access-list other-nbps**
**access-list within**
**access-list zone**
**appletalk access-group**
**appletalk distribute-list in**
**appletalk distribute-list out**
**appletalk getzonelist-filter**
**priority-list protocol**

## ACCESS-LIST INCLUDES

To define an AppleTalk access list that overlaps any part of a range of network numbers or cable ranges (for both extended and nonextended networks), use the **access-list includes** global configuration command. To remove an access list, use the **no** form of this command.

> **access-list** *access-list-number* {**deny** | **permit**} **includes** *cable-range*
>     [**broadcast-deny** | **broadcast-permit**]
> **no access-list** *access-list-number* [{**deny** | **permit**} **includes** *cable-range*
>     [**broadcast-deny** | **broadcast-permit**]]

| Syntax | Description |
| --- | --- |
| *access-list-number* | Number of the access list. This is a decimal number from 600 to 699. |
| **deny** | Denies access if the conditions are matched. |

| Syntax | Description |
|---|---|
| permit | Permits access if the conditions are matched. |
| *cable-range* | Cable range or network number. The argument specifies the start and end of the cable range, separated by a hyphen. These values are decimal numbers from 1 to 65279. The starting network number must be less than or equal to the ending network number. To specify a network number, set the starting and ending network numbers to the same value. |
| broadcast-deny | (Optional) Denies access to broadcast packets if the conditions are matched. |
| broadcast-permit | (Optional) Permits access to broadcast packets if the conditions are met. |

### Default

No access lists are predefined.

### Command Mode

Global configuration

### Usage Guidelines

This command first appeared in Cisco IOS Release 10.0.

When used as a routing update filter, the **access-list includes** command affects matching on extended and nonextended AppleTalk networks. The conditions defined by this access list are used when a cable range or network number overlaps, either partially or completely, one (or more) of those specified in the **access-list includes** command.

When used as a data-packet filter, the conditions defined by this access list are used when the packet's source network lies in the range defined in the **access-list includes** command.

You apply access lists defined with the **access-list includes** command to data-packet and routing-update filters (using the **appletalk access-group, appletalk distribute-list in,** and **appletalk distribute-list out**). You cannot apply them to GZL filters (using the **appletalk getzonelist-filter** command).

To delete an access list, specify the minimum number of keywords and arguments needed to delete the proper access list. For example, to delete the entire access list, use the following command:

> **no access-list** *access-list-number*

To delete the access list for a specific network, use the following command:

> **no access-list** *access-list-number* {**deny** | **permit**} **includes** *cable-range*

Priority queuing for AppleTalk operates on the destination network number, not the source network number.

*Example*

The following example defines an access list that permits access to any network or cable range that overlaps any part of the range from 10 to 20. This means, for example, that cable ranges 13 to 16 and 17 to 25 are permitted. This access list also permits all other ranges.

```
access-list 600 permit includes 10-20
access-list 600 permit other-access
```

*Related Commands*

Search online to find documentation for related commands.

**access-list additional-zones**
**access-list cable-range**
**access-list nbp**
**access-list network**
**access-list other-access**
**access-list other-nbps**
**access-list within**
**access-list zone**
**appletalk access-group**
**appletalk distribute-list in**
**appletalk distribute-list out**
**appletalk getzonelist-filter**
**priority-list protocol**

## ACCESS-LIST NBP

To define an AppleTalk access list entry for a particular Name Binding Protocol (NBP) named entity, class of NBP named entities, NBP packet type, or NBP named entities belonging to a specific zone, use the **access-list nbp** global configuration command. To remove an NBP access list entry from the access list, use the **no** form of this command.

> **access-list** *access-list-number* {**deny** | **permit**} **nbp** *sequence-number* {**BrRq** | **FwdRq** |
>     **Lookup** | **LkReply** |  **object** *string* | **type** *string* | **zone** *string*}
> **no access-list** *access-list-number* {**deny** | **permit**} **nbp** *sequence-number* {**BrRq** | **FwdRq** |
>     **Lookup** | **LkReply** |  **object** *string* | **type** *string* | **zone** *string*}

| Syntax | Description |
|---|---|
| *access-list-number* | Number of the access list. This is a decimal number from 600 to 699. |
| **deny** | Denies access if conditions are matched. |
| **permit** | Permits access if conditions are matched. |
| *sequence-number* | A number used to tie together two or three portions of an NBP name tuple and to keep track of the number of **access-list nbp** entries in an access list. Each command entry must have a sequence number. |

| Syntax | Description |
|--------|-------------|
| BrRq | Broadcast Request packet type. |
| FwdRq | Forward Request packet type. |
| Lookup | Lookup packet type. |
| LkReply | Lookup Reply packet type. |
| object | Characterizes *string* as the portion of an NBP name that identifies a particular **object** or named entity. |
| type | Characterizes *string* as the portion of an NBP name that identifies a category or **type** of named entity. |
| zone | Characterizes *string* as the portion of an NBP name that identifies an AppleTalk **zone**. |
| *string* | A portion of an NBP name identifying the **object, type,** or **zone** of a named entity. The name string can be up to 32 characters long, and it can include special characters from the Apple Macintosh character set. To include a special character, type a colon followed by two hexadecimal characters. For an NBP name with a leading space, enter the first character as the special sequence :20. |

## Default

No particular access list entry for an NBP named entity is defined, and the default filtering specified by the **access-list other-nbps** command takes effect.

## Command Mode

Global configuration

## Usage Guidelines

This command first appeared in Cisco IOS Release 11.0.

The **access-list nbp** command defines the action to take for filtering NBP packets from a particular **object** (particular named entity), **type** (class of named entities), or **zone** (AppleTalk zone in which named entities reside) or for a particular NBP packet type—superseding the default action for NBP packets from all named entities specified by the **access-list other-nbps** command. For each command that you enter, you must specify a sequence number.

The sequence number serves two purposes:

- Its principal purpose is to allow you to associate two or three portions of a NBP three-part name, referred to as a NBP tuple. To do this, you enter two or three commands having the same sequence number but each specifying a different keyword and NBP name portion: **object, type,** or **zone.** The same sequence number binds them together. This provides you with the ability to restrict forwarding of NBP packets at any level, down to a single named entity.

- Its second purpose is to allow you to keep track of the number of **access-list nbp** entries you have made. You must enter a sequence number even if you do not use it to associate portions of a NBP name.

## Examples

The following example adds entries to access list number 607 to allow forwarding of NBP packets from specific sources and deny forwarding of NBP packets from all other sources. The first command adds an entry that allows NBP packets from all printers of type *LaserWriter*. The second command adds an entry that allows NBP packets from all AppleTalk file servers of type *AFPServer*. The third command adds an entry that allows NBP packets from all applications called *HotShotPaint*. For example, there might be an application with a **zone** name of *Accounting* and an application with a **zone** name of *engineering*, both having the object name of *HotShotPaint*. NBP packets forwarded from both applications will be allowed.

The **access-list other-nbps** command denies forwarding of NBP packets from all other sources.

```
access-list 607 permit nbp 1 type LaserWriter
access-list 607 permit nbp 2 type AFPServer
access-list 607 permit nbp 3 object HotShotPaint
access-list 607 deny other-nbps
access-list 607 permit other-access
```

The following example adds entries to access list number 608 to deny forwarding of NBP packets from two specific servers whose fully qualified NBP names are specified. It permits forwarding of NBP packets from all other sources.

```
access-list 608 deny nbp 1 object ServerA
access-list 608 deny nbp 1 type AFPServer
access-list 608 deny nbp 1 zone Bld3
access-list 608 deny nbp 2 object ServerB
access-list 608 deny nbp 2 type AFPServer
access-list 608 deny nbp 2 zone Bld3
access-list 608 permit other-nbps
access-list 608 permit other-access
```

The following example denies forwarding of NBP Lookup Reply packets for all named entities. It permits forwarding of other NBP packet types from all other sources.

```
access-list 600 deny nbp 1 LkReply
access-list 600 permit other-nbps
access-list 600 permit other-access
```

The following example creates an access list that denies forwarding of these packets:

- All NBP Lookup Reply packets
- NBP packets from the server named *Bob's Server*
- Packets from all AppleTalk file servers of type *AFPServer*
- All NBP Lookup Reply packets that contain the specified named entities belonging to the zone *twilight*

```
access-list 600 deny nbp 1 LkReply
access-list 600 deny nbp 1 object Bob's Server
access-list 600 deny nbp 1 type AFPServer
access-list 600 deny nbp 1 zone twilight
access-list 600 permit other-nbps
access-list 600 permit other-access
```

### Related Commands

Search online to find documentation for related commands.

access-list additional-zones
access-list cable-range
access-list includes
access-list network
access-list other-access
access-list other-nbps
access-list within
access-list zone
appletalk access-group
appletalk distribute-list in
appletalk distribute-list out
appletalk getzonelist-filter
priority-list protocol

## ACCESS-LIST NETWORK

To define an AppleTalk access list for a single network number (that is, for a nonextended network), use the **access-list network** global configuration command. To remove an access list, use the **no** form of this command.

> access-list *access-list-number* {deny | permit} network *network*
>     [broadcast-deny | broadcast-permit]
> no access-list *access-list-number* [{deny | permit} network *network*
>     [broadcast-deny | broadcast-permit]]

| Syntax | Description |
| --- | --- |
| *access-list-number* | Number of the access list. This is a decimal number from 600 to 699. |
| deny | Denies access if the conditions are matched. |
| permit | Permits access if the conditions are matched. |
| *network* | AppleTalk network number. |

| Syntax | Description |
|---|---|
| **broadcast-deny** | (Optional) Denies access to broadcast packets if the conditions are matched. |
| **broadcast-permit** | (Optional) Permits access to broadcast packets if the conditions are met. |

### Default

No access lists are predefined.

### Command Mode

Global configuration

### Usage Guidelines

This command first appeared in Cisco IOS Release 10.0.

When used as a routing-update filter, the **access-list network** command affects matching on nonextended networks only. The conditions defined by this access list are used only when the nonextended number in a routing update matches a network number specified in one of the **access-list network** commands. The conditions are never used to match a cable range (for an extended network), even if the cable range has the same starting and ending number.

When used as a data-packet filter, the conditions defined by this access list are used only when the packet's source network matches the network number specified in the **access-list network** command.

You apply access lists defined with the **access-list network** command to data-packet and routing-update filters (using the **appletalk access-group, appletalk distribute-list in,** and **appletalk distribute-list out**). You cannot apply access lists to GZL filters (using the **appletalk getzonelist-filter** command).

In software releases before 9.0, the syntax of this command was **access-list** *access-list-number* {**deny** | **permit**} *network*. The current version of the software is still able to interpret commands in this format if it finds them in a configuration or boot file. However, it is recommended that you update the commands in your configuration or boot files to match the current syntax.

Use the **no access-list** command with the *access-list-number argument* only to remove an entire access list from the configuration. Specify the optional arguments to remove a particular clause.

To delete an access list, specify the minimum number of keywords and arguments needed to delete the proper access list. For example, to delete the entire access list, use the following command:

> **no access-list** *access-list-number*

To delete the access list for a specific network, use the following command:

> **no access-list** *access-list-number* {**deny** | **permit**} **network** *network*

Priority queuing for AppleTalk operates on the destination network number, not the source network number.

## Example

The following example defines an access list that forwards all packets except those destined for networks 1 and 2:

```
access-list 650 deny network 1
access-list 650 deny network 2
access-list 650 permit other-access
```

## Related Commands

Search online to find documentation for related commands.

**access-list additional-zones**
**access-list cable-range**
**access-list includes**
**access-list nbp**
**access-list other-access**
**access-list other-nbps**
**access-list within**
**access-list zone**
**appletalk access-group**
**appletalk distribute-list in**
**appletalk distribute-list out**
**appletalk getzonelist-filter**
**priority-list protocol**

## ACCESS-LIST OTHER-ACCESS

To define the default action to take for subsequent access checks that apply to networks or cable ranges, use the **access-list other-access** global configuration command. To remove an access list, use the **no** form of this command.

> **access-list** *access-list-number* {**deny** | **permit**} **other-access**

| Syntax | Description |
|--------|-------------|
| *access-list-number* | Number of the access list. This is a decimal number from 600 to 699. |
| **deny** | Denies access if the conditions are matched. |
| **permit** | Permits access if the conditions are matched. |

## Default

No access lists are predefined.

## Command Mode

Global configuration

## Usage Guidelines

This command first appeared in Cisco IOS Release 11.0.

The **access-list other-access** command defines the action to take for access checks not explicitly defined with an **access-list network, access-list cable-range, access-list includes,** or **access-list within** command. If you do not specify this command, the default action is to deny other access.

You apply access lists defined with the **access-list other-access** command to data-packet and routing- update filters (using the **appletalk access-group, appletalk distribute-list in,** and **appletalk distribute-list out**). You cannot apply them to GZL filters (using the **appletalk getzonelist-filter** command).

In software releases before 9.0, the syntax of this command was **access-list** *access-list-number* {**deny** | **permit**} **-1**. The current version of the software is still able to interpret commands in this format if it finds them in a configuration or boot file. However, it is recommended that you update the commands in your configuration or boot files to match the current syntax.

Priority queuing for AppleTalk operates on the destination network number, not the source network number.

## Example

The following example defines an access list that forwards all packets except those destined for networks 1 and 2:

```
access-list 650 deny network 1
access-list 650 deny network 2
access-list 650 permit other-access
```

## Related Commands

Search online to find documentation for related commands.

**access-list additional-zones**
**access-list cable-range**
**access-list includes**
**access-list nbp**
**access-list network**
**access-list other-nbps**
**access-list within**
**access-list zone**
**appletalk access-group**
**appletalk distribute-list in**
**appletalk distribute-list out**
**priority-list protocol**

## ACCESS-LIST OTHER-NBPS

To define the default action to take for access checks that apply to NBP packets from named entities not otherwise explicitly denied or permitted, use the **access-list other-nbps** global configuration command.

> **access-list** *access-list-number* {deny | permit} **other-nbps**
> **no access-list** *access-list-number* {deny | permit} **other-nbps**

| Syntax | Description |
|---|---|
| *access-list-number* | Number of the access list for AppleTalk. This is a decimal number from 600 to 699. |
| **deny** | Denies access if conditions are matched. |
| **permit** | Permits access if conditions are matched. |

### Default

Access is denied.

### Command Mode

Global configuration

### Usage Guidelines

This command first appeared in Cisco IOS Release 11.0.

The **access-list other-nbps** command defines the action to take for filtering of NBP packets from named entities not explicitly defined by an **access-list nbp** command. It allows you to implement the default AppleTalk network security state at the named entity level. Any **access-list nbp** commands you enter affect a particular named entity object, class of named entities, or all named entities within a zone. This command sets the security state for all other NBP named entities. If you do not specify this command, the default action is to deny access.

You can use this command to create an entry in an access list before or after you issue **access-list nbp** commands. The order of the command in the access list is irrelevant.

### Example

The following example permits forwarding of all NBP packets from all sources except AppleTalk file servers of type *AFPServer*:

```
access-list 607 deny nbp 2 type AFPServer
access-list 607 permit other-nbps
```

### Related Commands

Search online to find documentation for related commands.

access-list additional-zones
access-list cable-range
access-list includes
access-list nbp
access-list network
access-list other-access
access-list within
access-list zone
appletalk access-group
appletalk distribute-list in
appletalk distribute-list out
appletalk getzonelist-filter
priority-list protocol

## ACCESS-LIST WITHIN

To define an AppleTalk access list for an extended or a nonextended network whose network number or cable range is included entirely within the specified cable range, use the **access-list within** global configuration command. To remove this access list, use the **no** form of this command.

> **access-list** *access-list-number* {**deny** | **permit**} **within** *cable-range*
> **no access-list** *access-list-number* [{**deny** | **permit**} **within** *cable-range*]

| Syntax | Description |
|---|---|
| *access-list-number* | Number of the access list. This is a decimal number from 600 to 699. |
| **deny** | Denies access if the conditions are matched. |
| **permit** | Permits access if the conditions are matched. |
| *cable-range* | Cable range or network number. The argument specifies the start and end of the cable range, separated by a hyphen. These values are decimal numbers from 1 to 65279. The starting network number must be less than or equal to the ending network number. To specify a network number, set the starting and ending network numbers to the same value. |

### Default
No access lists are predefined.

### Command Mode
Global configuration

### Usage Guidelines
This command first appeared in Cisco IOS Release 10.0.

When used as a routing update filter, the **access-list within** command affects matching on extended and nonextended AppleTalk networks. The conditions defined by this access list are used when a cable range or network number overlaps, either partially or completely, one (or more) of those specified in the **access-list within** command.

When used as a data-packet filter, the conditions defined by this access list are used when the packet's source network lies in the range defined in the **access-list within** command.

You apply access lists defined with the **access-list within** command to data-packet and routing-update (using the **appletalk access-group, appletalk distribute-list in**, and **appletalk distribute-list out**). You cannot apply them to GZL filters (using the **appletalk getzonelist-filter** command).

To delete an access list, specify the minimum number of keywords and arguments needed to delete the proper access list. For example, to delete the entire access list, use the following command:

   **no access-list** *access-list-number*

To delete the access list for a specific network, use the following command:

   **no access-list** *access-list-number* {**deny** | **permit**} **within** *cable-range*

Priority queuing for AppleTalk operates on the destination network number, not the source network number.

## Example

The following example defines an access list that permits access to any network or cable range that is completely included in the range from 10 to 20. This means, for example, that cable range 13 to 16 is permitted, but cable range 17 to 25 is not. The second line of the access list permits all other packets.

```
access-list 600 permit within 10-20
access-list 600 permit other-access
```

## Related Commands

Search online to find documentation for related commands.

access-list additional-zones
access-list cable-range
access-list includes
access-list nbp
access-list network
access-list other-access
access-list other-nbps
access-list zone
appletalk access-group
appletalk distribute-list in
appletalk distribute-list out
appletalk getzonelist-filter
priority-list protocol

## ACCESS-LIST ZONE

To define an AppleTalk access list that applies to a zone, use the **access-list zone** global configuration command. To remove an access list, use the **no** form of this command.

> **access-list** *access-list-number* {**deny** | **permit**} **zone** *zone-name*
> **no access-list** *access-list-number* [{**deny** | **permit**} **zone** *zone-name*]

| Syntax | Description |
|---|---|
| *access-list number* | Number of the access list. This is a decimal number from 600 to 699. |
| **deny** | Denies access if the conditions are matched. |
| **permit** | Permits access if the conditions are matched. |
| *zone-name* | Name of the zone. The name can include special characters from the Apple Macintosh character set. To include a special character, type a colon followed by two hexadecimal characters. For zone names with a leading space character, enter the first character as the special sequence :20. |

### Default

No access lists are predefined.

### Command Mode

Global configuration

### Usage Guidelines

This command first appeared in Cisco IOS Release 10.0.

You apply access lists defined with the **access-list zones** command to outgoing routing update and GZL filters (using the **appletalk distribute-list out** and **appletalk getzonelist-filter** commands). You cannot apply them to data-packet filters (using the **appletalk access-group** command) or to incoming routing update filters (using the **appletalk distribute-list in** command).

To delete an access list, specify the minimum number of keywords and arguments needed to delete the proper access list. For example, to delete the entire access list, use the following command:

> **no access-list** *access-list-number*

To delete the access list for a specific network, use the following command:

> **no access-list** *access-list-number* {**deny** | **permit**} **zone** *zone-name*

Use the **access-list additional-zones** command to define the action to take for access checks not explicitly defined with the **access-list zone** command.

---

**NOTES** ——————————————————————————————

AppleTalk zone access lists on an Enhanced Internet Gateway Routing Protocol (Enhance IGRP) interface do not filter the distribution of Enhanced IGRP routes. When the **appletalk distribute-list out** command is applied to an Enhanced IGRP interface, any **access-list zone** commands in the specified access list are ignored.

---

### Example

The following example creates an access list based on AppleTalk zones:

```
access-list 610 deny zone Twilight
access-list 610 permit additional-zones
```

### Related Commands

Search online to find documentation for related commands.

access-list additional-zones
access-list cable-range
access-list includes
access-list nbp
access-list network
access-list other-access
access-list other-nbps
access-list within
appletalk access-group
appletalk distribute-list in
appletalk distribute-list out
appletalk getzonelist-filter
appletalk permit-partial-zones

## APPLETALK ACCESS-GROUP

To assign an access list to an interface, use the **appletalk access-group** interface configuration command. To remove the access list, use the **no** form of this command.

> **appletalk access-group** *access-list-number* [**in** | **out**]
> **no appletalk access-group** *access-list-number*

| Syntax | Description |
|---|---|
| *access-list-number* | Number of the access list. This is a decimal number from 600 to 699. |
| **in** | (Optional) Filters on incoming packets. |
| **out** | (Optional) Filters on outgoing packets. This is the default direction. |

### Default

No access lists are predefined. The default interface direction is out.

### Command Mode

Interface configuration

### Usage Guidelines

This command first appeared in Cisco IOS Release 10.0.

The **appletalk access-group** command applies data-packet filters or NBP-packet filters to an inbound or outbound interface. These filters check data packets being received or sent on an interface. If the source network of the packets has access denied, these packets are not processed and are discarded.

When you apply a data-packet filter to an interface, you should ensure that all networks or cable ranges within a zone are governed by the same filters.

### Examples

The following example applies access list 601 to outbound Ethernet interface 0:

```
access-list 601 deny cable-range 1-10
access-list 601 permit other-access
interface ethernet 0
 appletalk access-group 601
```

The following example applies access list 600 to inbound Ethernet interface 0:

```
interface ethernet 0
 appletalk access-group 600 in
```

### Related Commands

Search online to find documentation for related commands.

**access-list cable-range**
**access-list includes**
**access-list network**
**access-list other-access**
**access-list within**
**appletalk access-group**
**appletalk distribute-list in**
**appletalk distribute-list out**

## APPLETALK ADDRESS

To enable nonextended AppleTalk routing on an interface, use the **appletalk address** interface configuration command. To disable nonextended AppleTalk routing, use the **no** form of this command.

**appletalk address** *network.node*
**no appletalk address** [*network.node*]

| Syntax | Description |
|--------|-------------|
| *network.node* | AppleTalk network address assigned to the interface. The argument *network* is the 16-bit network number in the range from 0 to 65279. The argument *node* is the 8-bit node number in the range from 0 to 254. Both numbers are decimal and separated by a period. |

### Default

Disabled

### Command Mode

Interface configuration

### Usage Guidelines

This command first appeared in Cisco IOS Release 10.0.

You must enable routing on the interface before assigning zone names.

Specifying an address of 0.0, or 0.*node,* places the interface into *discovery mode.* When in this mode, the Cisco IOS software attempts to determine network address information from another router on the network. You also can enable discovery mode with the **appletalk discovery** command. Discovery mode does not run over serial lines.

### Example

The following example enables nonextended AppleTalk routing on Ethernet interface 0:

```
appletalk routing
interface ethernet 0
appletalk address 1.129
```

### Related Commands

Search online to find documentation for related commands.

**access-list cable-range**
**appletalk discovery**
**appletalk zone**

## APPLETALK ALTERNATE-ADDRESSING

To display network numbers in a two-octet format, use the **appletalk alternate-addressing** global configuration command. To return to displaying network numbers in the format *network.node,* use the **no** form of this command.

**appletalk alternate-addressing**
**no appletalk alternate-addressing**

*Syntax        Description*

This command has no arguments or keywords.

*Default*

Disabled

*Command Mode*

Global configuration

*Usage Guidelines*

This command first appeared in Cisco IOS Release 10.0.

The **appletalk alternate-addressing** command displays cable ranges in the alternate format wherever applicable. This format consists of printing the upper and lower bytes of a network number as 8-bit decimal values separated by a decimal point. For example, the cable range 511-512 would be printed as 1.255-2.0.

*Example*

The following example enables the display of network numbers in a two-octet format:

```
appletalk alternate-addressing
```

## APPLETALK ARP INTERVAL

To specify the time interval between retransmissions of Address Resolution Protocol (ARP) packets, use the **appletalk arp interval** global configuration command. To restore both default intervals, use the **no** form of this command.

**appletalk arp [probe | request] interval** *interval*
**no appletalk arp [probe | request] interval** *interval*

*Syntax*                    *Description*

probe                       (Optional) Interval to be used with AppleTalk Address Resolution Protocol (AARP) requests that are trying to determine the address of the local router when the Cisco IOS software is being configured. If you omit **probe** and **request, probe** is the default.

| Syntax | Description |
|--------|-------------|
| request | (Optional) Indicates that the interval specified is to be used when AARP is attempting to determine the hardware address of another node so that AARP can deliver a packet. |
| *interval* | Interval, in milliseconds, between AARP transmissions. The minimum value is 33 ms. When used with the **probe** keyword, the default interval is 200 ms. When used with the **request** keyword, the default interval is 1,000 ms. |

### Default

If you omit the keywords, probe is the default.

**probe**—200 ms
**request**—1000 ms

### Command Mode

Global configuration

### Usage Guidelines

This command first appeared in Cisco IOS Release 10.0.

The time interval you specify takes effect immediately.

Lengthening the interval between AARP transmissions permits responses from devices that respond slowly (such as printers and overloaded file servers) to be received.

AARP uses the **appletalk arp probe interval** value when obtaining the address of the local router. This is done when the Cisco IOS software is being configured. You should not change the default value of this interval unless absolutely necessary because this value directly modifies the AppleTalk dynamic node assignment algorithm.

AARP uses the **appletalk arp request interval** value when attempting to determine the hardware address of another node so that it can deliver a packet. You can change this interval as desired, although the default value is optimal for most sites.

The **no appletalk arp** command restores both the **probe** and **request** intervals specified in the **appletalk arp interval** and **appletalk arp retransmit-count** commands to their default values.

### Example

In the following example, the AppleTalk ARP retry interval is lengthened to 2,000 ms:

```
appletalk arp request interval 2000
```

### Related Commands

Search online to find documentation for related commands.

appletalk arp retransmit-count
appletalk arp-timeout
appletalk glean-packets
show appletalk globals

## APPLETALK ARP RETRANSMIT-COUNT

To specify the number of AARP probe or request transmissions, use the **appletalk arp retransmit-count** global configuration command. To restore both default values, use the **no** form of this command.

> **appletalk arp [probe | request] retransmit-count** *number*
> **no appletalk arp [probe | request] retransmit-count** *number*

| Syntax | Description |
| --- | --- |
| **probe** | (Optional) Indicates that the number specified is to be used with AARP requests that are trying to determine the address of the local router when the Cisco IOS software is being configured. If you omit **probe** and **request, probe** is the default. |
| **request** | (Optional) Indicates that the number specified is to be used when AARP is attempting to determine the hardware address of another node so that AARP can deliver a packet. |
| *number* | Number of AARP retransmissions that occur. The minimum number is 1. When used with the **probe** keyword, the default value is 10 retransmissions. When used with the **request** keyword, the default value is 5 retransmissions. Specifying 0 selects the default value. |

### Default

If you omit the keyword, probe is the default.

**probe**—10 transmissions
**request**—5 transmissions

### Command Mode

Global configuration

### Usage Guidelines

This command first appeared in Cisco IOS Release 10.0.

The value you specify takes effect immediately.

Increasing the number of retransmissions permits responses from devices that respond slowly (such as printers and overloaded file servers) to be received.

AARP uses the **appletalk arp probe retransmit-count** value when obtaining the address of the local router. This is done when the Cisco IOS software is being configured. You should not change the default value unless absolutely necessary because this value directly modifies the AppleTalk dynamic node assignment algorithm.

AARP uses the **appletalk arp request retransmit-count** value when attempting to determine the hardware address of another node so that it can deliver a packet. You can change this interval as desired, although the default value is optimal for most sites.

The **no appletalk arp** command restores both the **probe** and **request** intervals specified in the **appletalk arp interval** and **appletalk arp retransmit-count** commands to their default values.

### Example

The following example specifies an AARP retransmission count of 10 for AARP packets that are requesting the hardware address of another node on the network:

```
appletalk arp request retransmit-count 10
```

### Related Commands

Search online to find documentation for related commands.

**appletalk arp interval**
**appletalk arp-timeout**
**appletalk glean-packets**
**show appletalk globals**

### APPLETALK ARP-TIMEOUT

To specify the interval at which entries are aged out of the ARP table, use the **appletalk arp-timeout** interface configuration command. To return to the default timeout, use the **no** form of this command.

> **appletalk arp-timeout** *interval*
> **no appletalk arp-timeout** [*interval*]

### Syntax                    Description

*interval*                   Time, in minutes, after which an entry is removed from the AppleTalk ARP table. The default is 240 minutes (4 hours).

### Default

240 minutes (4 hours)

### Command Mode

Interface configuration

*Usage Guidelines*

This command first appeared in Cisco IOS Release 10.0.

*Example*

The following example changes the ARP timeout interval on Ethernet interface 0 to 2 hours:

```
interface ethernet 0
appletalk cable-range 2-2
appletalk arp-timeout 120
```

*Related Commands*

Search online to find documentation for related commands.

**appletalk arp interval**
**appletalk arp retransmit-count**
**appletalk glean-packets**

## APPLETALK AURP TICKLE-TIME

To set the Apple Update-Based Routing Protocol (AURP) last-heard-from timer value, use the **appletalk aurp tickle-time** interface configuration command. To return to the default last-heard-from timer value, use the **no** form of this command.

> **appletalk aurp tickle-time** *seconds*
> **no appletalk aurp tickle-time** [*seconds*]

| *Syntax* | *Description* |
|---|---|
| *seconds* | Timeout value, in seconds. This value can be a number in the range from 30 to infinity. The default is 90 seconds. |

*Default*

90 seconds

*Command Mode*

Interface configuration

*Usage Guidelines*

This command first appeared in Cisco IOS Release 10.3.

If the tunnel peer has not been heard from within the time specified by the least-heard-from timer value, the Cisco IOS software sends tickle packets to check that the tunnel peer is still up.

You can use this command only on tunnel interfaces.

*Example*

The following example changes the AURP last-heard-from timer value on tunnel interface 0 to 120 seconds:

```
interface tunnel 0
appletalk aurp tickle-time 120
```

*Related Commands*

Search online to find documentation for related commands.

**show appletalk interface tunnel**

## APPLETALK AURP UPDATE-INTERVAL

To set the minimum interval between AURP routing updates, use the **appletalk aurp update-interval** global configuration command. To return to the default interval, use the **no** form of this command.

**appletalk aurp update-interval** *seconds*
**no appletalk aurp update-interval** [*seconds*]

| *Syntax* | *Description* |
|---|---|
| *seconds* | AURP routing update interval, in seconds. This interval must be a multiple of 10. The default is 30 seconds. |

*Default*

30 seconds

*Command Mode*

Global configuration

*Usage Guidelines*

This command first appeared in Cisco IOS Release 10.3.

The AURP routing update interval applies only to tunnel interfaces.

*Example*

The following example changes the AURP routing update interval on tunnel interface 0 to 40 seconds:

```
interface tunnel 0
appletalk aurp update-interval 40
```

*Related Commands*

Search online to find documentation for related commands.

**show appletalk globals**

## APPLETALK CABLE-RANGE

To enable an extended AppleTalk network, use the **appletalk cable-range** interface configuration command. To disable an extended AppleTalk network, use the **no** form of this command.

> **appletalk cable-range** *cable-range* [*network.node*]
> **no appletalk cable-range** *cable-range* [*network.node*]

| Syntax | Description |
|--------|-------------|
| *cable-range* | Cable range value. The argument specifies the start and end of the cable range, separated by a hyphen. These values are decimal numbers from 0 to 65279. The starting network number must be less than or equal to the ending network number. |
| *network.node* | (Optional) Suggested AppleTalk address for the interface. The argument *network* is the 16-bit network number, and the argument *node* is the 8-bit node number. Both numbers are decimal and separated by a period. The suggested network number must fall within the specified range of network numbers. |

### Default

Disabled

### Command Mode

Interface configuration

### Usage Guidelines

This command first appeared in Cisco IOS Release 10.0.

You must enable routing on the interface before assigning zone names.

Specifying a cable range value of 0-0 places the interface into *discovery mode*. When in this mode, the Cisco IOS software attempts to determine cable range information from another router on the network. You can also enable discovery mode with the **appletalk discovery** command. Discovery mode does not run over serial lines.

### Example

The following example assigns a cable range of 3 to 3 to the interface:

```
interface ethernet 0
appletalk cable-range 3-3
```

*Related Commands*

Search online to find documentation for related commands.

**appletalk address**
**appletalk discovery**
**appletalk zone**

## APPLETALK CHECKSUM

To enable the generation and verification of checksums for all AppleTalk packets (except routed packets), use the **appletalk checksum** global configuration command. To disable checksum generation and verification, use the **no** form of this command.

>**appletalk checksum**
>**no appletalk checksum**

*Syntax      Description*

This command has no arguments or keywords.

*Default*

Enabled

*Command Mode*

Global configuration

*Usage Guidelines*

This command first appeared in Cisco IOS Release 10.0.

When the **appletalk checksum** command is enabled, the Cisco IOS software discards incoming Datagram Delivery Protocol (DDP) packets when the checksum is not zero and is incorrect and when the router is the final destination for the packet.

You might want to disable checksum generation and verification if you have very early devices (such as LaserWriter printers) that cannot receive packets that contain checksums.

The Cisco IOS software does not check checksums on routed packets, thereby eliminating the need to disable checksum to allow operation of some networking applications.

*Example*

The following example disables the generation and verification of checksums:

```
no appletalk checksum
```

*Command Reference*

*Related Commands*

Search online to find documentation for related commands.

**show appletalk globals**

## APPLETALK CLIENT-MODE

To allow users to access an AppleTalk zone when dialing into an asynchronous line (on Cisco routers, only via the auxiliary port), use the **appletalk client-mode** interface configuration command. To disable this function, use the **no** form of this command.

> **appletalk client-mode**
> **no appletalk client-mode**

*Syntax      Description*

This command has no arguments or keywords.

*Default*

Client mode is disabled.

*Command Mode*

Interface configuration

*Usage Guidelines*

This command first appeared in Cisco IOS Release 10.3.

The **appletalk client-mode** command allows a remote client to use an asynchronous interface to access AppleTalk zones, use networked peripherals, and share files with other Macintosh users.

This command works only on asynchronous interfaces on which Point-to-Point Protocol (PPP) encapsulation is enabled. Also, you must first create an internal network for the Macintosh client using the **appletalk virtual-net** global configuration command.

An interface configured with the **appletalk client-mode** and **appletalk virtual-net** global commands does not support routing.

*Example*

The following example allows a user to access AppleTalk functionality on an asynchronous line using PPP:

```
interface asynchronous 1
appletalk client-mode
```

## Related Commands

Search online to find documentation for related commands.

appletalk virtual-net
encapsulation
interface async
ppp

## APPLETALK DISCOVERY

To place an interface into discovery mode, use the **appletalk discovery** interface configuration command. To disable discovery mode, use the **no** form of this command.

> **appletalk discovery**
> **no appletalk discovery**

### Syntax    Description

This command has no arguments or keywords.

### Default

Disabled

### Command Mode

Interface configuration

### Usage Guidelines

This command first appeared in Cisco IOS Release 10.0.

If an interface is connected to a network that has at least one other operational AppleTalk router, you can dynamically configure the interface using *discovery mode*. In discovery mode, an interface acquires network address information about the attached network from an operational router and then uses this information to configure itself.

If you enable discovery mode on an interface, when the Cisco router starts up, that interface must acquire information to configure itself from another operational router on the attached network. If no operational router is present on the connected network, the interface will not start.

If you do not enable discovery mode, the interface must acquire its configuration from memory when the router starts. If the stored configuration is not complete, the interface will not start. If there is another operational router on the connected network, the router verifies the interface's stored configuration with that router. If there is any discrepancy, the interface does not start. If there are no neighboring operational routers, the router assumes the interface's stored configuration is correct and starts.

After an interface is operational, it can seed the configurations of other routers on the connected network regardless of whether you have enabled discovery mode on any of the routers.

If you enable **appletalk discovery** and the interface is restarted, another operational router must still be present on the directly connected network in order for the interface to start.

It is not advisable to have all routers on a network configured with discovery mode enabled. If all routers were to restart simultaneously (for instance, after a power failure), the network would become inaccessible until at least one router were restarted with discovery mode disabled.

You can also enable discovery mode by specifying an address of 0.0. in the **appletalk address** command or a cable range of 0-0 in the **appletalk cable-range** command.

Discovery mode is useful when you are changing a network configuration or when you are adding a router to an existing network.

Discovery mode does not run over serial lines.

Use the **no appletalk discovery** command to disable discovery mode. If the interface is not operational when you issue this command (that is, if you have not issued an **access-list zone** command on the interface), you must configure the zone name next. If the interface is operational when you issue the **no appletalk discovery** command, you can save the current configuration (in running memory) in nonvolatile memory by issuing the **copy running-config startup-config** command. (The **copy running-config startup-config** command replaces the write memory command. Refer to the description of the **copy running-config startup-config** command for more information.)

### Example

The following example enables discovery mode on Ethernet interface 0:

```
interface ethernet 0
appletalk discovery
```

### Related Commands

Search online to find documentation for related commands.

**appletalk address**
**appletalk cable-range**
**appletalk zone**
**copy running-config startup-config**
**show appletalk interface**

## APPLETALK DISTRIBUTE-LIST IN

To filter routing updates received from other routers over a specified interface, use the **appletalk distribute-list in** interface configuration command. To remove the routing table update filter, use the **no** form of this command.

> **appletalk distribute-list** *access-list-number* **in**
> **no appletalk distribute-list** [*access-list-number* **in**]

| Syntax | Description |
|--------|-------------|
| *access-list-number* | Number of the access list. This is a decimal number from 600 to 699. |

## Default

No routing filters are preconfigured.

## Command Mode

Interface configuration

## Usage Guidelines

This command first appeared in Cisco IOS Release 10.0.

The **appletalk distribute-list in** command controls which networks and cable ranges in routing updates are entered into the local routing table.

Filters for incoming routing updates use access lists that define conditions for networks and cable ranges only. They cannot use access lists that define conditions for zones. All zone information in an access list assigned to the interface with the **appletalk distribute-list in** command is ignored.

An input distribution list filters network numbers received in an incoming routing update. When AppleTalk routing updates are received on the specified interface, each network number and cable range in the update is checked against the access list. Only network numbers and cable ranges that are permitted by the access list are inserted into the Cisco IOS software AppleTalk routing table.

## Example

The following example prevents the router from accepting routing table updates received from network 10 and on Ethernet interface 3:

```
access-list 601 deny network 10
access-list 601 permit other-access
interface ethernet 3
appletalk distribute-list 601 in
```

## Related Commands

Search online to find documentation for related commands.

**access-list cable-range**
**access-list includes**
**access-list network**
**access-list other-access**
**access-list within**
**appletalk distribute-list out**

## APPLETALK DISTRIBUTE-LIST OUT

To filter routing updates transmitted to other routers, use the **appletalk distribute-list out** interface configuration command. To remove the routing table update filter, use the **no** form of this command.

> **appletalk distribute-list** *access-list-number* **out**
> **no appletalk distribute-list** [*access-list-number* **out**]

| Syntax | Description |
| --- | --- |
| *access-list-number* | Number of the access list. This is a decimal number from 600 to 699. |

### Default

No routing filters are preconfigured.

### Command Mode

Interface configuration

### Usage Guidelines

This command first appeared in Cisco IOS Release 10.0.

The **appletalk distribute-list out** command controls which network numbers and cable ranges are included in routing updates and which zones the local router includes in its GetZoneList (GZL) replies.

When an AppleTalk routing update is generated on the specified interface, each network number and cable range in the routing table is checked against the access list. If an undefined access list is used, all network numbers and cable ranges are added to the routing update. Otherwise, if an access list is defined, only network numbers and cable ranges that satisfy the following conditions are added to the routing update:

- The network number or cable range is not explicitly or implicitly denied.
- The network number or cable range is not a member of a zone that is explicitly or implicitly denied.
- If **appletalk permit-partial-zones** is disabled (the default), the network number or cable range is not a member of a zone that is partially obscured.

A zone is considered partially obscured when one or more network numbers or cable ranges that are members of the zone is explicitly or implicitly denied.

When a Zone Information Protocol (ZIP) GZL reply is generated, only zones that satisfy the following conditions are included:

- If **appletalk permit-partial-zones** is enabled, at least one network number or cable range that is a member of the zone is explicitly or implicitly permitted.

- If **appletalk permit-partial-zones** is disabled, all network numbers or cable ranges are explicitly or implicitly permitted.

- The zone is explicitly or implicitly permitted.

---

**NOTES**

---

AppleTalk zone access lists on an Enhanced IGRP interface do not filter the distribution of Enhanced IGRP routes. When the **appletalk distribute-list out** command is applied to an Enhanced IGRP interface, any **access-list zone** commands in the specified access list will be ignored.

---

### Example

The following example prevents routing updates sent on Ethernet 0 from mentioning any networks in zone Admin:

```
access-list 601 deny zone Admin
access-list 601 permit other-access
interface Ethernet 0
appletalk distribute-list 601 out
```

### Related Commands

Search online to find documentation for related commands.

**access-list additional-zones**
**access-list zone**
**appletalk distribute-list in**
**appletalk getzonelist-filter**
**appletalk permit-partial-zones**

## APPLETALK DOMAIN-GROUP

To assign a predefined domain number to an interface, use the **appletalk domain-group** interface configuration command. To remove an interface from a domain, use the **no** form of this command.

**appletalk domain-group** *domain-number*
**no appletalk domain-group** [*domain-number*]

| Syntax | Description |
|---|---|
| *domain-number* | Number of an AppleTalk domain. It can be a decimal integer from 1 to 1000000. |

### Default

No domain number is assigned to the interface.

## Command Mode

Interface configuration

## Usage Guidelines

This command first appeared in Cisco IOS Release 10.3.

Before you can assign a domain number to an interface, you must create a domain with that domain number using the **appletalk domain name** global configuration command.

One or more interfaces on a router can be members of the same domain. However, a given interface can be in only one domain.

After you assign AppleTalk interenterprise features to an AppleTalk domain, you can attribute those features to a tunnel interface configured for AURP by assigning the AppleTalk domain-group number to the tunnel interface.

## Examples

The following example assigns domain group 1 to Ethernet interface 0:

```
interface ethernet 0
appletalk domain-group 1
```

The following example assigns domain group 1 to tunnel interface 2. Assuming that domain group 1 is configured for AppleTalk interenterprise and that tunnel interface 2 is configured for AURP, any features configured for domain group 1 are ascribed to AURP on tunnel interface 2.

```
interface tunnel 2
appletalk domain-group 1
```

## Related Commands

Search online to find documentation for related commands.

**appletalk domain name**
**show appletalk domain**

## APPLETALK DOMAIN HOP-REDUCTION

To reduce the hop-count value in packets traveling between segments of domains, use the **appletalk domain hop-reduction** global configuration command. To disable the reduction of hop-count values, use the **no** form of this command.

> **appletalk domain** *domain-number* **hop-reduction**
> **no appletalk domain** *domain-number* **hop-reduction**

| Syntax | Description |
|---|---|
| *domain-number* | Number of an AppleTalk domain. It can be a decimal integer from 1 to 1000000. |

## Default

Reduction of hop-count values is disabled.

## Command Mode

Global configuration

## Usage Guidelines

This command first appeared in Cisco IOS Release 10.3.

Before you can specify the **appletalk domain hop-reduction** global configuration command, you must have created a domain with that domain number using the **appletalk domain name** global configuration command.

DDP and Routing Table Maintenance Protocol (RTMP) both impose a 15-hop limit when forwarding packets. A packet ages out and is no longer forwarded when its hop count reaches 16. To overcome RTMP's 15-hop limit, the domain router represents all networks accessible to routers on its local network as one hop away. This allows routers to maintain and send routing information about networks beyond the 15-hop limit and achieve full connectivity.

When you enable hop-count reduction, delivery of packets from networks that are farther than 15 hops apart is guaranteed.

When you enable hop-count reduction, the hop count in a packet is set to 1 as it passes from one domain to another. For example, if the hop count was 8 when the packet left one domain, its hop count is 1 when it enters the next segment of the domain.

## Example

The following example enables hop-count reduction for domain number 1:

```
appletalk domain 1 name Delta
appletalk domain 1 hop-reduction
```

## Related Commands

Search online to find documentation for related commands.

**appletalk domain name**
**show appletalk domain**

## APPLETALK DOMAIN NAME

To create a domain and assign it a name and number, use the **appletalk domain name** global configuration command. To remove a domain, use the **no** form of this command.

> **appletalk domain** *domain-number* **name** *domain-name*
> **no appletalk domain** *domain-number* **name** *domain-name*

| Syntax | Description |
|---|---|
| *domain-number* | Number of an AppleTalk domain. It can be a decimal integer from 1 to 1000000. |
| *domain-name* | Name of an AppleTalk domain. The name must be unique across the AppleTalk internetwork. It can be up to 32 characters long and can include special characters from the Apple Macintosh character set. To include a special character, type a colon, followed by two hexadecimal characters. For zone names with a leading space character, enter the first character as the special sequence :20. |

### Default

No domain is created.

### Command Mode

Global configuration

### Usage Guidelines

This command first appeared in Cisco IOS Release 10.3.

### Example

The following example creates domain number 1 and assigns it the domain name *Delta*:

```
appletalk domain 1 name Delta
```

### Related Commands

Search online to find documentation for related commands.

**appletalk routing**
**show appletalk domain**

## APPLETALK DOMAIN REMAP-RANGE

To remap ranges of AppleTalk network numbers or cable ranges between two segments of a domain, use the **appletalk domain remap-range** global configuration command. To disable remapping, use the **no** form of this command.

**appletalk domain** *domain-number* **remap-range** {**in** | **out**} *cable-range*
**no appletalk domain** *domain-number* **remap-range** {**in** | **out**} [*cable-range*]

| Syntax | Description |
| --- | --- |
| *domain-number* | Number of an AppleTalk domain. It can be a decimal integer from 1 to 1000000. |
| **in** | Specifies that the remapping is performed on inbound packets (that is, on packets arriving into the local interenterprise network). All network numbers or cable ranges coming from the domain are remapped into the specified range. |
| **out** | Specifies that the remapping is performed on outbound packets (that is, on packets exiting from the local interenterprise network). All network numbers or cable ranges going to the domain are remapped into the specified range. |
| *cable-range* | The argument specifies the start and end of the cable range, separated by a hyphen. The starting network must be the first AppleTalk network number or the beginning of the cable range to remap. The number must be immediately followed by a hyphen. The ending network must be the last AppleTalk network number or the end of the cable range to remap. |

### Default

No remapping is performed.

### Command Mode

Global configuration

### Usage Guidelines

This command first appeared in Cisco IOS Release 10.3.

Before you can specify the **appletalk domain remap-range** command, you must create a domain with that domain number using the **appletalk domain name** global configuration command.

Inbound and outbound packets are relative to the domain router.

Ensure that the domain range you specify does not overlap any network addresses or cable ranges that already exist in the AppleTalk interenterprise network.

Each domain can have two domain mapping ranges to which to remap all incoming or outgoing network numbers or cable ranges. Incoming remapping ranges cannot overlap. However, outbound remapping ranges can overlap.

When an AppleTalk network in a domain becomes inactive, its remapped entry is removed from the remapping table. This frees the space for another network to be remapped.

If there are more remote domains than available remapping range numbers, the Cisco IOS software displays an error message and shuts down domains.

## Example

The following example remaps all network addresses and cable ranges for packets inbound from domain 1 into the address range 1000 to 1999. It also remaps packets inbound from domain 2.

```
appletalk domain 1 name Delta
appletalk domain 2 name Echo
appletalk domain 1 remap-range in 10000-10999
appletalk domain 2 remap-range in 20000-20999
```

## Related Commands

Search online to find documentation for related commands.

**appletalk domain name**
**show appletalk remap**

## APPLETALK EIGRP ACTIVE-TIME

To specify the length of time that Enhanced IGRP routes can be active, use the **appletalk eigrp active-time** global configuration command. To return to the default value of one minute, use the **no** form of the command.

> **appletalk eigrp active-time** {*minutes* | **disabled**}
> **no appletalk eigrp active-time**

| Syntax | Description |
|---|---|
| *minutes* | Enhanced IGRP active state time (in minutes). Valid values are from 1 to 4294967295 minutes. |
| **disabled** | Disables the Enhanced IGRP active state time limit. Routes remain active indefinitely. |

## Default

1 minute

## Command Mode

Global configuration

## Usage Guidelines

This command first appeared in Cisco IOS Release 11.1.

The command allows you to configure the length of time that Enhanced IGRP routes can remain active. When a route reaches the active state time limit, the Cisco IOS software logs an error and removes the route from the routing table. You can view the current setting of the Enhanced IGRP active state time by using the **show appletalk globals** command.

## Example

The following example shows the current setting of the Enhanced IGRP active state time using the **show appletalk globals** command, changes the setting using the **appletalk eigrp active-time** command, and then displays the changed setting (using the **show appletalk globals** command again):

```
Router# show appletalk globals
AppleTalk global information:
  Internet is incompatible with older, AT Phase1, routers.
  There are 4 routes in the internet.
  There are 7 zones defined.
  Logging of significant AppleTalk events is disabled.
  ZIP resends queries every 10 seconds.
  RTMP updates are sent every 10 seconds.
  RTMP entries are considered BAD after 20 seconds.
  RTMP entries are discarded after 60 seconds.
  AARP probe retransmit count: 10, interval: 200 msec.
  AARP request retransmit count: 5, interval: 1000 msec.
  DDP datagrams will be checksummed.
  RTMP datagrams will be strictly checked.
  RTMP routes may not be propagated without zones.
  Routes will be distributed between routing protocols.
  Routing between local devices on an interface will not be performed.
  EIGRP router id is: 1
  EIGRP maximum active time is 1 minutes
  IPTalk uses the udp base port of 768 (Default).
  Alternate node address format will not be displayed.
  Access control of any networks of a zone hides the zone.
Router#
Router# configure terminal
Enter configuration commands, one per line.  End with CNTL/Z.
Router(config)# appletalk eigrp active-time 5
Router(config)# end
Router#

Router# show appletalk globals
AppleTalk global information:
  Internet is incompatible with older, AT Phase1, routers.
  There are 4 routes in the internet.
  There are 7 zones defined.
  Logging of significant AppleTalk events is disabled.
  ZIP resends queries every 10 seconds.
  RTMP updates are sent every 10 seconds.
  RTMP entries are considered BAD after 20 seconds.
  RTMP entries are discarded after 60 seconds.
  AARP probe retransmit count: 10, interval: 200 msec.
  AARP request retransmit count: 5, interval: 1000 msec.
  DDP datagrams will be checksummed.
  RTMP datagrams will be strictly checked.
  RTMP routes may not be propagated without zones.
```

```
Routes will be distributed between routing protocols.
Routing between local devices on an interface will not be performed.
EIGRP router id is: 1
EIGRP maximum active time is 5 minutes
IPTalk uses the udp base port of 768 (Default).
Alternate node address format will not be displayed.
Access control of any networks of a zone hides the zone.
```

### Related Commands

Search online to find documentation for related commands.

**show appletalk globals**

## APPLETALK EIGRP-BANDWIDTH-PERCENT

To configure the percentage of bandwidth that may be used by Enhanced IGRP on an interface, use the **appletalk eigrp-bandwidth-percent** interface configuration command. To restore the default value, use the **no** form of this command.

> **appletalk eigrp-bandwidth-percent** *percent*
> **no appletalk eigrp-bandwidth-percent**

| Syntax | Description |
|--------|-------------|
| *percent* | Percentage of bandwidth that Enhanced IGRP may use. |

### Default

50 percent

### Command Mode

Interface configuration

### Usage Guidelines

This command first appeared in Cisco IOS Release 11.2.

Enhanced IGRP uses up to 50 percent of the bandwidth of a link, as defined by the **bandwidth** interface configuration command. This command may be used if some other fraction of the bandwidth is desired. Note that values greater than 100 percent may be configured; this may be useful if the bandwidth is set artificially low for other reasons.

### Example

The following example allows Enhanced IGRP to use up to 75 percent (42 kbps) of a 56 kbps serial link.

```
interface serial 0
bandwidth 56
appletalk eigrp-bandwidth-percent 75
```

## Related Commands

Search online to find documentation for related commands.

**appletalk routing**
**bandwidth**

## APPLETALK EIGRP LOG-NEIGHBOR-CHANGES

To enable the logging of changes in Enhanced IGRP neighbor adjacencies, use the **appletalk eigrp log-neighbor-changes** global configuration command. To disable this function, use the **no** form of this command.

> **appletalk eigrp log-neighbor-changes**
> **no appletalk eigrp log-neighbor-changes**

## Syntax    Description

This command has no arguments or keywords.

## Default

No adjacency changes are logged.

## Command Mode

Global configuration

## Usage Guidelines

This command first appeared in Cisco IOS Release 11.2.

Enables the logging of neighbor adjacency changes to monitor the stability of the routing system and to help detect problems. Log messages are of the form:

```
%DUAL-5-NBRCHANGE: AT/EIGRP 1: Neighbor address (interface) is state: reason
```

The arguments have the following meanings:

| | |
|---|---|
| *address* | Neighbor address. |
| *state* | Up or down. |
| *reason* | Reason for change. |

## Example

The following configuration logs neighbor changes for AppleTalk Enhanced IGRP.

```
appletalk eigrp log-neighbor-changes
```

*Related Commands*

Search online to find documentation for related commands.

**appletalk routing**


## APPLETALK EIGRP-SPLITHORIZON

To enable split horizon, use the **appletalk eigrp-splithorizon** interface configuration command. To disable split horizon, use the **no** form of this command.

> **appletalk eigrp-splithorizon**
> **no appletalk eigrp-splithorizon**

*Syntax        Description*

This command has no arguments or keywords.


*Default*

Enabled


*Command Mode*

Interface configuration


*Usage Guidelines*

This command first appeared in Cisco IOS Release 10.3.

If you enable split horizon on an interface, AppleTalk Enhanced IGRP update and query packets are not sent if the interface is the next hop to that destination. This reduces the number of Enhanced IGRP packets of the network.

Split horizon blocks information about routes from being advertised by a router out any interface from which that information originated. This behavior usually optimizes communication among multiple routers, particularly when links are broken. However, with nonbroadcast networks, such as Frame Relay and Switched Multimegabit Data Service (SMDS), situations can arise for which this behavior is less than ideal. For these situations, you may want to disable split horizon.


*Example*

The following example disables split horizon on serial interface 0:

```
interface serial 0
no appletalk eigrp-splithorizon
```

## APPLETALK EIGRP-TIMERS

To configure the AppleTalk Enhanced IGRP hello packet interval and the route hold time, use the **appletalk eigrp-timers** interface configuration command. To return to the default values for these timers, use the **no** form of this command.

>**appletalk eigrp-timers** *hello-interval hold-time*
>**no appletalk eigrp-timers** *hello-interval hold-time*

| Syntax | Description |
|---|---|
| *hello-interval* | Interval between hello packets, in seconds. The default interval is 5 seconds. It can be a maximum of 30 seconds. |
| *hold-time* | Hold time, in seconds. The hold time is advertised in hello packets. It indicates to neighbors the length of time they should consider the sender valid. The hold time can be in the range from 15 to 90 seconds. |

### Default

*hello-interval*:
For low-speed NBMA networks: 60 seconds
For all other networks: 5 seconds

*hold-time*:
For low-speed NBMA networks: 180 seconds
For all other networks: 15 seconds

### Command Mode

Interface configuration

### Usage Guidelines

This command first appeared in Cisco IOS Release 10.3.

If the current value for the hold time is less than two times the hello interval, the hold time is reset to three times the hello interval.

If the Cisco IOS software does not receive a hello packet within the specified hold time, routes through this device are considered available.

Increasing the hold time delays route convergence across the network.

**NOTES**

Do not adjust the hold time without advising technical support.

The default of 180 seconds for *hold-time* applies only to low-speed, nonbroadcast, multiaccess (NBMA) media. Low speed is considered to be a rate of T1 or slower, as specified with the **bandwidth** interface configuration command.

The default of 60 seconds for *hello-interval* applies only to low-speed NBMA media. Low speed is considered to be a rate of T1 or slower, as specified with the **bandwidth** interface configuration command. Note that for purposes of Enhanced IGRP, Frame Relay and SMDS networks may or may not be considered to be NBMA. These networks are considered NBMA if the interface has not been configured to use physical multicasting; otherwise, they are considered not to be NBMA.

### Example

The following example changes the hello interval to 10 seconds:

```
interface ethernet 0
appletalk eigrp-timers 10 45
```

## APPLETALK EVENT-LOGGING

To log significant network events, use the **appletalk event-logging** global configuration command. To disable this function, use the **no** form of this command.

> **appletalk event-logging**
> **no appletalk event-logging**

### Syntax     Description

This command has no arguments or keywords.

### Default

Disabled

### Command Mode

Global configuration

### Usage Guidelines

This command first appeared in Cisco IOS Release 10.0.

The **appletalk event-logging** command logs a subset of messages produced by the **debug appletalk** command. These messages include routing changes, zone creation, port status, and address.

### Example

The following example enables logging of AppleTalk events:

```
appletalk routing
appletalk event-logging
```

## Related Commands

Search online to find documentation for related commands.

**show appletalk globals**

## APPLETALK FREE-TRADE-ZONE

To establish a free-trade zone, use the **appletalk free-trade-zone** interface configuration command. To disable a free-trade zone, use the **no** form of this command.

> **appletalk free-trade-zone**
> **no appletalk free-trade-zone**

### Syntax      Description

This command has no arguments or keywords.

### Default

Disabled

### Command Mode

Interface configuration

### Usage Guidelines

This command first appeared in Cisco IOS Release 10.0.

A *free-trade zone* is a part of an AppleTalk internetwork that is accessible by two other parts of the internetwork, neither of which can access the other. You might want to create a free-trade zone to allow the exchange of information between two organizations that otherwise want to keep their internetworks isolated from each other or that do not have physical connectivity with one another.

You apply the **appletalk free-trade-zone** command to each interface attached to the common-access network. This command has the following effect on the interface:

- All incoming RTMP updates are ignored.
- All outgoing RTMP updates contain no information.
- NBP conversion of BrRq packets to FwdReq packets is not performed.

The GZL for free-trade zone nodes will be empty.

### Example

The following example establishes a free-trade zone on Ethernet interface 0:

```
interface ethernet 0
appletalk cable-range 5-5
appletalk zone FreeAccessZone
appletalk free-trade-zone
```

## APPLETALK GETZONELIST-FILTER

To filter GZL replies, use the **appletalk getzonelist-filter** interface configuration command. To remove a filter, use the **no** form of this command.

> **appletalk getzonelist-filter** *access-list-number*
> **no appletalk getzonelist-filter** [*access-list-number*]

| Syntax | Description |
|---|---|
| *access-list-number* | Number of the access list. This is a decimal number from 600 to 699. |

### Default

No filters are preconfigured.

### Command Mode

Interface configuration

### Usage Guidelines

This command first appeared in Cisco IOS Release 10.0.

GZL filters define conditions for zones only. They cannot use access lists that define conditions for network numbers or cable ranges. All network number and cable range information in the access list assigned to an interface with the **appletalk getzonelist-filter** command is ignored.

Using a GZL filter is not a complete replacement for anonymous network numbers. In order to prevent users from seeing a zone, all routers must implement the GZL filter. If there are any routers from other vendors on the network, the GZL filter will not have a consistent effect.

The Macintosh Chooser uses ZIP GZL requests to compile a list of zones from which the user can select services. Any router on the same network as the Macintosh can respond to these requests with a GZL reply. You can create a GZL filter on the router to control which zones the router mentions in its GZL replies. This has the effect of controlling the list of zones that are displayed by the Chooser.

When defining GZL filters, you should ensure that all routers on the same internetwork filter the GZL reply identically. Otherwise, the Chooser lists different zones, depending upon which router responded to the request. Also, inconsistent filters can result in zones appearing and disappearing every few seconds when the user remains in the Chooser. Because of these inconsistencies, you should normally use the **appletalk getzonelist-filter** command only when all routers in the internetwork are Cisco routers, unless the routers from other vendors have a similar feature.

Replies to GZL requests are also filtered by any **appletalk distribute-list out** filter that has been applied to the same interface. You must specify an **appletalk getzonelist-filter** command only if you want additional filtering to be applied to GZL replies. This filter is rarely needed except to eliminate zones that do not contain user services.

## Example

The following example does not include the zone Engineering in GZL replies sent out Ethernet interface 0:

```
access-list 600 deny zone Engineering
interface ethernet 0
appletalk getzonelist-filter 600
```

## Related Commands

Search online to find documentation for related commands.

**access-list additional-zones**
**access-list zone**
**appletalk distribute-list out**
**appletalk permit-partial-zones**

## APPLETALK GLEAN-PACKETS

To derive AARP table entries from incoming packets, use the **appletalk glean-packets** interface configuration command. To disable this function, use the **no** form of this command.

> **appletalk glean-packets**
> **no appletalk glean-packets**

## Syntax      Description

This command has no arguments or keywords.

## Default

Enabled

## Command Mode

Interface configuration

## Usage Guidelines

This command first appeared in Cisco IOS Release 10.0.

The Cisco IOS software automatically derives AARP table entries from incoming packets. This process is referred to as *gleaning*, which speeds up the process of populating the AARP table.

Cisco's implementation of AppleTalk does not forward packets with local source and destination network addresses. This behavior does not conform with the definition of AppleTalk in Apple Computer's *Inside AppleTalk* publication. However, this behavior is designed to prevent any possible corruption of the AARP table in any AppleTalk node that is performing MAC-address gleaning.

*Example*

The following example disables the building of the AARP table using information derived from incoming packets:

```
interface ethernet 0
appletalk address 33
no appletalk glean-packets
```

## APPLETALK IGNORE-VERIFY-ERRORS

To allow the Cisco IOS software to start functioning even if the network is misconfigured, use the **appletalk ignore-verify-errors** global configuration command. To disable this function, use the **no** form of this command.

> **appletalk ignore-verify-errors**
> **no appletalk ignore-verify-errors**

*Syntax          Description*

This command has no arguments or keywords.

*Default*

Disabled

*Command Mode*

Global configuration

*Usage Guidelines*

This command first appeared in Cisco IOS Release 10.0.

Use this command only under the guidance of a customer engineer or other service representative. A router that starts routing in a misconfigured network serves only to make a bad situation worse; it does not correct other misconfigured routers.

*Example*

The following example allows a router to start functioning without verifying network misconfiguration:

```
appletalk ignore-verify-errors
```

## APPLETALK IPTALK

To enable IPTalk encapsulation on a tunnel interface, use the **appletalk iptalk** interface configuration command. To disable IPTalk encapsulation, use the **no** form of this command.

> **appletalk iptalk** *network zone*
> **no appletalk iptalk** [*network zone*]

| Syntax | Description |
|--------|-------------|
| *network* | AppleTalk network address assigned to the interface. The argument *network* is the 16-bit network number in decimal. |
| *zone* | Name of the zone for the connected AppleTalk network. |

### Default

Disabled

### Command Mode

Interface configuration

### Usage Guidelines

This command first appeared in Cisco IOS Release 10.0.

Use the **appletalk iptalk** command to enable IPTalk encapsulation on a tunnel interface. This command encapsulates AppleTalk in IP packets in a manner compatible with the Columbia AppleTalk Package (CAP) IPTalk and the Kinetics IPTalk implementations. IPTalk is configured on a tunnel interface.

This command allows AppleTalk communication with UNIX hosts running older versions of CAP that do not support native AppleTalk EtherTalk encapsulations. Typically, Apple Macintosh users wanting to communicate with these servers would have their connections routed through a Kinetics FastPath router running Kinetics IPTalk software.

This command is provided as a migration command; newer versions of CAP provide native AppleTalk EtherTalk encapsulations, and the IPTalk encapsulation is no longer required. Cisco's implementation of IPTalk assumes that AppleTalk is already being routed on the backbone; there is currently no LocalTalk hardware interface for Cisco routers.

Cisco's implementation of IPTalk does not support manually configured AppleTalk-to-IP address mapping (atab). The address mapping provided is the same as the Kinetics IPTalk implementation when the atab facility is not enabled. This address mapping functions as follows: The IP subnet mask used on the Ethernet interface on which IPTalk is enabled is inverted (ones complement). This result is then masked against 255 (0xFF hexadecimal). This is then masked against the low-order 8 bits of the IP address to obtain the AppleTalk node number.

### Example

The following example configuration illustrates how to configure IPTalk:

```
interface Ethernet0
ip address 131.108.1.118 255.255.255.0
interface Tunnel0
tunnel source Ethernet0
tunnel mode iptalk
appletalk iptalk 30 UDPZone
```

In this configuration, the IP subnet mask would be inverted:

```
255.255.255.0 inverted yields: 0.0.0.255
```

Masked with 255 it yields 255, and masked with the low-order 8 bits of the interface IP address it yields 118.

This means that the AppleTalk address of the Ethernet 0 interface seen in the UDPZone zone is 30.118. This caveat should be noted, however: Should the host field of an IP subnet mask for an interface be more than 8 bits wide, it is possible to obtain conflicting AppleTalk node numbers. For instance, consider a situation in which the subnet mask for the preceding Ethernet 0 interface is 255.255.240.0, meaning that the host field is 12 bits wide.

### Related Commands

Search online to find documentation for related commands.

**appletalk iptalk-baseport**
**tunnel mode**
**tunnel source**

## APPLETALK IPTALK-BASEPORT

To specify the User Datagram Protocol (UDP) port number when configuring IPTalk, use the **appletalk iptalk-baseport** global configuration command. To return to the default UDP port number, use the **no** form of this command.

> **appletalk iptalk-baseport** *port-number*
> **no appletalk iptalk-baseport** [*port-number*]

### Syntax

*port-number*

### Description

First UDP port number in the range of UDP ports used in mapping AppleTalk well-known DDP socket numbers to UDP ports.

### Default

768

### Command Mode

Global configuration

### Usage Guidelines

This command first appeared in Cisco IOS Release 10.0.

Implementations of IPTalk prior to April 1988 mapped well-known DDP socket numbers to privileged UDP ports starting at port number 768. In April 1988, the Network Information Center (NIC) assigned a range of UDP ports for the defined DDP well-known sockets starting at UDP port number 200 and assigned these ports the names at-nbp, at-rtmp, at-echo, and at-zis. Release 6 and later of the CAP program dynamically decides which port mapping to use. If there are no AppleTalk service entries in the UNIX system's */etc/services* file, CAP uses the older mapping, starting at UDP port number 768.

The default UDP port mapping supported by Cisco's implementation of IPTalk is 768. If there are AppleTalk service entries in the UNIX system's */etc/services* file, you should specify the beginning of the UDP port mapping range with the **appletalk iptalk-baseport** command.

### Example

The following example sets the base UDP port number to 200, which is the official NIC port number, and configures IPTalk on Ethernet interface 0:

```
appletalk routing
appletalk iptalk-baseport 200
!
interface Ethernet 0
ip address 131.108.1.118 255.255.255.0
appletalk address 20.129
appletalk zone Native AppleTalk
appletalk iptalk 30.0 UDPZone
```

### Related Commands

Search online to find documentation for related commands.

**appletalk iptalk**

### APPLETALK LOOKUP-TYPE

To specify which NBP service types are retained in the name cache, use the **appletalk lookup-type** global configuration command. To disable the caching of services, use the **no** form of this command.

> **appletalk lookup-type** *service-type*
> **no appletalk lookup-type** [*service-type*]

| Syntax | Description |
|--------|-------------|
| *service-type* | AppleTalk service types. The name of a service type can include special characters from the Apple Macintosh character set. To include a special character, type a colon, followed by two hexadecimal numbers. For zone names with a leading space character, enter the first character as the special sequence :20. For a list of possible types, see Table 3–2 in the "Usage Guidelines" section. |

### Default

The ciscoRouter entries are retained in the name cache.

### Command Mode

Global configuration

### Usage Guidelines

This command first appeared in Cisco IOS Release 10.0.

You can issue multiple **appletalk lookup-type** commands. The Cisco IOS software does not query the entire zone but instead polls only the connected networks. This reduces network overhead and means that the name cache contains entries only for selected services in a directly connected network or zone, not for all the selected services in a network or zone.

Table 3–1 lists some AppleTalk service types.

**Table 3–1** *AppleTalk Service Types*

| Service Type[*] | Description |
|---|---|
| **Services for Cisco Routers** | |
| ciscoRouter | Active adjacent Cisco routers. This service type is initially enabled by default. |
| IPADDRESS | Addresses of active MacIP server. |
| IPGATEWAY | Names of active MacIP server. |
| SNMP Agent | Active SNMP agents in Cisco routers. |
| **Services for Other Vendors' Routers** | |
| AppleRouter | Apple internetwork router. |
| FastPath | Shiva LocalTalk gateway. |
| GatorBox | Cayman LocalTalk gateway. |
| systemRouter | Cisco's OEM router name. |
| Workstation | Macintosh running System 7. The machine type also is defined, so it is possible to easily identify all user nodes. |

[*] Type all service names exactly as shown. Spaces are valid. Do not use leading or trailing spaces when entering service names.

If you omit the *service-type* argument from the **no appletalk lookup-type** command, no service types except those relating to Cisco devices are cached.

To display information that is stored in the name cache about the services being used by Cisco routers and other vendors' routers, use the **show appletalk name-cache** command.

If a neighboring router is not a Cisco device or is running Cisco software that is earlier than Release 9.0, it is possible that Cisco's device will be unable to determine the name of the neighbor. This is normal behavior, and there is no workaround.

If AppleTalk routing is enabled, enabling Simple Network Management Protocol (SNMP) will automatically enable SNMP over DDP.

Name cache entries are deleted after several interval periods expire without being refreshed. (You set the interval with the **appletalk name-lookup-interval** command.) At each interval, a single request is sent via each interface that has valid addresses.

### Example

The following example caches information about GatorBox services, Apple internetwork routers, MacIP services, and workstations. Information about Cisco devices is automatically cached.

```
appletalk lookup-type GatorBox
appletalk lookup-type AppleRouter
appletalk lookup-type IPGATEWAY
appletalk lookup-type Workstation
```

### Related Commands

Search online to find documentation for related commands.

**appletalk name-lookup-interval**
**show appletalk name-cache**
**show appletalk nbp**

## APPLETALK MACIP DYNAMIC

To allocate IP addresses to dynamic MacIP clients, use the **appletalk macip dynamic** global configuration command. To delete a MacIP dynamic address assignment, use the **no** form of this command.

> **appletalk macip dynamic** *ip-address* [*ip-address*] **zone** *server-zone*
> **no appletalk macip** [**dynamic** *ip-address* [*ip-address*] **zone** *server-zone*]

| Syntax | Description |
|---|---|
| *ip-address* | IP address, in four-part, dotted decimal notation. To specify a range, enter two IP addresses, which represent the first and last addresses in the range. |
| **zone** *server-zone* | Zone in which the MacIP server resides. The argument *server-zone* can include special characters from the Apple Macintosh character set. To include a special character, specify a colon followed by two hexadecimal characters. For zone names with a leading space character, enter the first character as the special sequence :20. For a list of Macintosh characters, refer to Apple Computer's *Inside AppleTalk* publication. |

## Default

No IP addresses are allocated.

## Command Mode

Global configuration

## Usage Guidelines

This command first appeared in Cisco IOS Release 10.0.

Use the **appletalk macip dynamic** command when configuring MacIP.

Dynamic clients are those that accept *any* IP address assignment within the dynamic range specified.

In general, it is recommended that you do not use fragmented address ranges in configuring ranges for MacIP. However, if this is unavoidable, use the **appletalk macip dynamic** command to specify as many addresses or ranges as required and use the **appletalk macip static** command to assign a specific address or address range.

To shut down all running MacIP services, use the following command:

> **no appletalk macip**

To delete a particular dynamic address assignment from the configuration, use the following command:

> **no appletalk macip dynamic** *ip-address* [*ip-address*] **zone** *server-zone*

## Example

The following example illustrates MacIP support for dynamically addressed MacIP clients with IP addresses in the range from 131.108.1.28 to 131.108.1.44:

```
!This global statement specifies the MacIP server address and zone:
appletalk macip server 131.108.1.27 zone Engineering
!
!This global statement identifies the dynamically addressed clients:
appletalk macip dynamic 131.108.1.28 131.108.1.44 zone Engineering
!
!These statements assign the IP address and subnet mask for Ethernet interface 0:
interface ethernet 0
ip address 131.108.1.27 255.255.255.0
!
!This global statement enables AppleTalk routing on the router.
appletalk routing
!
!These statements enable AppleTalk routing on the interface and
!set the zone name for the interface
interface ethernet 0
appletalk cable-range 69-69 69.128
appletalk zone Engineering
```

*Related Commands*

Search online to find documentation for related commands.

**appletalk macip server**
**appletalk macip static**
**ip address**
**show appletalk macip-servers**

## APPLETALK MACIP SERVER

To establish a MacIP server for a zone, use the **appletalk macip server** global configuration command. To shut down a MacIP server, use the **no** form of this command.

>   **appletalk macip server** *ip-address* zone *server-zone*
>   **no appletalk macip** [**server** *ip-address* zone *server-zone*]

| Syntax | Description |
|---|---|
| *ip-address* | IP address, in four-part, dotted decimal notation. It is suggested that this address match the address of an existing IP interface. |
| **zone** *server-zone* | Zone in which the MacIP server resides. The argument *server-zone* can include special characters from the Apple Macintosh character set. To include a special character, specify a colon followed by two hexadecimal characters. For zone names with a leading space character, enter the first character as the special sequence :20. For a list of Macintosh characters, refer to Apple Computer's *Inside AppleTalk* publication. |

*Default*

No MacIP server is established.

*Command Mode*

Global configuration

*Usage Guidelines*

This command first appeared in Cisco IOS Release 10.0.

Use the **appletalk macip server** command when configuring MacIP.

You can configure only one MacIP server per AppleTalk zone, and the server must reside in the default zone. A server is not registered via NBP until at least one MacIP resource is configured.

You can configure multiple MacIP servers for a router, but you can assign only one MacIP server to a particular zone and only one IP interface to each MacIP server. In general, you must be able to establish an alias between the IP address you assign with the **appletalk macip server** command and an existing IP interface. For implementation simplicity, it is suggested that the address specified in this command match an existing IP interface address.

To shut down all active MacIP servers, use the following command:

**no appletalk macip**

To delete a specific MacIP server from the MacIP configuration, use the following command:

**no appletalk macip server** *ip-address* **zone** *server-zone*

### Example

The following example establishes a MacIP server on Ethernet interface 0 in AppleTalk zone Engineering. It then assigns an IP address to the Ethernet interface and enables AppleTalk routing on a router and its Ethernet interface.

```
appletalk macip server 131.108.1.27 zone Engineering
ip address 131.108.1.27 255.255.255.0
appletalk routing
interface ethernet 0
appletalk cable-range 69-69 69.128
appletalk zone Engineering
```

### Related Commands

Search online to find documentation for related commands.

**appletalk macip dynamic**
**appletalk macip static**
**ip address**
**show appletalk macip-servers**

## APPLETALK MACIP STATIC

To allocate an IP address to be used by a MacIP client that has reserved a static IP address, use the **appletalk macip static** global configuration command. To delete a MacIP static address assignment, use the **no** form of this command.

**appletalk macip static** *ip-address* [*ip-address*] **zone** *server-zone*
**no appletalk macip** [**static** *ip-address* [*ip-address*] **zone** *server-zone*]

| Syntax | Description |
|--------|-------------|
| *ip-address* | IP address, in four-part, dotted decimal format. To specify a range, enter two IP addresses, which represent the first and last addresses in the range. |
| **zone** *server-zone* | Zone in which the MacIP server resides. The argument *server-zone* can include special characters from the Apple Macintosh character set. To include a special character, specify a colon followed by two hexadecimal characters. For zone names with a leading space character, enter the first character as the special sequence :20. For a list of Macintosh characters, refer to Apple Computer's *Inside AppleTalk* publication. |

### Default

No IP address is allocated.

### Command Mode

Global configuration

### Usage Guidelines

This command first appeared in Cisco IOS Release 10.0.

Use the **appletalk macip static** command when configuring MacIP.

Static addresses are for users who require fixed addresses for IP name domain name service and for administrators who do want addresses to change so that they can always know who has what IP address.

In general, it is recommended that you do not use fragmented address ranges in configuring ranges for MacIP. However, if this is unavoidable, use the **appletalk macip dynamic** command to specify as many addresses or ranges as required and then use the **appletalk macip static** command to assign a specific address or address range.

To shut down all running MacIP services, use the following command:

   **no appletalk macip**

To delete a particular static address assignment from the configuration, use the following command:

   **no appletalk macip static** *ip-address* [*ip-address*] **zone** *server-zone*

### Example

The following example illustrates MacIP support for MacIP clients with statically allocated IP addresses. The IP addresses range is from 131.108.1.50 to 131.108.1.66. The three nodes that have the specific addresses are 131.108.1.81, 131.108.1.92, and 131.108.1.101.

```
!This global statement specifies the MacIP server address and zone:
appletalk macip server 131.108.1.27 zone Engineering
!
!These global statements identify the statically addressed clients:
appletalk macip static 131.108.1.50 131.108.1.66 zone Engineering
appletalk macip static 131.108.1.81 zone Engineering
appletalk macip static 131.108.1.92 zone Engineering
appletalk macip static 131.108.1.101 zone Engineering
!
!These statements assign the IP address and subnet mask for Ethernet interface 0:
interface ethernet 0
ip address 131.108.1.27 255.255.255.0
!
!This global statement enables AppleTalk routing on the router.
appletalk routing
!
!These statements enable AppleTalk routing on the interface and
!set the zone name for the interface
interface ethernet 0
appletalk cable-range 69-69 69.128
appletalk zone Engineering
```

## Related Commands

Search online to find documentation for related commands.

**appletalk macip dynamic**
**appletalk macip server**
**ip address**
**show appletalk macip-servers**

## APPLETALK MAXIMUM-PATHS

To define the maximum number of equal-cost paths the router should use when balancing the traffic load, use the **appletalk maximum-paths** global configuration command. To restore the default value, use the **no** form of this command.

> **appletalk maximum-paths** [*paths*]
> **no appletalk maximum-paths** [*paths*]

| Syntax | Description |
|--------|-------------|
| *paths* | Maximum number of equal-cost paths to be used for balancing the traffic load. The *paths* argument is a decimal number in the range from 1 to 16. |

## Default

The default value is 1.

## Command Mode

Global configuration

## Usage Guidelines

This command first appeared in Cisco IOS Release 11.2.

Use the **appletalk maximum-paths** command when configuring AppleTalk load balancing.

The **appletalk maximum-paths** command increases throughput by allowing the software to choose among several equal-cost, parallel paths. (Note that when paths have differing costs, the software chooses lower-cost routes in preference to higher-cost routes.)

When the value of *paths* is greater than 1, packets are distributed over the multiple equal-cost paths in round-robin fashion on a packet-by-packet basis.

## Examples

The following example defines four equal-cost paths:

```
!Set the maximum number of equal-cost paths to 4
appletalk maximum-paths 4
```

The following example restores the default value:

```
!Restore the default value
no appletalk maximum-paths 4
```

## APPLETALK NAME-LOOKUP-INTERVAL

To set the interval between service pollings by the router on its AppleTalk interfaces, use the **appletalk name-lookup-interval** global configuration command. To purge the name cache and return to the default polling interval, use the **no** form of this command.

> **appletalk name-lookup-interval** *seconds*
> **no appletalk name-lookup-interval** [*seconds*]

| Syntax | Description |
|---|---|
| *seconds* | Interval, in seconds, between NBP lookup pollings. This can be any positive integer; there is no upper limit. It is recommended that you use an interval between 300 seconds (5 minutes) and 1,200 seconds (20 minutes). The smaller the interval, the more packets are generated to handle the names. Specifying an interval of 0 purges all entries from the name cache and disables the caching of service type information that is controlled by the **appletalk lookup-type** command, including the caching of information about Cisco routers. |

*Default*

The default is 0, which purges all entries from the name cache and disables the caching of service type information.

*Command Mode*

Global configuration

*Usage Guidelines*

This command first appeared in Cisco IOS Release 10.0.

The Cisco IOS software collects name information only for entities on connected AppleTalk networks. This reduces overhead.

If you enter an interval of 0, all polling for services (except ciscoRouter) is disabled. If you reenter a nonzero value, the configuration specified by the **appletalk lookup-type** command is reinstated. You cannot disable the lookup of ciscoRouter.

*Example*

The following example sets the lookup interval to 20 minutes:

```
appletalk name-lookup-interval 1200
```

*Related Commands*

Search online to find documentation for related commands.

**appletalk lookup-type**
**show appletalk name-cache**

## APPLETALK PERMIT-PARTIAL-ZONES

To permit access to the other networks in a zone when access to one of those networks is denied, use the **appletalk permit-partial-zones** global configuration command. To deny access to all networks in a zone if access to one of those networks is denied, use the **no** form of this command.

> **appletalk permit-partial-zones**
> **no appletalk permit-partial-zones**

*Syntax     Description*

This command has no arguments or keywords.

*Default*

Access denied.

## Command Mode

Global configuration

## Usage Guidelines

This command first appeared in Cisco IOS Release 10.0.

The permitting of partial zones provides IP-style access control.

When you enable the use of partial zones, the NBP protocol cannot ensure the consistency and uniqueness of name bindings.

If you enable the use of partial zones, access control behavior is compatible with that of Cisco IOS software Release 8.3.

## Example

The following example allows partial zones:

```
appletalk permit-partial-zones
```

## Related Commands

Search online to find documentation for related commands.

**access-list additional-zones**
**access-list zone**
**appletalk distribute-list out**
**appletalk getzonelist-filter**

## APPLETALK PRE-FDDITALK

To enable the recognition of pre-FDDITalk packets, use the **appletalk pre-fdditalk** global configuration command. To disable this function, use the **no** form of this command.

**appletalk pre-fdditalk**
**no appletalk pre-fdditalk**

## Syntax    Description

This command has no arguments or keywords.

## Default

Disabled

## Command Mode

Global configuration

## Usage Guidelines

This command first appeared in Cisco IOS Release 10.0.

Use this command to have the Cisco IOS software recognize AppleTalk packets sent on the FDDI ring from routers running Cisco software releases prior to Release 9.0(3) or Release 9.1(2).

## Example

The following example disables the recognition of pre-FDDITalk packets:

```
no appletalk pre-fdditalk
```

## APPLETALK PROTOCOL

To specify the routing protocol to use on an interface, use the **appletalk protocol** interface configuration command. To disable a routing protocol, use the **no** form of this command.

> **appletalk protocol** {aurp | eigrp | rtmp}
> **no appletalk protocol** {aurp | eigrp | rtmp}

| Syntax | Description |
| --- | --- |
| **aurp** | Specifies that the routing protocol to use is AURP. You can enable AURP only on tunnel interfaces. |
| **eigrp** | Specifies that the routing protocol to use is Enhanced IGRP. |
| **rtmp** | Specifies that the routing protocol to use is RTMP, which is enabled by default. |

## Default

RTMP

## Command Mode

Interface configuration

## Usage Guidelines

This command first appeared in Cisco IOS Release 10.3.

You can configure an interface to use both RTMP and Enhanced IGRP. If you do so, route information learned from Enhanced IGRP takes precedence over information learned from RTMP. The Cisco IOS software does, however, continue to send out RTMP routing updates.

You cannot disable RTMP without first enabling AURP or Enhanced IGRP.

Enabling AURP automatically disables RTMP.

You can enable AURP only on tunnel interfaces.

## Examples

The following example enables AURP on tunnel interface 1:

```
interface tunnel 1
appletalk protocol aurp
```

The following example enables AppleTalk Enhanced IGRP on serial interface 0:

```
interface serial 0
appletalk protocol eigrp
```

The following example disables RTMP on serial interface 0:

```
interface serial 0
no appletalk protocol rtmp
```

## Related Commands

Search online to find documentation for related commands.

**appletalk routing**

## APPLETALK PROXY-NBP

To assign a proxy network number for each zone in which there is a router that supports only non-extended AppleTalk, use the **appletalk proxy-nbp** global configuration command. To delete the proxy, use the **no** form of this command.

> **appletalk proxy-nbp** *network-number zone-name*
> **no appletalk proxy-nbp** [*network-number zone-name*]

| Syntax | Description |
|---|---|
| *network-number* | Network number of the proxy. It is a 16-bit decimal number and must be unique on the network. This is the network number that is advertised by the Cisco IOS software as if it were a real network number. |
| *zone-name* | Name of the zone that contains the devices that support only nonextended AppleTalk. The name can include special characters from the Apple Macintosh character set. To include a special character, type a colon, followed by two hexadecimal characters. For zone names with a leading space character, enter the first character as the special sequence :20. |

## Default

No proxy network number is assigned.

## Command Mode

Global configuration

*Usage Guidelines*

This command first appeared in Cisco IOS Release 10.0.

The **appletalk proxy-nbp** command provides compatibility between AppleTalk Phase 1 and Apple-Talk Phase 2 networks.

Proxy routes are included in outgoing RTMP updates as if they were directly connected routes, although they are not really directly connected, because they are not associated with any interface. Whenever an NBQ BrRq for the zone in question is generated by anyone anywhere in the internetwork, an NBP FwdReq is directed to any router connected to the proxy route. The Phase 2 router, which is the only router directly connected, converts the FwdReq to LkUps, which are understood by Phase 1 routers, and sends them to every network in the zone.

In an environment in which there are Phase 1 and Phase 2 networks, you must specify at least one **appletalk proxy-nbp** command for each zone that has a nonextended-only AppleTalk router.

The proxy network number you assign with the **appletalk proxy-nbp** command cannot also be assigned to a router, nor can it also be associated with a physical network.

You must assign only one proxy network number for each zone. However, you can define additional proxies with different network numbers to provide redundancy. Each proxy generates one or more packets for each forward request it receives. All other packets sent to the proxy network address are discarded. Defining redundant proxy network numbers increases the NBP traffic linearly.

*Example*

The following example defines network number 60 as an NBP proxy for the zone *Twilight*:

```
appletalk proxy-nbp 60 Twilight
```

*Related Commands*

Search online to find documentation for related commands.

**show appletalk route**


## APPLETALK REQUIRE-ROUTE-ZONES

To prevent the advertisement of routes (network numbers or cable ranges) that have no assigned zone, use the **appletalk require-route-zones** global configuration command. To disable this option and allow the Cisco IOS software to advertise to its neighbors routes that have no network-zone association, use the **no** form of this command.

> **appletalk require-route-zones**
> **no appletalk require-route-zones**

*Syntax     Description*

This command has no arguments or keywords.

## Default

Enabled

## Command Mode

Global configuration

## Usage Guidelines

This command first appeared in Cisco IOS Release 10.0.

The **appletalk require-route-zones** command ensures that all networks have zone names prior to advertisement to neighbors.

The **no appletalk require-route-zones** command enables behavior compatible with Cisco IOS Release 8.3.

Using this command helps prevent ZIP protocol storms. ZIP protocol storms can arise when corrupt routes are propagated and routers broadcast ZIP requests to determine the network/zone associations.

When the **appletalk require-route-zones** command is enabled, the Cisco IOS software will not advertise a route to its neighboring routers until it has obtained the network-zone associations. This effectively limits the storms to a single network rather than the entire internet.

As an alternative to disabling this option, use the **appletalk getzonelist-filter** interface configuration command to filter *empty* zones from the list presented to users.

You can configure different zone lists on different interfaces. However, you are discouraged from doing this because AppleTalk users expect to have the same user zone lists at any end node in the internet.

The filtering provided by the **appletalk require-route-zones** command does not prevent explicit access via programmatic methods but should be considered a user optimization to suppress unused zones. You should use other forms of AppleTalk access control lists to actually *secure* a zone or network.

## Example

The following example configures a router to prevent the advertisement of routes that have no assigned zone:

```
appletalk require-route-zones
```

## APPLETALK ROUTE-CACHE

To enable fast switching on all supported interfaces, use the **appletalk route-cache** interface configuration command. To disable fast switching, use the **no** form of this command.

**appletalk route-cache**
**no appletalk route-cache**

## Syntax     Description

This command has no arguments or keywords.

## Default

Enabled on all interfaces that support fast switching

## Command Mode

Interface configuration

## Usage Guidelines

This command first appeared in Cisco IOS Release 10.0.

Fast switching allows higher throughput by switching a packet using a cache created by previous packets. Fast switching is enabled by default on all interfaces that support fast switching, including Token Ring, Frame Relay, PPP, High-Level Data Link Control (HDLC), SMDS, and ATM. Note that fast switching is not supported over X.25 and Link Access Procedure Balance (LAPB), encapsulations, or on the CSC-R16, CSC-1R, or CSC-2R STR Token Ring adapters.

Packet transfer performance is generally better when fast switching is enabled. However, you may want to disable fast switching in order to save memory space on interface cards and to help avoid congestion when high-bandwidth interfaces are writing large amounts of information to low-bandwidth interfaces.

Fast switching of extended AppleTalk is supported on serial lines with several encapsulation types (for example, SMDS and HDLC). Fast switching of nonextended AppleTalk is not supported on serial lines.

## Example

The following example disables fast switching on an interface:

```
interface ethernet 0
appletalk cable-range 10-20
appletalk zone Twilight
no appletalk route-cache
```

## Related Commands

Search online to find documentation for related commands.

**show appletalk cache**

## APPLETALK ROUTE-REDISTRIBUTION

To redistribute RTMP routes into AppleTalk Enhanced IGRP and vice versa, use the **appletalk route-redistribution** global configuration command. To keep Enhanced IGRP and RTMP routes separate, use the **no** form of this command.

**appletalk route-redistribution**
**no appletalk route-redistribution**

## Syntax    Description

This command has no arguments or keywords.

## Default

Enabled when Enhanced IGRP is enabled.

## Command Mode

Global configuration

## Usage Guidelines

This command first appeared in Cisco IOS Release 10.3.

Redistribution allows routing information generated by one protocol to be advertised in another.

In the automatic redistribution of routes between Enhanced IGRP and RTMP, a RTMP hop is treated as having a slightly worse metric than an equivalent Enhanced IGRP hop on a 9.6-Kb link. This allows Enhanced IGRP to be preferred over RTMP except in the most extreme of circumstances. Typically, you see this only when using tunnels. If you want an Enhanced IGRP path in a tunnel to be preferred over an alternate RTMP path, you should set the interface delay and bandwidth parameters on the tunnel to bring the metric of the tunnel down to being better than a 9.6-Kb link.

## Example

In the following example, RTMP routing information is not redistributed:

```
appletalk routing eigrp 23
no appletalk route-redistribution
```

## APPLETALK ROUTING

To enable AppleTalk routing, use the **appletalk routing** global configuration command. To disable AppleTalk routing, use the **no** form of this command.

**appletalk routing** [**eigrp** *router-number*]
**no appletalk routing** [**eigrp** *router-number*]

| Syntax | Description |
|---|---|
| **eigrp** *router-number* | (Optional) Specifies the Enhanced IGRP routing protocol. The argument *router-number* is the router ID. It can be a decimal integer from 1 to 65535. It must be unique in your AppleTalk Enhanced IGRP internetwork. |

## Default
Disabled

## Command Mode
Global configuration

## Usage Guidelines
This command first appeared in Cisco IOS Release 10.0. The **eigrp** keyword first appeared in Cisco IOS Release 10.3.

If you do not specify the optional keyword and argument, this command enables AppleTalk routing using the RTMP routing protocol.

You can configure multiple AppleTalk Enhanced IGRP processes on a router. To do so, assign each a different router ID number. (Note that IP and IPX Enhanced IGRP use an autonomous system number to enable Enhanced IGRP, while AppleTalk Enhanced IGRP uses a router ID.)

If you configure a device with a router number that is the same as that of a neighboring router, the Cisco IOS software will refuse to start AppleTalk Enhanced IGRP on interfaces that connect with that neighboring router.

---
**CAUTION**

---
When disabling Enhanced IGRP routing with the **no appletalk routing eigrp** command, all interfaces enabled for only Enhanced IGRP (and not also RTMP) lose their AppleTalk configuration. If you want to disable Enhanced IGRP and use RTMP instead on specific interfaces, first enable RTMP on each interface using the **appletalk protocol rtmp** interface configuration command. Then, disable Enhanced IGRP routing using the **no appletalk routing eigrp** command. This process ensures that you do not lose AppleTalk configurations on interfaces for which you want to use RTMP.

---

## Examples
The following example enables AppleTalk protocol processing:

    appletalk routing

The following example enables AppleTalk Enhanced IGRP routing on router number 22:

    appletalk routing eigrp 22

## Related Commands
Search online to find documentation for related commands.

**appletalk address**
**appletalk cable-range**
**appletalk protocol**
**appletalk zone**

## APPLETALK RTMP-STUB

To enable AppleTalk RTMP stub mode, use the **appletalk rtmp-stub** interface configuration command. To disable this mode, use the **no** form of the command.

> **appletalk rtmp-stub**
> **no appletalk rtmp-stub**

*Syntax      Description*

This command has no arguments or keywords.

*Default*

Disabled

*Command Mode*

Interface configuration

*Usage Guidelines*

This command first appeared in Cisco IOS Release 11.1.

This command enables routers running Enhanced IGRP and RTMP to reduce the amount of CPU processing that RTMP modules use. RTMP modules send "stub" packets instead of full RTMP packets when you enable stub mode.

A stub packet is only the first tuple of an RTMP packet. The first tuple indicates the network number range assigned to that network. End nodes use stub packets to determine whether their node number is in the right network range.

Upon startup, an end node on an extended network uses stub packets to verify that its previous node number is still within the segment's network number range. If it is, the end node reuses the previous node number and stores the network number range information. If an end node learns upon startup that its previous node number does not fall within the segment's new network number range, the end node picks a new node number based on the new network number range and stores the new network number range information.

After startup, end nodes use subsequent stub packets to verify that the network number range sent in the stub packets precisely matches its stored network number range. In this way, stub packets keep end nodes alive.

When routers that have stub mode enabled receive full RTMP packets, they discard these packets because Enhanced IGRP (not RTMP) is expected to deliver routes. Discarding full RTMP packets when stub mode is enabled saves the overhead processing of RTMP routes.

You can also use stub mode on "end" networks. End networks are those to which no other routers attach. Because no other routers are listening for routes on these end segments, there is no need for the end router to send full RTMP packets to these end segments. The end router can send stub packet to keep end nodes alive.

*Example*

The following example turns on AppleTalk RTMP stub mode:

```
appletalk rtmp-stub
```

*Related Commands*

Search online to find documentation for related commands.

**show appletalk interface**

## APPLETALK SEND-RTMPS

To allow the Cisco IOS software to send routing updates to its neighbors, use the **appletalk send-rtmps** interface configuration command. To block updates from being sent, use the **no** form of this command.

> **appletalk send-rtmps**
> **no appletalk send-rtmps**

*Syntax       Description*

This command has no arguments or keywords.

*Default*

Send routing updates.

*Command Mode*

Interface configuration

*Usage Guidelines*

This command first appeared in Cisco IOS Release 10.0.

If you block the sending of routing updates, an interface on the network that has AppleTalk enabled is not "visible" to other routers on the network.

*Example*

The following example prevents a router from sending routing updates to its neighbors:

```
no appletalk send-rtmps
```

*Related Commands*

Search online to find documentation for related commands.

**appletalk require-route-zones**
**appletalk strict-rtmp-checking**
**appletalk timers**

## APPLETALK STATIC CABLE-RANGE

To define a static route or a floating static route on an extended network, use the **appletalk static cable-range** global configuration command. To remove a static route, use the **no** form of this command.

> **appletalk static cable-range** *cable-range* **to** *network.node* [**floating**] **zone** *zone-name*
> **no appletalk static cable-range** *cable-range* **to** *network.node* [**floating**] [**zone** *zone-name*]

| *Syntax* | *Description* |
|---|---|
| *cable-range* | Cable range value. The argument specifies the start and end of the cable range, separated by a hyphen. These values are decimal numbers from 0 to 65279. The starting network number must be less than or equal to the ending network number. |
| **to** *network.node* | AppleTalk network address of the remote router. The argument *network* is the 16-bit network number in the range from 0 to 65279. The argument *node* is the 8-bit node number in the range from 0 to 254. Both numbers are decimal. |
| **floating** | (Optional) Specifies that this route is a floating static route, which is a static route that can be overridden by a dynamically learned route. |
| **zone** *zone-name* | Name of the zone on the remote network. The name can include special characters from the Apple Macintosh character set. To include a special character, type a colon, followed by two hexadecimal characters. For zone names with a leading space character, enter the first character as the special sequence :20. |

### Default

No static routes are defined.

### Command Mode

Global configuration

### Usage Guidelines

This command first appeared in Cisco IOS Release 10.0.

You cannot delete a particular zone from the zone list without first deleting the static route.

When links associated with static routes are lost, traffic may stop being forwarded even though alternative paths might be available. For this reason, you should be careful when assigning static routes.

Floating static routes are a kind of static route that can be overridden by dynamically learned routes. Floating static routes allow you to switch to another path whenever routing information for a destination is lost. One application of floating static routes is to provide back-up routes in topologies where dial-on-demand routing is used.

If you configure a floating static route, the Cisco IOS software checks to see whether an entry for the route already exists in its routing table. If a dynamic route already exists, the floating static route is placed in reserve as part of a floating static route table. When the software detects that the dynamic route is no longer available, it replaces the dynamic route with the floating static route for that destination. If the route is later relearned dynamically, the dynamic route replaces the floating static route, and the floating static route is again placed in reserve.

To avoid the possibility of a routing loop occurring, by default floating static routes are not redistributed into other dynamic protocols.

### Examples

The following example creates a static route to the remote router whose address is 1.2 on the remote network 100-110 that is in the remote zone *Remote*:

```
appletalk static cable-range 100-110 to 1.2 zone Remote
```

The following example creates a floating static route to the remote router whose address is 1.3 on the remote network 100-110 that is in the remote zone *Remote*:

```
appletalk static cable-range 100-110 to 1.3 floating zone Remote
```

### Related Commands

Search online to find documentation for related commands.

**appletalk static network**
**show appletalk route**
**show appletalk static**

## APPLETALK STATIC NETWORK

To define a static route or a floating static route on a nonextended network, use the **appletalk static network** global configuration command. To remove a static route, use the **no** form of this command.

> **appletalk static network** *network-number* **to** *network.node* [**floating**] **zone** *zone-name*
> **no appletalk static network** *network-number* **to** *network.node* [**floating**] [**zone** *zone-name*]

| Syntax | Description |
|---|---|
| *network-number* | AppleTalk network number assigned to the interface. It is a 16-bit decimal number and must be unique on the network. This is the network number that is advertised by the Cisco IOS software as if it were a real network number. |
| **to** *network.node* | AppleTalk network address of the remote router. The argument *network* is the 16-bit network number in the range from 0 to 65279. The argument *node* is the 8-bit node number in the range from 0 to 254. Both numbers are decimal. |
| **floating** | (Optional) Specifies that this route is a floating static route, which is a static route that can be overridden by a dynamically learned route. |
| **zone** *zone-name* | Name of the zone on the remote network. The name can include special characters from the Apple Macintosh character set. To include a special character, type a colon, followed by two hexadecimal characters. For zone names with a leading space character, enter the first character as the special sequence :20. |

### Default

No static routes are defined.

### Command Mode

Global configuration

### Usage Guidelines

This command first appeared in Cisco IOS Release 10.0.

You cannot delete a particular zone from the zone list without first deleting the static route.

When links associated with static routes are lost, traffic may stop being forwarded even though alternative paths might be available. For this reason, you should be careful when assigning static routes.

A floating static route is a kind of static route that can be overridden by dynamically learned routes. Floating static routes allow you to switch to another path whenever routing information for a destination is lost. One application of floating static routes is to provide back-up routes in topologies where dial-on-demand routing is used.

If you configure a floating static route, the Cisco IOS software checks to see whether an entry for the route already exists in its routing table. If a dynamic route already exists, the floating static route is placed in reserve as part of a floating static route table. When the Cisco IOS software detects that the dynamic route is no longer available, it replaces the dynamic route with the floating static route for that destination. If the route is later relearned dynamically, the dynamic route replaces the floating static route, and the floating static route is again placed in reserve.

To avoid the possibility of a routing loop occurring, by default floating static routes are not redistributed into other dynamic protocols.

## Examples

The following example creates a static route to the remote router whose address is 1.2 on the remote network 200 that is in the remote zone *Remote*:

```
appletalk static network 200 to 1.2 zone Remote
```

The following example creates a floating static route to the remote router whose address is 1.3 on the remote network 200 that is in the remote zone *Remote*:

```
appletalk static network 200 to 1.3 floating zone Remote
```

## Related Commands

Search online to find documentation for related commands.

**appletalk static cable-range**
**show appletalk route**
**show appletalk static**


## APPLETALK STRICT-RTMP-CHECKING

To perform maximum checking of routing updates to ensure their validity, use the **appletalk strict-rtmp-checking** global configuration command. To disable the maximum checking, use the **no** form of this command.

> **appletalk strict-rtmp-checking**
> **no appletalk strict-rtmp-checking**

## Syntax       Description

This command has no arguments or keywords.


## Default

Provide maximum checking


## Command Mode

Global configuration


## Usage Guidelines

This command first appeared in Cisco IOS Release 10.0.

Strict RTMP checking discards any RTMP packets arriving from routers that are not directly connected to the local router. This means that the local router does not accept any routed RTMP packets. Note that RTMP packets that need to be forwarded are not discarded.

### Example

The following example disables strict checking of RTMP routing updates:

```
no appletalk strict-rtmp-checking
```

### Related Commands

Search online to find documentation for related commands.

**appletalk require-route-zones**
**appletalk send-rtmps**
**appletalk timers**

## APPLETALK TIMERS

To change the routing update timers, use the **appletalk timers** global configuration command. To return to the default routing update timers, use the **no** form of this command.

> **appletalk timers** *update-interval valid-interval invalid-interval*
> **no appletalk timers** [*update-interval valid-interval invalid-interval*]

| Syntax | Description |
|---|---|
| *update-interval* | Time, in seconds, between routing updates sent to other routers on the network. The default is 10 seconds. |
| *valid-interval* | Time, in seconds, that the Cisco IOS software considers a route valid without having heard a routing update for that route. The default is 20 seconds (two times the update interval). |
| *invalid-interval* | Time, in seconds, that the route is retained after the last update. The default is 60 seconds (three times the valid interval). |

### Default

*update-interval*: 10 seconds
*valid-interval*: 20 seconds
*invalid-interval*: 60 seconds

### Command Mode

Global configuration

### Usage Guidelines

This command first appeared in Cisco IOS Release 10.0.

Routes older than the time specified by *update-interval* are considered suspect. After the period of time specified by *valid-interval* has elapsed without having heard a routing update for a route, the route becomes bad and is eligible for replacement by a path with a higher (less favorable) metric. During the *invalid-interval* period, routing updates include this route with a special "*notify neighbor*" metric. If this timer expires, the route is deleted from the routing table.

Note that you should not attempt to modify the routing timers without fully understanding the ramifications of doing so. Many other AppleTalk router vendors provide no facility for modifying their routing timers; should you adjust the Cisco IOS software AppleTalk timers such that routing updates do not arrive at these other routers within the normal interval, it is possible to degrade or destroy AppleTalk network connectivity.

If you change the routing update interval, be sure to do so for *all* routers on the network.

In rare instances, you might want to change this interval, such as when a device is busy and cannot send routing updates every 10 seconds or when slower routers are incapable of processing received routing updates in a large network.

## Example

The following example increases the update interval to 20 seconds and the route-valid interval to 40 seconds:

```
appletalk timers 20 40 60
```

## APPLETALK VIRTUAL-NET

To add AppleTalk users logging in on an asynchronous line and using PPP encapsulation to an internal network, use the **appletalk virtual-net** global configuration command. To remove an internal network, use the **no** form of this command.

> **appletalk virtual-net** *network-number zone-name*
> **no appletalk virtual-net** *network-number zone-name*

| Syntax | Description |
| --- | --- |
| *network-number* | AppleTalk network address assigned to the interface. This is a 16-bit decimal network number in the range from 0 to 65279. The network address must be unique across your AppleTalk internetwork. |
| *zone-name* | Name of a new or existing zone to which the AppleTalk user belongs. |

## Default

No virtual networks are predefined.

## Command Mode

Global configuration

## Usage Guidelines

This command first appeared in Cisco IOS Release 10.3.

A virtual network is a logical network that exists only within the Cisco IOS software. It enables you—and by extension anyone who dials into the router—to add an asynchronous interface to either a new or an existing AppleTalk zone.

Virtual networks work with both extended and nonextended AppleTalk networks. On Cisco routers, you can only set a virtual network on an asynchronous line on the auxiliary port.

If you issue the **appletalk virtual-net** command and specify a new AppleTalk zone name, the network number you specify is the only one associated with this zone. If you issue this command and specify an existing AppleTalk zone, the network number you specify is added to the existing zone.

The selected AppleTalk zone (either new or existing) is highlighted when you open the Macintosh Chooser window. From this window, you can access all available zones.

## Example

The following example adds a user to the virtual network number 3 and specifies the zone name *renegade*:

```
apple virtual-net 3 renegade
```

## Related Commands

Search online to find documentation for related commands.

**appletalk address**
**appletalk cable-range**
**appletalk client-mode**
**appletalk zone**
**show appletalk zone**

## APPLETALK ZIP-QUERY-INTERVAL

To specify the interval at which the Cisco IOS software sends ZIP queries, use the **appletalk zip-query-interval** global configuration command. To return to the default interval, use the **no** form of this command.

> **appletalk zip-query-interval** *interval*
> **no zip-query-interval** [*interval*]

| Syntax | Description |
|---|---|
| *interval* | Interval, in seconds, at which the software sends ZIP queries. It can be any positive integer. The default is 10 seconds. |

*Default*

10 seconds

*Command Mode*

Global configuration

*Usage Guidelines*

This command first appeared in Cisco IOS Release 10.0.

The software uses the information received in response to its ZIP queries to update its zone table.

*Example*

The following example changes the ZIP query interval to 40 seconds:

```
appletalk zip-query-interval 40
```

## APPLETALK ZIP-REPLY-FILTER

To configure a ZIP reply filter, use the **appletalk zip-reply-filter** interface configuration command. To remove a filter, use the **no** form of this command.

> **appletalk zip-reply-filter** *access-list-number*
> **no appletalk zip-reply-filter** [*access-list-number*]

| Syntax | Description |
| --- | --- |
| *access-list-number* | Number of the access list. This is a decimal number from 600 to 699. |

*Default*

No access lists are predefined.

*Command Mode*

Interface configuration

*Usage Guidelines*

This command first appeared in Cisco IOS Release 10.3.

ZIP reply filters limit the visibility of zones from routers in unprivileged regions throughout the internetwork. These filters filter the zone list for each network provided by a router to neighboring routers to remove restricted zones.

ZIP reply filters apply to downstream routers, not to end stations on networks attached to the local router. With ZIP reply filters, when downstream routers request the names of zones in a network, the local router replies with the names of visible zones only. It does not reply with the names of zones that have been hidden with a ZIP reply filter. To filter zones from end stations, use GZL filters.

ZIP reply filters determine which networks and cable ranges the Cisco IOS software sends out in routing updates. Before sending out routing updates, the software excludes the networks and cable ranges whose zones have been completely denied access by ZIP reply filters. Excluding this information ensures that routers receiving these routing updates do not send unnecessary ZIP requests.

## Example

The following example assigns a ZIP reply filter to Ethernet interface 0:

```
interface ethernet 0
appletalk zip-reply-filter 600
```

## Related Commands

Search online to find documentation for related commands.

**access-list additional-zones**
**access-list zone**
**show appletalk interface**

## APPLETALK ZONE

To set the zone name for the connected AppleTalk network, use the **appletalk zone** interface configuration command. To delete a zone, use the **no** form of this command.

> **appletalk zone** *zone-name*
> **no appletalk zone** [*zone-name*]

| Syntax | Description |
|--------|-------------|
| *zone-name* | Name of the zone. The name can include special characters from the Apple Macintosh character set. To include a special character, type a colon, followed by two hexadecimal characters. For zone names with a leading space character, enter the first character as the special sequence :20. |

## Default

No zone name is set.

## Command Mode

Interface configuration

## Usage Guidelines

This command first appeared in Cisco IOS Release 10.0.

If discovery mode is not enabled, you can specify the **appletalk zone** command only after an **apple-talk address** or **appletalk cable-range** command. You can issue it multiple times if it follows the **appletalk cable-range** command.

On interfaces that have discovery mode disabled, you must assign a zone name in order for Apple-Talk routing to begin.

If an interface is using extended AppleTalk, the first zone specified in the list is the default zone. The Cisco IOS software always uses the default zone when registering NBP names for interfaces. Nodes in the network select the zone in which they operate from the list of zone names valid on the cable to which they are connected.

If an interface is using nonextended AppleTalk, repeated execution of the **appletalk zone** command replaces the interface's zone name with the newly specified zone name.

The **no** form of the command deletes a zone name from a zone list or deletes the entire zone list if you do not specify a zone name. For nonextended AppleTalk interfaces, the zone name argument is ignored. You should delete any existing zone-name list using the **no appletalk zone** interface sub-command before configuring a new zone list.

The zone list is cleared automatically when you issue an **appletalk address** or **appletalk cable-range** command. The list also is cleared if you issue the **appletalk zone** command on an *existing* network; this can occur when adding zones to a set of routers until all routers are in agreement.

### Examples

The following example assigns the zone name *Twilight* to an interface:

```
interface Ethernet 0
appletalk cable-range 10-20
appletalk zone Twilight
```

The following example uses AppleTalk special characters to set the zone name to *Cisco:A5Zone*.

```
appletalk zone Cisco:A5Zone
```

### Related Commands

Search online to find documentation for related commands.

**appletalk address**
**appletalk cable-range**
**show appletalk zone**

### CLEAR APPLETALK ARP

To delete all entries or a specified entry from the AARP table, use the **clear appletalk arp** EXEC command.

    **clear appletalk arp** [*network.node*]

| *Syntax* | *Description* |
|---|---|
| *network.node* | (Optional) AppleTalk network address to be deleted from the AARP table. The argument *network* is the 16-bit network number in the range from 0 to 65279. The argument *node* is the 8-bit node number in the range from 0 to 254. Both numbers are decimal. |

## *Command Mode*
EXEC

## *Usage Guidelines*
This command first appeared in Cisco IOS Release 10.0.

## *Example*
The following example deletes all entries from the AARP table:

```
clear appletalk arp
```

## *Related Commands*
Search online to find documentation for related commands.

**show appletalk arp**

## CLEAR APPLETALK NEIGHBOR

To delete all entries or a specified entry from the neighbor table, use the **clear appletalk neighbor** EXEC command.

**clear appletalk neighbor** [*neighbor-address*]

| *Syntax* | *Description* |
|---|---|
| *neighbor-address* | (Optional) Network address of the neighboring router to be deleted from the neighbor table. The address is in the format *network.node*. The argument *network* is the 16-bit network number in the range from 1 to 65279. The argument *node* is the 8-bit node number in the range from 0 to 254. Both numbers are decimal. |

## *Command Mode*
EXEC

## *Usage Guidelines*
This command first appeared in Cisco IOS Release 10.0.

You cannot clear the entry for an active neighbor—that is, for a neighbor that still has RTMP connectivity.

*Example*

The following example deletes the neighboring router 1.129 from the neighbor table:

```
clear appletalk neighbor 1.129
```

*Related Commands*

Search online to find documentation for related commands.

**show appletalk neighbors**

## CLEAR APPLETALK ROUTE

To delete entries from the routing table, use the **clear appletalk route** EXEC command.

> **clear appletalk route** [*network*]

| *Syntax* | *Description* |
|---|---|
| *network* | (Optional) Number of the network to which the route provides access. |

*Command Mode*

EXEC

*Usage Guidelines*

This command first appeared in Cisco IOS Release 10.0.

*Example*

The following example deletes the route to network 1:

```
clear appletalk route 1
```

*Related Commands*

Search online to find documentation for related commands.  ·

**show appletalk route**

## CLEAR APPLETALK TRAFFIC

To reset AppleTalk traffic counters, use the **clear appletalk traffic** EXEC command.

> **clear appletalk traffic**

*Syntax        Description*

This command has no arguments or keywords.

## Command Mode

EXEC

## Usage Guidelines

This command first appeared in Cisco IOS Release 10.0.

## Sample Display

The following is sample output after a **clear appletalk traffic** command was executed.

```
Router# clear appletalk traffic
Router# show appletalk traffic

AppleTalk statistics:
  Rcvd:  0 total, 0 checksum errors, 0 bad hop count
         0 local destination, 0 access denied
         0 for MacIP, 0 bad MacIP, 0 no client
         0 port disabled, 0 no listener
         0 ignored, 0 martians
  Bcast: 0 received, 0 sent
  Sent:  0 generated, 0 forwarded, 0 fast forwarded, 0 loopback
         0 forwarded from MacIP, 0 MacIP failures
         0 encapsulation failed, 0 no route, 0 no source
  DDP:   0 long, 0 short, 0 macip, 0 bad size
  NBP:   0 received, 0 invalid, 0 proxies
         0 replies sent, 0 forwards, 0 lookups, 0 failures
  RTMP:  0 received, 0 requests, 0 invalid, 0 ignored
         0 sent, 0 replies
  EIGRP: 0 received, 0 hellos, 0 updates, 0 replies, 0 queries
         0 sent,     0 hellos, 0 updates, 0 replies, 0 queries
         0 invalid, 0 ignored
  ATP:   0 received
  ZIP:   0 received, 0 sent, 0 netinfo
  Echo:  0 received, 0 discarded, 0 illegal
         0 generated, 0 replies sent
  Responder:  0 received, 0 illegal, 0 unknown
AppleTalk statistics:
         0 replies sent, 0 failures
  AARP:  0 requests, 0 replies, 0 probes
         0 martians, 0 bad encapsulation, 0 unknown
         0 sent, 0 failures, 0 delays, 0 drops
  Lost: 0 no buffers
  Unknown: 0 packets
  Discarded: 0 wrong encapsulation, 0 bad SNAP discriminator
```

Table 3–33 describes the fields shown in the **show appletalk traffic** display.

## Related Commands

Search online to find documentation for related commands.

**show appletalk macip-traffic**
**show appletalk traffic**

## CLEAR SMRP MCACHE

To remove all fast-switching entries in the Sample Multicast Routing Protocol (SMRP) fast-switching cache table, use the **clear smrp mcache** EXEC command.

    **clear smrp mcache**

### Syntax      Description

This command has no arguments or keywords.

### Command Mode

EXEC

### Usage Guidelines

This command first appeared in Cisco IOS Release 11.1.

Use this command to clear the SMRP fast-switching cache table. The SMRP fast-switching cache table contains the information needed to fast switch SMRP data packets. It is usually unnecessary to clear the table; however, you can do so to repopulate it or to clear a corrupted entry.

---

**NOTES**

---

Using this command clears the table of all entries, not just a single entry.

---

### Example

The following example shows the fast-switching cache table before and after the **clear smrp mcache** command clears the table of entries:

```
Router# show smrp mcache

SMRP Multicast Fast Switching Cache
Group       In  Parent      Child         MAC Header (Top)
Address     Use Interface   Interface(s)  Network Header (Bottom)
---------------------------------------------------------------

AT 11.121   Y   Ethernet0   Ethernet3     090007400b7900000c1740db
                                          001fed750000002aff020a0a0a
AT 11.122   Y   Ethernet0   Ethernet3     090007400b7a00000c1740db
                                          001f47750000002aff020a0a0a
```

```
      AT 11.123    Y    Ethernet0     Ethernet1     090007400b7b00000c1740d9
                                                    001fe77500000014ff020a0a0a
                                      Ethernet3     090007400b7b00000c1740db
                                                    001ffd750000002aff020a0a0a
      AT 11.124    N    Ethernet0     Ethernet1     090007400b7c00000c1740d9
                                                    001fef7500000014ff020a0a0a
      Router# clear smrp mcache
      Router# show smrp mcache

      SMRP Multicast Fast Switching Cache
      Group        In  Parent        Child         MAC Header (Top)
      Address      Use Interface     Interface(s)  Network Header (Bottom)
      --------------------------------------------------------------------
```

## Related Commands

Search online to find documentation for related commands.

**show smrp mcache**

## PING (PRIVILEGED)

To check host reachability and network connectivity, use the **ping** privileged EXEC command.

> **ping** [**appletalk**] [*network.node*]

| Syntax | Description |
|---|---|
| **appletalk** | (Optional) Specifies the AppleTalk protocol. |
| *network.node* | (Optional) AppleTalk address of the system to ping. |

## Command Mode

Privileged EXEC

## Usage Guidelines

This command first appeared in Cisco IOS Release 10.0.

The privileged **ping** (packet internet groper function) command provides a complete **ping** facility for users who have system privileges. The **ping** command sends AppleTalk Echo Protocol (AEP) datagrams to other AppleTalk nodes to verify connectivity and measure round-trip times.

Only an interface that supports *HearSelf* can respond to packets generated at a local console and directed to an interface on the same router. The Cisco IOS software only supports *HearSelf* on Ethernet.

If the system cannot map an address for a host name, it will return an "%Unrecognized host or address" error message.

To abort a **ping** session, type the escape sequence. By default, this is Ctrl-^ X. You enter this by simultaneously pressing the Ctrl, Shift, and 6 keys, letting go, and then pressing the X key.

Table 3–2 describes the test characters displayed in **ping** responses.

**Table 3–2**  *AppleTalk Ping Characters*

| Character | Meaning |
|-----------|---------|
| ! | Each exclamation point indicates the receipt of a reply (echo) from the target address. |
| . | Each period indicates the network server timed out while waiting for a reply from the target address. |
| B | The echo received from the target address was bad or malformed. |
| C | An echo with a bad DDP checksum was received. |
| E | Transmission of an echo packet to the target address failed. |
| R | Transmission of the echo packet to the target address failed because of lack of a route to the target address. |

### Sample Display of a Standard Ping

The following display shows a sample standard **appletalk ping** session:

```
Router# ping
Protocol [ip]: appletalk
Target Appletalk address: 1024.128
Repeat count [5]:
Datagram size [100]:
Timeout in seconds [2]:
Verbose [n]:
Sweep range of sizes [n]:
Type escape sequence to abort.
Sending 5, 100-byte AppleTalk Echos to 1024.128, timeout is 2 seconds:
!!!!!
Success rate is 100 percent, round-trip min/avg/max = 4/4/8 ms
```

### Sample Display Using Ping in Verbose Mode

When you answer y in response to the prompt Verbose [n], **ping** runs in verbose mode. The following display shows a sample **appletalk ping** session when verbose mode is enabled:

```
Router# ping
Protocol [ip]: appletalk
Target AppleTalk address: 4.129
Repeat count [5]:
Datagram size [100]:
Timeout in seconds [2]:
Verbose [n]: y
Sweep range of sizes [n]:
Type escape sequence to abort.
Sending 5, 100-byte AppleTalk Echos to 4.129, timeout is 2 seconds:
```

```
0 in 4 ms from 4.129 via 1 hop
1 in 8 ms from 4.129 via 1 hop
2 in 4 ms from 4.129 via 1 hop
3 in 8 ms from 4.129 via 1 hop
4 in 8 ms from 4.129 via 1 hop
Success rate is 100 percent, round-trip min/avg/max = 4/6/8 ms
```

Table 3–3 describes the fields in the verbose mode portion of the display.

**Table 3–3** *AppleTalk Ping Fields*

| Field | Meaning |
| --- | --- |
| 0 | Sequential number identifying the packet's relative position in the group of ping packets sent. |
| in 4 ms | Round-trip travel time of the ping packet, in milliseconds. |
| from 4.129 | Source address of the ping packet. |
| via 1 hop | Number of hops the ping packet traveled to the destination. |

### Related Commands

Search online to find documentation for related commands.

**clear smrp mcache**
**show appletalk zone**

## PING (USER)

To check host reachability and network connectivity, use the **ping** user EXEC command.

> **ping appletalk** *network.node*

| Syntax | Description |
| --- | --- |
| **appletalk** | Specifies the AppleTalk protocol. |
| *network.node* | AppleTalk address of the system to ping. |

### Command Mode

User EXEC

### Usage Guidelines

This command first appeared in Cisco IOS Release 10.3.

The user **ping** (packet internet groper function) command provides a basic ping facility for users who do not have system privileges. This command is equivalent to the nonverbose form of the privileged **ping** command. It sends five 100-byte ping packets. The **ping** command sends AppleTalk

Echo Protocol (AEP) datagrams to other AppleTalk nodes to verify connectivity and measure round-trip times.

Only an interface that supports *HearSelf* can respond to packets generated at a local console and directed to an interface on the same router. The Cisco IOS software supports only *HearSelf* on Ethernet.

If the system cannot map an address for a host name, it will return an "%Unrecognized host or address" error message.

To abort a **ping** session, type the escape sequence. By default, this is Ctrl-^ X. You enter this by simultaneously pressing the Ctrl, Shift, and 6 keys, letting go, and then pressing the X key.

Table 3–2 in the **ping (privileged)** command section describes the test characters displayed in **ping** responses.

### Sample Display

The following display shows input to and output from the user **ping** command.

```
Router> ping appletalk 1024.128

Type escape sequence to abort.
Sending 5, 100-byte AppleTalk Echoes to 1024.128, timeout is 2 seconds:
!!!!!
Success rate is 100 percent, round-trip min/avg/max = 4/4/8 ms
```

### Related Commands

Search online to find documentation for related commands.

**show appletalk access-lists**

## SHOW APPLETALK ACCESS-LISTS

To display the AppleTalk access lists currently defined, use the **show appletalk access-lists** user EXEC command.

**show appletalk access-lists**

### Syntax        Description

This command has no arguments or keywords.

### Command Mode

User EXEC

### Usage Guidelines

This command first appeared in Cisco IOS Release 10.0.

### Sample Display

The following is sample output from the **show appletalk access-lists** command:

```
Router> show appletalk access-lists

AppleTalk access list 601:
        permit zone ZoneA
        permit zone ZoneB
        deny additional-zones
        permit network 55
        permit network 500
        permit cable-range 900-950
        deny includes 970-990
        permit within 991-995
        deny other-access
```

Table 3–4 describes fields shown in the display.

**Table 3–4**  *Show AppleTalk Access-Lists Field Descriptions*

| Field | Description |
|---|---|
| AppleTalk access list 601: | Number of the AppleTalk access lists. |
| permit zone<br>deny zone | Indicates whether access to an AppleTalk zone has been explicitly permitted or denied with the **access-list zone** command. |
| permit additional-zones<br>deny additional-zones | Indicates whether additional zones have been permitted or denied with the **access-list additional-zones** command. |
| permit network<br>deny network | Indicates whether access to an AppleTalk network has been explicitly permitted or denied with the **access-list network** command. |
| permit cable-range<br>deny cable-range | Indicates the cable ranges to which access has been permitted or denied with the **access-list cable-range** command. |
| permit includes<br>deny includes | Indicates the cable ranges to which access has been permitted or denied with the **access-list includes** command. |
| permit within<br>deny within | Indicates the additional cable ranges to which access has been permitted or denied with the **access-list within** command. |
| permit other-access<br>deny other-access | Indicates whether additional networks or cable ranges have been permitted or denied with the **access-list other-access** command. |

### Related Commands

Search online to find documentation for related commands.

**access-list additional-zones**
**access-list cable-range**
**access-list includes**

access-list nbp
access-list network
access-list other-access
access-list other-nbps
access-list within
access-list zone
appletalk access-group
appletalk distribute-list in
appletalk distribute-list out
appletalk getzonelist-filter

## SHOW APPLETALK ADJACENT-ROUTES

To display routes to networks that are directly connected or that are one hop away, use the **show appletalk adjacent-routes** privileged EXEC command.

> show appletalk adjacent-routes

*Syntax       Description*

This command has no arguments or keywords.

*Command Mode*

Privileged EXEC

*Usage Guidelines*

This command first appeared in Cisco IOS Release 10.0.

The **show appletalk adjacent-routes** command provides a quick overview of the local environment that is especially useful when an AppleTalk internetwork consists of a large number of networks (typically, more then 600 networks).

You can use information provided by this command to determine whether any local routes are missing or are misconfigured.

*Sample Display*

The following is sample output from the **show appletalk adjacent-routes** command:

```
Router# show appletalk adjacent-routes

Codes: R - RTMP derived, E - EIGRP derived, C - connected, S - static, P - proxy, 67 routes
in internet

R Net 29-29 [1/G] via gatekeeper, 0 sec, Ethernet0, zone Engineering
C Net 2501-2501 directly connected, Ethernet1, no zone set
C Net 4160-4160 directly connected, Ethernet0, zone Low End SW Lab
C Net 4172-4172 directly connected, TokenRing0, zone Low End SW Lab
R Net 6160 [1/G] via urk, 0 sec, TokenRing0, zone Low End SW Lab
```

Table 3–5 describes the fields shown in the display.

**Table 3–5** *Show AppleTalk Adjacent-Routes Field Descriptions*

| Field | Description |
|---|---|
| Codes: | Codes defining source of route. |
| R - RTMP derived | Route derived from an RTMP update. |
| E - EIGRP derived | Route derived from an Enhanced IGRP. |
| C - Connected | Directly connected network RTMP update. |
| S - Static | Static route. |
| P - Proxy | Proxy route. |
| 67 routes in internet | Total number of known routes in the AppleTalk network. |
| Net 29-29 | Cable range or network to which the route goes. |
| [1/G] | Hop count, followed by the state of the route.<br><br>Possible values for state include the following:<br><br>• G—Good (update has been received within the last 10 seconds).<br><br>• S—Suspect (update has been received more than 10 seconds ago but less than 20 seconds ago).<br><br>• B—Bad (update was received more than 20 seconds ago). |
| via | NBP registered name or address of the router that sent the routing information. |
| 0 sec | Time, in seconds, since information about this network cable range was last received. |
| directly connected | Indicates that the network or cable range is directly connected to the router. |
| Ethernet0 | Possible interface through which updates to this NBP registered name or address are sent. |
| zone | Zone name assigned to the network or cable range sending this update. |

## SHOW APPLETALK ARP

To display the entries in the ARP cache, use the **show appletalk arp** privileged EXEC command.

**show appletalk arp**

## Syntax        Description

This command has no arguments or keywords.

## Command Mode

Privileged EXEC

## Usage Guidelines

This command first appeared in Cisco IOS Release 10.0.

ARP establishes associates between network addresses and hardware (MAC) addresses. This information is maintained in the ARP cache.

## Sample Display

The following is sample output from the **show appletalk arp** command:

```
Router# show appletalk arp

Address     Age (min) Type      Hardware Addr   Encap   Interface
2000.1            -   Hardware  0000.0c04.1111  SNAP    Ethernet1
2000.2            0   Dynamic   0000.0c04.2222  SNAP    Ethernet1
2000.3            0   Dynamic   0000.0c04.3333  SNAP    Ethernet3
2000.4            -   Hardware  0000.0c04.4444  SNAP    Ethernet3
```

Table 3–6 describes the fields shown in the display.

**Table 3–6**   *Show AppleTalk ARP Field Description*

| Field | Description |
|-------|-------------|
| Address | AppleTalk network address of the interface. |
| Age (min) | Time, in minutes, that this entry has been in the ARP table. Entries are purged after they have been in the table for 240 minutes (4 hours). A hyphen indicates that this is a new entry. |
| Type | Indicates how the ARP table entry was learned. It can be one of the following:<br><br>• Dynamic—Entry was learned via AARP.<br><br>• Hardware—Entry was learned from an adapter in the router.<br><br>• Pending—Entry for a destination for which the router does not yet know the address. When a packet requests to be sent to an address for which the router does not yet have the MAC-level address, the Cisco IOS software creates an AARP entry for that AppleTalk address and then sends an AARP Resolve packet to get the MAC-level address for that node. When the software gets the response, the entry is marked "Dynamic." A pending AARP entry times out after one minute. |

**Table 3-6** *Show AppleTalk ARP Field Description, Continued*

| Field | Description |
|---|---|
| Hardware Addr | MAC address of this interface. |
| Encap | Encapsulation type. It can be one of the following: <br><br> • ARPA—Ethernet-type encapsulation <br><br> • Subnetwork Access Protocol (SNAP)—IEEE 802.3 encapsulation |
| Interface | Type and number of the interface. |

## SHOW APPLETALK AURP EVENTS

To display the pending events in the AURP update-events queue, use the **show appletalk aurp events** privileged EXEC command.

**show appletalk aurp events**

*Syntax     Description*

This command has no arguments or keywords.

*Command Mode*

Privileged EXEC

*Usage Guidelines*

This command first appeared in Cisco IOS Release 10.3.

*Sample Display*

The following is sample output from the **show appletalk aurp events** command:

```
Router# show appletalk aurp events

100-100, NDC EVENT pending
17043-17043, ND EVENT pending
```

Table 3–7 explains the fields shown in the display.

**Table 3-7** *Show AppleTalk AURP Events Field Descriptions*

| Field | Description |
|---|---|
| 100-100 | Network number or cable range. |
| NCD EVENT pending | Type of update event that is pending. |

## SHOW APPLETALK AURP TOPOLOGY

To display entries in the AURP private path database, which consists of all paths learned from exterior routers, use the **show appletalk aurp topology** privileged EXEC command.

>**show appletalk aurp topology**

*Syntax      Description*

This command has no arguments or keywords.

*Command Mode*

Privileged EXEC

*Usage Guidelines*

This command first appeared in Cisco IOS Release 10.3.

*Sample Display*

The following is sample output from the **show appletalk aurp topology** command:

```
Router# show appletalk aurp topology

30
              via Tunnel0, 3 hops
80
              via Tunnel0, 3 hops
101-101
              via Tunnel0, 8 hops
102-102
              via Tunnel0, 8 hops
103-103
              via Tunnel0, 8 hops
104-104
              via Tunnel0, 8 hops
105-105
              via Tunnel0, 8 hops
108-108
              via Tunnel0, 8 hops
109-109
              via Tunnel0, 9 hops
120-120
              via Tunnel0, 10 hops
125-125
              via Tunnel0, 8 hops
169-169
              via Tunnel0, 7 hops
201-205
              via Tunnel0, 4 hops
```

Table 3–8 explains the field shown in the display.

**Table 3–8**  *Show AppleTalk AURP Topology Field Descriptions*

| Field | Description |
|-------|-------------|
| 30 | AppleTalk network number or cable range. |
| via Tunnel0 | Interface used to reach the network. |
| 3 hops | Number of hops to the network. |

## SHOW APPLETALK CACHE

To display the routes in the AppleTalk fast-switching table on an extended AppleTalk network, use the **show appletalk cache** EXEC command.

> **show appletalk cache**

*Syntax      Description*

This command has no arguments or keywords.

*Command Mode*

EXEC

*Usage Guidelines*

This command first appeared in Cisco IOS Release 10.0.

The **show appletalk cache** command displays information for all fast-switching route cache entries, regardless of whether they are valid.

Route entries are removed from the fast-switching cache if one of the following occurs:

- A route that was used has been deleted but has not yet been marked bad.
- A route that was used has gone bad.
- A route that was used has been replaced with a new route with a better metric.
- The state of a route to a neighbor has changed from suspect to bad.
- The hardware address corresponding to a node address in the AARP cache has changed.
- The node address corresponding to a hardware address has changed.
- The ARP cache has been flushed.
- An ARP cache entry has been deleted.
- You have entered the **no appletalk routing**, the **appletalk route-cache**, or an **access-list** command.
- The encapsulation on the line has changed.
- An interface has become operational or nonoperational.

*Sample Display*

The following is sample output from the **show appletalk cache** command:

```
Router> show appletalk cache

AppleTalk Routing Cache, * = active entry, cache version is 227
Destination    Interface    MAC Header
*      29.0    Ethernet0    00000C00008200000C00D8DD
*   1544.000   Ethernet1    AA000400013400000C000E8C809B84BE02
*     33.000   Ethernet1    AA000400013400000C000E8C809B84BE02
```

The following is sample output from the **show appletalk cache** command when AppleTalk load balancing is enabled. The output displayed shows additional MAC headers for parallel paths (for example, 6099.52):

```
Router> show appletalk cache

Appletalk Routing cache, * = active entry, cache version is 11021
Destination    Interface    MAC Header
*      82.36   Ethernet1/4  00000CF366A600000C12C52D
   17043.208   Ethernet1/5  00000C367B4000000C12C52E
*   60099.52   Ethernet1/5  00000C367B4000000C12C52E
               Ethernet1/2  00000C367B3D00000C12C52B
               Ethernet1/3  00000C367B3E00000C12C52C
```

Table 3–9 describes the fields shown in the display.

**Table 3–9**   *Show AppleTalk Cache Field Descriptions*

| Field | Description |
|-------|-------------|
| * | Indicates the entry is valid. |
| cache version is | Version number of the AppleTalk fast-switching cache. |
| Destination | Destination network for this packet. |
| Interface | Router interface through which this packet is transmitted. |
| MAC Header | First bytes of this packet's MAC header. |

*Related Commands*

Search online to find documentation for related commands.

**appletalk maximum-paths**
**appletalk route-cache**

## SHOW APPLETALK DOMAIN

To display all domain-related information, use the **show appletalk domain** EXEC command.

**show appletalk domain** [*domain-number*]

| Syntax | Description |
|--------|-------------|
| *domain-number* | (Optional) Number of an AppleTalk domain about which to display information. It can be a decimal integer from 1 to 1000000. |

## Command Mode

EXEC

## Usage Guidelines

This command first appeared in Cisco IOS Release 10.3.

If you omit the argument *domain-number*, the **show appletalk domain** command displays information about all domains.

## Sample Displays

The following is sample output from the **show appletalk domain** command:

```
Router# show appletalk domain

        AppleTalk   Domain   Information:

        Domain 1        Name : Xerxes
        - - - - - - - - - - - - - - - - - - - - - - - - - - - -
        State                : Active
        Inbound remap range  : 100-199
        Outbound remap range : 200-299
        Hop reduction        : OFF
        Interfaces in domain :
                Ethernet1    : Enabled

        Domain 2        Name : Desdemona
        - - - - - - - - - - - - - - - - - - - - - - - - - - - -
        State                : Active
        Inbound remap range  : 300-399
        Outbound remap range : 400-499
        Hop reduction        : OFF
        Interfaces in domain :
                Ethernet3    : Enabled
```

The following is sample output from the **show appletalk domain** command when you specify a domain number:

```
Router# show appletalk domain 1

        AppleTalk   Domain   Information:

        Domain 1        Name : Xerxes
        - - - - - - - - - - - - - - - - - - - - - - - - - - - -
        State                : Active
        Inbound remap range  : 100-199
```

```
Outbound remap range : 200-299
Hop reduction        : OFF
Interfaces in domain :
      Ethernet1      : Enabled
```

Table 3–10 explains the fields shown in the displays.

**Table 3–10**  *Show AppleTalk Domain Field Descriptions*

| Field | Description |
|---|---|
| Domain | Number of the domain as specified with the **appletalk domain name** global configuration command. |
| Name | Name of the domain as specified with the **appletalk domain name** global configuration command. |
| State | Status of the domain. It can be either Active or Nonactive. |
| Inbound remap range | Inbound mapping range as specified with the **appletalk domain remap-range in** global configuration command. |
| Outbound remap range | Outbound mapping range as specified with the **appletalk domain remap-range out** global configuration command. |
| Hop reduction | Indicates whether hop reduction has been enabled with the **appletalk domain hop-reduction** global configuration command. It can be either OFF or ON. |
| Interfaces in domain | Indicates which interfaces are in the domain as specified with the **appletalk domain-group** interface configuration command and whether they are enabled. |

### Related Commands

Search online to find documentation for related commands.

**appletalk domain-group**
**appletalk domain hop-reduction**
**appletalk domain name**
**appletalk domain remap-range**

### SHOW APPLETALK EIGRP INTERFACES

To display information about interfaces configured for Enhanced IGRP, use the **show appletalk eigrp interfaces** EXEC command.

**show appletalk eigrp interfaces** [*type  number*]

| Syntax | Description |
|--------|-------------|
| *type* | (Optional) Interface type. |
| *number* | (Optional) Interface number. |

## Command Mode

EXEC

## Usage Guidelines

This command first appeared in Cisco IOS Release 11.2.

Use the **show appletalk eigrp interfaces** command to determine on which interfaces Enhanced IGRP is active and to find out information about Enhanced IGRP relating to those interfaces.

If an interface is specified, only that interface is displayed. Otherwise, all interfaces on which Enhanced IGRP is running are displayed.

## Sample Display

The following is sample output from the **show appletalk eigrp interfaces** command:

```
Router> show appletalk eigrp interfaces
AT/EIGRP interfaces for process 1, router id 24096

                     Xmit Queue    Mean   Pacing Time   Multicast   Pending
Interface   Peers   Un/Reliable   SRTT   Un/Reliable   Flow Timer  Routes
Di0         0         0/0           0       11/434        0           0
Et0         1         0/0          337       0/10         0           0
SE0:1.16    1         0/0           10       1/63        103          0
Tu0         1         0/0          330       0/16         0           0
```

Table 3–11 describes the fields shown in the display.

**Table 3–11** *Show AppleTalk Enhanced IGRP Interfaces Field Descriptions*

| Field | Description |
|-------|-------------|
| process 1 | Autonomous system number of the process. |
| router id | Identification number of the router, as configured in the **appletalk routing eigrp** command. |
| Interface | Interface name. |
| Peers | Number of neighbors on the interface. |
| Xmit Queue | Count of unreliable and reliable packets queued for transmission. |
| Mean SRTT | Average round-trip time for all neighbors on the interface. |

**Table 3–11**   *Show AppleTalk Enhanced IGRP Interfaces Field Descriptions, Continued*

| Field | Description |
|---|---|
| Pacing Time | Number of milliseconds to wait after transmitting unreliable and reliable packets. |
| Multicast Flow Timer | Number of milliseconds to wait for acknowledgment of a multicast packet by all neighbors before transmitting the next multicast packet. |
| Pending Routes | Number of routes still to be transmitted on this interface. |

## Related Commands

Search online to find documentation for related commands.

**show appletalk eigrp neighbors**

## SHOW APPLETALK EIGRP NEIGHBORS

To display the neighbors discovered by Enhanced IGRP, use the **show appletalk eigrp neighbors** EXEC command.

> **show appletalk eigrp neighbors** [*interface*]

| *Syntax* | *Description* |
|---|---|
| *interface* | (Optional) Displays information about the specified neighbor router. |

## Command Mode

EXEC

## Usage Guidelines

This command first appeared in Cisco IOS Release 10.3.

The **show appletalk eigrp neighbors** command lists only the neighbors running AppleTalk Enhanced IGRP. To list all neighboring AppleTalk routers, use the **show appletalk neighbors** command.

## Sample Display

The following is sample output from the **show appletalk eigrp neighbors** command:

```
Router# show appletalk eigrp neighbors

AT/EIGRP Neighbors for process 1, router id 83
Address                 Interface     Holdtime Uptime   Q      Seq  SRTT  RTO
                                      (secs)   (h:m:s)  Count  Num  (ms)  (ms)
warp.Ethernet1          Ethernet2     41       0:02:48  0      282  4     20
master.Ethernet2        Ethernet2     40       1:16:46  0      333  4     20
```

Table 3–12 explains the fields shown in the display.

**Table 3–12** *Show AppleTalk Enhanced IGRP Neighbors Field Descriptions*

| Field | Description |
|---|---|
| process 1 | Number of the Enhanced IGRP routing process. |
| router id 83 | Autonomous system number specified in the **appletalk routing global** configuration command. |
| Address | AppleTalk address of the AppleTalk Enhanced IGRP peer. |
| Interface | Interface on which the router is receiving hello packets from the peer. |
| Holdtime | Length of time, in seconds, that the Cisco IOS software waits to hear from the peer before declaring it down. If the peer is using the default hold time, this number is less than 15. If the peer configures a nondefault hold time, it is reflected here. |
| Uptime | Elapsed time, in hours, minutes, and seconds, since the local router first heard from this neighbor. |
| Q Count | Number of AppleTalk Enhanced IGRP packets (update, query, and reply) that the Cisco IOS software is waiting to send. |
| Seq Num | Sequence number of the last update, query, or reply packet that was received from this neighbor. |
| SRTT | Smooth round-trip time. This is the number of milliseconds it takes for an AppleTalk Enhanced IGRP packet to be sent to this neighbor and for the local router to receive an acknowledgment of that packet. |
| RTO | Retransmission timeout, in milliseconds. This is the amount of time the Cisco IOS software waits before retransmitting a packet from the retransmission queue to a neighbor. |

### Related Commands

Search online to find documentation for related commands.

**appletalk routing**
**show appletalk neighbors**

### SHOW APPLETALK EIGRP TOPOLOGY

To display the AppleTalk Enhanced IGRP topology table, use the **show appletalk eigrp topology** EXEC command.

> **show appletalk eigrp topology** [*network-number* | **active** | **zero-successors**]

| *Syntax* | *Description* |
|---|---|
| *network-number* | (Optional) Number of the AppleTalk network whose topology table entry you want to display. |
| **active** | (Optional) Displays the entries for all active routes. |
| **zero-successors** | (Optional) Displays the entries for destinations for which no successors exist. These entries are destinations that the Cisco IOS software currently does not know how to reach via Enhanced IGRP. This option is useful for debugging network problems. |

## Command Mode

EXEC

## Usage Guidelines

This command first appeared in Cisco IOS Release 10.3.

All Enhanced IGRP routes that are received for a destination, regardless of metric, are placed in the topology table. The route to a destination that is currently in use is the first route listed. Routes that are listed as "connected" take precedence over any routes learned from any other source.

## Sample Displays

The following is sample output from the **show appletalk eigrp topology** command:

```
Router# show appletalk eigrp topology

IPX EIGRP Topology Table for process 1, router id 1

Codes: P - Passive, A - Active, U - Update, Q - Query, R - Reply,
       r - Reply status

P 3165-0, 1 successors, FD is 0
        via Redistributed (25601/0),
        via 100.1 (2198016/2195456), Fddi0
        via 4080.67 (2198016/53760), Serial4
P 3161-0, 1 successors, FD is 307200
        via Redistributed (1025850/0),
        via 100.1 (2198016/2195456), Fddi0
        via 4080.67 (2198016/1028410), Serial4
P 100-100, 1 successors, FD is 0
        via Connected, Fddi0
        via 4080.67 (2198016/28160), Serial4
P 4080-4080, 1 successors, FD is 0
        via Connected, Serial4
        via 100.1 (2172416/2169856), Fddi0
```

Table 3–13 explains the fields that may be displayed in the output.

**Table 3–13** *Show AppleTalk Enhanced IGRP Topology Field Descriptions*

| Field | Description |
|---|---|
| Codes | State of this topology table entry. Passive and Active refer to the Enhanced IGRP state with respect to this destination; Update, Query, and Reply refer to the type of packet that is being sent. |
| P – Passive | No Enhanced IGRP computations are being performed for this destination. |
| A – Active | Enhanced IGRP computations are being performed for this destination. |
| U – Update | Indicates that an update packet was sent to this destination. |
| Q – Query | Indicates that a query packet was sent to this destination. |
| R – Reply | Indicates that a reply packet was sent to this destination. |
| r – Reply status | Flag that is set after the Cisco IOS software has sent a query and is waiting for a reply. |
| 3165, 3161, and so on | Destination AppleTalk network number. |
| successors | Number of successors. This number corresponds to the number of next hops in the AppleTalk routing table. |
| FD | Feasible distance. This value is used in the feasibility condition check. If the neighbor's reported distance (the metric after the slash) is less than the feasible distance, the feasibility condition is met and that path is a feasible successor. After the software determines that it has a feasible successor, it does not have to send a query for that destination. |
| replies | Number of replies that are still outstanding (have not been received) with respect to this destination. This information appears only when the destination is in the Active state. |
| state | Exact Enhanced IGRP state that this destination is in. It can be the number 0, 1, 2, or 3. This information appears only when the destination is Active. |
| via | AppleTalk address of the peer who told the software about this destination. The first $n$ of these entries, where $n$ is the number of successors, is the current successor. The remaining entries on the list are feasible successors. |
| (345088/319488) | The first number is the Enhanced IGRP metric that represents the cost to the destination. The second number is the Enhanced IGRP metric that this peer advertised to us. |
| Ethernet0 | Interface from which this information was learned. |

The following is sample output from the **show appletalk eigrp topology** command when you specify an AppleTalk network number:

```
Router# show appletalk eigrp topology 3165

AT-EIGRP topology entry for 3165-0
State is Passive, Query origin flag is 1, 1 Successor(s)
Routing Descriptor Blocks:
0.0, from 0.0
  Composite metric is (25601/0), Send flag is 0x0, Route is Internal
  Vector metric:
    Minimum bandwidth is 2560000000 Kbit
    Total delay is 1000000 nanoseconds
    Reliability is 255/255
    Load is 1/255
    Minimum MTU is 1500
    Hop count is 0
100.1 (Fddi0), from 100.1
  Composite metric is (2198016/2195456), Send flag is 0x0, Route is External
  Vector metric:
    Minimum bandwidth is 1544 Kbit
    Total delay is 21100000 nanoseconds
    Reliability is 255/255
    Load is 1/255
    Minimum MTU is 1500
    Hop count is 2
4080.83 (Serial4), from 4080.83
    Composite metric is (2198016/53760), Send flag is 0x0, Route is Internal
    Vector metric:
    Minimum bandwidth is 1544 Kbit
    Total delay is 21100000 nanoseconds
    Reliability is 255/255
    Load is 1/255
    Minimum MTU is 1500
    Hop count is 2
```

Table 3–14 explains the fields that may appear in the output.

**Table 3–14**   *Show AppleTalk Enhanced IGRP Topology Field Descriptions for a Specified Network*

| Field | Description |
|-------|-------------|
| 3165 | AppleTalk network number of the destination. |
| State is... | State of this entry. It can be either Passive or Active. Passive means that no Enhanced IGRP computations are being performed for this destination, and Active means that they are being performed. |
| Query origin flag | Exact Enhanced IGRP state that this destination is in. It can be the number 0, 1, 2, or 3. This information appears only when the destination is Active. |

**Table 3–14** *Show AppleTalk Enhanced IGRP Topology Field Descriptions for a Specified Network, Continued*

| Field | Description |
|---|---|
| Successors | Number of successors. This number corresponds to the number of next hops in the IPX routing table. |
| Next hop is ... | Indicates how this destination was learned. It can be one of the following:<br><br>• Connected—The destination is on a network directly connected to this router.<br><br>• Redistributed—The destination was learned via RTMP or another routing protocol.<br><br>• AppleTalk host address—The destination was learned from that peer via this Enhanced IGRP process. |
| Ethernet0 | Interface from which this information was learned. |
| from | Peer from whom the information was learned. For connected and redistributed routers, this is 0.0. For information learned via Enhanced IGRP, this is the peer's address. Currently, for information learned via Enhanced IGRP, the peer's AppleTalk address always matches the address in the "Next hop is" field. |
| Composite metric is | Enhanced IGRP composite metric. The first number is this device's metric to the destination, and the second is the peer's metric to the destination. |
| Send flag | Numeric representation of the "flags" field. It is 0 when nothing is being sent, 1 when an Update is being sent, 3 when a Query is being sent, and 4 when a Reply is being sent. Currently, 2 is not used. |
| Route is ... | Type of router. It can be either internal or external. Internal routes are those that originated in an Enhanced IGRP autonomous system, and external routes are those that did not. Routes learned via RTMP are always external. |
| Vector metric: | This section describes the components of the Enhanced IGRP metric. |
| Minimum bandwidth | Minimum bandwidth of the network used to reach the next hop. |
| Total delay | Delay time to reach the next hop. |
| Reliability | Reliability value used to reach the next hop. |

**Table 3–14**  *Show AppleTalk Enhanced IGRP Topology Field Descriptions for a Specified Network, Continued*

| Field | Description |
|---|---|
| Load | Load value used to reach the next hop. |
| Minimum MTU | Smallest Maximum Transmission Unit (MTU) size of the network used to reach the next hop. |
| Hop count | Number of hops to the next hop. |
| External data | This section describes the original protocol from which this route was redistributed. It appears only for external routes. |
| Originating router | Network address of the router that first distributed this route into AppleTalk Enhanced IGRP. |
| External protocol metric delay | External protocol from which this route was learned. The metric matches the external hop count displayed by the **show appletalk route** command for this destination. The delay is the external delay. |
| Administrator tag | Currently not used. |
| Flag | Currently not used. |

*Related Commands*

Search online to find documentation for related commands.

**show appletalk route**

## SHOW APPLETALK GLOBALS

To display information and settings about the AppleTalk internetwork and other parameters, use the **show appletalk globals** EXEC command.

> **show appletalk globals**

*Syntax       Description*

This command has no arguments or keywords.

*Command Mode*

EXEC

*Usage Guidelines*

This command first appeared in Cisco IOS Release 10.0.

*Sample Display*

The following is sample output from the **show appletalk globals** command:

```
Router# show appletalk globals

AppleTalk global information:
        The router is a domain router.
        Internet is compatible with older, AT Phase1, routers.
        There are 67 routes in the internet.
        There are 25 zones defined.
        All significant events will be logged.
        ZIP resends queries every 10 seconds.
        RTMP updates are sent every 10 seconds.
        RTMP entries are considered BAD after 20 seconds.
        RTMP entries are discarded after 60 seconds.
        AARP probe retransmit count: 10, interval: 200.
        AARP request retransmit count: 5, interval: 1000.
        DDP datagrams will be checksummed.
        RTMP datagrams will be strictly checked.
        RTMP routes may not be propagated without zones.
        Alternate node address format will not be displayed.
```

Table 3–15 describes the fields shown in the display.

**Table 3–15** *Show AppleTalk Globals Filed Descriptions*

| Field | Description |
|---|---|
| AppleTalk global information: | Heading for the command output. |
| The router is a domain router. | Indicates whether this router is a domain router. |
| Internet is compatible with older, AT Phase1, routers. | Indicates whether the AppleTalk internetwork meets the criteria for interoperation with Phase 1 routers. |
| There are 67 routes in the internet. | Total number of routes in the AppleTalk internetwork from which this router has heard in routing updates. |
| There are 25 zones defined. | Total number of valid zones in the current AppleTalk internetwork configuration. |
| All significant events will be logged. | Indicates whether the router has been configured with the **appletalk event-logging** command. |
| ZIP resends queries every 10 seconds. | Interval, in seconds, at which zone name queries are retried. |
| RTMP updates are sent every 10 seconds. | Interval, in seconds, at which the Cisco IOS software sends routing updates. |

**Table 3–15**  *Show AppleTalk Globals Filed Descriptions, Continued*

| Field | Description |
|---|---|
| RTMP entries are considered BAD after 20 seconds. | Time after which routes for which the software has not received an update are marked as candidates for being deleted from the routing table. |
| RTMP entries are discarded after 60 seconds. | Time after which routes for which the software has not received an update are deleted from the routing table. |
| AARP probe retransmit count: 10, interval: 200. | Number of AARP probe retransmissions that are done before abandoning address negotiations and instead are using the selected AppleTalk address, followed by the time, in milliseconds, between retransmission of ARP probe packets. You set these values with the **appletalk arp retransmit-count** and **appletalk arp interval** commands, respectively. |
| AARP request retransmit count: 5, interval: 1000. | Number of AARP request retransmissions that are done before abandoning address negotiations and using the selected AppleTalk address, followed by the time, in milliseconds, between retransmission of ARP request packets. You set these values with the **appletalk arp retransmit-count** and **appletalk arp interval** commands, respectively. |
| DDP datagrams will be checksummed. | Indicates whether the **appletalk checksum** configuration command is enabled. When enabled, the software discards DDP packets when the checksum is incorrect and when the router is the final destination for the packet. |
| RTMP datagrams will be strictly checked. | Indicates whether the **appletalk strict-rtmp-checking** configuration command is enabled. When enabled, RTMP packets arriving from routers that are not directly connected to the router performing the check are discarded. |
| RTMP routes may not be propagated without zones. | Indicates whether the **appletalk require-route-zones** configuration command is enabled. When enabled, the Cisco IOS software does not advertise a route to its neighboring routers until it has obtained a network/zone association for that route. |
| Alternate node address format will not be displayed. | Indicates whether AppleTalk addresses are printed in numeric or name form. You configure this with the **appletalk lookup-type** and **appletalk name-lookup-interval** commands. |

## Related Commands

Search online to find documentation for related commands.

**appletalk arp interval**
**appletalk arp retransmit-count**
**appletalk checksum**
**appletalk event-logging**
**appletalk lookup-type**
**appletalk name-lookup-interval**
**appletalk require-route-zones**
**appletalk strict-rtmp-checking**

## SHOW APPLETALK INTERFACE

To display the status of the AppleTalk interfaces configured in the Cisco IOS software and the parameters configured on each interface, use the **show appletalk interface** privileged EXEC command.

    **show appletalk interface** [**brief**] [*type number*]

| Syntax | Description |
|--------|-------------|
| **brief** | (Optional) Displays a brief summary of the status of the AppleTalk interfaces. |
| *type* | (Optional) Interface type. It can be one of the following types: asynchronous, dialer, Ethernet (IEEE 802.3), Token Ring (IEEE 802.5), FDDI, High-Speed Serial Interface (HSSI), Virtual Interface, ISDN Basic Rate Interface (BRI), ATM interface, loopback, null, or serial. |
| *number* | (Optional) Interface number. |

## Command Mode

Privileged EXEC

## Usage Guidelines

This command first appeared in Cisco IOS Release 10.0.

The **show appletalk interface** is particularly useful when you first enable AppleTalk on a router interface.

*Sample Displays*

The following is sample output from the **show appletalk interface** command for an extended Apple-Talk network:

```
Router# show appletalk interface fddi 0

Fddi0 is up, line protocol is up
    AppleTalk cable range is 4199-4199
    AppleTalk address is 4199.82, Valid
    AppleTalk zone is "Low End SW Lab"
    AppleTalk address gleaning is disabled
    AppleTalk route cache is enabled
    Interface will not perform pre-FDDITalk compatibility
```

Table 3–16 describes the fields shown in the display as well as some fields that are not shown but that also may be displayed. Note that this command can show a node name in addition to the address, depending on how the software has been configured with the **appletalk lookup-type** and **appletalk name-lookup-interval** commands.

**Table 3–16**  *Show AppleTalk Interface Field Descriptions for an Extended Network*

| Field | Description |
|---|---|
| FDDI is ... | Type of interface and whether it is currently active and inserted into the network (up) or inactive and not inserted (down). |
| line protocol | Indicates whether the software processes that handle the line protocol believe the interface is usable (that is, whether *keepalives* are successful). |
| AppleTalk node | Indicates whether the node is up or down in the network. |
| AppleTalk cable range | Cable range of the interface. |
| AppleTalk address is ..., Valid | Address of the interface, and whether the address conflicts with any other address on the network ("Valid" means it does not). |
| AppleTalk zone | Name of the zone that this interface is in. |
| AppleTalk port configuration verified... | When Cisco access server implementation comes up on an interface, if there are other routers detected and the interface we are bringing up is not in discovery mode, Cisco access server "confirms" the configuration with the routers that are already on the cable. The address printed in this field is that of the router with which the local router has verified that the interface configuration matches that on the running network. |
| AppleTalk discarded...packets due to input errors | Number of packets the interface discarded because of input errors. These errors are usually incorrect encapsulations (that is, the packet has a malformed header format). |

Command Reference

**Table 3–16**  *Show AppleTalk Interface Field Descriptions for an Extended Network, Continued*

| Field | Description |
|---|---|
| AppleTalk address gleaning | Indicates whether the interface is automatically deriving ARP table entries from incoming packets (referred to as *gleaning*). |
| AppleTalk route cache | Indicates whether fast switching is enabled on the interface. |
| Interface will ... | Indicates that the AppleTalk interface checks to see whether AppleTalk packets sent on the FDDI ring from routers running Cisco software releases prior to Release 9.0(3) or 9.1(2) are recognized. |
| AppleTalk domain | AppleTalk domain of which this interface is a member. |

The following is sample output from the **show appletalk interface** command for a nonextended AppleTalk network:

```
Router# show appletalk interface ethernet 1

Ethernet 1 is up, line protocol is up
    AppleTalk address is 666.128, Valid
    AppleTalk zone is Underworld
    AppleTalk routing protocols enabled are RTMP
    AppleTalk address gleaning is enabled
    AppleTalk route cache is not initialized
```

Table 3–17 describes the fields shown in the display.

**Table 3–17**  *Show AppleTalk Interface Field Descriptions for a Nonextended Network*

| Field | Description |
|---|---|
| Ethernet 1 | Type of interface and whether it is currently active and inserted into the network (up) or inactive and not inserted (down). |
| line protocol | Indicates whether the software processes that handle the line protocol believe the interface is usable (that is, whether *keepalives* are successful). |
| AppleTalk address is ..., Valid | Address of the interface, and whether the address conflicts with any other address on the network ("Valid" means it does not). |
| AppleTalk zone | Name of the zone that this interface is in. |
| AppleTalk routing protocols enabled | AppleTalk routing protocols that are enabled on the interface. |

**Table 3–17** *Show AppleTalk Interface Field Descriptions for a Nonextended Network, Continued*

| Field | Description |
|---|---|
| AppleTalk address gleaning | Indicates whether the interface is automatically deriving ARP table entries from incoming packets (referred to as *gleaning*). |
| AppleTalk route cache | Indicates whether fast switching is enabled on the interface. |

The following is sample output from the **show appletalk interface brief** command:

```
Router# show appletalk interface brief

Interface    Address     Config         Status/Line Protocol     Atalk Protocol
TokenRing0   108.36      Extended       up                       down
TokenRing1   unassigned  not config'd   administratively down    n/a
Ethernet0    10.82       Extended       up                       up
Serial0      unassigned  not config'd   administratively down    n/a
Ethernet1    30.83       Extended       up                       up
Serial1      unassigned  not config'd   administratively down    n/a
Serial2      unassigned  not config'd   administratively down    n/a
Serial3      unassigned  not config'd   administratively down    n/a
Serial4      unassigned  not config'd   administratively down    n/a
Serial5      unassigned  not config'd   administratively down    n/a
Fddi0        50001.82    Extended       administratively down    down
Ethernet2    unassigned  not config'd   up                       n/a
Ethernet3    9993.137    Extended       up                       up
Ethernet4    40.82       Non-Extended   up                       up
Ethernet5    unassigned  not config'd   administratively down    n/a
Ethernet6    unassigned  not config'd   administratively down    n/a
Ethernet7    unassigned  not config'd   administratively down    n/a
```

Table 3–18 describes the fields shown in the display.

**Table 3–18** *Show AppleTalk Interface Brief Field Descriptions*

| Field | Description |
|---|---|
| Interface | Interface type and number. |
| Address | Address assigned to the interface. |
| Config | How the interface is configured. Possible values are extended, nonextended, and not configured. |
| Status/Line Protocol | Whether the software processes that handle the line protocol believe the interface is usable (that is, whether *keepalives* are successful). |
| Atalk Protocol | Whether AppleTalk routing is up and running on the interface. |

The following sample output displays the **show appletalk interface** command when AppleTalk RTMP stub mode is enabled. The last line of the output notes that this mode is turned on.

```
Router# show appletalk interface e 2
Ethernet2 is up, line protocol is up
  AppleTalk cable range is 30-30
  AppleTalk address is 30.1, Valid
  AppleTalk zone is "Zone30-30"
  AppleTalk address gleaning is disabled
  AppleTalk route cache is enabled
  AppleTalk RTMP stub mode is enabled
```

## *Related Commands*

Search online to find documentation for related commands.

**appletalk access-group**
**appletalk address**
**appletalk cable-range**
**appletalk client-mode**
**appletalk discovery**
**appletalk distribute-list in**
**appletalk distribute-list out**
**appletalk free-trade-zone**
**appletalk getzonelist-filter**
**appletalk glean-packets**
**appletalk pre-fdditalk**
**appletalk protocol**
**appletalk route-cache**
**appletalk rtmp-stub**
**appletalk send-rtmps**
**appletalk zip-reply-filter**
**appletalk zone**

## SHOW APPLETALK MACIP-CLIENTS

To display status information about all known MacIP clients, use the **show appletalk macip-clients** EXEC command.

> **show appletalk macip-clients**

## *Syntax      Description*

This command has no arguments or keywords.

## *Command Mode*

EXEC

*Usage Guidelines*

This command first appeared in Cisco IOS Release 10.0.

*Sample Display*

The following is sample output from the **show appletalk macip-clients** command:

```
Router# show appletalk macip-clients

131.108.199.1@[27001n,69a,72s] 45 secs    'S/W Test Lab'
```

Table 3–19 describes the fields shown in the display.

**Table 3–19**  *Show AppleTalk MacIP-Clients Field Descriptions*

| Field | Description |
|---|---|
| 131.108.199.1@ | Client IP address. |
| [2700ln,69a,72s] | DDP address of the registered entity, showing the network number, node address, and socket number. |
| 45 secs | Time (in seconds) since the last NBP confirmation was received. |
| 'S/W Test Lab' | Name of the zone to which the MacIP client is attached. |

*Related Commands*

Search online to find documentation for related commands.

**show appletalk traffic**

## SHOW APPLETALK MACIP-SERVERS

To display status information about related servers, use the **show appletalk macip-servers** EXEC command.

**show appletalk macip-servers**

*Syntax     Description*

This command has no arguments or keywords.

*Command Mode*

EXEC

*Usage Guidelines*

This command first appeared in Cisco IOS Release 10.0.

*Command Reference*

The information in the **show appletalk macip-servers** display can help you quickly determine the status of your MacIP configuration. In particular, the STATE field can help identify problems in your AppleTalk environment.

### Sample Display

The following is sample output from the **show appletalk macip-servers** command:

```
Router# show appletalk macip-servers

MACIP SERVER 1, IP 131.108.199.221,  ZONE 'S/W Test Lab' STATE is server_up
Resource #1 DYNAMIC 131.108.199.1-131.108.199.10, 1/10 IP in use
Resource #2 STATIC 131.108.199.11-131.108.199.20, 0/10 IP in use
```

Table 3–20 describes the fields shown in the display.

**Table 3–20**  *Show AppleTalk MacIP-Servers Field Descriptions*

| Field | Description |
|---|---|
| MACIP SERVER 1 | Number of the MacIP server. This number is assigned arbitrarily. |
| IP 131.108.199.221 | IP address of the MacIP server. |
| ZONE 'S/W Test Lab' | AppleTalk server zone specified with the **appletalk macip server** command. |
| STATE is server_up | State of the server. Table 3–22  lists the possible states. If the server remains in the "resource_wait" state, check that resources have been assigned to this server with either the **appletalk macip dynamic** or the **appletalk macip static** command. |
| Resource #1 DYNAMIC 131.108.199.1-131.108.199.10, 1/10 IP in use | Resource specifications defined in the **appletalk macip dynamic** and **appletalk macip static** commands. This list indicates whether the resource address was assigned dynamically or statically, identifies the IP address range associated with the resource specification, and indicates the number of active MacIP clients. |

Use the **show appletalk macip-servers** command with **show appletalk interface** to identify AppleTalk network problems, as follows.

**Step 1**  Determine the state of the MacIP server using **show macip-servers**. If the STATE field continues to indicate an anomalous status (something other than "server_up," such as "resource_wait" or "zone_wait"), there is a problem.

**Step 2**  Determine the status of AppleTalk routing and the specific interface using the **show appletalk interface** command.

**Step 3**    If the protocol and interface are up, check the MacIP configuration commands for inconsistencies in the IP address and zone.

The STATE field of the **show appletalk macip-servers** command indicates the current state of each configured MacIP server. Each server operates according to the finite-state machine table described in Table 3–21. Table 3–22 describes the state functions listed in Table 3–21. These are the states that are displayed by the **show appletalk macip-servers** command.

**Table 3–21**    *MacIP Finite-State Machine Table*

| State | Event | New State | Notes |
|---|---|---|---|
| initial | ADD_SERVER | resource_wait | Server configured |
| resource_wait | TIMEOUT | resource_wait | Wait for resources |
| resource_wait | ADD_RESOURCE | zone_wait | Wait for zone seeding |
| zone_wait | ZONE_SEEDED | server_start | Register server |
| zone_wait | TIMEOUT | zone_wait | Wait until seeded |
| server_start | START_OK | reg_wait | Wait for server register |
| server_start | START_FAIL | del_server | Could not start (possible configuration error) |
| reg_wait | REG_OK | server_up | Registration successful |
| reg_wait | REG_FAIL | del_server | Registration failed (possible duplicate IP address) |
| reg_wait | TIMEOUT | reg_wait | Wait until register |
| server_up | TIMEOUT | send_confirms | NBP confirm all clients |
| send_confirms | CONFIRM_OK | server_up | |
| send_confirms | ZONE_DOWN | zone_wait | Zone or IP interface down; restart |
| * | ADD_RESOURCE | * | Ignore, except resource_wait |
| * | DEL_SERVER | del_server | "No server" statement (HALT) |
| * | DEL_RESOURCE | ck_resource | Ignore |
| ck_resource | YES_RESOURCES | * | Return to previous state |
| ck_resource | NO_RESOURCES | resource_wait | Shut down and wait for resources |

**Table 3-22**  *Server States*

| State | Description |
|---|---|
| ck_resource | The server verifies that at least one client range is available. If not, it deregisters NBP names and returns to the resource_wait state. |
| del_server | State at which all servers end. In this state, the server deregisters all NBP names, purges all clients, and deallocates server resources. |
| initial | The state at which all servers start. |
| resource-wait | The server waits until a client range for the server has been configured. |
| send_confirms | The server tickles active clients every minute, deletes clients that have not responded within the last 5 minutes, and checks IP and AppleTalk interfaces used by MacIP server. If the interfaces are down or have been reconfigured, the server restarts. |
| server_start | The server registers configured IPADDRESS and registers as IPGATEWAY. It then opens an ATP socket to listen for IP address assignment requests, sends NBP lookup requests for existing IPADDRESSes, and automatically adds clients with addresses within one of the configured client ranges. |
| server_up | The server has registered. Being in this state enables routing to client ranges. The server now responds to IP address assignment requests. |
| zone_wait | The server waits until the configured AppleTalk zone name for the server is up. The server remains in this state if no such zone has been configured or if AppleTalk routing is not enabled. |
| * | An asterisk in the first column represents any state. An asterisk in the second column represents a return to the previous state. |

*Command Reference*

## Related Commands

Search online to find documentation for related commands.

appletalk macip dynamic
appletalk macip server
appletalk macip static
show appletalk interface
show appletalk traffic

## SHOW APPLETALK MACIP-TRAFFIC

To display statistics about MacIP traffic through the router, use the **show appletalk macip-traffic** privileged EXEC command.

> show appletalk macip-traffic

*Syntax     Description*

This command has no arguments or keywords.

*Command Mode*

Privileged EXEC

*Usage Guidelines*

This command first appeared in Cisco IOS Release 10.0.

Use the **show appletalk macip-traffic** command to obtain a detailed breakdown of MacIP traffic that is sent through a router from an AppleTalk to an IP network. The output from this command differs from that of the **show appletalk traffic** command, which shows normal AppleTalk traffic generated, received, or routed by the router.

*Sample Display*

The following is sample output from the **show appletalk macip-traffic** command:

```
Router# show appletalk macip-traffic

 -- MACIP Statistics
                MACIP_DDP_IN:    11062
           MACIP_DDP_IP_OUT:    10984
 MACIP_DDP_NO_CLIENT_SERVICE:      78
                MACIP_IP_IN:     7619
           MACIP_IP_DDP_OUT:     7619
            MACIP_SERVER_IN:       62
           MACIP_SERVER_OUT:       52
       MACIP_SERVER_BAD_ATP:       10
     MACIP_SERVER_ASSIGN_IN:       26
    MACIP_SERVER_ASSIGN_OUT:       26
      MACIP_SERVER_INFO_IN:        26
     MACIP_SERVER_INFO_OUT:        26
```

Table 3–23 describes the fields shown in the display.

**Table 3–23**   *Show AppleTalk MacIP-Traffic Field Descriptions*

| Field | Description |
|---|---|
| MACIP_DDP_IN | Number of DDP packets received. |
| MACIP_DDP_IP_OUT | Number of DDP packets received that were sent to the IP network. |
| MACIP_DDP_NO_CLIENT_ SERVICE | Number of DDP packets received for which there is no client. |

**Table 3-23** *Show AppleTalk MacIP-Traffic Field Descriptions, Continued*

| Field | Description |
|---|---|
| MACIP_IP_IN | Number of IP packets received. |
| MACIP_IP_DDP_OUT | Number of IP packets received that were sent to the AppleTalk network. |
| MACIP_SERVER_IN | Number of packets destined for MacIP servers. |
| MACIP_SERVER_OUT | Number of packets sent by MacIP servers. |
| MACIP_SERVER_BAD_ATP | Number of MacIP allocation requests received with a bad request. |
| MACIP_SERVER_ASSIGN_IN | Number of MacIP allocation requests received asking for an IP address. |
| MACIP_SERVER_ASSIGN_OUT | Number of IP addresses assigned. |
| MACIP_SERVER_INFO_IN | Number of MacIP packets received requesting server information. |
| MACIP_SERVER_INFO_OUT | Number of server information requests answered. |

*Related Commands*

Search online to find documentation for related commands.

**show appletalk traffic**

## SHOW APPLETALK NAME-CACHE

To display a list of NBP services offered by nearby routers and other devices that support NBP, use the **show appletalk name-cache** privileged EXEC command.

    **show appletalk name-cache**

*Syntax    Description*

This command has no arguments or keywords.

*Command Mode*

Privileged EXEC

*Usage Guidelines*

This command first appeared in Cisco IOS Release 10.0.

Command Reference

The **show appletalk name-cache** command displays the information currently in the NBP name cache.

Support for names enables you to easily identify and determine the status of any associated device. This can be important in AppleTalk internetworks where node numbers are dynamically generated.

You can authorize the **show appletalk name-cache** command to display any AppleTalk services of interest in local zones. This contrasts with the **show appletalk nbp** command, which you use to display services registered by routers.

### Sample Display

The following is sample output from the **show appletalk name-cache** command:

```
Router# show appletalk name-cache

AppleTalk Name Cache:
Net    Adr  Skt  Name                Type          Zone
4160   19   8    gatekeeper          SNMP Agent    Underworld
4160   19   254  gatekeeper.Ether4   ciscoRouter   Underworld
4160   86   8    bones               SNMP Agent    Underworld
4160   86   72   131.108.160.78      IPADDRESS     Underworld
4160   86   254  bones.Ethernet0     IPGATEWAY     Underworld
```

Table 3–24 describes the fields shown in the display.

**Table 3–24**   *Show AppleTalk Name-Cache Field Descriptions*

| Field | Description |
|-------|-------------|
| Net | AppleTalk network number or cable range. |
| Adr | Node address. |
| Skt | DDP socket number. |
| Name | Name of the service. |
| Type | Device type. The possible types vary, depending on the service. The following are the Cisco server types:<br>• ciscoRouter—Server is a Cisco router.<br>• SNMP Agent—Server is an SNMP agent.<br>• IPGATEWAY—Active MacIP server names.<br>• IPADDRESS—Active MacIP server addresses. |
| Zone | Name of the AppleTalk zone to which this address belongs. |

### Related Commands

Search online to find documentation for related commands.

**show appletalk nbp**

### SHOW APPLETALK NBP

To display the contents of the NBP name registration table, use the **show appletalk nbp** EXEC command.

> **show appletalk nbp**

*Syntax Description*

This command has no arguments or keywords.

*Command Mode*

EXEC

*Usage Guidelines*

This command first appeared in Cisco IOS Release 10.0.

The **show appletalk nbp** command lets you identify specific AppleTalk nodes. It displays services registered by the router. In contrast, use the **show appletalk name-cache** command to display any AppleTalk services of interest in local zones.

Routers with active AppleTalk interfaces register each interface separately. The Cisco IOS software generates a unique interface NBP name by appending the interface type name and unit number to the router name. For example, for the router named "router" that has AppleTalk enabled on Ethernet interface 0 in the zone Marketing, the NBP registered name is as follows:

```
router.Ethernet0:ciscoRouter@Marketing
```

Registering each interface on the router provides you with an indication that the device is configured and operating properly.

One name is registered for each interface. Other service types are registered once for each zone.

The Cisco IOS software deregisters the NBP name if AppleTalk is disabled on the interface for any reason.

*Sample Display*

The following is sample output from the **show appletalk nbp** command:

```
Router# show appletalk nbp

Net  Adr Skt Name                Type          Zone
4160 211 254 pag.Ethernet0       ciscoRouter   Low End SW Lab
4160 211   8 pag                 SNMP Agent    Low End SW Lab
4172  84 254 pag.TokenRing0      ciscoRouter   LES Tokenring
4172  84   8 pag                 SNMP Agent    LES Tokenring
 200  75 254 myrouter. Ethernet1 ciscoRouter   Marketing    *
```

Table 3–25 describes the fields shown in the display as well as some fields not shown that also may be displayed.

**Table 3–25**　*Show AppleTalk NBP Field Descriptions*

| Field | Description |
|---|---|
| Net | AppleTalk network number. |
| Adr | Node address. |
| Skt | DDP socket number. |
| Name | Name of the service. |
| Type | Device type. The possible types vary, depending on the service. The following are the Cisco server types:<br><br>• ciscoRouter—Cisco routers displayed by port.<br><br>• SNMP Agent—SNMP agents displayed by zone if AppleTalk SNMP-over-DDP is enabled.<br><br>• IPGATEWAY—Active MacIP server names.<br><br>• IPADDRESS—Active MacIP server addresses. |
| Zone | Name of the AppleTalk zone to which this address belongs. |
| * | An asterisk in the right margin indicates that the name registration is pending confirmation. |

## Related Commands

Search online to find documentation for related commands.

**show appletalk name-cache**

## SHOW APPLETALK NEIGHBORS

To display information about the AppleTalk routers that are directly connected to any of the networks to which this router is directly connected, use the **show appletalk neighbors** EXEC command.

**show appletalk neighbors** [*neighbor-address*]

*Syntax*　　　　　*Description*

*neighbor-address*　　(Optional) Displays information about the specified neighbor router.

## Command Mode

EXEC

## Usage Guidelines

This command first appeared in Cisco IOS Release 10.0.

If no neighbor address is specified, this command displays information about all AppleTalk routers.

The local router determines the AppleTalk network topology from its neighboring routers and learns from them most of the other information it needs to support the AppleTalk protocols.

## Sample Displays

The following is sample output from the **show appletalk neighbors** command:

```
Router# show appletalk neighbors

AppleTalk neighbors:
  17037.2      anger.Ethernet0/0      Ethernet0/0, uptime 8:33:27, 2 secs
            Neighbor is reachable as a RTMP peer
  17037.108    Ethernet0/0, uptime 8:33:21, 7 secs
            Neighbor is reachable as a RTMP peer
  17037.248    Ethernet0/0, uptime 8:33:30, 4 secs
            Neighbor is reachable as a RTMP peer
  17046.2      anger.Ethernet0/1      Ethernet0/1, uptime 8:33:27, 2 secs
            Neighbor is reachable as a RTMP peer
  17435.87     firewall.Ethernet0/0   Ethernet0/3, uptime 8:33:27, 6 secs
            Neighbor is reachable as a RTMP peer
  17435.186    the-wall.Ethernet0     Ethernet0/3, uptime 8:33:24, 5 secs
            Neighbor is reachable as a RTMP peer
  17435.233    teach-gw.Ethernet0     Ethernet0/3, uptime 8:33:24, 7 secs
            Neighbor is reachable as a RTMP peer
  17036.1      other-gw.Ethernet5 Ethernet0/5, uptime 8:33:29, 9 secs
            Neighbor is reachable as a RTMP peer
  4021.5       boojum.Hssi4/0   Hssi1/0, uptime 10:49:02, 0 secs
         Neighbor has restarted 1 time in 8:33:11.
         Neighbor is reachable as a static peer
```

Table 3–26 describes the fields shown in this display. Depending on the configuration of the **appletalk lookup-type** and **appletalk name-lookup-interval** commands, a node name as well as a node address also may be shown in this display.

**Table 3–26**  *Show AppleTalk Neighbors Field Descriptions*

| Field | Description |
|---|---|
| 31.86 | AppleTalk address of the neighbor router. |
| Ethernet0/0 | Router interface through which the neighbor router can be reached. |
| uptime 133:28:06 | Amount of time (in hours, minutes, and seconds) that the Cisco IOS software has received this neighboring router's routing updates. |

**Table 3–26**   *Show AppleTalk Neighbors Field Descriptions, Continued*

| Field | Description |
|---|---|
| 2 secs | Time (in seconds) since the software last received an update from the neighbor router. |
| Neighbor is reachable as a RTMP peer<br>Neighbor is reachable as a static peer | Indicates how the route to this neighbor was learned. |
| Neighbor is down.<br>Neighbor has restarted 1 time | Indicates whether neighbor is up or down and the number of times it has restarted in the specified time interval, displayed in the format hours:minutes:seconds. |

The following is sample output from the **show appletalk neighbor** command when you specify the AppleTalk address of a particular neighbor:

```
Router# show appletalk neighbors 69.163

Neighbor 69.163, Ethernet0, uptime 268:00:52, last update 7 secs ago
  We have sent queries for 299 nets via 214 packets.
  Last query was sent 4061 secs ago.
  We received 152 replies and 0 extended replies.
  We have received queries for 14304 nets in 4835 packets.
  We sent 157 replies and 28 extended replies.
  We received 0 ZIP notifies.
  We received 0 obsolete ZIP commands.
  We received 4 miscellaneous ZIP commands.
  We received 0 unrecognized ZIP commands.
  We have received 92943 routing updates.
  Of the 92943 valid updates, 1320 entries were invalid.
  We received 1 routing update which was very late.
  Last update had 0 extended and 2 nonextended routes.
  Last update detail: 2 old
```

Table 3–27 describes the fields shown in this display. Depending on the configuration of the **appletalk lookup-type** and **appletalk name-lookup-interval** commands, a node name as well as a node address can be shown in this display.

**Table 3–27**   *Show AppleTalk Neighbor Field Descriptions for a Specific Address*

| Field | Description |
|---|---|
| Neighbor 69.163 | AppleTalk address of the neighbor. |
| Ethernet0 | Interface through which the router receives this neighbor's routing updates. |

**Table 3–27** *Show AppleTalk Neighbor Field Descriptions for a Specific Address, Continued*

| Field | Description |
|---|---|
| uptime 268:00:52 | Amount of time (in hours, minutes, and seconds) that the Cisco IOS software has received this neighboring router's routing updates. |
| last update 7 secs ago | Time (in seconds) since the software last received an update from the neighbor router. |
| sent queries | Number of queries sent to neighbor networks and the number of query packets sent. |
| Last query was sent | Time (in seconds) since last query was sent. |
| received replies | Number of RTMP replies heard from this neighbor. |
| extended replies | Number of extended RTMP replies received from this neighbor. |
| ZIP notifies | Number of ZIP notify packets received from this neighbor. |
| obsolete ZIP commands | Number of nonextended-only (obsolete) ZIP commands received from this neighbor. |
| miscellaneous ZIP commands | Number of ZIP commands (for example, GNI, GZI, and GMZ) from end systems rather than from routers. |
| unrecognized ZIP commands | Number of bogus ZIP packets received from this neighbor. |
| routing updates | Number of RMTP updates received from this neighbor. |
| entries were invalid | Of the routing update packets received from this neighbor, the number of invalid entries discarded. |
| Last update detail | Of the routing update packets received from this neighbor, the number already known about. |

## Related Commands

Search online to find documentation for related commands.

**appletalk lookup-type**
**appletalk name-lookup-interval**

## SHOW APPLETALK REMAP

To display domain remapping information, use the **show appletalk remap** EXEC command.

> **show appletalk remap** [**domain** *domain-number* [{**in** | **out**} [{**to** | **from**} *domain-network*]]]

| Syntax | Description |
|---|---|
| **domain** *domain-number* | (Optional) Number of an AppleTalk domain about which to display remapping information. It can be a decimal integer from 1 through 1000000. |
| **in** | (Optional) Displays remapping information about inbound packets— that is, on packets entering the local segment of the domain. |
| **out** | (Optional) Displays remapping information about outbound packets—that is, on packets exiting from the local segment of the domain. |
| **to** | (Optional) Displays information about the network number or cable range to which an address has been remapped. |
| **from** | (Optional) Displays information about the original network number or cable range. |
| *domain-network* | (Optional) Number of an AppleTalk network. |

## Command Mode

EXEC

## Usage Guidelines

This command first appeared in Cisco IOS Release 10.3.

If you omit all options keywords and arguments, the **show appletalk remap** command displays all remapping information about all domains.

## Sample Displays

The following is sample output from the **show appletalk remap** command:

```
Router# show appletalk remap

    AppleTalk   Remapping   Table :
    -----------------------------

    Domain 1 : Domain 1   State : Active
    -------------------------------------------

    Direction : IN

    Domain Net(Cable)        Remapped to           Status
    3      - 3               100   - 100           Good

      Direction : OUT

    Domain Net(Cable)        Remapped to           Status
    1      - 1               200   - 200           Good
```

```
Domain 2 : Domain 2   State : Active
-----------------------------------------

Direction : IN

Domain Net(Cable)       Remapped to          Status

Direction : OUT

Domain Net(Cable)       Remapped to          Status
2      - 2              400   - 400          Good
100    - 100            401   - 401          Good
```

The following is sample output from the **show appletalk remap** command when you specify a domain number:

```
Router# show appletalk remap domain 1

AppleTalk   Remapping  Table :
----------------------------

Domain 1 : Domain 1   State : Active
-----------------------------------------

Direction : IN

Domain Net(Cable)       Remapped to          Status
3      - 3              100   - 100          Good

Direction : OUT

Domain Net(Cable)       Remapped to          Status
1      - 1              201   - 201          Good
```

The following is sample output from the **show appletalk remap** command to display inbound remappings for AppleTalk network 100:

```
Router# show appletalk remap domain 1 in from 100

AppleTalk   Remapping  Table :
----------------------------

For the Remap 100  the Domain  net is 3
```

Table 3–28 explains the fields shown in the display.

**Table 3–28**   *Show AppleTalk Remap Field Descriptions*

| Field | Description |
|-------|-------------|
| Domain | Number of the AppleTalk IP domain. |
| State | State of the domain. It can be either Active or Nonactive. |

**Table 3-28**　*Show AppleTalk Remap Field Descriptions, Continued*

| Field | Description |
|---|---|
| Direction | Indicates whether the mapping is an inbound one (for packets entering the local domain segment) or an outbound one (for packets leaving the local domain segment). |
| Domain Net (Cable) | Network number or cable range that is being remapped. |
| Remapped to | Number or range of numbers to which a network number or cable range has been remapped. |
| Status | It can be one of the following values:<br><br>• Unassigned—The network number or cable range was just remapped.<br><br>• Unzipped—The remapped network number or cable range is trying to acquire a zone list. This state is possible for inbound remapped network numbers only.<br><br>• Suspect—The Cisco IOS software suspects that it already has this entry in the routing table, and it is performing loop detection for this entry. This state is possible for inbound remappings only.<br><br>• Good—The remapped entry has a complete zone list and, for inbound remappings only, it is in the main routing table.<br><br>• Bad—The remapping entry is about to be deleted from the remapping table. |

### Related Commands

Search online to find documentation for related commands.

**appletalk domain remap-range**

### SHOW APPLETALK ROUTE

To display all entries or specified entries in the AppleTalk routing table, use the **show appletalk route** EXEC command.

　　　　**show appletalk route** [*network* | *type number*]

| Syntax | Description |
|---|---|
| *network* | (Optional) Displays the routing table entry for the specified network. |
| *type number* | (Optional) Displays the routing table entries for networks that can be reached via the specified interface type and number. |

### Command Mode

EXEC

### Usage Guidelines

This command first appeared in Cisco IOS Release 10.0.

If you omit the arguments, this command displays all entries in the routing table.

### Sample Displays

The following is sample output from the **show appletalk route** command for a nonextended Apple-Talk network:

```
Router#  show appletalk route

Codes: R - RTMP derived, E - EIGRP derived, C - connected, A - AURP
P - proxy, S - static
5 routes in internet
C Net 258 directly connected, 1431 uses, Ethernet0, zone Twilight
R Net 6 [1/G] via 258.179, 8 sec, 0 uses, Ethernet0, zone The O
C Net 11 directly connected, 472 uses, Ethernet1, zone No Parking
R Net 2154 [1/G] via 258.179, 8 sec, 6892 uses, Ethernet0, zone LocalTalk
S Net 1111 via 258.144, 0 uses, Ethernet0, no zone set
[hops/state] state can be one of G:Good, S:Suspect, B:Bad
```

The following is sample output from the **show appletalk route** command for an extended AppleTalk network:

```
Router#  show appletalk route

Codes: R - RTMP derived, E - EIGRP derived, C - connected, A - AURP
P - proxy, S - static
5 routes in internet
E Net 10000 -10000 [1/G] via 300.199, 275 sec, Ethernet2, zone France
R Net 890 [2/G] via 4.129, 1 sec, Ethernet0, zone release lab
R Net 901 [2/G] via 4.129, 1 sec, Ethernet0, zone Dave's House
C Net 999-999 directly connected, Serial3, zone Magnolia Estates
R Net 2003 [4/G] via 80.129, 6 sec, Ethernet4, zone Bldg-13
```

The following is sample output from the **show appletalk route** command when AppleTalk load balancing is enabled. The output displayed shows additional equal-cost path entries.

```
Router# show appletalk route

Codes: R - RTMP derived, E - EIGRP derived, C - connected, A - AURP
        P - proxy, S - static
759 routes in internet. Up to 4 parallel paths allowed.

The first zone listed for each entry is its default (primary) zone.

R Net 20-20 [2/G] via 60.172, 1 sec, Ethernet1/2,
                  via 1010.68 1 sec, Ethernet1/3,
                  via 70.199, 2 sec, Ethernet1/5, zone zone20
```

```
R Net 32-32 [9/G] via 60172, 2 sec, Ethernet1/2
                  via 1010.68, 2 sec, Ethernet1/3,
                  via 70.199, 2 sec, Ethernet1/5,
                  Zone: "Executive Briefing Center"
R Net 43-43 [7/G] via 60.172, 2 sec, Ethernet1/2,
                  via 1010.68, 2 sec, Ethernet1/3,
                  via 70.199, 2 sec, Ethernet1/5, zone ISDN Tunnel
R Net 57-57 [6/G] via 60.172, 2 sec, Ethernet1/2,
                  via 1010.68, 2 sec, Ethernet1/3,
                  via 70.199, 2 sec, Ethernet1/5, zone zone-home-bumi
```

Table 3–29 describes the fields shown in the two displays as well as some fields not shown, which may also be displayed. Depending on the configuration of the global configuration commands **appletalk lookup-type** and **appletalk name-lookup-interval**, a node name may appear in this display instead of a node address.

**Table 3–29**  *Show AppleTalk Route Field Descriptions*

| Field | Description |
|---|---|
| Codes: | Codes defining how the route was learned. |
| R - RTMP derived | Route learned from an RTMP update. |
| E - EIGRP derived | Route learned from an Enhanced IGRP update. |
| C - Connected | Directly connected network. |
| A - AURP | Route learned from an AURP update. |
| S - Static | Statically defined route. |
| P - Proxy | Proxy route. Proxy routes are included in outgoing RTMP updates as if they were directly connected routes (although they are not really directly connected) because they are not associated with any interface. Whenever an NBQ BrRq for the zone in question is generated by anyone anywhere in the internetwork, an NBP FwdReq is directed to any router connected to the proxy route. The Phase 2 router (which is the only router directly connected) converts the FwdReq to LkUps, which are understood by Phase 1 routers, and sends them to every network in the zone. |
| routes | Number of routes in the table. |
| Net | Network to which the route goes. |
| Net 999-999 | Cable range to which the route goes. |
| directly connected | Indicates that the network is directly connected to the router. |
| uses | Fair estimate of the number of times a route gets used. It actually indicates the number of times the route has been selected for use prior to operations such as access list filtering. |

**Table 3–29** *Show AppleTalk Route Field Descriptions, Continued*

| Field | Description |
|-------|-------------|
| Ethernet | Possible interface through which updates to the remote network will be sent. |
| zone | Name of zone of which the destination network is a member. |
| [1/G] | Number of hops to this network, followed by the state of the link to that network. The state can be one of the following letters:<br><br>• G—Link is good.<br><br>• S—Link is suspect.<br><br>• B—Link is bad.<br><br>The state is determined from the routing updates that occur at 10-second intervals. A separate and nonsynchronized event occurs at 20-second intervals, checking and flushing the ratings for particular routes that have not been updated. For each 20-second period that passes with no new routing information, a rating changes from G to S and then from S to B. After 1 minute with no updates, that route is flushed. Every time the Cisco IOS software receives a useful update, the status of the route in question is reset to G. Useful updates are those advertising a route that is as good or better than the one currently in the table.<br><br>When an AppleTalk route is poisoned by another router, its metric gets changed to poisoned (that is, 31 hops). The software then ages this route normally during a holddown period, during which the route is still visible in the routing table. |
| via 258.179 | Address of a router that is the next hop to the remote network. |
| via gatekeeper | Node name of a router that is the next hop to the remote network. |
| sec | Number of seconds that have elapsed since an RMTP update about this network was last received. |

The following is sample output from the **show appletalk route** command when you specify a network number:

```
Router#  show appletalk route 69

Codes: R - RTMP derived, E - EIGRP derived, C - connected, A - AURP
P - proxy, S - static

The first zone listed for each entry is its default (primary) zone.

R Net 69-69 [2/G] via gatekeeper, 0 sec, Ethernet0, zone Empty Guf
Route installed 125:20:21, updated 0 secs ago
```

```
Next hop: gatekeeper, 2 hops away
Zone list provided by gatekeeper
Route has been updated since last RTMP was sent
Valid zones: "Empty Guf"
```

Table 3–30 describes the fields shown in the display.

**Table 3–30**   *Show AppleTalk Route Field Descriptions for a Specified Network*

| Field | Description |
|---|---|
| Codes: | Codes defining how the route was learned. |
| R - RTMP derived | Route learned from an RTMP update. |
| E - EIGRP derived | Route learned from an Enhanced IGRP update. |
| C - Connected | Directly connected network. |
| A - AURP derived | Route learned from an AURP update. |
| P - Proxy | Proxy route. |
| S - Static | Static route. |
| routes in internet | Number of routes in the Apple Talk internet. |
| Net | Cable range to which the route goes. This is the number of the network you specified on the **show appletalk route** command line. |
| [2/G] | Number of hops to this network, followed by the state of the link to that network. The state can be one of the following letters:<br><br>• G—Link is good.<br><br>• S—Link is suspect.<br><br>• B—Link is bad.<br><br>The state is determined from the routing updates that occur at 10-second intervals. A separate and nonsynchronized event occurs at 20-second intervals, checking and flushing the ratings for particular routes that have not been updated. For each 20-second period that passes with no new routing information, a rating changes from G to S and then from S to B. After 1 minute with no updates, that route is flushed. Every time the Cisco IOS software receives a useful update, the status of the route in question is reset to G. Useful updates are those advertising a route that is as good or better than the one currently in the table.<br><br>When an AppleTalk route is poisoned by another router, its metric gets changed to poisoned (that is, 31 hops). The software then ages this route normally during a holddown period, during which the route is still visible in the routing table. |

**Table 3–30** *Show AppleTalk Route Field Descriptions for a Specified Network, Continued*

| Field | Description |
|-------|-------------|
| via gatekeeper | Address or node name of a router that is the next hop to the remote network. |
| 0 sec | Number of seconds that have elapsed since an RMTP update about this network was last received. |
| Ethernet0 | Possible interface through which updates to the remote network are sent. |
| zone Empty Guf | Name of zone of which the destination network is a member. |
| Route installed 125:20:21 | Length of time (in hours, minutes, and seconds) since this route was first learned about. |
| updated 0 secs ago | Time (in seconds) since the software received an update for this route. |
| Next hop: gatekeeper | Address or node name of the router that is one hop away. |
| 2 hops away | Number of hops to the network specified in the **show appletalk route** command line. |
| Zone list provided by gatekeeper | Address or node name of the router that provided the zone list included with the RTMP update. |
| Route has been updated since last RTMP was sent | Indicates whether the software has received a routing update from a neighboring router since the last time the software sent an RTMP update for this route. |
| Valid zones: "Empty Guf" | Zone names that are valid for this network. |

### Related Commands

Search online to find documentation for related commands.

**appletalk lookup-type**
**appletalk maximum-paths**
**appletalk name-lookup-interval**
**appletalk proxy-nbp**
**clear appletalk route**

### SHOW APPLETALK SOCKETS

To display all information or specified information about process-level operation in the sockets of an AppleTalk interface, use the **show appletalk sockets** privileged EXEC command.

> **show appletalk sockets** [*socket-number*]

| Syntax | Description |
|---|---|
| *socket-number* | (Optional) Displays information about the specified socket number. |

## Command Mode

Privileged EXEC

## Usage Guidelines

This command first appeared in Cisco IOS Release 10.0.

If no socket number is specified, this command displays information about all sockets.

## Sample Display

The following is sample output from the **show appletalk sockets** command when you do not specify a socket number:

```
Router# show appletalk sockets

Socket   Name     Owner          Waiting/Processed
1        RTMP     AT RTMP        0    148766
2        NIS      AT NBP         0    15642
4        AEP      AT Maintenance 0    0
6        ZIP      AT ZIP         0    13619
8        SNMP     AT SNMP        0    0
10       SMRP     SMRP Input     0    56393
253      PingServ AT Maintenance 0    0
```

The following is sample output from the **show appletalk sockets** command when you do specify a socket number:

```
Router# show appletalk sockets 6

6        ZIP      AT ZIP         0    13619
```

Table 3–31 describes the fields shown in these displays.

**Table 3–31**   *Show AppleTalk Socket Field Descriptions*

| Field | Description |
|---|---|
| Socket | Socket number. |
| Name | Name of the socket. |
| Owner | Process that is managing communication with this socket. |
| Waiting/Processed | Number of packets waiting to be processed by the socket and number of packets that have been processed by the socket since it was established. |

## SHOW APPLETALK STATIC

To display information about the statically defined routes, including floating static routes, use the **show appletalk static** EXEC command.

**show appletalk static**

*Syntax*     *Description*

This command has no arguments or keywords.

### Command Mode

EXEC

### Usage Guidelines

This command first appeared in Cisco IOS Release 10.0.

### Sample Display

The following is sample output from the **show appletalk static** command:

```
Router# show appletalk static

      AppleTalk    Static    Entries
    ---------------------------------------
    Network    NextIR    Zone     Status

    100-109    1.10      Zone100   A
    200        1.10      Zone200   A
    300-309    1.10      Zone300   A(Floating)
```

Table 3–32 describes the fields shown in the display.

**Table 3–32** *Show AppleTalk Static Field Descriptions*

| Field | Description |
| --- | --- |
| Network | For an extended AppleTalk network, the network range. For a nonextended AppleTalk network, the network number. |
| NextIR | The next internetwork router. |
| Zone | The AppleTalk zone name. |
| Status | The status of the route, which can be one of the following:<br>• A—The static route is active.<br>• A(Floating)—The floating static route is active.<br>• N/A—The static route is not active.<br>• N/A(Floating)—The floating static route is not active. |

*Related Commands*

Search online to find documentation for related commands.

**appletalk static cable-range**
**appletalk static network**
**show appletalk neighbors**
**show appletalk route**


## SHOW APPLETALK TRAFFIC

To display statistics about AppleTalk traffic, including MacIP traffic, use the **show appletalk traffic** EXEC command.

> **show appletalk traffic**

*Syntax        Description*

This command has no arguments or keywords.


*Command Mode*

EXEC


*Usage Guidelines*

This command first appeared in Cisco IOS Release 10.0.

For MacIP traffic, an IP alias is established for each MacIP client and for the IP address of the MacIP server if it does not match an existing IP interface address. To display the client aliases, use the **show ip aliases** command.


*Sample Display*

The following is sample output from the **show appletalk traffic** command:

```
Router# show appletalk traffic

AppleTalk statistics:
  Rcvd: 357471 total, 0 checksum errors, 264 bad hop count
        321006 local destination, 0 access denied
        0 for MacIP, 0 bad MacIP, 0 no client
        13510 port disabled, 2437 no listener
        0 ignored, 0 martians
  Bcast: 191881 received, 270406 sent
  Sent: 550293 generated, 66495 forwarded, 1840 fast forwarded, 0 loopback
        0 forwarded from MacIP, 0 MacIP failures
        436 encapsulation failed, 0 no route, 0 no source
  DDP:  387265 long, 0 short, 0 macip, 0 bad size
  NBP:  302779 received, 0 invalid, 0 proxies
        57875 replies sent, 59947 forwards, 418674 lookups, 432 failures
```

```
RTMP:  108454 received, 0 requests, 0 invalid, 40189 ignored
       90170 sent, 0 replies
EIGRP: 0 received, 0 hellos, 0 updates, 0 replies, 0 queries
       0 sent,     0 hellos, 0 updates, 0 replies, 0 queries
       0 invalid, 0 ignored
AURP:  0 Open Requests, 0 Router Downs
       0 Routing Information sent, 0 Routing Information received
       0 Zone Information sent, 0 Zone Information received
       0 Get Zone Nets sent, 0 Get Zone Nets received
       0 Get Domain Zone List sent, 0 Get Domain Zone List received
AppleTalk statistics:
       0 bad sequence
ATP:   0 received
ZIP:   13619 received, 33633 sent, 32 netinfo
Echo:  0 received, 0 discarded, 0 illegal
       0 generated, 0 replies sent
Responder:  0 received, 0 illegal, 0 unknown
       0 replies sent, 0 failures
AARP:  85 requests, 149 replies, 100 probes
       84 martians, 0 bad encapsulation, 0 unknown
       278 sent, 0 failures, 29 delays, 315 drops
Lost: 0 no buffers
Unknown: 0 packets
Discarded: 130475 wrong encapsulation, 0 bad SNAP discriminator
```

Table 3–33 describes the fields shown in the display.

**Table 3–33**   *Show AppleTalk Traffic Field Descriptions*

| Field | Description |
| --- | --- |
| Rcvd: | This section describes the packets received. |
| 357741 total | Total number of packets received. |
| 0 checksum errors | Number of packets that were discarded because their DDP checksum was incorrect. The DDP checksum is verified for packets that are directed to the router. It is not verified for forwarded packets. |
| 264 bad hop count | Number of packets discarded because they had traveled too many hops. |
| 321006 local destination | Number of packets addressed to the local router. |
| 0 access denied | Number of packets discarded because they were denied by an access list. |
| 0 for MacIP | Number of AppleTalk packets the Cisco IOS software received that were encapsulated within an IP packet. |

**Table 3-33** *Show AppleTalk Traffic Field Descriptions, Continued*

| Field | Description |
|---|---|
| 0 bad MacIP | Number of bad MacIP packets the software received and discarded. These packets may have been malformed or may not have included a destination address. |
| 0 no client | Number of packets discarded because they were directed to a nonexistent MacIP client. |
| 13510 port disabled | Number of packets discarded because routing was disabled for that port (extended AppleTalk only). This is the result of a configuration error or a packet's being received while the software is in verification/discovery mode. |
| 2437 no listener | Number of packets discarded because they were directed to a socket that had no services associated with it. |
| 0 ignored | Number of routing update packets ignored because they were from a misconfigured neighbor or because routing was disabled. |
| 0 martians | Number of packets discarded because they contained bogus information in the DDP header. What distinguishes this error from the others is that the data in the header is never valid, as opposed to not being valid at a given point in time. |
| Bcast: | Number of broadcast packets sent and received. |
| 191881 received | Number of broadcast packets received. |
| 270406 sent | Number of broadcast packets sent. |
| Sent: | Number of packets transmitted. |
| 550293 generated | Number of packets generated. |
| 66495 forwarded | Number of packets forwarded using routes derived from process switching. |
| 1840 fast forwarded | Number of packets sent using routes from the fast-switching cache. |
| 0 loopback | Number of packets that were broadcast out an interface on the router for which the device simulated reception of the packet because the interface does not support sending a broadcast packet to itself. The count is cumulative for all interfaces on the device. |

**Table 3–33** *Show AppleTalk Traffic Field Descriptions, Continued*

| Field | Description |
|-------|-------------|
| 0 forwarded from MacIP | Number of IP packets forwarded that were encapsulated within an AppleTalk DDP packet. |
| 0 MacIP failures | Number of MacIP packets sent that were corrupted during the MacIP encapsulation process. |
| 436 encapsulation failed | Number of packets the router could not send because encapsulation failed. This can happen because encapsulation of the DDP packet failed or because AARP address resolution failed. |
| 0 no route | Number of packets the router could not send because it knew of no route to the destination. |
| 0 no source | Number of packets the router sent when it did not know its own address. This should happen only if something is seriously wrong with the router or network configuration. |
| DDP: | This section describes DDP packets seen. |
| 387265 long | Number of DDP long packets. |
| 0 short | Number of DDP short packets. |
| 0 macip | Number of IP packets encapsulated in an AppleTalk DDP packet that the router sent. |
| 0 bad size | Number of packets whose physical packet length and claimed length differed. |
| NBP: | This section describes NBP packets. |
| 302779 received | Total number of NBP packets received. |
| 0 invalid | Number of invalid NBP packets received. Causes include invalid op code and invalid packet type. |
| 0 proxies | Number of NBP proxy lookup requests received by the router when it was configured for NBP proxy transition usage. |
| 57875 replies sent | Number of NBP replies sent. |
| 59947 forwards | Number of NBP forward requests received or sent. |
| 418674 lookups | Number of NBP lookups received. |
| 432 failures | Generic counter that increments any time the NBP process experiences a problem. |

*Command Reference*

**Table 3–33**   *Show AppleTalk Traffic Field Descriptions, Continued*

| Field | Description |
|---|---|
| RTMP: | This section describes RTMP packets. |
| 108454 received | Total number of RTMP packets received. |
| 0 requests | Number of RTMP requests received. |
| 0 invalid | Number of invalid RTMP packets received. Causes include invalid op code and invalid packet type. |
| 40189 ignored | Number of RTMP packets ignored. One reason for this is that the interface is still in discovery mode and is not yet initialized. |
| 90170 sent | Number of RTMP packets sent. |
| 0 replies | Number of RTMP replies sent. |
| EIGRP: | This section describes Enhanced IGRP packets. |
| 0 received | Number of EIGRP packets received. |
| 0 hellos | Number of EIGRP hello packets received. |
| 0 updates | Number of EIGRP update packets received. |
| 0 replies | Number of EIGRP reply packets received. |
| 0 queries | Number of EIGRP query packets received. |
| 0 sent | Number of EIGRP packets sent. |
| 0 hellos | Number of EIGRP hello packets sent. |
| 0 updates | Number of EIGRP update packets sent. |
| 0 replies | Number of EIGRP reply packets sent. |
| 0 queries | Number of EIGRP query packets sent. |
| 0 invalid | Number of invalid EIGRP packets sent. |
| 0 ignored | Number of packets ignored as a result of invalid EIGRP packets received. |
| ATP: | This section describes ATP packets. |
| 0 received | Number of ATP packets the router received. |
| ZIP: | This section describes ZIP packets. |
| 13619 received | Number of ZIP packets the router received. |
| 33633 sent | Number of ZIP packets the router sent. |

**Table 3–33** *Show AppleTalk Traffic Field Descriptions, Continued*

| Field | Description |
|---|---|
| 32 netinfo | Number of packets that requested port configuration via ZIP GetNetInfo requests. These are commonly used during node startup and are occasionally used by some AppleTalk network management software packages. |
| Echo: | This section describes AEP packets. |
| 0 received | Number of AEP packets the router received. |
| 0 discarded | Number of AEP packets the router discarded. |
| 0 illegal | Number of illegal AEP packets the router received. |
| 0 generated | Number of AEP packets the router generated. |
| 0 replies sent | Number of AEP replies the router sent. |
| Responder: | This section describes Responder Request packets. |
| 0 received | Number of Responder Request packets the router received. |
| 0 illegal | Number of illegal Responder Request packets the router received. |
| 0 unknown | Number of Responder Request packets the router received that it did not recognize. |
| 0 replies sent | Number of Responder Request replies the router sent. |
| 0 failures | Number of Responder Request replies the router could not send. |
| AARP: | This section describes AARP packets. |
| 85 requests | Number of AARP requests the router received. |
| 149 replies | Number of AARP replies the router received. |
| 100 probes | Number of AARP probe packets the router received. |
| 84 martians | Number of AARP packets the router did not recognize. If you start seeing an inordinate number of martians on an interface, check whether a bridge has been inserted into the network. When a bridge is starting up, it floods the network with AARP packets. |
| 0 bad encapsulation | Number of AARP packets received that had an unrecognizable encapsulation. |

*Command Reference*

**Table 3–33**   *Show AppleTalk Traffic Field Descriptions, Continued*

| Field | Description |
|---|---|
| 0 unknown | Number of AARP packets the router did not recognize. |
| 278 sent | Number of AARP packets the router sent. |
| 0 failures | Number of AARP packets the router could not send. |
| 29 delays | Number of AppleTalk packets delayed while waiting for the results of an AARP request. |
| 315 drops | Number of AppleTalk packets dropped because an AARP request failed. |
| Lost: 0 no buffers | Number of packets lost because of lack of buffer space. |
| Unknown: 0 packets | Number of packets whose protocol could not be determined. |
| Discarded: | This section describes the number of packets that were discarded. |
| 130475 wrong encapsulation | Number of packets discarded because they had the wrong encapsulation. That is, nonextended AppleTalk packets were on an extended AppleTalk network or vice versa. |
| 0 bad SNAP discrimination | Number of packets discarded because they had the wrong SNAP discriminator. This occurs when another AppleTalk device has implemented an obsolete or incorrect packet format. |
| AURP: | This section describes AppleTalk Update Routing Protocol packets. |
| 0 open requests | Total number of open requests. |
| 0 router downs | Number of router down packets received. |
| 0 routing information sent | Number of routing information packets sent. |
| 0 routing information received | Number of routing information packets received. |
| 0 zone information sent | Number of ZIP packets sent. |
| 0 zone information received | Number of ZIP packets received. |
| 0 get zone nets sent | Number of get zone network packets sent requesting zone information. |
| 0 get zone nets received | Number of get zone network packets received requesting zone information. |

**Table 3–33**  *Show AppleTalk Traffic Field Descriptions, Continued*

| Field | Description |
|---|---|
| 0 get domain zone list sent | Number of get domain zone list packets sent requesting domain zone list information. |
| 0 get domain zone list received | Number of get domain zone list packets received requesting domain zone list information. |
| 0 bad sequence | Number of AURP packets received out of sequence. |

## Related Commands

Search online to find documentation for related commands.

**clear appletalk traffic**
**show appletalk macip-traffic**
**show ip aliases**

## SHOW APPLETALK ZONE

To display all entries or specified entries in the zone information table, use the **show appletalk zone** EXEC command.

> **show appletalk zone** [*zone-name*]

| Syntax | Description |
|---|---|
| *zone-name* | (Optional) Displays the entry for the specified zone. |

## Command Mode

EXEC

## Usage Guidelines

This command first appeared in Cisco IOS Release 10.0.

If no zone name is specified, the command displays all entries in the zone information table.

You can use this command on extended and nonextended networks.

A zone name can be associated with multiple network addresses or cable ranges or both. There is not a one-to-one correspondence between a zone name and a LAN; a zone name may correspond to one or more networks (LANs or network interfaces). This means that a zone name will effectively replace multiple network addresses in zone filtering. This is reflected in the output of the **show appletalk zone** command. For example, the zone named *Mt. View 1* in the following sample display is associated with two network numbers and four cable ranges.

## Sample Display

The following is sample output from the **show appletalk zone** command:

```
Router# show appletalk zone

Name                    Network(s)
Gates of Hell           666-666
Engineering             3 29-29 4042-4042
customer eng            19-19
CISCO IP                4140-4140
Dave's House            3876 3924 5007
Narrow Beam             4013-4013 4023-4023 4037-4037 4038-4038
Low End SW Lab          6160 4172-4172 9555-9555 4160-4160
Tir'n na'Og             199-199
Mt. View 1              7010-7010 7122 7142 7020-7020 7040-7040 7060-7060
Mt. View 2              7152 7050-7050
UDP                     1112-12
Empty Guf               69-69
Light                   80
europe                  2010 3010 3034 5004
Bldg-13                 4032 5026 61669 3012 3025 3032 5025 5027
Bldg-17                 3004 3024 5002 5006
```

Table 3–34 describes the fields shown in the display.

The following is sample output from the **show appletalk zone** command when you specify a zone name:

```
Router# show appletalk zone CISCO IP

AppleTalk Zone Information for CISCO IP:
   Valid for nets: 4140-4140
   Not associated with any interface.
   Not associated with any access list.
```

**Table 3–34**   *Show AppleTalk Zone Field Descriptions for a Specific Zone Name*

| Field | Description |
| --- | --- |
| AppleTalk Zone Information for CISCO IP: | Name of the zone. |
| Valid for nets: 4140-4140 | Cable range(s) or network numbers assigned to this zone. |
| Not associated with any interface. | Interfaces that have been assigned to this zone. |
| Not associated with any access list. | Access lists that have been defined for this zone. |

## Related Commands

Search online to find documentation for related commands.

**appletalk zone**

## SHOW SMRP FORWARD

To display all entries or specific entries in the SMRP forwarding table, use the **show smrp forward** EXEC command.

> **show smrp forward** [**appletalk** [*group-address*]]

| Syntax | Description |
|---|---|
| **appletalk** | (Optional) Displays SMRP forwarding table entries for all AppleTalk networks. Currently SMRP services are supported over AppleTalk only. |
| *group-address* | (Optional) SMRP group address. All members of a group listen for multicast packets on this address. |

### Command Mode

EXEC

### Usage Guidelines

This command first appeared in Cisco IOS Release 11.0.

The SMRP forwarding table describes the relationship between the SMRP router and the distribution tree for each SMRP group on the internetwork. An SMRP router has an entry in this table for every SMRP group for which the router is forwarding data. When data for an SMRP group arrives on the parent interface, it is forwarded to each child interface.

Looking at child and parent interfaces in relation to members of an SMRP group, a child interface is a neighbor that is farther away from the SMRP creator node and a parent interface is one that is closer to the creator node.

If no SMRP group address is specified, then the **show smrp forward** command displays information for all entries in the SMRP forwarding table. For all entries, the **show smrp forward** command displays the SMRP group address, the state of the SMRP group, the parent interface and address, and one or more child interfaces and addresses.

If an SMRP group address is specified, the command displays additional information for that group showing the child count, the time elapsed since the entry was updated, and the next poll time.

— **NOTES** ————————————————————————————————

Because SMRP is currently supported over AppleTalk networks only, sample output resulting from the **show smrp forward** command is the same as output from the **show smrp forward appletalk** command.

*Sample Displays*

The following is sample output from the **show smrp forward** command showing all entries:

```
Router# show smrp forward

SMRP Forwarding Table

Group        State       Parent                  Child
Address                  Interface   Address   Interface    Address
- - - - - - - - - - - - - - - - - - - - - - - - - - - - - - - - - - - - -

AT 1.2       Fwd         Ethernet2   20.3      Ethernet3    30.2
AT 10.1      Fwd         Ethernet2   20.4      Ethernet4    40.2
AT 30.1      Fwd         Ethernet3   30.1      Ethernet2    20.2
```

The following is sample output from the **show smrp forward** command with the **appletalk** keyword and an SMRP group address specified:

```
Router# show smrp forward appletalk 10.1

Group        State       Parent                  Child
Address                  Interface   Address   Interface    Address
- - - - - - - - - - - - - - - - - - - - - - - - - - - - - - - - - - - - -

AT 10.1      Fwd         Ethernet2   20.4      Ethernet4    40.2

Child count: 1
Elapsed update time: 01:15:32
Next poll time (sec): 3
```

Table 3–35 describes the fields shown in the displays.

**Table 3–35**  *Show SMRP Forwarding Field Descriptions*

| Field | Description |
|-------|-------------|
| Group Address | Address of the SMRP group. |
| State | State of the group. Possible states are as follows:<br>• Join—Joining the group.<br>• Fwd—Forwarding data.<br>• Leave—Leaving the group. |
| Parent Interface | Interface that receives data to be forwarded. |
| Parent Address | Address of the parent interface. |
| Child Interface | One or more interfaces to which data is forwarded. |
| Child Address | Address of the interface. |
| Child Count | For a specific SMRP group address, the number of children for the group. |

**Table 3–35** *Show SMRP Forwarding Field Descriptions, Continued*

| Field | Description |
|-------|-------------|
| Elapsed update time | Time elapsed since the last change was made to the forwarding entry. |
| Next poll time | Time remaining before polling all child members. |

## SHOW SMRP GLOBALS

To display global information about SMRP—such as whether SMRP is enabled and running and settings for timers, most of which are used internally—use the **show smrp globals** EXEC command.

**show smrp globals**

*Syntax      Description*

This command has no arguments or keywords.

*Command Mode*

EXEC

*Usage Guidelines*

This command first appeared in Cisco IOS Release 11.0.

*Sample Display*

The following is sample output from the **show smrp globals** command:

```
Router# show smrp globals

SMRP global information:
  SMRP is running.
  Maximum number of retries for requests is 4 times.
  Request transactions are sent every 10 seconds.
  Response transactions are sent every 100 seconds.
  Creators are polled every 60 seconds.
  Members are polled every 30 seconds.
  Hellos are sent every 10 seconds.
  Neighbors are down after not being heard from for 30 seconds.
  Poisoned routes purged after 60 seconds.
  Primary requests sent every 1 second.
  Secondary requests sent every 1 second.
```

Table 3–36 describes the global information shown in the display.

**Table 3–36**  *Show SMRP Globals Fields Descriptions*

| Field | Description |
|---|---|
| SMRP is running. | SMRP is enabled. |
| Maximum number of retries for requests is 4. | This value is used internally. |
| Request transactions are sent every 10 seconds. | This timer is used internally. |
| Response transactions are sent every 100 seconds. | This timer is used internally. This is a variable value that is determined by the following formula: 2 * request-interval * (maximum-retries +1) |
| Creators are polled every 60 seconds. | Identifies how often the Cisco IOS software polls the SMRP group creator. This timer is used internally. |
| Members are polled every 30 seconds. | Identifies how often the software polls the SMRP group members. This timer is used internally. |
| Hellos are sent every 10 seconds. | Identifies how often the software sends hello packets to its neighbors. |
| Neighbors are down after not being heard from for 30 seconds. | Identifies the time in seconds that elapses after which neighbors that are not heard from are assumed to be down. |
| Poisoned routes are purged after 60 seconds. | Poisoned routes are bad routes having a distance of 255 hops. |
| Primary requests sent every 1 second. | Primary requests are requests from a secondary router requesting to become the primary router. Only a secondary router can become a primary router. |
| Secondary requests sent every 1 second. | Secondary requests are requests from a router in normal operation mode requesting to become a secondary router. Only a router in normal mode can become a secondary router. |

## SHOW SMRP GROUP

To display all entries or specific entries in the SMRP group table, use the **show smrp group** EXEC command.

   **show smrp group** [**appletalk** [*group-address*]]

| Syntax | Description |
|--------|------------|
| **appletalk** | (Optional) Displays SMRP group table entries for all AppleTalk networks. Currently, SMRP services are supported over AppleTalk networks only. |
| *group-address* | (Optional) SMRP group address. |

## Command Mode

EXEC

## Usage Guidelines

This command first appeared in Cisco IOS Release 11.0.

If no SMRP group address is specified, the command displays the group address, the state, and the parent and child information for all entries in the SMRP group table. If a group address is specified, the command displays the standard information, plus additional information for that group showing the child count, the elapsed update time, and the next poll time.

---

**NOTES**

---

Because SMRP is currently supported over AppleTalk networks only, sample output resulting from the **show smrp group** command is the same as output from the **show smrp group appletalk** command.

---

An SMRP group address is an address that is based on the local network address of the network to which the creator of the SMRP group belongs.

## Sample Displays

The following is sample output from the **show smrp group** command showing all group table entries:

```
Router# show smrp group

SMRP Group Table
Group        Creation  Next         Creator
Address      Time      Poll  Interface     Address
-----------------------------------------------------------

AT 30.1      0:04:37   22    Ethernet3     30.1
AT 40.2      0:04:35   24    Ethernet4     40.1
AT 40.1      0:04:36   23    Ethernet4     40.1
```

The following is sample output from the **show smrp group** command with the **appletalk** keyword and an SMRP group address specified:

```
Router# show smrp group appletalk 40.2

SMRP Group Table
Group       Creation  Next            Creator
Address     Time      Poll  Interface Address
- - - - - - - - - - - - - - - - - - - - - - - - - - - - - - - - - - - - - - - -

AT 40.2     0:05:58   1     Ethernet4   40.1
```

Table 3–37 describes the fields shown in the display.

**Table 3–37**  *Show SMRP Group Field Descriptions*

| Field | Description |
|-------|-------------|
| Group Address | SMRP group address. AT signifies that this is an AppleTalk network group. |
| Creation Time | Elapsed time since the group was created in hours, minutes, and seconds *(hh:mm:ss)*. |
| Next Poll | Time remaining until the next check is performed to determine whether the creator is still active. |
| Creator Interface | Interface that the creator of the SMRP group is on. |
| Creator Address | Address of the creator. |

## SHOW SMRP MCACHE

To display the SMRP fast-switching cache table, use the **show smrp mcache** EXEC command.

> **show smrp mcache** [**appletalk** [*group-address*]]

| *Syntax* | *Description* |
|----------|---------------|
| **appletalk** | (Optional) Displays the SMRP fast-switching cache table entries for all AppleTalk network groups. Currently, SMRP services are supported over AppleTalk only. |
| *group-address* | (Optional) SMRP group address. Use this argument to display only this group's fast-switching cache table entry. |

## *Command Mode*

EXEC

## *Usage Guidelines*

This command first appeared in Cisco IOS Release 11.1.

An SMRP router has an entry in its forwarding table for every SMRP group for which the router forwards data. For each group, the forwarding table lists the parent interface and address and one or more child interfaces and addresses. When data for an SMRP group arrives on the parent interface, the router forwards it to each child interface. The SMRP fast-switching cache table specifies whether or not to fast switch SMRP data packets out the interfaces specified by the forwarding table.

Use **show smrp mcache** command to view the SMRP fast-switching cache table. The command displays which interfaces are fast-switch enabled. If a parent interface is not fast-switch enabled, then there is no entry (row) in the table. If a child interface is not fast-switch enabled, then it is not in the list of child interfaces for an entry in the table.

If you do not specify an SMRP group address, then the **show smrp mcache** command displays information for all entries in the SMRP fast-switching cache table. If you specify an SMRP group address, the command displays cache entries for only that group.

SMRP fast-switching is enabled by default.

### Sample Display

The following is sample output from the **show smrp mcache** command:

```
Router# show smrp mcache

SMRP Multicast Fast Switching Cache
Group       In  Parent       Child         MAC Header (Top)
Address     Use Interface    Interface(s)  Network Header (Bottom)
------------------------------------------------------------------

AT 11.121   Y   Ethernet0    Ethernet3     090007400b7900000c1740db
                                           001fed750000002aff020a0a0a
AT 11.122   Y   Ethernet0    Ethernet3     090007400b7a00000c1740db
                                           001f47750000002aff020a0a0a
AT 11.123   Y   Ethernet0    Ethernet1     090007400b7b00000c1740d9
                                           001fe77500000014ff020a0a0a
                             Ethernet3     090007400b7b00000c1740db
                                           001ffd750000002aff020a0a0a
AT 11.124   N   Ethernet0    Ethernet1     090007400b7c00000c1740d9
                                           001fef7500000014ff020a0a0a
```

Table 3–38 describes the fields shown in the display.

**Table 3–38**  *Show SMRP Mcache Field Descriptions*

| Field | Description |
|---|---|
| Group Address | SMRP group address. AT signifies that this is an AppleTalk network group. |
| In Use | Y= Router can use the cache entry to fast-switch packets.<br><br>N= Router cannot use the cache entry to fast-switch packets. Router forwards packets via the process level. |
| Parent Interface | Interface that receives the SMRP data packet to send out. The interface must be fast-switch enabled. |
| Child Interface(s) | One or more interfaces to which the SMRP data packet is sent. At least one of the child interfaces must be fast-switch enabled. |
| MAC Header (Top) Network Header (Bottom) | MAC header and network header for only fast-switch enabled child interfaces. |

*Related Commands*

Search online to find documentation for related commands.

**clear smrp mcache**
**show smrp forward**

## SHOW SMRP NEIGHBOR

To display all entries or specific entries in the SMRP neighbor table, use the **show smrp neighbor** EXEC command.

> **show smrp neighbor** [**appletalk** [*network-address*]]

| *Syntax* | *Description* |
|---|---|
| **appletalk** | (Optional) Displays SMRP neighbor table entries for all AppleTalk networks. Currently SMRP services are supported over AppleTalk networks only. |
| *network-address* | (Optional) Network address of the neighbor router. |

*Command Mode*

EXEC

*Usage Guidelines*

This command first appeared in Cisco IOS Release 11.0.

A neighbor is an adjacent router. Neighboring routers keep track of one another by sending and receiving hello packets periodically. Using this method, the Cisco IOS software can determine if it has heard from a neighbor router within a certain amount of time. The software creates an entry in its neighbor table when it finds a neighboring route. The software maintains the entry, indicating, among other information, the current state of the neighbor. The software updates the entry if the state of the neighbor router changes; for example, a secondary router becomes a primary router. The secondary router is the router that becomes the primary router when the primary router is no longer heard from.

For all neighboring routers, the **show smrp neighbor** command displays the address of the neighbor router, the state of the neighbor, its interface, the last time it was heard from, its route version number, and whether or not routes need to be sent to the neighbor. If the network address of a specific neighbor is given as a command parameter, this information is displayed for that neighbor router only.

— **NOTES** ————————————————————————————————

Because SMRP is currently supported over AppleTalk networks only, sample output resulting from the **show smrp neighbor** command is the same as output from the **show smrp neighbor appletalk** command.

### Sample Displays

The following is sample output from the **show smrp neighbor** command displaying SMRP neighbor table entries for all neighbors:

```
Router# show smrp neighbor

SMRP Neighbor Table
                              Last
Neighbor  State Interface    Heard
- - - - - - - - - - - - - - - - - - - - - - - - -

20.3      (S)   Ethernet2    5
10.4      (N)   Ethernet1    3
11.5      (S)   Ethernet1    7
```

The following is sample output from the **show smrp neighbor** command with the **appletalk** keyword and the network address of a specific neighboring node:

```
Router# show smrp neighbor appletalk 20.3

SMRP Neighbor Table
                              Last
Neighbor  State Interface    Heard
- - - - - - - - - - - - - - - - - - - - - - - - -

20.3      (S)   Ethernet2    5

Route version: 0x0000000E
Routes needed: False
```

Table 3–39 describes the fields shown in the display.

**Table 3–39**   *Show SMRP Neighbor Field Descriptions*

| Field | Description |
|-------|-------------|
| Neighbor | Network address of the neighbor router. |
| State | State of the neighbor. Possible states are as follows:<br>• (P)   —Primary operation<br>• (S)   —Secondary operation<br>• (N)   —Normal operation<br>• PN..   —Primary negotiation<br>• SN..   —Secondary negotiation<br>• -D-   —Down |
| Interface | Interface to the neighbor router. |
| Last Heard | Last time in seconds that the neighbor was heard from. |
| Route Version | Route version number of the neighbor. If the route version number is less than the neighbor's route version, then the route is sent to that neighbor. |
| Route Needed | True if routes need to be sent to the neighbor; False if not. |

## SHOW SMRP PORT

To display all entries or specific entries in the SMRP port table, use the **show smrp port** EXEC command.

   **show smrp port** [**appletalk** [*type number*]]

| Syntax | Description |
|--------|-------------|
| **appletalk** | (Optional) Displays SMRP port table entries for all AppleTalk networks. Currently, SMRP services are supported over AppleTalk networks only. |
| *type* | (Optional) Interface type. |
| *number* | (Optional) Interface number. |

## Command Mode

EXEC

## Usage Guidelines

This command first appeared in Cisco IOS Release 11.0.

For all SMRP ports, the **show smrp port** command displays the interface of the SMRP port, the current state of the port, the network protocol type (currently, only AppleTalk is supported) and its address, the address of the primary router on the local network, the address of the secondary router on the local network, the current groups on the port, and the last group on the port.

If the interface of a specific SMRP port is given, this information is displayed for that port only.

---

**NOTES**

---

Because SMRP is currently supported over AppleTalk networks only, sample output resulting from the **show smrp port** command is the same as output from the **show smrp port appletalk** command.

---

## Sample Displays

The following is sample output from the **show smrp port** command:

```
Router# show smrp port

SMRP Port Table
Interface      State Network       Type Address   Primary   Secondary
- - - - - - - - - - - - - - - - - - - - - - - - - - - - - - - - - - - - - - - - -

Ethernet2      (P)   20-22         AT   20.2      20.2      20.3
Ethernet3      (P)   30-33         AT   30.2      30.2      0.0
Ethernet4      (S)   40-44         AT   40.3      40.2      40.0
```

The following is sample output from the **show smrp port** command with the **appletalk** keyword and the interface of a specific port:

```
Router# show smrp port appletalk ethernet 2
SMRP Port Table
Interface      State Network       Type Address   Primary   Secondary
- - - - - - - - - - - - - - - - - - - - - - - - - - - - - - - - - - - - - - - - -

Ethernet2      (P)   20-22         AT   20.2      20.2      20.3
Current groups:
Last group:
```

Table 3–40 describes the fields shown in the displays.

**Table 3–40**  *Show SMRP Port Field Descriptions*

| Field | Description |
|---|---|
| Interface | Interface of a specific SMRP port. |
| State | Current state of the port. Possible states are as follows: <br> • (P) — Primary operation <br> • (S) — Secondary operation <br> • (N) — Normal operation <br> • PN.. —Primary negotiation <br> • SN.. —Secondary negotiation <br> • -D- —Down |
| Network | Network range. |
| Type | Network protocol type. Currently only AppleTalk (AT) is supported. |
| Address | Network layer address. |
| Primary | Address of the primary SMRP router on the local network. |
| Secondary | Address of the secondary SMRP router on the local network. |

*Related Commands*

Search online to find documentation for related commands.

**smrp protocol appletalk**

## SHOW SMRP ROUTE

To display all entries or specific entries in the SMRP routing table, use the **show smrp route** EXEC command.

> **show smrp route** [**appletalk** [*network*] | *type number*]

| Syntax | Description |
|---|---|
| **appletalk** | (Optional) Displays SMRP route table entries for all AppleTalk networks. Currently, SMRP services are supported over AppleTalk networks only. |
| *network* | (Optional) SMRP network range. |
| *type* | (Optional) Interface type. |
| *number* | (Optional) Interface number. |

## Command Mode

EXEC

## Usage Guidelines

This command first appeared in Cisco IOS Release 11.0.

For all SMRP routes, the **show smrp route** command displays the number of SMRP routes in the internetwork. For each route, it shows the SMRP network range of the route, the version of the route, the elapsed time since the route was updated, the number of hops away the route is from the route's origin, the number of hops away the route is from the tunnel origin, the interface from which the route was received, and the router that sent the route.

If a specific network range is given, this information is displayed for that network range only.

If the interface is specified, the routes that came from this interface are displayed.

If the **appletalk** keyword is specified with or without an SMRP network range, the number of SMRP routes in the internetwork is not specified. Connected routes have a hop value of 0 and no address value.

---

**NOTES**

Because SMRP is currently supported over AppleTalk networks only, sample output resulting from the **show smrp port** command is the same as output from the **show smrp port appletalk** command.

---

## Sample Displays

The following is sample output from the **show smrp route** command:

```
Router# show smrp route

SMRP Route Table

5 routes in internet

Network        Hop Tunnel        Parent
                           Interface    Address
- - - - - - - - - - - - - - - - - - - - - - - - - - - - - - - - - - - - -

AT  1-1          1      0      Ethernet2    20.3
AT  10-11        1      0      Ethernet2    20.3
AT  20-22        0      0      Ethernet2
AT  40-44        0      0      Ethernet4
```

The following is sample output from the **show smrp route** command with the **appletalk** keyword and a specific SMRP network number within an SMRP network range:

```
Router# show smrp route appletalk 21

Network       Hop   Tunnel      Parent
                                Interface    Address
- - - - - - - - - - - - - - - - - - - - - - - - - - - - - - - - - - - - - - - -


AT 20-22       0    0          Ethernet2    20.3

Route version: 0x0000000E
Elapsed update time: 00:23:55
```

The following is sample output from the **show smrp route** command for a specific interface:

```
Router# show smrp route appletalk ethernet 2

Network       Hop Tunnel       Parent
                                Interface    Address
- - - - - - - - - - - - - - - - - - - - - - - - - - - - - - - - - - - - - - -


AT 1-1         1    0          Ethernet2    20.3
AT 10-11       1    0          Ethernet2    20.3
AT 20-22       0    0          Ethernet2
```

Table 3–41 describes the fields shown in the displays.

**Table 3–41**   *Show SMRP Route Field Descriptions*

| Field | Description |
|---|---|
| Network | SMRP network range (the route). "AT" indicates that this is an AppleTalk network. |
| Hop | Number of hops away from origin. |
| Tunnel | Number of hops away from the origin of this tunnel. |
| Parent Interface | Interface from which the route was received. |
| Parent Address | Address of the router that sent this route. |
| Route version | Version number of a route. If the route version is greater than the neighbor's route version, then the route is sent to that neighbor. |
| Elapsed update time | Time elapsed since the route was last updated. |

## SHOW SMRP TRAFFIC

To display all entries or specific entries in the SMRP traffic table, use the **show smrp traffic** EXEC command.

**show smrp traffic** [**all** | **group** | **neighbor** | **port** | **route** | **transaction**]

| Syntax | Description |
|--------|-------------|
| all | (Optional) Displays SMRP traffic for SMRP groups, neighbors, ports, routes, and transactions. |
| group | (Optional) Displays SMRP traffic for SMRP groups. |
| neighbor | (Optional) Displays SMRP traffic for neighbors. |
| port | (Optional) Displays SMRP traffic for ports. |
| route | (Optional) Displays SMRP traffic for routes. |
| transaction | (Optional) Displays SMRP traffic for transactions. |

### Command Mode

EXEC

### Usage Guidelines

This command first appeared in Cisco IOS Release 11.0.

To display general SMRP statistics, use the **show smrp traffic** command without keywords. To display traffic for all of the categories defined by the keywords, use the **show smrp traffic all** command. To display traffic for a specific category, specify the command and the keyword for the category.

### Sample Displays

The following is sample output from the **show smrp traffic all** command:

```
Router# show smrp traffic all

SMRP statistics:
 Rcvd:  350 total, 99 hellos, 0 mc data, 0 fast handled
        78 requests, 127 confirms, 1 reject
        3 primaries, 6 secondaries
        7 notifies, 2 distance vectors
        3 create groups, 0 delete groups
        4 join groups, 0 leave groups
        54 members
        0 add group entries, 0 remove group entries
        0 locates, 0 tunnels
 Sent:  547 total, 307 hellos
        0 duplicate mc data, 0 mc data, 0 fast forwarded
        176 requests, 62 confirms, 2 rejects
        3 primaries, 3 secondaries
        6 notifies, 1 distance vector
        0 joins, 0 leaves
        42 creators, 81 members
        0 add group entries, 0 remove group entries
```

```
Misc:   0 no buffers, 0 no forwards
        0 bad portids, 0 port downs
        0 bad versions, 0 runts
        0 bad packet types, 0 input errors

SMRP group statistics:
        Groups:  3 added, 0 removed,
        Forwards:  3 new, 1 recycled, 0 deleted
        Child Ports:  4 added, 1 freed,
        Misc: 0 range fulls, 0 not primary drops
              0 no routes

SMRP port statistics:
    Ports:  3 new, 0 recycled, 0 deleted

SMRP route statistics:
    Routes:  5 new, 0 recycled, 0 deleted
    Neighbor AT 20.3:
            1 received updates, 1 send updates
            3 received routes, 0 sent routes
            0 poisoned, 0 improved
            0 better parent interfaces, 0 worst parent interfaces
            0 better parent addresses, 0 worst parent addresses
            0 bad ranges, 0 overlaps

SMRP transaction statistics:
    Requests:  5 new, 135 recycled
            0 deleted, 0 freed
            9 timeouts, 36 resends
            0 duplicates, 0 incomplete duplicates
    Responses:  16 new, 62 recycled, 0 freed
            0 deleted, 0 freed
            0 unexpected, 0 bad
```

Table 3–42 describes the fields shown in the display.

**Table 3–42**   *Show SMRP Traffic Field Descriptions*

| Field | Description |
|---|---|
| **SMRP Statistics:** | |
| Rcvd: | |
| total | Total number of SMRP packets received. |
| hellos | Number of hello packets received from neighbors. |
| mc data | Number of packets of multicast data received. |
| fast handled | Number of input packets handled by the SMRP fast-switching function. |

**Table 3–42** *Show SMRP Traffic Field Descriptions, Continued*

| Field | Description |
|---|---|
| requests | Number of request transactions received from neighbors. |
| confirms | Number of confirm response transactions received. |
| reject | Number of reject response transactions received. |
| primaries | Number of primary request packets received. |
| secondaries | Number of secondary request packets received. |
| notifies | Number of notify packets received. A router sends a notify packet when it becomes an SMRP primary, secondary, or normal router. A router in normal operation mode can become a secondary router, and a router in secondary operation mode can become a primary router. |
| distance vectors | Number of route update packets received. |
| create groups | Number of create group packets received from the creator endpoint when it requests to create a group. |
| delete groups | Number of delete group packets received. These packets are sent when a group is deleted. |
| join groups | Number of join-group packets received. These packets are sent when members join a group. |
| leave groups | Number of leave-group packets received. These packets are sent when members leave a group. |
| members | Number of member-request packets for polling group members received. |
| add group entries | Number of packets received to add group entries. |
| remove group entries | Number of packets received to remove group entries. |
| locates | Number of locate packets received. Endpoints send locate packets to find the SMRP router on the local network. |
| tunnels | Number of SMRP tunnel packets received. |
| **Sent:** | |
| total | Total number of SMRP packets sent. |
| hellos | Number of hello packets sent to neighbors. |
| duplicate mc data | Number of packets of multicast data duplicated and forwarded. |

**Table 3–42**   *Show SMRP Traffic Field Descriptions, Continued*

| Field | Description |
|-------|-------------|
| mc data | Number of packets of multicast data forwarded. |
| fast forwarded | Number of packets that were fast-switched out of the fast-switch enabled interface. |
| requests | Number of request transaction packets sent to neighbors. |
| confirms | Number of confirm responses sent. |
| rejects | Number of reject responses sent. |
| primaries | Number of primary request packets sent. |
| secondaries | Number of secondary request packets sent. These are sent in attempt to become the secondary router. |
| notifies | The number of notify packets sent. A router sends a notify packet when it becomes an SMRP primary, secondary, or normal router. A router in normal operation mode can become a secondary router, and a router in secondary operation mode can become a primary router. |
| distance vectors | Number of route-update packets sent. |
| joins | Number of join-group packets sent. These packets are sent when members join a group. |
| leaves | Number of leave-group packets sent. These packets are sent when members leave a group. |
| creators | Number of creator-request packets sent to poll the creator endpoint to verify that it is still active. |
| members | Number of member request packets sent for polling group members. |
| add group entries | Number of packets sent to the secondary router to add group entries. |
| remove group entries | Number of packets sent to the secondary router to remove group entries. |
| **Misc:** | |
| no buffers | Number of times no system buffers available condition occurred. Memory allocation failure. |

**Table 3–42**  *Show SMRP Traffic Field Descriptions, Continued*

| Field | Description |
|---|---|
| no forwards | Number of packets for which there was no entry in the forwarding table for the packet's destination. |
| bad portids | Number of packets with invalid port IDs. |
| port downs | Number of packets for ports that were down. |
| bad versions | Number of packets with the wrong SMRP protocol version number. |
| runts | Number of truncated packet. |
| bad packet types | Number of packets with invalid type field values. |
| input errors | Number of packets received that failed network layer packet validation. |
| **SMRP group statistics:** | |
| Groups: | |
| added | Number of groups added. |
| removed | Number of groups removed. |
| Forwards: | |
| new | Number of new entries created in the forwarding table. |
| recycled | Number of forwarding table entries that were recycled. |
| deleted | Number of forwarding table entries that were deleted. |
| Child Ports: | |
| added | Number of child ports added to the forwarding table entries. |
| freed | Number of child ports removed from the forwarding table entries. |
| **Misc:** | |
| range fulls | Number of times attempts were made to create SMRP groups after the range of available SMRP addresses was exhausted. The number of SMRP group addresses available equals the SMRP network range times 254. |
| not primary drops | Number of packets received and dropped because this router is not the SMRP primary router and, therefore, not responsible for the packets. |

**Table 3–42**   *Show SMRP Traffic Field Descriptions, Continued*

| Field | Description |
|---|---|
| no routes | Number of times a route to the creator endpoint was not found in the routing table. |
| **SMRP port statistics:** | |
| Ports: | SMRP port traffic information |
| new | Number of new port entries added to the SMRP port table. |
| recycled | Number of recycled port entries added to the SMRP port table. |
| deleted | Number of port entries deleted from the SMRP port table. |
| **SMRP route statistics:** | |
| Routes: | Neighbor route statistics. |
| new | Number of new entries added to the SMRP routing table. |
| recycled | Number of recycled entries added to the SMRP routing table. |
| deleted | Number of entries deleted from the SMRP routing table. |
| Neighbor AT | AppleTalk neighbor information. |
| received updates | For each SMRP neighbor, the number of distance vector (routing update) packets received. |
| sent updates | For each SMRP neighbor, the number of distance vector (routing update) packets sent. |
| received routes | For each SMRP neighbor, the number of routes received. |
| sent routes | For each SMRP neighbor, the number of routes sent. |
| poisoned | Number of bad routes (with 255 hops) received in distance vector packets. |
| improved | Number of routes improved through updates received in distance vector packets. |
| better parent interfaces | Number of times the Cisco IOS software switches to a better parent interface when a tie condition exists. A tie exists when both routes have equal hop counts. A ties is broken by choosing the neighbor with the higher network address. |

**Table 3–42** *Show SMRP Traffic Field Descriptions, Continued*

| Field | Description |
|---|---|
| worst parent interfaces | Number of times the software does not switch interfaces in a tie condition. The software assesses a tie between two interfaces to choose the interface for the route when the hop count of both routes is equal. A tie is broken by choosing the neighbor with the higher network address. |
| better parent addresses | Number of times this software wins a tie to forward a packet when a tie condition exists. A tie condition occurs when two routers on the same local net have routes to the packet's destination with the same hop count. Whichever router has the highest network address wins and forwards the packet. |
| worst parent addresses | Number of times this software loses a tie to forward a packet when a tie condition exists. A tie condition occurs when two routers on the same local net have routes to the packet's destination with the same hop count. Whichever router has the highest network address wins and forwards the packet. |
| bad ranges | Number of times an invalid SMRP network range was received. |
| overlaps | Number of times an incoming SMRP network range overlapped with an existing SMRP routing entry. |
| **SMRP transaction statistics:** | |
| Requests: | |
| new | Number of new requests created. |
| recycled | Number of recycled requests. |
| deleted | Number of times data was allocated for requests. |
| freed | Number of times deleted requests are freed. |
| timeouts | Number of times requests timed out. |
| resends | Number of times requests were resent. |
| duplicates | Number of times a processed request arrived. |
| incomplete duplicates | Number of times requests were received while in incomplete state. |
| **Responses:** | |
| new | Number of new responses created. |

*Command Reference*

**Table 3–42**   *Show SMRP Traffic Field Descriptions, Continued*

| Field | Description |
|---|---|
| recycled | Number of recycled responses. |
| freed | Number of freed responses. |
| deleted | Number of times data was allocated for responses. |
| freed | Number of times deleted responses are freed. |
| unexpected | Number of unexpected responses. |
| bad | Number of bad responses. |

## SMRP MROUTE-CACHE PROTOCOL APPLETALK

To enable SMRP fast-switching on a port, use the **smrp mroute-cache protocol appletalk** interface configuration command. To disable SMRP fast-switching, use the **no** form of the command.

> **smrp mroute-cache protocol appletalk**
> **no smrp mroute-cache protocol appletalk**

### Syntax       Description

This command has no arguments or keywords.

### Default

Enabled

### Command Mode

Interface configuration

### Usage Guidelines

This command first appeared in Cisco IOS Release 11.1.

By default, fast-switching is enabled on all SMRP ports. A network protocol and interface compose an SMRP port. Fast switching improves the throughput rate by processing incoming packets more quickly than process switching.

SMRP uses the forwarding table to forward packets for a particular SMRP group. For each group, the forwarding table lists the parent interface and address and one or more child interfaces and addresses. When data for an SMRP group arrives on the parent interface, the router forwards it to each child interface. The SMRP fast-switching cache table specifies whether to fast switch SMRP data packets out the interfaces specified by the forwarding table.

SMRP fast switching requires that:

- A parent port is fast-switch enabled
- One or more child ports are fast-switch enabled

When the parent port is fast-switch enabled, the system populates and validates a fast-switching cache table when forwarding packets out child ports.

To populate the fast-switching cache table with fast-switching information, the first packets are process switched. Thus, the fast-switching cache table is populated with information about fast-switch enabled child ports. When succeeding packets arrive, the system uses the SMRP fast-switching cache table to fast switch the packets out those child ports.

If there are non-fast-switching ports in the forwarding table, then the system process switches the packet out those ports.

To validate the fast-switching cache table, the system validates each cache entry when it forwards the first packet out all child ports. If a cache entry is validated, the router can use the entry to fast switch succeeding packets out the child ports.

If a cache entry is invalidated, the router cannot use the entry to fast switch packets. The entry is removed from the fast-switching cache table, and the router process switches packets out the child ports. A cache entry is invalidated when one of these conditions is met:

- A child endpoint leaves the SMRP group
- A new child endpoint joins the SMRP group
- A port's fast-switching configuration is enabled or disabled
- A port is restarted

### Example

The following example disables SMRP fast-switching:

```
no smrp mroute-cache protocol appletalk
```

### SMRP PROTOCOL APPLETALK

To make SMRP multicast services available over AppleTalk for a specific interface, use the **smrp protocol appletalk** interface configuration command. To disable SMRP over AppleTalk for a specific interface, use the **no** form of the command.

**smrp protocol appletalk** [**network-range** *beginning-end*]
**no smrp protocol appletalk** [**network-range** *beginning-end*]

| Syntax | Description |
|---|---|
| **network-range** | (Optional) SMRP network range for the interface. We recommend that you do not specify an SMRP network range. When you omit the range, the Cisco IOS software uses the AppleTalk cable range configured for the interface as the SMRP network range. If you specify a range, it must fall within the SMRP network range from 1 to 65535. |
| *beginning-end* | (Optional) The beginning and end of the SMRP network range for this AppleTalk network. If you specify a range, it must fall within the SMRP network range from 1 to 65535. |

## Default

SMRP is disabled.

## Command Mode

Interface configuration

## Usage Guidelines

This command first appeared in Cisco IOS Release 11.0.

SMRP supports point-to-multipoint multicasting of packets for AppleTalk networks. This support provides the capability of sending data from a single source to multiple stations without having to send duplicate copies of the data.

The **smrp protocol appletalk** command configures SMRP support over an AppleTalk network on an interface basis. Before you use this command, you must issue the **smrp routing** command to enable SMRP. After you enable SMRP, you can use this command to make SMRP services available over AppleTalk for any number of individual interfaces.

We recommend that you do not specify an SMRP network range for the AppleTalk network. Because the upper limit of the AppleTalk network range is 65,535, AppleTalk network numbers always fit within the SMRP network range; SMRP network numbers are 3 bytes long, whereas AppleTalk network numbers are 2 bytes long. If the AppleTalk network is a nonextended network, which is defined by a single network number, the AppleTalk network is mapped to the SMRP network range using the single number to define both ends of the range (for example, 65,520-65,520).

To disable SMRP services for a specific AppleTalk network, use the **no** form of this command. To disable SMRP services globally (that is, for all AppleTalk networks whose interfaces you have configured for SMRP support), issue the **no smrp routing** command.

## Examples

The following example enables SMRP globally and turns on SMRP support over AppleTalk for the current interface:

```
smrp routing
interface ethernet 0
smrp protocol appletalk
```

The following example disables SMRP over AppleTalk for the current interface:

```
interface ethernet 0
no smrp protocol appletalk
```

## Related Commands

Search online to find documentation for related commands.

**show smrp port**
**smrp routing**

## SMRP ROUTING

To enable the use of the multicast transport services provided by the SMRP, use the **smrp routing** global configuration command. To disable SMRP services for all interfaces, use the **no** form of this command.

> **smrp routing**
> **no smrp routing**

## Syntax       Description

This command has no arguments or keywords.

## Default

SMRP is disabled.

## Command Mode

Global configuration

## Usage Guidelines

This command first appeared in Cisco IOS Release 11.0.

Currently, SMRP services are supported over AppleTalk only. The **smrp routing** command enables the use of SMRP. To enable SMRP for an AppleTalk network over a specific interface, you must use the **smrp protocol appletalk** interface configuration command after you issue this command. The **smrp routing** command has no effect until you enable SMRP at the interface level.

## Examples

The following example enables SMRP:

```
smrp routing
```

The following example disables SMRP:

```
no smrp routing
```

## Related Commands

Search online to find documentation for related commands.

**smrp protocol appletalk**

## TEST APPLETALK

To enter the test mode, use the **test appletalk** privileged EXEC command.

**test appletalk**

## Syntax    Description

This command has no arguments or keywords.

## Command Mode

Privileged EXEC

## Usage Guidelines

This command first appeared in Cisco IOS Release 11.1.

Use the **test appletalk** command to enter test mode. From test mode you can test the NBP protocol.

The following display shows how to enter Appletalk test mode:

```
Router# test appletalk
Router(atalk test)#
```

Type ? to display the following list of test options:

```
Router(atalk test)#?
end     Exit AppleTalk test mode
nbp     AppleTalk NBP test commands
```

Use the **test appletalk** command with the **nbp** options to test and to perform informational lookups of NBP-registered entities. Use the NBP options when you find that AppleTalk zones are listed in the Chooser, but services in these zones are unavailable.

Type **nbp** ? to learn what NBP test commands you can use:

```
Router(atalk test)# nbp ?
nbp confirm:        send out an NBP confirm packet to the specified entity
nbp lookup:         lookup an NVE. prompt for name, type and zone
nbp parameters:     display/change lookup parms (ntimes, ncecs, interval)
```

```
nbp poll:              for every zone, lookup all devices, using default
?:                     print command list
end:                   exit nbptest
```

The following list summarizes the **nbp** test commands you can use:

- **nbp confirm**—Sends out an NBP confirm packet to the specified entity.

- **nbp lookup**—Searches for NBP entities in a specific zone.

- **nbp parameters**—Sets the parameters used in subsequent lookup and pool tests.

- **nbp poll**—Searches for all devices in all zones.

- **?**—Displays the list of **nbp** tests.

- **end**—Exit from the **nbp** test commands.

The remainder of this section shows and explains the syntax and output of the various NBP test commands.

When running any of the NBP tests, you specify a nonprinting character by entering a three-character string that is the hexadecimal equivalent of the character. For example, type **:c5** to specify the test appletalk truncation wildcard.

This is the syntax of the **nbp confirm** command:

   **nbp confirm** *appletalk-address* [*:skt*] *object:type@zone*

| Syntax | Description |
|---|---|
| *appletalk-address* | AppleTalk network address in the form *network.node*. The argument *network* is the 16-bit network number in the range from 1 to 65,279. The argument *node* is the 8-bit node number in the range from 0 to 254. Both numbers are decimal. |
| *:skt* | (Optional) Name of socket. |
| *object:type* | Name of device and the type of service. The colon (:) between *object* and *type* is required. |
| *@zone* | Name of the AppleTalk zone where the entity *object:type* resides. |

The following display shows sample output of the **nbp confirm** command. In this example, the test sends a confirm packet to the entity *ciscoRouter* in zone *Engineering*.

```
Router(atalk test)# nbp confirm 24279.173 my-mac:AFPServer@Engineering
confirmed my-mac:AFPServer@Engineering at 24279n,173a,250s
```

This is the syntax of the **nbp lookup** command:

   **nbp lookup** *object:type@zone*

| Syntax | Description |
|---|---|
| *object:type* | Name of device and the type of service. The colon (:) between *object* and *type* is required. |
| *@zone* | Name of the AppleTalk zone where the entity *object:type* resides. |

The following display shows sample output of the **nbp lookup** command:

```
Router(atalk test)# nbp lookup =:macintosh:c5@engineering
(100n,50a,253s)[1]: 'userA:Macintosh IIcx@engineering'
(100n,16a,251s)[1]: 'userB:Macintosh II@engineering'
(200n,24a,253s)[1]: 'userC:Macintosh IIci@engineering'
(200n,36a,251s)[1]: 'userD:Macintosh II@engineering'
(300n,21a,252s)[1]: 'userE:Macintosh SE/30@engineering'
test appletalk lookup request timed out
Processed 6 replies, 7 events
```

Table 3–43 describes the fields shown in the display.

**Table 3–43**   *Test AppleTalk NBP Lookup Field Descriptions*

| Field | Description |
|---|---|
| (100n,50a,253s) [1] | AppleTalk DDP address of the registered entity, in the format network, node address, and socket number. The number in brackets is either the current value of the field (if this is the first time you have invoked **nbptest**) or the value the field had the last time you invoked **nbptest**. |
| 'userA:Macintosh IIcx@engineering' | NBP enumerator:NBP entity string of the registered entity. |
| test appletalk lookup request timed out | Indicates whether replies were heard within the timeout interval. |
| Processed 6 replies, 7 events | Number of NBP replies received. |

This is the syntax is of the **nbp parameters** command:

> **nbp parameters** *retransmissions replies interval*

| Syntax | Description |
|---|---|
| *retransmissions* | Maximum number of lookup retransmissions. This is a number from 1 to 5. The default value is 5. |
| *replies* | Maximum number of replies to accept for each lookup. This is a number from 1 to 500. The default is 1. |
| *interval* | Interval, in seconds, between each retry. This value is from 1 to 60 seconds. The default is 5 seconds. |

The following display shows sample output of the **nbp parameters** command. In this example, the maximum number of retransmission is 1, the maximum number of replies is 100, and there are 10 seconds between each retry.

```
Router(atalk test)# nbp parameters 1 100 10
```

The **nbp poll** command has no keywords or arguments. The following display shows sample output from the **nbp poll** command:

```
Router(atalk test)# nbp poll
poll: sent 2 lookups
(100n,82a,252s)[1]: 'userA:Macintosh IIci@Zone one'
(200n,75a,254s)[1]: 'userB:Macintosh IIcx@Zone two'
test appletalk polling completed.
Processed 2 replies, 2 events
```

Table 3–44 describes the fields shown in the display.

**Table 3–44**   *Test AppleTalk NBP Poll Field Descriptions*

| Field | Description |
| --- | --- |
| poll | Number of lookups the command sent. |
| (100n,82,252s) [1] | AppleTalk DDP address of the registered entity, in the format network, node address, and socket number. The number in brackets is either the current value of the field (if this is the first time you have invoked **nbptest**) or the value the field had the last time you invoked **nbptest**. |
| 'userA:Macintosh IIci@Zone one' | NBP enumerator:NBP entity string of the registered entity. |
| test appletalk polling completed. | Indicates that the polling completed successfully. |
| Processed 2 replies, 2 events | Number of NBP replies received. |

## Examples

The following example enables the **appletalk nbp polling** command, which does not use any keywords or arguments:

```
Router (atalk test)# nbp poll
```

## Related Commands

Search online to find documentation for related commands.

**test flash**
**test interfaces**
**test memory**

## TUNNEL MODE

To set the encapsulation mode for the tunnel interface, use the **tunnel mode** interface configuration command. To set to the default, use the **no** form of this command.

**tunnel mode** {aurp | cayman | dvmrp | eon | gre ip | nos}
**no tunnel mode**

| Syntax | Description |
|--------|-------------|
| **aurp** | AppleTalk Update Routing Protocol (AURP). |
| **cayman** | Cayman TunnelTalk AppleTalk encapsulation. |
| **dvmrp** | Distance Vector Multicast Routing Protocol (DVMRP). |
| **eon** | EON-compatible Connectionless Network Service (CLNS) tunnel. |
| **gre ip** | Generic routing encapsulation (GRE) protocol over IP. |
| **nos** | KA9Q/NOS compatible IP over IP. |

### Default

GRE tunneling

### Command Mode

Interface configuration

### Usage Guidelines

This command first appeared in Cisco IOS Release 11.2.

You cannot have two tunnels using the same encapsulation mode with exactly the same source and destination address. The workaround is to create a loopback interface and source packets off of the loopback interface.

Cayman tunneling implements tunneling as designed by Cayman Systems. This enables Cisco routers to interoperate with Cayman GatorBoxes. With Cayman tunneling, you can establish tunnels between two routers or between a Cisco router and a GatorBox. When using Cayman tunneling, you must not configure the tunnel with an AppleTalk network address. This means that there is no way to ping the other end of the tunnel.

Use DVMRP when a router connects to a mrouted router to run DVMRP over a tunnel. It is required to configure Protocol Independent Multicast (PIM) and an IP address on a DVMRP tunnel.

Generic route encapsulation (GRE) tunneling can be done between Cisco routers only. When using GRE tunneling for AppleTalk, you configure the tunnel with an AppleTalk network address. This means that you can ping the other end of the tunnel.

## Examples

The following example enables Cayman tunneling:

```
interface tunnel 0
tunnel source ethernet 0
tunnel destination 131.108.164.19
tunnel mode cayman
```

The following example enables GRE tunneling:

```
interface tunnel 0
appletalk cable-range 4160-4160 4160.19
appletalk zone Engineering
tunnel source ethernet0
tunnel destination 131.108.164.19
tunnel mode gre ip
```

## Related Commands

Search online to find documentation for related commands.

**appletalk cable-range**
**appletalk zone**
**tunnel destination**
**tunnel source**

## TUNNEL SOURCE

To set a tunnel interface's source address, use the **tunnel source** interface configuration command. To remove the source address, use the **no** form of this command.

> **tunnel source** {*ip-address* | *type number*}
> **no tunnel source**

| Syntax | Description |
|---|---|
| *ip-address* | IP address to use as the source address for packets in the tunnel. |
| *type* | All interface types. |
| *number* | Specifies the port, connector, or interface card number. The numbers are assigned at the factory at the time of installation or when added to a system, and they can be displayed with the show interfaces command. |

## Default

No tunnel interface's source address is set.

## Command Mode

Interface configuration

## Usage Guidelines

This command first appeared in Cisco IOS Release 11.2.

You cannot have two tunnels using the same encapsulation mode with exactly the same source and destination address. The workaround is to create a loopback interface and source packets off of the loopback interface.

When using tunnels to Cayman boxes, you must set the **tunnel source** to an explicit IP address on the same subnet as the Cayman box, not the tunnel itself.

## Examples

The following example enables Cayman tunneling:

```
interface tunnel0
tunnel source ethernet0
tunnel destination 131.108.164.19
tunnel mode cayman
```

The following example enables GRE tunneling:

```
interface tunnel0
appletalk cable-range 4160-4160 4160.19
appletalk zone Engineering
tunnel source ethernet0
tunnel destination 131.108.164.19
tunnel mode gre ip
```

## Related Commands

Search online to find documentation for related commands.

**appletalk cable-range**
**appletalk iptalk**
**appletalk zone**
**tunnel mode**

# CHAPTER 4

# Configuring Novell IPX

This chapter describes how to configure Novell Internet Packet Exchange (IPX) and provides configuration examples. For a complete description of the IPX commands in this chapter, see Chapter 5, "Novell IPX Commands."

## IPX ADDRESSES

An IPX network address consists of a network number and a node number expressed in the format *network.node*.

### Network Numbers

The network number identifies a physical network. It is a 4-byte (32-bit) quantity that must be unique throughout the entire IPX internetwork. The network number is expressed as hexadecimal digits. The maximum number of digits allowed is eight.

The Cisco IOS software does not require that you enter all eight digits; you can omit leading zeros.

### Node Numbers

The node number identifies a node on the network. It is a 48-bit quantity, represented by dotted triplets of 4-digit hexadecimal numbers.

If you do not specify a node number for a router to be used on WAN links, the Cisco IOS software uses the hardware Media Access Control (MAC) address currently assigned to it as its node address. This is the MAC address of the first Ethernet, Token Ring, or FDDI interface card. If there are no valid IEEE interfaces, then the Cisco IOS software randomly assigns a node number using a number that is based on the system clock.

## IPX Address Example

The following is an example of an IPX network address:

```
4a.0000.0c00.23fe
```

In this example, the network number is 4a (more specifically, it is 0000004a), and the node number is 0000.0c00.23fe. All digits in the address are hexadecimal.

## IPX CONFIGURATION TASK LIST

To configure IPX routing, complete the tasks in the following sections. At a minimum, you must enable IPX routing. The remaining tasks are optional.

- Enabling IPX Routing
- Configuring IPX Enhanced IGRP
- Configuring NLSP
- Configuring Next Hop Resolution Protocol
- Configuring IPX and SPX over WANs
- Controlling Access to IPX Networks
- Tuning IPX Network Performance
- Shutting Down an IPX Network
- Configuring IPX Accounting
- Monitoring and Maintaining the IPX Network

See the "Novell IPX Configuration Examples" section later in this chapter for configuration examples.

## ENABLING IPX ROUTING

You enable IPX routing by first enabling it on the router and then configuring it on each interface.

Optionally, you can route IPX on some interfaces and transparently bridge it on other interfaces. You can also route IPX traffic between routed interfaces and bridge groups or route IPX traffic between bridge groups.

## IPX Default Routes

In IPX, a *default route* is the network where all packets for which the route to the destination address is unknown are forwarded.

Original RIP implementations allowed the use of network -2 (0xFFFFFFFE) as a regular network number in a network. With the inception of NLSP, network -2 is reserved as the default route for NLSP and RIP. Both NLSP and RIP routers should treat network -2 as a default route. Therefore, you should implement network -2 as the default route regardless of whether you configure NLSP in your IPX network.

By default, Cisco IOS software treats network -2 as the default route. You should ensure that your IPX network does not use network -2 as a regular network. If, for some reason, you must use network -2 as a regular network, you can disable the default behavior. To do so, see the "Adjust Default Routes" section later in this chapter.

For more background information on how to handle IPX default routes, refer to Novell's *NetWare Link Services Protocol (NLSP) Specification, Revision 1.1*.

## Enable IPX Routing Task List

Complete the tasks in the following sections to enable IPX routing. The first two tasks are required; the rest are optional.

- Enable IPX Routing
- Assign Network Numbers to Individual Interfaces
- Enable Concurrent Routing and Bridging
- Configure Integrated Routing and Bridging

## Enable IPX Routing

The first step in enabling IPX routing is to enable it on the router. If you do not specify the node number of the router to be used on WAN links, the Cisco IOS software uses the hardware Media Access Control (MAC) address currently assigned to it as its node address. This is the MAC address of the first Ethernet, Token Ring, or FDDI interface card. If there are no valid IEEE interfaces, then the Cisco IOS software randomly assigns a node number using a number that is based on the system clock.

To enable IPX routing, perform the following global configuration task:

| Task | Command |
| --- | --- |
| Enable IPX routing. | **ipx routing** [*node*] |

For an example of how to enable IPX routing, see the "IPX Routing Examples" section near the end of this chapter.

---

**CAUTION**

If you plan to use DECnet and IPX routing concurrently on the same interface, you should enable DECnet routing first and then enable IPX routing without specifying the optional MAC node number. If you enable IPX before enabling DECnet routing, routing for IPX is disrupted because DECnet forces a change in the MAC-level node number.

---

## Assign Network Numbers to Individual Interfaces

After you have enabled IPX routing, you assign network numbers to individual interfaces. This enables IPX routing on those interfaces.

You enable IPX routing on interfaces that support a single network or on those that support multiple networks.

When you enable IPX routing on an interface, you can also specify an encapsulation (frame type) to use for packets being transmitted on that network. Table 4–1 lists the encapsulation types you can use on IEEE interfaces and shows the correspondence between Cisco naming conventions and Novell naming conventions for the encapsulation types.

**Table 4–1**    *Cisco and Novell IPX Encapsulation Names on IEEE Interfaces*

| Interface Type | Cisco Name | Novell Name |
|---|---|---|
| Ethernet | novell-ether (Cisco IOS default)<br>arpa<br>sap<br>snap | Ethernet_802.3<br>Ethernet_II<br>Ethernet_802.2<br>Ethernet_Snap |
| Token Ring | sap (Cisco IOS default)<br>snap | Token-Ring<br>Token-Ring_Snap |
| FDDI | snap (Cisco IOS default)<br>sap<br>novell-fddi | Fddi_Snap<br>Fddi_802.2<br>Fddi_Raw |

### *Assign Network Numbers to Individual Interfaces Task List*

The following sections describe how to enable IPX routing on interfaces that support a single network and on those that support multiple networks. You must perform one of the tasks to enable IPX routing on an interface in these sections:

- Assign Network Numbers to Interfaces That Support a Single Network
- Assign Network Numbers to Interfaces That Support Multiple Networks

### *Assign Network Numbers to Interfaces That Support a Single Network*

A single interface can support a single network or multiple logical networks. For a single network, you can configure any encapsulation type. Of course, it should match the encapsulation type of the servers and clients using that network number.

To assign a network number to an interface that supports a single network, perform the following interface configuration task:

| Task | Command |
|------|---------|
| Enable IPX routing on an interface. | ipx network *network* [encapsulation *encapsulation-type*] |

If you specify an encapsulation type, be sure to choose the one that matches the one used by the servers and clients on that network. Refer to Table 4–1 for a list of encapsulation types you can use on IEEE interfaces.

For an example of how to enable IPX routing, see the "IPX Routing Examples" section near the end of this chapter.

## Assign Network Numbers to Interfaces That Support Multiple Networks

When assigning network numbers to an interface that supports multiple networks, you must specify a different encapsulation type for each network. Because multiple networks share the physical medium, this allows the Cisco IOS software to identify the packets that belong to each network. For example, you can configure up to four IPX networks on a single Ethernet cable because four encapsulation types are supported for Ethernet. Again, the encapsulation type should match the servers and clients using the same network number. Refer to Table 4–1 for a list of encapsulation types you can use on IEEE interfaces.

There are two ways to assign network numbers to interfaces that support multiple networks. You can use subinterfaces or primary and secondary networks.

### Subinterfaces

You typically use subinterfaces to assign network numbers to interfaces that support multiple networks.

A *subinterface* is a mechanism that allows a single physical interface to support multiple logical interfaces or networks. That is, several logical interfaces or networks can be associated with a single hardware interface. Each subinterface must use a distinct encapsulation, and the encapsulation must match that of the clients and servers using the same network number.

— **NOTES**

When enabling NLSP and configuring multiple encapsulations on the same physical LAN interface, you must use subinterfaces. You cannot use secondary networks.

Any interface configuration parameters that you specify on an individual subinterface are applied to that subinterface only.

To configure multiple IPX networks on a physical interface using subinterfaces, perform the following tasks, starting in global configuration mode:

| Task | Command |
|------|---------|
| **Step 1** Specify a subinterface. | **interface** *type number.subinterface-number* |
| **Step 2** Enable IPX routing, specifying the first encapsulation type. | **ipx network** *network* [**encapsulation** *encapsulation-type*] |

To configure more than one subinterface, repeat these two steps. Refer to Table 4–1 for a list of encapsulation types you can use on IEEE interfaces.

For examples of configuring multiple IPX networks on an interface, see the "IPX Routing on Multiple Networks Examples" section near the end of this chapter.

### Primary and Secondary Networks

When assigning network numbers to interfaces that support multiple networks, you can also configure primary and secondary networks.

---
**NOTES**
---

In future Cisco IOS software releases, primary and secondary networks will not be supported.

---

The first logical network you configure on an interface is considered the *primary network*. Any additional networks are considered *secondary networks*. Again, each network on an interface must use a distinct encapsulation, and it should match that of the clients and servers using the same network number.

Any interface configuration parameters that you specify on this interface are applied to all the logical networks. For example, if you set the routing update timer to 120 seconds, this value is used on all four networks.

To use primary and secondary networks to configure multiple IPX networks on an interface, perform the following tasks in interface configuration mode:

| Task | Command |
|------|---------|
| **Step 1** Enable IPX routing on the primary network. | **ipx network** *network* [**encapsulation** *encapsulation-type*] |
| **Step 2** Enable IPX routing on a secondary network. | **ipx network** *network* [**encapsulation** *encapsulation-type*] [**secondary**] |

To configure more than one secondary network, repeat Step 2 as appropriate. Refer to Table 4–1 for a list of encapsulation types you can use on IEEE interfaces.

---

**NOTES**

When enabling NLSP and configuring multiple encapsulations on the same physical LAN interface, you must use subinterfaces. You cannot use secondary networks.

---

## Enable Concurrent Routing and Bridging

You can route IPX on some interfaces and transparently bridge it on other interfaces simultaneously. To do this, you must enable concurrent routing and bridging. To enable concurrent routing and bridging, perform the following task in global configuration mode:

| Task | Command |
|------|---------|
| Enable concurrent routing and bridging. | **bridge crb** |

## Configure Integrated Routing and Bridging

Integrated routing and bridging (IRB) enables a user to route IPX traffic between routed interfaces and bridge groups or route IPX traffic between bridge groups. Specifically, local or unroutable traffic is bridged among the bridged interfaces in the same bridge group. Routable traffic is routed to other routed interfaces or bridge groups. Using IRB, you can do the following:

- Switch packets from a bridged interface to a routed interface
- Switch packets from a routed interface to a bridged interface
- Switch packets within the same bridge group

## CONFIGURING IPX ENHANCED IGRP

Enhanced IGRP is an enhanced version of the Interior Gateway Routing Protocol (IGRP) developed by Cisco Systems, Inc. Enhanced IGRP uses the same distance vector algorithm and distance information as IGRP. However, the convergence properties and the operating efficiency of Enhanced IGRP have improved significantly over IGRP.

The convergence technology is based on research conducted at SRI International. It employs an algorithm referred to as the Diffusing Update Algorithm (DUAL). This algorithm guarantees loop-free operation at every instant throughout a route computation and allows all routers involved in a topology change to synchronize at the same time. Routers that are not affected by topology changes are not involved in recomputations. The convergence time with DUAL rivals that of any other existing routing protocol.

## Enhanced IGRP Features

Enhanced IGRP offers the following features:

- Fast convergence—The DUAL algorithm allows routing information to converge as quickly as any currently available routing protocol.

- Partial updates—Enhanced IGRP sends incremental updates when the state of a destination changes instead of sending the entire contents of the routing table. This feature minimizes the bandwidth required for Enhanced IGRP packets.

- Less CPU usage than IGRP—This occurs because full update packets do not have to be processed each time they are received.

- Neighbor discovery mechanism—This is a simple hello mechanism used to learn about neighboring routers. It is protocol-independent.

- Scaling—Enhanced IGRP scales to large networks.

## Enhanced IGRP Components

Enhanced IGRP has four basic components, which are discussed in the following sections:

- Neighbor Discovery/Recovery
- Reliable Transport Protocol
- DUAL Finite-State Machine
- Protocol-Dependent Modules

### Neighbor Discovery/Recovery

Neighbor discovery/recovery is the process that routers use to dynamically learn of other routers on their directly attached networks. Routers must also discover when their neighbors become unreachable or inoperative. Neighbor discovery/recovery is achieved with low overhead by periodically sending small hello packets. As long as hello packets are received, a router can determine that a neighbor is alive and functioning. After this status is determined, the neighboring devices can exchange routing information.

### Reliable Transport Protocol

The reliable transport protocol is responsible for guaranteed, ordered delivery of Enhanced IGRP packets to all neighbors. It supports intermixed transmission of multicast and unicast packets. Some Enhanced IGRP packets must be transmitted reliably, and others need not be. For efficiency, reliability is provided only when necessary. For example, on a multiaccess network that has multicast capabilities (such as Ethernet), it is not necessary to send hellos reliably to all neighbors individually. Therefore, Enhanced IGRP sends a single multicast hello with an indication in the packet informing the receivers that the packet need not be acknowledged. Other types of packets (such as updates) require acknowledgment, and this is indicated in the packet. The reliable transport has a provision to send multicast packets quickly when there are unacknowledged packets pending. Doing so helps ensure that convergence time remains low in the presence of varying speed links.

### DUAL Finite-State Machine

The DUAL finite-state machine embodies the decision process for all route computations. It tracks all routes advertised by all neighbors. DUAL uses the distance information (known as a metric) to select efficient, loop-free paths. DUAL selects routes to be inserted into a routing table based on feasible successors. A *successor* is a neighboring router used for packet forwarding that has a least-cost path to a destination that is guaranteed not to be part of a routing loop. When there are no feasible successors but there are neighbors advertising the destination, a recomputation must occur. This is the process whereby a new successor is determined. The amount of time it takes to recompute the route affects the convergence time. Recomputation is processor intensive. It is advantageous to avoid recomputation if it is not necessary. When a topology change occurs, DUAL tests for feasible successors. If there are feasible successors, it uses any it finds in order to avoid unnecessary recomputation.

### Protocol-Dependent Modules

The protocol-dependent modules are responsible for network layer protocol-specific tasks. They are also responsible for parsing Enhanced IGRP packets and informing DUAL of the new information received. Enhanced IGRP asks DUAL to make routing decisions, but the results are stored in the IPX routing table. Also, Enhanced IGRP is responsible for redistributing routes learned by other IPX routing protocols.

## Configure IPX Enhanced IGRP Task List

To enable IPX Enhanced IGRP, complete the tasks in the following sections. Only the first task is required; the remaining tasks are optional.

- Enable IPX Enhanced IGRP
- Customize Link Characteristics
- Customize the Exchange of Routing and Service Information
- Query the Backup Server

## Enable IPX Enhanced IGRP

To create an IPX Enhanced IGRP routing process, perform the following tasks:

| Task | Command |
|------|---------|
| **Step 1** Enable an Enhanced IGRP routing process in global configuration mode. | **ipx router eigrp** *autonomous-system-number* |
| **Step 2** Enable Enhanced IGRP on a network in IPX router configuration mode. | **network** {*network-number* \| **all**} |

To associate multiple networks with an Enhanced IGRP routing process, you can repeat Step 2.

For an example of how to enable Enhanced IGRP, see the "IPX Enhanced IGRP Example" section near the end of this chapter.

## Customize Link Characteristics

You might want to customize the Enhanced IGRP link characteristics. The following sections describe these customization tasks:

- Configure the Percentage of Link Bandwidth Used by Enhanced IGRP
- Configure Maximum Hop Count
- Adjust the Interval between Hello Packets and the Hold Time

### Configure the Percentage of Link Bandwidth Used by Enhanced IGRP

By default, Enhanced IGRP packets consume a maximum of 50 percent of the link bandwidth, as configured with the **bandwidth** interface subcommand. If a different value is desired, use the **ipx bandwidth-percent** command. This command may be useful if a different level of link utilization is required, or if the configured bandwidth does not match the actual link bandwidth (it may have been configured to influence route metric calculations).

To configure the percentage of bandwidth that may be used by Enhanced IGRP on an interface, perform the following task in interface configuration mode:

| Task | Command |
| --- | --- |
| Configure the percentage of bandwidth that may be used by Enhanced IGRP on an interface. | **ipx bandwidth-percent eigrp** *as-number percent* |

For an example of how to configure the percentage of Enhanced IGRP bandwidth, see the "IPX Enhanced IGRP Bandwidth Configuration Examples" section near the end of this chapter.

### Configure Maximum Hop Count

 **NOTES**

While adjusting the maximum hop count is possible, it is not recommended for Enhanced IGRP. Cisco recommends that you use the default value for the maximum hop count of Enhanced IGRP.

By default, IPX packets whose hop count exceeds 15 are discarded. In larger internetworks, this may be insufficient. You can increase the hop count to a maximum of 254 hops for Enhanced IGRP. To modify the maximum hop count, perform the following task in global configuration mode:

| Task | Command |
|------|---------|
| Set the maximum hop count accepted from RIP update packets. | **ipx maximum-hops** *hop* |

## Adjust the Interval between Hello Packets and the Hold Time

You can adjust the interval between hello packets and the hold time.

Routers periodically send hello packets to each other to dynamically learn of other devices on their directly attached networks. Routers use this information to discover who their neighbors are and to discover when their neighbors become unreachable or inoperative.

By default, hello packets are sent every 5 seconds. The exception is on low-speed, nonbroadcast, multiaccess (NBMA) media, on which the default hello interval is 60 seconds. Low speed is considered to be a rate of T1 or slower, as specified with the bandwidth interface configuration command. The default hello interval remains 5 seconds for high-speed NBMA networks.

---
**NOTES**
---

For the purposes of Enhanced IGRP, Frame Relay and SMDS networks may or may not be considered to be NBMA. These networks are considered NBMA if the interface has not been configured to use physical multicasting; otherwise, they are considered not to be NBMA.

---

You can configure the hold time on a specified interface for a particular Enhanced IGRP routing process designated by the autonomous system number. The hold time is advertised in hello packets. It indicates to neighbors the length of time they should consider the sender valid. The default hold time is 3 times the hello interval, or 15 seconds.

To change the interval between hello packets, perform the following task in interface configuration mode:

| Task | Command |
|------|---------|
| Set the interval between hello packets. | **ipx hello-interval eigrp** *autonomous-system-number seconds* |

On very congested and large networks, 15 seconds may not be sufficient time for all routers to receive hello packets from their neighbors. In this case, you may want to increase the hold time. To do this, perform the following task in interface configuration mode:

| Task | Command |
| --- | --- |
| Set the hold time. | ipx hold-time eigrp *autonomous-system-number seconds* |

**NOTES**

Do not adjust the hold time without consulting with Cisco technical support.

## Customize the Exchange of Routing and Service Information

You might want to customize the exchange of routing and service information. The following sections describe these customization tasks:

- Redistribute Routing Information
- Disable Split Horizon
- Control the Advertising of Routes in Routing Updates
- Control the Processing of Routing Updates
- Control SAP Updates
- Control the Advertising of Services in SAP Updates
- Control the Processing of SAP Updates

### *Redistribute Routing Information*

By default, the Cisco IOS software redistributes IPX RIP routes into Enhanced IGRP and vice versa.

To disable route redistribution, perform the following task in IPX router configuration mode:

| Task | Command |
| --- | --- |
| Disable redistribution of RIP routes into Enhanced IGRP and Enhanced IGRP routes into RIP. | no redistribute {rip \| eigrp *autonomous-system-number* \| connected \| static} |

The Cisco IOS software does not automatically redistribute NLSP routes into Enhanced IGRP routes and vice versa. You must configure this type of redistribution. To do so, perform the following tasks, beginning in global configuration mode:

| Task | Command |
| --- | --- |
| **Step 1** From global configuration mode, enable Enhanced IGRP. | **ipx router eigrp** *autonomous-system-number* |
| **Step 2** From IPX-router configuration mode, enable redistribution of NLSP into Enhanced IGRP. | **redistribute nlsp** [*tag*] |
| **Step 3** Enable NLSP. | **ipx router nlsp** [*tag*] |
| **Step 4** From IPX-router configuration mode, enable redistribution of Enhanced IGRP into NLSP. | **redistribute eigrp** *autonomous-system-number* |

For an example of how to enable redistribution of Enhanced IGRP and NLSP, see the "Enhanced IGRP and NLSP Route Redistribution Example" section near the end of this chapter.

### Disable Split Horizon

Split horizon controls the sending of Enhanced IGRP update and query packets. When split horizon is enabled on an interface, these packets are not sent for destinations if this interface is the next hop to that destination.

By default, split horizon is enabled on all interfaces.

Split horizon blocks information about routes from being advertised by the Cisco IOS software out any interface from which that information originated. This behavior usually optimizes communication among multiple routers, particularly when links are broken. However, with nonbroadcast networks (such as Frame Relay and SMDS), situations can arise for which this behavior is less than ideal. For these situations, you can disable split horizon.

To disable split horizon, perform the following task in interface configuration mode:

| Task | Command |
| --- | --- |
| Disable split horizon. | **no ipx split-horizon eigrp** *autonomous-system-number* |

---
**NOTES**
---

Split horizon cannot be disabled for RIP or SAP—only for Enhanced IGRP.

### Control the Advertising of Routes in Routing Updates

To control which devices learn about routes, you can control the advertising of routes in routing updates. To do this, perform the following task in router configuration mode:

| Task | Command |
|------|---------|
| Control the advertising of routes in routing updates. | distribute-list *access-list-number* out [*interface-name* \| *routing-process*] |

### Control the Processing of Routing Updates

To control the processing of routes listed in incoming updates, perform the following task in router configuration mode:

| Task | Command |
|------|---------|
| Control which incoming route updates are processed. | distribute-list *access-list-number* in [*interface-name*] |

### Control SAP Updates

If IPX Enhanced IGRP peers are found on an interface, you can configure the Cisco IOS software to send SAP updates either periodically or when a change occurs in the SAP table. When no IPX Enhanced IGRP peer is present on the interface, periodic SAPs are always sent.

On serial lines, by default, if an Enhanced IGRP neighbor is present, the Cisco IOS software sends SAP updates only when the SAP table changes. On Ethernet, Token Ring, and FDDI interfaces, by default, the software sends SAP updates periodically. To reduce the amount of bandwidth required to send SAP updates, you might want to disable the periodic sending of SAP updates on LAN interfaces. Do this only when all nodes out this interface are Enhanced IGRP peers; otherwise, loss of SAP information on the other nodes results.

To send SAP updates only when a change occurs in the SAP table and to send only the SAP changes, perform the following task in interface configuration mode:

| Task | Command |
|------|---------|
| Send SAP updates only when a change in the SAP table occurs, and send only the SAP changes. | ipx sap-incremental eigrp *autonomous-system-number* rsup-only |

When you enable incremental SAP using the ipx sap-incremental eigrp rsup-only command, Cisco IOS software disables the exchange of route information via Enhanced IGRP for that interface.

To send periodic SAP updates, perform the following task in interface configuration mode:

| Task | Command |
| --- | --- |
| Send SAP updates periodically. | **no ipx sap-incremental eigrp** *autonomous-system-number* |

For an example of how to configure SAP updates, see the "Enhanced IGRP SAP Update Examples" section near the end of this chapter.

### Control the Advertising of Services in SAP Updates

To control which devices learn about services, you can control the advertising of these services in SAP updates. To do this, perform the following task in router configuration mode:

| Task | Command |
| --- | --- |
| Control the advertising of services in SAP updates. | **distribute-sap-list** *access-list-number* **out** [*interface-name* l *routing-process*] |

For a configuration example of controlling the advertisement of SAP updates, see the "Advertisement and Processing of SAP Update Examples" section near the end of this chapter.

### Control the Processing of SAP Updates

To control the processing of routes listed in incoming updates, perform the following task in router configuration mode:

| Task | Command |
| --- | --- |
| Control which incoming SAP updates are processed. | **distribute-sap-list** *access-list-number* **in** [*interface-name*] |

For a configuration example of controlling the processing of SAP updates, see the "Advertisement and Processing of SAP Update Examples" section near the end of this chapter.

### Query the Backup Server

The backup server table is a table kept for each Enhanced IGRP peer. It lists the IPX servers that have been advertised by that peer. If a server is removed from the main server table at any time and for any reason, the Cisco IOS software examines the backup server table to see if this just-removed server is known by any of the Enhanced IGRP peers. If it is, the information from that peer is advertised back into the main server table just as if that peer had re-advertised the server information to this router. Using this method to allow the router to keep the backup server table consistent with what is advertised by each peer means that only changes to the table must be advertised between Enhanced IGRP routers; full periodic updates do not need to be sent.

By default, the Cisco IOS software queries its own copy of each Enhanced IGRP neighbor's backup server table every 60 seconds. To change this interval, perform the following task in global configuration mode:

| Task | Command |
| --- | --- |
| Specify the minimum period of time between successive queries of a neighbor's backup server table. | **ipx backup-server-query-interval** *interval* |

## CONFIGURING NLSP

The NetWare Link Services Protocol (NLSP) is a link-state routing protocol based on the Open System Interconnection (OSI) Intermediate System to Intermediate System (IS-IS) protocol.

NLSP is designed to be used in a hierarchical routing environment, in which networked systems are grouped into routing areas. Routing areas can then be grouped into routing domains, and domains can be grouped into an internetwork.

### Understand Level 1, 2, and 3 Routers

Level 1 routers connect networked systems within a given routing area. Areas are connected to each other by Level 2 routers, and domains are connected by Level 3 routers. A Level 2 router also acts as a Level 1 router within its own area; likewise, a Level 3 router also acts as a Level 2 router within its own domain.

The router at each level of the topology stores complete information for its level. For instance, Level 1 routers store complete link-state information about their entire area. This information includes a record of all the routers in the area, the links connecting them, the operational status of the devices and their links, and other related parameters. For each point-to-point link, the database records the end-point devices and the state of the link. For each LAN, the database records which routers are connected to the LAN. Similarly, Level 2 routers would store information about all the areas in the routing domain, and Level 3 routers would store information about all the domains in the internetwork.

Although NLSP is designed for hierarchical routing environments containing Level 1, 2, and 3 routers, only Level 1 routing with area route aggregation and route redistribution has been defined in a specification.

## Understand NLSP Databases

NLSP is a link-state protocol. This means that every router in a routing area maintains an identical copy of the link-state database, which contains all information about the topology of the area. All routers synchronize their views of the databases among themselves to keep their copies of the link-state databases consistent. NLSP has the following three major databases:

- Adjacency—Keeps track of the router's immediate neighbors and the operational status of the directly attached links by exchanging hello packets. Adjacencies are created upon receipt of periodic hello packets. If a link or router goes down, adjacencies time out and are deleted from the database.

- Link state—Tracks the connectivity of an entire routing area by aggregating the immediate neighborhood information from all routers into link-state packets (LSPs). LSPs contain lists of adjacencies. They are flooded to all other devices via a reliable flooding algorithm every time a link state changes. LSPs are refreshed every two hours. To keep the size of the link-state database reasonable, NLSP uses fictitious pseudonodes, which represent the LAN as a whole, and designated routers, which originate LSPs on behalf of the pseudonode.

- Forwarding—Calculated from the adjacency and link-state databases using Dijkstra's shortest path first (SPF) algorithm.

## Cisco Support of NLSP

Cisco's implementation of NLSP supports the Novell NLSP specification, version 1.1. Cisco's implementation of NLSP also includes read-only NLSP MIB variables.

## Configure NLSP Task List

To configure NLSP, you must have configured IPX routing on your router, as described previously in this chapter. Then, you must perform the tasks described in the following sections:

- Define an Internal Network
- Enable NLSP Routing
- Configure NLSP on an Interface

You can optionally perform the tasks described in the following sections:

- Customize Link Characteristics
- Configure Route Aggregation
- Customize the Exchange of Routing Information

For an example of enabling NLSP, see the "IPX Routing Protocols Examples" section near the end of this chapter.

## Define an Internal Network

An internal network number is an IPX network number assigned to the router. For NLSP to operate, you must configure an internal network number for each device.

To enable IPX routing and to define an internal network number, perform the following tasks in global configuration mode:

| Task | Command |
|------|---------|
| Enable IPX routing. | **ipx routing** |
| Define an internal network number. | **ipx internal-network** *network-number* |

## Enable NLSP Routing

To enable NLSP, perform the following tasks, starting in global configuration mode:

| Task | Command |
|------|---------|
| **Step 1** Enable NLSP. | **ipx router nlsp** [*tag*] |
| **Step 2** Define a set of network numbers to be part of the current NLSP area. | **area-address** *address mask* |

## Configure NLSP on an Interface

You configure NLSP differently on LAN and WAN interfaces, as described in the following sections:

- Configure NLSP on a LAN interface
- Configure NLSP on a WAN interface

### Configure NLSP on a LAN Interface

To configure NLSP on a LAN interface, perform the following tasks in interface configuration mode:

| Task | Command |
|------|---------|
| **Step 1** Enable IPX routing on an interface. | **ipx network** *network* [encapsulation *encapsulation-type*] |
| **Step 2** Enable NLSP on the interface. | **ipx nlsp** [*tag*] **enable** |

To configure multiple encapsulations on the same physical LAN interfaces, you must configure subinterfaces. Each subinterface must have a different encapsulation type. To do this, perform the following tasks, starting in global configuration mode:

| Task | Command |
|---|---|
| **Step 1** Specify a subinterface. | **interface** *type number.subinterface-number* |
| **Step 2** Enable IPX routing, specifying the first encapsulation type. | **ipx network** *network* [**encapsulation** *encapsulation-type*] |
| **Step 3** Enable NLSP on the subinterface. | **ipx nlsp** [*tag*] **enable** |

Repeat these three steps for each subinterface.

— **NOTES** —

When enabling NLSP and configuring multiple encapsulations on the same physical LAN interface, you must use subinterfaces. You cannot use secondary networks.

### Configure NLSP on a WAN Interface

To configure NLSP on a WAN interface, perform the following tasks, starting in global configuration mode:

| Task | Command |
|---|---|
| **Step 1** Specify a serial interface. | **interface serial** *number* |
| **Step 2** Enable IPXWAN. | **ipx ipxwan** [*local-node* **unnumbered** *local-server-name retry-interval retry-limit*] |
| **Step 3** Enable NLSP on the interface. | **ipx nlsp** [*tag*] **enable** |

## Customize Link Characteristics

You might want to customize the NLSP link characteristics. The following sections describe these customization tasks:

- Enable NLSP Multicast Addressing
- Configure the Metric Value
- Configure the Link Delay and Throughput
- Configure the Maximum Hop Count
- Specify a Designated Router

- Configure Transmission and Retransmission Intervals
- Modify Link-State Packet Parameters
- Limit Partial Route Calculations

## Enable NLSP Multicast Addressing

Cisco IOS supports the use of NLSP multicast addressing for Ethernet, Token Ring, and FDDI router interfaces. This capability is only possible when the underlying Cisco hardware device or driver supports multicast addressing.

With this feature, the router defaults to using multicasts on Ethernet, Token Ring, and FDDI interfaces, instead of broadcasts, to address all NLSP routers on the network. If an adjacent neighbor does not support NLSP multicasting, the router reverts to using broadcasts on the affected interface.

This feature is only available on routers running Cisco IOS Release 11.3 or later software. When routers running prior versions of Cisco IOS software are present on the same network with routers running Cisco IOS Release 11.3 software, broadcasts are used on any segment shared by the two routers.

### Benefits of NLSP Multicast Addressing

The NLSP multicast addressing offers the following benefits:

- Increases overall efficiency and performance by reducing broadcast traffic
- Reduces CPU cycles on devices that use NLSP multicast addressing
- Increases Cisco's level of compliance with the Novell NLSP specification, version 1.1

### Enable NLSP Multicast Addressing Task List

The following sections describe configuration tasks associated with the NLSP multicast addressing:

- Enable NLSP Multicast Addressing
- Disable NLSP Multicast Addressing

### Enable NLSP Multicast Addressing

By default, NLSP multicast addressing is enabled. You do not need to configure anything to turn on NLSP multicasting.

### Disable NLSP Multicast Addressing

Typically, you do not want to substitute broadcast addressing where NLSP multicast addressing is available. NLSP multicast addressing uses network bandwidth more efficiently than broadcast addressing. However, there are circumstances in which you might want to disable NLSP multicast addressing.

For example, you might want to disable NLSP multicast addressing in favor of broadcast addressing when one or more devices on a segment do not support NLSP multicast addressing. You might also want to disable it for testing purposes.

If you want to disable NLSP multicast addressing, you can do so for the entire router or for a particular interface.

To disable multicast addressing for the entire router, perform the following steps in IPX-router configuration mode:

| Task | Command |
| --- | --- |
| **Step 1** Enter NLSP router configuration mode. | **ipx router nlsp** |
| **Step 2** Disable NLSP multicast addressing on the router. | **no multicast** |

To disable multicast addressing on a particular router interface, perform the following task in interface configuration mode:

| Task | Command |
| --- | --- |
| Disable multicast addressing on the interface. | **no ipx nlsp** [*tag*] **multicast** |

For examples of how to disable NLSP multicast addressing, see the "NLSP Multicast Addressing Examples" section near the end of this chapter.

### Configure the Metric Value

NLSP assigns a default link cost (metric) based on the link throughput. If desired, you can set the link cost manually.

Typically, you do not need to set the link cost manually; however, there are some cases in which you might want to. For example, in highly redundant networks, you might want to favor one route over another for certain kinds of traffic. As another example, you might want to ensure load sharing. Changing the metric value can help achieve these design goals.

To set the NLSP link cost for an interface, perform the following task in interface configuration mode:

| Task | Command |
| --- | --- |
| Set the metric value for an interface. | **ipx nlsp** [*tag*] **metric** *metric-number* |

### Configure the Link Delay and Throughput

The delay and throughput of each link are used by NLSP as part of its route calculations. By default, these parameters are set to appropriate values or, in the case of IPXWAN, are dynamically measured.

Typically, you do not need to change the link delay and throughput; however, there are some cases in which you might want to change these parameters. For example, in highly redundant networks, you might want to favor one route over another for certain kinds of traffic. To do this, you would change the metric on the less-desirable path to make it slightly worse by assigning it a higher metric value using the **ipx-link-delay** command. This forces the traffic to route over the favorable path. As another example, you might want to ensure load sharing. To load share, you ensure that the metrics on the equal paths are the same.

The link delay and throughput you specify replaces the default value or overrides the value measured by IPXWAN when it starts. The value is also supplied to NLSP for use in metric calculations.

To change the link delay, perform the following task in interface configuration mode:

| Task | Command |
|------|---------|
| Specify the link delay. | **ipx link-delay** *microseconds* |

To change the throughput, perform the following task in interface configuration mode:

| Task | Command |
|------|---------|
| Specify the throughput. | **ipx throughput** *bits-per-second* |

### Configure the Maximum Hop Count

By default, IPX packets whose hop count exceeds 15 are discarded. In larger internetworks, this may be insufficient. You can increase the hop count to a maximum of 127 hops for NLSP.

For example, if you have a network with end nodes separated by more than 15 hops, you can set the maximum hop count to a value between 16 and 127.

To modify the maximum hop count, perform the following task in global configuration mode:

| Task | Command |
|------|---------|
| Set the maximum hop count accepted from RIP update packets. | **ipx maximum-hops** *hop* |

### Specify a Designated Router

---
**NOTES**
---

In the context of this discussion, the term *designated router* can refer to an access server or a router.

---

NLSP elects a designated router on each LAN interface. The designated router represents all routers that are connected to the same LAN segment. It creates a virtual router called a *pseudonode*, which generates routing information on behalf of the LAN and transmits it to the remainder of the routing area. The routing information generated includes adjacencies and RIP routes. The use of a designated router significantly reduces the number of entries in the LSP database.

By default, electing a designated router is done automatically. However, you can manually affect the identity of the designated router by changing the priority of the system; the system with the highest priority is elected to be the designated router.

By default, the priority of the system is 44. To change it, perform the following task in interface configuration mode:

| Task | Command |
|---|---|
| Configure the designated router election priority. | **ipx nlsp** [*tag*] **priority** *priority-number* |

### Configure Transmission and Retransmission Intervals

You can configure the hello transmission interval and holding time multiplier, the complete sequence number PDU (CSNP) transmission interval, the LSP transmission interval, and the LSP retransmission interval.

The hello transmission interval and holding time multiplier used together determine how long a neighboring system should wait after a link or system failure (the "holding time") before declaring this system to be unreachable. The holding time is equal to the hello transmission interval multiplied by the holding time multiplier.

To configure the hello transmission interval on an interface, perform the following task in interface configuration mode:

| Task | Command |
|---|---|
| Configure the hello transmission interval. | **ipx nlsp** [*tag*] **hello-interval** *seconds* |

To specify the holding time multiplier used on an interface, perform the following task in interface configuration mode:

| Task | Command |
|---|---|
| Configure the hello multiplier. | **ipx nlsp** [*tag*] **hello-multiplier** *multiplier* |

Although not typically necessary, you can configure the CSNP transmission interval. To do so, perform the following task in interface configuration mode:

| Task | Command |
|---|---|
| Configure the CSNP transmission interval. | **ipx nlsp** [*tag*] **csnp-interval** *seconds* |

You can specify how fast LSPs can be flooded out an interface by configuring the LSP transmission interval. To configure the LSP transmission interval, perform the following task in interface configuration mode:

| Task | Command |
|---|---|
| Configure the LSP transmission interval. | **ipx nlsp** [*tag*] **lsp-interval** *interval* |

You can set the maximum amount of time that can pass before an LSP is retransmitted on a WAN link when no acknowledgment is received. To configure this LSP retransmission interval, perform the following task in interface configuration mode:

| Task | Command |
|---|---|
| Configure the LSP retransmission interval. | **ipx nlsp** [*tag*] **retransmit-interval** *seconds* |

## Modify Link-State Packet Parameters

To modify link-state packet (LSP) parameters, perform one or more of the following tasks in router configuration mode:

| Task | Command |
|---|---|
| **Step 1** Set the minimum LSP generation interval. | **lsp-gen-interval** *seconds* |
| **Step 2** Set the maximum time the LSP persists. | **max-lsp-lifetime** [**hours**] *value* |

| Task | Command |
|------|---------|
| **Step 3** Set the LSP refresh time. | **lsp-refresh-interval** *seconds* |
| **Step 4** Set the maximum size of a link-state packet. | **lsp-mtu** *bytes* |
| **Step 5** Set the minimum time between SPF calculations. | **spf-interval** *seconds* |

### Limit Partial Route Calculations

You can control how often the Cisco IOS software performs a partial route calculation (PRC). Because the partial route calculation is processor intensive, it may be useful to limit how often this is done, especially on slower router models. Increasing the PRC interval reduces the processor load of the router, but it also potentially slows down the rate of convergence.

To modify the partial route calculation, perform the following task in router configuration mode:

| Task | Command |
|------|---------|
| Set the holddown period between partial route calculations. | **prc-interval** *seconds* |

## Configure Route Aggregation

Prior to Cisco IOS Release 11.1, you could segregate IPX internetworks into distinct NLSP areas only by interconnecting them with IPX RIP. With Release 11.1 or later software, you can easily perform the following tasks:

- Divide large IPX internetworks into multiple NLSP areas
- Redistribute route and service information directly from one NLSP area into other areas
- Enable route summarization

In this document, these independent capabilities are known collectively as the *route aggregation* feature. Cisco has designed the route aggregation feature to be compatible with Novell's *NetWare Link Services Protocol (NLSP) Specification, Revision 1.1*.

**NOTES**

In the sections that follow, "NLSP version 1.1 routers" refers to routers that support the route aggregation feature, while "NLSP version 1.0 routers" refers to routers that do not. Additionally, all NLSP instances configured on a router running Release 11.1 are NLSP 1.1 instances. They are all capable of generating and using aggregated routes. However, in the text and examples that follow, an "NLSP 1.0 instance" refers to an instance of NLSP that is in an area that includes NLSP version 1.0 routers.

## Benefits of Route Summarization

NLSP route summarization provides the following benefits to well-designed IPX networks:

- Compact address representation—A single aggregated route efficiently represents many explicit routes.

- Reduced update bandwidth—Most changes in the explicit routes represented by an aggregated route do not need to be propagated to neighboring areas.

- Reduced computational overhead—Because the routers in one area are unaffected by most changes in adjacent areas, the SPF algorithm runs less often.

- Improved information management—Filtering of route and service information may be done at area boundaries.

As a result, you can build larger IPX networks using route aggregation.

## Understand Area Addresses, Route Summaries, and Aggregated Routes

This section discusses area addresses, route summaries, and aggregated routes. It also describes how area addresses relate to route summaries.

### Area Addresses

An *area address* uniquely identifies an NLSP area. The area addresses configured on each router determine the areas to which a router belongs.

An area address consists of a pair of 32-bit hexadecimal numbers that include an area number and a corresponding mask. The mask indicates how much of the area number identifies the area and how much identifies individual networks in the area. For example, the area address pair *12345600 FFFFFF00* describes an area composed of 256 networks in the range from 12345600 to 123456FF.

You can configure up to three area addresses per NLSP process on the router. Adjacencies are formed only between routers that share at least one common area address.

### Route Summaries

A *route summary* defines a set of explicit routes that the router uses to generate an aggregated route. A route summary tells the router how to summarize the set of explicit routes into a single summarized route.

A route summary is similar in form to an area address. That is, the route summary described by *12345600 FFFFFF00* summarizes the 256 networks in the range from 12345600 to 123456FF.

### Aggregated Routes

An *aggregated route* is the single, compact data structure that describes many IPX network numbers simultaneously. The aggregated route represents all the explicit routes defined by the route summary. In an LSP, the router expresses an aggregated route as a 1-byte number that gives the length, in bits, of the portion of the 32-bit network number common to all summarized addresses. The aggregated route for *12345600 FFFFFF00* is *18 12345600*.

### Relationship between Area Addresses and Route Summaries

When you enable route summarization in Release 11.1 while running multiple instances of NLSP, the router performs default route summarization based on the area address configured in each NLSP area. That is, explicit routes that match the area address in a given area are not redistributed individually into neighboring NLSP areas. Instead, the router redistributes a single aggregated route that is equivalent to the area address into neighboring areas.

## Understand NLSP Areas

This section describes single versus multiple NLSP areas and discusses the router's behavior when you mix NLSP versions within a single NLSP area.

### Single Versus Multiple NLSP Areas

NLSP version 1.0 routers support only a single, Level 1 area. Two routers form an adjacency only if they share at least one configured area address in common. The union of routers with adjacencies in common form an area.

Each router within the NLSP area has its own adjacencies, link-state, and forwarding databases. Further, each router's link-state database is identical. Within the router, these databases operate collectively as a single *process* or *instance* to discover, select, and maintain route information about the area. NLSP version 1.0 routers and NLSP version 1.1 routers that exist within a single area use a single NLSP instance.

With NLSP version 1.1 and Cisco IOS Release 11.1, multiple instances of NLSP may exist on a given router. Each instance discovers, selects, and maintains route information for a separate NLSP area. Each instance has its own copy of the NLSP adjacency and link-state database for its area. However, all instances (along with other routing protocols, such as RIP and Enhanced IGRP) share a single copy of the forwarding table.

### Mixing NLSP Versions in a Single Area

You can have NLSP version 1.1 routers and NLSP version 1.0 routers in the same area. However, NLSP version 1.0 routers do not recognize aggregated routes. For this reason, the default behavior of Cisco IOS Release 11.1 software is to not generate aggregated routes. To prevent routing loops in a mixed environment, packets routed via an aggregated route by an NLSP version 1.1 router are dropped if the next hop is an NLSP version 1.0 router.

— **NOTES** ———————————————————————

In general, you should ensure that all routers in an area are running NLSP version 1.1-capable software before you enable route summarization on any of the routers in an area.

### Understand Route Redistribution

Because you can configure multiple NLSP areas, you must understand how the router passes route information from one area to another. Passing route information from one area to another, or from one protocol to another, is known as *route redistribution*. Additionally, you must understand the router's default route redistribution behavior before configuring route summarization.

This section describes the default route redistribution behavior between multiple NLSP areas, between NLSP and Enhanced IGRP, and between NLSP and RIP.

#### Default Redistribution between Multiple NLSP Areas

Regardless of the NLSP version, Cisco IOS Release 11.1 redistributes routes between multiple NLSP areas by default. That is, redistribution between multiple NLSP version 1.1 areas, between multiple NLSP version 1.0 areas, and between NLSP version 1.1 and NLSP version 1.0 areas is enabled by default. All routes are redistributed as individual, explicit routes.

#### Default Redistribution between NLSP and Enhanced IGRP

Route redistribution between instances of NLSP (version 1.1 or version 1.0) and Enhanced IGRP is disabled by default. You must explicitly configure this type of redistribution. Refer to the "Redistribute Routing Information" section earlier in this chapter for information about configuring redistribution between NLSP and Enhanced IGRP.

#### Default Redistribution between NLSP and RIP

Route redistribution between instances of NLSP (version 1.1 or version 1.0) and RIP is enabled by default. All routes are redistributed as individual, explicit routes.

### Understand Route Summarization

Route summarization is disabled by default to avoid the generation of aggregated routes in an area running mixed versions of NLSP. You can explicitly enable route summarization on a router running Cisco IOS Release 11.1. This section describes default route summarization, customized route summarization, and the relationship between filtering and route summarization.

#### Default Route Summarization

When you explicitly enable route summarization, the default route summarization depends on the following circumstances:

- All routers use NLSP version 1.1—The area address for each NLSP instance is used as the basis for generating aggregated routes.
- Some routers use NLSP version 1.1 and some use NLSP version 1.0—The area address for each NLSP instance is used as the basis for generating aggregated routes; however, NLSP version 1.0 routers do not recognize aggregated routes. You must not enable route aggregation on the NLSP version 1.0 instance or you must configure customized route

summarization to prevent generation of aggregated routes from the NLSP version 1.0 areas. See the "Customized Route Summarization" section.

- Some routers use Enhanced IGRP and NLSP version 1.1—There is no default route summarization. You must configure customized route summarization to generate aggregated routes from Enhanced IGRP to NLSP version 1.1. See the "Customized Route Summarization" section.

- Some routers use RIP and NLSP version 1.1—There is no default route summarization. You must configure customized route summarization to generate aggregated routes from RIP to NLSP version 1.1. See the "Customized Route Summarization" section.

In the first two circumstances, the area address for each NLSP instance is used as the basis for generating aggregated routes. That is, all explicit routes that match a local area address generate a common aggregated route. The router redistributes only the aggregated route into other NLSP areas; explicit routes (and more specific aggregated routes) represented by a particular aggregated route are filtered.

---

**NOTES**

The router continues to redistribute into other areas the explicit routes that do *not* match the area address.

---

### Customized Route Summarization

You can also customize the router's route summarization behavior using the **redistribute** IPX-router subcommand with an access list. The access list specifies in detail which routes to summarize and which routes to redistribute explicitly. In this case, the router ignores area addresses and uses only the access list as a template to control summarization and redistribution. You can use numbered or named access lists to control summarization and redistribution.

In addition, you must use customized route summarization in environments that use either of the following combinations:

- Enhanced IGRP and NLSP version 1.1
- RIP and NLSP version 1.1

Route summarization between Enhanced IGRP and NLSP is controlled by the access list. Route summarization is possible only in the Enhanced IGRP-to-NLSP direction. Routes redistributed from NLSP to Enhanced IGRP are always explicit routes.

Route summarization between RIP and NLSP is also controlled by the access list. Route summarization is possible only in the RIP-to-NLSP direction. Routes redistributed from NLSP to RIP are always explicit routes. Use the default route instead to minimize routing update overhead, yet maximize reachability in a RIP-only area.

---

**NOTES**

---

Before introducing the default route into a RIP-only area, be sure that all routers and servers in the area are upgraded to understand and use the default route.

---

In a well-designed network, within each NLSP area, most external networks are reachable by a few aggregated routes, while all other external networks are reachable either by individual explicit routes or by the default route.

### Relationship between Filtering and Route Summarization

Redistribution of routes and services into and out of an NLSP area may be modified using filters. Filters are available for both input and output directions. Refer to the **distribute-list in, distribute-list out, distribute-sap-list in,** and **distribute-sap-list out** commands in Chapter 5, "Novell IPX Commands."

Filtering is independent of route summarization but may affect it indirectly because filters are always applied before the aggregation algorithm is applied. It is possible to filter all explicit routes that could generate aggregated routes, making the router unable to generate aggregated routes even though route aggregation is turned on.

## Understand Service and Path Selection

The router always accepts service information as long as the service's network is reachable by an explicit route, an aggregated route, or the default route. When choosing a server for a Get Nearest Server (GNS) response, the tick value of the route to each eligible server is used as the metric. No distinction is made between explicit and summary routes in this determination. If the tick values are equal, then the hop count is used as a tiebreaker. However, because there is no hop value associated with an aggregated route, services reachable via an explicit route are always preferred over those reachable via only an aggregated route.

An NLSP version 1.1 router always uses the most explicit match to route packets. That is, the router always uses an explicit route if possible. If not, then a matching aggregated route is used. If multiple aggregated routes match, then the most explicit (longest match) is used. If no aggregated route is present, then the default route is used as a last resort.

## Configure Route Aggregation Task List

To configure the route aggregation feature, perform one or more of the tasks in the following sections:

- Configure Route Aggregation for Multiple NLSP Version 1.1 Areas
- Configure Route Aggregation for NLSP Version 1.1 and NLSP Version 1.0 Areas
- Configure Route Aggregation for Enhanced IGRP and NLSP Version 1.1 Environments
- Configure Route Aggregation for RIP and NLSP Version 1.1 Environments

### Configure Route Aggregation for Multiple NLSP Version 1.1 Areas

Redistribution between multiple NLSP 1.1 areas is enabled by default. Because multiple NLSP processes are present on the router, a *tag* or label identifies each. For each instance, configure an appropriate area address and, optionally, enable route summarization. Finally, enable NLSP on appropriate interfaces. Be sure to use the correct tag (process) identifier to associate that interface with the appropriate NLSP area.

---

**NOTES**

---

Note that the tag used to identify an NLSP instance is meaningful only locally within the router. NLSP adjacencies and areas are determined by the area address and interfaces configured for each instance of NLSP running on each router. There is no need (other than administrative convenience) to ensure that individual tags match between routers.

---

The following sections describe how to configure route aggregation for multiple NLSP Version 1.1 areas:

- Configure Route Aggregation with Default Route Summarization
- Configure Route Aggregation with Customized Route Summarization Using Numbered Access Lists
- Configure Route Aggregation with Customized Route Summarization Using Named Access Lists

### Configure Route Aggregation with Default Route Summarization

To configure the route aggregation feature with the default route summarization behavior, perform these tasks for each NLSP process:

| Task | Command |
|------|---------|
| **Step 1** Enable NLSP routing and identify the process with a unique tag. | **ipx router nlsp** [*tag*] |
| **Step 2** From router configuration mode, define up to three area addresses for the process. | **area-address** *address mask* |
| **Step 3** (Optional.) From router configuration mode, enable route summarization. | **route-aggregation** |
| **Step 4** From interface configuration mode, enable NLSP on each network in the area described by the *tag* argument. | **ipx nlsp** [*tag*] **enable** |

For an example of how to configure this type of route aggregation, see "NLSP Route Aggregation for NLSP Version 1.1 and Version 1.0 Areas Example" section near the end of this chapter.

### Configure Route Aggregation with Customized Route Summarization Using Numbered Access Lists

To configure the route aggregation feature with customized route summarization behavior (using numbered access lists), perform these tasks for each NLSP process:

| Task | Command |
|------|---------|
| **Step 1** Enable NLSP routing and identify the process with a unique tag. | **ipx router nlsp** [*tag*] |
| **Step 2** From router configuration mode, define up to three area addresses for the process. | **area-address** *address mask* |
| **Step 3** Enable route summarization from router configuration mode. | **route-aggregation** |
| **Step 4** From router configuration mode, use the **redistribute** command with an access list in the range of 1200 to 1299. In this case, the *tag* argument identifies a unique NLSP process. | **redistribute nlsp** [*tag*] **access-list** *access-list-number* |
| **Step 5** From interface configuration mode, enable NLSP on each network in the area described by the *tag* argument. | **ipx nlsp** [*tag*] **enable** |
| **Step 6** From global configuration mode, define the access list to redistribute an aggregated route instead of the explicit route. For each address range you want to summarize, use the **deny** keyword. | **access-list** *access-list-number* **deny** *network network-mask* [**ticks** *ticks*] [**area-count** *area-count*] |
| **Step 7** (Optional.) Terminate the access list with a "permit all" statement to redistribute all other routes as explicit routes. | **access-list** *access-list-number* **permit -1** |

### Configure Route Aggregation with Customized Route Summarization Using Named Access Lists

To configure the route aggregation feature with customized route summarization behavior (using named access lists), perform these tasks for each NLSP process:

| Task | | Command |
|------|------|---------|
| Step 1 | Enable NLSP routing and identify the process with a unique tag. | **ipx router nlsp** [*tag*] |
| Step 2 | From router configuration mode, define up to three area addresses for the process. | **area-address** *address mask* |
| Step 3 | Enable route summarization from router configuration mode. | **route-aggregation** |
| Step 4 | From router configuration mode, use the **redistribute** command with a named access list. In this case, the *tag* argument identifies a unique NLSP process. | **redistribute nlsp** [*tag*] **access-list** *name* |
| Step 5 | From interface configuration mode, enable NLSP on each network in the area described by the *tag* argument. | **ipx nlsp** [*tag*] **enable** |
| Step 6 | From global configuration mode, specify a named IPX access list for NLSP route aggregation. | **ipx access-list summary** *name* |
| Step 7 | In access-list configuration mode, specify the redistribution of aggregated routes instead of explicit routes. For each address range you want to summarize, enter a **deny** statement. | **deny** *network network-mask* [**ticks** *ticks*] [**area-count** *area-count*] |
| Step 8 | (Optional.) Terminate the access list with a "permit all" statement to redistribute all other routes as explicit routes. | **permit -1** |

### Configure Route Aggregation for NLSP Version 1.1 and NLSP Version 1.0 Areas

By default, redistribution is enabled between multiple instances of NLSP. Route summarization, when enabled, is possible in one direction only—from NLSP version 1.0 to NLSP version 1.1.

The following sections describe how to configure route aggregation for NLSP Version 1.1 and NLSP Version 1.0 areas:

- Configure Route Aggregation with Default Route Summarization
- Configure Route Aggregation with Customized Route Summarization Using Numbered Access Lists
- Configure Route Aggregation with Customized Route Summarization Using Named Access Lists

#### Configure Route Aggregation with Default Route Summarization

To configure the route aggregation feature with default route summarization behavior, perform the following tasks for each NLSP process:

| Task | Command |
| --- | --- |
| **Step 1** Enable NLSP routing and identify the process with a unique tag. | **ipx router nlsp** [*tag*] |
| **Step 2** From router configuration mode, define up to three area addresses for the process. | **area-address** *address mask* |
| **Step 3** For NLSP version 1.1 areas, enable route summarization from router configuration mode. Skip this step for NLSP version 1.0 areas. | **route-aggregation** |
| **Step 4** From interface configuration mode, enable NLSP on each network in the area described by the *tag* argument. | **ipx nlsp** [*tag*] **enable** |

#### Configure Route Aggregation with Customized Route Summarization Using Numbered Access Lists

To configure the route aggregation feature with customized route summarization behavior (using numbered access lists), perform the tasks in the following two tables.

For the NLSP version 1.1 process, perform these tasks:

| Task | | Command |
|------|---|---------|
| Step 1 | Enable NLSP routing and identify the process with a unique tag. | **ipx router nlsp** [*tag*] |
| Step 2 | From router configuration mode, define up to three area addresses for the process. | **area-address** *address mask* |
| Step 3 | For NLSP version 1.1 areas, enable route summarization from router configuration mode. | **route-aggregation** |
| Step 4 | (Optional.) From router configuration mode, redistribute NLSP version 1.0 into the NLSP version 1.1 area. Include an access list number between 1200 and 1299. | **redistribute nlsp** [*tag*] **access-list** *access-list-number* |
| Step 5 | From interface configuration mode, enable NLSP on each network in the area described by the *tag* argument. | **ipx nlsp** [*tag*] **enable** |
| Step 6 | (Optional.) From global configuration mode, define the access list to redistribute an aggregated route instead of explicit routes learned from the NLSP version 1.0 area. For each address range you want to summarize, use the **deny** keyword. | **access-list** *access-list-number* **deny** *network network-mask* [**ticks** *ticks*] [**area-count** *area-count*] |
| Step 7 | (Optional.) Terminate the access list with a "permit all" statement to redistribute all other routes as explicit routes. | **access-list** *access-list-number* **permit -1** |

For the NLSP version 1.0 process, perform these tasks:

| Task | | Command |
|------|---|---------|
| Step 1 | Enable NLSP routing and identify the process with a unique tag. | **ipx router nlsp** [*tag*] |

| | | |
|---|---|---|
| **Step 2** | From router configuration mode, define up to three area addresses for the process. | **area-address** *address mask* |
| **Step 3** | From interface configuration mode, enable NLSP on each network in the area described by the *tag* argument. | **ipx nlsp** [*tag*] **enable** |

For an example of how to configure the route aggregation feature with this type of customized route summarization, refer to the "NLSP Route Aggregation for NLSP Version 1.1 and Version 1.0 Areas Example" section near the end of this chapter.

### Configure Route Aggregation with Customized Route Summarization Using Named Access Lists

To configure the route aggregation feature with customized route summarization behavior (using named access lists), perform the tasks in the following two tables.

For the NLSP version 1.1 process, perform these tasks:

| Task | | Command |
|---|---|---|
| **Step 1** | Enable NLSP routing and identify the process with a unique tag. | **ipx router nlsp** [*tag*] |
| **Step 2** | From router configuration mode, define up to three area addresses for the process. | **area-address** *address mask* |
| **Step 3** | For NLSP version 1.1 areas, enable route summarization from router configuration mode. | **route-aggregation** |
| **Step 4** | (Optional.) From router configuration mode, redistribute NLSP version 1.0 into the NLSP version 1.1 area. | **redistribute nlsp** [*tag*] **access-list** *name* |
| **Step 5** | From interface configuration mode, enable NLSP on each network in the area described by the *tag* argument. | **ipx nlsp** [*tag*] **enable** |
| **Step 6** | (Optional.) From global configuration mode, specify a named IPX access list for NLSP route aggregation. | **ipx access-list summary** *name* |

| Task | Command |
|------|---------|
| **Step 7** (Optional.) From access-list configuration mode, define the access list to redistribute an aggregated route instead of explicit routes learned from the NLSP version 1.0 area. For each address range you want to summarize, enter a **deny** statement. | **deny** *network network-mask* [**ticks** *ticks*] [**area-count** *area-count*] |
| **Step 8** (Optional.) Terminate the access list with a "permit all" statement to redistribute all other routes as explicit routes. | **permit -1** |

For the NLSP version 1.0 process, perform these tasks:

| Task | Command |
|------|---------|
| **Step 1** Enable NLSP routing and identify the process with a unique tag. | **ipx router nlsp** [*tag*] |
| **Step 2** From router configuration mode, define up to three area addresses for the process. | **area-address** *address mask* |
| **Step 3** From interface configuration mode, enable NLSP on each network in the area described by the *tag* argument. | **ipx nlsp** [*tag*] **enable** |

### Configure Route Aggregation for Enhanced IGRP and NLSP Version 1.1 Environments

Redistribution is not enabled by default. Additionally, summarization is possible in the Enhanced IGRP to NLSP direction only.

The following sections describe how to configure route aggregation for Enhanced IGRP and NLSP Version 1.1 environments:

- Configure Route Aggregation Using Numbered Access Lists
- Configure Route Aggregation Using Named Access Lists

*Configure Route Aggregation Using Numbered Access Lists*

For each NLSP version 1.1 process, perform these tasks, beginning in global configuration mode:

| Task | Command |
|------|---------|
| **Step 1** Enable NLSP routing and identify the process with a unique tag. | **ipx router nlsp** [*tag*] |
| **Step 2** From router configuration mode, define up to three area addresses for the process. | **area-address** *address mask* |
| **Step 3** (Optional.) From router configuration mode, enable route summarization. | **route-aggregation** |
| **Step 4** (Optional.) From router configuration mode, redistribute Enhanced IGRP into the NLSP version 1.1 area. Include an access list number between 1200 and 1299. | **redistribute** {**eigrp** *autonomous-system-number*} [**access-list** *access-list-number* |
| **Step 5** From interface configuration mode, enable NLSP on each network in the area described by the *tag* argument. | **ipx nlsp** [*tag*] **enable** |
| **Step 6** (Optional.) From global configuration mode, define the access list to redistribute an aggregated route instead of explicit routes learned from Enhanced IGRP. For each address range you want to summarize, use the **deny** keyword. | **access-list** *access-list-number* **deny** *network network-mask* [**ticks** *ticks*] [**area-count** *area-count*] |
| **Step 7** (Optional.) Terminate the access list with a "permit all" statement to redistribute all other Enhanced IGRP routes as explicit routes. | **access-list** *access-list-number* **permit -1** |

For each Enhanced IGRP autonomous system, perform these tasks, beginning in global configuration mode:

| Task | Command |
| --- | --- |
| **Step 1** Enable Enhanced IGRP. | **ipx router eigrp** *autonomous-system-number* |
| **Step 2** From router configuration mode, specify the networks to be enabled for Enhanced IGRP. | **network** {*network-number* \| **all**} |
| **Step 3** From router configuration mode, redistribute NLSP version 1.1 into Enhanced IGRP. | **redistribute nlsp** [*tag*] |

For an example of how to configure this type of route aggregation, refer to the "NLSP Route Aggregation for NLSP Version 1.1, Enhanced IGRP, and RIP Example" section near the end of this chapter.

### Configure Route Aggregation Using Named Access Lists

For each NLSP version 1.1 process, perform these tasks, beginning in global configuration mode:

| Task | Command |
| --- | --- |
| **Step 1** Enable NLSP routing and identify the process with a unique tag. | **ipx router nlsp** [*tag*] |
| **Step 2** From router configuration mode, define up to three area addresses for the process. | **area-address** *address mask* |
| **Step 3** (Optional.) From router configuration mode, enable route summarization. | **route-aggregation** |
| **Step 4** (Optional.) From router configuration mode, redistribute Enhanced IGRP into the NLSP version 1.1 area. | **redistribute** {**eigrp** *autonomous-system-number*} **access-list** *name* |
| **Step 5** From interface configuration mode, enable NLSP on each network in the area described by the *tag* argument. | **ipx nlsp** [*tag*] **enable** |
| **Step 6** (Optional.) From global configuration mode, specify a named IPX access list for NLSP route aggregation. | **ipx access-list summary** *name* |

| | | |
|---|---|---|
| Step 7 | (Optional.) From access-list configuration mode, define the access list to redistribute an aggregated route instead of explicit routes learned from Enhanced IGRP. For each address range you want to summarize, enter a **deny** statement. | **deny** *network network-mask* [**ticks** *ticks*] [**area-count** *area-count*] |
| Step 8 | (Optional.) Terminate the access list with a "permit all" statement to redistribute all other Enhanced IGRP routes as explicit routes. | **permit -1** |

For each Enhanced IGRP autonomous system, perform these tasks, beginning in global configuration mode:

| Task | Command |
|---|---|
| Step 1 Enable Enhanced IGRP. | **ipx router eigrp** *autonomous-system-number* |
| Step 2 From router configuration mode, specify the networks to be enabled for Enhanced IGRP. | **network** {*network-number* | **all**} |
| Step 3 From router configuration mode, redistribute NLSP version 1.1 into Enhanced IGRP. | **redistribute nlsp** [*tag*] |

### Configure Route Aggregation for RIP and NLSP Version 1.1 Environments

Because redistribution between RIP and NLSP is enabled by default, you only need to enable the route summarization, if desired, to configure all the capabilities of the route aggregation feature.

The following sections describe how to configure route aggregation for RIP and NLSP Version 1.1 environments:

* Configure Route Aggregation Using Numbered Access Lists
* Configure Route Aggregation Using Named Access Lists

## Configure Route Aggregation Using Numbered Access Lists

For each NLSP version 1.1 process, perform these tasks, beginning in global configuration mode:

| Task | Command |
|---|---|
| **Step 1** Enable NLSP routing and identify the process with a unique tag. | **ipx router nlsp** [*tag*] |
| **Step 2** From router configuration mode, define up to three area addresses for the process. | **area-address** *address mask* |
| **Step 3** (Optional.) From router configuration mode, enable route summarization. | **route-aggregation** |
| **Step 4** (Optional.) From router configuration mode, redistribute RIP routes into the NLSP version 1.1 area. Include an access list number between 1200 and 1299. | **redistribute rip** [**access-list** *access-list-number*] |
| **Step 5** From interface configuration mode, enable NLSP on each network in the area described by the *tag* argument. | **ipx nlsp** [*tag*] **enable** |
| **Step 6** (Optional.) From global configuration mode, define the access list to redistribute an aggregated route instead of explicit RIP routes. For each address range you want to summarize, use the **deny** keyword. | **access-list** *access-list-number* **deny** *network network-mask* [**ticks** *ticks*] [**area-count** *area-count*] |
| **Step 7** (Optional.) Terminate the access list with a "permit all" statement to redistribute all other RIP routes as explicit routes. | **access-list** *access-list-number* **permit -1** |

For an example of how to configure this type of route aggregation, refer to the "NLSP Route Aggregation for NLSP Version 1.1, Enhanced IGRP, and RIP Example" section near the end of this chapter.

*Configure Route Aggregation Using Named Access Lists*

For each NLSP version 1.1 process, perform these tasks, beginning in global configuration mode:

| Task | | Command |
|------|---|---------|
| Step 1 | Enable NLSP routing and identify the process with a unique tag. | **ipx router nlsp** [*tag*] |
| Step 2 | From router configuration mode, define up to three area addresses for the process. | **area-address** *address mask* |
| Step 3 | (Optional.) From router configuration mode, enable route summarization. | **route-aggregation** |
| Step 4 | (Optional.) From router configuration mode, redistribute RIP routes into the NLSP version 1.1 area. | **redistribute rip access-list** *name* |
| Step 5 | From interface configuration mode, enable NLSP on each network in the area described by the *tag* argument. | **ipx nlsp** [*tag*] **enable** |
| Step 6 | (Optional.) From global configuration mode, specify a named IPX access list for NLSP route aggregation. | **ipx access-list summary** *name* |
| Step 7 | (Optional.) From access-list configuration mode, define the access list to redistribute an aggregated route instead of explicit RIP routes. For each address range you want to summarize, enter a **deny** statement. | **deny** *network network-mask* [**ticks** *ticks*] [**area-count** *area-count*] |
| Step 8 | (Optional.) Terminate the access list with a "permit all" statement to redistribute all other RIP routes as explicit routes. | **permit -1** |

## Customize the Exchange of Routing Information

You might want to customize the exchange of routing information. The following sections describe customization tasks:

- Configure RIP and SAP Compatibility
- Redistribute Routing Information

### Configure RIP and SAP Compatibility

Routing Information Protocol (RIP) and Service Advertising Protocol (SAP) are enabled by default on all interfaces configured for IPX, and these interfaces always respond to RIP and SAP requests. When you also enable NLSP on an interface, the interface, by default, generates and sends RIP and SAP periodic traffic only if another RIP router or SAP service is sending RIP or SAP traffic.

To modify the generation of periodic RIP updates on a network enabled for NLSP, perform one of the following tasks in interface configuration mode:

| Task | Command |
| --- | --- |
| **Step 1** Never generate RIP periodic traffic. | **ipx nlsp** [*tag*] **rip off** |
| **Step 2** Always generate RIP periodic traffic. | **ipx nlsp** [*tag*] **rip on** |
| **Step 3** Send RIP periodic traffic only if another RIP router is sending periodic RIP traffic. (This is the default on interfaces configured for NLSP.) | **ipx nlsp** [*tag*] **rip auto** |

To modify the generation of periodic SAP updates on a network enabled for NLSP, perform one of the following tasks in interface configuration mode:

| Task | Command |
| --- | --- |
| **Step 1** Never generate SAP periodic traffic. | **ipx nlsp** [*tag*] **sap off** |
| **Step 2** Always generate SAP periodic traffic. | **ipx nlsp** [*tag*] **sap on** |
| **Step 3** Send SAP periodic traffic only if another SAP service is sending periodic SAP traffic. (This is the default on interfaces configured for NLSP.) | **ipx nlsp** [*tag*] **sap auto** |

### Redistribute Routing Information

Automatic redistribution of one routing protocol into another provides a simple and effective means for building IPX networks in a heterogeneous routing protocol environment. Redistribution is usually effective as soon as you enable an IPX routing protocol. One exception is NLSP and Enhanced IGRP. You must configure the redistribution of Enhanced IGRP into NLSP and vice versa.

After you enable Enhanced IGRP and NLSP redistribution, the router makes path decisions based on a predefined, nonconfigurable administrative distance and prevents redistribution feedback loops without filtering via a stored, external hop count.

To enable redistribution of Enhanced IGRP into NLSP and vice versa, perform the following tasks, beginning in global configuration mode:

| Task | Command |
|------|---------|
| **Step 1** Enable NLSP. | **ipx router nlsp** [*tag*] |
| **Step 2** From IPX-router configuration mode, enable redistribution of Enhanced IGRP into NLSP. | **redistribute eigrp** *autonomous-system-number* |
| **Step 3** From global configuration mode, enable Enhanced IGRP. | **ipx router eigrp** *autonomous-system-number* |
| **Step 4** From IPX-router configuration mode, enable redistribution of NLSP into Enhanced IGRP. | **redistribute nlsp** [*tag*] |

For an example of how to enable redistribution of Enhanced IGRP and NLSP, see the "Enhanced IGRP and NLSP Route Redistribution Example" section near the end of this chapter.

## CONFIGURING NEXT HOP RESOLUTION PROTOCOL

Routers, access servers, and hosts can use Next Hop Resolution Protocol (NHRP) to discover the addresses of other routers and hosts connected to a nonbroadcast, multiaccess (NBMA) network. NHRP provides an ARP-like solution that alleviates some NBMA network problems. With NHRP, systems attached to an NBMA network can dynamically learn the NBMA address of the other systems that are part of that network. These systems can then directly communicate without requiring traffic to use an intermediate hop.

### NHRP Configuration Task List

To configure NHRP, perform the tasks described in the following sections. The first task is required; the remainder are optional.

- Enable NHRP on an Interface
- Configure a Station's Static IPX-to-NBMA Address Mapping
- Statically Configure a Next Hop Server
- Configure NHRP Authentication
- Control NHRP Initiation
- Control NHRP Packet Rate
- Suppress Forward and Reverse Record Options
- Specify the NHRP Responder Address
- Change the Time Period NBMA Addresses Are Advertised as Valid

For NHRP configuration examples, see the "NHRP Examples" section near the end of this chapter.

## Enable NHRP on an Interface

To enable NHRP for an interface on a router, perform the following task in interface configuration mode. In general, all NHRP stations within a logical NBMA network must be configured with the same network identifier.

| Task | Command |
| --- | --- |
| Enable NHRP on an interface. | **ipx nhrp network-id** *number* |

For an example of enabling NHRP, see the "NHRP Examples" section near the end of this chapter.

## Configure a Station's Static IPX-to-NBMA Address Mapping

To participate in NHRP, a station connected to an NBMA network must be configured with the IPX and NBMA addresses of its Next Hop Servers. The format of the NBMA address depends on the medium you are using. For example, ATM uses a network-layer service access point (NSAP) address, Ethernet uses a MAC address, and SMDS uses an E.164 address.

These Next Hop Servers are most likely the stations's default or peer routers, so their IPX addresses are obtained from the station's network layer forwarding table.

If the station is attached to several link layer networks (including logical NBMA networks), the station should also be configured to receive routing information from its Next Hop Servers and peer routers so that it can determine which IPX networks are reachable through which link layer networks.

To configure static IPX-to-NBMA address mapping on a station (host or router), perform the following task in interface configuration mode:

| Task | Command |
| --- | --- |
| Configure static IPX-to-NBMA address mapping. | **ipx nhrp map** *ipx-address nbma-address* |

## Statically Configure a Next Hop Server

A Next Hop Server normally uses the network layer forwarding table to determine where to forward NHRP packets and to find the egress point from an NBMA network. A Next Hop Server may alternately be statically configured with a set of IPX address prefixes that correspond to the IPX addresses of the stations it serves and their logical NBMA network identifiers.

To statically configure a Next Hop Server, perform the following task in interface configuration mode:

| Task | Command |
|------|---------|
| Statically configure a Next Hop Server. | **ipx nhrp nhs** *nhs-address* [*net-number*] |

To configure multiple networks that the Next Hop Server serves, repeat the **ipx nhrp nhs** command with the same Next Hop Server address, but different IPX network addresses. To configure additional Next Hop Servers, repeat the **ipx nhrp nhs** command.

## Configure NHRP Authentication

Configuring an authentication string ensures that only routers configured with the same string can intercommunicate using NHRP. Therefore, if the authentication scheme is to be used, the same string must be configured in all devices configured for NHRP on a fabric. To specify the authentication string for NHRP on an interface, perform the following task in interface configuration mode:

| Task | Command |
|------|---------|
| Specify an authentication string. | **ipx nhrp authentication** *string* |

## Control NHRP Initiation

Complete one of the tasks in the following sections to control when NHRP is initiated:

- Trigger NHRP by IPX Packet
- Trigger NHRP on a Per-Destination Basis

### Trigger NHRP by IPX Packet

You can specify an IPX access list that is used to decide which IPX packets trigger the sending of NHRP requests. By default, all non-NHRP packets can trigger NHRP requests. To limit which IPX packets trigger NHRP requests, you must define an access list and then apply it to the interface.

To define an access list, perform one of the following tasks in global configuration mode:

| Task | Command |
|------|---------|
| **Step 1** Define a standard IPX access list. | **access-list** *access-list-number* {**deny** \| **permit**} *source-network*[.*source-node*[*source-node-mask*]] [*destination-network*[.*destination-node* [*destination-node-mask*]]] |

| Task | Command |
|---|---|
| **Step 2** Define an extended IPX access list. | **access-list** *access-list-number* {**deny** \| **permit**} *protocol* [*source-network*] [[[.*source-node*] *source-node-mask*] \| [.*source-node source-network-mask.source-node-mask*]] [*source-socket*] [*destination.network*] [[[.*destination-node*] *destination-node-mask*] \| [.*destination-node destination-network-mask .destination-nodemask*]] [*destination-socket*] |

Then apply the IPX access list to the interface by performing the following task in interface configuration mode:

| Task | Command |
|---|---|
| Specify an IPX access list that controls NHRP requests. | **ipx nhrp interest** *access-list-number* |

### Trigger NHRP on a Per-Destination Basis

By default, when the software attempts to transmit a data packet to a destination for which it has determined that NHRP can be used, it transmits an NHRP request for that destination. You can configure the system to wait until a specified number of data packets have been sent to a particular destination before NHRP is attempted. To do so, perform the following task in interface configuration mode:

| Task | Command |
|---|---|
| Specify how many data packets are sent to a destination before NHRP is attempted. | **ipx nhrp use** *usage-count* |

### Control NHRP Packet Rate

By default, the maximum rate at which the software sends NHRP packets is 5 packets per 10 seconds. The software maintains a per-interface quota of NHRP packets (whether generated locally or forwarded) that can be transmitted. To change this maximum rate, perform the following task in interface configuration mode:

| Task | Command |
|---|---|
| Change the NHRP packet rate per interface. | **ipx nhrp max-send** *pkt-count* **every** *interval* |

## Suppress Forward and Reverse Record Options

To dynamically detect link-layer filtering in NBMA networks (for example, SMDS address screens) and to provide loop detection and diagnostic capabilities, NHRP incorporates a route record in requests and replies. The route record options contain the network (and link layer) addresses of all intermediate Next Hop Servers between source and destination (in the forward direction) and between destination and source (in the reverse direction).

By default, forward record options and reverse record options are included in NHRP request and reply packets. To suppress the use of these options, perform the following task in interface configuration mode:

| Task | Command |
|------|---------|
| Suppress forward and reverse record options. | **no ipx nhrp record** |

## Specify the NHRP Responder Address

If an NHRP requester wants to know which Next Hop Server generates an NHRP reply packet, it can request that information by including the responder address option in its NHRP request packet. The Next Hop Server that generates the NHRP reply packet then complies by inserting its own IPX address in the NHRP reply. The Next Hop Server uses the primary IPX address of the specified interface.

To specify which interface the Next Hop Server uses for the NHRP responder IPX address, perform the following task in interface configuration mode:

| Task | Command |
|------|---------|
| Specify which interface the Next Hop Server uses to determine the NHRP responder address. | **ipx nhrp responder** *type number* |

If an NHRP reply packet being forwarded by a Next Hop Server contains that Next Hop Server's own IPX address, the Next Hop Server generates an "NHRP Loop Detected" error indication and discards the reply.

## Change the Time Period NBMA Addresses Are Advertised as Valid

You can change the length of time that NBMA addresses are advertised as valid in positive and negative NHRP responses. In this context, advertised means how long the Cisco IOS software tells other routers to keep the addresses it is providing in NHRP responses. The default length of time for each response is 7,200 seconds (2 hours). To change the length of time, perform the following task in interface configuration mode:

| Task | Command |
|------|---------|
| Specify the number of seconds that NBMA addresses are advertised as valid in positive or negative NHRP responses. | **ipx nhrp holdtime** *seconds-positive* [*seconds-negative*] |

## CONFIGURING IPX AND SPX OVER WANS

You can configure IPX over dial-on-demand routing (DDR), Frame Relay, Point-to-Point Protocol (PPP), Switched Multimegabit Data Service (SMDS), and X.25 networks. To do this, you configure address mappings as described in the appropriate chapter.

When you configure IPX over PPP, address maps are not necessary for this protocol. Also, you can enable IPX header compression over point-to-point links to increase available useful bandwidth of the link and reduce response time for interactive uses of the link.

You can use fast-switching IPX serial interfaces configured for Frame Relay and SMDS, and you can use fast-switching SNAP-encapsulated packets over interfaces configured for ATM.

Additionally, you can configure the IPXWAN protocol.

For an example of how to configure IPX over a WAN interface, see the "IPX over a WAN Interface Example" section near the end of this chapter.

### Configure IPX over DDR

IPX sends periodic watchdog (keepalive) packets. These are keepalive packets that are sent from servers to clients after a client session has been idle for approximately 5 minutes. On a DDR link, this means that a call would be made every 5 minutes, regardless of whether there were data packets to send. You can prevent these calls from being made by configuring the Cisco IOS software to respond to the server's watchdog packets on a remote client's behalf. This is sometimes referred to as *spoofing the server*.

When configuring IPX over DDR, you might want to disable the generation of these packets so that a call is not made every 5 minutes. This is not an issue for the other WAN protocols because they establish dedicated connections rather than establishing connections only as needed.

For an example of configuring IPX over DDR, see the "IPX over DDR Example" section near the end of this chapter.

### Configure SPX Spoofing over DDR

Sequenced Packet Exchange (SPX) sends periodic keepalive packets between clients and servers. Similar to IPX watchdog packets, these are keepalive packets that are sent between servers and clients after the data has stopped being transferred. On pay-per-packet or byte networks, these packets can incur large customer telephone connection charges for idle time. You can prevent these calls from being made by configuring the Cisco IOS software to respond to the keepalive packets on behalf of a remote system.

When configuring SPX over DDR, you might want to disable the generation of these packets so that a call has the opportunity to go idle. This may not be an issue for the other WAN protocols because they establish dedicated connections rather than establishing connections only as needed.

For an example of how to configure SPX spoofing over DDR, see the "IPX over DDR Example" section near the end of this chapter.

### Configure IPX Header Compression

You can configure IPX header compression over point-to-point links. With IPX header compression, a point-to-point link can compress IPX headers only or the combined IPX and NetWare Core Protocol headers. Currently, point-to-point links must first negotiate IPX header compression via IPXCP or IXPWAN. The Cisco IOS software supports IPX header compression as defined by RFC 1553.

### Configure the IPXWAN Protocol

The Cisco IOS software supports the IPXWAN protocol, as defined in RFC 1634. IPXWAN allows a router that is running IPX routing to connect via a serial link to another router, possibly from another manufacturer, that is also routing IPX and using IPXWAN.

IPXWAN is a connection start-up protocol. After a link has been established, IPXWAN incurs little or no overhead.

You can use the IPXWAN protocol over PPP. You can also use it over HDLC; however, the devices at both ends of the serial link must be Cisco routers.

To configure IPXWAN, perform the following tasks in interface configuration mode on a serial interface:

| Task | Command |
| --- | --- |
| **Step 1** Ensure that you have not configured an IPX network number on the interface. | no ipx network |
| **Step 2** Enable PPP. | encapsulation ppp |
| **Step 3** Enable IPXWAN. | ipx ipxwan [*local-node* {*network-number* \| unnumbered} *local-server-name retry-interval retry-limit*] |

| Task | Command |
|------|---------|
| **Step 4** Optionally, define how to handle IPXWAN when a serial link fails. | **ipx ipxwan error [reset | resume | shutdown]** |
| **Step 5** Optionally, enable static routing with IPXWAN. Note that the remote site must also use static routing. | **ipx ipxwan static** |

## CONTROLLING ACCESS TO IPX NETWORKS

To control access to IPX networks, you create access lists and then apply them to individual interfaces using filters.

### Types of Access Lists

You can create the following IPX access lists to filter various kinds of traffic:

- Standard access list—Restricts traffic based on the source network number. You can further restrict traffic by specifying a destination address and a source and destination address mask. Standard IPX access lists use numbers from 800 to 899 or names to identify them.

- Extended access list—Restricts traffic based on the IPX protocol type. You can further restrict traffic by specifying source and destination addresses and address masks and source and destination sockets. Extended IPX access lists use numbers from 900 to 999 or names to identify them.

- SAP access list—Restricts traffic based on the IPX Service Advertising Protocol (SAP) type. These lists are used for SAP filters and Get Nearest Server (GNS) response filters. Novell SAP access lists use numbers from 1,000 to 1,099 or names to identify them.

- IPX NetBIOS access list—Restricts IPX NetBIOS traffic based on NetBIOS names, not numbers.

- NLSP route aggregation access list—Specifies in detail which routes to summarize and which routes to redistribute explicitly. Route aggregation is discussed in detail in the "Configure Route Aggregation" section. Refer to that section for more information.

### Types of Filters

There are more than 14 different IPX filters that you can define for IPX interfaces. They fall into the following six groups:

- Generic filters—Control which data packets are routed in or out of an interface based on the packet's source and destination addresses and IPX protocol type.

- Routing table filters—Control which Routing Information Protocol (RIP) updates are accepted and advertised by the Cisco IOS software and from which devices the local router accepts RIP updates.

- SAP filters—Control which SAP services the Cisco IOS software accepts and advertises and which Get Nearest Server (GNS) response messages it sends out.

- IPX NetBIOS filters—Control incoming and outgoing IPX NetBIOS packets.

- Broadcast filters—Control which broadcast packets are forwarded.

- NLSP route aggregation filters—Control the redistribution of routes and services into and out of an NLSP area.

Table 4–2 summarizes the filters, the access lists they use, and the commands used to define the filters in the first five groups. Use the **show ipx interfaces** command to display the filters defined on an interface. Route aggregation is discussed in detail in the "Configure Route Aggregation" section. Refer to that section for additional information.

**Table 4–2**   *IPX Filters*

| Filter Type | Access List Used by Filter | Command to Define Filter |
|---|---|---|
| **Generic filters** | | |
| Filter inbound or outbound packets based on the contents of the IPX network header. | Standard or Extended | **ipx access-group** {*access-list-number* \| *name*} [**in** \| **out**] |
| **Routing table filters** | | |
| Control which networks are added to the routing table. | Standard or Extended | **ipx input-network-filter** {*access-list-number* \| *name*} |
| Control which networks are advertised in routing updates. | Standard or Extended | **ipx output-network-filter** {*access-list-number* \| *name*} |
| Control which networks are advertised in the Enhanced IGRP routing updates sent out by the Cisco IOS software. | Standard or Extended | **distribute-list** {*access-list-number* \| *name*} **out** [*interface-name* \| *routing-process*] |
| Control the routers from which updates are accepted. | Standard or Extended | **ipx router-filter** {*access-list-number* \| *name*} |
| **SAP filters** | | |
| Filter incoming service advertisements. | SAP | **ipx input-sap-filter** {*access-list-number* \| *name*} |

**Table 4–2**  *IPX Filters*

| Filter Type | Access List Used by Filter | Command to Define Filter |
|---|---|---|
| Filter outgoing service advertisements. | SAP | **ipx output-sap-filter** {*access-list-number* \| *name*} |
| Control the routers from which SAP updates are accepted. | SAP | **ipx router-sap-filter** {*access-list-number* \| *name*} |
| Filter list of servers in GNS response messages. | SAP | **ipx output-gns-filter** {*access-list-number* \| *name*} |
| **IPX NetBIOS filters** | | |
| Filter incoming packets by node name. | IPX NetBIOS | **ipx netbios input-access-filter host** *name* |
| Filter incoming packets by byte pattern. | IPX NetBIOS | **ipx netbios input-access-filter bytes** *name* |
| Filter outgoing packets by node name. | IPX NetBIOS | **ipx netbios output-access-filter host** *name* |
| Filter outgoing packets by byte pattern. | IPX NetBIOS | **ipx netbios output-access-filter bytes** *name* |
| **Broadcast filters** | | |
| Control which broadcast packets are forwarded. | Standard or Extended | **ipx helper-list** {*access-list-number* \| *name*} |

## Implementation Considerations

Keep the following information in mind when configuring IPX network access control:

- Access lists entries are scanned in the order you enter them. The first matching entry is used. To improve performance, it is recommended that you place the most commonly used entries near the beginning of the access list.

- An implicit *deny everything* entry is defined near the end of an access list unless you include an explicit *permit everything* entry near the end of the list.

- For numbered access lists, all new entries to an existing list are placed near the end of the list. You cannot add an entry to the middle of a list. This means that if you have previously included an explicit *permit everything* entry, new entries are never scanned. The solution is to delete the access list and re-enter it with the new entries.

  For named access lists, all new entries to an existing list are placed near the end of the list. You cannot add entries to the middle of a list. However, you can remove specific entries using the **no deny** and **no permit** commands, rather than deleting the entire access list.

- Do not to set up conditions that result in packets getting lost. One way this can happen is when a device or interface is configured to advertise services on a network that has access lists that deny these packets.

- You cannot filter SAP packets within an NLSP area. You can filter them at the boundary of NLSP and RIP/SAP areas, though restrictions do apply.

## Control Access to IPX Networks Task List

You perform the required tasks in the following section to control access to IPX networks:

- Create Access Lists
- Create Filters

## Create Access Lists

You can create access lists using numbers or names. You can choose which method you prefer. If you use numbers to identify your access lists, you are limited to 100 access lists per filter type. If you use names to identify your access lists, you can have an unlimited number of access lists per filter type.

The following sections describe how to perform these tasks:

- Create Access Lists Using Numbers
- Create Access Lists Using Names

### Create Access Lists Using Numbers

To create access lists using numbers, you can perform one or more of the following tasks in global configuration mode:

| Task | | Command |
|------|---|---------|
| **Step 1** | Create a standard IPX access list using a number. (Generic, routing, and broadcast filters use this type of access list.) | **access-list** *access-list-number* {**deny** \| **permit**} *source-network*[*.source-node*[*source-node-mask*]] [*destination-network*[*.destination-node* [*destination-node-mask*]]] |
| **Step 2** | Create an extended IPX access list using a number. (Generic, routing, and broadcast filters use this type of access list.) | **access-list** *access-list-number* {**deny** \| **permit**} *protocol* [*source-network*[*.source-node* [*source-network-mask.source-node-mask*]] *source-socket* [*destination-network* [*.destination-node* [*destination-network-mask.destination-node-mas k*] *destination-socket*] [**log**] |

| Task | Command |
|------|---------|
| **Step 3** Create a SAP filtering access list using a number. (SAP and GNS response filters use this type of access list). | **access-list** *access-list-number* {**deny** \| **permit**} *network*[*.node*] [*network-mask node-mask*] [*service-type* [*server-name*]] |

After you have created an access list using numbers, apply it to the appropriate interfaces using filters, as described in the "Create Filters" section of this chapter. This activates the access list.

## Create Access Lists Using Names

IPX named access lists enable you to identify IPX access lists with an alphanumeric string (a name) rather than a number. You can configure an unlimited number of the following types of IPX named access lists:

- Standard
- Extended
- SAP
- NLSP route aggregation (summarization)
- NetBIOS

If you identify your access list with a name rather than a number, the mode and command syntax are slightly different.

### Benefits of IPX Named Access Lists

Using IPX named access lists enables you to maintain security by using a separate and easily identifiable access list for each user or interface. IPX named access lists also remove the limit of 100 lists per filter type.

### Implementation Considerations for Configuring IPX Named Access Lists

Consider the following information before configuring IPX named access lists:

- Except for NetBIOS access lists, access lists specified by name are not compatible with releases prior to Cisco IOS Release 11.2(4)F.
- Access list names must be unique across all protocols.
- Except for NetBIOS access lists, numbered access lists are also available.

### IPX Named Access List Configuration Task List

To configure IPX named access lists for standard, extended, SAP, NLSP route aggregation (summarization), or NetBIOS access lists, complete one or more of the tasks in the following sections:

- Create a Named Standard Access List
- Create a Named Extended Access List

- Create a Named SAP Filtering Access List
- Create a Named NLSP Route Aggregation Access List
- Create a NetBIOS Access List

### Create a Named Standard Access List

To create a named standard access list, perform the following tasks, beginning in global configuration mode:

| Task | Command |
|------|---------|
| **Step 1** Define a standard IPX access list using a name. (Generic, routing, and broadcast filters use this type of access list.) | **ipx access-list standard** *name* |
| **Step 2** In access-list configuration mode, specify one or more conditions allowed or denied. This determines whether the packet is passed or dropped. | {**deny** \| **permit**} *source-network*[.*source-node* [*source-node-mask*]] [*destination-network* [.*destination-node* [*destination-node-mask*]]] |
| **Step 3** Exit access-list configuration mode. | **exit** |

For an example of creating a named standard access list, see the "Standard Named Access List Example" section near the end of this chapter.

### Create a Named Extended Access List

To create a named extended access list, perform the following tasks, beginning in global configuration mode:

| Task | Command |
|------|---------|
| **Step 1** Define an extended IPX access list using a name. (Generic, routing, and broadcast filters use this type of access list.) | **ipx access-list extended** *name* |

| Task | Command |
|------|---------|
| **Step 2** In access-list configuration mode, specify the conditions allowed or denied. Use the **log** keyword to get access list logging messages, including violations. | {**deny** | **permit**} *protocol* [*source-network*] [[[.*source-node*] *source-node-mask*] | [.*source-node source-network-mask.source-node-mask*]] [*source-socket*] [*destination.network*] [[[.*destination-node*] *destination-node-mask*] |[.*destination-node destination-network-mask.destination-node-mask*]] [*destination-socket*] [**log**] |
| **Step 3** Exit access-list configuration mode. | **exit** |

### Create a Named SAP Filtering Access List

To create a named access list for filtering SAP requests, perform the following tasks, beginning in global configuration mode:

| Task | Command |
|------|---------|
| **Step 1** Define a SAP filtering access list using a name. (SAP and GNS response filters use this type of access list.) | **ipx access-list sap** *name* |
| **Step 2** In access-list configuration mode, specify the conditions allowed or denied. | {**deny** | **permit**} *network*[.*node*] [*network-mask.node-mask*] [*service-type* [*server-name*]] |
| **Step 3** Exit access-list configuration mode. | **exit** |

### Create a Named NLSP Route Aggregation Access List

NLSP route aggregation access lists perform one of the following functions:

- Permit networks to be redistributed as explicit networks, without summarization
- Deny the redistribution of explicit networks and generate an appropriate aggregating (summary) route for redistribution

To create a named access list for NLSP route aggregation, perform the following tasks, beginning in global configuration mode:

| Task | Command |
|------|---------|
| **Step 1** Define an IPX access list for NLSP route aggregation using a name. | **ipx access-list summary** *name* |
| **Step 2** In access-list configuration mode, specify the conditions allowed or denied. For each address range you want to redistribute as a single aggregated route, use the **deny** keyword. For each address that you want to redistribute explicitly, use the **permit** keyword. | {**deny** \| **permit**} *network network-mask* [**ticks** *ticks*] [**area-count** *area-count*] |
| **Step 3** Exit access-list configuration mode. | **exit** |

For information on how to use a named access list when configuring route aggregation, refer to the tasks listed in the "Configure Route Aggregation Task List" section earlier in this chapter.

### Create a NetBIOS Access List

To create a NetBIOS access list, perform one or more of the following tasks in global configuration mode:

| Task | Commands |
|------|----------|
| **Step 1** Create an access list for filtering IPX NetBIOS packets by node name. (NetBIOS filters use this type of access list.) | **netbios access-list host** *name* {**deny** \| **permit**} *string* |
| **Step 2** Create an access list for filtering IPX NetBIOS packets by arbitrary byte pattern. (NetBIOS filters use this type of access list.) | **netbios access-list bytes** *name* {**deny** \| **permit**} *offset byte-pattern* |

### Modifying IPX Named Access Lists

After you initially create an access list, you place any subsequent additions (possibly entered from the terminal) near the end of the list. In other words, you cannot selectively add access list command lines to the middle of a specific access list. However, you can use **no permit** and **no deny** commands to remove entries from a named access list.

---

**NOTES**

---

When creating access lists, remember that, by default, the end of the access list contains an implicit deny statement for everything if it did not find a match before reaching the end.

---

For an example of creating a generic filter, see the "IPX Network Access Examples" section near the end of this chapter.

### Applying Named Access Lists to Interfaces

After creating an access list, you must apply it to the appropriate interface using filters as described in the "Create Filters" section of this chapter. This activates the access list.

## Create Filters

Filters allow you to control which traffic is forwarded or blocked at a router's interfaces. Filters apply specific numbered or named access lists to interfaces.

The following sections describe how to perform the tasks for creating filters:

- Create Generic Filters
- Create Filters for Updating the Routing Table
- Create SAP Filters
- Create GNS Response Filters
- Create IPX NetBIOS Filters
- Create Broadcast Message Filters

### Create Generic Filters

Generic filters determine which data packets to receive from or send to an interface, based on the packet's source and destination addresses, IPX protocol type, and source and destination socket numbers.

To create generic filters, perform the following tasks:

| Step 1 | Create a standard or an extended access list as described in the "Create Access Lists" section of this chapter. |
| Step 2 | Apply a filter to an interface. |

To apply a generic filter to an interface, perform the following task in interface configuration mode:

| Task | Command |
|---|---|
| Apply a generic filter to an interface. | **ipx access-group** {*access-list-number* | *name*} [**in** | **out**] |

You can apply only one input filter and one output filter per interface or subinterface. You cannot configure an output filter on an interface on which autonomous switching is already configured. Similarly, you cannot configure autonomous switching on an interface on which an output filter is already present. You cannot configure an input filter on an interface if autonomous switching is already configured on *any* interface. Likewise, you cannot configure input filters if autonomous switching is already enabled on *any* interface.

For an example of creating a generic filter, see the "IPX Network Access Examples" section near the end of this chapter.

### Create Filters for Updating the Routing Table

Routing table update filters control the entries that the Cisco IOS software accepts for its routing table, and the networks that it advertises in its routing updates.

To create filters to control updating of the routing table, perform the following tasks:

**Step 1**    Create a standard or an extended access list as described in the "Create Access Lists" section of this chapter.

**Step 2**    Apply one or more routing filters to an interface.

To apply routing table update filters to an interface, perform one or more of the following tasks in interface configuration mode:

| Task | Command |
| --- | --- |
| **Step 1** Control which networks are added to the routing table when IPX routing updates are received. | **ipx input-network-filter** {*access-list-number* \| *name*} |
| **Step 2** Control which networks are advertised in RIP routing updates sent out by the Cisco IOS software. | **ipx output-network-filter** {*access-list-number* \| *name*} |
| **Step 3** Control which networks are advertised in the Enhanced IGRP routing updates sent out by the Cisco IOS software. | **distribute-list** {*access-list-number* \| *name*} **out** [*interface-name* \| *routing-process*] |
| **Step 4** Control the routers from which routing updates are accepted. | **ipx router-filter** {*access-list-number* \| *name*} |

> **NOTES**
>
> The **ipx output-network-filter** command applies to the IPX RIP only. To control the advertising of routes when filtering routing updates in Enhanced IGRP, use the **distribute-list out** command. See the "Control the Advertising of Routes in Routing Updates" section in this chapter for more information.

### Create SAP Filters

A common source of traffic on Novell networks is SAP messages, which are generated by NetWare servers and the Cisco IOS software when they broadcast their available services. To control how SAP messages from network segments or specific servers are routed among IPX networks, perform the following steps:

**Step 1** Create a SAP filtering access list as described in the "Create Access Lists" section of this chapter.

**Step 2** Apply one or more filters to an interface.

To apply SAP filters to an interface, perform one or more of the following tasks in interface configuration mode:

| Task | Command |
| --- | --- |
| **Step 1** Filter incoming service advertisements. | **ipx input-sap-filter** {*access-list-number* | *name*} |
| **Step 2** Filter outgoing service advertisements. | **ipx output-sap-filter** {*access-list-number* | *name*} |
| **Step 3** Filter service advertisements received from a particular router. | **ipx router-sap-filter** {*access-list-number* | *name*} |

You can apply one of each SAP filter to each interface.

For examples of creating and applying SAP filters, see the "SAP Input Filter Example" and "SAP Output Filter Example" sections near the end of this chapter.

### Create GNS Response Filters

To create filters for controlling which servers are included in the GNS responses sent by the Cisco IOS software, perform the following tasks:

**Step 1** Create a SAP filtering access list as described in the "Create Access Lists" section of this chapter.

**Step 2** Apply a GNS filter to an interface.

To apply a GNS filter to an interface, perform the following task in interface configuration mode:

| Task | Command |
| --- | --- |
| Filter the list of servers in GNS response messages. | **ipx output-gns-filter** {*access-list-number* | *name*} |

## Create IPX NetBIOS Filters

Novell's IPX NetBIOS allows messages to be exchanged between nodes using alphanumeric names and node addresses. Therefore, the Cisco IOS software lets you filter incoming and outgoing NetBIOS FindName packets by the node name or by an arbitrary byte pattern (such as the node address) in the packet.

---

**NOTES**

---

These filters apply to IPX NetBIOS FindName packets only. They have no effect on LLC2 NetBIOS packets.

---

### Implementation Considerations

Keep the following in mind when configuring IPX NetBIOS access control:

- Host (node) names are case sensitive.
- Host and byte access lists can have the same names because the two types of lists are independent of each other.
- When filtering by node name, the names in the access lists are compared with the destination name field for IPX NetBIOS "find name" requests.
- Access filters that filter by byte offset can have a significant impact on the packet transmission rate because each packet must be examined. You should use these access lists only when absolutely necessary.
- If a node name is not found in an access list, the default action is to deny access.

### IPX NetBIOS Filters Configuration Tasks

To create filters for controlling IPX NetBIOS access, perform the following tasks:

**Step 1**    Create a NetBIOS access list as described in the "Create Access Lists" section of this chapter.

**Step 2**    Apply the access list to an interface.

To apply a NetBIOS access list to an interface, perform one or more of the following tasks in interface configuration mode:

| Task | Command |
| --- | --- |
| **Step 1** Filter incoming packets by node name. | **ipx netbios input-access-filter host** *name* |
| **Step 2** Filter incoming packets by byte pattern. | **ipx netbios input-access-filter bytes** *name* |

| Task | Command |
|------|---------|
| **Step 3** Filter outgoing packets by node name. | **ipx netbios output-access-filter host** *name* |
| **Step 4** Filter outgoing packets by byte pattern. | **ipx netbios output-access-filter bytes** *name* |

You can apply one of each of these four filters to each interface.

For an example of how to create filters for controlling IPX NetBIOS, see the "IPX NetBIOS Filter Examples" section near the end of this chapter.

## Create Broadcast Message Filters

Routers normally block all broadcast requests and do not forward them to other network segments. This is done to prevent the degradation of performance inherent in broadcast traffic over the entire network. You can define which broadcast messages get forwarded to other networks by applying a broadcast message filter to an interface.

To create filters for controlling broadcast messages, perform the following tasks:

**Step 1**   Create a standard or an extended access list as described in the "Create Access Lists" section of this chapter.

**Step 2**   Apply a broadcast message filter to an interface.

To apply a broadcast message filter to an interface, perform the following tasks in interface configuration mode:

| Task | Command |
|------|---------|
| **Step 1** Specify a helper address for forwarding broadcast messages. | **ipx helper-address** *network.node* |
| **Step 2** Apply a broadcast message filter to an interface. | **ipx helper-list** {*access-list-number* \| *name*} |

### NOTES

A broadcast message filter has no effect unless you have issued an **ipx helper-address** or an **ipx type-20-propagation** command on the interface to enable and control the forwarding of broadcast messages. These commands are discussed later in this chapter.

For examples of creating and applying broadcast message filters, see the "Helper Facilities to Control Broadcast Examples" section near the end of this chapter.

## Tuning IPX Network Performance

You can tune IPX network performance by completing the tasks in one or more of the following sections:

- Control Novell IPX Compliance
- Adjust RIP and SAP Information
- Configure Load Sharing
- Specify the Use of Broadcast Messages
- Disable IPX Fast Switching
- Adjust the Route Cache
- Adjust Default Routes
- Pad Odd-Length Packets

## Control Novell IPX Compliance

Cisco's implementation of Novell's IPX protocol is certified to provide full IPX router functionality, as defined by Novell's IPX Router Specification, Version 1.10, published November 17, 1992.

You can control compliance to Novell specifications by performing the tasks in these sections:

- Control the Forwarding of Type 20 Packets
- Control Interpacket Delay
- Shut Down an IPX Network
- Achieve Full Novell Compliance

### Control the Forwarding of Type 20 Packets

NetBIOS over IPX uses type 20 propagation broadcast packets flooded to all networks to get information about the named nodes on the network. NetBIOS uses a broadcast mechanism to get this information because it does not implement a network layer.

Routers normally block all broadcast requests. By enabling type 20 packet propagation, IPX interfaces on the router may accept and forward type 20 packets.

#### How Type 20 Packet Propagation Works

When an interface configured for type 20 propagation receives a type 20 packet, Cisco IOS software processes the packet according to Novell specifications. Cisco IOS software propagates the packet to the next interface. The type 20 packet can be propagated for up to eight hop counts.

#### Loop Detection and Other Checks

Before forwarding (flooding) the packets, the router performs loop detection as described by the IPX router specification.

You can configure the Cisco IOS software to apply extra checks to type 20 propagation packets above and beyond the loop detection described in the IPX specification. These checks are the same ones that are applied to helpered all-nets broadcast packets. They can limit unnecessary duplication of type 20 broadcast packets. The extra helper checks are as follows:

- Accept type 20 propagation packets only on the primary network, which is the network that is the primary path back to the source network.
- Forward type 20 propagation packets only via networks that do not lead back to the source network.

While this extra checking increases the robustness of type 20 propagation packet handling by decreasing the amount of unnecessary packet replication, it has the following two side effects:

- If type 20 packet propagation is not configured on all interfaces, these packets might be blocked when the primary interface changes.
- It might be impossible to configure an arbitrary, manual spanning tree for type 20 packet propagation.

### Relationship between Type 20 Propagation and Helper Addresses

You use helper addresses to forward non-type 20 broadcast packets to other network segments. For information on forwarding other broadcast packets, see the "Use Helper Addresses to Forward Broadcast Packets" section in this chapter.

You can use helper addresses and type 20 propagation together in your network. Use helper addresses to forward non-type 20 broadcast packets and use type 20 propagation to forward type 20 broadcast packets.

### Type 20 Packets Configuration Task List

You can enable the forwarding of type 20 packets on individual interfaces. Additionally, you can restrict the acceptance and forwarding of type 20 packets. You can also choose to not comply with Novell specifications and forward type 20 packets using helper addresses rather than using type 20 propagation. The following sections describe these tasks:

- Enable the Forwarding of Type 20 Packets
- Restrict the Acceptance of Incoming Type 20 Packets
- Restrict the Forwarding of Outgoing Type 20 Packets
- Forward Type 20 Packets Using Helper Addresses

### Enable the Forwarding of Type 20 Packets

By default, type 20 propagation packets are dropped by the Cisco IOS software. You can configure the software to receive type 20 propagation broadcast packets and forward (flood) them to other network segments, subject to loop detection.

To enable the receipt and forwarding of type 20 packets, perform the following task in interface configuration mode:

| Task | Command |
| --- | --- |
| Forward IPX type 20 propagation packet broadcasts to other network segments. | ipx type-20-propagation |

When you enable type 20 propagation, Cisco IOS propagates the broadcast to the next interface up to eight hops.

### Restrict the Acceptance of Incoming Type 20 Packets

For incoming type 20 propagation packets, the Cisco IOS software is configured by default to accept packets on all interfaces enabled to receive type 20 propagation packets. You can configure the software to accept packets only from the single network that is the primary route back to the source network. This means that similar packets from the same source that are received via other networks are dropped.

Checking of incoming type 20 propagation broadcast packets is done only if the interface is configured to receive and forward type 20 packets.

To impose restrictions on the receipt of incoming type 20 propagation packets in addition to the checks defined in the IPX specification, perform the following task in global configuration mode:

| Task | Command |
| --- | --- |
| Restrict the acceptance of IPX type 20 propagation packets. | ipx type-20-input-checks |

### Restrict the Forwarding of Outgoing Type 20 Packets

For outgoing type 20 propagation packets, the Cisco IOS software is configured by default to send packets on all interfaces enabled to send type 20 propagation packets, subject to loop detection. You can configure the software to send these packets only to networks that are not routes back to the source network. (The software uses the current routing table to determine routes.)

Checking of outgoing type 20 propagation broadcast packets is done only if the interface is configured to receive and forward type 20 packets.

To impose restrictions on the transmission of type 20 propagation packets and to forward these packets to all networks using only the checks defined in the IPX specification, perform the following task in global configuration mode:

| Task | Command |
| --- | --- |
| Restrict the forwarding of IPX type 20 propagation packets. | ipx type-20-output-checks |

### Forward Type 20 Packets Using Helper Addresses

You can also forward type 20 packets to specific network segments using helper addresses rather than using the type 20 packet propagation.

You may want to forward type 20 packets using helper addresses when some routers in your network are running versions of Cisco IOS that do not support type 20 propagation. When some routers in your network support type 20 propagation and others do not, you can avoid flooding packets everywhere in the network by using helper addresses to direct packets to certain segments only.

Cisco IOS Release 9.1 and earlier versions do not support type 20 propagation.

— **NOTES** ————————————————————————————

Forwarding type 20 packets using helper addresses does not comply with the Novell IPX router specification.

To forward type 20 packets addresses using helper addresses, perform the following tasks beginning in global configuration mode:

| Task | Command |
| --- | --- |
| **Step 1** Forward IPX type 20 packets to specific network segments. This step turns off type 20 propagation. | ipx type-20-helpered |
| **Step 2** From interface configuration mode, specify a helper address for forwarding broadcast messages, including IPX type 20 packets. | ipx helper-address *network.node* |

The Cisco IOS software forwards type 20 packets to only those nodes specified by the **ipx helper-address** command.

---

Using the **ipx type-20-helpered** command disables the receipt and forwarding of type 20 propagation packets as directed by the **ipx type-20-propagation** command.

---

### Control Interpacket Delay

To control interpacket delay, you can use a combination of global configuration and interface configuration commands.

You can perform one or more of the following tasks in global configuration mode:

| Task | | Command |
|---|---|---|
| **Step 1** | Set the interpacket delay of multiple-packet routing updates sent on all interfaces. | **ipx default-output-rip-delay** *delay* |
| **Step 2** | Set the interpacket delay of multiple-packet triggered routing updates sent on all interfaces. | **ipx default-triggered-rip-delay** *delay* |
| **Step 3** | Set the interpacket delay of multiple-packet SAP updates sent on all interfaces. | **ipx default-output-sap-delay** *delay* |
| **Step 4** | Set the interpacket delay of multiple-packet triggered SAP updates sent on all interfaces. | **ipx default-triggered-sap-delay** *delay* |

You can also perform one or more of the following tasks in interface configuration mode:

| Task | | Command |
|---|---|---|
| **Step 1** | Set the interpacket delay of multiple-packet routing updates sent on a single interface. | **ipx output-rip-delay** *delay* |
| **Step 2** | Set the interpacket delay of multiple-packet triggered routing updates sent on a single interface. | **ipx triggered-rip-delay** *delay* |
| **Step 3** | Set the interpacket delay of multiple-packet SAP updates sent on a single interface. | **ipx output-sap-delay** *delay* |
| **Step 4** | Set the interpacket delay of multiple-packet triggered SAP updates sent on a single interface. | **ipx triggered-sap-delay** *delay* |

---

**NOTES**

We recommend that you use an **ipx output-rip-delay** and **ipx output-sap-delay** on slower speed WAN interfaces.The default delay for Cisco IOS Release 11.1 and later versions is 55 ms.

---

### Shut Down an IPX Network

To shut down an IPX network using a Novell-compliant method, perform the following task in interface configuration mode:

| Task | Command |
|------|---------|
| Administratively shut down an IPX network on an interface. This removes the network from the interface. | ipx down *network* |

Convergence is faster when you shut down an IPX network using the **ipx down** command than when using the **shutdown** command.

### Achieve Full Novell Compliance

To achieve full compliance, issue the following interface configuration commands on each interface configured for IPX:

| Task | | Command |
|------|---|---------|
| Step 1 | Set the interpacket delay of multiple-packet routing updates to 55 ms. | ipx output-rip-delay 55 |
| Step 2 | Set the interpacket delay of multiple-packet SAP updates to 55 ms. | ipx output-sap-delay 55 |
| Step 3 | Optionally enable type 20 packet propagation if you want to forward type 20 broadcast traffic across the router. | ipx type-20-propagation |

You can also globally set interpacket delays for multiple-packet RIP and SAP updates to achieve full compliance, eliminating the need to set delays on each interface. To do so, issue the following commands from global configuration mode:

| Task | | Command |
|------|---|---------|
| Step 1 | Set the interpacket delay of multiple-packet routing updates sent on all interfaces to 55 ms. | ipx default-output-rip-delay 55 |

| Task | Command |
|------|---------|
| **Step 2** Set the interpacket delay of multiple-packet SAP updates sent on all interfaces to 55 ms. | ipx default-output-sap-delay 55 |

 **NOTES**

The default delay for Cisco IOS Release 11.1 and later versions is 55 ms.

## Adjust RIP and SAP Information

You can adjust RIP and SAP information by completing one or more of the optional tasks in the following sections:

- Configure Static Routes
- Adjust the RIP Delay Field
- Adjust RIP Update Timers
- Configure RIP Update Packet Size
- Configure Static SAP Table Entries
- Configure the Queue Length for SAP Requests
- Adjust SAP Update Timers
- Configure SAP Update Packet Size
- Enable SAP-after-RIP
- Disable Sending of General RIP or SAP Queries
- Control Responses to GNS Requests

### Configure Static Routes

IPX uses RIP, Enhanced IGRP, or NLSP to determine the best path when several paths to a destination exist. The routing protocol then dynamically updates the routing table. However, you might want to add static routes to the routing table to explicitly specify paths to certain destinations. Static routes always override any dynamically learned paths.

Be careful when assigning static routes. When links associated with static routes are lost, traffic may stop being forwarded or traffic may be forwarded to a nonexistent destination, even though an alternative path might be available.

To add a static route to the routing table, perform the following task in global configuration mode:

| Task | Command |
| --- | --- |
| Add a static route to the routing table. | ipx route {*network* I **default**} {*network.node* I *interface*} [**floating-static**] |

You can configure static routes that can be overridden by dynamically learned routes. These routes are referred to as floating static routes. You can use a floating static route to create a path of last resort that is used only when no dynamic routing information is available.

— **NOTES** —————————————————————————————————————

By default, floating static routes are not redistributed into other dynamic protocols.

To add a floating static route to the routing table, perform the following task in global configuration mode:

| Task | Command |
| --- | --- |
| Add a floating static route to the routing table. | ipx route {*network* I **default**} {*network.node* I *interface*} [**floating-static**] |

### Adjust the RIP Delay Field

By default, all LAN interfaces have a RIP delay of 1 and all WAN interfaces have a RIP delay of 6. Leaving the delay at its default value is sufficient for most interfaces. However, you can adjust the RIP delay field by setting the tick count. To set the tick count, perform the following task in interface configuration mode:

| Task | Command |
| --- | --- |
| Set the tick count, which is used in the IPX RIP delay field. | ipx delay *number* |

### Adjust RIP Update Timers

You can set the interval between IPX RIP updates on a per-interface basis. You can also specify the delay between the packets of a multiple-packet RIP update on a per-interface or global basis. Additionally, you can specify the delay between packets of a multiple-packet triggered RIP update on a per-interface or global basis.

You can set RIP update timers only in a configuration in which all routers are Cisco routers or in which the IPX routers allow configurable timers. The timers should be the same for all devices connected to the same cable segment. The update value you choose affects internal IPX timers as follows:

- IPX routes are marked invalid if no routing updates are heard within three times the value of the update interval (3 * *interval*) and are advertised with a metric of infinity.

- IPX routes are removed from the routing table if no routing updates are heard within four times the value of the update interval (4 * *interval*).

- If you define a timer for more than one interface in a router, the granularity of the timer is determined by the lowest value defined for one of the interfaces in the router. The router "wakes up" at this granularity interval and sends out updates as appropriate.

You might want to set a delay between the packets in a multiple-packet update if there are some slower PCs on the network or on slower-speed interfaces.

To adjust RIP update timers on a per-interface basis, perform any or all of the following tasks in interface configuration mode:

| Task | Command |
|------|---------|
| **Step 1**  Adjust the RIP update timer. | **ipx update interval** {**rip** I **sap**} {*value* I **changes-only**} |
| **Step 2**  Adjust the delay between multiple-packet routing updates sent on a single interface. | **ipx output-rip-delay** *delay* |
| **Step 3**  Adjust the delay between multiple-packet triggered routing updates sent on a single interface. | **ipx triggered-rip-delay** *delay* |

To adjust RIP update timers on a global basis, perform any or all of the following tasks in global configuration mode:

| Task | Command |
|------|---------|
| **Step 1**  Adjust the delay between multiple-packet routing updates sent on all interfaces. | **ipx default-output-rip-delay** *delay* |
| **Step 2**  Adjust the delay between multiple-packet triggered routing updates sent on all interfaces. | **ipx default-triggered-rip-delay** *delay* |

By default, the RIP entry for a network or server ages out at an interval equal to three times the RIP timer. To configure the multiplier that controls the interval, perform the following task in interface configuration mode:

| Task | Command |
|------|---------|
| Configure the interval at which a network RIP entry ages out. | **ipx rip-multiplier** *multiplier* |

### Configure RIP Update Packet Size

By default, the maximum size of RIP updates sent out an interface is 432 bytes. This size allows for 50 routes at 8 bytes each, plus a 32-byte IPX RIP header. To modify the maximum packet size, perform the following task in interface configuration mode:

| Task | Command |
|------|---------|
| Configure the maximum packet size of RIP updates sent out an interface. | **ipx rip-max-packetsize** *bytes* |

### Configure Static SAP Table Entries

Servers use SAP to advertise their services via broadcast packets. The Cisco IOS software stores this information in the SAP table, also known as the Server Information Table. This table is updated dynamically. You might want to explicitly add an entry to the Server Information Table so that clients always use the services of a particular server. Static SAP assignments always override any identical entries in the SAP table that are learned dynamically, regardless of hop count. If a dynamic route that is associated with a static SAP entry is lost or deleted, the software does not announce the static SAP entry until it relearns the route.

To add a static entry to the SAP table, perform the following task in global configuration mode:

| Task | Command |
|------|---------|
| Specify a static SAP table entry. | **ipx sap** *service-type name network.node socket hop-count* |

### Configure the Queue Length for SAP Requests

The Cisco IOS software maintains a list of SAP requests to process, including all pending GNS queries from clients attempting to reach servers. When the network is restarted following a power failure or other unexpected event, the router can be inundated with hundreds of requests for servers. Typically, many of these are repeated requests from the same clients. You can configure the maximum length allowed for the pending SAP requests queue. SAP requests received when the queue is full are dropped, and the client must resend them.

To set the queue length for SAP requests, perform the following task in global configuration mode:

| Task | Command |
|------|---------|
| Configure the maximum SAP queue length. | **ipx sap-queue-maximum** *number* |

### Adjust SAP Update Timers

You can adjust the interval at which SAP updates are sent. You can also set the delay between packets of a multiple-packet SAP update on a per-interface or global basis. Additionally, you can specify the delay between packets of a multiple-packet triggered SAP update on a per-interface or global basis.

Changing the interval at which SAP updates are sent is most useful on limited-bandwidth, point-to-point links, such as slower-speed interfaces. You should ensure that all IPX servers and routers on a given network have the same SAP interval. Otherwise, they might decide that a server is down when it is really up.

It is not possible to change the interval at which SAP updates are sent on most PC-based servers. This means that you should never change the interval for an Ethernet or Token Ring network that has servers on it.

You can set the router to send an update only when changes have occurred. Using the **changes-only** keyword specifies the sending of a SAP update only when the link comes up, when the link is downed administratively, or when the databases change. The **changes-only** keyword causes the router to do the following:

- Send a single, full broadcast update when the link comes up
- Send appropriate triggered updates when the link is shut down
- Send appropriate triggered updates when specific service information changes

To modify the SAP update timers on a per-interface basis, perform any or all of the following tasks in interface configuration mode:

| Task | Command |
|------|---------|
| **Step 1** Adjust the interval at which SAP updates are sent. | **ipx update interval** {**rip** \| **sap**} {*value* \| **changes-only**} |
| **Step 2** Adjust the interpacket delay of multiple-packet SAP updates sent on a single interface. | **ipx output-sap-delay** *delay* |

| Task | Command |
|------|---------|
| **Step 3** Adjust the interpacket delay of multiple-packet triggered SAP updates sent on a single interface. | **ipx triggered-sap-delay** *delay* |

To adjust SAP update timers on a global basis (eliminating the need to configure delays on a per-interface basis), perform any or all of the following tasks in global configuration mode:

| Task | Command |
|------|---------|
| **Step 1** Adjust the interpacket delay of multiple-packet SAP updates sent on all interfaces. | **ipx default-output-sap-delay** *delay* |
| **Step 2** Adjust the interpacket delay of multiple-packet triggered SAP updates sent on all interfaces. | **ipx default-triggered-sap-delay** *delay* |

By default, the SAP entry of a network or server ages out at an interval equal to three times the SAP update interval. To configure the multiplier that controls the interval, perform the following task in interface configuration mode:

| Task | Command |
|------|---------|
| Configure the interval at which a network's or server's SAP entry ages out. | **ipx sap-multiplier** *multiplier* |

### Configure SAP Update Packet Size

By default, the maximum size of SAP updates sent out an interface is 480 bytes. This size allows for 7 servers (64 bytes each), plus a 32-byte IPX SAP header. To modify the maximum packet size, perform the following task in interface configuration mode:

| Task | Command |
|------|---------|
| Configure the maximum packet size of SAP updates sent out an interface. | **ipx sap-max-packetsize** *bytes* |

### Enable SAP-after-RIP

The IPX SAP-after-RIP feature links Service Advertising Protocol (SAP) updates to Routing Information Protocol (RIP) updates so that SAP broadcast and unicast updates automatically occur immediately after the completion of the corresponding RIP update. This feature ensures that a remote router does not reject service information because it lacks a valid route to the service. As a result of this feature, periodic SAP updates are sent at the same interval as RIP updates.

The default behavior of the router is to send RIP and SAP periodic updates, with each using its own update interval, depending on the configuration. In addition, RIP and SAP periodic updates are jittered slightly, such that they tend to diverge from each other over time. This feature synchronizes SAP and RIP updates.

### Benefits of SAP-after-RIP

Sending all SAP and RIP information in a single update reduces bandwidth demands and eliminates erroneous rejections of SAP broadcasts.

Linking SAP and RIP updates populates the remote router's service table more quickly because services are not rejected due to the lack of a route to the service. This can be especially useful on WAN circuits on which the update intervals have been greatly increased to reduce the overall level of periodic update traffic on the link.

### Send a SAP Update after RIP Broadcast

To configure the router to send a SAP update following a RIP broadcast, perform the following task in interface configuration mode:

| Task | Command |
| --- | --- |
| Configure the router to send a SAP broadcast immediately following a RIP broadcast. | **ipx update sap-after-rip** |

## Disable Sending of General RIP or SAP Queries

You can disable the sending of general RIP and/or SAP queries on a link when it first comes up to reduce traffic and save bandwidth.

RIP and SAP general queries are normally sent by remote routers when a circuit first comes up. On WAN circuits, two full updates of each kind are often sent across the link. The first update is a full broadcast update, triggered locally by the link-up event. The second update is a specific (unicast) reply triggered by the general query received from the remote router. By disabling the sending of general queries when the link first comes up, it is possible to reduce traffic to a single update and save bandwidth.

To disable the sending of a general RIP and/or SAP query when an interface comes up, perform the following task in interface configuration mode:

| Task | Command |
|------|---------|
| Disable the sending of a general RIP and/or SAP query when an interface comes up. | no ipx linkup-request {rip \| sap} |

To re-enable the sending of a general RIP and/or SAP query, use the positive form of the command.

## Control Responses to GNS Requests

You can set the method in which the router responds to SAP GNS requests, you can set the delay time in responding to these requests, or you can disable the sending of responses to these requests altogether.

By default, the router responds to GNS requests if appropriate. For example, if a local server with a better metric exists, then the router does not respond to the GNS request on that segment.

The default method of responding to GNS requests is to respond with the server whose availability was learned most recently.

To control responses to GNS requests, perform one or both of the following tasks in global configuration mode:

| Task | | Command |
|------|--|---------|
| Step 1 | Respond to GNS requests using a round-robin selection method. | ipx gns-round-robin |
| Step 2 | Set the delay when responding to GNS requests. | ipx gns-response-delay [*milliseconds*] |

---

**NOTES**

The **ipx gns-response-delay** command is also supported as an interface configuration command. To override the global delay value for a specific interface, use the **ipx gns-response-delay** command in interface configuration mode.

---

You can also disable GNS queries on a per-interface basis. To do so, perform the following task from interface configuration mode:

| Task | Command |
|------|---------|
| Disable the sending of replies to GNS queries. | ipx gns-reply-disable |

## Configure Load Sharing

You can configure IPX to perform round-robin or per-host load sharing, as described in the following sections:

- Enable Round-Robin Load Sharing
- Enable Per-Host Load Sharing

### Enable Round-Robin Load Sharing

You can set the maximum number of equal-cost, parallel paths to a destination. (Note that when paths have differing costs, the Cisco IOS software chooses lower-cost routes in preference to higher-cost routes.) The software then distributes output on a packet-by-packet basis in round-robin fashion. That is, the first packet is sent along the first path, the second packet along the second path, and so on. When the final path is reached, the next packet is sent to the first path, the next to the second path, and so on. This round-robin scheme is used regardless of whether fast switching is enabled.

Limiting the number of equal-cost paths can save memory on routers with limited memory or very large configurations. Additionally, in networks with a large number of multiple paths and systems with limited capability to cache out-of-sequence packets, performance might suffer when traffic is split between many paths.

To set the maximum number of paths, perform the following task in global configuration mode:

| Task | Command |
| --- | --- |
| Set the maximum number of equal-cost paths to a destination. | **ipx maximum-paths** *paths* |

### Enable Per-Host Load Sharing

Round-robin load sharing is the default behavior when you configure **ipx maximum-paths** to a value greater than 1. Round-robin load sharing works by sending data packets over successive equal cost paths without regard to individual end hosts or user sessions. Path utilization is good, but, because packets destined for a given end host may take different paths, they might arrive out of order.

You can address the possibility of packets arriving out of order by enabling per-host load sharing. With per-host load sharing, the router still uses multiple, equal-cost paths to achieve load sharing; however, packets for a given end host are guaranteed to take the same path, even if multiple equal-cost paths are available. Traffic for different end hosts tend to take different paths, but true load balancing is not guaranteed. The exact degree of load balancing achieved depends on the exact nature of the workload.

To enable per-host load sharing, perform the following tasks in global configuration mode:

| Task | Command |
|------|---------|
| **Step 1** Set the maximum number of equal-cost paths to a destination to a value greater than 1. | **ipx maximum-paths** *paths* |
| **Step 2** Enable per-host load sharing. | **ipx per-host-load-share** |

## Specify the Use of Broadcast Messages

You can specify the use of broadcast messages as described in the following sections:

- Use Helper Addresses to Forward Broadcast Packets
- Enable Fast Switching of IPX Directed Broadcast Packets

### Use Helper Addresses to Forward Broadcast Packets

Routers normally block all broadcast requests and do not forward them to other network segments. This is done to prevent the degradation of performance over the entire network. However, you can enable the router to forward broadcast packets to helper addresses on other network segments.

#### How Helper Addresses Work

Helper addresses specify the network and node on another segment that can receive unrecognized broadcast packets. Unrecognized broadcast packets are non-RIP and non-SAP packets that are not addressed to the local network.

When the interface configured with helper addresses receives an unrecognized broadcast packet, Cisco IOS software changes the broadcast packet to a unicast and sends the packet to the specified network and node on the other network segment. Unrecognized broadcast packets are not flooded everywhere in your network.

With helper addresses, there is no limit on the number of hops that the broadcast packet can make.

#### Fast Switching Support

Cisco IOS supports fast switching of helpered broadcast packets.

#### When to Use Helper Addresses

You use helper addresses when you want to forward broadcast packets (except type 20 packets) to other network segments.

Forwarding broadcast packets to helper addresses is sometimes useful when a network segment does not have an end host capable of servicing a particular type of broadcast request. You can specify the address of a server, network, or networks that can process the broadcast packet.

### Relationship between Helper Addresses and Type 20 Propagation

You use type 20 packet propagation to forward type 20 packets to other network segments. For information on forwarding type 20 packets, see the "Control the Forwarding of Type 20 Packets" section in this chapter.

You can use helper addresses and type 20 propagation together in your network. Use helper addresses to forward non-type 20 broadcast packets and use type 20 propagation to forward type 20 broadcast packets.

### Implementation Considerations

Using helper addresses is not Novell-compliant; however, it does allow routers to forward broadcast packets to network segments that can process them without flooding the network. It also allows routers running versions of Cisco IOS that do not support type 20 propagation to forward type 20 packets.

The Cisco IOS software supports all-networks flooded broadcasts (sometimes referred to as *all-nets flooding*). These are broadcast messages that are forwarded to all networks. Use all-nets flooding carefully and only when necessary because the receiving networks may be overwhelmed to the point that no other traffic can traverse them.

Use the **ipx helper-list** command, described earlier in this chapter, to define access lists that control which broadcast packets get forwarded.

### Use Helper Addresses

To specify a helper address for forwarding broadcast packets, perform the following task in interface configuration mode:

| Task | Command |
| --- | --- |
| Specify a helper address for forwarding broadcast messages. | **ipx helper-address** *network.node* |

You can specify multiple helper addresses on an interface.

For an example of using helper addresses to forward broadcast messages, see the "Helper Facilities to Control Broadcast Examples" section near the end of this chapter.

### Enable Fast Switching of IPX Directed Broadcast Packets

By default, Cisco IOS software switches packets that have been helpered to the broadcast address. To enable fast switching of these IPX-directed broadcast packets, perform the following task in global configuration mode:

| Task | Command |
| --- | --- |
| Enable fast switching of IPX directed broadcast packets. | ipx broadcast-fastswitching |

## Disable IPX Fast Switching

By default, fast switching is enabled on all interfaces that support fast switching. However, you might want to turn off fast switching.

Fast switching allows higher throughput by switching a packet using a cache created by previous packets. Fast switching is enabled by default on all interfaces that support fast switching.

Packet transfer performance is generally better when fast switching is enabled. However, you might want to disable fast switching in order to save memory space on interface cards and to help avoid congestion when high-bandwidth interfaces are writing large amounts of information to low-bandwidth interfaces.

---

**CAUTION**

Turning off fast switching increases system overhead.

---

To disable IPX fast switching, perform the following task in interface configuration mode:

| Task | Command |
| --- | --- |
| Disable IPX fast switching. | no ipx route-cache |

## Adjust the Route Cache

Adjusting the route cache enables you to control the size of the route cache, reduce memory consumption, and improve router performance. You accomplish these tasks by controlling the route cache size and invalidation. The following sections describe these optional tasks:

- Control Route Cache Size
- Control Route Cache Invalidation

### Control Route Cache Size

You can limit the number of entries stored in the IPX route cache to free up router memory and aid router processing.

Storing too many entries in the route cache can use a significant amount of router memory, causing router processing to slow. This situation is most common on large networks that run network management applications for NetWare.

For example, if a network management station is responsible for managing all clients and servers in a very large (greater than 50,000 nodes) Novell network, the routers on the local segment can become inundated with route cache entries. You can set a maximum number of route cache entries on these routers to free up router memory and aid router processing.

To set a maximum limit on the number of entries in the IPX route cache, complete this task in global configuration mode:

| Task | Command |
| --- | --- |
| Set a maximum limit on the number of entries in the IPX route cache. | **ipx route-cache max-size** *size* |

If the route cache has more entries than the specified limit, the extra entries are not deleted. However, they may be removed if route cache invalidation is in use. See the "Control Route Cache Invalidation" section in this chapter for more information on invalidating route cache entries.

### Control Route Cache Invalidation

You can configure the router to invalidate fast switch cache entries that are inactive. If these entries remain invalidated for one minute, the router purges the entries from the route cache.

Purging invalidated entries reduces the size of the route cache, reduces memory consumption, and improves router performance. Also, purging entries helps ensure accurate route cache information.

You specify the period of time that valid fast switch cache entries must be inactive before the router invalidates them. You can also specify the number of cache entries that the router can invalidate per minute.

To configure the router to invalidate fast switch cache entries that are inactive, complete this task in global configuration mode:

| Task | Command |
| --- | --- |
| Invalidate fast switch cache entries that are inactive. | **ipx route-cache inactivity-timeout** *period* [*rate*] |

When you use the **ipx route-cache inactivity-timeout** command with the **ipx route-cache max-size** command, you can ensure a small route cache with fresh entries.

## Adjust Default Routes

You can adjust the use of default routes in your IPX network. You can turn off the use of network number -2 as the default route. You can also specify that the router advertise only default RIP routes out an interface. The following sections describe these optional tasks:

- Disable Network Number -2 as the Default Route
- Advertise Only Default RIP Routes

### *Disable Network Number -2 as the Default Route*

The default route is used when a route to any destination network is unknown. All packets for which a route to the destination address is unknown are forwarded to the default route. By default, IPX treats network number -2 (0xFFFFFFFE) as the default route.

For an introduction to default routes, see the "IPX Default Routes" section earlier in this chapter.

By default, Cisco IOS software treats network -2 as the default route. You can disable this default behavior and use network -2 as a regular network number in your network.

To disable the use of network number -2 as the default route, perform the following task in global configuration mode:

| Task | Command |
| --- | --- |
| Disable default route handling. | **no ipx default-route** |

### *Advertise Only Default RIP Routes*

Unless configured otherwise, all known RIP routes are advertised out each interface. However, you can choose to advertise only the default RIP route if it is known. This greatly reduces the CPU overhead when routing tables are large.

To advertise only the default route via an interface, perform the following task in interface configuration mode:

| Task | Command |
| --- | --- |
| Advertise only the default RIP route. | **ipx advertise-default-route-only** *network* |

## Pad Odd-Length Packets

Some IPX end hosts accept only even-length Ethernet packets. If the length of a packet is odd, the packet must be padded with an extra byte so that the end host can receive it. By default, Cisco IOS pads odd-length Ethernet packets.

However, there are cases in certain topologies in which non-padded Ethernet packets are being forwarded onto a remote Ethernet network. Under specific conditions, you can enable padding on intermediate media as a temporary workaround for this problem. Note that you should perform this task only under the guidance of a customer engineer or other service representative.

To enable the padding of odd-length packets, perform the following tasks in interface configuration mode:

| Task | Command |
| --- | --- |
| **Step 1**  Disable fast switching. | **no ipx route-cache** |
| **Step 2**  Enable the padding of odd-length packets. | **ipx pad-process-switched-packets** |

## SHUTTING DOWN AN IPX NETWORK

You can administratively shut down an IPX network in two ways. In the first way, the network still exists in the configuration but is not active. When shutting down, the network sends out update packets informing its neighbors that it is shutting down. This allows the neighboring systems to update their routing, SAP, and other tables without having to wait for routes and services learned via this network to time out.

To shut down an IPX network such that the network still exists in the configuration, perform the following task in interface configuration mode:

| Task | Command |
| --- | --- |
| Shut down an IPX network, but have the network still exist in the configuration. | **ipx down** *network* |

In the second way, you shut down an IPX network and remove it from the configuration. To do this, perform one of the following tasks in interface configuration mode:

| Task | Command |
| --- | --- |
| **Step 1**  Shut down an IPX network and remove it from the configuration. | **no ipx network** |

| Task | Command |
|------|---------|
| **Step 2** When multiple networks are configured on an interface, shut down all networks and remove them from the interface. | **no ipx network** *network* (where *network* is 1, the primary interface) |
| **Step 3** When multiple networks are configured on an interface, shut down one of the secondary networks and remove it from the interface. | **no ipx network** *network* (where *network* is the number of the secondary interface [not 1]) |

When multiple networks are configured on an interface and you want to shut down one of the secondary networks and remove it from the interface, perform the second task in the previous table, specifying the network number of one of the secondary networks.

**NOTES**

In future Cisco IOS software releases, primary and secondary networks will not be supported.

For an example of shutting down an IPX network, see the "IPX Routing Examples" section near the end of this chapter.

## CONFIGURING IPX ACCOUNTING

IPX accounting enables you to collect information about IPX packets and the number of bytes that are switched through the Cisco IOS software. You collect information based on the source and destination IPX address. IPX accounting tracks only IPX traffic that is routed out an interface on which IPX accounting is configured; it does not track traffic generated by or terminated at the router itself.

The Cisco IOS software maintains two accounting databases: an active database and a checkpoint database. The active database contains accounting data tracked until the database is cleared. When the active database is cleared, its contents are copied to the checkpoint database. Using these two databases together enables you to monitor both current traffic and traffic that has previously traversed the router.

### Switching Support

Process and fast switching support IPX accounting statistics. Autonomous and SSE switching do not support IPX accounting statistics.

### Access List Support

IPX access lists support IPX accounting statistics.

## IPX Accounting Task List

You can configure IPX accounting by completing the tasks in the following sections. The first task is required. The remaining tasks are optional.

- Enable IPX Accounting
- Customize IPX Accounting
- Monitor and Maintain IPX Accounting

## Enable IPX Accounting

To enable IPX accounting, perform the following task in interface configuration mode:

| Task | Command |
|---|---|
| Enable IPX accounting. | **ipx accounting** |

## Customize IPX Accounting

To customize IPX accounting, perform one or more of the following tasks in global configuration mode:

| Task | | Command |
|---|---|---|
| **Step 1** | Set the maximum number of accounting entries. | **ipx accounting-threshold** *threshold* |
| **Step 2** | Set the maximum number of transit entries. | **ipx accounting-transits** *count* |
| **Step 3** | Filter networks for which IPX accounting information is kept. Enter one command for each network. | **ipx accounting-list** *number mask* |

Transit entries are entries in the database that do not match any of the networks specified by the **ipx accounting-list** commands.

If you enable IPX accounting on an interface but do not specify an accounting list, IPX accounting tracks all traffic through the interface (all transit entries) up to the accounting threshold limit.

For an example of how to configure IPX accounting, see the "IPX Accounting Example" section near the end of this chapter.

## MONITORING AND MAINTAINING THE IPX NETWORK

You can monitor and maintain your IPX network by performing the optional tasks described in the following sections:

- Perform General Monitoring and Maintaining Tasks
- Monitor and Maintain IPX Enhanced IGRP
- Monitor and Maintain NLSP
- Monitor and Maintain NHRP
- Monitor and Maintain IPX Accounting

## Perform General Monitoring and Maintaining Tasks

You can perform one or more of these general monitoring and maintaining tasks as described in the following sections:

- Monitor and Maintain Caches, Tables, Interfaces, and Statistics
- Specify the Type and Use of Ping Packets
- Repair Corrupted Network Numbers

### Monitor and Maintain Caches, Tables, Interfaces, and Statistics

To monitor and maintain caches, tables, interfaces, or statistics in a Novell IPX network, perform one or more of the following tasks at the EXEC prompt:

| Task | | Command |
|------|------|---------|
| Step 1 | Delete all entries in the IPX fast-switching cache. | clear ipx cache |
| Step 2 | Delete entries in the IPX routing table. | clear ipx route [*network* \| *] |
| Step 3 | List the entries in the IPX fast-switching cache. | show ipx cache |
| Step 4 | Display the status of the IPX interfaces configured in the router and the parameters configured on each interface. | show ipx interface [*type number*] |
| Step 5 | List the entries in the IPX routing table. | show ipx route [*network*] [default] [detailed] |
| Step 6 | List the servers discovered through SAP advertisements. | show ipx servers [unsorted \| sorted [name \| net \| type]] [regexp *name*] |

| Task | Command |
|---|---|
| **Step 7** Display information about the number and type of IPX packets transmitted and received. | show ipx traffic |
| **Step 8** Display a summary of SSP statistics. | show sse summary |

## Specify the Type and Use of Ping Packets

The Cisco IOS software can transmit Cisco pings or standard Novell pings as defined in the NLSP specification. By default, the software generates Cisco pings. To choose the ping type, perform the following task in global configuration mode:

| Task | Command |
|---|---|
| Select the ping type. | ipx ping-default {cisco I novell} |

To initiate a ping, perform one of the following tasks in EXEC mode:

| Task | Command |
|---|---|
| **Step 1** Diagnose basic IPX network connectivity (user-level command). | ping ipx *network.node* |
| **Step 2** Diagnose basic IPX network connectivity (privileged command). | ping [ipx] [*network.node*] |

## Repair Corrupted Network Numbers

To repair corrupted network numbers on an interface, perform the following tasks in interface configuration mode:

| Task | Command |
|---|---|
| **Step 1** Disable fast switching. | no ipx route-cache |
| **Step 2** Repair corrupted network numbers. | ipx source-network-update |

---

**CAUTION**

The **ipx source-network-update** interface configuration command interferes with the proper working of OS/2 Requestors. Do not use this command in a network that has OS/2 Requestors.

---

---

**CAUTION**

Do not use the **ipx source-network-update** interface configuration command on interfaces on which NetWare servers are using internal network numbers (that is, all NetWare 3.1*x*, 4.*x*, and NetWare IntraNetWare servers).

---

## Monitor and Maintain IPX Enhanced IGRP

To monitor and maintain Enhanced IGRP on an IPX network, perform one or more of the following tasks at the EXEC prompt:

| Task | Command |
|------|---------|
| **Step 1** List the neighbors discovered by IPX Enhanced IGRP. | **show ipx eigrp neighbors** [**servers**] [*autonomous-system-number* \| *interface*] |
| **Step 2** Display information about interfaces configured for Enhanced IGRP. | **show ipx eigrp interfaces** [*interface*] [*as-number*] |
| **Step 3** Display the contents of the IPX Enhanced IGRP topology table. | **show ipx eigrp topology** [*network-number*] |
| **Step 4** Display the contents of the IPX routing table, including Enhanced IGRP entries. | **show ipx route** [*network-number*] |
| **Step 5** Display information about IPX traffic, including Enhanced IGRP traffic. | **show ipx traffic** |

### *Log Enhanced IGRP Neighbor Adjacency Changes*

You can enable the logging of neighbor adjacency changes to monitor the stability of the routing system and to help you detect problems. By default, adjacency changes are not logged.

To enable logging of Enhanced IGRP neighbor adjacency changes, perform the following task in global configuration mode:

| Task | Command |
|------|---------|
| Enable logging of Enhanced IGRP neighbor adjacency changes. | **log-neighbor-changes** |

## Monitor and Maintain NLSP

To monitor and maintain NLSP on an IPX network, perform one or more of the following tasks at the EXEC prompt:

| Task | Command |
|------|---------|
| **Step 1** Delete all NLSP adjacencies from the adjacency database. | **clear ipx nlsp** [*tag*] **neighbors** |
| **Step 2** Display the entries in the link-state packet (LSP) database. | **show ipx nlsp** [*tag*] **database** [*lspid*] [**detail**] |
| **Step 3** Display the device's NLSP neighbors and their states. | **show ipx nlsp** [*tag*] **neighbors** [*interface*] [**detail**] |
| **Step 4** Display a history of the SPF calculations for NLSP. | **show ipx nlsp** [*tag*] **spf-log** |

### Log Adjacency State Changes

You can allow NLSP to generate a log message when an NLSP adjacency changes state (up or down). This may be very useful when monitoring large networks. Messages are logged using the system error message facility. Messages are of the following form:

```
%CLNS-5-ADJCHANGE: NLSP: Adjacency to 0000.0000.0034 (Serial0) Up, new adjacency
%CLNS-5-ADJCHANGE: NLSP: Adjacency to 0000.0000.0034 (Serial0) Down, hold time expired
```

To generate log messages when an NLSP adjacency changes state, perform the following task in router configuration mode:

| Task | Command |
|------|---------|
| Log NLSP adjacency state changes. | **log-adjacency-changes** |

## Monitor and Maintain NHRP

To monitor the NHRP cache or traffic, perform either of the following tasks in EXEC mode:

| Task | Command |
|------|---------|
| Display the IPX NHRP cache, optionally limited to dynamic or static cache entries for a specific interface. | **show ipx nhrp** [**dynamic** \| **static**] [*type number*] |
| Display NHRP traffic statistics. | **show ipx nhrp traffic** |

The NHRP cache can contain static entries caused by statically configured addresses and dynamic entries caused by the Cisco IOS software learning addresses from NHRP packets. To clear static entries, use the **no ipx nhrp map** command. To clear the NHRP cache of dynamic entries, perform the following task in EXEC mode:

| Task | Command |
| --- | --- |
| Clear the IPX NHRP cache of dynamic entries. | **clear ipx nhrp** |

## Monitor and Maintain IPX Accounting

To monitor and maintain IPX accounting in your IPX network, perform the following tasks in EXEC mode:

| Task | | Command |
| --- | --- | --- |
| **Step 1** | Delete all entries in the IPX accounting or accounting checkpoint database. | **clear ipx accounting** [checkpoint] |
| **Step 2** | List the entries in the IPX accounting or accounting checkpoint database. | **show ipx accounting** [checkpoint] |

## NOVELL IPX CONFIGURATION EXAMPLES

This section provides configuration examples for the following IPX configuration situations:

- IPX Routing Examples
- Enhanced IGRP Examples
- NLSP Examples
- NHRP Examples
- IPX over WAN Examples
- IPX Network Access Examples
- Helper Facilities to Control Broadcast Examples
- IPX Accounting Example

## IPX Routing Examples

This section shows examples for enabling IPX routing on interfaces with a single network and with multiple networks. It also shows how to enable and disable various combinations of routing protocols.

The following sections contain these examples:

- IPX Routing on a Single Network Example
- IPX Routing on Multiple Networks Examples
- IPX Routing Protocols Examples

## IPX Routing on a Single Network Example

The following configuration commands enable IPX routing, defaulting the IPX host address to that of the first IEEE-conformance interface (in this example, Ethernet 0). Routing is then enabled on Ethernet 0 and Ethernet 1 for IPX networks 2abc and 1def, respectively.

```
ipx routing
interface ethernet 0
 ipx network 2abc
interface ethernet 1
 ipx network 1def
```

## IPX Routing on Multiple Networks Examples

There are two ways to enable IPX on an interface that supports multiple networks. You can use subinterfaces or primary and secondary networks. This section gives an example of each.

### Subinterfaces Example

The following example uses subinterfaces to create four logical networks on Ethernet interface 0. Each subinterface has a different encapsulation. Any interface configuration parameters that you specify on an individual subinterface are applied to that subinterface only.

```
ipx routing
interface ethernet 0.1
 ipx network 1 encapsulation novell-ether
interface ethernet 0.2
 ipx network 2 encapsulation snap
interface ethernet 0.3
 ipx network 3 encapsulation arpa
interface ethernet 0.4
 ipx network 4 encapsulation sap
```

**NOTES**

When enabling NLSP and configuring multiple encapsulations on the same physical LAN interface, you must use subinterfaces. You cannot use secondary networks.

You can administratively shut down each of the four subinterfaces separately by using the **shutdown** interface configuration command for each subinterface. For example, the following commands administratively shut down a subinterface:

```
interface ethernet 0.3
 shutdown
```

To bring down network 1, use the following commands:

```
interface ethernet 0.1
 ipx down 1
```

To bring network 1 back up, use the following commands:

```
interface ethernet 0.1
 no ipx down 1
```

To remove all the networks on the interface, use the following interface configuration commands:

```
interface ethernet 0.1
 no ipx network
interface ethernet 0.2
 no ipx network
interface ethernet 0.3
 no ipx network
interface ethernet 0.4
 no ipx network
```

### *Primary and Secondary Networks Examples*

**NOTES**

The following examples discuss primary and secondary networks. In future Cisco IOS software releases, primary and secondary networks will not be supported. Use subinterfaces.

The following example uses primary and secondary networks to create the same four logical networks, as shown earlier in this section. Any interface configuration parameters that you specify on this interface are applied to all the logical networks. For example, if you set the routing update timer to 120 seconds, this value is used on all four networks.

```
ipx routing
interface ethernet 0
 ipx network 1 encapsulation novell-ether
 ipx network 2 encapsulation snap secondary
 ipx network 3 encapsulation arpa secondary
 ipx network 4 encapsulation sap secondary
```

Using this method to configure logical networks, if you administratively shut down Ethernet interface 0 using the **shutdown** interface configuration command, all four logical networks are shut down. You cannot bring down each logical network independently using the **shutdown** command; however, you can do this using the **ipx down** command.

To shut down network 1, use the following command:

```
interface ethernet 0
 ipx down 1
```

To bring the network back up, use the following command:

```
interface ethernet 0
 no ipx down 1
```

To shut down all four networks on the interface and remove all the networks on the interface, use one of the following interface configuration commands:

```
no ipx network

no ipx network 1
```

To remove one of the secondary networks on the interface (in this case, network 2), use the following interface configuration command:

```
no ipx network 2
```

The following example enables IPX routing on FDDI interfaces 0.2 and 0.3. On FDDI interface 0.2, the encapsulation type is SNAP. On FDDI interface 0.3, the encapsulation type is Novell's FDDI_RAW.

```
ipx routing
interface fddi 0.2
 ipx network f02 encapsulation snap
interface fddi 0.3
 ipx network f03 encapsulation novell-fddi
```

### IPX Routing Protocols Examples

Three routing protocols can run over interfaces configured for IPX: RIP, Enhanced IGRP, and NLSP. This section provides examples of how to enable and disable various combinations of routing protocols.

When you enable IPX routing with the **ipx routing** global configuration command, the RIP routing protocol is automatically enabled. The following example enables RIP on networks 1 and 2:

```
ipx routing
!
interface ethernet 0
 ipx network 1
!
interface ethernet 1
 ipx network 2
```

The following example enables RIP on networks 1 and 2 and Enhanced IGRP on network 1:

```
ipx routing
!
interface ethernet 0
 ipx network 1
!
interface ethernet 1
 ipx network 2
!
ipx router eigrp 100
 network 1
```

The following example enables RIP on network 2 and Enhanced IGRP on network 1:

```
ipx routing
!
```

```
interface ethernet 0
 ipx network 1
!
interface ethernet 1
 ipx network 2
!
ipx router eigrp 100
 ipx network 1
!
ipx router rip
 no ipx network 1
```

The following example configures NLSP on two of a router's Ethernet interfaces. Note that RIP is automatically enabled on both of these interfaces. This example assumes that the encapsulation type is Ethernet 802.2.

```
ipx routing
 ipx internal-network 3
!
ipx router nlsp area1
area-address 0 0
!
interface ethernet 0
 ipx network e0 encapsulation sap
ipx nlsp area1 enable
!
interface ethernet 1
 ipx network e1 encapsulation sap
ipx nlsp area1 enable
```

## Enhanced IGRP Examples

This section shows several examples for configuring IPX Enhanced IGRP routing. The following sections contain these examples:

- IPX Enhanced IGRP Example
- Enhanced IGRP SAP Update Examples
- Advertisement and Processing of SAP Update Examples
- IPX Enhanced IGRP Bandwidth Configuration Examples

### *IPX Enhanced IGRP Example*

The following example configures two interfaces for Enhanced IGRP routing in autonomous system 1:

```
ipx routing
!
interface ethernet 0
 ipx network 10
```

```
!
interface serial 0
 ipx network 20
!
ipx router eigrp 1
 network 10
 network 20
```

## Enhanced IGRP SAP Update Examples

If an Ethernet interface has neighbors that are all configured for Enhanced IGRP, you might want to reduce the bandwidth used by SAP packets by sending SAP updates incrementally. To do this, you would configure the interface as follows:

```
ipx routing
!
interface ethernet 0
 ipx network 10
 ipx sap-incremental eigrp 1
!
interface serial 0
 ipx network 20
!
ipx router eigrp 1
 network 10
 network 20
```

If you want to send only incremental SAP updates on a serial line that is configured for Enhanced IGRP, but periodic RIP updates, use the following commands:

```
ipx routing
!
interface ethernet 0
 ipx network 10
!
interface serial 0
 ipx network 20
 ipx sap-incremental eigrp 1 rsup-only
!
ipx router eigrp 1
 network 10
 network 20
```

## Advertisement and Processing of SAP Update Examples

The following example causes only services from network 3 to be advertised by an Enhanced IGRP routing process:

```
access-list 1010 permit 3
access-list 1010 deny -1
!
ipx router eigrp 100
 network 3
 distribute-sap-list 1010 out
```

In the following example, the router redistributes Enhanced IGRP into NLSP *area1*. Only services for networks 2 and 3 are accepted by the NLSP routing process.

```
access-list 1000 permit 2
access-list 1000 permit 3
access-list 1000 deny -1
!
ipx router nlsp area1
 redistribute eigrp
 distribute-sap-list 1000 in
```

### IPX Enhanced IGRP Bandwidth Configuration Examples

The following example shows how to configure the bandwidth used by IPX Enhanced IGRP. In this example, Enhanced IGRP process 109 is configured to use a maximum of 25 percent (or 32 kbps) of a 128 kbps circuit:

```
interface serial 0
 bandwidth 128
 ipx bandwidth-percent eigrp 109 25
```

In the following example, the bandwidth of a 56 kbps circuit has been configured to be 20 kbps for routing policy reasons. The Enhanced IGRP process 109 is configured to use a maximum of 200 percent (or 40 kbps) of the circuit.

```
interface serial 1
 bandwidth 20
 ipx bandwidth-percent eigrp 109 200
```

## NLSP Examples

This section shows several examples for configuring NSLP. The following sections contain these examples:

- NLSP Multicast Addressing Examples
- Enhanced IGRP and NLSP Route Redistribution Example
- NLSP Route Aggregation for Multiple NLSP Version 1.1 Areas Example
- NLSP Route Aggregation for NLSP Version 1.1 and Version 1.0 Areas Example
- NLSP Route Aggregation for NLSP Version 1.1, Enhanced IGRP, and RIP Example

### NLSP Multicast Addressing Examples

By default, NLSP multicast addressing is enabled. You do not need to configure anything to turn on NLSP multicasting.

Typically, you do not want to substitute broadcast addressing where NLSP multicast addressing is available. NLSP multicast addressing uses network bandwidth more efficiently than broadcast addressing. However, there are circumstances in which you might want to disable NLSP multicast addressing.

For example, you might want to disable NLSP multicast addressing in favor of broadcast addressing when one or more devices on a segment do not support NLSP multicast addressing. You might also want to disable it for testing purposes.

If you want to disable NLSP multicast addressing, you can do so for the entire router or for a particular interface.

The following sections provide sample configurations for disabling multicast addressing:

- Disable NLSP Multicasting on the Router Example
- Disable NLSP Multicasting on an Interface Example

### Disable NLSP Multicasting on the Router Example

The following example disables multicast addressing on the router:

```
ipx router nlsp
no multicast
```

### Disable NLSP Multicasting on an Interface Example

The following example disables multicast addressing on Ethernet interface 1.2:

```
interface ethernet1.2
 no ipx nlsp multicast
```

## Enhanced IGRP and NLSP Route Redistribution Example

The following example configures a router to redistribute NLSP into Enhanced IGRP autonomous system 100 and Enhanced IGRP autonomous system 100 into NLSP:

```
!
ipx router eigrp 100
 redistribute nlsp
!
ipx router nlsp
 redistribute eigrp 100
!
```

## NLSP Route Aggregation for Multiple NLSP Version 1.1 Areas Example

The following example shows the route aggregation configuration for a router connecting multiple NLSP version 1.1 areas. In this example, the two areas are *area1* and *area2*. Because both areas are NLSP version 1.1 areas, redistribution of aggregated routes or explicit routes between the two areas is automatic.

```
ipx routing
ipx internal-network 2000
!
interface ethernet 1
 ipx network 1001
 ipx nlsp area1 enable
```

```
!
interface ethernet 2
 ipx network 2001
 ipx nlsp area2 enable
!
ipx router nlsp area1
 area-address 1000 fffff000
 route-aggregation
!
ipx router nlsp area2
 area-address 2000 fffff000
 route-aggregation
```

### NLSP Route Aggregation for NLSP Version 1.1 and Version 1.0 Areas Example

The following example configures the route aggregation feature with customized route summarization. In this example, *area1* is an NLSP version 1.0 area and *area2* is an NLSP version 1.1 area. Any explicit routes learned in *area1* that fall in the range of *aaaa0000 ffff0000* are redistributed into *area2* as an aggregated route. Explicit routes from *area1* that do not fall in that range are redistributed into *area2* as an explicit route.

Because *area1* is an NLSP version 1.0 area, it cannot accept aggregated routes learned in *area2*. Thus, when redistribution into *area1* occurs, the router sends explicit routes instead of aggregated routes.

```
ipx routing
ipx internal-network 2000
!
interface ethernet 1
 ipx network 1001
 ipx nlsp area1 enable
!
interface ethernet 2
 ipx network 2001
 ipx nlsp area2 enable
!
access-list 1200 deny aaaa0000 ffff0000
access-list 1200 permit -1
!
ipx router nlsp area1
 area-address 1000 fffff000
!
ipx router nlsp area2
 area-address 2000 fffff000
 route-aggregation
 redistribute nlsp area1 access-list 1200
```

### NLSP Route Aggregation for NLSP Version 1.1, Enhanced IGRP, and RIP Example

In the following example, the router connects two NLSP version 1.1 areas, one Enhanced IGRP area, and one RIP area.

Any routes learned via NLSP *a1* that are represented by *aaaa0000 ffff0000* are not redistributed into NLSP *a2* as explicit routes. Instead, the router generates an aggregated route. Any routes learned via NLSP *a2* that are represented by *bbbb0000 ffff0000* are not redistributed as explicit routes into NLSP *a1*. Again, the router generates an aggregated route. Any routes learned via RIP that are represented by *cccc0000 ffff0000* are not redistributed as explicit routes into NLSP *a1* or NLSP *a2*. Instead, the router sends an aggregated route. Likewise, any routes learned via Enhanced IGRP 129 that are represented by *dddd0000 ffff0000* are not redistributed into NLSP *a1* or NLSP *a2*. Again, the router sends an aggregated route.

```
ipx routing
ipx internal-network 2000
!
interface ethernet 0
 ipx network aaaa0000
 ipx nlsp a1 enable
!
interface ethernet 1
 ipx network bbbb0000
 ipx nlsp a2 enable
!
interface ethernet 2
 ipx network cccc0000
!
interface ethernet 3
 ipx network dddd0000
!
access-list 1200 deny aaaa0000 ffff0000
access-list 1200 permit -1
!
access-list 1201 deny bbbb0000 ffff0000
access-list 1201 permit -1
!
access-list 1202 deny cccc0000 ffff0000
access-list 1202 permit -1
!
access-list 1203 deny dddd0000 ffff0000
access-list 1203 permit -1
!
ipx router nlsp a1
 area-address 10000 fffff000
 route-aggregation
 redistribute nlsp a2 access-list 1201
 redistribute rip access-list 1202
 redistribute eigrp 129 access-list 1203
!
ipx router nlsp a2
 area-address 2000 fffff000
 route-aggregation
 redistribute nlsp a1 access-list 1200
 redistribute rip access-list 1202
 redistribute eigrp 129 access-list 1203
```

```
!
ipx router eigrp 129
 network dddd0000
 redistribute nlsp a1
 redistribute nlsp a2
```

## NHRP Examples

This section shows examples for configuring NHRP. The following sections contain these examples:

- NHRP Example
- NHRP over ATM Example

### NHRP Example

A logical NBMA network is considered the group of interfaces and hosts participating in NHRP and having the same network identifier. Figure 4–1 illustrates two logical NBMA networks (shown as circles) configured over a single physical NBMA network. Router A communicates with Routers B and C because they share the same network identifier (2). Router C also communicates with Routers D and E because they share network identifier 7. After address resolution is complete, Router A sends IPX packets to Router C in one hop, and Router C sends them to Router E in one hop, as shown by the dotted lines.

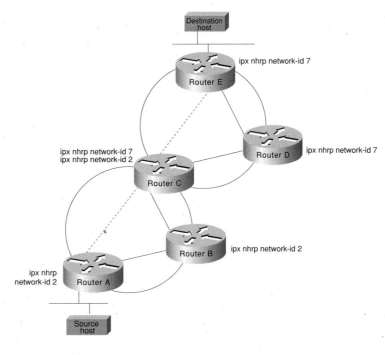

*Figure 4–1*
*Two Logical NBMA Networks over One Physical NBMA Network.*

— = Statically configured tunnel end points or permanent virtual circuits

----- = Dynamically created virtual circuits

The physical configuration of the five routers in Figure 4–1 might actually be that shown in Figure 4–2. The source host is connected to Router A, and the destination host is connected to Router E. The same switch serves all five routers, making one physical NBMA network.

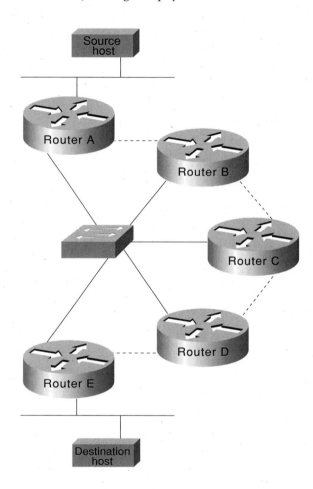

**Figure 4–2**

*Physical Configuration of a Sample NBMA Network.*

Refer again to Figure 4–1. Initially, before NHRP resolves any NBMA addresses, IPX packets from the source host to the destination host travel through all five routers connected to the switch before reaching the destination. When Router A first forwards the IPX packet toward the destination host, Router A also generates an NHRP request for the destination host's IPX address. The request is forwarded to Router C, where a reply is generated. Router C replies because it is the egress router between the two logical NBMA networks.

Similarly, Router C generates an NHRP request of its own, to which Router E replies. In this example, subsequent IPX traffic between the source and the destination still requires two hops to traverse the NBMA network because the IPX traffic must be forwarded between the two logical NBMA networks. Only one hop would be required if the NBMA network was not logically divided.

### NHRP over ATM Example

The following example shows a configuration of three routers using NHRP over ATM. Router A is configured with a static route, which it uses to reach the IPX network where Router B resides. Router A initially reaches Router B through Router C. Router A and Router B directly communicate without Router C once NHRP resolves Router A's and Router C's respective NSAP addresses.

The significant portions of the configurations for Routers A, B, and C follow:

### Router A

```
interface ATM0/0
 map-group a
 atm nsap-address 11.1111.11.111111.1111.1111.1111.1111.1111.1111.11
 atm rate-queue 1 10
 atm pvc 1 0 5 qsaal
 ipx network 1
 ipx nhrp network-id 1

map-list a
ipx 1.0000.0c15.3588 atm-nsap 33.3333.33.333333.3333.3333.3333.3333.3333.3333.33

ipx route 2 1.0000.0c15.3588
```

### Router B

```
interface ATM0/0
 map-group a
 atm nsap-address 22.2222.22.222222.2222.2222.2222.2222.2222.2222.22
 atm rate-queue 1 10
 atm pvc 2 0 5 qsaal
 ipx network 2
 ipx nhrp network-id 1

map-list a
ipx 2.0000.0c15.3628 atm-nsap 33.3333.33.333333.3333.3333.3333.3333.3333.3333.33

ipx route 1 2.0000.0c15.3628
```

### Router C

```
interface ATM0/0
atm rate-queue 1 10
 atm pvc 2 0 5 qsaal

interface ATM0/0.1 multipoint
 map-group a
 atm nsap-address 33.3333.33.333333.3333.3333.3333.3333.3333.3333.33
 ipx network 1
 ipx nhrp network-id 1
```

```
interface ATM0/0.2 multipoint
 map-group b
 atm nsap-address 33.3333.33.333333.3333.3333.3333.3333.3333.3333.33
 ipx network 2
 ipx nhrp network-id 2

map-list a
ipx 1.0000.0c15.4f80 atm-nsap 11.1111.11.111111.1111.1111.1111.1111.1111.1111.11

map-list b
ipx 2.0000.0c15.5021 atm-nsap 22.2222.22.222222.2222.2222.2222.2222.2222.2222.22
```

## IPX over WAN Examples

This section shows examples for configuring IPX over WAN and dial interfaces. The following sections contain these examples:

- IPX over a WAN Interface Example
- IPX over DDR Example

### IPX over a WAN Interface Example

When you configure the Cisco IOS software to transport IPX packets over a serial interface that is running a WAN protocol such as X.25 or PPP, you specify how the packet is encapsulated for transport. This encapsulation is not the same as the encapsulation used on an IPX LAN interface. Figure 4–3 illustrates IPX over a WAN interface.

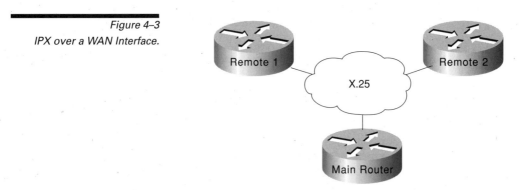

Figure 4–3

IPX over a WAN Interface.

The following examples configure a serial interface for X.25 encapsulation and for several IPX subinterfaces used in a nonmeshed topology:

### Configuration for Main Router

```
hostname Main
!
no ip routing
```

```
novell routing 0000.0c17.d726
!
interface ethernet 0
 no ip address
 Novell network 100
 media-type 10BaseT
!
interface serial 0
 no ip address
 shutdown
!
interface serial 1
 no ip address
 encapsulation x25
 x25 address 33333
 x25 htc 28
!
interface serial 1.1 point-to-point
 no ip address
 novell network 2
 x25 map novell 2.0000.0c03.a4ad 11111 BROADCAST
!
interface serial 1.2 point-to-point
 no ip address
 novell network 3
 x25 map novell 3.0000.0c07.5e26 55555 BROADCAST
```

## Configuration for Router 1

```
hostname Remote1
!
no ip routing
novell routing 0000.0c03.a4ad
!
interface ethernet 0
 no ip address
 novell network 1
!
interface serial 0
 no ip address
 encapsulation x25
 novell network 2
 x25 address 11111
 x25 htc 28
 x25 map novell 2.0000.0c17.d726 33333 BROADCAST
```

## Configuration for Router 2

```
hostname Remote2
!
no ip routing
novell routing 0000.0c07.5e26
```

```
!
interface ethernet 0
 no ip address
 novell network 4
 media-type 10BaseT
!
interface serial 0
 no ip address
 shutdown
!
interface serial 1
 no ip address
 encapsulation x25
 novell network 3
 x25 address 55555
 x25 htc 28
 x25 map novell 3.0000.0c17.d726 33333 BROADCAST
```

### IPX over DDR Example

In the configuration shown in Figure 4–4, an IPX client is separated from its server by a DDR telephone line.

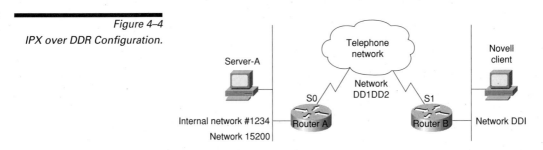

**Figure 4–4**
*IPX over DDR Configuration.*

Routing and service information is sent every minute. The output RIP and SAP filters defined in this example filter these updates, preventing them from being sent between Routers A and B. If you were to forward these packets, the two routers would each have to telephone the other once a minute. On a serial link that charges based on the number of packets transmitted, this is generally not desirable. This might not be an issue on a dedicated serial line.

After the server and client have established contact, the server sends keepalive (watchdog) packets regularly. When SPX is used, both the server and the client send keepalive packets. The purpose of these packets is to ensure that the connection between the server and the client is still functional; these packets contain no other information. Servers send watchdog packets approximately every 5 minutes.

If you were to allow Router A to forward the server's keepalive packets to Router B, Router A would have to telephone Router B every 5 minutes just to send these packets. Again, on a serial link that charges based on the number of packets transmitted, this is generally not desirable. Instead of having Router A telephone Router B only to send keepalive packets, you can enable watchdog spoofing on Router A. This way, when the server connected to this router sends keepalive packets, Router A responds on behalf of the remote client (the client connected to Router B). When SPX is used, you must enable spoofing of SPX keepalive packets on both Router A and Router B to inhibit the sending of them because both the server and the client send keepalive packets.

### Configuration for Router A

```
novell routing 0000.0c04.4878
!
interface Ethernet0
 novell network 15200
!
interface Serial0
!ppp encap for DDR(recommended)
 encapsulation ppp
 novell network DD1DD2
!kill all rip updates
 novell output-network-filter 801
!kill all sap updates
 novell output-sap-filter 1001
! fast-switching off for watchdog spoofing
 no novell route-cache
!don't listen to rip
 novell router-filter 866
!novell watchdog spoofing
 novell watchdog-spoof
!SPX watchdog spoofing
 ipx spx-spoof
!turn on DDR
 dialer in-band
 dialer idle-timeout 200
 dialer map IP 198.92.96.132 name R13 7917
 dialer map NOVELL DD1DD2.0000.0c03.e3c3 7917
 dialer-group 1
 ppp authentication chap
!chap authentication required
 pulse-time 1
!
access-list 801 deny  FFFFFFFF
access-list 866 deny  FFFFFFFF
!serialization packets
access-list 900 deny  0 FFFFFFFF 0 FFFFFFFF 457
!RIP packets
access-list 900 deny  1 FFFFFFFF 453 FFFFFFFF 453
!SAP packets
access-list 900 deny  4 FFFFFFFF 452 FFFFFFFF 452
!permit everything else
access-list 900 permit -1 FFFFFFFF 0 FFFFFFFF 0
```

```
!
access-list 1001 deny  FFFFFFFF
!
!static novell route for remote network
novell route DD1 DD1DD2.0000.0c03.e3c3
!
!
!IPX will trigger the line up (9.21 and later)
dialer-list 1 list 900
```

## Configuration for Router B

```
novell routing 0000.0c03.e3c3
!
interface Ethernet1/0
 novell network DD1
!
interface Serial2/0
 encapsulation ppp
 novell network DD1DD2
 novell output-network-filter 801
 novell output-sap-filter 1001
 no novell route-cache
 novell router-filter 866
 ipx spx-spoof
 dialer in-band
 dialer idle-timeout 200
 dialer map IP 198.92.96.129 name R5 7919
 dialer map NOVELL DD1DD2.0000.0c04.4878 7919
 dialer-group 1
 ppp authentication chap
 pulse-time 1
!
access-list 801 deny -1
access-list 866 deny -1
access-list 900 deny  0 FFFFFFFF 0 FFFFFFFF 457
access-list 900 deny  1 FFFFFFFF 453 FFFFFFFF 453
access-list 900 deny  4 FFFFFFFF 452 FFFFFFFF 452
access-list 900 permit -1 FFFFFFFF 0 FFFFFFFF 0
access-list 1001 deny  FFFFFFFF
!
!static novell route for server's internal network
novell route 1234 DD1DD2.0000.0c04.4878
novell route 15200 DD1DD2.0000.0c04.4878
!static route
!The following line is the static novell sap required to get to the remote server.
!It informs the router of the next hop.
novell sap 4 CE1-LAB 1234.0000.0000.0001 451 4 <====
!
dialer-list 1 list 900
```

## IPX Network Access Examples

This section contains examples for controlling access to your IPX network. It shows the configurations for various access lists and filters. The following sections contain these examples:

- IPX Network Access Example
- Standard Named Access List Example
- SAP Input Filter Example
- SAP Output Filter Example
- IPX NetBIOS Filter Examples

### IPX Network Access Example

Using access lists to manage traffic routing is a powerful tool in overall network control. However, it requires a certain amount of planning and the appropriate application of several related commands. Figure 4–5 illustrates a network featuring two routers on two network segments.

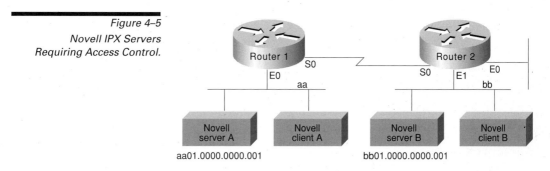

Figure 4–5
Novell IPX Servers
Requiring Access Control.

Router 1
S0
E0
aa

Router 2
S0  E1  E0
bb

Novell server A
Novell client A

Novell server B
Novell client B

aa01.0000.0000.001

bb01.0000.0000.001

Suppose you want to prevent clients and servers on Network *aa* from using the services on Network *bb*, but you want to allow the clients and servers on Network *bb* to use the services on Network *aa*. To do this, you would need an access list on Ethernet interface 1 on Router 2 that blocks all packets coming from Network *aa* and destined for Network *bb*. You would not need any access list on Ethernet interface 0 on Router 1.

You would configure Ethernet interface 1 on Router 2 with the following commands:

```
ipx routing
access-list 800 deny aa bb01
access-list 800 permit -1 -1
interface ethernet 1
 ipx network bb
 ipx access-group 800
```

You can accomplish the same result as the previous example more efficiently. For example, you can place the same output filter on Router 1, interface serial 0. Alternatively, you could also place an input filter on interface Ethernet 0 of Router 1, as follows:

```
ipx routing
access-list 800 deny aa bb01
access-list 800 permit -1 -1
interface ethernet 0
 ipx network aa
 ipx access-group 800 in
```

**NOTES**

When using access control list logging on an interface with fast switching turned on, packets that match the access list (and thus need to be logged) are slow switched, not fast switched.

### Logging Access Control List Violations

You can keep a log of all access control list violations by using the keyword **log** near the end of the **access-list** command, as follows:

```
access-list 907 deny -1 -1 0 100 0 log
```

The previous example denies and logs all packets that arrive at the router from any source in any protocol from any socket to any destination on network 100.

The following is an example of a log entry for the **access-list** command:

```
%IPX-6-ACL: 907 deny SPX B5A8 50.0000.0000.0001 B5A8 100.0000.0000.0001 10 pkts
```

In this example, 10 SPX packets were denied because they matched access list number 907. The packets were coming from socket B5A8 on network 50.0000.0000.0001 and were destined for socket B5A8 on network 100.0000.0000.0001.

## Standard Named Access List Example

The following example creates a standard access list named *fred*. It denies communication with only IPX network number 5678.

```
ipx access-list standard fred
 deny 5678 any
 permit any
```

## SAP Input Filter Example

SAP input filters allow a router to determine whether to accept information about a service. Router C1, illustrated in Figure 4–6, does not accept and, consequently does not advertise, any information about Novell server F. However, Router C1 accepts information about all other servers on the network 3c. Router C2 receives information about servers D and B.

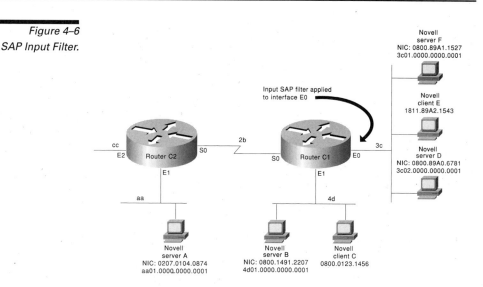

*Figure 4–6*
*SAP Input Filter.*

The following example configures Router C1. The first line denies server F, and the second line accepts all other servers.

```
access-list 1000 deny 3c01.0000.0000.0001
access-list 1000 permit -1
interface ethernet 0
 ipx network 3c
 ipx input-sap-filter 1000
interface ethernet 1
 ipx network 4d
interface serial 0
 ipx network 2b
```

**NOTES**

NetWare Versions 3.11 and later use an internal network and node number as their address for access list commands (the first configuration command in this example).

## SAP Output Filter Example

SAP output filters are applied prior to the Cisco IOS software sending information out a specific interface. In the example that follows, Router C1 (illustrated in Figure 4–7) is prevented from advertising information about Novell server A out interface Ethernet 1 but can advertise server A on network 3c.

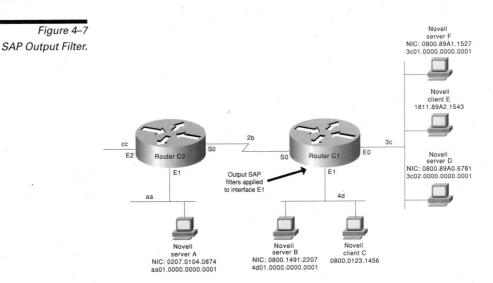

*Figure 4–7*
*SAP Output Filter.*

The following example refers to Router C1. The first line denies server A. All other servers are permitted.

```
access-list 1000 deny aa01.0000.0000.0001
access-list 1000 permit -1
interface ethernet 0
 novell net 3c
interface ethernet 1
 ipx network 4d
 ipx output-sap-filter 1000
interface serial 0
 ipx network 2b
```

## IPX NetBIOS Filter Examples

The following is an example of using a NetBIOS host name to filter IPX NetBIOS frames. The example denies all outgoing IPX NetBIOS frames with a NetBIOS host name of *Boston* on Ethernet interface 0:

```
netbios access-list host token deny Boston
netbios access-list host token permit *
!
ipx routing 0000.0c17.d45d
!
interface ethernet 0
 ipx network 155 encapsulation ARPA
 ipx output-rip-delay 60
 ipx triggered-rip-delay 30
 ipx output-sap-delay 60
 ipx triggered-sap-delay 30
```

```
 ipx type-20-propagation
 ipx netbios output-access-filter host token
 no mop enabled
!
interface ethernet 1
 no ip address
 ipx network 105
!
interface fddi 0
 no ip address
 no keepalive
ipx network 305 encapsulation SAP
!
interface serial 0
 no ip address
 shutdown
!
interface serial 1
 no ip address
 no keepalive
 ipx network 600
 ipx output-rip-delay 100
 ipx triggered-rip-delay 60
 ipx output-sap-delay 100
 ipx triggered-sap-delay 60
 ipx type-20-propagation
```

The following is an example of using a byte pattern to filter IPX NetBIOS frames. This example permits IPX NetBIOS frames from IPX network numbers that end in 05. This means that all IPX NetBIOS frames from Ethernet interface 1 (network 105) and FDDI interface 0 (network 305) are forwarded by serial interface 0. However, this interface filters out and does not forward all frames from Ethernet interface 0 (network 155).

```
netbios access-list bytes finigan permit 2 **05
!
ipx routing 0000.0c17.d45d
!
ipx default-output-rip-delay 1000
ipx default-triggered-rip-delay 100
ipx default-output-sap-delay 1000
ipx default-triggered-sap-delay 100
!
interface ethernet 0
 ipx network 155 encapsulation ARPA
 ipx output-rip-delay 55
 ipx triggered-rip-delay 55
 ipx output-sap-delay 55
 ipx triggered-sap-delay 55
 ipx type-20-propagation
 media-type 10BaseT
!
interface ethernet 1
```

```
  no ip address
  ipx network 105
  ipx output-rip-delay 55
  ipx triggered-rip-delay 55
  ipx output-sap-delay 55
  ipx triggered-sap-delay 55
  media-type 10BaseT
!
interface fddi 0
 no ip address
 no keepalive
 ipx network 305 encapsulation SAP
 ipx output-sap-delay 55
 ipx triggered-sap-delay 55
!
interface serial 0
 no ip address
 shutdown
!
interface serial 1
 no ip address
 no keepalive
 ipx network 600
 ipx type-20-propagation
 ipx netbios input-access-filter bytes finigan
```

## Helper Facilities to Control Broadcast Examples

The following examples illustrate how to control broadcast messages on IPX networks. The following sections contain these examples:

- Forwarding to an Address Example
- Forwarding to All Networks Example
- All-Nets Flooded Broadcast Example

Note that in the following examples, packet type 2 is used. This type has been chosen arbitrarily; the actual type to use depends on the specific application.

### Forwarding to an Address Example

All broadcast packets are normally blocked by the Cisco IOS software. However, type 20 propagation packets may be forwarded, subject to certain loop-prevention checks. Other broadcasts may be directed to a set of networks or a specific host (node) on a segment. The following examples illustrate these options.

Figure 4–8 shows a router (*C1*) connected to several Ethernet interfaces. In this environment, all IPX clients are attached to segment *aa*, while all servers are attached to segments *bb* and *dd*. In controlling broadcasts, the following conditions are to be applied:

- Only type 2 and type 20 broadcasts are to be forwarded.

- The IPX clients on network *aa* are allowed to broadcast via type 2 to any server on networks *bb* and *dd*.

- The IPX clients are allowed to broadcast via type 20 to any server on network *dd*.

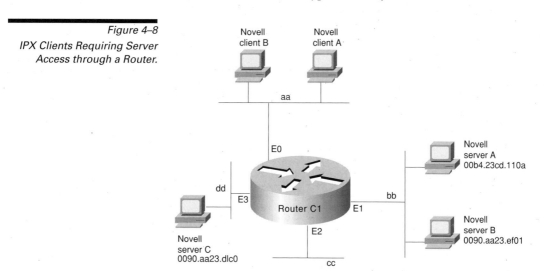

*Figure 4–8*
*IPX Clients Requiring Server Access through a Router.*

The following example configures the router shown in Figure 4–8. The first line permits broadcast traffic of type 2 from network *aa*. The interface and network commands configure each specific interface. The **ipx helper-address** commands permit broadcast forwarding from network *aa* to *bb* and from network *aa* to *dd*. The helper list allows type 2 broadcasts to be forwarded. (Note that type 2 broadcasts are chosen as an example only. The actual type to use depends on the application.) The **ipx type-20-propagation** command is also required to allow type 20 broadcasts, usually IPX NetBIOS, to be forwarded to all networks where type-20-propagation is enabled. The ipx helper-list filter is applied to both the type 2 packets forwarded by the helper-address mechanism and the type 20 packets forwarded by type-20 propagation.

```
access-list 900 permit 2 aa
interface ethernet 0
 ipx network aa
 ipx type-20-propagation
 ipx helper-address bb.ffff.ffff.ffff
 ipx helper-address dd.ffff.ffff.ffff
 ipx helper-list 900
interface ethernet 1
 ipx network bb
interface ethernet 3
 ipx network dd
 ipx type-20-propagation
```

This configuration means that any network that is downstream from network *aa* (for example, some arbitrary network *aa1*) cannot broadcast (type 2) to network *bb* through Router *C1* unless the routers partitioning networks *aa* and *aa1* are configured to forward these broadcasts with a series of configuration entries analogous to the example provided for Figure 4–8. These entries must be applied to the input interface and be set to forward broadcasts between directly connected networks. In this way, such traffic can be passed along in a directed manner from network to network. A similar situation exists for type 20 packets.

The following example rewrites the **ipx helper-address** interface configuration command line to direct broadcasts to server A:

```
ipx helper-address bb.00b4.23cd.110a
! Permits node-specific broadcast forwarding to
! Server A at address 00b4.23cd.110a on network bb
```

### Forwarding to All Networks Example

In some networks, it might be necessary to allow client nodes to broadcast to servers on multiple networks. If you configure your router to forward broadcasts to all attached networks, you are flooding the interfaces. In the environment illustrated in Figure 4–9, client nodes on network 2b1 must obtain services from IPX servers on networks 3c2, 4a1, and 5bb through Router C1. To support this requirement, use the flooding address (-1.ffff.ffff.ffff) in your **ipx helper-address** interface configuration command specifications.

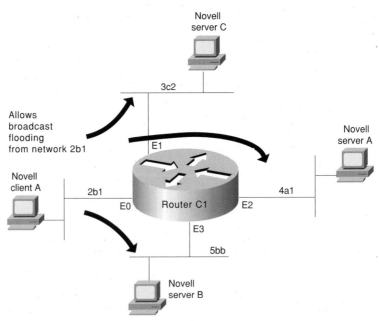

*Figure 4–9*
*Type 2 Broadcast Flooding.*

In the following example, the first line permits traffic of type 2 from network 2b1. Then the first interface is configured with a network number. The all-nets helper address is defined and the helper list limits forwarding to type 2 traffic. Type 2 broadcasts from network 2b1 are forwarded to all directly connected networks. All other broadcasts, including type 20, are blocked. To permit broadcasts, delete the **ipx helper-list** entry. To allow type 20 broadcasts, enable the **ipx type-20-propagation** interface configuration command on all interfaces.

```
access-list 901 permit 2 2b1
interface ethernet 0
 ipx network 2b1
 ipx helper-address -1.ffff.ffff.ffff
 ipx helper-list 901
interface ethernet 1
 ipx network 3c2
interface ethernet 2
 ipx network 4a1
interface ethernet 3
 ipx network 5bb
```

### All-Nets Flooded Broadcast Example

The following example configures all-nets flooding on an interface. As a result of this configuration, Ethernet interface 0 forwards all broadcast messages (except type 20) to all the networks it knows how to reach. This flooding of broadcast messages might overwhelm these networks with so much broadcast traffic that no other traffic may be able to pass on them.

```
interface ethernet 0
 ipx network 23
 ipx helper-address -1.FFFF.FFFF.FFFF
```

## IPX Accounting Example

The following example configures two Ethernet network segments that are connected via a serial link (see Figure 4–10). On Router A, IPX accounting is enabled on both the input and output interfaces (that is, on Ethernet interface 0 and serial interface 0). This means that statistics are gathered for traffic traveling in both directions (that is, out to the Ethernet network and out the serial link).

On Router B, IPX accounting is enabled only on the serial interface and not on the Ethernet interface. This means that statistics are gathered only for traffic that passes out the router on the serial link. Also the accounting threshold is set to 1000, which means that IPX accounting tracks all IPX traffic passing through the router up to 1000 source and destination pairs.

*Figure 4–10*
*IPX Accounting Example.*

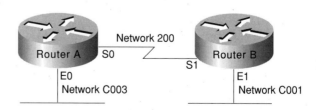

## *Configuration for Router A*

```
ipx routing
interface ethernet 0
 no ip address
 ipx network C003
 ipx accounting
interface serial 0
 no ip address
 ipx network 200
 ipx accounting
```

## *Configuration for Router B*

```
ipx routing
interface ethernet 1
 no ip address
 no keepalive
 ipx network C001
 no mop enabled
interface serial 1
 no ip address
 ipx network 200
 ipx accounting
 ipx accounting-threshold 1000
```

# CHAPTER 5

# Novell IPX Commands

Novell Internet Packet Exchange (IPX) is derived from the Xerox Network Systems (XNS) Internet Datagram Protocol (IDP). One major difference between IPX and XNS is that they do not always use the same Ethernet encapsulation format. A second difference is that IPX uses Novell's proprietary Service Advertising Protocol (SAP) to advertise special network services.

Cisco's implementation of Novell's IPX protocol has been certified as providing full IPX router functionality.

Use the commands in this chapter to configure and monitor Novell IPX networks. For IPX configuration information and examples, see Chapter 4, "Configuring Novell IPX."

---
**NOTES**
---

For all commands that previously used the keyword **novell**, this keyword has been changed to **ipx**. You can still use the keyword **novell** in all commands.

---

## ACCESS-LIST (EXTENDED)

To define an extended Novell IPX access list, use the extended version of the **access-list** global configuration command. To remove an extended access list, use the **no** form of this command.

> **access-list** *access-list-number* {**deny** | **permit**} *protocol* [*source-network*][[[.*source-node*]
> *source-node-mask*] | [.*source-node source-network-mask.source-node-mask*]]
> [*source-socket*] [*destination.network*][[[.*destination-node*] *destination-node-mask*] |
> [.*destination-node destination-network-mask.destination-nodemask*]]
> [*destination-socket*][**log**]

**no access-list** *access-list-number* {**deny** | **permit**} *protocol source-network*][[[*.source-node*]
*source-node-mask*] | [*.source-node source-network-mask.source-node-mask*]]
[*source-socket*] [*destination.network*][[[*.destination-node*] *destination-node-mask*] |
[*.destination-node destination-network-mask.destination-nodemask*]]
[*destination-socket*]

[**log**]

| Syntax | Description |
| --- | --- |
| *access-list-number* | Number of the access list. This is a number from 900 to 999. |
| **deny** | Denies access if the conditions are matched. |
| **permit** | Permits access if the conditions are matched. |
| *protocol* | Name or number of an IPX protocol type. This is sometimes referred to as the packet type. Table 5–1 in the "Usage Guidelines" section lists some IPX protocol names and numbers. |
| *source-network* | (Optional) Number of the network from which the packet is being sent. This is an eight-digit hexadecimal number that uniquely identifies a network cable segment. It can be a number in the range 1 to FFFFFFFE. A network number of 0 matches the local network. A network number of -1 matches all networks. You do not need to specify leading zeros in the network number; for example, for the network number 000000AA, you can enter AA. |
| *.source-node* | (Optional) Node on *source-network* from which the packet is being sent. This is a 48-bit value represented by a dotted triplet of four-digit hexadecimal numbers (*xxxx.xxxx.xxxx*). |
| *source-network-mask.* | (Optional) Mask to be applied to *source-network*. This is an eight-digit hexadecimal mask. Place ones in the bit positions you want to mask. The mask must immediately be followed by a period, which must in turn immediately be followed by *source-node-mask*. |
| *source-node-mask* | (Optional) Mask to be applied to *source-node*. This is a 48-bit value represented as a dotted triplet of four-digit hexadecimal numbers (*xxxx.xxxx.xxxx*). Place ones in the bit positions you want to mask. |
| *source-socket* | (Optional) Socket name or number (hexadecimal) from which the packet is being sent. Table 5–2 in the "Usage Guidelines" section lists some IPX socket names and numbers. |

| Syntax | Description |
|---|---|
| *destination.network* | (Optional) Number of the network to which the packet is being sent. This is an eight-digit hexadecimal number that uniquely identifies a network cable segment. It can be a number in the range 1 to FFFFFFFE. A network number of 0 matches the local network. A network number of -1 matches all networks. |
| | You do not need to specify leading zeros in the network number. For example, for the network number 000000AA, you can enter AA. |
| *.destination-node* | (Optional) Node on *destination-network* to which the packet is being sent. This is a 48-bit value represented by a dotted triplet of four-digit hexadecimal numbers (*xxxx.xxxx.xxxx*). |
| *destination-network-mask.* | (Optional) Mask to be applied to *destination-network*. This is an eight-digit hexadecimal mask. Place ones in the bit positions you want to mask. |
| | The mask must immediately be followed by a period, which must in turn immediately be followed by *destination-node-mask*. |
| *destination-node-mask* | (Optional) Mask to be applied to *destination-node*. This is a 48-bit value represented as a dotted triplet of four-digit hexadecimal numbers (*xxxx.xxxx.xxxx*). Place ones in the bit positions you want to mask. |
| *destination-socket* | (Optional) Socket name or number (hexadecimal) to which the packet is being sent. Table 5–3 in the "Usage Guidelines" section lists some IPX socket names and numbers. |
| **log** | (Optional) Logs IPX access control list violations whenever a packet matches a particular access list entry. The information logged includes source address, destination address, source socket, destination socket, protocol type, and action taken (permit/deny). |

### Default

No access lists are predefined.

### Command Mode

Global configuration

### Usage Guidelines

This command first appeared in Cisco IOS Release 10.0. The **log** keyword first appeared in Cisco IOS Release 11.2.

Extended IPX access lists filter on protocol type. All other parameters are optional.

If a network mask is used, all other fields are required.

Use the **ipx access-group** command to assign an access list to an interface. You can apply only one extended or one standard access list to an interface. The access list filters all outgoing packets on the interface.

---

**NOTES**

For some versions of NetWare, the protocol type field is not a reliable indicator of the type of packet encapsulated by the IPX header. In these cases, use the source and destination socket fields to make this determination. For additional information, contact Novell.

---

Table 5–1 lists some IPX protocol names and numbers. Table 5–2 lists some IPX socket names and numbers. For additional information about IPX protocol numbers and socket numbers, contact Novell.

**Table 5–1**   *Some IPX Protocol Names and Numbers*

| IPX Protocol Number (Decimal) | IPX Protocol Name | Protocol (Packet Type) |
|---|---|---|
| -1 | any | Wildcard; matches any packet type in 900 lists |
| 0 | | Undefined; refer to the socket number to determine the packet type |
| 1 | rip | Routing Information Protocol (RIP) |
| 4 | sap | Service Advertising Protocol (SAP) |
| 5 | spx | Sequenced Packet Exchange (SPX) |
| 17 | ncp | NetWare Core Protocol (NCP) |
| 20 | netbios | IPX NetBIOS |

**Table 5–2**   *Some IPX Socket Names and Numbers*

| IPX Socket Number (Hexadecimal) | IPX Socket Name | Socket |
|---|---|---|
| 0 | all | All sockets; wildcard used to match all sockets |
| 2 | cping | Cisco IPX ping packet |
| 451 | ncp | NetWare Core Protocol (NCP) process |
| 452 | sap | Service Advertising Protocol (SAP) process |
| 453 | rip | Routing Information Protocol (RIP) process |

**Table 5–2**  *Some IPX Socket Names and Numbers, Continued*

| IPX Socket Number (Hexadecimal) | IPX Socket Name | Socket |
|---|---|---|
| 455 | netbios | Novell NetBIOS process |
| 456 | diagnostic | Novell diagnostic packet |
| 457 | | Novell serialization socket |
| 4000-7FFF | | Dynamic sockets; used by workstations for interaction with file servers and other network servers |
| 8000-FFFF | | Sockets as assigned by Novell, Inc. |
| 85BE | eigrp | IPX Enhanced Interior Gateway Routing Protocol (Enhanced IGRP) |
| 9001 | nlsp | NetWare Link Services Protocol |
| 9086 | nping | Novell standard ping packet |

*Command Reference*

To delete an extended access list, specify the minimum number of keywords and arguments needed to delete the proper access list. For example, to delete the entire access list, use the following command:

**no access-list** *access-list-number*

To delete the access list for a specific protocol, use the following command:

**no access-list** *access-list-number* {**deny** | **permit**} *protocol*

### Examples

The following example denies access to all RIP packets from the RIP process socket on source network 1 that are destined for the RIP process socket on network 2. It permits all other traffic. This example uses protocol and socket names rather than hexadecimal numbers.

```
access-list  900  deny  -1 1 rip 2 rip
access-list  900  permit  -1
```

The following example permits type 2 packets from any socket from host 10.0000.0C01.5234 to access any sockets on any node on networks 1000 through 100F. It denies all other traffic (with an implicit deny all):

**NOTES**

This type is chosen only as an example. The actual type to use depends on the specific application.

```
access-list 910 permit 2 10.0000.0C01.5234 0000.0000.0000 0
    1000.0000.0000.0000 F.FFFF.FFFF.FFFF 0
```

*Related Commands*

Search online to find documentation for related commands.

**access-list (standard)**
**deny (extended)**
**ipx access-group**
**ipx access-list**
**ipx input-network-filter**
**ipx output-network-filter**
**ipx router-filter**
**permit (extended)**
**priority-list protocol**

## ACCESS-LIST (NLSP ROUTE AGGREGATION SUMMARIZATION)

To define an access list that denies or permits area addresses that summarize routes, use the NLSP route aggregation version of the **access-list** global configuration command. To remove an NLSP route aggregation access list, use the **no** form of this command.

> **access-list** *access-list-number* {**deny** | **permit**} *network network-mask* [ticks *ticks*]
>     [**area-count** *area-count*]
> **no access-list** *access-list-number* {**deny** | **permit**} *network network-mask* [ticks *ticks*]
>     [**area-count** *area-count*]

| *Syntax* | *Description* |
|---|---|
| *access-list-number* | Number of the access list. This is a number from 1200 to 1299. |
| **deny** | Denies redistribution of explicit routes if the conditions are matched. If you have enabled route summarization with route-aggregation command, the router redistributes an aggregated route instead. |
| **permit** | Permits redistribution of explicit routes if the conditions are matched. |
| *network* | Network number to summarize. An IPX network number is an eight-digit hexadecimal number that uniquely identifies a network cable segment. It can be a number in the range 1 to FFFFFFFE. A network number of 0 matches the local network. A network number of -1 matches all networks. |
| | You do not need to specify leading zeros in the network number. For example, for the network number 000000AA, you can enter AA. |
| *network-mask* | Specifies the portion of the network address that is common to all addresses in the route summary. The high-order bits of *network-mask* must be contiguous Fs, while the low-order bits must be contiguous zeros (0). An arbitrary mix of Fs and 0s is not permitted. |

| Syntax | Description |
|---|---|
| **ticks** *ticks* | (Optional) Metric assigned to the route summary. The default is 1 tick. |
| **area-count** *area-count* | (Optional) Maximum number of NLSP areas to which the route summary can be redistributed. The default is 6 areas. |

## Default

No access lists are predefined.

## Command Mode

Global configuration

## Usage Guidelines

This command first appeared in Cisco IOS Release 11.1.

Use the NLSP route aggregation access list in the following situations:

- When redistributing from an Enhanced IGRP or RIP area into a new NLSP area.

  Use the access list to instruct the router to redistribute an aggregated route instead of the explicit route. The access list also contains a "permit all" statement that instructs the router to redistribute explicit routes that are not subsumed by a route summary.

- When redistributing from an NLSP version 1.0 area into an NLSP version 1.1 area, and vice versa.

  ○ From an NLSP version 1.0 area into an NLSP version 1.1 area, use the access list to instruct the router to redistribute an aggregated route instead of an explicit route and to redistribute explicit routes that are not subsumed by a route summary.

  ○ From an NLSP version 1.1 area into an NLSP version 1.0 area, use the access list to instruct the router to filter aggregated routes from passing into the NLSP version 1.0 areas and to redistribute explicit routes instead.

---

**NOTES**

---

NLSP version 1.1 routers refer to routers that support the route aggregation feature, while NLSP version 1.0 routers refer to routers that do not.

---

## Example

The following example uses NLSP route aggregation access lists to redistribute routes learned from RIP to NLSP area1. Routes learned via RIP are redistributed into NLSP area1. Any routes learned via RIP that are subsumed by aaaa0000 ffff0000 are not redistributed. An address summary is generated instead.

```
ipx routing
ipx internal-network 2000

interface ethernet 1
 ipx network 1001
 ipx nlsp area1 enable

interface ethernet 2
 ipx network 2001

access-list 1200 deny aaaa0000 ffff0000
access-list 1200 permit -1

ipx router nlsp area
 area-address 1000 fffff000
 route-aggregation
 redistribute rip access-list 1200
```

### Related Commands

Search online to find documentation for related commands.

**area-address**
**deny (NLSP route aggregation summarization)**
**ipx access-list**
**ipx nlsp enable**
**ipx router**
**permit (NLSP route aggregation summarization)**
**redistribute**

## ACCESS-LIST (SAP FILTERING)

To define an access list for filtering Service Advertising Protocol (SAP) requests, use the SAP filtering form of the **access-list** global configuration command. To remove the access list, use the **no** form of this command.

> **access-list** *access-list-number* {**deny** | **permit**} *network*[*.node*] [*network-mask.node-mask*]
>     [*service-type* [*server-name*]]
> **no access-list** *access-list-number* {**deny** | **permit**} *network*[*.node*] [*network-mask.node-mask*]
>     [*service-type* [*server-name*]]

| Syntax | Description |
| --- | --- |
| *access-list-number* | Number of the SAP access list. This is a number from 1000 to 1099. |
| **deny** | Denies access if the conditions are matched. |
| **permit** | Permits access if the conditions are matched. |

| Syntax | Description |
|---|---|
| *network* | Network number. This is an eight-digit hexadecimal number that uniquely identifies a network cable segment. It can be a number in the range 1 to FFFFFFFE. A network number of 0 matches the local network. A network number of –1 matches all networks. |
| | You do not need to specify leading zeros in the network number. For example, for the network number 000000AA, you can enter AA. |
| *.node* | (Optional) Node on *network*. This is a 48-bit value represented by a dotted triplet of four-digit hexadecimal numbers (*xxxx.xxxx.xxxx*). |
| *network-mask.node-mask* | (Optional) Mask to be applied to *network* and *node*. Place ones in the bit positions to be masked. |
| *service-type* | (Optional) Service type on which to filter. This is a hexadecimal number. A value of 0 means all services. |
| | Table 5–3 in the "Usage Guidelines" section lists examples of service types. |
| *server-name* | (Optional) Name of the server providing the specified service type. This can be any contiguous string of printable ASCII characters. Use double quotation marks (" ") to enclose strings containing embedded spaces. You can use an asterisk (*) at the end of the name as a wildcard to match one or more trailing characters. |

## Default

No access lists are predefined.

## Command Mode

Global configuration

## Usage Guidelines

This command first appeared in Cisco IOS Release 10.0.

When configuring SAP filters for NetWare 3.11 and later servers, use the server's internal network and node number (the node number is always 0000.0000.0001) as its address in the **access-list** command. Do not use the *network.node* address of the particular interface board.

Table 5–3 lists some sample IPX SAP types. For more information about SAP types, contact Novell. Note that in the filter (specified by the *service-type* argument), we define a value of 0 to filter all SAP services. If, however, you receive a SAP packet with a SAP type of 0, this indicates an unknown service.

**Table 5–3** *Sample IPX SAP Services*

| Service Type (Hexadecimal) | Description |
| --- | --- |
| 1 | User |
| 2 | User group |
| 3 | Print server queue |
| 4 | File server |
| 5 | Job server |
| 7 | Print server |
| 9 | Archive server |
| A | Queue for job servers |
| 21 | Network Application Support Systems Network Architecture (NASSNA) gateway |
| 2D | Time Synchronization value-added process (VAP) |
| 2E | Dynamic SAP |
| 47 | Advertising print server |
| 4B | Btrieve VAP 5.0 |
| 4C | SQL VAP |
| 7A | TES—NetWare for Virtual Memory System (VMS) |
| 98 | NetWare access server |
| 9A | Named Pipes server |
| 9E | Portable NetWare—UNIX |
| 107 | RCONSOLE |
| 111 | Test server |
| 166 | NetWare management (Novell's Network Management Station [NMS]) |
| 26A | NetWare management (NMS console) |

To delete a SAP access list, specify the minimum number of keywords and arguments needed to delete the proper access list. For example, to delete the entire access list, use the following command:

**no access-list** *access-list-number*

To delete the access list for a specific network, use the following command:

> **no access-list** *access-list-number* {**deny** | **permit**} *network*

## Example

The following access list blocks all access to a file server (service Type 4) on the directly attached network by resources on other Novell networks, but allows access to all other available services on the interface:

```
access-list 1001 deny -1 4
access-list 1001 permit -1
```

## Related Commands

Search online to find documentation for related commands.

**deny (SAP filtering)**
**ipx access-list**
**ipx input-sap-filter**
**ipx output-gns-filter**
**ipx output-sap-filter**
**ipx router-sap-filter**
**permit (SAP filtering)**
**priority-list protocol**

## ACCESS-LIST (STANDARD)

To define a standard IPX access list, use the standard version of the **access-list** global configuration command. To remove a standard access list, use the **no** form of this command.

> **access-list** *access-list-number* {**deny** | **permit**} *source-network*[*.source-node*
>    [*source-node-mask*]] [*destination-network*[*.destination-node* [*destination-node-mask*]]]
> **no access-list** *access-list-number* {**deny** | **permit**} *source-network*[*.source-node*
>    [*source-node-mask*]] [*destination-network*[*.destination-node* [*destination-node-mask*]]]

| Syntax | Description |
| --- | --- |
| *access-list-number* | Number of the access list. This is a number from 800 to 899. |
| deny | Denies access if the conditions are matched. |
| permit | Permits access if the conditions are matched. |

| Syntax | Description |
|--------|-------------|
| *source-network* | Number of the network from which the packet is being sent. This is an eight-digit hexadecimal number that uniquely identifies a network cable segment. It can be a number in the range 1 to FFFFFFFE. A network number of 0 matches the local network. A network number of -1 matches all networks. |
| | You do not need to specify leading zeros in the network number. For example, for the network number 000000AA, you can enter AA. |
| *.source-node* | (Optional) Node on *source-network* from which the packet is being sent. This is a 48-bit value represented by a dotted triplet of four-digit hexadecimal numbers (*xxxx.xxxx.xxxx*). |
| *source-node-mask* | (Optional) Mask to be applied to *source-node*. This is a 48-bit value represented as a dotted triplet of four-digit hexadecimal numbers (*xxxx.xxxx.xxxx*). Place ones in the bit positions you want to mask. |
| *destination-network* | (Optional) Number of the network to which the packet is being sent. This is an eight-digit hexadecimal number that uniquely identifies a network cable segment. It can be a number in the range 1 to FFFFFFFE. A network number of 0 matches the local network. A network number of -1 matches all networks. |
| | You do not need to specify leading zeros in the network number. For example, for the network number 000000AA, you can enter AA. |
| *.destination-node* | (Optional) Node on *destination-network* to which the packet is being sent. This is a 48-bit value represented by a dotted triplet of four-digit hexadecimal numbers (*xxxx.xxxx.xxxx*). |
| *destination-node-mask* | (Optional) Mask to be applied to *destination-node*. This is a 48-bit value represented as a dotted triplet of four-digit hexadecimal numbers (*xxxx.xxxx.xxxx*). Place ones in the bit positions you want to mask. |

## Default

No access lists are predefined.

## Command Mode

Global configuration

## Usage Guidelines

This command first appeared in Cisco IOS Release 10.0.

Standard IPX access lists filter on the source network. All other parameters are optional.

Use the **ipx access-group** command to assign an access list to an interface. You can apply only one extended or one standard access list to an interface. The access list filters all outgoing packets on the interface.

To delete a standard access list, specify the minimum number of keywords and arguments needed to delete the proper access list. For example, to delete the entire access list, use the following command:

> **no access-list** *access-list-number*

To delete the access list for a specific network, use the following command:

> **no access-list** *access-list-number* {**deny** | **permit**} *source-network*

### Examples

The following example denies access to traffic from all IPX networks (-1) to destination network 2:

```
access-list 800 deny -1 2
```

The following example denies access to all traffic from IPX address 1.0000.0c00.1111:

```
access-list 800 deny 1.0000.0c00.1111
```

The following example denies access from all nodes on network 1 that have a source address beginning with 0000.0c:

```
access-list 800 deny 1.0000.0c00.0000 0000.00ff.ffff
```

The following example denies access from source address 1111.1111.1111 on network 1 to destination address 2222.2222.2222 on network 2:

```
access-list 800 deny 1.1111.1111.1111 0000.0000.0000 2.2222.2222.2222 0000.0000.0000
```

> or

```
access-list 800 deny 1.1111.1111.1111 2.2222.2222.2222
```

### Related Commands

Search online to find documentation for related commands.

**access-list (extended)**
**deny (standard)**
**ipx access-group**
**ipx access-list**
**ipx input-network-filter**
**ipx output-network-filter**
**ipx router-filter**
**permit (standard)**
**priority-list protocol**

## AREA-ADDRESS

To define a set of network numbers to be part of the current NLSP area, use the **area-address** router configuration command. To remove a set of network numbers from the current NLSP area, use the **no** form of this command.

>**area-address** *address mask*
>**no area-address** *address mask*

| Syntax | Description |
|---|---|
| *address* | Network number prefix. This is a 32-bit hexadecimal number. |
| *mask* | Mask that defines the length of the network number prefix. This is a 32-bit hexadecimal number. |

### Default

No area address is defined by default.

### Command Mode

Router configuration

### Usage Guidelines

This command first appeared in Cisco IOS Release 10.3.

You must configure at least one area address before NLSP will operate.

The **area-address** command defines a prefix that includes all networks in the area. This prefix allows a single route to an area address to substitute for a longer list of networks.

All networks on which NLSP is enabled must fall under the area address prefix. This configuration is for future compatibility. When Level 2 NLSP becomes available, the only route advertised for the area will be the area address prefix (the prefix represents all networks within the area).

All routers in an NLSP area must be configured with a common area address, or they will form separate areas. You can configure up to three area addresses on the router.

The area address must have zero bits in all bit positions where the mask has zero bits. The mask must consist of only left-justified contiguous one bits.

### Examples

The following example defines an area address that includes networks AAAABBC0 through AAAABBDF:

```
area-address AAAABBC0 FFFFFFE0
```

The following example defines an area address that includes all networks:

```
area-address 0 0
```

### Related Commands

Search online to find documentation for related commands.

**ipx router nlsp**

## CLEAR IPX ACCOUNTING

To delete all entries in the accounting database when IPX accounting is enabled, use the **clear ipx accounting** EXEC command.

**clear ipx accounting** [checkpoint]

| Syntax | Description |
| --- | --- |
| **checkpoint** | (Optional) Clears the checkpoint database. |

### Command Mode

EXEC

### Usage Guidelines

This command first appeared in Cisco IOS Release 10.0.

Specifying the **clear ipx accounting** command with no keywords copies the active database to the checkpoint database and clears all entries in the active database. When cleared, active database entries and static entries, such as those set by the **ipx accounting-list** command, are reset to zero. Dynamically found entries are deleted.

Any traffic that traverses the router after you issue the **clear ipx accounting** command is saved in the active database. Accounting information in the checkpoint database at that time reflects traffic prior to the most recent **clear ipx accounting** command.

You can also delete all entries in the active and checkpoint database by issuing the **clear ipx accounting** command twice in succession.

### Example

The following example first displays the contents of the active database before the contents are cleared. Then, the **clear ipx accounting** command clears all entries in the active database. As a result, the **show ipx accounting** command shows that there is no accounting information in the active database. Lastly, the **show ipx accounting checkpoint** command shows that the contents of the active database were copied to the checkpoint database when the **clear ipx accounting** command was issued.

```
Router# show ipx accounting

Source                  Destination             Packets     Bytes
0000C003.0000.0c05.6030 0000C003.0260.8c9b.4e33      72      2880
0000C001.0260.8c8d.da75 0000C003.0260.8c9b.4e33      14       624
```

```
0000C003.0260.8c9b.4e33 0000C001.0260.8c8d.da75        62            3110
0000C001.0260.8c8d.e7c6 0000C003.0260.8c9b.4e33        20            1470
0000C003.0260.8c9b.4e33 0000C001.0260.8c8d.e7c6        20            1470

Accounting data age is    6

Router# clear ipx accounting
Router# show ipx accounting

Source                  Destination           Packets          Bytes

Accounting data age is 0
Router# show ipx accounting checkpoint

Source                  Destination           Packets          Bytes
0000C003.0000.0c05.6030 0000C003.0260.8c9b.4e33        72            2880
0000C001.0260.8c8d.da75 0000C003.0260.8c9b.4e33        14             624
0000C003.0260.8c9b.4e33 0000C001.0260.8c8d.da75        62            3110
0000C001.0260.8c8d.e7c6 0000C003.0260.8c9b.4e33        20            1470
0000C003.0260.8c9b.4e33 0000C001.0260.8c8d.e7c6        20            1470

Accounting data age is    6
```

## Related Commands

Search online to find documentation for related commands.

**ipx accounting**
**ipx accounting-list**
**ipx accounting-threshold**
**ipx accounting-transits**
**show ipx accounting**

## CLEAR IPX CACHE

To delete entries from the IPX fast-switching cache, use the **clear ipx cache** EXEC command.

    **clear ipx cache**

## Syntax     Description

This command has no arguments or keywords.

## Command Mode

EXEC

## Usage Guidelines

This command first appeared in Cisco IOS Release 10.0.

The **clear ipx cache** command clears entries used for fast switching and autonomous switching.

## Example

The following example deletes all entries from the IPX fast-switching cache:

```
clear ipx cache
```

## Related Commands

Search online to find documentation for related commands.

**ipx route-cache**
**show ipx cache**

### CLEAR IPX NHRP

To clear all dynamic entries from the Next Hop Resolution Protocol (NHRP) cache, use the **clear ipx nhrp** EXEC command.

**clear ipx nhrp**

## Syntax    Description

This command has no arguments or keywords.

## Command Mode

EXEC

## Usage Guidelines

This command first appeared in Cisco IOS Release 11.1.

This command does not clear any static (configured) IPX-to-NBMA address mappings from the NHRP cache.

## Example

The following example clears all dynamic entries from the NHRP cache for the interface:

```
clear ipx nhrp
```

## Related Commands

Search online to find documentation for related commands.

**show ipx nhrp**

## CLEAR IPX NLSP NEIGHBORS

To delete all NetWare Link Services Protocol (NLSP) adjacencies from the Cisco IOS software's adjacency database, use the **clear ipx nlsp neighbors** EXEC command.

    **clear ipx nlsp** [*tag*] **neighbors**

| *Syntax* | *Description* |
|---|---|
| *tag* | (Optional) Names the NLSP process. The *tag* can be any combination of printable characters. |

### Command Mode

EXEC

### Usage Guidelines

This command first appeared in Cisco IOS Release 10.3.

Deleting all entries from the adjacency database forces all routers in the area to perform the shortest path first (SPF) calculation.

When you specify an NLSP *tag*, the router clears all NLSP adjacencies discovered by that NLSP process. An NLSP *process* is a router's databases working together to manage route information about an area. NLSP version 1.0 routers are always in the same area. Each router has its own adjacencies, link-state, and forwarding databases. These databases operate collectively as a single *process* to discover, select, and maintain route information about the area. NLSP version 1.1 routers that exist within a single area also use a single process.

NLSP version 1.1 routers that interconnect multiple areas use multiple processes to discover, select, and maintain route information about the areas they interconnect. These routers manage an adjacencies, link-state, and area address database for each area to which they attach. Collectively, these databases are still referred to as a *process*. The forwarding database is shared among processes within a router. The sharing of entries in the forwarding database is automatic when all processes interconnect NLSP version 1.1 areas.

Configure multiple NLSP processes when a router interconnects multiple NLSP areas.

— **NOTES** ————————————————————————————————————

NLSP version 1.1 routers refer to routers that support the route aggregation feature, while NLSP version 1.0 routers refer to routers that do not.

### Examples

The following example deletes all NLSP adjacencies from the adjacency database:

```
clear ipx nlsp neighbors
```

The following example deletes the NLSP adjacencies for process *area2*:

```
clear ipx nlsp area2 neighbors
```

### Related Commands

Search online to find documentation for related commands.

**ipx router nlsp**
**spf-interval**

## CLEAR IPX ROUTE

To delete routes from the IPX routing table, use the **clear ipx route** EXEC command.

**clear ipx route** {*network* [*network-mask*] | **default** | *}

| Syntax | Description |
| --- | --- |
| *network* | Number of the network whose routing table entry you want to delete. This is an eight-digit hexadecimal number that uniquely identifies a network cable segment. It can be a number in the range 1 to FFFFFFFD. You do not need to specify leading zeros in the network number. For example, for the network number 000000AA, you can enter AA. |
| *network-mask* | (Optional) Specifies the portion of the network address that is common to all addresses in an NLSP route summary. When used with the *network* argument, it specifies the NLSP route summary to clear. |
| | The high-order bits of *network-mask* must be contiguous Fs, while the low-order bits must be contiguous zeros (0). An arbitrary mix of Fs and 0s is not permitted. |
| **default** | Deletes the default route from the routing table. |
| * | Deletes all routes in the routing table. |

### Command Mode

EXEC

### Usage Guidelines

This command first appeared in Cisco IOS Release 10.0. The *network-mask* argument and **default** keyword first appeared in Cisco IOS Release 11.1.

After you use the **clear ipx route** command, RIP/SAP general requests are issued on all IPX interfaces.

For routers configured for NLSP route aggregation, use this command to clear an aggregated route from the routing table.

*Command Reference*

## Examples

The following example clears the entry for network 3 from the IPX routing table:

```
clear ipx route 3
```

The following example clears a route summary entry from the IPX routing table:

```
clear ipx route ccc00000 fff00000
```

## Related Commands

Search online to find documentation for related commands.

**show ipx route**


## DENY (EXTENDED)

To set conditions for a named IPX extended access list, use the **deny** (**extended**)access-list configuration command. To remove a deny condition from an access list, use the **no** form of this command.

> **deny** *protocol* [*source-network*][[[.*source-node*] *source-node-mask*] | [.*source-node*
> *source-network-mask.source-node-mask*]] [*source-socket*] [*destination-network*]
> [[[.*destination-node*] *destination-node-mask*] | [.*destination-node*
> *destination-network-mask.destination-node-mask*]] [*destination-socket*] [**log**]
> **no deny** *protocol* [*source-network*][[[.*source-node*] *source-node-mask*] | [.*source-node*
> *source-network-mask.source-node-mask*]] [*source-socket*] [*destination-network*]
> [[[.*destination-node*] *destination-node-mask*] | [.*destination-node*
> *destination-network-mask.destination-node-mask*]] [*destination-socket*] [**log**]

| Syntax | Description |
|---|---|
| *protocol* | Name or number of an IPX protocol type. This is sometimes referred to as the packet type. You can also use the word **any** to match all protocol types. |
| *source-network* | (Optional) Number of the network from which the packet is being sent. This is an eight-digit hexadecimal number that uniquely identifies a network cable segment. It can be a number in the range 1 to FFFFFFFE. A network number of 0 matches the local network. A network number of -1 matches all networks. You can also use the keyword **any** to match all networks. |
| | You do not need to specify leading zeros in the network number; for example, for the network number 000000AA, you can enter AA. |
| *.source-node* | (Optional) Node on *source-network* from which the packet is being sent. This is a 48-bit value represented by a dotted triplet of four-digit hexadecimal numbers (*xxxx.xxxx.xxxx*). |

| Syntax | Description |
|---|---|
| *source-node-mask* | (Optional) Mask to be applied to *source-node*. This is a 48-bit value represented as a dotted triplet of four-digit hexadecimal numbers (*xxxx.xxxx.xxxx*). Place ones in the bit positions you want to mask. |
| *source-network-mask.* | (Optional) Mask to be applied to *source-network*. This is an eight-digit hexadecimal mask. Place ones in the bit positions you want to mask.<br><br>The mask must immediately be followed by a period, which must in turn immediately be followed by *source-node-mask*. |
| *source-socket* | (Optional) Socket name or number (hexadecimal) from which the packet is being sent. You can also use the keyword **all** to match all sockets. |
| *destination-network* | (Optional) Number of the network to which the packet is being sent. This is an eight-digit hexadecimal number that uniquely identifies a network cable segment. It can be a number in the range 1 to FFFFFFFE. A network number of 0 matches the local network. A network number of -1 matches all networks. You can also use the keyword **any** to match all networks.<br><br>You do not need to specify leading zeros in the network number. For example, for the network number 000000AA, you can enter AA. |
| *.destination-node* | (Optional) Node on *destination-network* to which the packet is being sent. This is a 48-bit value represented by a dotted triplet of four-digit hexadecimal numbers (*xxxx.xxxx.xxxx*). |
| *destination-node-mask* | (Optional) Mask to be applied to *destination-node*. This is a 48-bit value represented as a dotted triplet of four-digit hexadecimal numbers (*xxxx.xxxx.xxxx*). Place ones in the bit positions you want to mask. |
| *destination-network-mask.* | (Optional) Mask to be applied to *destination-network*. This is an eight-digit hexadecimal mask. Place ones in the bit positions you want to mask.<br><br>The mask must immediately be followed by a period, which must in turn immediately be followed by *destination-node-mask*. |
| *destination-socket* | (Optional) Socket name or number (hexadecimal) to which the packet is being sent. |
| **log** | (Optional) Logs IPX access control list violations whenever a packet matches a particular access list entry. The information logged includes source address, destination address, source socket, destination socket, protocol type, and action taken (permit/deny). |

*Command Reference*

### Default
No access lists are defined.

### Command Mode
Access-list configuration

### Usage Guidelines
This command first appeared in Cisco IOS Release 11.3.

Use this command following the **ipx access-list** command to specify conditions under which a packet cannot pass the named access list.

For additional information on IPX protocol names and numbers, and IPX socket names and numbers, see the **access-list (extended)** command.

### Example
The following example creates an extended access list named *sal* that denies all SPX packets:

```
ipx access-list extended sal
  deny spx any all any all log
  permit any
```

### Related Commands
Search online to find documentation for related commands.

**access-list (extended)**
**ipx access-group**
**ipx access-list**
**permit (extended)**
**show ipx access-list**

## DENY (NLSP ROUTE AGGREGATION SUMMARIZATION)

To filter explicit routes and generate an aggregated route for a named NLSP route aggregation access list, use the **deny** access-list configuration command. To remove a deny condition from an access list, use the **no** form of this command.

> **deny** *network network-mask* [**ticks** *ticks*] [**area-count** *area-count*]
> **no deny** *network network-mask* [**ticks** *ticks*] [**area-count** *area-count*]

| Syntax | Description |
|---|---|
| *network* | Network number to summarize. An IPX network number is an eight-digit hexadecimal number that uniquely identifies a network cable segment. It can be a number in the range 1 to FFFFFFFE. A network number of 0 matches the local network. A network number of -1 matches all networks. |
| | You do not need to specify leading zeros in the network number. For example, for the network number 000000AA, you can enter AA. |
| *network-mask* | Specifies the portion of the network address that is common to all addresses in the route summary, expressed as an 8-digit hexadecimal number. The high-order bits of *network-mask* must be contiguous 1s, while the low-order bits must be contiguous zeros (0). An arbitrary mix of 1s and 0s is not permitted. |
| **ticks** *ticks* | (Optional) Metric assigned to the route summary. The default is 1 tick. |
| **area-count** *area-count* | (Optional) Maximum number of NLSP areas to which the route summary can be redistributed. The default is 6 areas. |

*Command Reference*

## Default

No access lists are defined.

## Command Mode

Access-list configuration

## Usage Guidelines

This command first appeared in Cisco IOS Release 11.3.

Use this command following the **ipx access-list** command to prevent the redistribution of explicit networks that are denied by the access list entry and, instead, generate an appropriate aggregated (summary) route.

For additional information on creating access lists that deny or permit area addresses that summarize routes, see the **access-list (NLSP route aggregation summarization)** command.

## Example

The following example from a configuration file defines the access list named *finance* for NLSP route aggregation. This access list prevents redistribution of explicit routes in the range 12345600 to 123456FF and, instead, summarizes these routes into a single aggregated route. The access list allows explicit route redistribution of all other routes.

```
ipx access-list summary finance
 deny 12345600 ffffff00
 permit -1
```

*Related Commands*

Search online to find documentation for related commands.

**access-list (NLSP route aggregation summarization)**
**ipx access-group**
**ipx access-list**
**permit (NLSP route aggregation summarization)**
**show ipx access-list**

## DENY (SAP FILTERING)

To set conditions for a named IPX SAP filtering access list, use the **deny** access-list configuration command. To remove a deny condition from an access list, use the **no** form of this command.

> **deny** *network*[.*node*] [*network-mask.node-mask*] [*service-type* [*server-name*]]
> **no deny** *network*[.*node*] [*network-mask.node-mask*] [*service-type* [*server-name*]]

| Syntax | Description |
|---|---|
| *network* | Network number. This is an eight-digit hexadecimal number that uniquely identifies a network cable segment. It can be a number in the range 1 to FFFFFFFE. A network number of 0 matches the local network. A network number of –1 matches all networks. |
| | You do not need to specify leading zeros in the network number. For example, for the network number 000000AA, you can enter AA. |
| .*node* | (Optional) Node on *network*. This is a 48-bit value represented by a dotted triplet of four-digit hexadecimal numbers (*xxxx.xxxx.xxxx*). |
| *network-mask.node-mask* | (Optional) Mask to be applied to *network* and *node*. Place ones in the bit positions to be masked. |
| *service-type* | (Optional) Service type on which to filter. This is a hexadecimal number. A value of 0 means all services. |
| *server-name* | (Optional) Name of the server providing the specified service type. This can be any contiguous string of printable ASCII characters. Use double quotation marks (" ") to enclose strings containing embedded spaces. You can use an asterisk (*) at the end of the name as a wildcard to match one or more trailing characters. |

*Default*

No access lists are defined.

*Command Mode*

Access-list configuration

## Usage Guidelines

This command first appeared in Cisco IOS Release 11.3.

Use this command following the **ipx access-list** command to specify conditions under which a packet cannot pass the named access list.

For additional information on IPX SAP service types, see the **access-list (SAP filtering)** command.

## Example

The following example creates a SAP access list named *MyServer* that denies MyServer to be sent in SAP advertisements:

```
ipx access-list sap MyServer
  deny 1234 4 MyServer
```

## Related Commands

Search online to find documentation for related commands.

**access-list (SAP filtering)**
**ipx access-group**
**ipx access-list**
**permit (SAP filtering)**
**show ipx access-list**

## DENY (STANDARD)

To set conditions for a named IPX access list, use the **deny** access-list configuration command. To remove a deny condition from an access list, use the **no** form of this command.

> **deny** *source-network*[.*source-node* [*source-node-mask*]]
>   [*destination-network*[.*destination-node* [*destination-node-mask*]]]
> **no deny** *source-network*[.*source-node* [*source-node-mask*]]
>   [*destination-network*[.*destination-node* [*destination-node-mask*]]]

| Syntax | Description |
|---|---|
| *source-network* | Number of the network from which the packet is being sent. This is an eight-digit hexadecimal number that uniquely identifies a network cable segment. It can be a number in the range 1 to FFFFFFFE. A network number of 0 matches the local network. A network number of -1 matches all networks. |
| | You do not need to specify leading zeros in the network number. For example, for the network number 000000AA, you can enter AA. |
| *.source-node* | (Optional) Node on *source-network* from which the packet is being sent. This is a 48-bit value represented by a dotted triplet of four-digit hexadecimal numbers (*xxxx.xxxx.xxxx*). |

| Syntax | Description |
|---|---|
| *source-node-mask* | (Optional) Mask to be applied to *source-node*. This is a 48-bit value represented as a dotted triplet of four-digit hexadecimal numbers (*xxxx.xxxx.xxxx*). Place ones in the bit positions you want to mask. |
| *destination-network* | (Optional) Number of the network to which the packet is being sent. This is an eight-digit hexadecimal number that uniquely identifies a network cable segment. It can be a number in the range 1 to FFFFFFFE. A network number of 0 matches the local network. A network number of -1 matches all networks.

You do not need to specify leading zeros in the network number. For example, for the network number 000000AA, you can enter AA. |
| *.destination-node* | (Optional) Node on *destination-network* to which the packet is being sent. This is a 48-bit value represented by a dotted triplet of four-digit hexadecimal numbers (*xxxx.xxxx.xxxx*). |
| *destination-node-mask* | (Optional) Mask to be applied to *destination-node*. This is a 48-bit value represented as a dotted triplet of four-digit hexadecimal numbers (*xxxx.xxxx.xxxx*). Place ones in the bit positions you want to mask. |

### Default

No access lists are defined.

### Command Mode

Access-list configuration

### Usage Guidelines

This command first appeared in Cisco IOS Release 11.3.

Use this command following the **ipx access-list** command to specify conditions under which a packet cannot pass the named access list.

For additional information on creating IPX access lists, see the **access-list (standard)** command.

### Example

The following example creates a standard access list named *fred*. It denies communication with only IPX network number 5678.

```
ipx access-list standard fred
  deny 5678 any
  permit any
```

### Related Commands

Search online to find documentation for related commands.

**access-list (standard)**
**ipx access-group**
**ipx access-list**
**permit (standard)**
**show ipx access-list**

## DISTRIBUTE-LIST IN

To filter networks received in updates, use the **distribute-list in** router configuration command. To change or cancel the filter, use the **no** form of this command.

> **distribute-list** {*access-list-number* | *name*} **in** [*interface-name*]
> **no distribute-list** {*access-list-number* | *name*} **in** [*interface-name*]

| Syntax | Description |
| --- | --- |
| *access-list-number* | Standard IPX access list number in the range 800 to 899 or NLSP access list number in the range 1200 to 1299. The list explicitly specifies which networks are to be received and which are to be suppressed. |
| *name* | Name of the access list. Names cannot contain a space or quotation mark and must begin with an alphabetic character to prevent ambiguity with numbered access lists. |
| **in** | Applies the access list to incoming routing updates. |
| *interface-name* | (Optional) Interface on which the access list should be applied to incoming updates. If no interface is specified, the access list is applied to all incoming updates. |

### Default

Disabled

### Command Mode

Router configuration

### Usage Guidelines

This command first appeared in Cisco IOS Release 10.0.

*Command Reference*

*Example*

The following example causes only two networks—network 2 and network 3—to be accepted by an Enhanced IGRP routing process:

```
access-list 800 permit 2
access-list 800 permit 3
access-list 800 deny -1
!
ipx router eigrp 100
 network 3
 distribute-list 800 in
```

*Related Commands*

Search online to find documentation for related commands.

**access-list (NLSP route aggregation summarization)**
**access-list (standard)**
**deny (NLSP route aggregation summarization)**
**deny (standard)**
**distribute-list out**
**ipx access-list**
**permit (NLSP route aggregation summarization)**
**permit (standard)**
**redistribute**

## DISTRIBUTE-LIST OUT

To suppress networks from being advertised in updates, use the **distribute-list out** router configuration command. To cancel this function, use the **no** form of this command.

**distribute-list** {*access-list-number* | *name*} **out** [*interface-name* | *routing-process*]
**no distribute-list** {*access-list-number* | *name*} **out** [*interface-name* | *routing-process*]

| *Syntax* | *Description* |
|---|---|
| *access-list-number* | Standard IPX access list number in the range 800 to 899 or NLSP access list number in the range 1200 to 1299. The list explicitly specifies which networks are to be sent and which are to be suppressed in routing updates. |
| *name* | Name of the access list. Names cannot contain a space or quotation mark and must begin with an alphabetic character to prevent ambiguity with numbered access lists. |
| **out** | Applies the access list to outgoing routing updates. |

| Syntax | Description |
|--------|-------------|
| *interface-name* | (Optional) Interface on which the access list should be applied to outgoing updates. If no interface is specified, the access list is applied to all outgoing updates. |
| *routing-process* | (Optional) Name of a particular routing process as follows: |

- **eigrp** *autonomous-system-number*
- **rip**
- **nlsp** [*tag*]

### Default

Disabled

### Command Mode

Router configuration

### Usage Guidelines

This command first appeared in Cisco IOS Release 10.0.

When redistributing networks, a routing process name can be specified as an optional trailing argument to the **distribute-list out** command. This causes the access list to be applied to only those routes derived from the specified routing process. After the process-specific access list is applied, any access list specified by a **distribute-list out** command without a process name argument is applied. Addresses not specified in the **distribute-list out** command are not advertised in outgoing routing updates.

### Example

The following example causes only one network—network 3—to be advertised by an Enhanced IGRP routing process:

```
access-list 800 permit 3
access-list 800 deny -1
!
ipx router eigrp 100
 network 3
 distribute-list 800 out
```

### Related Commands

Search online to find documentation for related commands.

access-list (NLSP route aggregation summarization)
access-list (standard)
deny (NLSP route aggregation summarization)
deny (standard)
distribute-list in
ipx access-list
permit (NLSP route aggregation summarization)
permit (standard)
redistribute

## DISTRIBUTE-SAP-LIST IN

To filter services received in updates, use the **distribute-sap-list in** router configuration command. To change or cancel the filter, use the **no** form of this command.

**distribute-sap-list** {*access-list-number* | *name*} **in** [*interface-name*]
**no distribute-sap-list** {*access-list-number* | *name*} **in** [*interface-name*]

| Syntax | Description |
|---|---|
| *access-list-number* | SAP access list number in the range 1000 to 1099. The list explicitly specifies which services are to be received and which are to be suppressed. |
| *name* | Name of the access list. Names cannot contain a space or quotation mark and must begin with an alphabetic character to prevent ambiguity with numbered access lists. |
| **in** | Applies the access list to incoming routing updates. |
| *interface-name* | (Optional) Interface on which the access list should be applied to incoming updates. If no interface is specified, the access list is applied to all incoming updates. |

### Default

Disabled

### Command Mode

Router configuration

### Usage Guidelines

This command first appeared in Cisco IOS Release 11.1.

*Example*

In the following example, the router redistributes Enhanced IGRP into NLSP *area1*. Only services for networks 2 and 3 are accepted by the NLSP routing process.

```
access-list 1000 permit 2
access-list 1000 permit 3
access-list 1000 deny -1
!
ipx router nlsp area1
 redistribute eigrp
 distribute-sap-list 1000 in
```

*Related Commands*

Search online to find documentation for related commands.

access-list (SAP filtering)
deny (SAP filtering)
distribute-list out
ipx access-list
permit (SAP filtering)
redistribute

## DISTRIBUTE-SAP-LIST OUT

To suppress services from being advertised in SAP updates, use the **distribute-sap-list out** router configuration command. To cancel this function, use the **no** form of this command.

**distribute-sap-list** {*access-list-number* | *name*} **out** [*interface-name* | *routing-process*]
**no distribute-sap-list** {*access-list-number* | *name*} **out** [*interface-name* | *routing-process*]

| *Syntax* | *Description* |
| --- | --- |
| *access-list-number* | SAP access list number in the range 1000 to 1099. The list explicitly specifies which networks are to be sent and which are to be suppressed in routing updates. |
| *name* | Name of the access list. Names cannot contain a space or quotation mark and must begin with an alphabetic character to prevent ambiguity with numbered access lists. |
| **out** | Applies the access list to outgoing routing updates. |
| *interface-name* | (Optional) Interface on which the access list should be applied to outgoing updates. If no interface is specified, the access list is applied to all outgoing updates. |
| *routing-process* | (Optional) Name of a particular routing process as follows: |
| | • **eigrp** *autonomous-system-number* |
| | • **nlsp** [*tag*] |
| | • **rip** |

*Default*

Disabled

*Command Mode*

Router configuration

*Usage Guidelines*

This command first appeared in Cisco IOS Release 11.1.

When redistributing networks, a routing process name can be specified as an optional trailing argument to the **distribute-sap-list out** command. This causes the access list to be applied to only those routes derived from the specified routing process. After the process-specific access list is applied, any access list specified by a **distribute-sap-list out** command without a process name argument is applied. Addresses not specified in the **distribute-sap-list out** command are not advertised in outgoing routing updates.

*Example*

The following example causes only services from network 3 to be advertised by an Enhanced IGRP routing process:

```
access-list 1010 permit 3
access-list 1010 deny -1
!
ipx router eigrp 100
 network 3
 distribute-sap-list 1010 out
```

*Related Commands*

Search online to find documentation for related commands.

**access-list (SAP filtering)**
**deny (SAP filtering)**
**distribute-sap-list in**
**ipx access-list**
**permit (SAP filtering)**
**redistribute**

## IPX ACCESS-GROUP

To apply generic input and output filters to an interface, use the **ipx access-group** interface configuration command. To remove filters, use the **no** form of this command.

ipx access-group {*access-list-number* | *name*} [in | out]
no ipx access-group {*access-list-number* | *name*} [in | out]

| Syntax | Description |
|---|---|
| *access-list-number* | Number of the access list. For standard access lists, *access-list-number* is a number from 800 to 899. For extended access lists, *access-list-number* is a number from 900 to 999. |
| *name* | Name of the access list. Names cannot contain a space or quotation mark and must begin with an alphabetic character to prevent ambiguity with numbered access lists. |
| in | (Optional) Filters inbound packets. All incoming packets defined with either standard or extended access lists are filtered by the entries in this access list. |
| out | (Optional) Filters outbound packets. All outgoing packets defined with either standard or extended access lists and forwarded through the interface are filtered by the entries in this access list. This is the default when you do not specify an input (in) or output (out) keyword in the command line. |

### Default

No filters are predefined.

### Command Mode

Interface configuration

### Usage Guidelines

This command first appeared in Cisco IOS Release 10.0.

Generic filters control which data packets an interface receives or sends out based on the packet's source and destination addresses, IPX protocol type, and source and destination socket numbers. You use the standard **access-list** and extended **access-list** commands to specify the filtering conditions.

You can apply only one input filter and one output filter per interface or subinterface.

When you do not specify an input (in) or output (out) filter in the command line, the default is an output filter.

You cannot configure an output filter on an interface where autonomous switching is already configured. Similarly, you cannot configure autonomous switching on an interface where an output filter is already present. You cannot configure an input filter on an interface if autonomous switching is already configured on *any* interface. Likewise, you cannot configure input filters if autonomous switching is already enabled on *any* interface.

### Examples

In the following example, access list 801 is applied to Ethernet interface 1. Because the command line does not specify an input filter or output filter with the keywords **in** or **out**, the software assumes that it is an output filter.

```
interface ethernet 1
 ipx access-group 801
```

In the following example, access list 901 is applied to Ethernet interface 0. The access list is an input filter access list as specified by the keyword **in**.

```
interface ethernet 0
 ipx access-group 901 in
```

To remove the input access list filter in the previous example, you must specify the **in** keyword when you use the **no** form of the command. The following example correctly removes the access list:

```
interface ethernet 0
 no ipx access-group 901 in
```

### Related Commands

Search online to find documentation for related commands.

access-list (extended)
access-list (standard)
deny (extended)
deny (standard)
ipx access-list
permit (extended)
permit (standard)
priority-list protocol

## IPX ACCESS-LIST

To define an IPX access list by name, use the **ipx access-list** global configuration command. To remove a named IPX access list, use the **no** form of this command.

**ipx access-list** {**standard** | **extended** | **sap** | **summary**} *name*
**no ipx access-list** {**standard** | **extended** | **sap** | **summary**} *name*

---

— **CAUTION** ————————————————————————

Named access lists will not be recognized by any software release prior to Cisco IOS Release 11.3.

---

| Syntax | Description |
|---|---|
| **standard** | Specifies a standard IPX access list. |
| **extended** | Specifies an extended IPX access list. |
| **sap** | Specifies a SAP access list. |
| **summary** | Specifies area addresses that summarize routes using NLSP route aggregation filtering. |
| *name* | Name of the access list. Names cannot contain a space or quotation mark, and they must begin with an alphabetic character to prevent ambiguity with numbered access lists. |

### Default

There is no default named IPX access list.

### Command Mode

Global configuration

### Usage Guidelines

This command first appeared in Cisco IOS Release 11.3.

Use this command to configure a named IPX access list as opposed to a numbered IPX access list. This command will take you into access-list configuration mode, where you must define the denied or permitted access conditions with the **deny** and **permit** commands.

Specifying **standard, extended, sap,** or **summary** with the **ipx access-list** command determines the prompt you get when you enter access-list configuration mode.

Named access lists are not compatible with Cisco IOS releases prior to Release 11.3.

### Examples

The following example creates a standard access list named *fred*. It permits communication with only IPX network number 5678.

```
ipx access-list standard fred
  permit 5678 any
  deny any
```

The following example creates an extended access list named *sal* that denies all SPX packets:

```
ipx access-list extended sal
  deny spx any all any all log
  permit any
```

*Command Reference*

The following example creates a SAP access list named *MyServer* that allows only MyServer to be sent in SAP advertisements:

```
ipx access-list sap MyServer
 permit 1234 4 MyServer
```

The following example creates a summary access list named *finance* that allows the redistribution of all explicit routes every 64 ticks:

```
ipx access-list summary finance
 permit -1 ticks 64
```

### Related Commands

Search online to find documentation for related commands.

access-list (extended)
access-list (NLSP route aggregation summarization)
access-list (SAP filtering)
access-list (standard)
deny (extended)
deny (NLSP route aggregation summarization)
deny (SAP filtering)
deny (standard)
permit (extended)
permit (NLSP route aggregation summarization)
permit (SAP filtering)
permit (standard)
show ipx access-list

## IPX ACCOUNTING

To enable IPX accounting, use the **ipx accounting** interface configuration command. To disable IPX accounting, use the **no** form of this command.

**ipx accounting**
**no ipx accounting**

### Syntax        Description

This command has no arguments or keywords.

### Default

Disabled

### Command Mode

Interface configuration

### Usage Guidelines

This command first appeared in Cisco IOS Release 10.0.

IPX accounting allows you to collect information about IPX packets and the number of bytes that are switched through the Cisco IOS software. You collect information based on the source and destination IPX address. IPX accounting tracks only IPX traffic that is routed out an interface on which IPX accounting is configured; it does not track traffic generated by or terminated at the router itself.

The Cisco IOS software maintains two accounting databases: an active database and a checkpoint database. The active database contains accounting data tracked until the database is cleared. When the active database is cleared, its contents are copied to the checkpoint database. Using these two databases together allows you to monitor both current traffic and traffic that has previously traversed the router.

IPX accounting statistics will be accurate even if IPX access lists are being used or if IPX fast switching is enabled. Enabling IPX accounting significantly decreases performance of a fast switched interface.

IPX accounting does not keep statistics if autonomous switching is enabled. In fact, IPX accounting is disabled if autonomous or SSE switching is enabled.

### Example

The following example enables IPX accounting on Ethernet interface 0:

```
interface ethernet 0
  ipx accounting
```

### Related Commands

Search online to find documentation for related commands.

**clear ipx accounting**
**ipx accounting-list**
**ipx accounting-threshold**
**ipx accounting-transits**
**show ipx accounting**

## IPX ACCOUNTING-LIST

To filter networks for which IPX accounting information is kept, use the **ipx accounting-list** global configuration command. To remove the filter, use the **no** form of this command.

**ipx accounting-list** *number mask*
**no ipx accounting-list** *number mask*

| Syntax | Description |
|--------|-------------|
| *number* | Network number. This is an eight-digit hexadecimal number that uniquely identifies a network cable segment. It can be a number in the range 1 to FFFFFFFD. |
| | You do not need to specify leading zeros in the network number. For example, for the network number 000000AA you can enter AA. |
| *mask* | Network mask. |

### Default

No filters are predefined.

### Command Mode

Global configuration

### Usage Guidelines

This command first appeared in Cisco IOS Release 10.0.

The source and destination addresses of each IPX packet traversing the router are compared with the network numbers in the filter. If there is a match, accounting information about the IPX packet is entered into the active accounting database. If there is no match, the IPX packet is considered to be a transit packet and may be counted, depending on the setting of the **ipx accounting-transits** global configuration command.

### Example

The following example adds all networks with IPX network numbers beginning with 1 to the list of networks for which accounting information is kept:

```
ipx accounting-list 1 0000.0000.0000
```

### Related Commands

Search online to find documentation for related commands.

**clear ipx accounting**
**ipx accounting**
**ipx accounting-threshold**
**ipx accounting-transits**
**show ipx accounting**

## IPX ACCOUNTING-THRESHOLD

To set the maximum number of accounting database entries, use the **ipx accounting-threshold** global configuration command. To restore the default, use the **no** form of this command.

> **ipx accounting-threshold** *threshold*
> **no ipx accounting-threshold** *threshold*

| Syntax | Description |
|--------|-------------|
| *threshold* | Maximum number of entries (source and destination address pairs) that the Cisco IOS software can accumulate. |

### Default

512 entries

### Command Mode

Global configuration

### Usage Guidelines

This command first appeared in Cisco IOS Release 10.0.

The accounting threshold defines the maximum number of entries (source and destination address pairs) that the software accumulates. The threshold is designed to prevent IPX accounting from consuming all available free memory. This level of memory consumption could occur in a router that is switching traffic for many hosts. To determine whether overflows have occurred, use the **show ipx accounting** EXEC command.

### Example

The following example sets the IPX accounting database threshold to 500 entries:

```
ipx accounting-threshold 500
```

### Related Commands

Search online to find documentation for related commands.

**clear ipx accounting**
**ipx accounting**
**ipx accounting-list**
**ipx accounting-transits**
**show ipx accounting**

## IPX ACCOUNTING-TRANSITS

To set the maximum number of transit entries that will be stored in the IPX accounting database, use the **ipx accounting-transits** global configuration command. To disable this function, use the **no** form of this command.

> **ipx accounting-transits** *count*
> **no ipx accounting-transits**

*Syntax*

*count*

*Description*

Number of transit entries that will be stored in the IPX accounting database.

### Default

0 entries

### Command Mode

Global configuration

### Usage Guidelines

This command first appeared in Cisco IOS Release 10.0.

Transit entries are those that do not match any of the networks specified by **ipx accounting-list** global configuration commands. If you have not defined networks with **ipx accounting-list** commands, IPX accounting tracks all traffic through the interface (all transit entries) up to the accounting threshold limit.

### Example

The following example specifies a maximum of 100 transit records to be stored in the IPX accounting database:

```
ipx accounting-transits 100
```

### Related Commands

Search online to find documentation for related commands.

**clear ipx accounting**
**ipx accounting-list**
**ipx accounting-threshold**
**show ipx accounting**

## IPX ADVERTISE-DEFAULT-ROUTE-ONLY

To advertise only the default RIP route via the specified network, use the **ipx advertise-default-route-only** interface configuration command. To advertise all known RIP routes out the interface, use the **no** form of this command.

> **ipx advertise-default-route-only** *network*
> **no ipx advertise-default-route-only** *network*

| Syntax | Description |
|--------|-------------|
| *network* | Number of the network via which to advertise the default route. |

### Default

Disabled (that is, all known routes are advertised out the interface)

### Command Mode

Interface configuration

### Usage Guidelines

This command first appeared in Cisco IOS Release 10.3.

If you specify the **ipx advertise-default-route-only** command, only a known default RIP route is advertised out the interface; no other networks will be advertised. If you have a large number of routes in the routing table, for example, on the order of 1,000 routes, none of them will be advertised out the interface. However, if the default route is known, it will be advertised. Nodes on the interface can still reach any of the 1,000 networks via the default route.

Specifying the **ipx advertise-default-route-only** command results in a significant reduction in CPU processing overhead when there are many routes and many interfaces. It also reduces the load on downstream routers.

This command applies only to RIP. NLSP and Enhanced IGRP are not affected when you enable this command. They continue to advertise all routes that they know about.

— **NOTES** ——————————————————————————————

Not all routers recognize and support the default route. Use this command with caution if you are not sure if all routers in your network support the default route.

### Example

The following example enables the advertising of the default route only:

```
interface ethernet 1
 ipx network 1234
 ipx advertise-default-route-only 1234
```

*Command Reference*

*Related Commands*

Search online to find documentation for related commands.

ipx default-route

## IPX BACKUP-SERVER-QUERY-INTERVAL

To change the time between successive queries of each Enhanced IGRP neighbor's backup server table, use the **ipx backup-server-query-interval** global configuration command. To restore the default time, use the **no** form of this command.

    ipx backup-server-query-interval *interval*
    no ipx backup-server-query-interval

| *Syntax* | *Description* |
|----------|---------------|
| *interval* | Minimum time, in seconds, between successive queries of each Enhanced IGRP neighbor's backup server table. The default is 15 seconds. |

*Default*

15 seconds

*Command Mode*

Global configuration

*Usage Guidelines*

This command first appeared in Cisco IOS Release 10.0.

A lower interval may use more CPU resources, but may cause lost server information to be retrieved from other servers' tables sooner.

*Example*

The following example changes the server query time to 5 seconds:

```
ipx backup-server-query-interval 5
```

## IPX BANDWIDTH-PERCENT EIGRP

To configure the percentage of bandwidth that may be used by Enhanced IGRP on an interface, use the **ipx bandwidth-percent eigrp** interface configuration command. To restore the default value, use the **no** form of this command.

ipx bandwidth-percent eigrp *as-number percent*
no ipx bandwidth-percent eigrp *as-number*

| Syntax | Description |
|--------|-------------|
| *as-number* | Autonomous system number. |
| *percent* | Percentage of bandwidth that Enhanced IGRP may use. |

### Default

50 percent

### Command Mode

Interface configuration

### Usage Guidelines

This command first appeared in Cisco IOS Release 11.2.

Enhanced IGRP will use up to 50 percent of the bandwidth of a link, as defined by the **bandwidth** interface configuration command. This command may be used if some other fraction of the bandwidth is desired. Note that values greater than 100 percent may be configured; this may be useful if the bandwidth is set artificially low for other reasons.

### Example

The following example allows Enhanced IGRP to use up to 75 percent (42 Kbps) of a 56 Kbps serial link in autonomous system 209:

```
interface serial 0
 bandwidth 56
 ipx bandwidth-percent eigrp 209 75
```

### Related Commands

Search online to find documentation for related commands.

**bandwidth**
**ipx router**

## IPX BROADCAST-FASTSWITCHING

To enable the router to fast switch IPX directed broadcast packets, use the **ipx broadcast-fastswitching** global configuration command. To disable fast switching of IPX directed broadcast packets, use the **no** form of the command.

ipx broadcast-fastswitching
no ipx broadcast-fastswitching

*Syntax       Description*

This command has no arguments or keywords.

*Default*

Disabled

The default behavior is to process-switch directed broadcast packets.

*Command Mode*

Global configuration

*Usage Guidelines*

This command first appeared in Cisco IOS Release 11.1.

A directed broadcast is one with a network layer destination address of the form net.ffff.ffff.ffff. The **ipx broadcast-fastswitching** command permits the router to fast switch IPX directed broadcast packets. This may be useful in certain broadcast-based applications that rely on helpering.

Note that the router never uses autonomous switching for eligible directed broadcast packets, even if autonomous switching is enabled on the output interface. Also note that routing and service updates are always exempt from this treatment.

*Example*

The following example enables the router to fast switch IPX directed broadcast packets:

```
ipx broadcast-fastswitching
```

*Related Commands*

Search online to find documentation for related commands.

**ipx helper-address**

## IPX DEFAULT-OUTPUT-RIP-DELAY

To set the default interpacket delay for RIP updates sent on all interfaces, use the **ipx default-output-rip-delay** global configuration command. To return to the initial default delay value, use the **no** form of this command.

ipx default-output-rip-delay *delay*
no ipx default-output-rip-delay [*delay*]

| Syntax | Description |
|--------|-------------|
| *delay* | Delay, in milliseconds, between packets in a multiple-packet RIP update. The default delay is 55 ms. Novell recommends a delay of 55 ms. |

## Default

55 ms

## Command Mode

Global configuration

## Usage Guidelines

This command first appeared in Cisco IOS Release 11.1.

The interpacket delay is the delay between the individual packets sent in a multiple-packet routing update. The **ipx default-output-rip-delay** command sets a default interpacket delay for all interfaces.

The system uses the delay specified by the **ipx default-output-rip-delay** command for periodic and triggered routing updates when no delay is set for periodic and triggered routing updates on an interface. When you set a delay for triggered routing updates, the system uses the delay specified by the **ipx default-output-rip-delay** command for only the periodic routing updates sent on all interfaces.

To set a delay for triggered routing updates, see the **ipx triggered-rip-delay** or **ipx default-triggered-rip-delay** commands.

Novell recommends a delay of 55 ms for compatibility with older and slower IPX machines. These machines may lose RIP updates because they process packets more slowly than the router sends them. The delay imposed by this command forces the router to pace its output to the slower-processing needs of these IPX machines.

The default delay on a NetWare 3.11 server is about 100 ms.

This command is also useful on limited bandwidth point-to-point links or X.25 and Frame Relay multipoint interfaces.

## Example

The following example sets a default interpacket delay of 55 ms for RIP updates sent on all interfaces:

```
ipx default-output-rip-delay 55
```

Command Reference

*Related Commands*

Search online to find documentation for related commands.

**ipx default-triggered-rip-delay**
**ipx output-rip-delay**
**ipx triggered-rip-delay**

## IPX DEFAULT-OUTPUT-SAP-DELAY

To set a default interpacket delay for SAP updates sent on all interfaces, use the **ipx default-output-sap-delay** global configuration command. To return to the initial default delay value, use the **no** form of this command.

> **ipx default-output-sap-delay** *delay*
> **no ipx default-output-sap-delay** [*delay*]

| Syntax | Description |
|--------|-------------|
| *delay* | Delay, in milliseconds, between packets in a multiple-packet SAP update. The default delay is 55 ms. Novell recommends a delay of 55 ms. |

*Default*

55 ms

*Command Mode*

Global configuration

*Usage Guidelines*

This command first appeared in Cisco IOS Release 11.1.

The interpacket delay is the delay between the individual packets sent in a multiple-packet SAP update. The **ipx default-output-sap-delay** command sets a default interpacket delay for all interfaces.

The system uses the delay specified by the **ipx default-output-sap-delay** command for periodic and triggered SAP updates when no delay is set for periodic and triggered updates on an interface. When you set a delay for triggered updates, the system uses the delay specified by the **ipx default-output-sap-delay** command only for the periodic SAP updates sent on all interfaces.

To set a delay for triggered updates, see the **ipx triggered-sap-delay** or **ipx default-triggered-sap-delay** commands.

Novell recommends a delay of 55 ms for compatibility with older and slower IPX servers. These servers may lose SAP updates because they process packets more slowly than the router sends them.

The delay imposed by this command forces the router to pace its output to the slower-processing needs of these servers.

The default delay on a NetWare 3.11 server is about 100 ms.

This command is also useful on limited bandwidth point-to-point links or X.25 interfaces.

### Example

The following example sets a default interpacket delay of 55 ms for SAP updates sent on all interfaces:

```
ipx default-output-sap-delay 55
```

### Related Commands

Search online to find documentation for related commands.

ipx default-triggered-sap-delay
ipx output-sap-delay
ipx triggered-sap-delay

## IPX DEFAULT-ROUTE

To forward to the default network all packets for which a route to the destination network is unknown, use the **ipx default-route** global configuration command. To disable the use of the default network, use the **no** form of this command.

**ipx default-route**
**no ipx default-route**

### Syntax    Description

This command has no arguments or keywords.

### Default

Enabled; that is, all packets for which a route to the destination is unknown are forwarded to the default network, which is -2 (0xFFFFFFFE).

### Command Mode

Global configuration

### Usage Guidelines

This command first appeared in Cisco IOS Release 10.3.

When you use the **no ipx default-route** command, Cisco IOS software no longer uses -2 as the default network. Instead, the software interprets -2 as a regular network and packets for which a route to the destination network is unknown are dropped.

*Command Reference*

*Example*

The following example disables the forwarding of packets towards the default network:

```
no ipx default-route
```

*Related Commands*

Search online to find documentation for related commands.

ipx advertise-default-route-only

## IPX DEFAULT-TRIGGERED-RIP-DELAY

To set the default interpacket delay for triggered RIP updates sent on all interfaces, use the **ipx default-triggered-rip-delay** global configuration command. To return to the system default delay, use the **no** form of this command.

> **ipx default-triggered-rip-delay** *delay*
> **no ipx default-triggered-rip-delay** [*delay*]

| Syntax | Description |
|--------|-------------|
| *delay* | Delay, in milliseconds, between packets in a multiple-packet RIP update. The default delay is 55 ms. Novell recommends a delay of 55 ms. |

*Default*

55 ms

*Command Mode*

Global configuration

*Usage Guidelines*

This command first appeared in Cisco IOS Release 11.1.

The interpacket delay is the delay between the individual packets sent in a multiple-packet routing update. A triggered routing update is one that the system sends in response to a "trigger" event, such as a request packet, interface up/down, route up/down, or server up/down.

The **ipx default-triggered-rip-delay** command sets the default interpacket delay for triggered routing updates sent on all interfaces. On a single interface, you can override this global default delay for triggered routing updates using the **ipx triggered-rip-delay** interface command.

The global default delay for triggered routing updates overrides the delay value set by the **ipx output-rip-delay** or **ipx default-output-rip-delay** command for triggered routing updates.

If the delay value set by the **ipx output-rip-delay** or **ipx default-output-rip-delay** command is high, then we strongly recommend a low delay value for triggered routing updates so that updates triggered by special events are sent in a more timely manner than periodic routing updates.

Novell recommends a delay of 55 ms for compatibility with older and slower IPX machines. These machines may lose RIP updates because they process packets more slowly than the router sends them. The delay imposed by this command forces the router to pace its output to the slower-processing needs of these IPX machines.

The default delay on a NetWare 3.11 server is approximately 100 ms.

When you do not set the interpacket delay for triggered routing updates, the system uses the delay specified by the **ipx output-rip-delay** or **ipx default-output-rip-delay** command for both periodic and triggered routing updates.

When you use the **no** form of the **ipx default-triggered-rip-delay** command, the system uses the delay set by the **ipx output-rip-delay** or **ipx default-output-rip-delay** command for triggered RIP updates, if set. Otherwise, the system uses the initial default delay as described in the "Default" section.

This command is also useful on limited bandwidth point-to-point links, or X.25 and Frame Relay multipoint interfaces.

### Example

The following example sets an interpacket delay of 55 ms for triggered routing updates sent on all interfaces:

```
ipx default-triggered-rip-delay 55
```

### Related Commands

Search online to find documentation for related commands.

**ipx default-output-rip-delay**
**ipx output-rip-delay**
**ipx triggered-rip-delay**

## IPX DEFAULT-TRIGGERED-SAP-DELAY

To set the default interpacket delay for triggered SAP updates sent on all interfaces, use the **ipx default-triggered-sap-delay** global configuration command. To return to the system default delay, use the **no** form of this command.

> **ipx default-triggered-sap-delay** *delay*
> **no ipx default-triggered-sap-delay** [*delay*]

*Command Reference*

| Syntax | Description |
|--------|-------------|
| *delay* | Delay, in milliseconds, between packets in a multiple-packet SAP update. The default delay is 55 ms. Novell recommends a delay of 55 ms. |

## Default

55 ms

## Command Mode

Global configuration

## Usage Guidelines

This command first appeared in Cisco IOS Release 11.1.

The interpacket delay is the delay between the individual packets sent in a multiple-packet SAP update. A triggered SAP update is one that the system sends in response to a "trigger" event, such as a request packet, interface up/down, route up/down, or server up/down.

The **ipx default-triggered-sap-delay** command sets the default interpacket delay for triggered SAP updates sent on all interfaces. On a single interface, you can override this global default delay for triggered updates using the **ipx triggered-sap-delay** interface command.

The global default delay for triggered updates overrides the delay value set by the **ipx output-sap-delay** or **ipx default-output-sap-delay** command for triggered updates.

If the delay value set by the **ipx output-sap-delay** or **ipx default-output-sap-delay** command is high, then we strongly recommend a low delay value for triggered updates so that updates triggered by special events are sent in a more timely manner than periodic updates.

Novell recommends a delay of 55 ms for compatibility with older and slower IPX servers. These servers may lose SAP updates because they process packets more slowly than the router sends them. The delay imposed by this command forces the router to pace its output to the slower-processing needs of these IPX servers.

The default delay on a NetWare 3.11 server is approximately 100 ms.

When you do not set the interpacket delay for triggered SAP updates, the system uses the delay specified by the **ipx output-sap-delay** or **ipx default-output-sap-delay** command for both periodic and triggered SAP updates.

When you use the **no** form of the **ipx default-triggered-sap-delay** command, the system uses the delay set by the **ipx output-sap-delay** or **ipx default-output-sap-delay** command for triggered SAP updates, if set. Otherwise, the system uses the initial default delay as described in the "Default" section.

This command is also useful on limited bandwidth point-to-point links, or X.25 and Frame Relay multipoint interfaces.

### Example

The following example sets an interpacket delay of 55 ms for triggered SAP updates sent on all interfaces:

```
ipx default-triggered-sap-delay 55
```

### Related Commands

Search online to find documentation for related commands.

**ipx default-output-sap-delay**
**ipx output-sap-delay**
**ipx triggered-sap-delay**

## IPX DELAY

To set the tick count, use the **ipx delay** interface configuration command. To reset the default increment in the delay field, use the **no** form of this command.

> **ipx delay** *ticks*
> **no ipx delay**

| Syntax | Description |
|--------|-------------|
| *ticks* | Number of IBM clock ticks of delay to use. One clock tick is 1/18 of a second (approximately 55 ms). |

### Default

The default delay is determined from the delay configured on the interface with the **delay** command. It is (interface delay + 333) / 334. Therefore, unless you change the delay by a value greater than 334, you will not notice a difference.

### Command Mode

Interface configuration

### Usage Guidelines

This command first appeared in Cisco IOS Release 10.0.

The **ipx delay** command sets the count used in the IPX RIP delay field, which is also known as the *ticks field*.

IPXWAN links determine their delay dynamically. If you do not specify the **ipx delay** command on an interface and you have not changed the interface delays with the **interface delay** interface configuration command, all LAN interfaces have a delay of 1 and all WAN interfaces have a delay of 6. The preferred method of adjusting delays is to use the **ipx delay** command, not the **interface delay** command. The **show ipx interface** EXEC command displays only the delay value configured with the **ipx delay** command.

With IPXWAN, if you change the interface delay with the **interface delay** command, the **ipx delay** command uses that delay when calculating a delay to use. Also, when changing delays with IPX-WAN, the changes affect only the link's calculated delay on the side considered to be the master.

Leaving the delay at its default value is sufficient for most interfaces.

### Example

The following example changes the delay for serial interface 0 to 10 ticks:

```
interface serial 0
  ipx delay 10
```

### Related Commands

Search online to find documentation for related commands.

**delay**
**ipx maximum-paths**
**ipx output-network-filter**
**ipx output-rip-delay**

### IPX DOWN

To administratively shut down an IPX network, use the **ipx down** interface configuration command. To restart the network, use the **no** form of this command.

> **ipx down** *network*
> **no ipx down**

| Syntax | Description |
|---|---|
| *network* | Number of the network to shut down. This is an eight-digit hexadecimal number that uniquely identifies a network cable segment. It can be a number in the range 1 to FFFFFFFD. You do not need to specify leading zeros in the network number. For example, for the network number 000000AA, you can enter AA. |

### Default

Disabled

### Command Mode

Interface configuration

### Usage Guidelines

This command first appeared in Cisco IOS Release 10.0.

The **ipx down** command administratively shuts down the specified network. The network still exists in the configuration, but is not active. When shutting down, the network sends out update packets informing its neighbors that it is shutting down. This allows the neighboring systems to update their routing, SAP, and other tables without having to wait for routes and services learned via this network to time out.

To shut down an interface in a manner that is considerate of one's neighbor, use **ipx down** before using the **shutdown** command.

### Example

The following example administratively shuts down network AA on Ethernet interface 0:

```
interface ethernet 0
  ipx down AA
```

## IPX GNS-REPLY-DISABLE

To disable the sending of replies to IPX Get Nearest Server (GNS) queries, use the **ipx gns-reply-disable** interface configuration command. To return to the default, use the **no** form of this command.

**ipx gns-reply-disable**
**no ipx gns-reply-disable**

### Syntax      Description

This command has no arguments or keywords.

### Default

Replies are sent to IPX GNS queries.

### Command Mode

Interface configuration

### Usage Guidelines

This command first appeared in Cisco IOS Release 10.0.

### Example

The following example disables the sending of replies to GNS queries on Ethernet interface 0:

```
interface ethernet 0
  ipx gns-reply-disable
```

### Related Commands

Search online to find documentation for related commands.

**ipx gns-response-delay**

## IPX GNS-RESPONSE-DELAY

To change the delay when responding to Get Nearest Server (GNS) requests, use the **ipx gns-response-delay** global or interface configuration command. To return to the default delay, use the **no** form of this command.

> **ipx gns-response-delay** [*milliseconds*]
> **no ipx gns-response-delay**

| Syntax | Description |
|---|---|
| *milliseconds* | (Optional) Time, in milliseconds, that the Cisco IOS software waits after receiving a GNS request from an IPX client before responding with a server name to that client. The default is zero, which indicates no delay. |

### Default

0 (no delay)

### Command Mode

Global configuration (globally changes the delay for the router)
Interface configuration (overrides the globally configured delay for an interface)

### Usage Guidelines

This command first appeared in Cisco IOS Release 10.0.

This command can be used in two modes: global configuration or interface configuration. In both modes, the command syntax is the same. A delay in responding to GNS requests might be imposed so that, in certain topologies, any local Novell IPX servers respond to the GNS requests before Cisco software does. It is desirable to have these end-host server systems get their reply to the client before the router does because the client typically takes the first response, not the best response. In this case the best response is the one from the local server.

NetWare 2.*x* has a problem with dual-connected servers in parallel with a router. If you are using this version of NetWare, you should set a GNS delay. A value of 500 ms is recommended.

In situations in which servers are always located across routers from their clients, there is no need for a delay to be imposed.

### Example

The following example sets the delay in responding to GNS requests to 500 ms (0.5 second):

```
ipx gns-response-delay 500
```

### Related Commands

Search online to find documentation for related commands.

**ipx gns-reply-disable**

### IPX GNS-ROUND-ROBIN

To rotate using a round-robin selection method through a set of eligible servers when responding to Get Nearest Server (GNS) requests, use the **ipx gns-round-robin** global configuration command. To use the most recently learned server, use the **no** form of this command.

> **ipx gns-round-robin**
> **no ipx gns-round-robin**

*Syntax      Description*

This command has no arguments or keywords.

*Default*

The most recently learned, eligible server is used.

*Command Mode*

Global configuration

*Usage Guidelines*

This command first appeared in Cisco IOS Release 10.0.

In the normal server selection process, requests for service are responded to with the most recently learned, closest server. If you enable the round-robin method, the Cisco IOS software maintains a list of the nearest servers eligible to provide specific services. It uses this list when responding to GNS requests. Responses to requests are distributed in a round-robin fashion across all active IPX interfaces on the router.

Eligible servers are those that satisfy the "nearest" requirement for a given request and that are not filtered either by a SAP filter or by a GNS filter.

*Example*

The following example responds to GNS requests using a round-robin selection method from a list of eligible nearest servers:

```
ipx gns-round-robin
```

*Related Commands*

Search online to find documentation for related commands.

**ipx output-gns-filter**
**ipx output-sap-delay**

**IPX HELLO-INTERVAL EIGRP**

To configure the interval between Enhanced IGRP hello packets, use the **ipx hello-interval eigrp** interface configuration command. To restore the default interval, use the **no** form of this command.

> **ipx hello-interval eigrp** *autonomous-system-number seconds*
> **no ipx hello-interval eigrp** *autonomous-system-number seconds*

| Syntax | Description |
|--------|-------------|
| *autonomous-system-number* | Enhanced IGRP autonomous system number. It can be a number from 1 to 65535. |
| *seconds* | Interval between hello packets, in seconds. The default interval is 5 seconds, which is one-third of the default hold time. |

*Default*

For low-speed NBMA networks: 60 seconds
For all other networks: 5 seconds

*Command Mode*

Interface configuration

*Usage Guidelines*

This command first appeared in Cisco IOS Release 10.0.

The default of 60 seconds applies only to low-speed, nonbroadcast, multiaccess (NBMA) media. Low speed is considered to be a rate of T1 or slower, as specified with the **bandwidth** interface configuration command. Note that for purposes of Enhanced IGRP, Frame Relay and SMDS networks may or may not be considered to be NBMA. These networks are considered NBMA if the interface has not been configured to use physical multicasting; otherwise they are considered not to be NBMA.

*Example*

The following example changes the hello interval to 10 seconds:

```
interface ethernet 0
  ipx network 10
  ipx hello-interval eigrp 4 10
```

*Related Commands*

Search online to find documentation for related commands.

**ipx hold-down eigrp**

## IPX HELPER-ADDRESS

To forward broadcast packets to a specified server, use the **ipx helper-address** interface configuration command. To disable this function, use the **no** form of this command.

```
ipx helper-address network.node
no ipx helper-address network.node
```

| Syntax | Description |
|--------|-------------|
| *network* | Network on which the target IPX server resides. This is an eight-digit hexadecimal number that uniquely identifies a network cable segment. It can be a number in the range 1 to FFFFFFFD. A network number of -1 indicates all-nets flooding. You do not need to specify leading zeros in the network number. For example, for the network number 000000AA, you can enter AA. |
| *.node* | Node number of the target Novell server. This is a 48-bit value represented by a dotted triplet of four-digit hexadecimal numbers (*xxxx.xxxx.xxxx*). A node number of FFFF.FFFF.FFFF matches all servers. |

### Default
Disabled

### Command Mode
Interface configuration

### Usage Guidelines
This command first appeared prior to Cisco IOS Release 10.0.

Routers normally block all broadcast requests and do not forward them to other network segments. This is done to prevent the degradation of performance over the entire network. The **ipx helper-address** command allows broadcasts to be forwarded to other networks. This is useful when a network segment does not have an end-host capable of servicing a particular type of broadcast request. This command lets you forward the broadcasts to a server, network, or networks that can process them. Incoming unrecognized broadcast packets that match the access list created with the **ipx helper-list** command, if it is present, are forwarded.

You can specify multiple **ipx helper-address** commands on a given interface.

The Cisco IOS software supports all-networks flooded broadcasts (sometimes referred to as *all-nets flooding*). These are broadcast messages that are forwarded to all networks. To configure the all-nets flooding, define the IPX helper address for an interface as follows:

```
ipx helper-address -1.FFFF.FFFF.FFFF
```

On systems configured for IPX routing, this helper address is displayed as follows (via the **show ipx interface** command):

```
FFFFFFFF.FFFF.FFFF.FFFF
```

Although Cisco software takes care to keep broadcast traffic to a minimum, some duplication is unavoidable. When loops exist, all-nets flooding can propagate bursts of excess traffic that will eventually age out when the hop count reaches its limit (16 hops). Use all-nets flooding carefully and only when necessary. Note that you can apply additional restrictions by defining a helper list.

To forward type 20 packets to only those nodes specified by the **ipx helper-address** command, use the **ipx helper-address** command in conjunction with the **ipx type-20-helpered** global configuration command.

To forward type 20 packets to all nodes on the network, use the **ipx type-20-propagation** command. See the **ipx type-20-propagation** command for more information.

### Example

In the following example, all-nets broadcasts on Ethernet interface 0 (except type 20 propagation packets) are forwarded to IPX server 00b4.23cd.110a on network bb:

```
interface ethernet 0
  ipx helper-address bb.00b4.23cd.110a
```

### Related Commands

Search online to find documentation for related commands.

ipx helper-list
ipx type-20-propagation

## IPX HELPER-LIST

To assign an access list to an interface to control broadcast traffic (including type 20 propagation packets), use the **ipx helper-list** interface configuration command. To remove the access list from an interface, use the **no** form of this command.

> **ipx helper-list** {*access-list-number* | *name*}
> **no ipx helper-list** {*access-list-number* | *name*}

| Syntax | Description |
|---|---|
| *access-list-number* | Number of the access list. All outgoing packets defined with either standard or extended access lists are filtered by the entries in this access list. For standard access lists, *access-list-number* is a number from 800 to 899. For extended access lists, it is a number from 900 to 999. |
| *name* | Name of the access list. Names cannot contain a space or quotation mark and must begin with an alphabetic character to prevent ambiguity with numbered access lists. |

## Default

No access list is preassigned.

## Command Mode

Interface configuration

## Usage Guidelines

This command first appeared prior to Cisco IOS Release 10.0.

The **ipx helper-list** command specifies an access list to use in forwarding broadcast packets. One use of this command is to prevent client nodes from discovering services they should not use.

Because the destination address of a broadcast packet is by definition the broadcast address, this command is useful only for filtering based on the source address of the broadcast packet.

The helper list, if present, is applied to both all-nets broadcast packets and type 20 propagation packets.

The helper list on the input interface is applied to packets before they are output via either the helper address or type 20 propagation packet mechanism.

## Example

The following example assigns access list 900 to Ethernet interface 0 to control broadcast traffic:

```
interface ethernet 0
  ipx helper-list 900
```

## Related Commands

Search online to find documentation for related commands.

**access-list (extended)**
**access-list (standard)**
**deny (extended)**
**deny (standard)**
**ipx access-list**
**ipx helper-address**
**ipx type-20-propagation**
**permit (extended)**
**permit (standard)**

## IPX HOLD-DOWN EIGRP

To specify the length of time a lost Enhanced IGRP route is placed in the hold-down state, use the **ipx hold-down eigrp** interface configuration command. To restore the default time, use the **no** form of this command.

*Command Reference*

ipx hold-down eigrp *autonomous-system-number seconds*
no ipx hold-down eigrp *autonomous-system-number seconds*

| Syntax | Description |
| --- | --- |
| *autonomous-system-number* | Enhanced IGRP autonomous system number. It can be a number from 1 to 65535. |
| *seconds* | Hold-down time, in seconds. The default hold time is 5 seconds. |

### Default

5 seconds

### Command Mode

Interface configuration

### Usage Guidelines

This command first appeared in Cisco IOS Release 10.0.

When an Enhanced IGRP route is lost, it is placed into a hold-down state for a period of time. The purpose of the hold-down state is to ensure the validity of any new routes for the same destination.

The amount of time a lost Enhanced IGRP route is placed in the hold-down state is configurable. Set the amount of time to a value longer than the default of 5 seconds if your network requires a longer time for the unreachable route information to propagate.

### Example

The following example changes the hold-down time for autonomous system 4 to 45 seconds:

```
interface ethernet 0
 ipx network 10
 ipx hold-down eigrp 4 45
```

## IPX HOLD-TIME EIGRP

To specify the length of time a neighbor should consider Enhanced IGRP hello packets valid, use the ipx hold-time eigrp interface configuration command. To restore the default time, use the no form of this command.

ipx hold-time eigrp *autonomous-system-number seconds*
no ipx hold-time eigrp *autonomous-system-number seconds*

| Syntax | Description |
| --- | --- |
| *autonomous-system-number* | Enhanced IGRP autonomous system number. It can be a number from 1 to 65535. |
| *seconds* | Hold time, in seconds. The hold time is advertised in hello packets and indicates to neighbors the length of time they should consider the sender valid. The default hold time is 15 seconds, which is 3 times the hello interval. |

## Default

For low-speed NBMA networks: 180 seconds
For all other networks: 15 seconds

## Command Mode

Interface configuration

## Usage Guidelines

This command first appeared in Cisco IOS Release 10.0.

If the current value for the hold time is less than two times the interval between hello packets, the hold time will be reset to three times the hello interval.

If a router does not receive a hello packet within the specified hold time, routes through the router are considered available.

Increasing the hold time delays route convergence across the network.

The default of 180 seconds applies only to low-speed, nonbroadcast, multiaccess (NBMA) media. Low speed is considered to be a rate of T1 or slower, as specified with the **bandwidth** interface configuration command.

## Example

The following example changes the hold time to 45 seconds:

```
interface ethernet 0
 ipx network 10
 ipx hold-time eigrp 4 45
```

## Related Commands

Search online to find documentation for related commands.

**ipx hello-interval eigrp**

**IPX INPUT-NETWORK-FILTER**

To control which networks are added to the Cisco IOS software's routing table, use the **ipx input-network-filter** interface configuration command. To remove the filter from the interface, use the **no** form of this command.

> **ipx input-network-filter** {*access-list-number* | *name*}
> **no ipx input-network-filter** {*access-list-number* | *name*}

| Syntax | Description |
|---|---|
| *access-list-number* | Number of the access list. All incoming packets defined with either standard or extended access lists are filtered by the entries in this access list. For standard access lists, *access-list-number* is a number from 800 to 899. For extended access lists, it is a number from 900 to 999. |
| *name* | Name of the access list. Names cannot contain a space or quotation mark and must begin with an alphabetic character to prevent ambiguity with numbered access lists. |

*Default*

No filters are predefined.

*Command Mode*

Interface configuration

*Usage Guidelines*

This command first appeared in Cisco IOS Release 10.0.

The **ipx input-network-filter** command controls which networks are added to the routing table based on the networks learned in incoming IPX routing updates (RIP updates) on the interface.

You can issue only one **ipx input-network-filter** command on each interface.

*Examples*

In the following example, access list 876 controls which networks are added to the routing table when IPX routing updates are received on Ethernet interface 1. Routing updates for network 1b will be accepted. Routing updates for all other networks are implicitly denied and are not added to the routing table.

```
access-list 876 permit 1b
interface ethernet 1
  ipx input-network-filter 876
```

The following example is a variation of the preceding that explicitly denies network 1a and explicitly allows updates for all other networks:

```
access-list 876 deny 1a
access-list 876 permit -1
```

## Related Commands

Search online to find documentation for related commands.

**access-list (extended)**
**access-list (standard)**
**deny (extended)**
**deny (standard)**
**ipx access-list**
**ipx output-network-filter**
**ipx router-filter**
**permit (extended)**
**permit (standard)**

## IPX INPUT-SAP-FILTER

To control which services are added to the Cisco IOS software's SAP table, use the **ipx input-sap-filter** interface configuration command. To remove the filter, use the **no** form of this command.

> **ipx input-sap-filter** {*access-list-number* | *name*}
> **no ipx input-sap-filter** {*access-list-number* | *name*}

| Syntax | Description |
|---|---|
| *access-list-number* | Number of the SAP access list. All incoming packets are filtered by the entries in this access list. The argument *access-list-number* is a number from 1000 to 1099. |
| *name* | Name of the access list. Names cannot contain a space or quotation mark, and they must begin with an alphabetic character to prevent ambiguity with numbered access lists. |

## Default

No filters are predefined.

## Command Mode

Interface configuration

## Usage Guidelines

This command first appeared in Cisco IOS Release 10.0.

*Command Reference*

The **ipx input-sap-filter** command filters all incoming service advertisements received by the router. This is done prior to accepting information about a service.

You can issue only one **ipx input-sap-filter** command on each interface.

When configuring SAP filters for NetWare 3.11 and later servers, use the server's internal network and node number (the node number is always 0000.0000.0001) as its address in the **access-list (SAP filtering)** command. Do not use the *network.node* address of the particular interface board.

### Example

The following example denies service advertisements about the server at address 3c.0800.89a1.1527, but accepts information about all other services on all other networks:

```
access-list 1000 deny 3c.0800.89a1.1527
access-list 1000 permit -1
!
interface ethernet 0
 ipx input-sap-filter 1000
```

### Related Commands

Search online to find documentation for related commands.

**access-list (SAP filtering)**
**deny (SAP filtering)**
**ipx access-list**
**ipx output-sap-filter**
**ipx router-sap-filter**
**permit (SAP filtering)**

## IPX INTERNAL-NETWORK

To set an internal network number for use by NLSP and IPXWAN, use the **ipx internal-network** global configuration command. To remove an internal network number, use the **no** form of this command.

> **ipx internal-network** *network-number*
> **no ipx internal-network** [*network-number*]

### Syntax

| Syntax | Description |
|---|---|
| *network-number* | Number of the internal network. |

### Default

No internal network number is set.

### Command Mode

Global configuration

## Usage Guidelines

This command first appeared in Cisco IOS Release 10.3.

An internal network number is a network number assigned to the router. This network number must be unique within the internetwork.

You must configure an internal network number on each device on an NLSP-capable network for NLSP to operate.

When you set an internal network number, the Cisco IOS software advertises the specified network out all interfaces. It accepts packets destined to that network at the address *internal-network*.0000.0000.0001.

## Example

The following example assigns internal network number e001 to the local router:

```
ipx routing
ipx internal-network e001
```

## Related Commands

Search online to find documentation for related commands.

**ipx router nlsp**
**ipx routing**

### IPX IPXWAN

To enable the IPXWAN protocol on a serial interface, use the **ipx ipxwan** interface configuration command. To disable the IPXWAN protocol, use the **no** form of this command.

    **ipx ipxwan** [*local-node* {*network-number* | **unnumbered**} *local-server-name retry-interval retry-limit*]
    **no ipx ipxwan**

*Command Reference*

| Syntax | Description |
|---|---|
| *local-node* | (Optional) Primary network number of the router. This is an IPX network number that is unique across the entire internetwork. On NetWare 3.*x* servers, the primary network number is called the internal network number. The device with the higher number is determined to be the link master. A value of 0 causes the Cisco IOS software to use the configured internal network number. |
| *network-number* | (Optional) IPX network number to be used for the link if this router is the one determined to be the link master. The number is an eight-digit hexadecimal number that uniquely identifies a network cable segment. It can be a number in the range 0 to FFFFFFFD. A value 0 is equivalent to specifying the keyword **unnumbered**.<br><br>You do not need to specify leading zeros in the network number. For example, for the network number 000000AA, you can enter AA. |
| **unnumbered** | (Optional) Specifies that no IPX network number is defined for the link. This is equivalent to specifying a value of 0 for the *network-number* argument. |
| *local-server-name* | (Optional) Name of the local router. It can be up to 47 characters long, and can contain uppercase letters, digits, underscores (_), hyphens (-), and at signs (@). On NetWare 3.*x* servers, this is the router name. For Cisco routers, this is the name of the router as configured via the **hostname** command; that is, the name that precedes the standard prompt, which is an angle bracket (>) for EXEC mode or a pound sign (#) for privileged EXEC mode. |
| *retry-interval* | (Optional) Retry interval, in seconds. This interval defines how often the software will retry the IPXWAN start-up negotiation if a start-up failure occurs. Retries will occur until the retry limit defined by the *retry-limit* argument is reached. It can be a value from 1 to 600. The default is 20 seconds. |
| *retry-limit* | (Optional) Maximum number of times the software retries the IPXWAN start-up negotiation before taking the action defined by the **ipx ipxwan error** command. It can be a value from 1 through 100. The default is 3. |

### Default

IPXWAN is disabled.

If you enable IPXWAN, the default is **unnumbered**.

### Command Mode

Interface configuration

### Usage Guidelines

This command first appeared in Cisco IOS Release 10.0. The **unnumbered** keyword and *retry-interval* argument first appeared in Cisco IOS Release 10.3.

If you omit all optional arguments and keywords, the **ipx ipxwan** command defaults to **ipx ipxwan 0 unnumbered** *router-name* (which is equivalent to **ipx ipxwan 0** *local-server-name*), where *router-name* is the name of the router as configured with the **hostname** global configuration command. For this configuration, the **show ipx interface** command displays `ipx ipxwan 0 0 local-server-name`.

If you enter a value of 0 for the *network-number* argument, the output of the **show running-config** EXEC command does not show the 0 but rather reports this value as "unnumbered."

The name of each device on each side of the link must be different.

IPXWAN is a start-up end-to-end options negotiations protocol. When a link comes up, the first IPX packets sent across are IPXWAN packets negotiating the options for the link. When the IPX-WAN options have been successfully determined, normal IPX traffic starts. The three options negotiated are the link IPX network number, internal network number, and link delay (ticks) characteristics. The side of the link with the higher local-node number (internal network number) gives the IPX network number and delay to use for the link to the other side. Once IPXWAN finishes, no IPX-WAN packets are sent unless link characteristics change or the connection fails. For example, if the IPX delay is changed from the default setting, an IPXWAN restart will be forced.

To enable the IPXWAN protocol on a serial interface, you must not have configured an IPX network number (using the **ipx network** interface configuration command) on that interface.

To control the delay on a link, use the **ipx delay** interface configuration command. If you issue this command when the serial link is already up, the state of the link will be reset and renegotiated.

### Examples

The following example enables IPXWAN on serial interface 0:

```
interface serial 0
 encapsulation ppp
 ipx ipxwan
```

The following example enables IPXWAN on serial interface 1 on device CHICAGO-AS. When the link comes up, CHICAGO-AS will be the master because it has a larger internal network number. It will give the IPX number 100 to NYC-AS to use as the network number for the link. The link delay, in ticks, will be determined by the exchange of packets between the two access servers.

On the local access server (CHICAGO-AS):

```
interface serial 1
  no ipx network
  encapsulation ppp
  ipx ipxwan 6666 100 CHICAGO-AS
```

On the remote router (NYC-AS):

```
interface serial 0
  no ipx network
  encapsulation ppp
  ipx ipxwan 1000 101 NYC-AS
```

## Related Commands

Search online to find documentation for related commands.

**encapsulation ppp**
**hostname**
**ipx delay**
**ipx internal-network**
**ipx ipxwan error**
**ipx ipxwan static**
**ipx network**
**show ipx interface**

## IPX IPXWAN ERROR

To define how to handle IPXWAN when IPX fails to negotiate properly at link startup, use the **ipx ipxwan error** interface configuration command. To restore the default, use the **no** form of this command.

> **ipx ipxwan error** [**reset** | **resume** | **shutdown**]
> **no ipx ipxwan error** [**reset** | **resume** | **shutdown**]

| Syntax | Description |
|---|---|
| **reset** | (Optional) Resets the link when negotiations fail. This is the default action. |
| **resume** | (Optional) When negotiations fail, IPXWAN ignores the failure, takes no special action, and resumes the start-up negotiation attempt. |
| **shutdown** | (Optional) Shuts down the link when negotiations fail. |

## Default

The link is reset.

## Command Mode

Interface configuration

*Usage Guidelines*

This command first appeared in Cisco IOS Release 10.3.

Use the **ipx ipxwan error** command to define what action to take if the IPXWAN startup negotiation fails.

*Example*

In the following example, the serial link will be shut down if the IPXWAN startup negotiation fails after three attempts spaced 20 seconds apart:

```
interface serial 0
 encapsulation ppp
 ipx ipxwan
 ipx ipxwan error shutdown
```

*Related Commands*

Search online to find documentation for related commands.

ipx ipxwan
ipx ipxwan static

## IPX IPXWAN STATIC

To negotiate static routes on a link configured for IPXWAN, use the **ipx ipxwan static** interface configuration command. To disable static route negotiation, use the **no** form of this command.

> **ipx ipxwan static**
> **no ipx ipxwan static**

*Syntax       Description*

This command has no arguments or keywords.

*Default*

Static routing is disabled.

*Command Mode*

Interface configuration

*Usage Guidelines*

This command first appeared in Cisco IOS Release 10.3.

When you specify the **ipx ipxwan static** command, the interface negotiates static routing on the link. If the router at the other side of the link is not configured to negotiate for static routing, the link will not initialize.

## Example

The following example enables static routing with IPXWAN:

```
interface serial 0
  encapsulation ppp
  ipx ipxwan
  ipx ipxwan static
```

## Related Commands

Search online to find documentation for related commands.

**ipx ipxwan**
**ipx ipxwan error**

### IPX LINK-DELAY

To specify the link delay, use the **ipx link-delay** interface configuration command. To return to the default link delay, use the **no** form of this command.

> **ipx link-delay** *microseconds*
> **no ipx link-delay** *microseconds*

| Syntax | Description |
|--------|-------------|
| *microseconds* | Delay, in microseconds. |

## Default

No link delay (delay of 0)

## Command Mode

Interface configuration

## Usage Guidelines

This command first appeared in Cisco IOS Release 10.3.

The link delay you specify replaces the default value or overrides the value measured by IPXWAN when it starts. The value is also supplied to NLSP for use in metric calculations.

## Example

The following example sets the link delay to 20 microseconds:

```
ipx link-delay 20
```

## Related Commands

Search online to find documentation for related commands.

ipx ipxwan
ipx spx-idle-time

## IPX LINKUP-REQUEST

To enable the sending of a general RIP and/or SAP query when an interface comes up, use the **ipx linkup-request** interface configuration command. To disable the sending of a general RIP and/or SAP query when an interface comes up, use the **no** form of this command.

> **ipx linkup-request** {**rip** | **sap**}
> **no ipx linkup-request** {**rip** | **sap**}

| *Syntax* | *Description* |
| --- | --- |
| rip | Enables the sending of a general RIP query when an interface comes up. |
| sap | Enables the sending of a general SAP query when an interface comes up. |

### Default

General RIP and SAP queries are sent.

### Command Mode

Interface configuration

### Usage Guidelines

This command first appeared in Cisco IOS Release 11.3.

Under normal operation, when using serial or other point-to-point links, the router sends RIP and SAP information twice when an interface comes up. The RIP and SAP information is sent as soon as the link is up and is sent again when the router receives a general RIP query from the other end of the connection. By disabling the **ipx linkup-request** command, the router sends the RIP and SAP information once, instead of twice.

### Example

The following example configures the router to disable the general query for both RIP and SAP on serial interface 0:

```
interface serial 0
  no ipx linkup-request rip
  no ipx linkup-request sap
```

### Related Commands

Search online to find documentation for related commands.

**ipx update interval**
**ipx update sap-after-rip**

## IPX MAXIMUM-HOPS

To set the maximum hop count allowed for IPX packets, use the **ipx maximum-hop** global configuration command. To return to the default number of hops, use the **no** form of this command.

> **ipx maximum-hops** *hops*
> **no ipx maximum-hops** *hops*

| Syntax | Description |
| --- | --- |
| *hops* | Maximum number of hops considered to be reachable by non-RIP routing protocols. Also, maximum number of routers that an IPX packet can traverse before being dropped. It can be a value from 16 to 254. The default is 16 hops. |

### Default

16 hops

### Command Mode

Global configuration

### Usage Guidelines

This command first appeared in Cisco IOS Release 10.3.

Packets whose hop count is equal to or greater than that specified by the **ipx maximum-hops** command are dropped.

In periodic RIP updates, the Cisco IOS software never advertises any network with a hop count greater than 15. However, using protocols other than RIP, the software might learn routes that are farther away than 15 hops. The **ipx maximum-hops** command defines the maximum number of hops that the software will accept as reachable, as well as the maximum number of hops that an IPX packet can traverse before it is dropped by the software. Also, the software will respond to a specific RIP request for a network that is reachable at a distance of greater than 15 hops.

### Example

The following command configures the software to accept routes that are up to 64 hops away:

```
ipx maximum-hops 64
```

## IPX MAXIMUM-PATHS

To set the maximum number of equal-cost paths the Cisco IOS software uses when forwarding packets, use the **ipx maximum-paths** global configuration command. To restore the default value, use the **no** form of this command.

ipx maximum-paths *paths*
no ipx maximum-paths

| *Syntax* | *Description* |
|---|---|
| *paths* | Maximum number of equal-cost paths which the Cisco IOS software will use. It can be a number from 1 to 512. The default value is 1. |

## Default

1 path

## Command Mode

Global configuration

## Usage Guidelines

This command first appeared in Cisco IOS Release 10.0.

The **ipx maximum-paths** command increases throughput by allowing the software to choose among several equal-cost, parallel paths. (Note that when paths have differing costs, the software chooses lower-cost routes in preference to higher-cost routes.)

When per-host load sharing is disabled, IPX performs load sharing on a packet-by-packet basis in round-robin fashion, regardless of whether you are using fast switching or process switching. That is, the first packet is sent along the first path, the second packet along the second path, and so on. When the final path is reached, the next packet is sent to the first path, the next to the second path, and so on.

Limiting the number of equal-cost paths can save memory on routers with limited memory or with very large configurations. Additionally, in networks with a large number of multiple paths and systems with limited ability to cache out-of-sequence packets, performance might suffer when traffic is split between many paths.

When you enable per-host load sharing, IPX performs load sharing by transmitting traffic across multiple, equal-cost paths while guaranteeing that packets for a given end host always take the same path. Per-host load sharing decreases the possibility that successive packets to a given end host will arrive out of order.

With per-host load balancing, the number of equal-cost paths set by the **ipx maximum-paths** command must be greater than one; otherwise, per-host load sharing has no effect.

## Example

In the following example, the software uses up to three parallel paths:

```
ipx maximum-paths 3
```

*Related Commands*

Search online to find documentation for related commands.

**ipx delay**
**ipx per-host-load-share**
**show ipx route**


## IPX NETBIOS INPUT-ACCESS-FILTER

To control incoming IPX NetBIOS FindName messages, use the **ipx netbios input-access-filter** interface configuration command. To remove the filter, use the **no** form of this command.

> **ipx netbios input-access-filter** {**host** | **bytes**} *name*
> **no ipx netbios input-access-filter** {**host** | **bytes**} *name*

| Syntax | Description |
|--------|-------------|
| **host** | Indicates that the following argument is the name of a NetBIOS access filter previously defined with one or more **netbios access-list host** commands. |
| **bytes** | Indicates that the following argument is the name of a NetBIOS access filter previously defined with one or more **netbios access-list bytes** commands. |
| *name* | Name of a NetBIOS access list. |


*Default*

No filters are predefined.


*Command Mode*

Interface configuration


*Usage Guidelines*

This command first appeared in Cisco IOS Release 10.0.

You can issue only one **ipx netbios input-access-filter host** and one **ipx netbios input-access-filter bytes** command on each interface.

These filters apply only to IPX NetBIOS FindName packets. They have no effect on LLC2 NetBIOS packets.


*Example*

The following example filters packets arriving on Token Ring interface 1 using the NetBIOS access list named *engineering*:

```
netbios access-list host engineering permit eng*
netbios access-list host engineering deny manu*
```

```
interface tokenring 1
  ipx netbios input-access-filter engineering
```

## Related Commands

Search online to find documentation for related commands.

**ipx netbios output-access-filter**
**netbios access-list**
**show ipx interface**

## IPX NETBIOS OUTPUT-ACCESS-FILTER

To control outgoing NetBIOS FindName messages, use the **ipx netbios output-access-filter** interface configuration command. To remove the filter, use the **no** form of this command.

> **ipx netbios output-access-filter** {**host** | **bytes**} *name*
> **no ipx netbios output-access-filter** {**host** | **bytes**} *name*

| Syntax | Description |
|--------|-------------|
| **host** | Indicates that the following argument is the name of a NetBIOS access filter previously defined with one or more **netbios access-list host** commands. |
| **bytes** | Indicates that the following argument is the name of a NetBIOS access filter previously defined with one or more **netbios access-list bytes** commands. |
| *name* | Name of a previously defined NetBIOS access list. |

## Default

No filters are predefined.

## Command Mode

Interface configuration

## Usage Guidelines

This command first appeared in Cisco IOS Release 10.0.

You can issue only one **ipx netbios output-access-filter host** and one **ipx netbios output-access-filter bytes** command on each interface.

These filters apply only to IPX NetBIOS FindName packets. They have no effect on LLC2 NetBIOS packets.

*Command Reference*

*Example*

The following example filters packets leaving Token Ring interface 1 using the NetBIOS access list named *engineering*:

```
netbios access-list bytes engineering permit 20 AA**04

interface token 1
 ipx netbios output-access-filter bytes engineering
```

*Related Commands*

Search online to find documentation for related commands.

**ipx netbios input-access-filter**
**netbios access-list**
**show ipx interface**

## IPX NETWORK

To enable IPX routing on a particular interface and to optionally select the type of encapsulation (framing), use the **ipx network** interface configuration command. To disable IPX routing, use the **no** form of this command.

> **ipx network** *network* [**encapsulation** *encapsulation-type* [**secondary**]]
> **no ipx network** *network* [**encapsulation** *encapsulation-type*]

| Syntax | Description |
| --- | --- |
| *network* | Network number. This is an eight-digit hexadecimal number that uniquely identifies a network cable segment. It can be a number in the range 1 to FFFFFFFD. |
| | You do not need to specify leading zeros in the network number. For example, for the network number 000000AA you can enter AA. |
| **encapsulation** *encapsulation-type* | (Optional) Type of encapsulation (framing). It can be one of the following values: |

- **arpa** (for Ethernet interfaces only)—Use Novell's Ethernet_II encapsulation. This encapsulation is recommended for networks that handle both TCP/IP and IPX traffic.
- **hdlc** (for serial interfaces only)—Use HDLC encapsulation.
- **novell-ether** (for Ethernet interfaces only)—Use Novell's "Ethernet_802.3" encapsulation. This encapsulation consists of a standard 802.3 Media Access Control (MAC) header followed directly by the IPX header with a checksum of FFFF. It is the default encapsulation used by all versions of NetWare up to and including Version 3.11.

*Syntax*

**encapsulation**
*encapsulation-type*
(*Continued*)

*Description*

- **novell-fddi** (for FDDI interfaces only)—Use Novell's "FDDI_RAW" encapsulation. This encapsulation consists of a standard FDDI MAC header followed directly by the IPX header with a checksum of 0xFFFF.

- **sap** (for Ethernet interfaces)—Use Novell's Ethernet_802.2 encapsulation. This encapsulation consists of a standard 802.3 MAC header followed by an 802.2 LLC header. This is the default encapsulation used by NetWare Version 3.12 and 4.0.
  — Token Ring interfaces—This encapsulation consists of a standard 802.5 MAC header followed by an 802.2 LLC header.
  —FDDI interfaces—This encapsulation consists of a standard FDDI MAC header followed by an 802.2 LLC header.

- **snap** (for Ethernet interfaces)—Use Novell Ethernet_Snap encapsulation. This encapsulation consists of a standard 802.3 MAC header followed by an 802.2 SNAP LLC header.
  — Token Ring and FDDI interfaces—This encapsulation consists of a standard 802.5 or FDDI MAC header followed by an 802.2 SNAP LLC header.

**secondary**

(Optional) Indicates an additional (secondary) network configured after the first (primary) network.

*Default*

IPX routing is disabled.

Encapsulation types:
  For Ethernet: **novell-ether**
  For Token Ring: **sap**
  For FDDI: **snap**

If you use NetWare Version 4.0 and Ethernet, you must change the default encapsulation type from **novell-ether** to **sap**.

*Command Mode*

Interface configuration

*Usage Guidelines*

This command first appeared in Cisco IOS Release 10.0.

The **ipx network** command allows you to configure a single logical network on a physical network or more than one logical network on the same physical network (network cable segment). Each network on a given interface must have a different encapsulation type.

*Command Reference*

The first network you configure on an interface is considered to be the primary network. Any additional networks are considered to be secondary networks; these must include the **secondary** keyword.

---

**NOTES**

In future Cisco IOS software releases, primary and secondary networks will not be supported.

---

NLSP does not support secondary networks. You must use subinterfaces in order to use multiple encapsulations with NLSP.

---

**NOTES**

When enabling NLSP and configuring multiple encapsulations on the same physical LAN interface, you must use subinterfaces. You cannot use secondary networks.

---

You can configure an IPX network on any supported interface as long as all the networks on the same physical interface use a distinct encapsulation type. For example, you can configure up to four IPX networks on a single Ethernet cable because Ethernet supports four encapsulation types.

The interface processes only packets with the correct encapsulation and the correct network number. IPX networks using other encapsulations can be present on the physical network. The only effect on the router is that it uses some processing time to examine packets to determine whether they have the correct encapsulation.

All logical networks on an interface share the same set of configuration parameters. For example, if you change the IPX RIP update time on an interface, you change it for all networks on that interface.

When you define multiple logical networks on the same physical network, IPX treats each encapsulation as if it were a separate physical network. This means, for example, that IPX sends RIP updates and SAP updates for each logical network.

The **ipx network** command is useful when migrating from one type of encapsulation to another. If you are using it for this purpose, you should define the new encapsulation on the primary network.

To delete all networks on an interface, use the following command:

    **no ipx network**

Deleting the primary network with the following command also deletes all networks on that interface. The argument *number* is the number of the primary network.

    **no ipx network** *number*

To delete a secondary network on an interface, use one of the following commands. The argument *number* is the number of a secondary network.

    **no ipx network** *number*
    **no ipx network** *number* **encapsulation** *encapsulation-type*

Novell's FDDI_RAW encapsulation is common in bridged or switched environments that connect Ethernet-based Novell end hosts via a FDDI backbone. Packets with FDDI_RAW encapsulation are classified as Novell packets, and are not automatically bridged when you enable both bridging and IPX routing. Additionally, you cannot configure FDDI_RAW encapsulation on an interface configured for IPX autonomous or SSE switching. Similarly, you cannot enable IPX autonomous or SSE switching on an interface configured with FDDI_RAW encapsulation.

With FDDI_RAW encapsulation, platforms that do not use CBUS architecture support fast switching. Platforms using CBUS architecture support only process switching of **novell-fddi** packets received on an FDDI interface.

### Examples

The following example uses subinterfaces to create four logical networks on Ethernet interface 0. Each subinterface has a different encapsulation. Any interface configuration parameters that you specify on an individual subinterface are applied to that subinterface only.

```
ipx routing
interface ethernet 0

interface ethernet 0.1
 ipx network 1 encapsulation novell-ether

interface ethernet 0.2
 ipx network 2 encapsulation snap

interface ethernet 0.3
 ipx network 3 encapsulation arpa

interface ethernet 0.4
 ipx network 4 encapsulation sap
```

The following example uses primary and secondary networks to create the same four logical networks as shown previously in this section. Any interface configuration parameters that you specify on this interface are applied to all the logical networks. For example, if you set the routing update timer to 120 seconds, this value is used on all four networks.

```
ipx routing
ipx network 1 encapsulation novell-ether
ipx network 2 encapsulation snap secondary
ipx network 3 encapsulation arpa secondary
ipx network 4 encapsulation sap secondary
```

The following example enables IPX routing on FDDI interfaces 0.2 and 0.3. On FDDI interface 0.2, the encapsulation type is SNAP. On FDDI interface 0.3, the encapsulation type is Novell's FDDI_RAW.

```
ipx routing

interface fddi 0.2
 ipx network f02 encapsulation snap
```

*Command Reference*

```
interface fddi 0.3
 ipx network f03 encapsulation novell-fddi
```

## Related Commands

Search online to find documentation for related commands.

**ipx routing**

## IPX NHRP AUTHENTICATION

To configure the authentication string for an interface using Next Hop Resolution Protocol (NHRP), use the **ipx nhrp authentication** interface configuration command. To remove the authentication string, use the **no** form of this command.

> **ipx nhrp authentication** *string*
> **no ipx nhrp authentication** [*string*]

| Syntax | Description |
|--------|-------------|
| *string* | Authentication string configured for the source and destination stations that controls whether NHRP stations allow intercommunication. The string can be up to eight characters long. |

### Default

No authentication string is configured; the Cisco IOS software adds no authentication option to NHRP packets it generates.

### Command Mode

Interface configuration

### Usage Guidelines

This command first appeared in Cisco IOS Release 11.1.

All routers configured with NHRP on a fabric (for an interface) must share the same authentication string.

### Example

In the following example, the authentication string *specialxx* must be configured in all devices using NHRP on the interface before NHRP communication occurs:

```
ipx nhrp authentication specialxx
```

## IPX NHRP HOLDTIME

To change the number of seconds that NHRP nonbroadcast, multiaccess (NBMA) addresses are advertised as valid in authoritative NHRP responses, use the **ipx nhrp holdtime** interface configuration command. To restore the default value, use the **no** form of this command.

>   **ipx nhrp holdtime** *seconds-positive* [*seconds-negative*]
>   **no ipx nhrp holdtime** [*seconds-positive* [*seconds-negative*]]

| Syntax | Description |
|---|---|
| *seconds-positive* | Time in seconds that NBMA addresses are advertised as valid in positive authoritative NHRP responses. |
| *seconds-negative* | (Optional) Time in seconds that NBMA addresses are advertised as valid in negative authoritative NHRP responses. |

### Default

7200 seconds (2 hours) for both arguments

### Command Mode

Interface configuration

### Usage Guidelines

This command first appeared in Cisco IOS Release 11.1.

The **ipx nhrp holdtime** command affects authoritative responses only. The advertised holding time is the length of time the Cisco IOS software tells other routers to keep information that it is provided in authoritative NHRP responses. The cached IPX-to-NBMA address mapping entries are discarded after the holding time expires.

The NHRP cache can contain static and dynamic entries. The static entries never expire. Dynamic entries expire regardless of whether they are authoritative or nonauthoritative.

If you want to change the valid time period for negative NHRP responses, you must also include a value for positive NHRP responses, as the arguments are position-dependent.

### Examples

In the following example, NHRP NBMA addresses are advertised as valid in positive authoritative NHRP responses for one hour:

```
ipx nhrp holdtime 3600
```

In the following example, NHRP NBMA addresses are advertised as valid in negative authoritative NHRP responses for one hour and in positive authoritative NHRP responses for two hours:

```
ipx nhrp holdtime 7200 3600
```

Command Reference

## IPX NHRP INTEREST

To control which IPX packets can trigger sending a Next Hop Resolution Protocol (NHRP) Request, use the **ipx nhrp interest** interface configuration command. To restore the default value, use the **no** form of this command.

> **ipx nhrp interest** *access-list-number*
> **no ipx nhrp interest** [*access-list-number*]

| Syntax | Description |
|--------|-------------|
| *access-list-number* | Standard or extended IPX access list number from 800 through 999. |

### Default

All non-NHRP packets can trigger NHRP requests.

### Command Mode

Interface configuration

### Usage Guidelines

This command first appeared in Cisco IOS Release 11.1.

Use this command with the **access-list** command to control which IPX packets trigger NHRP Requests.

### Example

In the following example, any NetBIOS traffic can cause NHRP requests to be sent, but no other IPX packets will cause NHRP requests:

```
ipx nhrp interest 901
access-list 901 permit 20
```

### Related Commands

Search online to find documentation for related commands.

**access-list (extended)**
**access-list (standard)**

## IPX NHRP MAP

To statically configure the IPX-to-NBMA address mapping of IPX destinations connected to a non-broadcast, multiaccess (NBMA) network, use the **ipx nhrp map** interface configuration command. To remove the static entry from the NHRP cache, use the **no** form of this command.

ipx nhrp map *ipx-address nbma-address*
no ipx nhrp map *ipx-address nbma-address*

| Syntax | Description |
|---|---|
| *ipx-address* | IPX address of the destinations reachable through the NBMA network. This address is mapped to the NBMA address. |
| *nbma-address* | NBMA address that is directly reachable through the NBMA network. The address format varies depending on the medium you are using. For example, ATM has a network-service access point (NSAP) address, and SMDS has an E.164 address. This address is mapped to the IPX address. |

### Default

No static IPX-to-NBMA cache entries exist.

### Command Mode

Interface configuration

### Usage Guidelines

This command first appeared in Cisco IOS Release 11.1.

You will probably have to configure at least one static mapping in order to reach the Next Hop Server. Repeat this command to statically configure multiple IPX-to-NBMA address mappings.

### Example

In the following example, this station in an SMDS network is statically configured to be served by two Next Hop Servers 1.0000.0c14.59ef and 1.0000.0c14.59d0. The NBMA address for 1.0000.0c14.59ef is statically configured to be c141.0001.0001 and the NBMA address for 1.0000.0c14.59d0 is c141.0001.0002.

```
interface serial 0
 ipx nhrp nhs 1.0000.0c14.59ef
 ipx nhrp nhs 1.0000.0c14.59d0
 ipx nhrp map 1.0000.0c14.59ef c141.0001.0001
 ipx nhrp map 1.0000.0c14.59d0 c141.0001.0002
```

### Related Commands

Search online to find documentation for related commands.

**clear ipx nhrp**

## IPX NHRP MAX-SEND

To change the maximum frequency at which NHRP packets can be sent, use the **ipx nhrp max-send** interface configuration command. To restore this frequency to the default value, use the **no** form of this command.

> **ipx nhrp max-send** *pkt-count* **every** *interval*
> **no ipx nhrp max-send**

| Syntax | Description |
| --- | --- |
| *pkt-count* | Number of packets which can be transmitted in the range 1 to 65535. |
| *interval* | Time (in seconds) in the range 10 to 65535. |

### Default

*pkt-count* = 5 packets
*interval* = 10 seconds

### Command Mode

Interface configuration

### Usage Guidelines

This command first appeared in Cisco IOS Release 11.1.

The software maintains a per interface quota of NHRP packets that can be transmitted. NHRP traffic, whether locally generated, or forwarded, cannot be sent at a rate that exceeds this quota. The quota is replenished at the rate specified by *interval*.

### Example

In the following example, only one NHRP packet can be sent out serial interface 0 each minute:

```
interface serial 0
 ipx nhrp max-send 1 every 60
```

### Related Commands

Search online to find documentation for related commands.

**ipx nhrp interest**
**ipx nhrp use**

## IPX NHRP NETWORK-ID

To enable the Next Hop Resolution Protocol (NHRP) on an interface, use the **ipx nhrp network-id** interface configuration command. To disable NHRP on the interface, use the **no** form of this command.

**ipx nhrp network-id** *number*
**no ipx nhrp network-id** [*number*]

| Syntax | Description |
|---|---|
| *number* | Globally unique, 32-bit network identifier for a nonbroadcast, multiaccess (NBMA) network. The range is 1 to 4294967295. |

### Default

NHRP is disabled on the interface.

### Command Mode

Interface configuration

### Usage Guidelines

This command first appeared in Cisco IOS Release 11.1.

In general, all NHRP stations within a fabric must be configured with the same network identifier.

### Example

The following example enables NHRP on the interface:

```
ipx nhrp network-id 1
```

## IPX NHRP NHS

To specify the address of one or more NHRP Next Hop Servers, use the **ipx nhrp nhs** interface configuration command. To remove the address, use the **no** form of this command.

**ipx nhrp nhs** *nhs-address* [*net-address*]
**no ipx nhrp nhs** *nhs-address* [*net-address*]

| Syntax | Description |
|---|---|
| *nhs-address* | Address of the Next Hop Server being specified. |
| *net-address* | (Optional) IPX address of a network served by the Next Hop Server. |

### Default

No Next Hop Servers are explicitly configured, so normal network layer routing decisions forward NHRP traffic.

### Command Mode

Interface configuration

## Usage Guidelines

This command first appeared in Cisco IOS Release 11.1.

Use this command to specify the address of a Next Hop Server and the networks it serves. Normally, NHRP consults the network layer forwarding table to determine how to forward NHRP packets. When Next Hop Servers are configured, the next hop addresses specified with the **ipx nhrp nhs** command override the forwarding path specified by the network layer forwarding table that would usually be used for NHRP traffic.

For any Next Hop Server that is configured, you can specify multiple networks that it serves by repeating this command with the same *nhs-address* address, but different *net-address* IPX network numbers.

## Example

In the following example, the Next Hop Server with address 1.0000.0c00.1234 serves IPX network 2:

```
ipx nhrp nhs 1.0000.0c00.1234 2
```

## IPX NHRP RECORD

To re-enable the use of forward record and reverse record options in NHRP Request and Reply packets, use the **ipx nhrp record** interface configuration command. To suppress the use of such options, use the **no** form of this command.

> **ipx nhrp record**
> **no ipx nhrp record**

## Syntax     Description

This command has no arguments or keywords.

## Default

Forward record and reverse record options are enabled by default.

## Command Mode

Interface configuration

## Usage Guidelines

This command first appeared in Cisco IOS Release 11.1.

Forward record and reverse record options provide loop detection and are used in NHRP Request and Reply packets. Using the **no** form of this command disables this method of loop detection. For another method of loop detection, see the **ipx nhrp responder** command.

## Example

The following example suppresses forward record and reverse record options:

```
no ipx nhrp record
```

## Related Commands

Search online to find documentation for related commands.

**ipx nhrp responder**

## IPX NHRP RESPONDER

To designate which interface's primary IPX address that the Next Hop Server uses in NHRP Reply packets when the NHRP requestor uses the Responder Address option, use the **ipx nhrp responder** interface configuration command. To remove the designation, use the **no** form of this command.

**ipx nhrp responder** *type number*
**no ipx nhrp responder** [*type*] [*number*]

| Syntax | Description |
|--------|-------------|
| *type* | Interface type whose primary IPX address is used when a Next Hop Server complies with a Responder Address option. Valid options are **atm, serial,** and **tunnel.** |
| *number* | Interface number whose primary IPX address is used when a Next Hop Server complies with a Responder Address option. |

## Default

The Next Hop Server uses the IPX address of the interface where the NHRP Request was received.

## Command Mode

Interface configuration

## Usage Guidelines

This command first appeared in Cisco IOS Release 11.1.

If an NHRP requestor wants to know which Next Hop Server generates an NHRP Reply packet, it can request that information through the Responder Address option. The Next Hop Server that generates the NHRP Reply packet then complies by inserting its own IPX address in the Responder Address option of the NHRP Reply. The Next Hop Server uses the primary IPX address of the specified interface.

If an NHRP Reply packet being forwarded by a Next Hop Server contains that Next Hop Server's own IPX address, the Next Hop Server generates an Error Indication of type "NHRP Loop Detected" and discards the Reply.

*Command Reference*

*Example*

In the following example, any NHRP requests for the Responder Address will cause this router acting as a Next Hop Server to supply the primary IPX address of interface serial 0 in the NHRP Reply packet:

```
ipx nhrp responder serial 0
```

## IPX NHRP USE

To configure the software so that NHRP is deferred until the system has attempted to send data traffic to a particular destination multiple times, use the **ipx nhrp use** interface configuration command. To restore the default value, use the **no** form of this command.

> **ipx nhrp use** *usage-count*
> **no ipx nhrp use** *usage-count*

*Syntax Description*

*usage-count*              Packet count in the range 1 to 65535.

*Default*

*usage-count* = 1. The first time a data packet is sent to a destination for which the system determines NHRP can be used, an NHRP request is sent.

*Command Mode*

Interface configuration

*Usage Guidelines*

This command first appeared in Cisco IOS Release 11.1.

When the software attempts to transmit a data packet to a destination for which it has determined that NHRP address resolution can be used, an NHRP request for that destination is normally transmitted right away. Configuring the *usage-count* causes the system to wait until that many data packets have been sent to a particular destination before it attempts NHRP. The *usage-count* for a particular destination is measured over 1-minute intervals (the NHRP cache expiration interval).

The usage-count applies *per destination*. So if *usage-count* is configured to be 3, and 4 data packets are sent toward 10.0.0.1 and 1 packet toward 10.0.0.2, then an NHRP request is generated for 10.0.0.1 only.

If the system continues to need to forward data packets to a particular destination, but no NHRP response has been received, retransmission of NHRP requests are performed. This retransmission occurs only if data traffic continues to be sent to a destination.

The **ipx nhrp interest** command controls *which* packets cause NHRP address resolution to take place; the **ipx nhrp use** command controls *how readily* the system attempts such address resolution.

## Example

In the following example, if in the first minute four packets are sent to one IPX address and five packets are sent to a second IPX address, then a single NHRP request is generated for the second IPX address. If in the second minute the same traffic is generated and no NHRP responses have been received, then the system retransmits its request for the second IPX address.

```
ipx nhrp use 5
```

## Related Commands

Search online to find documentation for related commands.

**ipx nhrp interest**
**ipx nhrp max-send**

### IPX NLSP CSNP-INTERVAL

To configure the NLSP complete sequence number PDU (CSNP) interval, use the **ipx nlsp csnp-interval** interface configuration command. To restore the default value, use the **no** form of this command.

> **ipx nlsp** [*tag*] **csnp-interval** *seconds*
> **no ipx nlsp** [*tag*] **csnp-interval** *seconds*

| Syntax | Description |
|--------|-------------|
| *tag* | (Optional) Names the NLSP process. The *tag* can be any combination of printable characters. |
| *seconds* | Time, in seconds, between the transmission of CSNPs on multiaccess networks. This interval applies to the designated router only. The interval can be a number in the range 1 to 600. The default is 30 seconds. |

## Default

30 seconds

## Command Mode

Interface configuration

## Usage Guidelines

This command first appeared in Cisco IOS Release 10.3.

The **ipx nlsp csnp-interval** command applies only to the designated router for the specified interface only. This is because only designated routers send CSNP packets, which are used to synchronize the database.

CSNP does not apply to serial point-to-point interfaces. However, it does apply to WAN connections if the WAN is viewed as a multiaccess meshed network.

### Example

The following example configures Ethernet interface 0 to transmit CSNPs every 10 seconds:

```
interface ethernet 0
 ipx network 101
 ipx nlsp enable
 ipx nlsp csnp-interval 10
```

### Related Commands

Search online to find documentation for related commands.

**ipx nlsp hello-interval**
**ipx nlsp retransmit-interval**

## IPX NLSP ENABLE

To enable NLSP routing on the primary network configured on this interface or subinterface, use the **ipx nlsp enable** interface configuration command. To disable NLSP routing on the primary network configured on this interface or subinterface, use the **no** form of this command.

> **ipx nlsp** [*tag*] **enable**
> **no ipx nlsp** [*tag*] **enable**

| Syntax | Description |
|--------|-------------|
| *tag*  | (Optional) Names the NLSP process. The *tag* can be any combination of printable characters. |

### Default

NLSP is disabled on all interfaces.

### Command Mode

Interface configuration

### Usage Guidelines

This command first appeared in Cisco IOS Release 10.3.

When you enable NLSP routing, the current settings for RIP and SAP compatibility modes as specified with the **ipx nlsp rip** and **ipx nlsp sap** interface configuration commands take effect automatically.

When you specify an NLSP *tag*, the router enables NLSP on the specified process. An NLSP *process* is a router's databases working together to manage route information about an area. NLSP version 1.0 routers are always in the same area. Each router has its own adjacencies, link-state, and forwarding databases. These databases operate collectively as a single *process* to discover, select, and maintain route information about the area. NLSP version 1.1 routers that exist within a single area also use a single process.

NLSP version 1.1 routers that interconnect multiple areas use multiple processes to discover, select, and maintain route information about the areas they interconnect. These routers manage an adjacencies, link-state, and area address database for each area to which they attach. Collectively, these databases are still referred to as a *process*. The forwarding database is shared among processes within a router. The sharing of entries in the forwarding database is automatic when all processes interconnect NLSP version 1.1 areas.

Configure multiple NLSP processes when a router interconnects multiple NLSP areas.

— **NOTES** —————————————————————————————

NLSP version 1.1 routers refer to routers that support the route aggregation feature, while NLSP version 1.0 routers refer to routers that do not.

### *Examples*

The following example enables NLSP routing on Ethernet interface 0:

```
interface ethernet 0
  ipx nlsp enable
```

The following example enables NLSP routing on serial interface 0:

```
interface serial 0
  ipx ipxwan 2442 unnumbered local1
  ipx nlsp enable
```

The following example enables NLSP routing for process *area3* on Ethernet interface 0:

```
interface ethernet 0
  ipx nlsp area3 enable
```

### *Related Commands*

Search online to find documentation for related commands.

**ipx nlsp rip**
**ipx nlsp sap**

### IPX NLSP HELLO-INTERVAL

To configure the interval between the transmission of hello packets, use the **ipx nlsp hello-interval** interface configuration command. To restore the default value, use the **no** form of this command.

**ipx nlsp** [*tag*] **hello-interval** *seconds*
**no ipx nlsp** [*tag*] **hello-interval** *seconds*

| Syntax | Description |
|--------|-------------|
| *tag* | (Optional) Names the NLSP process. The *tag* can be any combination of printable characters. |
| *seconds* | Time, in seconds, between the transmission of hello packets on the interface. It can be a number in the range 1 to 1600. The default is 10 seconds for the designated router and 20 seconds for nondesignated routers. |

### Default

10 seconds for the designated router
20 seconds for nondesignated routers

### Command Mode

Interface configuration

### Usage Guidelines

This command first appeared in Cisco IOS Release 10.3.

The designated router sends hello packets at an interval equal to one-half the configured value.

Use this command to improve the speed at which a failed router or link is detected. A router is declared to be down if a hello has not been received from it for the time determined by the holding time (the hello interval multiplied by the holding time multiplier; by default, 60 seconds for non-designated routers and 30 seconds for designated routers). You can reduce this time by lowering the hello-interval setting, at the cost of increased traffic overhead.

You may also use this command to reduce link overhead on very slow links by raising the hello interval. This will reduce the traffic on the link at the cost of increasing the time required to detect a failed router or link.

### Example

The following example configures serial interface 0 to transmit hello packets every 30 seconds:

```
interface serial 0
  ipx ipxwan 2442 unnumbered local1
  ipx nlsp enable
  ipx nlsp hello-interval 30
```

### Related Commands

Search online to find documentation for related commands.

Command Reference

ipx nlsp csnp-interval
ipx nlsp hello-multiplier
ipx nlsp retransmit-interval

## IPX NLSP HELLO-MULTIPLIER

To specify the hello multiplier used on an interface, use the **ipx nlsp hello-multiplier** interface configuration command. To restore the default value, use the **no** form of this command.

> **ipx nlsp** [*tag*] **hello-multiplier** *multiplier*
> **no nlsp** [*tag*] **hello-multiplier**

| Syntax | Description |
|---|---|
| *tag* | (Optional) Names the NLSP process. The *tag* can be any combination of printable characters. |
| *multiplier* | Value by which to multiply the hello interval. It can be a number in the range 3 to 1000. The default is 3. |

### Default

The default multiplier is 3.

### Command Mode

Interface configuration

### Usage Guidelines

This command first appeared in Cisco IOS Release 11.1.

You use the hello modifier in conjunction with the hello interval to determine the holding time value sent in a hello packet. The holding time is equal to the hello interval multiplied by the hello multiplier.

The holding time tells the neighboring router how long to wait for another hello packet from the sending router. If the neighboring router does not receive another hello packet in the specified time, then the neighboring router declares that the sending router is down.

You can use this method of determining the holding time when hello packets are lost with some frequency and NLSP adjacencies are failing unnecessarily. You raise the hello multiplier and lower the hello interval correspondingly to make the hello protocol more reliable without increasing the time required to detect a link failure.

### Example

In the following example, serial interface 0 will advertise hello packets every 15 seconds. The multiplier is 5. These values determine that the hello packet holding time is 75 seconds.

```
interface serial 0
```

```
ipx nlsp hello-interval 15
ipx nlsp hello-multiplier 5
```

## Related Commands

Search online to find documentation for related commands.

**ipx nlsp hello-interval**

### IPX NLSP LSP-INTERVAL

To configure the time delay between successive NLSP link-state packet (LSP) transmissions, use the **ipx nlsp lsp-interval** interface configuration command. To restore the default time delay, use the **no** form of the command.

> **ipx nlsp** [*tag*] **lsp-interval** *interval*
> **no ipx nlsp** [*tag*] **lsp-interval**

| Syntax | Description |
|---|---|
| *tag* | (Optional) Names the NLSP process. The *tag* can be any combination of printable characters. |
| *interval* | Time, in milliseconds, between successive LSP transmissions. The interval can be a number in the range 55 and 5000. The default interval is 55 milliseconds. |

### Default

55 milliseconds

### Command Mode

Interface configuration

### Usage Guidelines

This command first appeared in Cisco IOS Release 11.1.

This command allows you to control how fast LSPs can be flooded out an interface.

In topologies with a large number of NLSP neighbors and interfaces, a router may have difficulty with the CPU load imposed by LSP transmission and reception. This command allows you to reduce the LSP transmission rate (and by implication the reception rate of other systems).

### Example

The following example causes the system to transmit LSPs every 100 milliseconds (10 packets per second) on Ethernet interface 0:

```
interface Ethernet 0
ipx nlsp lsp-interval 100
```

*Related Commands*

Search online to find documentation for related commands.

**ipx nlsp retransmit-interval**

## IPX NLSP METRIC

To configure the NLSP cost for an interface, use the **ipx nlsp metric** interface configuration command. To restore the default cost, use the **no** form of this command.

**ipx nlsp** [*tag*] **metric** *metric-number*
**no ipx** nlsp [*tag*] **metric** *metric-number*

| Syntax | Description |
|---|---|
| *tag* | (Optional) Names the NLSP process. The *tag* can be any combination of printable characters. |
| *metric-number* | Metric value for the interface. It can be a number from 0 to 63. |

*Default*

The default varies based on the throughput of the link connected to the interface.

*Command Mode*

Interface configuration

*Usage Guidelines*

This command first appeared in Cisco IOS Release 10.3.

Use the **ipx nlsp metric** command to cause NLSP to prefer some links over others. A link with a lower metric is more preferable than one with a higher metric.

Typically, it is not necessary to configure the metric; however, it may be desirable in some cases when there are wide differences in link bandwidths. For example, using the default metrics, a single 64-kbps ISDN link will be preferable to two 1544-Kbps T1 links.

*Example*

The following example configures a metric of 10 on serial interface 0:

```
interface serial 0
  ipx network 107
  ipx nlsp enable
  ipx nlsp metric 10
```

*Related Commands*

Search online to find documentation for related commands.

**ipx nlsp enable**

**IPX NLSP MULTICAST**

To configure an interface to use multicast addressing, use the **ipx nlsp multicast** interface configuration command. To configure the interface to use broadcast addressing, use the **no** form of this command.

> **ipx nlsp** [*tag*] **multicast**
> **no ipx nlsp** [*tag*] **multicast**

| Syntax | Description |
|--------|-------------|
| *tag* | (Optional) Names the NLSP process. The *tag* can be any combination of printable characters. |

*Default*

Multicast addressing is enabled.

*Command Mode*

Interface configuration

*Usage Guidelines*

This command first appeared in Cisco IOS Release 11.3.

This command allows the router interface to use NLSP multicast addressing. If an adjacent neighbor does not support NLSP multicast addressing, the router will revert to using broadcasts on the affected interface.

The router will also revert to using broadcasts if multicast addressing is not supported by the hardware or driver.

*Example*

The following example disables multicast addressing on Ethernet interface 0:

```
interface ethernet0
  no ipx nlsp multicast
```

**IPX NLSP PRIORITY**

To configure the election priority of the specified interface for designated router election, use the **ipx nlsp priority** interface configuration command. To restore the default priority, use the **no** form of this command.

> **ipx nlsp** [*tag*] **priority** *priority-number*
> **no ipx nlsp** [*tag*] **priority** *priority-number*

| Syntax | Description |
|---|---|
| *tag* | (Optional) Names the NLSP process. The *tag* can be any combination of printable characters. |
| *priority-number* | Election priority of the designated router for the specified interface. This can be a number in the range 0 to 127. This value is unitless. The default is 44. |

## Default

44

## Command Mode

Interface configuration

## Usage Guidelines

This command first appeared in Cisco IOS Release 10.3.

Use the **ipx nlsp priority** command to control which router is elected designated router. The device with the highest priority number is selected as the designated router.

The designated router increases its own priority by 20 in order to keep its state as of the designated router more stable. To have a particular router be selected as the designated router, configure its priority to be at least 65.

## Example

The following example sets the designated router election priority to 65:

```
interface ethernet 0
  ipx network 101
  ipx nlsp enable
  ipx nlsp priority 65
```

## IPX NLSP RETRANSMIT-INTERVAL

To configure the link-state packet (LSP) retransmission interval on WAN links, use the **ipx nlsp retransmit-interval** interface configuration command. To restore the default interval, use the **no** form of this command.

ipx nlsp [*tag*] retransmit-interval *seconds*
no ipx nlsp [*tag*] retransmit-interval *seconds*

| Syntax | Description |
|--------|-------------|
| *tag* | (Optional) Names the NLSP process. The *tag* can be any combination of printable characters. |
| *seconds* | LSP retransmission interval, in seconds. This can be a number in the range 1 to 30. The default is 5 seconds. |

### Default

5 seconds

### Command Mode

Interface configuration

### Usage Guidelines

This command first appeared in Cisco IOS Release 10.3.

This command sets the maximum amount of time that can pass before an LSP will be sent again (retransmitted) on a WAN link, if no acknowledgment is received.

Reducing the retransmission interval can improve the convergence rate of the network in the face of lost WAN links. The cost of reducing the retransmission interval is the potential increase in link utilization.

### Example

The following example configures the LSP retransmission interval to 2 seconds:

```
ipx nlsp retransmit-interval 2
```

### Related Commands

Search online to find documentation for related commands.

**ipx nlsp csnp-interval**
**ipx nlsp hello-interval**

## IPX NLSP RIP

To configure RIP compatibility when NLSP is enabled, use the **ipx nlsp rip** interface configuration command. To restore the default, use the **no** form of this command.

**ipx nlsp** [*tag*] **rip** [**on** | **off** | **auto**]
**no ipx nlsp** [*tag*] **rip** [**on** | **off** | **auto**]

| Syntax | Description |
|--------|-------------|
| *tag* | (Optional) Names the NLSP process. The *tag* can be any combination of printable characters. |
| **on** | (Optional) Always generates and sends RIP periodic traffic. |
| **off** | (Optional) Never generates and sends RIP periodic traffic. |
| **auto** | (Optional) Sends RIP periodic traffic only if another RIP router in sending periodic RIP traffic. This is the default. |

### Default

RIP periodic traffic is sent only if another router in sending periodic RIP traffic.

### Command Mode

Interface configuration

### Usage Guidelines

This command first appeared in Cisco IOS Release 10.3.

The **ipx nlsp rip** command is meaningful only on networks on which NLSP is enabled. (RIP and SAP are always on by default on other interfaces.) Because the default mode is **auto,** no action is normally required to fully support RIP compatibility on an NLSP network.

### Example

In the following example, the interface never generates or sends RIP periodic traffic:

```
interface ethernet 0
  ipx nlsp rip off
```

### Related Commands

Search online to find documentation for related commands.

**ipx nlsp enable**
**ipx nlsp sap**

## IPX NLSP SAP

To configure SAP compatibility when NLSP in enabled, use the **ipx nlsp sap** interface configuration command. To restore the default, use the **no** form of this command.

**ipx nlsp** [*tag*] **sap** [**on** | **off** | **auto**]
**no ipx nlsp** [*tag*] **sap** [**on** | **off** | **auto**]

| Syntax | Description |
|--------|-------------|
| *tag* | (Optional) Names the NLSP process. The *tag* can be any combination of printable characters. |
| **on** | (Optional) Always generates and sends SAP periodic traffic. |
| **off** | (Optional) Never generates and sends SAP periodic traffic. |
| **auto** | (Optional) Sends SAP periodic traffic only if another SAP router in sending periodic SAP traffic. This is the default. |

## Default

SAP periodic traffic is sent only if another router in sending periodic SAP traffic.

## Command Mode

Interface configuration

## Usage Guidelines

This command first appeared in Cisco IOS Release 10.3.

The **ipx nlsp sap** command is meaningful only on networks on which NLSP is enabled. Because the default mode is **auto,** no action is normally required to fully support SAP compatibility on an NLSP network.

## Example

In the following example, the interface never generates or sends SAP periodic traffic:

```
interface ethernet 0
  ipx nlsp sap off
```

## Related Commands

Search online to find documentation for related commands.

**ipx nlsp enable**
**ipx nlsp rip**

## IPX OUTPUT-GNS-FILTER

To control which servers are included in the Get Nearest Server (GNS) responses sent by the Cisco IOS software, use the **ipx output-gns-filter** interface configuration command. To remove the filter from the interface, use the **no** form of this command.

**ipx output-gns-filter** {*access-list-number* | *name*}
**no ipx output-gns-filter** {*access-list-number* | *name*}

| Syntax | Description |
|--------|-------------|
| *access-list-number* | Number of the SAP access list. All outgoing GNS packets are filtered by the entries in this access list. The argument *access-list-number* is a number from 1000 to 1099. |
| *name* | Name of the access list. Names cannot contain a space or quotation mark, and they must begin with an alphabetic character to prevent ambiguity with numbered access lists. |

## Default

No filters are predefined.

## Command Mode

Interface configuration

## Usage Guidelines

This command first appeared in Cisco IOS Release 10.0.

You can issue only one **ipx output-gns-filter** command on each interface.

## Example

The following example excludes the server at address 3c.0800.89a1.1527 from GNS responses sent on Ethernet interface 0, but allows all other servers:

```
access-list 1000 deny 3c.0800.89a1.1527
access-list 1000 permit -1
ipx routing

interface ethernet 0
 ipx network 2B
 ipx output-gns-filter 1000
```

## Related Commands

Search online to find documentation for related commands.

**access-list (SAP filtering)**
**deny (SAP filtering)**
**ipx access-list**
**ipx gns-round-robin**
**permit (SAP filtering)**

### IPX OUTPUT-NETWORK-FILTER

To control the list of networks included in routing updates sent out an interface, use the **ipx output-network-filter** interface configuration command. To remove the filter from the interface, use the **no** form of this command.

> **ipx output-network-filter** {*access-list-number* | *name*}
> **no ipx output-network-filter** {*access-list-number* | *name*}

| Syntax | Description |
|---|---|
| *access-list-number* | Number of the access list. All outgoing packets defined with either standard or extended access lists are filtered by the entries in this access list. For standard access lists, *access-list-number* is a number from 800 to 899. For extended access lists, it is a number from 900 to 999. |
| *name* | Name of the access list. Names cannot contain a space or quotation mark, and they must begin with an alphabetic character to prevent ambiguity with numbered access lists. |

### Default

No filters are predefined.

### Command Mode

Interface configuration

### Usage Guidelines

This command first appeared in Cisco IOS Release 10.0.

The **ipx output-network-filter** command controls which networks the Cisco IOS software advertises in its IPX routing updates (RIP updates).

You can issue only one **ipx output-network-filter** command on each interface.

### Example

In the following example, access list 896 controls which networks are specified in routing updates sent out the serial 1 interface. This configuration causes network 2b to be the only network advertised in Novell routing updates sent on the specified serial interface.

```
access-list 896 permit 2b

interface serial 1
 ipx output-network-filter 896
```

### Related Commands

Search online to find documentation for related commands.

access-list (extended)
access-list (standard)
deny (extended)
deny (standard)
ipx access-list
ipx input-network-filter
ipx router-filter
permit (extended)
permit (standard)

## IPX OUTPUT-RIP-DELAY

To set the interpacket delay for RIP updates sent on a single interface, use the **ipx output-rip-delay** interface configuration command. To return to the default value, use the **no** form of this command.

> **ipx output-rip-delay** *delay*
> **no ipx output-rip-delay** [*delay*]

| Syntax | Description |
|--------|-------------|
| *delay* | Delay, in milliseconds, between packets in a multiple-packet RIP update. The default delay is 55 ms. Novell recommends a delay of 55 ms. |

### Default

55 ms

### Command Mode

Interface configuration

### Usage Guidelines

This command first appeared in Cisco IOS Release 10.0.

The interpacket delay is the delay between the individual packets sent in a multiple-packet routing update. The **ipx output-rip-delay** command sets the interpacket delay for a single interface.

The system uses the interpacket delay specified by the **ipx output-rip-delay** command for periodic and triggered routing updates when no delay is set for triggered routing updates. When you set a delay for triggered routing updates, the system uses the delay specified by the **ipx output-rip-delay** command for only the periodic routing updates sent on the interface.

To set a delay for triggered routing updates, see the **ipx triggered-rip-delay** or **ipx default-triggered-rip-delay** commands.

You can also set a default RIP interpacket delay for all interfaces. See the **ipx default-output-rip-delay** command for more information.

Novell recommends a delay of 55 ms for compatibility with older and slower IPX machines. These machines may lose RIP updates because they process packets more slowly than the router sends them. The delay imposed by this command forces the router to pace its output to the slower-processing needs of these IPX machines.

The default delay on a NetWare 3.11 server is about 100 ms.

This command is also useful on limited bandwidth point-to-point links or X.25 and Frame Relay multipoint interfaces.

### Example

The following example establishes a 55-ms interpacket delay on serial interface 0:

```
interface serial 0
 ipx network 106A
 ipx output-rip-delay 55
```

### Related Commands

Search online to find documentation for related commands.

**ipx default-output-rip-delay**
**ipx default-triggered-rip-delay**
**ipx triggered-rip-delay**
**ipx update sap-after-rip**

## IPX OUTPUT-SAP-DELAY

To set the interpacket delay for Service Advertising Protocol (SAP) updates sent on a single interface, use the **ipx output-sap-delay** interface configuration command. To return to the default delay value, use the **no** form of this command.

> **ipx output-sap-delay** *delay*
> **no ipx output-sap-delay** [*delay*]

| Syntax | Description |
|---|---|
| *delay* | Delay, in milliseconds, between packets in a multiple-packet SAP update. The default delay is 55 ms. Novell recommends a delay of 55 ms. |

### Default

55 ms

### Command Mode

Interface configuration

*Usage Guidelines*

This command first appeared in Cisco IOS Release 10.0.

The interpacket delay is the delay between the individual packets sent in a multiple-packet SAP update. The **ipx output-sap-delay** command sets the interpacket delay for a single interface.

The system uses the interpacket delay specified by the **ipx output-sap-delay** command for periodic and triggered SAP updates when no delay is set for triggered updates. When you set a delay for triggered updates, the system uses the delay specified by the **ipx output-sap-delay** command only for the periodic updates sent on the interface.

To set a delay for triggered updates, see the **ipx triggered-sap-delay** or **ipx default-triggered-sap-delay** commands.

You can also set a default SAP interpacket delay for all interfaces. See the **ipx default-output-sap-delay** command for more information.

Novell recommends a delay of 55 ms for compatibility with older and slower IPX servers. These servers may lose SAP updates because they process packets more slowly than the router sends them. The delay imposed by the **ipx output-sap-delay** command forces the router to pace its output to the slower-processing needs of these servers.

The default delay on a NetWare 3.11 server is about 100 ms.

This command is also useful on limited bandwidth point-to-point links or X.25 and Frame Relay multipoint interfaces.

*Example*

The following example establishes a 55-ms delay between packets in multiple-packet SAP updates on Ethernet interface 0:

```
interface ethernet 0
 ipx network 106A
 ipx output-sap-delay 55
```

*Related Commands*

Search online to find documentation for related commands.

ipx default-output-sap-delay
ipx default-triggered-sap-delay
ipx linkup-request
ipx triggered-sap-delay

## IPX OUTPUT-SAP-FILTER

To control which services are included in SAP updates sent by the Cisco IOS software, use the **ipx output-network-filter** interface configuration command. To remove the filter, use the **no** form of this command.

*Command Reference*

ipx output-sap-filter {*access-list-number* | *name*}
no ipx output-sap-filter {*access-list-number* | *name*}

| Syntax | Description |
|---|---|
| *access-list-number* | Number of the SAP access list. All outgoing service advertisements are filtered by the entries in this access list. The argument *access-list-number* is a number from 1000 to 1099. |
| *name* | Name of the access list. Names cannot contain a space or quotation mark, and must begin with an alphabetic character to prevent ambiguity with numbered access lists. |

### Default

No filters are predefined.

### Command Mode

Interface configuration

### Usage Guidelines

This command first appeared in Cisco IOS Release 10.0.

The Cisco IOS software applies output SAP filters prior to sending SAP packets.

You can issue only one **ipx output-sap-filter** command on each interface.

When configuring SAP filters for NetWare 3.11 and later servers, use the server's internal network and node number (the node number is always 0000.0000.0001) as its address in the SAP **access-list** command. Do not use the *network.node* address of the particular interface board.

### Example

The following example denies service advertisements about server 0000.0000.0001 on network aa from being sent on network 4d (via Ethernet interface 1). All other services are advertised via this network. All services, included those from server aa.0000.0000.0001, are advertised via networks 3c and 2b.

```
access-list 1000 deny aa.0000.0000.0001
access-list 1000 permit -1

interface ethernet 0
 ipx network 3c

interface ethernet 1
 ipx network 4d
 ipx output-sap-filter 1000

interface serial 0
 ipx network 2b
```

*Related Commands*

Search online to find documentation for related commands.

**access-list (SAP filtering)**
**deny (SAP filtering)**
**ipx access-list**
**ipx gns-round-robin**
**ipx input-sap-filter**
**ipx router-sap-filter**
**permit (SAP filtering)**

## IPX PAD-PROCESS-SWITCHED-PACKETS

To control whether odd-length packets are padded so as to be sent as even-length packets on an interface, use the **ipx pad-process-switched-packets** interface configuration command. To disable padding, use the **no** form of this command.

    ipx pad-process-switched-packets
    no ipx pad-process-switched-packets

*Syntax      Description*

This command has no arguments or keywords.

*Default*

Enabled on Ethernet interfaces
Disabled on Token Ring, FDDI, and serial interfaces

*Command Mode*

Interface configuration

*Usage Guidelines*

This command first appeared in Cisco IOS Release 10.0.

Use this command only under the guidance of a customer engineer or other service representative.

The **ipx pad-process-switched-packets** command affects process-switched packets only, so you must disable fast switching before the **ipx pad-process-switched-packets** command has any effect.

Some IPX end hosts reject Ethernet packets that are not padded. Certain topologies can result in such packets being forwarded onto a remote Ethernet network. Under specific conditions, padding on intermediate media can be used as a temporary workaround for this problem.

## Example

The following example configures the Cisco IOS software to pad odd-length packets so that they are sent as even-length packets on FDDI interface 1.

```
interface fddi 1
  ipx network 2A
  no ipx route-cache
  ipx pad-process-switched-packets
```

## Related Commands

Search online to find documentation for related commands.

ipx route-cache


## IPX PER-HOST-LOAD-SHARE

To enable per-host load sharing, use the **ipx per-host-load-share** global configuration command. To disable per-host load sharing, use the **no** form of the command.

**ipx per-host-load-share**
**no ipx per-host-load-share**

## Syntax       Description

This command has no arguments or keywords.


## Default

Disabled


## Command Mode

Global configuration


## Usage Guidelines

This command first appeared in Cisco IOS Release 11.1.

Use this command to enable per-host load sharing. Per-host load sharing transmits traffic across multiple, equal-cost paths while guaranteeing that packets for a given end host always take the same path.

When you do not enable per-host load sharing, the software uses a round-robin algorithm to accomplish load sharing. Round-robin load sharing transmits successive packets over alternate, equal-cost paths, regardless of the destination host. With round-robin load sharing, successive packets destined for the same end host might take different paths. Thus, round-robin load sharing increases the possibility that successive packets to a given end host might arrive out of order or be dropped, but ensures true load balancing of a given workload across multiple links.

In contrast, per-host load sharing decreases the possibility that successive packets to a given end host will arrive out of order; but, there is a potential decrease in true load balancing across multiple links. True load sharing occurs only when different end hosts utilize different paths; equal link utilization cannot be guaranteed.

With per-host load balancing, the number of equal-cost paths set by the **ipx maximum-paths** command must be greater than one; otherwise, per-host load sharing has no effect.

### Example

The following command globally enables per-host load sharing:

```
ipx per-host-load share
```

### Related Commands

Search online to find documentation for related commands.

**ipx maximum-paths**

### IPX PING-DEFAULT

To select the ping type that the Cisco IOS software transmits, use the **ipx ping-default** global configuration command. To return to the default ping type, use the **no** form of this command.

> **ipx ping-default** {cisco | novell}
> **no ipx ping-default** {cisco | novell}

| Syntax | Description |
|--------|-------------|
| cisco | Transmits Cisco pings. |
| novell | Transmits standard Novell pings. |

### Default

Cisco pings

### Command Mode

Global configuration

### Usage Guidelines

This command first appeared in Cisco IOS Release 10.3.

Standard Novell pings conform to the definition in the Novell NLSP specification.

### Example

The following example enables standard Novell pings:

```
ipx ping-default novell
```

*Related Commands*

Search online to find documentation for related commands.

**ping (user)**

## IPX RIP-MAX-PACKETSIZE

To configure the maximum packet size of RIP updates sent out the interface, use the **ipx rip-max-packetsize** interface configuration command. To restore the default packet size, use the **no** form of this command.

> **ipx rip-max-packetsize** *bytes*
> **no ipx rip-max-packetsize** *bytes*

| *Syntax* | *Description* |
|---|---|
| *bytes* | Maximum packet size in bytes. The default is 432 bytes, which allows for 50 routes at 8 bytes each, plus 32 bytes of IPX network and RIP header information. |

*Default*

432 bytes

*Command Mode*

Interface configuration

*Usage Guidelines*

This command first appeared in Cisco IOS Release 10.3.

The maximum size is for the IPX packet including the IPX network and RIP header information.

Do not allow the maximum packet size to exceed the allowed maximum size of packets for the interface.

*Example*

The following example sets the maximum RIP update packet to 832 bytes:

```
ipx rip-max-packetsize 832
```

*Related Commands*

Search online to find documentation for related commands.

**ipx sap-max-packetsize**

## IPX RIP-MULTIPLIER

To configure the interval at which a network's RIP entry ages out, use the **ipx rip-multiplier** interface configuration command. To restore the default interval, use the **no** form of this command.

> **ipx rip-multiplier** *multiplier*
> **no ipx rip-multiplier** *multiplier*

| Syntax | Description |
|---|---|
| *multiplier* | Multiplier used to calculate the interval at which to age out RIP routing table entries. This can be any positive number. The value you specify is multiplied by the RIP update interval to determine the aging-out interval. The default is three times the RIP update interval. |

*Default*

Three times the RIP update interval

*Command Mode*

Interface configuration

*Usage Guidelines*

This command first appeared in Cisco IOS Release 10.3.

All routers on the same physical cable should use the same multiplier value.

*Example*

In the following example, in a configuration where RIP updates are sent once every 2 minutes, the interval at which RIP entries age out is set to 10 minutes:

```
interface ethernet 0
  ipx rip-multiplier 5
```

*Related Commands*

Search online to find documentation for related commands.

**ipx update sap-after-rip**

## IPX ROUTE

To add a static route or static NLSP route summary to the routing table, use the **ipx route** global configuration command. To remove a route from the routing table, use the **no** form of this command.

> **ipx route** {*network* [*network-mask*] | **default**} {*network.node* | *interface*} [*ticks*] [*hops*]
>     [**floating-static**]
> **no ipx route**

| Syntax | Description |
| --- | --- |
| *network* | Network to which you want to establish a static route. |
| | This is an eight-digit hexadecimal number that uniquely identifies a network cable segment. It can be a number in the range 1 to FFFFFFFD. You do not need to specify leading zeros in the network number. For example, for the network number 000000AA, you can enter AA. |
| *network-mask* | (Optional) Specifies the portion of the network address that is common to all addresses in an NLSP route summary. When used with the *network* argument, it specifies the static route summary. |
| | The high-order bits of *network-mask* must be contiguous Fs, while the low-order bits must be contiguous zeros (0). An arbitrary mix of Fs and 0s is not permitted. |
| **default** | Creates a static entry for the "default route." The router forwards all nonlocal packets for which no explicit route is known via the specified next hop address (*network.node*) or interface. |
| *network.node* | Router to which to forward packets destined for the specified network. |
| | The argument *network* is an eight-digit hexadecimal number that uniquely identifies a network cable segment. It can be a number in the range 1 to FFFFFFFD. You do not need to specify leading zeros in the network number. For example, for the network number 000000AA, you can enter AA. |
| | The argument *node* is the node number of the target router. This is a 48-bit value represented by a dotted triplet of four-digit hexadecimal numbers (*xxxx.xxxx.xxxx*). |
| *interface* | Network interface to which to forward packets destined for the specified network. Interface is serial 0 or serial 0.2. Specifying an interface instead of a network node is intended for use on IPXWAN unnumbered interfaces. The specified interface can be a null interface. |
| *ticks* | (Optional) Number of IBM clock ticks of delay to the network for which you are establishing a static route. One clock tick is 1/18 of a second (approximately 55 ms). Valid values are 1 through 65534. |
| *hops* | (Optional) Number of hops to the network for which you are establishing a static route. Valid values are 1 through 254. |
| **floating-static** | (Optional) Specifies that this route is a floating static route, which is a static route that can be overridden by a dynamically learned route. |

*Default*

No static routes are predefined.

## Command Mode

Global configuration

## Usage Guidelines

This command first appeared in Cisco IOS Release 10.0. The following arguments and keywords first appeared in Cisco IOS 10.3: *network-mask*, **default**, *interface*, **floating-static**.

The **ipx route** command forwards packets destined for the specified network (*network*) via the specified router (*network.node*) or an interface (*interface*) on that network regardless of whether that router is sending dynamic routing information.

Floating static routes are static routes that can be overridden by dynamically learned routes. Floating static routes allow you to switch to another path whenever routing information for a destination is lost. One application of floating static routes is to provide back-up routes in topologies where dial-on-demand routing is used.

If you configure a floating static route, the Cisco IOS software checks to see if an entry for the route already exists in its routing table. If a dynamic route already exists, the floating static route is placed in reserve as part of a floating static route table. When the software detects that the dynamic route is no longer available, it replaces the dynamic route with the floating static route for that destination. If the route is later relearned dynamically, the dynamic route replaces the floating static route and the floating static route is again placed in reserve.

If you specify an interface instead of a network node address, the interface must be an IPXWAN unnumbered interface. For IPXWAN interfaces, the network number need not be preassigned; instead, the nodes may negotiate the network number dynamically.

Note that by default, floating static routes are not redistributed into other dynamic protocols.

## Examples

In the following example, a router at address 3abc.0000.0c00.1ac9 handles all traffic destined for network 5e:

```
ipx routing
ipx route 5e 3abc.0000.0c00.1ac9
```

The following example defines a static NLSP route summary:

```
ipx routing
ipx route aaaa0000 ffff0000
```

## Related Commands

Search online to find documentation for related commands.

**ipx default-route**
**show ipx route**

*Command Reference*

## IPX ROUTE-CACHE

To enable IPX fast switching, use the **ipx route-cache** interface configuration command. To disable fast switching, use the **no** form of this command.

    **ipx route-cache**
    **no ipx route-cache**

### Syntax      Description

This command has no arguments or keywords.

### Default

Fast switching is enabled.

### Command Mode

Interface configuration

### Usage Guidelines

This command first appeared in Cisco IOS Release 10.0.

Fast switching allows higher throughput by switching packets using a cache created by previous transit packets. Fast switching is enabled by default on all interfaces that support fast switching, including Token Ring, Frame Relay, PPP, SMDS, and ATM.

On ciscoBus-2 interface cards, fast switching is done between all encapsulation types. On other interface cards, fast switching is done in all cases *except* the following: transfer of packets with sap encapsulation from an Ethernet, a Token Ring, or an FDDI network to a standard serial line.

You might want to disable fast switching in two situations. One is if you want to save memory on the interface cards: fast-switching caches require more memory than those used for standard switching. The second situation is to avoid congestion on interface cards when a high-bandwidth interface is writing large amounts of information to a low-bandwidth interface.

### Examples

The following example enables fast switching:

```
interface ethernet 0
 ipx route-cache
```

In the following example, fast switching is turned off on an interface:

```
interface ethernet 0
 no ipx route-cache
```

### Related Commands

Search online to find documentation for related commands.

clear ipx cache
ipx source-network-update
ipx watchdog-spoof
show ipx cache
show ipx interface

## IPX ROUTE-CACHE INACTIVITY-TIMEOUT

To adjust the period and rate of route cache invalidation because of inactivity, use the **ipx route-cache inactivity-timeout** global configuration command. To return to the default values, use the **no** form of this command.

> **ipx route-cache inactivity-timeout** *period* [*rate*]
> **no ipx route-cache inactivity-timeout**

| Syntax | Description |
|--------|-------------|
| *period* | Number of minutes that a valid cache entry may be inactive before it is invalidated. Valid values are 0 through 65535. A value of zero disables this feature. |
| *rate* | (Optional) The maximum number of inactive entries that may be invalidated per minute. Valid values are 0 through 65535. A value of zero means no limit. |

### Defaults

The default period is 2 minutes. The default rate is 0 (cache entries do not age).

### Command Mode

Global configuration

### Usage Guidelines

This command first appeared in Cisco IOS Release 10.3.

IPX fast-switch cache entries that are not in use may be invalidated after a configurable period of time. If no new activity occurs, these entries will be purged from the route cache after one additional minute.

Cache entries that have been uploaded to the switch processor when autonomous switching is configured are always exempt from this treatment.

This command has no effect if silicon switching is configured.

*Command Reference*

*Example*

The following example sets the inactivity period to 5 minutes, and sets a maximum of 10 entries that can be invalidated per minute:

```
ipx route-cache inactivity-timeout 5 10
```

*Related Commands*

Search online to find documentation for related commands.

clear ipx cache
ipx route-cache
ipx route-cache update-timeout
show ipx cache

## IPX ROUTE-CACHE MAX-SIZE

To set a maximum limit on the number of entries in the IPX route cache, use the **ipx route-cache max-size** global configuration command. To return to the default setting, use the **no** form of this command.

> **ipx route-cache max-size** *size*
> **no ipx route-cache max-size**

| Syntax | Description |
|--------|-------------|
| *size* | Maximum number of entries allowed in the IPX route cache. |

*Default*

The default setting is no limit on the number of entries.

*Command Mode*

Global configuration

*Usage Guidelines*

This command first appeared in Cisco IOS Release 10.3.

On large networks, storing too many entries in the route cache can use a significant amount of router memory, causing router processing to slow. This situation is most common on large networks that run network management applications for NetWare. If the network management station is responsible for managing all clients and servers in a very large (greater than 50,000 nodes) Novell network, the routers on the local segment can become inundated with route cache entries. The **ipx route-cache max-size** command allows you to set a maximum number of entries for the route cache.

If the route cache already has more entries than the specified limit, the extra entries are not deleted. However, all route cache entries are subject to being removed via the parameter set for route cache aging via the **ipx route-cache inactivity-timeout** command.

### Example

The following example sets the maximum route cache size to 10,000 entries.

```
ipx route-cache max-size 10000
```

### Related Commands

Search online to find documentation for related commands.

**ipx route-cache**
**ipx route-cache inactivity-timeout**
**ipx route-cache update-timeout**
**show ipx cache**

## IPX ROUTE-CACHE UPDATE-TIMEOUT

To adjust the period and rate of route cache invalidation because of aging, use the **ipx route-cache update-timeout** global configuration command. To return to the default values, use the **no** form of this command.

**ipx route-cache update-timeout** *period* [*rate*]
**no ipx route-cache update-timeout**

| Syntax | Description |
|--------|-------------|
| *period* | Number of minutes since a valid cache entry was created before it may be invalidated. A value of zero disables this feature. |
| *rate* | (Optional) The maximum number of aged entries that may be invalidated per minute. A value of zero means no limit. |

### Default

The default setting is disabled.

### Command Mode

Global configuration

### Usage Guidelines

This command first appeared in Cisco IOS Release 11.2.

IPX fast-switch cache entries that exceed a minimum age may be invalidated after a configurable period of time. Invalidation occurs unless the cache entry was marked as active during the last minute. Following invalidation, if no new activity occurs, these entries will be purged from the route cache after one additional minute.

This capability is primarily useful when autonomous switching or silicon switching is enabled. In both cases, activity is not recorded for entries in the route cache, because data is being switched by the Switch Processor (SP) or Silicon Switch Processor (SSP). In this case, it may be desirable to periodically invalidate a limited number of older cache entries each minute.

If the end hosts have become inactive, the cache entries will be purged after one additional minute. If the end hosts are still active, the route cache and autonomous or SSP cache entries will be revalidated instead of being purged.

### Example

The following example sets the update timeout period to 5 minutes and sets a maximum of 10 entries that can be invalidated per minute:

```
ipx route-cache update-timeout 5 10
```

### Related Commands

Search online to find documentation for related commands.

**clear ipx cache**
**ipx route-cache**
**ipx route-cache inactivity-timeout**
**show ipx cache**

## IPX ROUTER

To specify the routing protocol to use, use the **ipx router** global configuration command. To disable a particular routing protocol on the router, use the **no** form of this command.

> **ipx router** {**eigrp** *autonomous-system-number* | **nlsp** [*tag*] | **rip**}
> **no ipx router** {**eigrp** *autonomous-system-number* | **nlsp** [*tag*] | **rip**}

| Syntax | Description |
| --- | --- |
| **eigrp** *autonomous-system-number* | Enables the Enhanced IGRP routing protocol. The argument *autonomous-system-number* is the Enhanced IGRP autonomous system number. It can be a number from 1 to 65535. |
| **nlsp** [*tag*] | Enables the NLSP routing protocol. The optional argument *tag* names the NLSP process to which you are assigning the NLSP protocol. If the router has only one process, defining a *tag* is optional. A maximum of three NLSP processes may be configured on the router at the same time. The *tag* can be any combination of printable characters. |
| **rip** | Enables the RIP routing protocol. It is on by default. |

## Default

RIP is enabled.

## Command Mode

Global configuration

## Usage Guidelines

This command first appeared in Cisco IOS Release 10.0. The **nlsp** keyword and *tag* argument first appeared in Cisco IOS Release 11.0.

You must explicitly disable RIP by issuing the **no ipx router rip** command if you do not want to use this routing protocol.

You can configure multiple Enhanced IGRP processes on a router. To do so, assign each a different autonomous system number.

---

**NOTES**

---

NLSP version 1.1 routers refer to routers that support the route aggregation feature, while NLSP version 1.0 routers refer to routers that do not.

---

When you specify an NLSP *tag*, you configure the NLSP routing protocol for a particular NLSP process. An NLSP *process* is a router's databases working together to manage route information about an area. NLSP version 1.0 routers are always in the same area. Each router has its own adjacencies, link-state, and forwarding databases. These databases operate collectively as a single *process* to discover, select, and maintain route information about the area. NLSP version 1.1 routers that exist within a single area also use a single process.

NLSP version 1.1 routers that interconnect multiple areas use multiple processes to discover, select, and maintain route information about the areas they interconnect. These routers manage an adjacencies, link-state, and area address database for each area to which they attach. Collectively, these databases are still referred to as a *process*. The forwarding database is shared among processes within a router. The sharing of entries in the forwarding database is automatic when all processes interconnect NLSP version 1.1 areas.

Configure multiple NLSP processes when a router interconnects multiple NLSP areas.

## Examples

The following example enables Enhanced IGRP:

```
ipx router eigrp 4
```

The following example enables NLSP on process *area1*. This process handles routing for NLSP area 1.

```
ipx router nlsp area1
```

*Related Commands*

Search online to find documentation for related commands.

**network**
**redistribute**

## IPX ROUTER-FILTER

To filter the routers from which packets are accepted, use the **ipx router-filter** interface configuration command. To remove the filter from the interface, use the **no** form of this command.

> **ipx router-filter** {*access-list-number* | *name*}
> **no ipx router-filter**

| Syntax | Description |
|---|---|
| *access-list-number* | Number of the access list. All incoming packets defined with either standard or extended access lists are filtered by the entries in this access list. For standard access lists, *access-list-number* is a number from 800 to 899. For extended access lists, it is a number from 900 to 999. |
| *name* | Name of the access list. Names cannot contain a space or quotation mark, and must begin with an alphabetic character to prevent ambiguity with numbered access lists. |

*Default*

No filters are predefined.

*Command Mode*

Interface configuration

*Usage Guidelines*

This command first appeared in Cisco IOS Release 10.0.

You can issue only one **ipx router-filter** command on each interface.

*Example*

In the following example, access list 866 controls the routers from which packets are accepted. For Ethernet interface 0, only packets from the router at 3c.0000.00c0.047d are accepted. All other packets are implicitly denied.

```
access-list 866 permit 3c.0000.00c0.047d

interface ethernet 0
 ipx router-filter 866
```

*Related Commands*

Search online to find documentation for related commands.

**access-list (extended)**
**access-list (standard)**
**deny (extended)**
**deny (standard)**
**ipx access-list**
**ipx input-network-filter**
**ipx output-network-filter**
**permit (extended)**
**permit (standard)**

## IPX ROUTER-SAP-FILTER

To filter Service Advertising Protocol (SAP) messages received from a particular router, use the **ipx router-sap-filter** interface configuration command. To remove the filter, use the **no** form of this command.

> **ipx router-sap-filter** {*access-list-number* | *name*}
> **no ipx router-sap-filter** {*access-list-number* | *name*}

| *Syntax* | *Description* |
|---|---|
| *access-list-number* | Number of the access list. All incoming service advertisements are filtered by the entries in this access list. The argument *access-list-number* is a number from 1000 to 1099. |
| *name* | Name of the access list. Names cannot contain a space or quotation mark, and must begin with an alphabetic character to prevent ambiguity with numbered access lists. |

*Default*

No filters are predefined.

*Command Mode*

Interface configuration

*Usage Guidelines*

This command first appeared in Cisco IOS Release 10.0.

You can issue only one **ipx router-sap-filter** command on each interface.

## Example

In the following example, the Cisco IOS software will receive service advertisements only from router aa.0207.0104.0874:

```
access-list 1000 permit aa.0207.0104.0874
access-list 1000 deny -1

interface ethernet 0
 ipx router-sap-filter 1000
```

## Related Commands

Search online to find documentation for related commands.

access-list (SAP filtering)
deny (SAP filtering)
ipx access-list
ipx input-sap-filter
ipx output-sap-filter
ipx sap
permit (SAP filtering)
show ipx interface

## IPX ROUTING

To enable IPX routing, use the **ipx routing** global configuration command. To disable IPX routing, use the **no** form of this command.

    **ipx routing** [*node*]
    **no ipx routing**

| Syntax | Description |
|---|---|
| *node* | (Optional) Node number of the router. This is a 48-bit value represented by a dotted triplet of four-digit hexadecimal numbers (*xxxx.xxxx.xxxx*). It must not be a multicast address. |
| | If you omit *node*, the Cisco IOS software uses the hardware MAC address currently assigned to it as its node address. This is the MAC address of the first Ethernet, Token Ring, or FDDI interface card. If no satisfactory interfaces are present in the router (such as only serial interfaces), you must specify *node*. |

## Default

Disabled

## Command Mode

Global configuration

## Usage Guidelines

This command first appeared in Cisco IOS Release 10.0.

The **ipx routing** command enables IPX Routing Information Protocol (RIP) and Service Advertising Protocol (SAP) services.

If you omit the argument *node* and if the MAC address later changes, the IPX node address automatically changes to the new address. However, connectivity may be lost between the time that the MAC address changes and the time that the IPX clients and servers learn the router's new address.

If you plan to use DECnet and IPX routing concurrently on the same interface, you should enable DECnet router first, then enable IPX routing without specifying the optional MAC node number. If you enable IPX before enabling DECnet routing, routing for IPX will be disrupted.

## Example

The following example enables IPX routing:

```
ipx routing
```

## Related Commands

Search online to find documentation for related commands.

**ipx network**

## IPX SAP

To specify static Service Advertising Protocol (SAP) entries, use the **ipx sap** global configuration command. To remove static SAP entries, use the **no** form of this command.

> **ipx sap** *service-type name network.node socket hop-count*
> **no ipx sap** *service-type name network.node socket hop-count*

| Syntax | Description |
|---|---|
| *service-type* | SAP service-type number. Table 5–3 earlier in this chapter lists some IPX SAP services. |
| *name* | Name of the server that provides the service. |
| *network.node* | Network number and node address of the server. |
| | *The argument network is an eight-digit hexadecimal number that uniquely identifies a network cable segment. It can be a number in the range 1 to FFFFFFFD. You do not need to specify leading zeros in the network number. For example, for the network number 000000AA you can enter AA.* |
| | *The argument node is the node number of the target Novell server. This is a 48-bit value represented by a dotted triplet of four-digit hexadecimal numbers (xxxx.xxxx.xxxx).* |

*Command Reference*

| Syntax | Description |
|--------|-------------|
| *socket* | Socket number for this service. Table 5–2 earlier in this chapter lists some IPX socket numbers. |
| *hop-count* | Number of hops to the server. |

## Default

Disabled

## Command Mode

Global configuration

## Usage Guidelines

This command first appeared in Cisco IOS Release 10.0.

The **ipx sap** command allows you to add static entries into the SAP table. Each entry has a SAP service associated with it. Static SAP assignments always override any identical entries in the SAP table that are learned dynamically, regardless of hop count. The router will not announce a static SAP entry unless it has a route to that network.

## Example

In the following example, the route to JOES_SERVER is not yet learned, so the system displays an informational message. The JOES_SERVER service will not be announced in the regular SAP updates until the Cisco IOS software learns the route to it either by means of a RIP update from a neighbor or an **ipx sap** command.

```
ipx sap 107 MAILSERV 160.0000.0c01.2b72 8104 1
ipx sap 4 FILESERV 165.0000.0c01.3d1b 451 1
ipx sap 143 JOES_SERVER A1.0000.0c01.1234 8170 2
no route to A1, JOES_SERVER won't be announced until route is learned
```

## Related Commands

Search online to find documentation for related commands.

**ipx input-sap-filter**
**ipx output-sap-filter**
**ipx router-sap-filter**
**show ipx servers**

## IPX SAP-INCREMENTAL

To send Service Advertising Protocol (SAP) updates only when a change occurs in the SAP table, use the **ipx sap-incremental** interface configuration command. To send periodic SAP updates, use the **no** form of this command.

ipx sap-incremental eigrp *autonomous-system-number* [**rsup-only**]
no ipx sap-incremental eigrp *autonomous-system-number* [**rsup-only**]

| Syntax | Description |
|---|---|
| eigrp *autonomous-system-number* | IPX Enhanced IGRP autonomous system number. It can be a number from 1 to 65535. |
| rsup-only | (Optional) Indicates that the system uses Enhanced IGRP on this interface to carry reliable SAP update information only. RIP routing updates are used, and Enhanced IGRP routing updates are ignored. |

### Default

Enabled on serial interfaces
Disabled on LAN media (Ethernet, Token Ring, FDDI)

### Command Mode

Interface configuration

### Usage Guidelines

This command first appeared in Cisco IOS Release 10.0.

To use the **ipx sap-incremental** command, you must enable Enhanced IGRP. This is the case even if you want to use only RIP routing. You must do this because the incremental SAP feature requires the Enhanced IGRP reliable transport mechanisms.

With this functionality enabled, if an IPX Enhanced IGRP peer is found on the interface, SAP updates will be sent only when a change occurs in the SAP table. Periodic SAP updates are not sent. When no IPX Enhanced IGRP peer is present on the interface, periodic SAPs are always sent, regardless of how this command is set.

If you configure the local router to send incremental SAP updates on an Ethernet, and if the local device has at least one IPX Enhanced IGRP neighbor and any servers, clients, or routers that do not have IPX Enhanced IGRP configured on the Ethernet interface, these devices will not receive complete SAP information from the local router.

If the incremental sending of SAP updates on an interface is configured and no IPX Enhanced IGRP peer is found, SAP updates will be sent periodically until a peer is found. Then, updates will be sent only when changes occur in the SAP table.

To take advantage of Enhanced IGRP's incremental SAP update mechanism while using the RIP routing protocol instead of the Enhanced IGRP routing protocol, specify the **rsup-only** keyword. SAP updates are then sent only when changes occur, and only changes are sent. Use this feature only when you want to use RIP routing; Cisco IOS software disables the exchange of route information via Enhanced IGRP for that interface.

## Example

The following example sends SAP updates on Ethernet interface 0 only when there is a change in the SAP table:

```
interface ethernet 0
  ipx sap-incremental eigrp 200
```

## IPX SAP-MAX-PACKETSIZE

To configure the maximum packet size of Service Advertising Protocol (SAP) updates sent out the interface, use the **ipx sap-max-packetsize** interface configuration command. To restore the default packet size, use the **no** form of this command.

**ipx sap-max-packetsize** *bytes*
**no ipx sap-max-packetsize** *bytes*

| Syntax | Description |
| --- | --- |
| *bytes* | Maximum packet size in bytes. The default is 480 bytes, which allows for 7 servers (64 bytes each), plus 32 bytes of IPX network and SAP header information. |

## Default

480 bytes

## Command Mode

Interface configuration

## Usage Guidelines

This command first appeared in Cisco IOS Release 10.3.

The maximum size is for the IPX packet including the IPX network and SAP header information. For example, to allow 10 servers per SAP packet, you would configure (32 + (10 x 64)), or 672 bytes for the maximum packet size.

You are responsible for guaranteeing that the maximum packet size does not exceed the allowed maximum size of packets for the interface.

## Example

The following example sets the maximum SAP update packet size to 672 bytes:

```
ipx sap-max-packetsize 672
```

## Related Commands

Search online to find documentation for related commands.

**ipx rip-max-packetsize**

## IPX SAP-MULTIPLIER

To configure the interval at which a network's or server's Service Advertising Protocol (SAP) entry ages out, use the **ipx sap-multiplier** interface configuration command. To restore the default interval, use the **no** form of this command.

> **ipx sap-multiplier** *multiplier*
> **no ipx sap-multiplier** *multiplier*

| Syntax | Description |
| --- | --- |
| *multiplier* | Multiplier used to calculate the interval at which to age out SAP routing table entries. This can be any positive number. The value you specify is multiplied by the SAP update interval to determine the aging-out interval. The default is three times the SAP update interval. |

### Default

Three times the SAP update interval.

### Command Mode

Interface configuration

### Usage Guidelines

This command first appeared in Cisco IOS Release 10.3.

All routers on the same physical cable should use the same multiplier value.

### Example

In the following example, in a configuration where SAP updates are sent once every 1 minute, the interval at which SAP entries age out is set to 10 minutes:

```
interface ethernet 0
  ipx sap-multiplier 10
```

### Related Commands

Search online to find documentation for related commands.

**ipx sap-max-packetsize**

## IPX SAP-QUEUE-MAXIMUM

To configure the maximum length of the queue of pending input Service Advertising Protocol (SAP) GNS requests and SAP query packets, use the **ipx sap-queue-maximum** global configuration command. To return to the default value, use the **no** form of this command.

> **ipx sap-queue-maximum** *number*
> **no ipx sap-queue-maximum**

Command Reference

| *Syntax* | *Description* |
|----------|---------------|
| *number* | Maximum length of the queue of pending SAP requests. By default, there is no limit to the number of pending SAP requests that the Cisco IOS software stores in this queue. |

## Default

No maximum queue size

## Command Mode

Global configuration

## Usage Guidelines

This command first appeared in Cisco IOS Release 10.0.

The Cisco IOS software maintains a list of SAP requests to process, including all pending GNS queries from clients attempting to reach servers. When the network is restarted, the software can be inundated with hundreds of requests for servers. Most of these can be repeated requests from the same clients. The **ipx sap-queue-maximum** command allows you to configure the maximum length allowed for the pending SAP requests queue. Packets received when the queue is full are dropped.

## Example

The following example sets the length of the queue of pending SAP requests to 20:

```
ipx sap-queue-maximum 20
```

## IPX SOURCE-NETWORK-UPDATE

To repair corrupted network numbers, use the **ipx source-network-update** interface configuration command. To disable this feature, use the **no** form of this command.

> **ipx source-network-update**
> **no ipx source-network-update**

*Syntax*      *Description*

This command has no arguments or keywords.

## Default

Disabled

## Command Mode

Interface configuration

## Usage Guidelines

This command first appeared in Cisco IOS Release 10.0.

In some early implementations of IPX client software, it was possible for the client's network number to become corrupted. The **ipx source-network-update** command repairs this number by setting the source network field of any packet on the local network that has a hop count of zero.

You must disable fast switching with the **no ipx route-cache** command before using the **ipx source-network-update** command.

> **CAUTION**
>
> The **ipx source-network-update** command interferes with the proper working of OS/2 Requestors. Do not use this command in a network that has OS/2 Requestors.

> **CAUTION**
>
> Do not use the **ipx source-network-update** command on interfaces on which NetWare (NetWare 3.1x or 4.0 or later) servers are using internal network numbers.

## Example

In the following example, corrupted network numbers on serial interface 0 are repaired:

```
interface serial 0
  no ipx route-cache
  ipx source-network-update
```

## Related Commands

Search online to find documentation for related commands.

ipx route-cache

### IPX SPLIT-HORIZON EIGRP

To configure split horizon, use the **ipx split-horizon eigrp** interface configuration command. To disable split horizon, use the **no** form of this command.

> **ipx split-horizon eigrp** *autonomous-system-number*
> **no ipx split-horizon eigrp** *autonomous-system-number*

| Syntax | Description |
| --- | --- |
| *autonomous-system-number* | Enhanced IGRP autonomous system number. It can be a number from 1 to 65535. |

*Default*

Enabled

*Command Mode*

Interface configuration

*Usage Guidelines*

This command first appeared in Cisco IOS Release 10.0.

When split horizon is enabled, Enhanced IGRP update and query packets are not sent for destinations that have next hops on this interface. This reduces the number of Enhanced IGRP packets on the network.

Split horizon blocks information about routes from being advertised by a router out any interface from which that information originated. Typically, this behavior optimizes communication among multiple routers, particularly when links are broken. However, with nonbroadcast networks, such as Frame Relay and SMDS, situations can arise for which this behavior is less than ideal. For these situations, you may wish to disable split horizon.

*Example*

The following example disables split horizon on serial interface 0:

```
interface serial 0
 no ipx split-horizon eigrp 200
```

## IPX SPX-IDLE-TIME

To set the amount of time to wait before starting the spoofing of SPX keepalive packets following inactive data transfer, use the **ipx spx-idle-time** interface configuration command. To disable the current delay time set by this command, use the **no** form of this command.

    **ipx spx-idle-time** *delay-in-seconds*
    **no ipx spx-idle-time**

| *Syntax* | *Description* |
|---|---|
| *delay-in-seconds* | The amount of time in seconds to wait before spoofing SPX keepalives after data transfer has stopped. |

*Default*

60 seconds

*Command Mode*

Interface configuration

### Usage Guidelines

This command first appeared in Cisco IOS Release 11.0.

This command sets the elapsed time in seconds after which spoofing of keepalive packets occurs, following the end of data transfer; that is, after the acknowledgment and sequence numbers of the data being transferred have stopped increasing. By default, SPX keepalive packets are sent from servers to clients every 15 to 20 seconds.

If you turn on SPX spoofing and you do not set an idle time, the default of 60 seconds is assumed. This means that the dialer idle time begins when SPX spoofing begins. For example, if the dialer idle time is 3 minutes, the elapse time before SPX spoofing begins is 4 minutes: 3 minutes of dialer idle time plus 1 minute of SPX spoofing idle time.

For this command to take effect, you must first use the **ipx spx-spoof** interface configuration command to enable SPX spoofing for the interface.

### Example

The following example enables spoofing on serial interface 0 and sets the idle timer to 300 seconds:

```
interface serial 0
ipx spx-spoof
no ipx route-cache
ipx spx-idle-time 300
```

### Related Commands

Search online to find documentation for related commands.

**ipx spx-spoof**
**show ipx spx-spoof**

## IPX SPX-SPOOF

To configure the Cisco IOS software to respond to a client or server's SPX keepalive packets on behalf of a remote system so that a dial-on-demand (DDR) link will go idle when data has stopped being transferred, use the **ipx spx-spoof** interface configuration command. To disable spoofing, use the **no** form of this command.

> **ipx spx-spoof**
> **no ipx spx-spoof**

### Syntax       Description

This command has no arguments or keywords.

### Default

Disabled

## Command Mode

Interface configuration

## Usage Guidelines

This command first appeared in Cisco IOS Release 11.0.

You can use the **ipx spx-spoof** command on any serial dialer or point-to-point interface. Fast switching and autonomous switching must be disabled on the interface; otherwise, SPX spoofing will not be permitted.

SPX keepalive packets are sent from servers to clients every 15 to 20 seconds after a client session has been idle for a certain period of time following the end of data transfer and after which only unsolicited acknowledgments are sent. The idle time may vary, depending on parameters set by the client and server.

Because of acknowledgment packets, a session would never go idle on a DDR link. On pay-per-packet or byte networks, these keepalive packets can incur for the customer large phone connection charges for idle time. You can prevent these calls from being made by configuring the software to respond to the server's keepalive packets on a remote client's behalf. This is sometimes referred to as "spoofing the server."

You can use the **ipx spx-idle-time** command to set the elapsed time in seconds after which spoofing of keepalive packets occurs, following the end of data transfer. If you turn on SPX spoofing and you do not set an idle time, the default of 60 seconds is assumed. This means that the dialer idle time begins when SPX spoofing begins. For example, if the dialer idle time is 3 minutes, the elapse time before the line goes "idle-spoofing" is 4 minutes: 3 minutes of dialer idle time plus 1 minute of SPX spoofing idle time.

## Example

The following example enables spoofing on serial interface 0:

```
interface serial 0
 ipx spx-spoof
 no ipx route-cache
```

## Related Commands

Search online to find documentation for related commands.

**ipx throughput**
**show ipx spx-spoof**

## IPX THROUGHPUT

To configure the throughput, use the **ipx throughput** interface configuration command. To revert to the current bandwidth setting for the interface, use the **no** form of this command.

ipx throughput *bits-per-second*
no ipx throughput *bits-per-second*

*Syntax*                     *Description*

*bits-per-second*            Throughput, in bits per second.

*Default*

Current bandwidth setting for the interface

*Command Mode*

Interface configuration

*Usage Guidelines*

This command first appeared in Cisco IOS Release 10.3.

The value you specify with the **ipx throughput** command overrides the value measured by IPXWAN when it starts. This value is also supplied to NLSP for use in its metric calculations.

*Example*

The following example changes the throughput to 1,000,000 bits per second:

```
ipx throughput 1000000
```

*Related Commands*

Search online to find documentation for related commands.

**ipx ipxwan**

### IPX TRIGGERED-RIP-DELAY

To set the interpacket delay for triggered RIP updates sent on a single interface, use the **ipx triggered-rip-delay** interface configuration command. To return to the default delay, use the **no** form of this command.

ipx triggered-rip-delay *delay*
no ipx triggered-rip-delay [*delay*]

*Syntax*                     *Description*

*delay*                      Delay, in milliseconds, between packets in a multiple-packet RIP update. The default delay is 55 ms. Novell recommends a delay of 55 ms.

*Default*

55 ms

*Command Mode*

Interface configuration

*Usage Guidelines*

This command first appeared in Cisco IOS Release 11.1.

The interpacket delay is the delay between the individual packets sent in a multiple-packet routing update. A triggered routing update is one that the system sends in response to a "trigger" event, such as a request packet, interface up/down, route up/down, or server up/down.

The **ipx triggered-rip-delay** command sets the interpacket delay for triggered routing updates sent on a single interface. The delay value set by this command overrides the delay value set by the **ipx output-rip-delay** or **ipx default-output-rip-delay** command for triggered routing updates sent on the interface.

If the delay value set by the **ipx output-rip-delay** or **ipx default-output-rip-delay** command is high, then we strongly recommend a low delay value for triggered routing updates so that updates triggered by special events are sent in a more timely manner than periodic routing updates.

Novell recommends a delay of 55 ms for compatibility with older and slower IPX machines. These machines may lose RIP updates because they process packets more slowly than the router sends them. The delay imposed by this command forces the router to pace its output to the slower-processing needs of these IPX machines.

The default delay on a NetWare 3.11 server is about 100 ms.

When you do not set the interpacket delay for triggered routing updates, the system uses the delay specified by the **ipx output-rip-delay** or **ipx default-output-rip-delay** command for both periodic and triggered routing updates.

When you use the **no** form of the **ipx triggered-rip-delay** command, the system uses the global default delay set by the **ipx default-triggered-rip-delay** command for triggered RIP updates, if it is set. If it is not set, the system uses the delay set by the **ipx output-rip-delay** or **ipx default-output-rip-delay** command for triggered RIP updates, if set. Otherwise, the system uses the initial default delay as described in the "Default" section.

This command is also useful on limited bandwidth point-to-point links, or X.25 and Frame Relay multipoint interfaces.

*Example*

The following example sets an interpacket delay of 55 ms for triggered routing updates sent on interface FDDI 0:

```
interface FDDI 0
 ipx triggered-rip-delay 55
```

*Related Commands*

Search online to find documentation for related commands.

ipx default-output-rip-delay
ipx default-triggered-rip-delay
ipx output-rip-delay

### IPX TRIGGERED-SAP-DELAY

To set the interpacket delay for triggered Service Advertising Protocol (SAP) updates sent on a single interface, use the **ipx triggered-sap-delay** interface configuration command. To return to the default delay, use the **no** form of this command.

> ipx triggered-sap-delay *delay*
> no ipx triggered-sap-delay [*delay*]

| *Syntax* | *Description* |
|---|---|
| *delay* | Delay, in milliseconds, between packets in a multiple-packet SAP update. The default delay is 55 ms. Novell recommends a delay of 55 ms. |

*Default*

55 ms

*Command Mode*

Interface configuration

*Usage Guidelines*

This command first appeared in Cisco IOS Release 11.1.

The interpacket delay is the delay between the individual packets sent in a multiple-packet SAP update. A triggered SAP update is one that the system sends in response to a "trigger" event, such as a request packet, interface up/down, route up/down, or server up/down.

The **ipx triggered-sap-delay** command sets the interpacket delay for triggered updates sent on a single interface. The delay value set by this command overrides the delay value set by the **ipx output-sap-delay** or **ipx default-output-sap-delay** command for triggered updates sent on the interface.

If the delay value set by the **ipx output-sap-delay** or **ipx default-output-sap-delay** command is high, then we strongly recommend a low delay value for triggered updates so that updates triggered by special events are sent in a more timely manner than periodic updates.

Novell recommends a delay of 55 ms for compatibility with older and slower IPX servers. These servers may lose SAP updates because they process packets more slowly than the router sends them.

*Command Reference*

The delay imposed by this command forces the router to pace its output to the slower-processing needs of these IPX servers.

The default delay on a NetWare 3.11 server is about 100 ms.

When you do not set the interpacket delay for triggered updates, the system uses the delay specified by the **ipx output-sap-delay** or **ipx default-output-sap-delay** command for both periodic and triggered SAP updates.

When you use the **no** form of the **ipx triggered-sap-delay** command, the system uses the global default delay set by the **ipx default-triggered-sap-delay** command for triggered SAP updates, if it is set. If it is not set, the system uses the delay set by the **ipx output-sap-delay** or **ipx default-output-sap-delay** command for triggered SAP updates, if set. Otherwise, the system uses the initial default delay as described in the "Default" section.

This command is also useful on limited bandwidth point-to-point links, or X.25 and Frame Relay multipoint interfaces.

### Example

The following example sets an interpacket delay of 55 ms for triggered SAP updates sent on interface FDDI 0:

```
interface FDDI 0
 ipx triggered-sap-delay 55
```

### Related Commands

Search online to find documentation for related commands.

**ipx default-output-sap-delay**
**ipx default-triggered-sap-delay**
**ipx linkup-request**
**ipx output-sap-delay**
**ipx update sap-after-rip**

## IPX TYPE-20-HELPERED

To forward IPX type 20 propagation packet broadcasts to specific network segments, use the **ipx type-20-helpered** global configuration command. To disable this function, use the **no** form of this command.

> **ipx type-20-helpered**
> **no ipx type-20-helpered**

### Syntax    Description

This command has no arguments or keywords.

*Default*

Disabled

*Command Mode*

Global configuration

*Usage Guidelines*

This command first appeared in Cisco IOS Release 10.3.

The **ipx type-20-helpered** command disables the input and output of type 20 propagation packets as done by the **ipx type-20-propagation** interface configuration command.

The **ipx type-20-propagation** command broadcasts type 20 packets to all nodes on the network and imposes a hop-count limit of eight routers for broadcasting these packets. These functions are in compliance with the Novell IPX router specification. In contrast, the **ipx type-20-helpered** command broadcasts type 20 packets to only those nodes indicated by the **ipx helper-address** interface configuration command and extends the hop-count limit to 16 routers.

Use of the **ipx type-20-helpered** command does not comply with the Novell IPX router specification; however, you may need to use this command if you have a mixed internetwork that contains routers running Software Release 9.1 and routers running later versions of Cisco IOS software.

*Example*

The following example forwards IPX type 20 propagation packet broadcasts to specific network segments:

```
interface ethernet 0
 ipx network aa
 ipx type-20-helpered
 ipx helper-address bb.ffff.ffff.ffff
```

*Related Commands*

Search online to find documentation for related commands.

**ipx helper-address**
**ipx type-20-propagation**

## IPX TYPE-20-INPUT-CHECKS

To restrict the acceptance of IPX type 20 propagation packet broadcasts, use the **ipx type-20-input-checks** global configuration command. To remove these restrictions, use the **no** form of this command.

> **ipx type-20-input-checks**
> **no ipx type-20-input-checks**

*Syntax     Description*

This command has no arguments or keywords.

*Default*

Disabled

*Command Mode*

Global configuration

*Usage Guidelines*

This command first appeared in Cisco IOS Release 10.0.

By default, the Cisco IOS software is configured to block type 20 propagation packets. When type 20 packet handling is enabled on multiple interfaces, you can use the **ipx type-20-input-checks** command to impose additional restrictions on the acceptance of type 20 packets. Specifically, the software will accept type 20 propagation packets only on the single network that is the primary route back to the source network. Similar packets received via other networks will be dropped. This behavior can be advantageous in redundant topologies, because it reduces unnecessary duplication of type 20 packets.

*Example*

The following example imposes additional restrictions on incoming type 20 broadcasts:

```
ipx type-20-input-checks
```

*Related Commands*

Search online to find documentation for related commands.

**ipx type-20-output-checks**
**ipx type-20-propagation**

## IPX TYPE-20-OUTPUT-CHECKS

To restrict the forwarding of IPX type 20 propagation packet broadcasts, use the **ipx type-20-output-checks** global configuration command. To remove these restrictions, use the **no** form of this command.

> **ipx type-20-output-checks**
> **no ipx type-20-output-checks**

*Syntax     Description*

This command has no arguments or keywords.

### Default

Disabled

### Command Mode

Global configuration

### Usage Guidelines

This command first appeared in Cisco IOS Release 10.0.

By default, the Cisco IOS software is configured to block type 20 propagation packets. When type 20 packet handling is enabled on multiple interfaces, you can use the **ipx type-20-output-checks** command to impose additional restrictions on outgoing type 20 packets. Specifically, the software will forward these packets only to networks that are not routes back to the source network. (The software uses the current routing table to determine routes.) This behavior can be advantageous in redundant topologies, because it reduces unnecessary duplication of type 20 packets.

### Example

The following example imposes restrictions on outgoing type 20 broadcasts:

```
ipx type-20-output-checks
```

### Related Commands

Search online to find documentation for related commands.

**ipx type-20-input-checks**
**ipx type-20-propagation**

## IPX TYPE-20-PROPAGATION

To forward IPX type 20 propagation packet broadcasts to other network segments, use the **ipx type-20-propagation** interface configuration command. To disable both the reception and forwarding of type 20 broadcasts on an interface, use the **no** form of this command.

> **ipx type-20-propagation**
> **no ipx type-20-propagation**

### Syntax      Description

This command has no arguments or keywords.

### Default

Disabled

### Command Mode

Interface configuration

## Usage Guidelines

This command first appeared in Cisco IOS Release 10.0.

Routers normally block all broadcast requests. To allow input and output of type 20 propagation packets on an interface, use the **ipx type-20-propagation** command. Note that type 20 packets are subject to loop detection and control as specified in the IPX router specification.

Additional input and output checks may be imposed by the **ipx type-20-input-checks** and **ipx type-20-output-checks** commands.

IPX type 20 propagation packet broadcasts are subject to any filtering defined by the **ipx helper-list** command.

## Examples

The following example enables both the reception and forwarding of type 20 broadcasts on Ethernet interface 0:

```
interface ethernet 0
 ipx type-20-propagation
```

The following example enables the reception and forwarding of type 20 broadcasts between networks 123 and 456, but does not enable reception and forwarding of these broadcasts to and from network 789:

```
interface ethernet 0
 ipx network 123
 ipx type-20-propagation
 !
interface ethernet 1
 ipx network 456
 ipx type-20-propagation
 !
interface ethernet 2
 ipx network 789
```

## Related Commands

Search online to find documentation for related commands.

ipx helper-list
ipx type-20-input-checks
ipx type-20-output-checks

## IPX UPDATE INTERVAL

To adjust the RIP or SAP update interval, use the **ipx update interval** interface configuration command. To restore the default values, use the **no** form of this command.

> ipx update interval {rip | sap} {*value* | changes-only}
> no ipx update interval {rip | sap}

| Syntax | Description |
|--------|-------------|
| **rip** | Adjusts the interval at which RIP updates are sent. The minimum interval is 10 seconds. |
| **sap** | Adjusts the interval at which SAP updates are sent. The minimum interval is 10 seconds. |
| *value* | The interval specified in seconds. |
| **changes-only** | Specifies the sending of a SAP update only when the link comes up, when the link is downed administratively, or when service information changes. This parameter is supported for SAP updates only. |

### Default

The default interval is 60 seconds for both IPX routing updates and SAP updates.

### Command Mode

Interface configuration

### Usage Guidelines

This command first appeared in Cisco IOS Release 11.3.

This command replaces two commands found in previous releases of the Cisco IOS software: **ipx sap-interval** and **ipx update-time**.

Routers exchange information about routes by sending broadcast messages when they are started up and shut down, and periodically while they are running. The **ipx update interval** command enables you to modify the periodic update interval. By default, this interval is 60 seconds (this default is defined by Novell).

You should set RIP timers only in a configuration in which all routers are Cisco routers or in which all other IPX routers allow configurable timers. The timers should be the same for all devices connected to the same cable segment.

The update value you choose affects the internal IPX timers as follows:

- IPX routes are marked invalid if no routing updates are heard within three times the value of the update interval and are advertised with a metric of infinity.

- IPX routes are removed from the routing table if no routing updates are heard within four times the value of the update interval.

Setting the interval at which SAP updates are sent is most useful on limited-bandwidth links, such as slower-speed serial interfaces.

You should ensure that all IPX servers and routers on a given network have the same SAP interval. Otherwise, they may decide that a server is down when it is really up.

It is not possible to change the interval at which SAP updates are sent on most PC-based servers. This means that you should never change the interval for an Ethernet or Token Ring network that has servers on it.

You can set the router to send an update only when changes have occurred. Using the **changes-only** keyword specifies the sending of a SAP update only when the link comes up, when the link is downed administratively, or when the databases change. The **changes-only** keyword causes the router to do the following:

- Send a single, full broadcast update when the link comes up
- Send appropriate triggered updates when the link is shut down
- Send appropriate triggered updates when specific service information changes

### Examples

The following example configures the update timers for RIP updates on two interfaces in a router:

```
interface serial 0
 ipx update interval rip 40

interface ethernet 0
 ipx update interval rip 20
```

The following example configures SAP updates to be sent (and expected) on serial interface 0 every 300 seconds (5 minutes) to reduce periodic update overhead on a slow-speed link:

```
interface serial 0
 ipx update interval sap 300
```

### Related Commands

Search online to find documentation for related commands.

**ipx linkup-request**
**ipx output-sap-delay**
**ipx update sap-after-rip**
**show ipx interface**

## IPX UPDATE SAP-AFTER-RIP

To configure the router to send a SAP update immediately following a RIP broadcast, use the **ipx update sap-after-rip** interface configuration command. To restore the default value, use the **no** form of this command.

> **ipx update sap-after-rip**
> **no ipx update sap-after-rip**

### Syntax      Description

This command has no arguments or keywords.

### Default

RIP and SAP updates are sent every 60 seconds.

### Command Mode

Interface configuration

### Usage Guidelines

This command first appeared in Cisco IOS Release 11.3.

The **ipx update sap-after-rip** command causes the router to issue a SAP update immediately following a RIP broadcast. This ensures that the SAP update follows the RIP broadcast, and that the SAP update is sent using the RIP update interval. It also ensures that the receiving router has learned the route to the service interface via RIP prior to getting the SAP broadcast.

### Example

The following example configures the router to issue a SAP broadcast immediately following a RIP broadcast on serial interface 0.

```
interface serial 0
  ipx update sap-after-rip
```

### Related Commands

Search online to find documentation for related commands.

**ipx linkup-request**
**ipx update interval**
**show ipx interface**


## IPX WATCHDOG-SPOOF

To have the Cisco IOS software respond to a server's watchdog packets on behalf of a remote client, use the **ipx watchdog-spoof** interface configuration command. To disable spoofing, use the **no** form of this command.

> **ipx watchdog-spoof**
> **no ipx watchdog-spoof**

### Syntax      Description

This command has no arguments or keywords.

### Default

Disabled

*Command Reference*

## Command Mode

Interface configuration

## Usage Guidelines

This command first appeared in Cisco IOS Release 10.0.

You can use the **ipx watchdog-spoof** command only on a serial interface on which dial-on-demand routing (DDR) has been enabled. Also, fast switching and autonomous switching must be disabled on the interface.

IPX watchdog packets are keepalive packets that are sent from servers to clients after a client session has been idle for approximately 5 minutes. On a DDR link, this would mean that a call would be made every 5 minutes, regardless of whether there were data packets to send. You can prevent these calls from being made by configuring the software to respond to the server's watchdog packets on a remote client's behalf. This is sometimes referred to as "spoofing the server."

## Example

The following example enables spoofing on serial interface 0:

```
interface serial 0
 ipx watchdog-spoof
 no ipx route-cache
```

## Related Commands

Search online to find documentation for related commands.

**ipx route-cache**
**ipx spx-spoof**

## LOG-ADJACENCY-CHANGES

To generate a log message when an NLSP adjacency changes state (up or down), use the **log-adjacency-changes** IPX-router configuration command. Use the **no** form of this command to disable this function.

```
log-adjacency-changes
no log-adjacency-changes
```

## Syntax     Description

This command has no arguments or keywords.

## Default

Adjacency changes are not logged.

## Command Mode

IPX-router configuration

## Usage Guidelines

This command first appeared in Cisco IOS Release 11.1.

This command allows the monitoring of NLSP adjacency state changes. Adjacency state monitoring can be very useful when monitoring large networks. Messages are logged using the system error message facility. Messages are of the form:

```
%CLNS-5-ADJCHANGE: NLSP: Adjacency to 0000.0000.0034 (Serial0) Up, new adjacency
%CLNS-5-ADJCHANGE: NLSP: Adjacency to 0000.0000.0034 (Serial0) Down, hold time expired
```

Messages regarding the use of NLSP multicast and broadcast addressing are also logged. For example, if broadcast addressing is in use on Ethernet interface 1.2, and the last neighbor requiring broadcasts goes down, the following messages will be logged:

```
%CLNS-5-ADJCHANGE: NLSP: Adjacency to 0000.0C34.D838 (Ethernet1.2) Down, hold time expired
%CLNS-5-MULTICAST: NLSP: Multicast address in use on Ethernet1.2
```

If multicast addressing is in use and a new neighbor that supports only broadcast addressing comes up, the following messages will be logged:

```
%CLNS-5-ADJCHANGE: NLSP: Adjaocency to 0000.0C34.D838 (Ethernet1.2) Up, new adjacency
%CLNS-5-MULTICAST: NLSP Broadcast address is in use on Ethernet1.2
```

## Example

The following example instructs the router to log adjacency changes for the NLSP process *area1*:

```
ipx router nlsp area1
  log-adjacency-changes
```

## Related Commands

Search online to find documentation for related commands.

**logging**

## LOG-NEIGHBOR-CHANGES

To enable the logging of changes in Enhanced IGRP neighbor adjacencies, use the **log-neighbor-changes** IPX-router configuration command. Use the no form of the command to disable this function.

> **log-neighbor-changes**
> **no log-neighbor-changes**

## Syntax     Description

This command has no arguments or keywords.

## Default

No adjacency changes are logged.

## Command Mode

IPX-router configuration

## Usage Guidelines

This command first appeared in Cisco IOS Release 11.2.

Enable the logging of neighbor adjacency changes in order to monitor the stability of the routing system and to help detect problems. Log messages are of the following form:

```
%DUAL-5-NBRCHANGE: IPX EIGRP as-number: Neighbor address (interface) is state: reason
```

where the arguments have the following meanings:

| | |
|---|---|
| *as-number* | Autonomous system number |
| *address* | Neighbor address |
| *state* | Up or down |
| *reason* | Reason for change |

## Example

The following configuration will log neighbor changes for Enhanced IGRP process 209:

```
ipx router eigrp 209
 log-neighbor-changes
```

## Related Commands

Search online to find documentation for related commands.

**ipx router**

## LSP-GEN-INTERVAL

To set the minimum interval at which link-state packets (LSPs) are generated, use the **lsp-gen-interval** router configuration command. To restore the default interval, use the **no** form of this command.

> **lsp-gen-interval** *seconds*
> **no lsp-gen-interval** *seconds*

| Syntax | Description |
|---|---|
| *seconds* | Minimum interval, in seconds. It can be a number in the range 0 to 120. The default is 5 seconds. |

*Default*

5 seconds

*Command Mode*

Router configuration

*Usage Guidelines*

This command first appeared in Cisco IOS Release 10.3.

The **lsp-gen-interval** command controls the rate at which LSPs are generated on a per-LSP basis. For instance, if a link is changing state at a high rate, the default value of the LSP generation interval limits the signaling of this change to once every 5 seconds. Because the generation of an LSP may cause all routers in the area to perform the SPF calculation, controlling this interval may have area-wide impact. Raising this interval can reduce the load on the network imposed by a rapidly changing link.

*Example*

The following example sets the minimum interval at which LSPs are generated to 10 seconds:

```
lsp-gen-interval 10
```

*Related Commands*

Search online to find documentation for related commands.

**ipx router nlsp**
**spf-interval**

## LSP-MTU

To set the maximum size of a link-state packet (LSP) generated by the Cisco IOS software, use the **lsp-mtu** router configuration command. To restore the default MTU size, use the **no** form of this command.

> **lsp-mtu** bytes
> **no lsp-mtu** *bytes*

| Syntax | Description |
|---|---|
| *bytes* | MTU size, in bytes. It can be a number in the range 512 to 4096. The default is 512 bytes. |

*Default*

512 bytes

Command Reference

## Command Mode

Router configuration

## Usage Guidelines

This command first appeared in Cisco IOS Release 10.3.

You can increase the LSP MTU if there is a very large amount of information generated by a single router, because each device is limited to approximately 250 LSPs. In practice, this should never be necessary.

The LSP MTU must never be larger than the smallest MTU of any link in the area. This is because LSPs are flooded throughout the area.

The **lsp-mtu** command limits the size of LSPs generated by this router only; the Cisco IOS software can receive LSPs of any size up to the maximum.

## Example

The following example sets the maximum LSP size to 1500 bytes:

```
lsp-mtu 1500
```

## Related Commands

Search online to find documentation for related commands.

**ipx router nlsp**

## LSP-REFRESH-INTERVAL

To set the link-state packet (LSP) refresh interval, use the **lsp-refresh-interval** router configuration command. To restore the default refresh interval, use the **no** form of this command.

> **lsp-refresh-interval** *seconds*
> **no lsp-refresh-interval** *seconds*

| Syntax | Description |
| --- | --- |
| *seconds* | Refresh interval, in seconds. It can be a value in the range 1 to 50000 seconds. The default is 7200 seconds (2 hours). |

## Default

7,200 seconds (2 hours)

## Command Mode

Router configuration

## Usage Guidelines

This command first appeared in Cisco IOS Release 10.3.

The refresh interval determines the rate at which the Cisco IOS software periodically transmits the route topology information that it originates. This is done in order to keep the information from becoming too old. By default, the refresh interval is 2 hours.

LSPs must be periodically refreshed before their lifetimes expire. The refresh interval must be less than the LSP lifetime specified with the **max-lsp-lifetime** router configuration command. Reducing the refresh interval reduces the amount of time that undetected link state database corruption can persist at the cost of increased link utilization. (This is an extremely unlikely event, however, because there are other safeguards against corruption.) Increasing the interval reduces the link utilization caused by the flooding of refreshed packets (although this utilization is very small).

## Example

The following example changes the LSP refresh interval to 10,800 seconds (3 hours):

```
lsp-refresh-interval 10800
```

## Related Commands

Search online to find documentation for related commands.

**ipx router nlsp**
**max-lsp-lifetime**

## MAX-LSP-LIFETIME

To set the maximum time that link-state packets (LSPs) persist without being refreshed, use the **max-lsp-lifetime** router configuration command. To restore the default time, use the **no** form of this command.

> **max-lsp-lifetime [hours]** *value*
> **no max-lsp-lifetime**

| Syntax | Description |
|--------|-------------|
| **hours** | (Optional) If specified, the lifetime of the LSP is set in hours. If not specified, the lifetime is set in seconds. |
| *value* | Lifetime of LSP in hours or seconds. It can be a number in the range 1 to 32767. The default is 7500 seconds. |

## Default

7500 seconds (2 hours, 5 minutes)

## Command Mode

Router configuration

## Usage Guidelines

This command first appeared in Cisco IOS Release 10.3.

The **hours** keyword enables the router to interpret the maximum lifetime field in hours, allowing the router to keep LSPs for a much longer time. Keeping LSPs longer reduces overhead on slower-speed serial links and keeps ISDN links from becoming active unnecessarily.

You might need to adjust the maximum LSP lifetime if you change the LSP refresh interval with the **lsp-refresh-interval** router configuration command. The maximum LSP lifetime must be greater than the LSP refresh interval.

## Examples

The following example sets the maximum time that the LSP persists to 11,000 seconds (more than 3 hours):

```
max-lsp-lifetime 11000
```

The following example sets the maximum time that the LSP persists to 15 hours:

```
max-lsp-lifetime hours 15
```

## Related Commands

Search online to find documentation for related commands.

**ipx router nlsp**
**lsp-refresh-interval**

## MULTICAST

To configure the router to use multicast addressing, use the **multicast** router configuration command. To configure the router to use broadcast addressing, use the **no** form of this command.

> **multicast**
> **no multicast**

## Syntax      Description

This command has no arguments or keywords.

## Default

Multicast addressing is enabled.

## Command Mode

Router configuration

### Usage Guidelines

This command first appeared in Cisco IOS Release 11.3.

This command allows the router to use NLSP multicast addressing. If an adjacent neighbor does not support NLSP multicast addressing, the router will revert to using broadcasts on the affected interface.

The router will also revert to using broadcasts on any interface where multicast addressing is not supported by the hardware or driver.

### Example

The following example disables multicast addressing on the router:

```
ipx router nlsp
no multicast
```

## NETBIOS ACCESS-LIST

To define an IPX NetBIOS FindName access list filter, use the **netbios access-list** global configuration command. To remove a filter, use the **no** form of the command.

> **netbios access-list host** *name* {**deny** | **permit**} *string*
> **no netbios access-list host** *name* {**deny** | **permit**} *string*
>
> **netbios access-list bytes** *name* {**deny** | **permit**} *offset byte-pattern*
> **no netbios access-list bytes** *name* {**deny** | **permit**} *offset byte-pattern*

| Syntax | Description |
|---|---|
| **host** | Indicates that the following argument is the name of a NetBIOS access filter previously defined with one or more **netbios access-list host** commands. |
| **bytes** | Indicates that the following argument is the name of a NetBIOS access filter previously defined with one or more **netbios access-list bytes** commands. |
| *name* | Name of the access list being defined. The name can be an alphanumeric string. |
| **deny** | Denies access if the conditions are matched. |
| **permit** | Permits access if the conditions are matched. |
| *string* | Character string that identifies one or more NetBIOS host names. It can be up to 14 characters long. The argument *string* can include the following wildcard characters: |
| | • *—Match one or more characters. You can use this wildcard character only at the end of a string. |
| | • ?—Match any single character. |

| Syntax | Description |
|---|---|
| *offset* | Decimal number that indicates the number of bytes into the packet at which the byte comparison should begin. An offset of 0 indicates the beginning of the NetBIOS packet header, which is at the end of the IPX header. |
| *byte-pattern* | Hexadecimal pattern that represents the byte pattern to match. It can be up to 16 bytes (32 digits) long and must be an even number of digits. The argument *byte-pattern* can include the double asterisk (**) wildcard character to match any digits for that byte. |

### Default

No filters are predefined.

### Command Mode

Global configuration

### Usage Guidelines

This command first appeared in Cisco IOS Release 10.0.

Keep the following points in mind when configuring IPX NetBIOS access control:

- Host (node) names are case-sensitive.
- Host and byte access lists can have the same names. They are independent of each other.
- When filtering by node name for IPX NetBIOS, the names in the access lists are compared with the destination name field for IPX NetBIOS "find name" requests.
- When filtering by byte offset, note that these access filters can have a significant impact on the packets' transmission rate across the bridge because each packet must be examined. You should use these access lists only when absolutely necessary.
- If a node name is not found in an access list, the default action is to deny access.

These filters apply only to IPX NetBIOS FindName packets. They have no effect on LLC2 NetBIOS packets.

To delete an IPX NetBIOS access list, specify the minimum number of keywords and arguments needed to delete the proper list. For example, to delete the entire list, use the following command:

**no netbios access-list {host | bytes}** *name*

To delete a single entry from the list, use the following command:

**no netbios access-list host** *name* **{permit | deny}** *string*

## Examples

The following example defines the IPX NetBIOS access list *engineering*:

```
netbios access-list host engineering permit eng-ws1 eng-ws2 eng-ws3
```

The following example removes a single entry from the *engineering* access list:

```
netbios access-list host engineering deny eng-ws3
```

The following example removes the entire *engineering* NetBIOS access list:

```
no netbios access-list host engineering
```

## Related Commands

Search online to find documentation for related commands.

**ipx netbios input-access-filter**
**ipx netbios output-access-filter**
**show ipx interface**

## NETWORK

To enable Enhanced IGRP, use the **network** router configuration command. To disable Enhanced IGRP, use the **no** form of this command.

> **network** {*network-number* | **all**}
> **no network** {*network-number* | **all**}

| Syntax | Description |
|--------|-------------|
| *network-number* | IPX network number. |
| **all** | Enables the routing protocol for all IPX networks configured on the router. |

## Default

Disabled

## Command Mode

Router configuration

## Usage Guidelines

This command first appeared in Cisco IOS Release 10.3.

Use the **network** command to enable the routing protocol specified in the **ipx router** command on each network.

*Example*

The following commands disable RIP on network 10 and enable Enhanced IGRP on networks 10 and 20:

```
ipx router rip
 no network 10

ipx router eigrp 12
 network 10
 network 20
```

*Related Commands*

Search online to find documentation for related commands.

**ipx router**


## PERMIT (EXTENDED)

To set conditions for a named IPX extended access list, use the **permit** access-list configuration command. To remove a permit condition from an access list, use the **no** form of this command.

> **permit** *protocol* [*source-network*][[[.*source-node*] *source-node-mask*] | [.*source-node*]
> *source-network-mask.source-node-mask*]] [*source-socket*] [*destination-network*]
> [[[.*destination-node*] *destination-node-mask*] | [.*destination-node*]
> *destination-network-mask.destination-nodemask*]] [*destination-socket*] [**log**]
> **no permit** *protocol* [*source-network*][[[.*source-node*] *source-node-mask*] | [.*source-node*]
> *source-network-mask.source-node-mask*]] [*source-socket*] [*destination-network*]
> [[[.*destination-node*] *destination-node-mask*] | [.*destination-node*]
> *destination-network-mask.destination-nodemask*]] [*destination-socket*] [**log**]

| Syntax | Description |
|---|---|
| *protocol* | Name or number of an IPX protocol type. This is sometimes referred to as the packet type. You can also use the word **any** to match all protocol types. |
| *source-network* | (Optional) Number of the network from which the packet is being sent. This is an eight-digit hexadecimal number that uniquely identifies a network cable segment. It can be a number in the range 1 to FFFFFFFE. A network number of 0 matches the local network. A network number of -1 matches all networks. You can also use the word **any** to match all networks.<br><br>You do not need to specify leading zeros in the network number; for example, for the network number 000000AA, you can enter AA. |
| .*source-node* | (Optional) Node on *source-network* from which the packet is being sent. This is a 48-bit value represented by a dotted triplet of four-digit hexadecimal numbers (*xxxx.xxxx.xxxx*). |

| Syntax | Description |
|---|---|
| *source-network-mask.* | (Optional) Mask to be applied to *source-network*. This is an eight-digit hexadecimal mask. Place ones in the bit positions you want to mask. |
| | The mask must immediately be followed by a period, which must in turn immediately be followed by *source-node-mask*. |
| *source-node-mask* | (Optional) Mask to be applied to *source-node*. This is a 48-bit value represented as a dotted triplet of four-digit hexadecimal numbers (*xxxx.xxxx.xxxx*). Place ones in the bit positions you want to mask. |
| *source-socket* | Socket name or number (hexadecimal) from which the packet is being sent. You can also use the word **all** to match all sockets. |
| *destination-network* | (Optional) Number of the network to which the packet is being sent. This is an eight-digit hexadecimal number that uniquely identifies a network cable segment. It can be a number in the range 1 to FFFFFFFE. A network number of 0 matches the local network. A network number of -1 matches all networks. You can also use the word **any** to match all networks. |
| | You do not need to specify leading zeros in the network number. For example, for the network number 000000AA, you can enter AA. |
| *.destination-node* | (Optional) Node on *destination-network* to which the packet is being sent. This is a 48-bit value represented by a dotted triplet of four-digit hexadecimal numbers (*xxxx.xxxx.xxxx*). |
| *destination-network-mask.* | (Optional) Mask to be applied to *destination-network*. This is an eight-digit hexadecimal mask. Place ones in the bit positions you want to mask. |
| | The mask must immediately be followed by a period, which must in turn immediately be followed by *destination-node-mask*. |
| *destination-nodemask* | (Optional) Mask to be applied to *destination-node*. This is a 48-bit value represented as a dotted triplet of four-digit hexadecimal numbers (*xxxx.xxxx.xxxx*). Place ones in the bit positions you want to mask. |
| *destination-socket* | (Optional) Socket name or number (hexadecimal) to which the packet is being sent. |
| *log* | (Optional) Logs IPX access control list violations whenever a packet matches a particular access list entry. The information logged includes source address, destination address, source socket, destination socket, protocol type, and action taken (permit/deny). |

*Command Reference*

## Default

There is no specific condition under which a packet passes the named access list.

## Command Mode

Access-list configuration

## Usage Guidelines

This command first appeared in Cisco IOS Release 11.3.

Use this command following the **ipx access-list** command to specify conditions under which a packet passes the named access list.

For additional information on IPX protocol names and numbers, and IPX socket names and numbers, see the **access-list (extended)** command.

## Example

The following example creates an extended access list named *sal* that denies all SPX packets and permits all others:

```
ipx access-list extended sal
  deny spx any all any all log
  permit any
```

## Related Commands

Search online to find documentation for related commands.

**access-list (extended)**
**deny (extended)**
**ipx access-group**
**ipx access-list**
**show ipx access-list**

## PERMIT (NLSP ROUTE AGGREGATION SUMMARIZATION)

To allow explicit route redistribution in a named NLSP route aggregation access list, use the **permit** access-list configuration command. To remove a permit condition, use the **no** form of this command.

> **permit** *network network-mask* [**ticks** *ticks*] [**area-count** *area-count*]
> **no permit** *network network-mask* [**ticks** *ticks*] [**area-count** *area-count*]

| Syntax | Description |
| --- | --- |
| *network* | Network number to summarize. An IPX network number is an eight-digit hexadecimal number that uniquely identifies a network cable segment. It can be a number in the range 1 to FFFFFFFE. A network number of 0 matches the local network. A network number of -1 matches all networks.<br><br>You do not need to specify leading zeros in the network number. For example, for the network number 000000AA, you can enter AA. |

| Syntax | Description |
|---|---|
| *network-mask* | Specifies the portion of the network address that is common to all addresses in the route summary, expressed as an eight-digit hexadecimal number. The high-order bits of *network-mask* must be contiguous 1s, while the low-order bits must be contiguous zeros (0). An arbitrary mix of 1s and 0s is not permitted. |
| **ticks** *ticks* | (Optional) Metric assigned to the route summary. The default is 1 tick. |
| **area-count** *area-count* | (Optional) Maximum number of NLSP areas to which the route summary can be redistributed. The default is 6 areas. |

## Default

No access lists are defined.

## Command Mode

Access-list configuration

## Usage Guidelines

This command first appeared in Cisco IOS Release 11.3.

Use this command following the **ipx access-list** command to specify conditions under which networks that are permitted by the access list entry can be redistributed as explicit networks, without summarization.

For additional information on creating access lists that deny or permit area addresses that summarize routes, see the **access-list (NLSP route aggregation summarization)** command.

## Example

The following example allows networks 12345600 and 12345601 to be redistributed explicitly. Other routes in the range 12345600 to 123456FF are summarized into a single aggregated route. All other routes will be redistributed as explicit routes.

```
ipx access-list summary finance
  permit 12345600
  permit 12345601
  deny 12345600 ffffff00
  permit -1
```

## Related Commands

Search online to find documentation for related commands.

**access-list (NLSP route aggregation summarization)**
**deny (NLSP route aggregation summarization)**
**ipx access-group**
**ipx access-list**
**show ipx access-list**

## PERMIT (SAP FILTERING)

To set conditions for a named IPX SAP filtering access list, use the **permit** access-list configuration command. To remove a permit condition from an access list, use the **no** form of this command.

**permit** *network*[.*node*] [*network-mask.node-mask*] [*service-type* [*server-name*]]
**no permit** *network*[.*node*] [*network-mask.node-mask*] [*service-type* [*server-name*]]

| Syntax | Description |
| --- | --- |
| *network* | Network number. This is an eight-digit hexadecimal number that uniquely identifies a network cable segment. It can be a number in the range 1 to FFFFFFFE. A network number of 0 matches the local network. A network number of –1 matches all networks. |
| | You do not need to specify leading zeros in the network number. For example, for the network number 000000AA, you can enter AA. |
| *.node* | (Optional) Node on *network*. This is a 48-bit value represented by a dotted triplet of four-digit hexadecimal numbers (*xxxx.xxxx.xxxx*). |
| *network-mask.node-mask* | (Optional) Mask to be applied to *network* and *node*. Place ones in the bit positions to be masked. |
| *service-type* | (Optional) Service type on which to filter. This is a hexadecimal number. A value of 0 means all services. |
| *server-name* | (Optional) Name of the server providing the specified service type. This can be any contiguous string of printable ASCII characters. Use double quotation marks (" ") to enclose strings containing embedded spaces. You can use an asterisk (*) at the end of the name as a wildcard to match one or more trailing characters. |

### Default

No access lists are defined.

### Command Mode

Access-list configuration

### Usage Guidelines

This command first appeared in Cisco IOS Release 11.3.

Use this command following the **ipx access-list** command to specify conditions under which a packet passes the named access list.

For additional information on IPX SAP service types, see the **access-list (SAP filtering)** command.

## Example

The following example creates a SAP access list named *MyServer* that allows only MyServer to be sent in SAP advertisements:

```
ipx access-list sap MyServer
 permit 1234 4 MyServer
```

## Related Commands

Search online to find documentation for related commands.

**access-list (SAP filtering)**
**deny (SAP filtering)**
**ipx access-group**
**ipx access-list**
**show ipx access-list**

## PERMIT (STANDARD)

To set conditions for a named IPX access list, use the **permit** access-list configuration command. To remove a permit condition from an access list, use the **no** form of this command.

> **permit** *source-network*[.*source-node* [*source-node-mask*]]
> [*destination-network*[.*destination-node* [*destination-node-mask*]]]
> **no permit** *source-network*[.*source-node* [*source-node-mask*]]
> [*destination-network*[.*destination-node* [*destination-node-mask*]]]

| Syntax | Description |
|---|---|
| *source-network* | Number of the network from which the packet is being sent. This is an eight-digit hexadecimal number that uniquely identifies a network cable segment. It can be a number in the range 1 to FFFFFFFE. A network number of 0 matches the local network. A network number of -1 matches all networks. |
| | You do not need to specify leading zeros in the network number. For example, for the network number 000000AA, you can enter AA. |
| *.source-node* | (Optional) Node on *source-network* from which the packet is being sent. This is a 48-bit value represented by a dotted triplet of four-digit hexadecimal numbers (*xxxx.xxxx.xxxx*). |
| *source-node-mask* | (Optional) Mask to be applied to *source-node*. This is a 48-bit value represented as a dotted triplet of four-digit hexadecimal numbers (*xxxx.xxxx.xxxx*). Place ones in the bit positions you want to mask. |

| Syntax | Description |
|--------|-------------|
| *destination-network* | (Optional) Number of the network to which the packet is being sent. This is an eight-digit hexadecimal number that uniquely identifies a network cable segment. It can be a number in the range 1 to FFFFFFFE. A network number of 0 matches the local network. A network number of -1 matches all networks. |
| | You do not need to specify leading zeros in the network number. For example, for the network number 000000AA, you can enter AA. |
| *.destination-node* | (Optional) Node on *destination-network* to which the packet is being sent. This is a 48-bit value represented by a dotted triplet of four-digit hexadecimal numbers (*xxxx.xxxx.xxxx*). |
| *destination-node-mask* | (Optional) Mask to be applied to *destination-node*. This is a 48-bit value represented as a dotted triplet of four-digit hexadecimal numbers (*xxxx.xxxx.xxxx*). Place ones in the bit positions you want to mask. |

## Default

No access lists are defined.

## Command Mode

Access-list configuration

## Usage Guidelines

This command first appeared in Cisco IOS Release 11.3.

Use this command following the **ipx access-list** command to specify conditions under which a packet passes the named access list.

For additional information on creating IPX access lists, see the **access-list (standard)** command.

## Example

The following example creates a standard access list named *fred*. It permits communication with only IPX network number 5678.

```
ipx access-list standard fred
 permit 5678 any
 deny any
```

### Related Commands

Search online to find documentation for related commands.

access-list (standard)
deny (standard)
ipx access-group
ipx access-list
show ipx access-list

## PING (PRIVILEGED)

To check host reachability and network connectivity, use the **ping** privileged EXEC command.

ping [ipx] [*network.node*]

| Syntax | Description |
|---|---|
| ipx | (Optional) Specifies the IPX protocol. |
| *network.node* | (Optional) Address of the system to ping. |

### Command Mode

Privileged EXEC

### Usage Guidelines

This command first appeared in Cisco IOS Release 10.0.

The privileged **ping** (IPX echo) command provides a complete **ping** facility for users who have system privileges.

The **ping** command with **ipx ping-default** set to Cisco works only on Cisco routers running Software Release 8.2 or later.

Novell IPX devices that support the echo function defined in version 1.0 of the NLSP specification will respond to this command if you answer **Y** to the prompt Novell Standard Echo that is displayed when you use the privileged ping command or if **ipx ping-default** is set to Novell. If you answer **N** to this prompt, Novell IPX devices will not respond.

To abort a **ping** session, type the escape sequence. By default, this is Ctrl-^ X. You enter this by simultaneously pressing the Ctrl, Shift, and 6 keys, letting go, and then pressing the X key.

Table 5–4 describes the test characters displayed in **ping** responses.

**Table 5–4** *Ping Test Characters*

| Character | Meaning |
|-----------|---------|
| ! | Each exclamation point indicates the receipt of a reply from the target address. |
| . | Each period indicates the network server timed out while waiting for a reply from the target address. |
| U | A destination unreachable error PDU was received. |
| C | A congestion experienced packet was received. |
| I | User interrupted the test. |
| ? | Unknown packet type. |
| & | Packet lifetime exceeded. |

## Sample Display

The following sample display shows input to and output from the **ping** command:

```
Router# ping

Protocol [ip]: ipx
Target IPX address: 211.0000.0c01.f4cf
Repeat count [5]:
Datagram size [100]:
Timeout in seconds [2]:
Verbose [n]:
Novell Standard Echo [n]:
Type escape sequence to abort.
Sending 5 100-byte IPX echoes to 211.0000.0c01.f4cf, timeout is 2 seconds.
!!!!!
Success rate is 100 percent (0/5)
```

## Related Commands

Search online to find documentation for related commands.

**ipx ping-default**
**ping (user)**

## PING (USER)

To check host reachability and network connectivity, use the **ping** user EXEC command.

> **ping ipx** {*host* | *address*}

| *Syntax* | *Description* |
|----------|---------------|
| **ipx** | Specifies the IPX protocol. |
| *host* | Host name of system to ping. |
| *address* | Address of system to ping. |

## Command Mode

User EXEC

## Usage Guidelines

This command first appeared in Cisco IOS Release 10.0.

The user-level **ping** (packet internet groper function) command provides a basic ping facility for users who do not have system privileges. This command is equivalent to the nonverbose form of the privileged **ping** command. It sends five 100-byte ping packets.

The **ping** command with **ipx ping-default** set to Cisco works only on Cisco routers running Cisco IOS software Release 8.2 or later. Novell IPX devices will not respond to this command.

If the system cannot map an address for a host name, it will return an "%Unrecognized host or address" error message.

To abort a **ping** session, type the escape sequence. By default, this is Ctrl-^ X. You enter this by simultaneously pressing the Ctrl, Shift, and 6 keys, letting go, and then pressing the X key.

Table 5–4 in the **ping (privileged)** command section describes the test characters displayed in **ping** responses.

## Sample Display

The following sample display shows input to and output from the user **ping** command:

```
Router> ping ipx 211.0000.0c01.f4cf

Type escape sequence to abort.
Sending 5, 100-byte Novell Echoes to 211.0000.0c01.f4cf, timeout is 2 seconds:
.....
Success rate is 0 percent (0/5)
```

## Related Commands

Search online to find documentation for related commands.

**ipx ping-default**
**ping (privileged)**

*Command Reference*

## PRC-INTERVAL

To control the holddown period between partial route calculations, use the **prc-interval** router configuration command. To restore the default interval, use the **no** form of this command.

> **prc-interval** *seconds*
> **no prc-interval** *seconds*

*Syntax*

*Description*

*seconds*

Minimum amount of time between partial route calculations, in seconds. It can be a number in the range 1 to 120. The default is 5 seconds.

### Default

5 seconds

### Command Mode

Router configuration

### Usage Guidelines

This command first appeared in Cisco IOS Release 10.3.

The **prc-interval** command controls how often the Cisco IOS software can perform a partial route (PRC) calculation. The PRC calculation is processor-intensive. Therefore, it may be useful to limit how often this is done, especially on slower router models. Increasing the PRC interval reduces the processor load of the router, but potentially slows down the rate of convergence.

This command is analogous to the **spf-interval** command, which controls the holddown period between shortest path first calculations.

### Example

The following example sets the PRC calculation interval to 20 seconds:

```
prc-interval 20
```

### Related Commands

Search online to find documentation for related commands.

**ipx router nlsp**
**spf-interval**

## REDISTRIBUTE

To redistribute from one routing domain into another, and vice versa, use one of the following **redistribute** router configuration commands. To disable this feature, use the **no** form of the commands.

For Enhanced IGRP or RIP environments, use the following command to redistribute from one routing domain into another, and vice versa:

> **redistribute** {**connected** | **eigrp** *autonomous-system-number* | **floating-static** | **nlsp** [*tag*] | **rip static**}
>
> **no redistribute** {**connected** | **eigrp** *autonomous-system-number* | **floating-static** | **nlsp** [*tag*] | **rip** | **static**}

For NLSP environments, use the following command to redistribute from one routing domain into another, and vice versa:

> **redistribute** {**eigrp** *autonomous-system-number* | **nlsp** [*tag*] | **rip** | **static**}
> [**access-list** {*access-list-number* | *name*}]
>
> **no redistribute** {**eigrp** *autonomous-system-number* | **nlsp** [*tag*] | **rip** | **static**}
> [**access-list** {*access-list-number* | *name*}]

| Syntax | Description |
|---|---|
| connected | Specifies connected routes. |
| eigrp *autonomous-system-number* | Specifies the Enhanced IGRP protocol and the Enhanced IGRP autonomous system number. It can be a number from 1 to 65535. |
| floating-static | Specifies a floating static route. This is a static route that can be overridden by a dynamically learned route. |
| nlsp [*tag*] | Specifies the NLSP protocol and, optionally, names the NLSP process (*tag*). The *tag* can be any combination of printable characters. |
| rip | Specifies the RIP protocol. You can configure only one RIP process on the router. Thus, you cannot redistribute RIP into RIP. |
| static | Specifies static routes. |
| access-list *access-list-number* | Specifies an NLSP route summary access list. The *access-list-number* is a number from 1200 to 1299. |
| access-list *name* | Name of the access list. Names cannot contain a space or quotation mark, and must begin with an alphabetic character to prevent ambiguity with numbered access lists. |

### Defaults

Redistribution is enabled between all routing domains except between separate Enhanced IGRP processes.

Redistribution of floating static routes is disabled.

Redistribution between NLSP and Enhanced IGRP is disabled.

## Command Mode

Router configuration

## Usage Guidelines

This command first appeared in Cisco IOS Release 11.1.

Redistribution provides for routing information generated by one protocol to be advertised in another.

The only connected routes affected by this redistribute command are the routes not specified by the **network** command.

If you have enabled floating static routes by specifying the **floating** keyword in the **ipx route** global configuration command and you redistribute floating static routes into a dynamic IPX routing protocol, any nonhierarchical topology causes the floating static destination to be redistributed immediately via a dynamic protocol back to the originating router, causing a routing loop. This occurs because dynamic protocol information overrides floating static routes. For this reason, automatic redistribution of floating static routes is off by default. If you redistribute floating static routes, you should specify filters to eliminate routing loops.

For NLSP environments, you can use the NLSP **redistribute** command to configure IPX route aggregation with customized route summarization. Configure IPX route aggregation with customized route summarization in

- Enhanced IGRP and NLSP version 1.1 environments
- RIP and NLSP version 1.1 environments

— **NOTES** ———————————————————————————————

NLSP version 1.1 routers refer to routers that support the route aggregation feature, while NLSP version 1.0 routers refer to routers that do not.

An NLSP *process* is a router's databases working together to manage route information about an area. NLSP version 1.0 routers are always in the same area. Each router has its own adjacencies, link-state, and forwarding databases. These databases operate collectively as a single *process* to discover, select, and maintain route information about the area. NLSP version 1.1 routers that exist within a single area also use a single process.

NLSP version 1.1 routers that interconnect multiple areas use multiple processes to discover, select, and maintain route information about the areas they interconnect. These routers manage an adjacencies, link-state, and area address database for each area to which they attach. Collectively, these databases are still referred to as a *process*. The forwarding database is shared among processes within a router. The sharing of entries in the forwarding database is automatic when all processes interconnect NLSP version 1.1 areas.

### Examples

In the following example, RIP routing information is not redistributed:

```
ipx router eigrp 222
  no redistribute rip
```

In the following example, Enhanced IGRP routes from autonomous system 100 are redistributed into Enhanced IGRP autonomous system 300:

```
ipx router eigrp 300
  redistribute eigrp 100
```

In the following example, Enhanced IGRP routes from autonomous system 300 are redistributed into the NLSP process *area3*:

```
ipx router nlsp area3
  redistribute eigrp 300
```

The following example enables route summarization and redistributes routes learned from one NLSP instance to another. Any routes learned via NLSP *a1* that are subsumed by route summary *aaaa0000 ffff0000* are not redistributed into NLSP *a2*. Instead, an aggregated route is generated. Likewise, any routes learned via NLSP *a2* that are subsumed by route summary *bbbb0000 ffff0000* are not redistributed into NLSP *a1*—an aggregated route is generated.

```
ipx routing
ipx internal-network 2000
!
interface ethernet 1
 ipx network 1001
 ipx nlsp a1 enable
!
interface ethernet 2
 ipx network 2001
 ipx nlsp a2 enable
!
access-list 1200 deny aaaa0000 ffff0000
access-list 1200 permit -1
access-list 1201 deny bbbb0000 ffff0000
access-list 1201 permit -1
!
ipx router nlsp a1
 area-address 1000 fffff000
 route-aggregation
 redistribute nlsp a2 access-list 1201
!
ipx router nlsp a2
 area-address 2000 fffff000
 route-aggregation
 redistribute nlsp a1 access-list 1200
```

*Related Commands*

Search online to find documentation for related commands.

**access-list (NLSP route aggregation summarization)**
**deny (NLSP route aggregation summarization)**
**ipx access-list**
**ipx router**
**permit (NLSP route aggregation summarization)**

## ROUTE-AGGREGATION

To enable the generation of aggregated routes in an NLSP area, use the **route-aggregation** router configuration command. To disable generation, use the **no** form of this command.

    **route-aggregation**
    **no route-aggregation**

*Syntax      Description*

This command has no arguments or keywords.

*Default*

Route summarization is disabled by default.

*Command Mode*

Router configuration

*Usage Guidelines*

This command first appeared in Cisco IOS Release 11.1.

When route summarization is disabled, all routes redistributed into an NLSP area will be explicit routes.

When route summarization is enabled, the router uses the access list associated with the **redistribute** command (if one exists) for the routing process associated with each route as a template for route summarization. Explicit routes that match a range denied by the access list trigger generation of an aggregated route instead. Routes permitted by the access list are redistributed as explicit routes.

If no access list exists, the router instead uses the area address (if one exists) of the routing process associated with each route as a template for route summarization. Explicit routes that match the area address trigger the generation of an aggregated route instead.

---

**NOTES**

Because an Enhanced IGRP or RIP routing process cannot have an area address, it is not possible to generate aggregated routes without the use of an access list.

---

### Example

The following example enables route summarization between two NLSP areas. Route summarization is based on the area addresses configured for each area.

```
ipx routing
ipx internal-network 123
!
interface ethernet 1
 ipx nlsp area1 enable
!
interface ethernet 2
 ipx nlsp area2 enable
!
ipx router nlsp area1
 area-address 1000 fffff000
 route-aggregation
!
ipx router nlsp area2
 area-address 2000 fffff000
 route-aggregation
```

### Related Commands

Search online to find documentation for related commands.

**ipx router nlsp**
**redistribute**

### SHOW IPX ACCESS-LIST

To display the contents of all current IPX access lists, use the **show ipx access-list** EXEC command.

**show ipx access-list** [*access-list-number* | *name*]

### Syntax Description

*access-list-number*   (Optional) Number of the IPX access list to display. This is a number from 800 to 899, 900 to 999, 1000 to 1099, or 1200 to 1299.

*name*   (Optional) Name of the IPX access list to display.

### Default

Displays all standard, extended, SAP, and NLSP route aggregation summary IPX access lists.

*Command Reference*

*Command Mode*

EXEC

*Usage Guidelines*

This command first appeared in Cisco IOS Release 11.3.

The **show ipx access-list** command provides output identical to the **show access-lists** command, except that it is IPX specific and allows you to specify a particular access list.

*Sample Displays*

The following is sample output from the **show ipx access-list** command when all access lists are requested:

```
Router# show ipx access-list
IPX extended access list 900
 deny any 1
IPX sap access list London
 deny FFFFFFFF 107
 deny FFFFFFFF 301C
 permit FFFFFFFF 0
```

The following is sample output from the **show ipx access-list** command when the name of a specific access list is requested:

```
Router# show ipx access-list London
IPX sap access list London
 deny FFFFFFFF 107
 deny FFFFFFFF 301C
 permit FFFFFFFF 0
```

## SHOW IPX ACCOUNTING

To display the active or checkpoint accounting database, use the **show ipx accounting** EXEC command.

   **show ipx accounting [checkpoint]**

| Syntax | Description |
|---|---|
| checkpoint | (Optional) Displays entries in the checkpoint database. |

*Command Mode*

EXEC

*Usage Guidelines*

This command first appeared in Cisco IOS Release 10.0.

### Sample Display

The following is sample output from the **show ipx accounting** command:

```
Router# show ipx accounting

Source                   Destination              Packets      Bytes
0000C003.0000.0c05.6030 0000C003.0260.8c9b.4e33       72       2880
0000C001.0260.8c8d.da75 0000C003.0260.8c9b.4e33       14        624
0000C003.0260.8c9b.4e33 0000C001.0260.8c8d.da75       62       3110
0000C001.0260.8c8d.e7c6 0000C003.0260.8c9b.4e33       20       1470
0000C003.0260.8c9b.4e33 0000C001.0260.8c8d.e7c6       20       1470

Accounting data age is   6
```

Table 5–5 describes the fields shown in the display.

**Table 5–5**  *Show IPX Accounting Field Descriptions*

| Field | Description |
|---|---|
| Source | Source address of the packet. |
| Destination | Destination address of the packet. |
| Packets | Number of packets transmitted from the source address to the destination address. |
| Bytes | Number of bytes transmitted from the source address to the destination address. |
| Accounting data age is ... | Time since the accounting database has been cleared. It can be in one of the following formats: *mm*, *hh:mm*, *dd:hh*, and *ww dd*, where *m* is minutes, *h* is hours, *d* is days, and *w* is weeks. |

### Related Commands

Search online to find documentation for related commands.

**clear ipx accounting**
**ipx accounting**
**ipx accounting-list**
**ipx accounting-threshold**
**ipx accounting-transits**

## SHOW IPX CACHE

To display the contents of the IPX fast-switching cache, use the **show ipx cache** EXEC command.

    **show ipx cache**

### Syntax    Description

This command has no arguments or keywords.

## Command Mode

EXEC

## Usage Guidelines

This command first appeared in Cisco IOS Release 10.0.

## Sample Display

The following is sample output from the **show ipx cache** command:

```
Router# show ipx cache

Novell routing cache version is 9
Destination          Interface            MAC Header
*1006A               Ethernet 0           00000C0062E600000C003EB0064
*14BB                Ethernet 1           00000C003E2A00000C003EB0064
```

Table 5–6 describes the fields shown in the display.

**Table 5–6**   *Show IPX Cache Field Descriptions*

| Field | Description |
|---|---|
| Novell routing cache version is ... | Number identifying the version of the fast-switching cache table. It increments each time the table changes. |
| Destination | Destination network for this packet. Valid entries are marked by an asterisk (*). |
| Interface | Route interface through which this packet is transmitted. |
| MAC Header | Contents of this packet's MAC header. |

## Related Commands

Search online to find documentation for related commands.

**clear ipx cache**
**ipx route-cache**

## SHOW IPX EIGRP INTERFACES

To display information about interfaces configured for Enhanced IGRP, use the **show ipx eigrp interfaces** EXEC command.

> **show ipx eigrp interfaces** [*type number*] [*as-number*]

| Syntax | Description |
|---|---|
| *type* | (Optional) Interface type. |
| *number* | (Optional) Interface number. |
| *as-number* | (Optional) Autonomous system number. |

## Command Mode

EXEC

## Usage Guidelines

This command first appeared in Cisco IOS Release 11.2.

Use the **show ipx eigrp interfaces** command to determine on which interfaces Enhanced IGRP is active and to find out information about Enhanced IGRP relating to those interfaces.

If an interface is specified, only that interface is displayed. Otherwise, all interfaces on which Enhanced IGRP is running are displayed.

If an autonomous system is specified, only the routing process for the specified autonomous system is displayed. Otherwise, all Enhanced IGRP processes are displayed.

## Sample Display

The following is sample output from the **show ipx eigrp interfaces** command:

```
Router> show ipx eigrp interfaces
IPX EIGRP interfaces for process 109

                   Xmit Queue    Mean   Pacing Time   Multicast   Pending
Interface   Peers  Un/Reliable   SRTT   Un/Reliable   Flow Timer  Routes
Di0         0      0/0           0      11/434        0           0
Et0         1      0/0           337    0/10          0           0
SE0:1.16    1      0/0           10     1/63          103         0
Tu0         1      0/0           330    0/16          0           0
```

Table 5–7 describes the fields shown in the display.

**Table 5–7**  *Show IPX EIGRP Interfaces Field Descriptions*

| Field | Description |
|---|---|
| process 109 | Autonomous system number of the process. |
| Interface | Interface name. |
| Peers | Number of neighbors on the interface. |
| Xmit Queue | Count of unreliable and reliable packets queued for transmission. |
| Mean SRTT | Average round-trip time for all neighbors on the interface. |

**Table 5–7**   *Show IPX EIGRP Interfaces Field Descriptions, Continued*

| Field | Description |
|---|---|
| Pacing Time | Number of milliseconds to wait after transmitting unreliable and reliable packets. |
| Multicast Flow Timer | Number of milliseconds to wait for acknowledgment of a multicast packet by all neighbors before transmitting the next multicast packet. |
| Pending Routes | Number of routes still to be transmitted on this interface. |

## Related Commands

Search online to find documentation for related commands.

**show ipx eigrp neighbors**

## SHOW IPX EIGRP NEIGHBORS

To display the neighbors discovered by Enhanced IGRP, use the **show ipx eigrp neighbors** EXEC command.

> **show ipx eigrp neighbors** [**servers**] [*autonomous-system-number* | *interface*]

| Syntax | Description |
|---|---|
| **servers** | (Optional) Displays the server list advertised by each neighbor. This is displayed only if the **ipx sap incremental** command is enabled on the interface on which the neighbor resides. |
| *autonomous-system-number* | (Optional) Autonomous system number. It can be a number from 1 to 65535. |
| *interface* | (Optional) Interface type and number. |

## Command Mode

EXEC

## Usage Guidelines

This command first appeared in Cisco IOS Release 10.0.

## Sample Display

The following is sample output from the **show ipx eigrp neighbors** command:

```
Router# show ipx eigrp neighbors

IPX EIGRP Neighbors for process 200
```

```
     H   Address                 Interface      Hold   Uptime    Q    Seq    SRTT   RTO
                                                (secs) (h:m:s)   Cnt  Num    (ms)   (ms)
     6   90.0000.0c02.096e       Tunnel44444    13     0:30:57   0    21     9      20
     5   80.0000.0c02.34f2       Fddi0          12     0:31:17   0    62     14     28
     4   83.5500.2000.a83c       TokenRing2     13     0:32:36   0    626    16     32
     3   98.0000.3040.a6b0       TokenRing1     12     0:32:37   0    43     9      20
     2   80.0000.0c08.cbf9       Fddi0          12     0:32:37   0    624    19     38
     1   85.aa00.0400.153c       Ethernet2      12     0:32:37   0    627    15     30
     0   82.0000.0c03.4d4b       Hssi0          12     0:32:38   0    629    12     24
```

Table 5–8 explains the fields in the display.

**Table 5–8**   *Show IPX Enhanced IGRP Neighbors Field Descriptions*

| Field | Description |
|---|---|
| process 200 | Autonomous system number specified in the **ipx router** configuration command. |
| H | Handle. An arbitrary and unique number inside this router that identifies the neighbor. |
| Address | IPX address of the Enhanced IGRP peer. |
| Interface | Interface on which the router is receiving hello packets from the peer. |
| Hold | Length of time, in seconds, that the Cisco IOS software will wait to hear from the peer before declaring it down. If the peer is using the default hold time, this number will be less than 15. If the peer configures a nondefault hold time, it will be reflected here. |
| Uptime | Elapsed time (in hours, minutes, and seconds) since the local router first heard from this neighbor. |
| Q Cnt | Number of IPX Enhanced IGRP packets (Update, Query, and Reply) that the Cisco IOS software is waiting to send. |
| Seq Num | Sequence number of the last Update, Query, or Reply packet that was received from this neighbor. |
| SRTT | Smooth round-trip time. This is the number of milliseconds it takes for an IPX Enhanced IGRP packet to be sent to this neighbor and for the local router to receive an acknowledgment of that packet. |
| RTO | Retransmission timeout, in milliseconds. This is the amount of time the Cisco IOS software waits before retransmitting a packet from the retransmission queue to a neighbor. |

## SHOW IPX EIGRP TOPOLOGY

To display the Enhanced IGRP topology table, use the **show ipx eigrp topology** EXEC command.

    **show ipx eigrp topology** [*network-number*]

---

*Syntax*

*network-number*

*Description*

(Optional) IPX network number whose topology table entry to display.

## Command Mode

EXEC

## Usage Guidelines

This command first appeared in Cisco IOS Release 10.0.

## Sample Displays

The following is sample output from the **show ipx eigrp topology** command:

```
Router# show ipx eigrp topology

IPX EIGRP Topology Table for process 109
Codes: P - Passive, A - Active, U - Update, Q - Query, R - Reply,
r - Reply status
P 42, 1 successors, FD is 0
     via 160.0000.0c00.8ea9 (345088/319488), Ethernet0
P 160, 1 successor via Connected, Ethernet
   · via 160.0000.0c00.8ea9 (307200/281600), Ethernet0
P 165, 1 successors, FD is 307200
     via Redistributed (287744/0)
     via 160.0000.0c00.8ea9 (313344/287744), Ethernet0
P 164, 1 successors, flags: U, FD is 200
     via 160.0000.0c00.8ea9 (307200/281600), Ethernet1
     via 160.0000.0c01.2b71 (332800/307200), Ethernet1
P A112, 1 successors, FD is 0
     via Connected, Ethernet2
     via 160.0000.0c00.8ea9 (332800/307200), Ethernet0
P AAABBB, 1 successors, FD is 10003
     via Redistributed (287744/0),
     via 160.0000.0c00.8ea9 (313344/287744), Ethernet0
A A112, 0 successors, 1 replies, state: 0, FD is 0
     via 160.0000.0c01.2b71 (307200/281600), Ethernet1
     via 160.0000.0c00.8ea9 (332800/307200), r, Ethernet1
```

Table 5–9 explains the fields in the output.

**Table 5–9** *Show IPX Enhanced IGRP Topology Field Descriptions*

| Field | Description |
|---|---|
| Codes | State of this topology table entry. Passive and Active refer to the Enhanced IGRP state with respect to this destination; Update, Query, and Reply refer to the type of packet that is being sent. |
| P – Passive | No Enhanced IGRP computations are being performed for this destination. |
| A – Active | Enhanced IGRP computations are being performed for this destination. |
| U – Update | Indicates that an update packet was sent to this destination. |
| Q – Query | Indicates that a query packet was sent to this destination. |
| R – Reply | Indicates that a reply packet was sent to this destination. |
| r – Reply status | Flag that is set after the Cisco IOS software has sent a query and is waiting for a reply. |
| 42, 160, and so on | Destination IPX network number. |
| successors | Number of successors. This number corresponds to the number of next hops in the IPX routing table. |
| FD | Feasible distance. This value is used in the feasibility condition check. If the neighbor's reported distance (the metric after the slash) is less than the feasible distance, the feasibility condition is met and that path is a feasible successor. Once the router determines it has a feasible successor, it does not have to send a query for that destination. |
| replies | Number of replies that are still outstanding (have not been received) with respect to this destination. This information appears only when the destination is in Active state. |
| state | Exact Enhanced IGRP state that this destination is in. It can be the number 0, 1, 2, or 3. This information appears only when the destination is Active. |
| via | IPX address of the peer who told the Cisco IOS software about this destination. The first $n$ of these entries, where $n$ is the number of successors, are the current successors. The remaining entries on the list are feasible successors. |
| (345088/319488) | The first number is the Enhanced IGRP metric that represents the cost to the destination. The second number is the Enhanced IGRP metric that this peer advertised. |
| Ethernet0 | Interface from which this information was learned. |

The following is sample output from the **show ipx eigrp topology** command when you specify an IPX network number:

```
Router# show ipx eigrp topology 160

IPX-EIGRP topology entry for 160
State is Passive, Query origin flag is 1, 1 Successor(s)
Routing Descriptor Blocks:
  Next hop is Connected (Ethernet0), from 0.0000.0000.0000
  Composite metric is (0/0), Send flag is 0x0, Route is Internal
  Vector metric:
    Minimum bandwidth is 10000 Kbit
    Total delay is 1000000 nanoseconds
    Reliability is 255/255
    Load is 1/255
    Minimum MTU is 1500
    Hop count is 0
Next hop is 164.0000.0c00.8ea9 (Ethernet1), from 164.0000.0c00.8ea9
  Composite metric is (307200/281600), Send flag is 0x0, Route is External
  This is an ignored route
  Vector metric:
    Minimum bandwidth is 10000 Kbit
    Total delay is 2000000 nanoseconds
    Reliability is 255/255
    Load is 1/255
    Minimum MTU is 1500
    Hop count is 1
  External data:
    Originating router is 0000.0c00.8ea9
    External protocol is RIP, metric is 1, delay 2
    Administrator tag is 0 (0x00000000)
    Flag is 0x00000000
```

Table 5–10 explains the fields in the output

**Table 5–10**  *Show IPX Enhanced IGRP Topology Field Descriptions for a Specific Network*

| Field | Description |
|---|---|
| 160 | IPX network number of the destination. |
| State is ... | State of this entry. It can be either Passive or Active. Passive means that no Enhanced IGRP computations are being performed for this destination, and Active means that they are being performed. |
| Query origin flag | Exact Enhanced IGRP state that this destination is in. It can be the number 0, 1, 2, or 3. This information appears only when the destination is Active. |
| Successor(s) | Number of successors. This number corresponds to the number of next hops in the IPX routing table. |

**Table 5–10**  *Show IPX Enhanced IGRP Topology Field Descriptions for a Specific Network, Continued*

| Field | Description |
|-------|-------------|
| Next hop is ... | Indicates how this destination was learned. It can be one of the following:<br><br>• Connected—The destination is on a network directly connected to this router.<br><br>• Redistributed—The destination was learned via RIP or another Enhanced IGRP process.<br><br>• IPX host address—The destination was learned from that peer via this Enhanced IGRP process. |
| Ethernet0 | Interface from which this information was learned. |
| from | Peer from whom the information was learned. For connected and redistributed routers, this is 0.0000.0000.0000. For information learned via Enhanced IGRP, this is the peer's address. Currently, for information learned via Enhanced IGRP, the peer's IPX address always matches the address in the "Next hop is" field. |
| Composite metric is | Enhanced IGRP composite metric. The first number is this device's metric to the destination, and the second is the peer's metric to the destination. |
| Send flag | Numeric representation of the "flags" field described in Table 5–8. It is 0 when nothing is being sent, 1 when an Update is being sent, 3 when a Query is being sent, and 4 when a Reply is being sent. Currently, 2 is not used. |
| Route is ... | Type of router. It can be either internal or external. Internal routes are those that originated in an Enhanced IGRP autonomous system, and external are routes that did not. Routes learned via RIP are always external. |
| This is an ignored route | Indicates that this path is being ignored because of filtering. |
| Vector metric: | This section describes the components of the Enhanced IGRP metric. |
| Minimum bandwidth | Minimum bandwidth of the network used to reach the next hop. |
| Total delay | Delay time to reach the next hop. |
| Reliability | Reliability value used to reach the next hop. |

**Table 5–10** *Show IPX Enhanced IGRP Topology Field Descriptions for a Specific Network, Continued*

| Field | Description |
|---|---|
| Load | Load value used to reach the next hop. |
| Minimum MTU | Minimum MTU size of the network used to reach the next hop. |
| Hop count | Number of hops to the next hop. |
| External data: | This section describes the original protocol from which this route was redistributed. It appears only for external routes. |
| Originating router | Network address of the router that first distributed this route into Enhanced IGRP. |
| External protocol..metric..delay | External protocol from which this route was learned. The metric will match the external hop count displayed by the **show ipx route** command for this destination. The delay is the external delay. |
| Administrator tag | Not currently used. |
| Flag | Not currently used. |

*Related Commands*

Search online to find documentation for related commands.

**show ipx route**

## SHOW IPX INTERFACE

To display the status of the IPX interfaces configured in the Cisco IOS software and the parameters configured on each interface, use the **show ipx interface** EXEC command.

       **show ipx interface** [*type number*]

| *Syntax* | *Description* |
|---|---|
| *type* | (Optional) Interface type. It can be one of the following types: asynchronous, dialer, Ethernet (IEEE 802.3), FDDI, loopback, null, serial, Token Ring, or tunnel. |
| *number* | (Optional) Interface number. |

*Command Mode*

EXEC

## Usage Guidelines

This command first appeared in Cisco IOS Release 10.0.

## Sample Displays

The following is sample output from the **show ipx interface** command:

```
Router# show ipx interface ethernet 1

Ethernet1 is up, line protocol is up
  IPX address is C03.0000.0c05.6030, NOVELL-ETHER [up] line-up, RIPPQ: 0, SAPPQ : 0
  Delay of this Novell network, in ticks is 1
  IPXWAN processing not enabled on this interface.
  IPX SAP update interval is 1 minute(s)
  IPX type 20 propagation packet forwarding is disabled
  Outgoing access list is not set
  IPX Helper access list is not set
  SAP Input filter list is not set
  SAP Output filter list is not set
  SAP Router filter list is not set
  SAP GNS output filter list is not set
  Input filter list is not set
  Output filter list is not set
  Router filter list is not set
  Netbios Input host access list is not set
  Netbios Input bytes access list is not set
  Netbios Output host access list is not set
  Netbios Output bytes access list is not set
  Update time is 60 seconds
  IPX accounting is enabled
  IPX fast switching is configured (enabled)
  IPX SSE switching is disabled
```

The following is sample output from the **show ipx interface** command when NLSP is enabled:

```
Router# show ipx interface ethernet 1

Ethernet0 is up, line protocol is up
  IPX address is E001.0000.0c02.8cf9, SAP [up] line-up, RIPPQ: 0, SAPPQ : 0
  Delay of this IPX network, in ticks is 1 throughput 0 link delay 0
  IPXWAN processing not enabled on this interface.
  IPX SAP update interval is 1 minute(s)
  IPX type 20 propagation packet forwarding is disabled
  Outgoing access list is not set
  IPX Helper access list is not set
  SAP Input filter list is not set
  SAP Output filter list is not set
  SAP Router filter list is not set
  SAP GNS output filter list is not set
  Input filter list is not set
  Output filter list is not set
  Router filter list is not set
```

```
Netbios Input host access list is not set
Netbios Input bytes access list is not set
Netbios Output host access list is not set
Netbios Output bytes access list is not set
Update time is 60 seconds
IPX accounting is enabled
IPX fast switching is configured (enabled)
IPX SSE switching is disabled
IPX NLSP is running on primary network E001
RIP compatibility mode is AUTO (OFF)
SAP compatibility mode is AUTO (OFF)
Level 1 Hello interval 20 sec
Level 1 Designated Router Hello interval 10 sec
Level 1 CSNP interval 30 sec
Level 1 LSP retransmit interval 5 sec, LSP (pacing) interval 1000 mSec
Level 1 adjacency count is 1
Level 1 circuit ID is 0000.0C02.8CF9.02
```

Table 5–11 describes the fields shown in the display.

**Table 5–11**   *Show IPX Interface Field Descriptions*

| Field | Description |
|---|---|
| Ethernet1 is ..., line protocol is ... | Type of interface and whether it is currently active and inserted into the network (up) or inactive and not inserted (down). |
| IPX address is ... | Network and node address of the local router interface, followed by the type of encapsulation configured on the interface and the interface's status. Refer to the **ipx network** command for a list of possible values. |
| NOVELL-ETHER | Type of encapsulation being used on the interface, if any. |
| [up] line-up | Indicates whether IPX routing is enabled or disabled on the interface. The "line-up" indicates that IPX routing has been enabled with the **ipx routing** command. The "line-down" indicates that it is not enabled. The word in square brackets provides more detail about the status of IPX routing when it is in the process of being enabled or disabled. |
| RIPPQ | Number of packets in the RIP queue. |
| SAPPQ | Number of packets in the SAP queue. |

**Table 5–11** *Show IPX Interface Field Descriptions, Continued*

| Field | Description |
|-------|-------------|
| Secondary address is ... | Address of a secondary network configured on this interface, if any, followed by the type of encapsulation configured on the interface and the interface's status. Refer to the **ipx routing** command for a list of possible values. This line is displayed only if you have configured a secondary address with the **ipx routing** command. |
| Delay of this IPX network, in ticks, ... | Value of the ticks field (configured with the **ipx delay** command). |
| throughput | Throughput of the interface (configured with the **ipx spx-idle-time** interface configuration command). |
| link delay | Link delay of the interface (configured with the **ipx link-delay** interface configuration command). |
| IPXWAN processing... | Indicates whether IPXWAN processing has been enabled on this interface with the **ipx ipxwan** command. |
| IPX SAP update interval | Indicates the frequency of outgoing SAP updates (configured with the **ipx update interval** command). |
| IPX type 20 propagation packet forwarding... | Indicates whether forwarding of IPX type 20 propagation packets (used by NetBIOS) is enabled or disabled on this interface, as configured with the **ipx type-20-propagation** command. |
| Outgoing access list | Indicates whether an access list has been enabled with the **ipx access-group** command. |
| IPX Helper access list | Number of the broadcast helper list applied to the interface with the **ipx helper-list** command. |
| SAP Input filter list | Number of the input SAP filter applied to the interface with the **ipx input-sap-filter** command. |
| SAP Output filter list | Number of the output SAP filter applied to the interface with the **ipx output-sap-filter** command. |
| SAP Router filter list | Number of the router SAP filter applied to the interface with the **ipx router-sap-filter** command. |
| SAP GNS output filter list | Number of the Get Nearest Server (GNS) response filter applied to the interface with the **ipx output-gns-filter** command. |

**Table 5–11**  *Show IPX Interface Field Descriptions, Continued*

| Field | Description |
|---|---|
| Input filter list | Number of the input filter applied to the interface with the **ipx input-network-filter** command. |
| Output filter list | Number of the output filter applied to the interface with the **ipx output-network-filter** command. |
| Router filter list | Number of the router entry filter applied to the interface with the **ipx router-filter** command. |
| Netbios Input host access list | Name of the IPX NetBIOS input host filter applied to the interface with the **ipx netbios input-access-filter host** command. |
| Netbios Input bytes access list | Name of the IPX NetBIOS input bytes filter applied to the interface with the **ipx netbios input-access-filter bytes** command. |
| Netbios Output host access list | Name of the IPX NetBIOS output host filter applied to the interface with the **ipx netbios input-access-filter host** command. |
| Netbios Output bytes access list | Name of the IPX NetBIOS output bytes filter applied to the interface with the **ipx netbios input-access-filter bytes** command. |
| Update time | How often the Cisco IOS software sends RIP updates, as configured with the **ipx update sap-after-rip** command. |
| Watchdog spoofing ... | Indicates whether watchdog spoofing is enabled or disabled for this interface, as configured with the **ipx watchdog-spoof** command. This information is displayed only on serial interfaces. |
| IPX accounting | Indicates whether IPX accounting has been enabled with the **ipx accounting** command. |
| IPX fast switching IPX autonomous switching | Indicates whether IPX fast switching is enabled (default) or disabled for this interface, as configured with **ipx route-cache** command. (If IPX autonomous switching is enabled, it is configured with the **ipx route-cache cbus** command.) |
| IPX SSE switching | Indicates whether IPX SSE switching is enabled for this interface, as configured with the **ipx route-cache sse** command. |

**Table 5–11** *Show IPX Interface Field Descriptions, Continued*

| Field | Description |
|---|---|
| IPX NLSP is running on primary network E001 | Indicates that NLSP is running and the number of the primary IPX network on which it is running. |
| RIP compatibility mode | State of RIP compatibility (configured by the **ipx nlsp rip** interface configuration command). |
| SAP compatibility mode | State of SAP compatibility (configured by the **ipx nlsp sap** interface configuration command). |
| Level 1 Hello interval | Interval between transmission of hello packets for nondesignated routers (configured by the **ipx nlsp hello-interval** interface configuration command). |
| Level 1 Designated Router Hello interval | Interval between transmission of hello packets for designated routers (configured by the **ipx nlsp hello-interval** interface configuration command). |
| Level 1 CSNP interval | CSNP interval (as configured by the **ipx nlsp csnp-interval** interface configuration command). |
| Level 1 LSP retransmit interval | LSP retransmission interval (as configured by the **ipx nlsp retransmit-interval** interface configuration command). |
| LSP (pacing) interval | LSP transmission interval (as configured by the **ipx nlsp lsp-interval** interface configuration command). |
| Level 1 adjacency count | Number of Level 1 adjacencies in the adjacency database. |
| Level 1 circuit ID | System ID and pseudonode number of the designated router. In this example, 0000.0C02.8CF9 is the system ID, and 02 is the pseudonode number. |

*Command Reference*

### Related Commands

Search online to find documentation for related commands.

**access-list (SAP filtering)**
**access-list (standard)**
**ipx accounting**
**ipx delay**
**ipx helper-list**
**ipx input-network-filter**
**ipx input-sap-filter**
**ipx ipxwan**
**ipx netbios input-access-filter**

ipx netbios output-access-filter
ipx network
ipx output-gns-filter
ipx output-network-filter
ipx output-rip-delay
ipx output-sap-filter
ipx route-cache
ipx router-filter
ipx router-sap-filter
ipx routing
ipx update sap-after-rip
ipx watchdog-spoof
netbios access-list

## SHOW IPX NHRP

To display the Next Hop Resolution Protocol (NHRP) cache, use the **show ipx nhrp** EXEC command.

> show ipx nhrp [dynamic | static] [*type number*]

| Syntax | Description |
|---|---|
| **dynamic** | (Optional) Displays only the dynamic (learned) IPX-to-NBMA address cache entries. |
| **static** | (Optional) Displays only the static IPX-to-NBMA address entries in the cache (configured through the **ipx nhrp map** command). |
| *type* | (Optional) Interface type about which to display the NHRP cache. Valid options are **atm**, **serial**, and **tunnel**). |
| *number* | (Optional) Interface number about which to display the NHRP cache. |

### Command Mode

EXEC

### Usage Guidelines

This command first appeared in Cisco IOS Release 11.1.

### Sample Display

The following is sample output from the **show ipx nhrp** command:

```
Router# show ipx nhrp

1.0000.0c35.de01, Serial1 created 0:00:43 expire 1:59:16
  Type: dynamic Flags: authoritative
  NBMA address: c141.0001.0001
```

```
  1.0000.0c35.e605, Serial1 created 0:10:03 expire 1:49:56
    Type: static Flags: authoritative
    NBMA address: c141.0001.0002
  Router#
```

Table 5–12 describes the fields in the display.

**Table 5–12** *Show IP NHRP Field Descriptions*

| Field | Description |
|---|---|
| 1.0000.0c35.de01 | IPX address in the IPX-to-NBMA address cache. |
| Serial1 created 0:00:43 | Interface type and number and how long ago it was created (hours:minutes:seconds). |
| expire 1:59:16 | Time in which the positive and negative authoritative NBMA address will expire (hours:minutes:seconds). This value is based on the **ipx nhrp holdtime** command. |
| Type | Value can be one of the following:<br>• dynamic—NBMA address was obtained from NHRP Request packet.<br>• static—NBMA address was statically configured. |
| Flags | Value can be one of the following:<br>• authoritative—Indicates that the NHRP information was obtained from the Next Hop Server or router that maintains the NBMA-to-IPX address mapping for a particular destination.<br>• implicit—Indicates that the information was learned not from an NHRP request generated from the local router, but from an NHRP packet being forwarded or from an NHRP request being received by the local router.<br>• negative—For negative caching; indicates that the requested NBMA mapping could not be obtained. |
| NBMA address | Nonbroadcast, multiaccess address. The address format is appropriate for the type of network being used (for example, ATM, Ethernet, SMDS, multipoint tunnel). |

*Command Reference*

## Related Commands

Search online to find documentation for related commands.

**ipx nhrp map**

## SHOW IPX NHRP TRAFFIC

To display Next Hop Resolution Protocol (NHRP) traffic statistics, use the **show ipx nhrp traffic** EXEC command.

> **show ipx nhrp traffic**

*Syntax    Description*

This command has no arguments or keywords.

*Command Mode*

EXEC

*Usage Guidelines*

This command first appeared in Cisco IOS Release 11.1.

*Sample Display*

The following is sample output from the **show ipx nhrp traffic** command:

```
Router# show ipx nhrp traffic

Tunnel0
  request packets sent: 2
  request packets received: 4
  reply packets sent: 4
  reply packets received: 2
  register packets sent: 0
  register packets received: 0
  error packets sent: 0
  error packets received: 0
Router#
```

Table 5–13 describes the fields in the display.

**Table 5–13**   *Show IP NHRP Traffic Field Descriptions*

| Field | Description |
|---|---|
| Tunnel 0 | Interface type and number. |
| request packets sent | Number of NHRP Request packets originated from this station. |
| request packets received | Number of NHRP Request packets received by this station. |
| reply packets sent | Number of NHRP Reply packets originated from this station. |
| reply packets received | Number of NHRP Reply packets received by this station. |

**Table 5–13** *Show IP NHRP Traffic Field Descriptions, Continued*

| Field | Description |
|---|---|
| register packets sent | Number of NHRP Register packets originated from this station. Currently, Cisco routers do not send Register packets, so this value is 0. |
| register packets received | Number of NHRP Register packets received by this station. Currently, Cisco routers do not send Register packets, so this value is 0. |
| error packets sent | Number of NHRP Error packets originated by this station. |
| error packets received | Number of NHRP Error packets received by this station. |

## SHOW IPX NLSP DATABASE

To display the entries in the link-state packet (LSP) database, use the **show ipx nlsp database** EXEC command.

  **show ipx nlsp** [*tag*] **database** [*lspid*] [**detail**]

| Syntax | Description |
|---|---|
| *tag* | (Optional) Names the NLSP process. The *tag* can be any combination of printable characters. |
| *lspid* | (Optional) Link-state protocol ID (LSPID). You must specify this in the format *xxxx.xxxx.xxxx.yy-zz*. The components of this argument have the following meaning: |
| | • *xxxx.xxxx.xxxx* is the system identifier. |
| | • *yy* is the pseudo identifier. |
| | • *zz* is the LSP number. |
| **detail** | (Optional) Displays the contents of the LSP database entries. If you omit this keyword, only a summary display is shown. |

*Command Mode*

EXEC

*Usage Guidelines*

This command first appeared in Cisco IOS Release 10.3.

When you specify an NLSP *tag*, the router displays the link-state packet database entries for that NLSP process. An NLSP *process* is a router's databases working together to manage route information about an area. NLSP version 1.0 routers are always in the same area. Each router has its own adjacencies, link-state, and forwarding databases. These databases operate collectively as a single *process* to discover, select, and maintain route information about the area. NLSP version 1.1 routers that exist within a single area also use a single process.

NLSP version 1.1 routers that interconnect multiple areas use multiple processes to discover, select, and maintain route information about the areas they interconnect. These routers manage an adjacencies, link-state, and area address database for each area to which they attach. Collectively, these databases are still referred to as a *process*. The forwarding database is shared among processes within a router. The sharing of entries in the forwarding database is automatic when all processes interconnect NLSP version 1.1 areas.

Configure multiple NLSP processes when a router interconnects multiple NLSP areas.

---

**NOTES** ——————————————————————————————

NLSP version 1.1 routers refer to routers that support the route aggregation feature, while NLSP version 1.0 routers refer to routers that do not.

---

If you omit all options, a summary display is shown.

*Sample Display*

The following is sample output from the **show ipx nlsp database** command:

```
Router# show ipx nlsp database detail

LSPID                  LSP Seq Num  LSP Checksum  LSP Holdtime  ATT/P/OL
0000.0C00.3097.00-00*  0x00000042   0xC512        699           0/0/0
0000.0C00.3097.06-00*  0x00000027   0x0C27        698           0/0/0
0000.0C02.7471.00-00   0x0000003A   0x4A0F        702           0/0/0
0000.0C02.7471.08-00   0x00000027   0x0AF0        702           0/0/0
0000.0C02.7471.0A-00   0x00000027   0xC589        702           0/0/0
0000.0C02.747D.00-00   0x0000002E   0xC489        715           0/0/0
0000.0C02.747D.06-00   0x00000027   0xEEFE        716           0/0/0
0000.0C02.747D.0A-00   0x00000027   0xFE38        716           0/0/0
0000.0C02.74AB.00-00   0x00000035   0xE4AF        1059          0/0/0
0000.0C02.74AB.0A-00   0x00000027   0x34A4        705           0/0/0
0000.0C06.FBEE.00-00   0x00000038   0x3838        1056          0/0/0
0000.0C06.FBEE.0D-00   0x0000002C   0xD248        1056          0/0/0
0000.0C06.FBEE.0E-00   0x0000002D   0x7DD2        1056          0/0/0
0000.0C06.FBEE.17-00   0x00000029   0x32FB        1056          0/0/0

0000.0C00.AECC.00-00*  0x000000B6   0x62A8        7497          0/0/0
   IPX Area Address: 00000000 00000000
   IPX Mgmt Info 87.0000.0000.0001  Ver 1  Name oscar
   Metric: 45 Lnk 0000.0C00.AECC.06  MTU 1500  Dly 8000  Thru 64K    PPP
   Metric: 20 Lnk 0000.0C00.AECC.02  MTU 1500  Dly 1000  Thru 10000K  802.3 Raw
   Metric: 20 Lnk 0000.0C01.EF90.0C  MTU 1500  Dly 1000  Thru 10000K  802.3 Raw
0000.0C00.AECC.02-00*  0x00000002   0xDA74        3118          0/0/0
   IPX Mgmt Info E0.0000.0c00.aecc  Ver 1  Name Ethernet0
   Metric: 0  Lnk 0000.0C00.AECC.00  MTU 0  Dly 0  Thru 0K   802.3 Raw
```

```
0000.0C00.AECC.06-00* 0x00000002   0x5DB9      7494          0/0/0
  IPX Mgmt Info 0.0000.0000.0000  Ver 1  Name Serial0
  Metric: 0  Lnk 0000.0C00.AECC.00  MTU 0  Dly 0  Thru 0K  PPP
  Metric: 1  IPX Ext D001  Ticks 0
  Metric: 1  IPX SVC Second-floor-printer  D001.0000.0000.0001  Sock 1  Type 4
```

Table 5–14 explains the fields in the display.

**Table 5–14** *Show IPX NLSP Database Field Descriptions*

| Field | Description |
|---|---|
| LSPID | System ID (network number), pseudonode circuit identifier, and fragment number. |
| LSP Seq Num | Sequence number of this LSP. |
| LSP Checksum | Checksum of this LSP. |
| LSP Holdtime | Time until this LSP expires, in hours or seconds. |
| ATT/P/OL | Indicates which of three bits are set. A "1" means the bit is set, and a "0" means it is not set.<br>ATT is the L2-attached bit.<br>OL is the overload bit.<br>P is the partition repair bit. This bit is not used in NLSP. |
| IPX Area Address: | Area address of the router advertising the LSP. |
| IPX Mgmt Info | Management information. For nonpseudonode LSPs, the internal network number is advertised in this field. For pseudonode LSPs, the network number of the associated interface is advertised. |
| Ver | NLSP version running on the advertising router. |
| Name | For nonpseudonode LSPs, the name of the router. For pseudonode LSPs, the name (or description, if configured) of the associated interface. |
| Link Information | Information about the link. |
| Metric: | NLSP metric (cost) for the link. Links from a pseudonode to real nodes have a cost of 0 so that this link cost is not counted twice. |
| Lnk | System ID of the adjacent node. |
| MTU | MTU of the link in bytes. For pseudonode LSPs, the value in this field is always 0. |
| Dly | Delay of the link in microseconds. For pseudonode LSPs, the value in this field is always 0. |

**Table 5–14**   *Show IPX NLSP Database Field Descriptions, Continued*

| Field | Description |
|---|---|
| Thru | Throughput of the link in bits per second. For pseudonode LSPs, the value in this field is always 0. |
| 802.3 Raw, Generic LAN | Link media type. |
| External (RIP) Networks | Information about an external (RIP) network. |
| Metric: | Received RIP hop count. |
| IPX Ext | IPX network number. |
| Ticks | Received RIP tick count. |
| SAP Services | Information about SAP services. |
| Metric: | Received SAP hop count. |
| IPX SVC | Name of the IPX service. |
| D001.000.0000.0001 | IPX address of the server advertising this service. |
| Sock | Socket number of the service. |
| Type | Type of service. |

## SHOW IPX NLSP NEIGHBORS

To display NLSP neighbors and their states, use the **show ipx nlsp neighbors** EXEC command.

> **show ipx nlsp** [*tag*] **neighbors** [*interface*] [**detail**]

| Syntax | Description |
|---|---|
| *tag* | (Optional) Names the NLSP process. The *tag* value can be any combination of printable characters. |
| *interface* | (Optional) Interface type and number. |
| **detail** | (Optional) Displays detailed information about the neighbor. If you omit this keyword, only a summary display is shown. |

### Command Mode

EXEC

### Usage Guidelines

This command first appeared in Cisco IOS Release 10.3.

When you specify an NLSP *tag* value, the router displays the NLSP neighbors for that NLSP process. An NLSP process is a router's databases working together to manage route information about an area. NLSP version 1.0 routers must be in a single area. Each router has its own adjacencies, link-state, and forwarding databases. These databases operate collectively as a single process to discover, select, and maintain route information about the area. NLSP version 1.1 routers that exist within a single area also use a single process.

NLSP version 1.1 routers that interconnect multiple areas use multiple processes to discover, select, and maintain route information about the areas they interconnect. These routers manage adjacencies, link-state, and area address databases for each area to which they attach. Collectively, these databases are still referred to as a process. The forwarding database is shared among processes within a router. The sharing of entries in the forwarding database is automatic when all processes interconnect NLSP version 1.1 areas.

You must configure multiple NLSP processes when a router interconnects multiple NLSP areas.

Command Reference

---

**NOTES**

NLSP version 1.1 routers refer to routers that support the route aggregation feature, while NLSP version 1.0 routers refer to routers that do not.

---

If you omit the keyword **detail**, a summary display is shown.

### Sample Displays

The following command output for the **show ipx nlsp neighbors** shows a summary display of three adjacencies on two circuits:

```
Router# show ipx nlsp neighbors

System Id   Interface   State   Holdtime   Priority   Cir   Adj   Circuit Id
dtp-37      Et1.2       Up      21         64         mc    mc    dtp-37.03
dtp-37      Et1.1       Up      58         44         bc    mc    dtp-17.02
dtp-17      ET1.1       Up      27         64         bc    bc    dtp-17.02
```

This display indicates the following information about the first circuit (Circuit Id = dtp-37.03):

- Multicast addressing is in use (Cir = mc).
- The neighbor supports multicast addressing (Adj = mc).

This display indicates the following information about the second circuit (Circuit Id = dtp-17.02):

- The broadcast address is in use (Cir = bc).
- The first neighbor (System Id = dtp-37) supports multicast addressing (Adj = mc).
- The second neighbor (System Id = dtp-17) does not support multicast addressing (Adj = bc). This adjacency explains why the broadcast address is in use on the second circuit.

Table 5–19 explains the fields in the display.

The following is sample output from the **show ipx nlsp neighbors detail** command:

```
Router# show ipx nlsp neighbors detail

System Id       Interface State  Holdtime  Priority  Cir  Adj  Circuit Id
0000.0C01.EF90  Ethernet1 Up     25        64        mc   mc   0000.0C01.EF90.0C
   IPX Address: E1.0000.0c01.ef91
   IPX Areas:  00000000/00000000
   Uptime: 2:59:11
```

Table 5–15 explains the fields in the display.

**Table 5–15**   *Show IPX NLSP Neighbors Fields*

| Field | Description |
|---|---|
| System Id | System ID of the neighbor. |
| Interface | Interface on which the neighbor was discovered. |
| State | State of the neighbor adjacency. |
| Holdtime | Remaining time before the router assumes that the neighbor has failed. |
| Priority | Designated router election priority. |
| Cir | NLSP addressing state (multicast or broadcast) of the interface. |
| Adj | NSLP addressing state (multicast or broadcast) of the adjacent neighbor. |
| Circuit Id | Neighbor's internal identifier for the circuit. |
| IPX Address: | IPX address on this network of the neighbor. |
| IPX Areas: | IPX area addresses configured on the neighbor. |
| Uptime: | Time since the router discovered the neighbor. Time is formatted in *hh:mm:ss*. |

## SHOW IPX NLSP SPF-LOG

To display a history of the shortest path first (SPF) calculations for NLSP, use the **show ipx nlsp spf-log** EXEC command.

   **show ipx nlsp** [*tag*] **spf-log**

| Syntax | Description |
|---|---|
| *tag* | (Optional) Names the NLSP process. The *tag* can be any combination of printable characters. |

*Command Mode*

EXEC

## Usage Guidelines

This command first appeared in Cisco IOS Release 11.1.

## Sample Display

The following is sample output from the **show ipx nlsp spf-log** command:

```
Router> show ipx nlsp spf-log

        Level 1 SPF log
   When   Duration  Nodes  Count  Triggers
  0:30:59    1028     84      1    TLVCONTENT
  0:27:09    1016     84      1    TLVCONTENT
  0:26:30    1136     84      1    TLVCONTENT
  0:23:11    1244     84      1    TLVCONTENT
  0:22:39     924     84      2    TLVCONTENT
  0:22:08    1036     84      1    TLVCONTENT
  0:20:02    1096     84      1    TLVCONTENT
  0:19:31    1140     84      1    TLVCONTENT
  0:17:25     964     84      2    PERIODIC TLVCONTENT
  0:16:54     996     84      1    TLVCONTENT
  0:16:23     984     84      1    TLVCONTENT
  0:15:52    1052     84      1    TLVCONTENT
  0:14:34    1112     84      1    TLVCONTENT
  0:13:37     992     84      1    TLVCONTENT
  0:13:06    1036     84      1    TLVCONTENT
  0:12:35    1008     84      1    TLVCONTENT
  0:02:52    1032     84      1    TLVCONTENT
  0:02:16    1032     84      1    PERIODIC
  0:01:44    1000     84      3    TLVCONTENT
```

Table 5–16 describes the fields shown in the display.

**Table 5–16**   *Show ISIS SPF Log Field Descriptions*

| Field | Description |
|---|---|
| When | Amount of time since the SPF calculation took place. |
| Duration | Amount of time (in milliseconds) that the calculation required. |
| Nodes | Number of link state packets (LSPs) encountered during the calculation. |
| Count | Number of times that the SPF calculation was triggered before it actually took place. An SPF calculation is normally delayed for a short time after the event that triggers it. |

*Command Reference*

**Table 5–16**   *Show ISIS SPF Log Field Descriptions, Continued*

| Field | Description |
|---|---|
| Triggers | List of the types of triggers that were recorded before the SPF calculation occurred (more than one type may be displayed): |
| | PERIODIC—Periodic SPF calculation (every 15 minutes). |
| | NEWSYSID—New system ID was assigned. |
| | NEWAREA—New area address was configured. |
| | RTCLEARED—IPX routing table was manually cleared. |
| | NEWMETRIC—Link metric of an interface was reconfigured. |
| | ATTACHFLAG—Level 2 router has become attached or unattached from the rest of the level 2 topology. |
| | LSPEXPIRED—LSP has expired. |
| | NEWLSP—New LSP has been received. |
| | LSPHEADER—LSP with changed header fields was received. |
| | TLVCODE—LSP with a changed (Type-Length-Value) TLV code field was received. |
| | TLVCONTENT—LSP with changed TLV contents was received. |
| | AREASET—Calculated area address set has changed. |
| | NEWADJ—New neighbor adjacency came up. |
| | DBCHANGED—NLSP link state database was manually cleared. |

## SHOW IPX ROUTE

To display the contents of the IPX routing table, use the **show ipx route** user EXEC command.

   **show ipx route** [*network*] [**default**] [**detailed**]

| Syntax | Description |
|---|---|
| *network* | (Optional) Number of the network whose routing table entry you want to display. This is an eight-digit hexadecimal number that uniquely identifies a network cable segment. It can be a number in the range 1 to FFFFFFFD. You do not need to specify leading zeros in the network number. For example, for the network number 000000AA, you can enter AA. |
| **default** | (Optional) Displays the default route. This is equivalent to specifying a value of FFFFFFFE for the argument *network*. |
| **detailed** | (Optional) Displays detailed route information. |

## Command Mode

EXEC

## Usage Guidelines

This command first appeared in Cisco IOS Release 10.0. The **default** and **detailed** keywords first appeared in Cisco IOS Release 10.0.

## Sample Displays

The following is sample output from the **show ipx route** command:

```
Router# show ipx route

Codes: C - Connected primary network,    c - Connected secondary network
       S - Static, F - Floating static, L - Local (internal), W - IPXWAN
       R - RIP, E - EIGRP, N - NLSP, X - External, A - Aggregate
       s - seconds, u - uses

8 Total IPX routes. Up to 1 parallel paths and 16 hops allowed.

No default route known.

L        D40 is the internal network
C        100 (NOVELL-ETHER), Et1
C       7000 (TUNNEL),        Tu1
S        200 via      7000.0000.0c05.6023,        Tu1
R        300 [02/01] via      100.0260.8c8d.e748,    19s, Et1
S       2008 via      7000.0000.0c05.6023,        Tu1
R     CC0001 [02/01] via      100.0260.8c8d.e748,    19s, Et1
```

Table 5–17 describes the fields shown in the display.

**Table 5–17**   *Show IPX Route Field Descriptions*

| Field | Description |
|---|---|
| Codes | Codes defining how the route was learned. |
| L - Local | Internal network number. |
| C - Connected primary network | Directly connected primary network |
| c - connected secondary network | Directly connected secondary network |
| S - Static | Statically defined route via the **ipx route** command. |
| R - RIP | Route learned from a RIP update. |
| E - EIGRP | Route learned from an Enhanced IGRP (EIGRP) update. |
| W - IPXWAN | Directly connected route determined via IPXWAN. |

**Table 5–17**    *Show IPX Route Field Descriptions, Continued*

| Field | Description |
|---|---|
| 8 Total IPX routes | Number of routes in the IPX routing table. |
| No parallel paths allowed | Maximum number of parallel paths for which the Cisco IOS software has been configured with the **ipx maximum-paths** command. |
| Novell routing algorithm variant in use | Indicates whether the Cisco IOS software is using the IPX-compliant routing algorithms (default). |
| Net 1 | Network to which the route goes. |
| [3/2] | Delay/Metric. Delay is the number of IBM clock ticks (each tick is 1/18 seconds) reported to the destination network. Metric is the number of hops reported to the same network. Delay is used as the primary routing metric, and the metric (hop count) is used as a tie breaker. |
| via *network.node* | Address of a router that is the next hop to the remote network. |
| age | Amount of time (in hours, minutes, and seconds) that has elapsed since information about this network was last received. |
| uses | Number of times this network has been looked up in the route table. This field is incremented when a packet is process-switched, even if the packet is eventually filtered and not sent. As such, this field represents a fair estimate of the number of times a route gets used. |
| Ethernet0 | Interface through which packets to the remote network will be sent. |
| (NOVELL-ETHER) | Encapsulation (frame) type. This is shown only for directly connected networks. |
| is directly connected | Indicates that the network is directly connected to the router. |

When the Cisco IOS software generates an aggregated route, the **show ipx route** command displays a line item similar to the following:

```
    NA      1000 FFFFF000 [**][**/06] via        0.0000.0000.0000,  163s, Nu0
```

In the following example, the router that sends the aggregated route also generates the aggregated route line item in its table. But the entry in the table points to the null interface (*Nu0*), indicating that if this aggregated route is the most-specific route when a packet is being forwarded, the router drops the packet instead.

```
Router# show ipx route
Codes: C - Connected primary network,   c - Connected secondary network
       S - Static, F - Floating static, L - Local (internal), W - IPXWAN
       R - RIP, E - EIGRP, N - NLSP, X - External, A - Aggregate
       s - seconds, u - uses

13 Total IPX routes. Up to 4 parallel paths and 16 hops allowed.

No default route known.

NA     1000 FFFFF000 [**][**/06] via      0.0000.0000.0000,   163s, Nu0
L      2008 is the internal network
C         1 (NOVELL-ETHER),   Et0
C        89 (SAP),            To0
C        91 (SAP),            To1
C       100 (NOVELL-ETHER),   Et1
N         2 [19][01/01]          via      91.0000.30a0.51cd,  317s, To1
N         3 [19][01/01]          via      91.0000.30a0.51cd,  327s, To1
N        20 [20][01/01]          via      1.0000.0c05.8b24,  2024s, Et0
N       101 [19][01/01]          via      91.0000.30a0.51cd,  327s, To1
NX     1000 [20][02/02][01/01]   via      1.0000.0c05.8b24,  2024s, Et0
N      2010 [20][02/01]          via      1.0000.0c05.8b24,  2025s, Et0
N      2011 [19][02/01]          via      91.0000.30a0.51cd,  328s, To1
```

The following is sample output from the **show ipx route detailed** command:

```
Router# show ipx route detailed

Codes: C - Connected primary network,   c - Connected secondary network
       S - Static, F - Floating static, L - Local (internal), W - IPXWAN
       R - RIP, E - EIGRP, N - NLSP, X - External, s - seconds, u - uses

9 Total IPX routes. Up to 1 parallel paths and 16 hops allowed.

No default route known.

L        D35 is the internal network
C        E001 (SAP),          Et0
C        D35E2 (NOVELL-ETHER), Et2
R        D34 [02/01]
          -- via     E001.0000.0c02.8cf9,  43s,      1u, Et0
N        D36 [20][02/01]
          -- via     D35E2.0000.0c02.8cfc, 704s,     1u, Et2
                  10000000:1000:1500:0000.0c02.8cfb:6:0000.0c02.8cfc
NX       D40 [20][03/02][02/01]
          -- via     D35E2.0000.0c02.8cfc, 704s,     1u, Et2
                  10000000:2000:1500:0000.0c02.8cfb:6:0000.0c02.8cfc
R        D34E1 [01/01]
          -- via     E001.0000.0c02.8cf9,  43s,      1u, Et0
```

```
NX     D40E1 [20][02/02][01/01]
          -- via    D35E2.0000.0c02.8cfc, 704s,    3u, Et2
                10000000:2000:1500:0000.0c02.8cfb:6:0000.0c02.8cfc
N      D36E02 [20][01/01]
          -- via    D35E2.0000.0c02.8cfc, 705s,    2u, Et2
                10000000:2000:1500:0000.0c02.8cfb:6:0000.0c02.8cfc
```

Table 5–18 explains the additional fields shown in the display.

**Table 5–18**   *Show IPX Route Detailed Field Descriptions*

| Field | Description |
|---|---|
| 1u | Number of times this network has been looked up in the route table. This field is incremented when a packet is process-switched, even if the packet is eventually filtered and not sent. As such, this field represents a fair estimate of the number of times a route gets used. |
| 10000000 | (NLSP only) Throughput (end to end). |
| 3000 | (NLSP only) Link delay (end to end). |
| 1500 | (NLSP only) MTU (end to end). |
| 0000.0c02.8cfb | (NLSP only) System ID of the next-hop router. |
| 6 | (NLSP only) Local circuit ID. |
| 0000.0c02.8cfc | (NLSP only) MAC address of the next-hop router. |

## Related Commands

Search online to find documentation for related commands.

**clear ipx route**
**ipx maximum-paths**
**ipx nlsp metric**
**ipx route**

## SHOW IPX SERVERS

To list the IPX servers discovered through Service Advertising Protocol (SAP) advertisements, use the **show ipx servers** EXEC command.

**show ipx servers [unsorted | [sorted [name | net | type]] [regexp** *name*]

| Syntax | Description |
|---|---|
| **unsorted** | (Optional) Does not sort entries when displaying IPX servers. |
| **sorted** | (Optional) Sorts the display of IPX servers according to the keyword that follows. |

| Syntax | Description |
|---|---|
| **name** | (Optional) Displays the IPX servers alphabetically by server name. |
| **net** | (Optional) Displays the IPX servers numerically by network number. |
| **type** | (Optional) Displays the IPX servers numerically by SAP service type. This is the default. |
| **regexp** *name* | (Optional) Displays the IPX servers whose names match the regular expression. |

## Default

IPX servers are displayed numerically by SAP service type.

## Command Mode

EXEC

## Usage Guidelines

This command first appeared in Cisco IOS Release 10.0. The **unsorted** keyword first appeared in Cisco IOS Release 11.0

## Sample Displays

The following is sample output from the **show ipx servers** command when NLSP is enabled:

```
Router# show ipx servers

Codes: S - Static, P - Periodic, E - EIGRP, N - NLSP, H - Holddown, + = detail
9 Total IPX Servers

Table ordering is based on routing and server info

Type Name                       Net Address            Port Route Hops Itf
N+   4 MERLIN1-VIA-E03           E03E03.0002.0004.0006:0451 4/03   4    Et0
N+   4 merlin                    E03E03.0002.0004.0006:0451 4/03   3    Et0
N+   4 merlin 123456789012345    E03E03.0002.0004.0006:0451 4/03   3    Et0
S    4 WIZARD1--VIA-E0           E0.0002.0004.0006:0451      none   2
N+   4 dtp-15-AB                 E002.0002.0004.0006:0451    none   4    Et0
N+   4 dtp-15-ABC                E002.0002.0004.0006:0451    none   4    Et0
N+   4 dtp-15-ABCD               E002.0002.0004.0006:0451    none   4    Et0
N+   4 merlin                    E03E03.0002.0004.0006:0451 4/03   3    Et0
N+   4 dtp-15-ABC                E002.0002.0004.0006:0451    none   4    Et0
```

Table 5–19 describes the fields shown in the display.

**Table 5–19**  *Show IPX Servers Field Descriptions*

| Field | Description |
|---|---|
| Codes: | Codes defining how the service was learned. |
| S - Static | Statically defined service via the **ipx sap** command. |
| P - Periodic | Service learned via a SAP update. |
| E - EIGRP | Service learned via Enhanced IGRP. |
| N - NLSP | Service learned via NLSP. |
| H- Holddown | Indicates that the entry is in holddown mode and is not reachable. |
| + - detail | Indicates that multiple paths to the server exist. Use the **show ipx servers detailed** EXEC command to display more detailed information about the paths. |
| Type | Contains codes from Codes field to indicate how service was learned. |
| Name | Name of server. |
| Net | Network on which server is located. |
| Address | Network address of server. |
| Port | Source socket number. |
| Route | Ticks/hops (from the routing table). |
| Hops | Hops (from the SAP protocol). |
| Itf | Interface through which to reach server. |

The following example uses a regular expression to display SAP table entries corresponding to a particular group of servers in the accounting department of a company:

```
Router# show ipx servers regexp ACCT\_SERV.+

Codes: S - Static, P - Periodic, E - EIGRP, N - NLSP, H - Holddown, + = detail
9 Total IPX Servers

Table ordering is based on routing and server info

  Type  Name          Net  Address           Port  Route  Hops Itf
S 108   ACCT_SERV_1   7001.0000.0000.0001:0001  1/01    2   Et0
S 108   ACCT_SERV_2   7001.0000.0000.0001:0001  1/01    2   Et0
S 108   ACCT_SERV_3   7001.0000.0000.0001:0001  1/01    2   Et0
```

See Table 5–19 for **show IPX servers** field descriptions.

---

**NOTES**

---

For more information on regular expressions, see the "Regular Expressions" appendix in the *Dial Solutions Command Reference*.

---

*Related Commands*

Search online to find documentation for related commands.

**ipx sap**

## SHOW IPX SPX-SPOOF

To display the table of SPX connections through interfaces for which SPX spoofing is enabled, use the **show ipx spx-spoof** EXEC command.

    **show ipx spx-spoof**

*Syntax    Description*

This command has no arguments or keywords.

*Default*

Disabled

*Command Mode*

EXEC

*Usage Guidelines*

This command first appeared in Cisco IOS Release 11.0.

*Sample Display*

The following is sample output from the **show ipx spx-spoof** command:

```
Router> show ipx spx-spoof

Local SPX Network.Host:sock Cid  Remote SPX Network.Host:sock Cid  Seq  Ack  Idle
CC0001.0000.0000.0001:8104  0D08 200.0260.8c8d.e7c6:4017      7204 09   0021 120
CC0001.0000.0000.0001:8104  0C08 200.0260.8c8d.c558:4016      7304 07   0025 120
```

Table 5–20 describes the fields shown in the display.

**Table 5–20**   *Show SPX Spoofing Field Descriptions*

| Field | Description |
| --- | --- |
| Local SPX Network.Host:sock | Address of the local end of the SPX connection. The address is composed of the SPX network number, host, and socket. |
| Cid | Connection identification of the local end of the SPX connection. |
| Remote SPX Network.Host:sock | Address of the remote end of the SPX connection. The address is composed of the SPX network number, host, and socket. |
| Cid | Connection identification of the remote end of the SPX connection. |
| Seq | Sequence number of the last data packet transferred. |
| Ack | Number of the last solicited acknowledge received. |
| Idle | Amount of time elapsed since the last data packet was transferred. |

## Related Commands

Search online to find documentation for related commands.

**ipx spx-idle-time**
**ipx spx-spoof**

## SHOW IPX TRAFFIC

To display information about the number and type of IPX packets transmitted and received, use the **show ipx traffic** user EXEC command.

        show ipx traffic

## Syntax      Description

This command has no arguments or keywords.

## Command Mode

EXEC

## Usage Guidelines

This command first appeared prior to Cisco IOS Release 10.0.

## Sample Display

The following is sample output from the **show ipx traffic** command:

```
Router> show ipx traffic

Rcvd:     593135 total, 38792 format errors, 0 checksum errors, 0 bad hop count,
          21542 packets pitched, 295493 local destination, 0 multicast
Bcast:    295465 received, 346725 sent
Sent:     429393 generated, 276100 forwarded
          0 encapsulation failed, 0 no route
SAP:      4259 SAP requests, 0 SAP replies, 35 servers
          0 SAP Nearest Name requests, 0 replies
          0 SAP General Name requests, 0 replies
          191636 SAP advertisements received, 277136 sent
          115 SAP flash updates sent, 0 SAP format errors
RIP:      4676 RIP requests, 336 RIP replies, 18 routes
          87274 RIP advertisements received, 69438 sent
          74 RIP flash updates sent, 0 RIP format errors
Echo:     Rcvd 0 requests, 0 replies
          Sent 0 requests, 0 replies
          7648 unknown: 0 no socket, 0 filtered, 7648 no helper
          0 SAPs throttled, freed NDB len 0
Watchdog:
          0 packets received, 0 replies spoofed
Queue lengths:
          IPX input: 0, SAP 0, RIP 0, GNS 0
          SAP throttling length: 0/(no limit), 0 nets pending lost route reply
          Delayed process creation: 0
EIGRP:    Total received 0, sent 0
          Updates received 0, sent 0
          Queries received 0, sent 0
          Replies received 0, sent 0
          SAPs received 0, sent 0
NLSP:     Level-1 Hellos received 0, sent 0
          PTP Hello received 0, sent 0
          Level-1 LSPs received 0, sent 0
          LSP Retransmissions: 0
          LSP checksum errors received: 0
          LSP HT=0 checksum errors received: 0
          Level-1 CSNPs received 0, sent 0
          Level-1 PSNPs received 0, sent 0
          Level-1 DR Elections: 0
          Level-1 SPF Calculations: 0
          Level-1 Partial Route Calculations: 0
```

Table 5–21 describes the fields that might possibly be shown in the display.

**Table 5–21**  *Show IPX Traffic Field Descriptions*

| Field | Description |
| --- | --- |
| Rcvd: | Description of the packets received. |
| 593135 total | Total number of packets received. |
| 38792 format errors | Number of bad packets discarded (for example, packets with a corrupted header). Includes IPX packets received in an encapsulation that this interface is not configured for. |
| 0 checksum errors | Number of packets containing a checksum error. This number should always be 0, because IPX rarely uses a checksum. |
| 0 bad hop count | Number of packets discarded because their hop count exceeded 16. |
| 21542 packets pitched | Number of times the device received its own broadcast packet. |
| 295493 local destination | Number of packets sent to the local broadcast address or specifically to the router. |
| 0 multicast | Number of packets received that were addressed to an IPX multicast address. |
| Bcast: | Description of the broadcast packets the router has received and sent. |
| 295465 received | Number of broadcast packets received. |
| 346725 sent | Number of broadcast packets sent. It includes broadcast packets the router is either forwarding or has generated. |
| Sent: | Description of those packets that the software generated and then sent, and also those the software has received and then routed to other destinations. |
| 429393 generated | Number of packets transmitted that it generated itself. |
| 276100 forwarded | Number of packets transmitted that it forwarded from other sources. |
| 0 encapsulation failed | Number of packets the software was unable to encapsulate. |
| 0 no route | Number of times the software could not locate a route to the destination in the routing table. |
| SAP: | Description of the SAP packets sent and received. |
| 4259 SAP requests | Number of SAP requests received. |
| 0 SAP replies | Number of SAP replies sent in response to SAP requests. |

**Table 5–21** *Show IPX Traffic Field Descriptions, Continued*

| Field | Description |
|---|---|
| 35 servers | Number of servers in the SAP table. |
| 0 SAP Nearest Name requests    0 replies | Number of SAP Nearest Name requests and replies. This field applies to Cisco IOS Release 11.2. |
| 0 SAP General Name requests    0 replies | Number of SAP General Name requests and replies. This field applies to Cisco IOS Release 11.2. |
| 191636 SAP advertisements received | Number of SAP advertisements received from another router. |
| 277136 sent | Number of SAP advertisements generated and then sent. |
| 115 SAP flash updates sent | Number of SAP advertisements generated and then sent as a result of a change in its routing or service tables. |
| 0 SAP format errors | Number of SAP advertisements received that were incorrectly formatted. |
| RIP: | Description of the RIP packets sent and received. |
| 4676 RIP requests | Number of RIP requests received. |
| 336 RIP replies | Number of RIP replies sent in response to RIP requests. |
| 18 routes | Number of RIP routes in the current routing table. |
| 87274 RIP advertisements received | Number of RIP advertisements received from another router. |
| 69438 sent | Number of RIP advertisements generated and then sent. |
| 74 RIP flash updates sent | Number of RIP advertisements generated and then sent as a result of a change in its routing table. |
| 0 RIP format errors | Number of RIP packets received that were incorrectly formatted. |
| freed NDB length | Number of Network Descriptor Blocks (NDBs) that have been removed from the network but still need to be removed from the router's routing table. |
| Watchdog: | Description of the watchdog packets the software has handled. |

*Command Reference*

**Table 5-21**  *Show IPX Traffic Field Descriptions, Continued*

| Field | Description |
|---|---|
| 0 packets received | Number of watchdog packets received from IPX servers on the local network. |
| 0 replies spoofed | Number of times the software has responded to a watchdog packet on behalf of the remote client. |
| Queue lengths | Description of outgoing packets currently in buffers that are waiting to be processed. |
| IPX input | Number of incoming packets waiting to be processed. |
| SAP | Number of outgoing SAP packets waiting to be processed. |
| RIP | Number of outgoing RIP packets waiting to be processed. |
| GNS | Number of outgoing GNS packets waiting to be processed. |
| SAP throttling length | Maximum number of outgoing SAP packets allowed in the buffer. Any packets received beyond this number are discarded. |
| Echo: | Description of the ping replies and requests sent and received. |
| Rcvd 55 requests, 0 replies | Number of ping requests and replies received. |
| Sent 0 requests, 0 replies | Number of ping requests and replies sent. |
| 7648 unknown | Number of packets received on socket that are not supported. |
| 0 SAPs throttled | Number of sap packets discarded because they exceeded buffer capacity. |
| EIGRP totals: | Description of the Enhanced IGRP packets the router has sent and received. |
| Updates received | Number of Enhanced IGRP updates sent and received. |
| Queries received | Number of Enhanced IGRP queries sent and received. |
| Replies received | Number of Enhanced IGRP replies sent and received. |
| SAPs received | Number of SAP packets sent to and received from Enhanced IGRP neighbors. |
| 0 unknown: 0 socket, 0 filtered, 0 no helper | Number of packets the software was unable to forward, for example, because of a misconfigured helper address or because no route was available. |
| NLSP: | Description of the NLSP packets the router has sent and received. |

**Table 5–21** *Show IPX Traffic Field Descriptions, Continued*

| Field | Description |
|-------|-------------|
| Level-1 Hellos | Number of LAN hello packets sent and received. |
| PTP Hello | Number of point-to-point packets sent and received. |
| Level-1 LSPs | Number of link-state packets (LSPs) sent and received. |
| Level-1 CSNPs | Number of complete sequence number PDU (CSNP) packets sent and received. |
| Level-1 PSNPs | Number of partial sequence number PDU (PSNP) packets sent and received. |
| Level-1 DR Elections | Number of times the software has calculated its designated router election priority. |
| Level-1 SPF Calculations | Number of times the software has perform the shortest path first (SPF) calculation. |
| Level-1 Partial Route Calculations | Number of times the software has recalculated routes without running SPF. |

## SHOW SSE SUMMARY

To display a summary of Silicon Switch Processor (SSP) statistics, use the **show sse summary** EXEC command.

> **show sse summary**

*Syntax      Description*

This command has no arguments or keywords.

*Command Mode*

EXEC

*Usage Guidelines*

This command first appeared in Cisco IOS Release 11.0.

*Sample Display*

The following is sample output from the **show sse summary** command:

```
Router# show sse summary

SSE utilization statistics
```

```
                Program words  Rewrite bytes  Internal nodes  Depth
Overhead              499             1              8
IP                      0             0              0           0
IPX                     0             0              0           0
SRB                     0             0              0           0
CLNP                    0             0              0           0
IP access lists         0             0              0
Total used            499             1              8
Total free          65037        262143
Total available     65536        262144

Free program memory
  [499..65535]
Free rewrite memory
  [1..262143]

Internals
  75032 internal nodes allocated, 75024 freed
  SSE manager process enabled, microcode enabled, 0 hangs
  Longest cache computation 4ms, longest quantum 160ms at 0x53AC8
```

## SPF-INTERVAL

To control how often the Cisco IOS software performs the Shortest Path First (SPF) calculation, use the **spf-interval** router configuration command. To restore the default interval, use the **no** form of this command.

> **spf-interval** *seconds*
> **no spf-interval** *seconds*

| Syntax | Description |
|---|---|
| *seconds* | Minimum amount of time between SPF calculations, in seconds. It can be a number in the range 1 to 120. The default is 5 seconds. |

### Default

5 seconds

### Command Mode

Router configuration

### Usage Guidelines

This command first appeared in Cisco IOS Release 10.3.

SPF calculations are performed only when the topology changes. They are not performed when external routes change.

The **spf-interval** command controls how often the Cisco IOS software can perform the SPF calculation. The SPF calculation is processor-intensive. Therefore, it may be useful to limit how often this is done, especially when the area is large and the topology changes often. Increasing the SPF interval reduces the processor load of the router, but potentially slows down the rate of convergence.

## Example

The following example sets the SPF calculation interval to 30 seconds:

```
spf-interval 30
```

## Related Commands

Search online to find documentation for related commands.

**ipx router nlsp**
**log-neighbor-changes**
**prc-interval**

# CHAPTER 6

# Network Protocols Overview

The Cisco IOS software supports a variety of network protocols, from popular protocols such as Internet Protocol (IP) to less frequently used protocols such as Apollo Domain and XNS.

This section of the book describes the following network protocols:

- Apollo Domain
- Banyan VINES
- DECNet
- ISO CLNS
- XNS

This overview chapter provides a high-level description of each technology.

Not all Cisco access servers support the protocols described in this publication. For a model-by-model list of supported protocols, refer to the release notes for the current Cisco IOS release.

## APOLLO DOMAIN

The Cisco IOS software implementation supports packet forwarding and routing for the Apollo Domain network protocols on Ethernet, Fiber Distributed Data Interface (FDDI), and serial interfaces using High-Level Data Link Control (HDLC) or X.25 encapsulation. The software implementation does not support direct attachment to the 12-MB Domain Token Ring. The following restrictions apply to the Cisco implementation of Apollo Domain:

- When both bridging and Apollo Domain routing are enabled on an Ethernet network, you must specify an Ethernet type code access list that filters out datagrams with the Apollo Domain-type code (hexadecimal 8019). This restriction applies to MCI cards running microcode Version 1.5 or earlier.

- You must set IP addresses on all networks that use the IP Address Resolution Protocol (ARP)—for example, Ethernet and FDDI. This is necessary because Domain ARP (sometimes called D-ARP) uses the same Ethernet-type value as IP ARP.

- The Cisco implementation of Apollo Domain routing assumes that ARP can be used to locate workstations on the local cable. The following workstations and versions of the Apollo operating system support Domain ARP:

  - DN3000 and DN3010 nodes need Version 9.7.4.1, which is available from local Apollo field offices on patch tape 186.

  - DN3500, 4000, and 4500 nodes need Version 9.7.5.1, which is available from local Apollo field offices on patch tape 185.

  - Version 9.7, which provides ARP for DN5xx-T nodes, needs Version 9.7.4.b101. No patch is available for these workstations. The software is provided only on a DECnet tape.

---

**NOTES**

---

Release10.0 of the Apollo Domain operating system does not provide ARP. You must migrate to Release10.1 and later versions before you can operate with Cisco routers. Cisco routers support neither the **rtchk** and **lcnode** commands nor Domain ARP in Apollo's 802.5 implementation.

---

## BANYAN VINES

The Banyan Virtual Network Service (VINES) protocol is a networking system for personal computers. This proprietary protocol was developed by Banyan Systems, Inc., and is derived from the Xerox Network System (XNS) protocol. Cisco's implementation of VINES has been designed in conjunction with Banyan.

Cisco's implementation of Banyan VINES provides routing of VINES packets on all media. Although the software automatically determines a metric value that it uses for routing updates based on the delay set for the interface, this software implementation allows you to customize the metric. Cisco's implementation also offers address resolution to respond to address requests and broadcast address propagation. Echo support at the Media Access Control (MAC) level is also available for Ethernet, IEEE 802.2, Token Ring, and FDDI media. Name-to-address mapping for VINES host names also is supported, as are access lists to filter packets to or from a specific network.

## DECNET

Digital Equipment Corporation designed the DECnet stack of protocols in the 1970s as part of its Digital Network Architecture (DNA). DNA supports DECnet routing over Ethernet, Token Ring, FDDI, HDLC, Point-to-Point Protocol (PPP), Frame Relay, Switched Multimegabit Data Service (SMDS), X.25, and IEEE 802.2.

DECnet supports both connectionless and connection-oriented network layers implemented by Open System Interconnection (OSI) protocols. DECnet's most recent product release is called Phase V, which is equivalent to International Organization for Standardization (ISO) Connectionless Network Service (CLNS). Phase V is compatible with the previous release, Phase IV. Phase IV was similar to OSI routing, but Phase V implements full OSI routing, including support for End System-to-Intermediate System (ES-IS) and Intermediate System-to-Intermediate System (IS-IS) connections. An end system (ES) is a nonrouting network node; an intermediate system (IS) refers to a router. ES-IS support allows ESs and ISs to discover each other. IS-IS provides routing between ISs only.

DECnet Phase IV Prime supports inherent MAC addresses, which allows DECnet nodes to coexist with systems running other protocols that have MAC address restrictions.

DECnet support on Cisco routers includes local-area and wide-area DECnet Phase IV routing over Ethernet, Token Ring, FDDI, and serial lines (X.25, Frame Relay, SMDS). The following are the specifics of Cisco's support:

- Cisco routers interoperate with Digital routers, and Digital hosts do not differentiate between a Cisco router and a Digital router.

- The Cisco IOS software uses HDLC framing rather than Digital Data Communications Message Protocol (DDCMP) framing for point-to-point lines.

- If you construct a network using both Cisco and Digital equipment, you must ensure that each point-to-point line has the same type of equipment on both ends.

- Cisco and DECnet Phase IV routers have incompatible X.25 support.

- As with point-to-point lines, you must use a single vendor's equipment on the X.25 portion of your network.

- You can configure your Cisco router running Software Release 9.1 or later to interoperate with Digital equipment, or you can configure your Cisco router to operate with other Cisco routers that use prior versions of Cisco IOS software.

- The Cisco IOS software gives you additional security options through access lists.

- The Cisco IOS software supports the address translation gateway (ATG), which allows the router to participate in multiple, independent DECnet networks. In case of duplicate addressing, ATG establishes a user-specified address translation table for selected nodes between networks.

- Digital uses some nonroutable protocols that are not part of the DECnet stack. For example, neither Cisco nor Digital routers can route the Maintenance Operation Protocol (MOP) and local-area transport (LAT); instead, these protocols must be bridged.

- The parameters in Cisco's implementation of DECnet are a subset of the parameters you can modify in Digital's Network Control Program (NCP). Cisco uses the same names, the same range of allowable values, and the same defaults wherever possible. You must use the configuration commands to set DECnet parameters. Cisco's DECnet implementation does not set parameters by communicating with NCP.

- Cisco supports DECnet Phase IV-to-Phase V conversion:
  - Cost information is represented in native mode for the Phase IV or Phase V protocols.
  - Digital has defined algorithms for mapping a subset of the Phase V address space onto the Phase IV address space, and for converting Phase IV and Phase V packets back and forth to support Phase IV hosts in Phase V networks, and vice versa.
- Cisco's implementation differs from Digital's in the following ways:
  - You can add Phase V support without modifying your existing Phase IV support.
  - Cisco's implementation delays converting packets from Phase IV to Phase V, while Digital's implementation converts as soon as possible.

## ISO CLNS

The Cisco IOS software supports packet forwarding and routing for ISO CLNS on networks using a variety of data link layers: Ethernet, Token Ring, FDDI, and serial.

You can use CLNS routing on serial interfaces with HDLC, PPP, Link Access Procedure, Balanced (LAPB), X.25, SMDS, or Frame Relay encapsulation To use HDLC encapsulation, you must have a router at both ends of the link. If you use X.25 encapsulation, you must manually enter the network service access point (NSAP)-to-X.121 mapping. The LAPB, X.25, Frame Relay, and SMDS encapsulations interoperate with other vendors.

Cisco's CLNS implementation also is compliant with the Government Open Systems Interconnection Profile (GOSIP) Version 2.

As part of its CLNS support, Cisco routers fully support the following ISO and American National Standards Institute (ANSI) standard:

- ISO 9542—Documents the ES-IS routing exchange protocol.
- ISO 8473—Documents the ISO Connectionless Network Protocol (CLNP).
- ISO 8348/Ad2—Documents NSAP addresses.
- ISO 10589—Documents IS-IS Intra-domain Routing Exchange Protocol.

Both the ISO-developed IS-IS routing protocol and Cisco's ISO Interior Gateway Routing Protocol (IGRP) are supported for dynamic routing of ISO CLNS. In addition, static routing for ISO CLNS is supported.

— **NOTES** —————————————————————————————————————

Cisco access servers currently support only ES-IS, but not IS-IS.

_____

## XNS

The XNS protocols, which were developed by the Xerox Corporation, are designed to be used across a variety of communication media, processors, and office applications. Ungermann-Bass,

Inc., (now a part of Tandem Computers) adopted XNS in developing its Net/One XNS routing protocol. Standard XNS routing uses the Routing Information Protocol (RIP) update packets and the hop count metric. Ungermann-Bass Net/One uses hello packets and a path-delay metric.

Cisco provides a subset of the XNS protocol stack to support XNS routing. XNS traffic can be routed over Ethernet, FDDI, and Token Ring LANs, as well as over point-to-point serial lines running HDLC, LAPB, X.25, Frame Relay, or SMDS.

# CHAPTER 7

# Configuring
# Apollo Domain

The Apollo Domain routing protocol is the native-mode networking protocol for Apollo workstations. This chapter describes how to configure Apollo Domain routing and provides configuration examples.

Not all Cisco access servers support the Apollo Domain protocol. For more information, refer to the release notes for the current Cisco IOS release.

## APOLLO DOMAIN ADDRESSES

Apollo Domain network addresses are 32-bit quantities represented in hexadecimal numbers in the format *network.host*. Each host has a single address that is used for all its network connections.

The network number is a 12-bit number, expressed in hexadecimal, that identifies a physical network. Network numbers must be unique throughout an Apollo Domain internetwork. The host number is a 20-bit quantity expressed in hexadecimal. An Apollo Domain host can have interfaces on more than one physical network (Ethernet, Domain Token Ring, serial line, and so on).

In the following example of a network address, the number 5fe identifies a physical network and the number 1293c identifies a host (see Figure 7–1):

    5fe.1293c

---

*Figure 7–1*
*Apollo domain Addresses.*

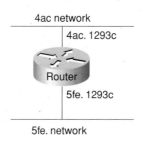

4ac network

4ac. 1293c

Router

5fe. 1293c

5fe. network

607

## APOLLO DOMAIN CONFIGURATION TASK LIST

To configure Apollo Domain routing, complete the tasks in the following sections. At a minimum, you must enable routing.

- Enabling Apollo Domain Routing
- Controlling Access to the Apollo Domain Network
- Tuning Apollo Domain Network Performance
- Monitoring the Apollo Domain Network
- Monitoring the Apollo Domain Network

### NOTES

See the "Apollo Domain Configuration Examples" section at the end of this chapter for configuration examples.

## ENABLING APOLLO DOMAIN ROUTING

To enable the Apollo Domain routing protocol, first enable it on the router, then configure each interface for Apollo Domain. These are the only tasks you must perform when configuring Apollo Domain routing.

You can route Apollo Domain on some interfaces and transparently bridge it on other interfaces simultaneously. To do this, you must enable concurrent routing and bridging. To configure an interface for concurrent routing and bridging, you use the **bridge crb** command to enable concurrent routing and bridging on the router.

### Enable Apollo Domain Routing

To enable Apollo Domain routing, perform the following task in global configuration mode:

| Task | Command |
|------|---------|
| Enable Apollo Domain routing. | **apollo routing** *host* |

For an example of how to enable Apollo Domain routing, see the "Apollo Domain Routing Example" section at the end of this chapter.

## Enable Apollo Domain Routing on an Interface

To enable Apollo Domain routing on an interface, perform the following tasks in interface configuration mode:

| Task | Command |
|------|---------|
| Enable Apollo Domain routing on an interface. | **apollo network** *number* |

For an example of how to enable Apollo Domain routing, see the "Apollo Domain Routing Example" section at the end of this chapter.

## Enable Concurrent Routing and Bridging

To enable concurrent routing and bridging, perform the following task in global configuration mode:

| Task | Command |
|------|---------|
| Enable concurrent routing and bridging. | **bridge crb** |

## CONTROLLING ACCESS TO THE APOLLO DOMAIN NETWORK

To control access to Apollo Domain networks, you create access lists and then apply them to individual interfaces. Apollo Domain access lists control access based on a range of network numbers. The conditions defined in access lists are applied to outgoing routed packets.

Keep the following in mind when configuring Apollo Domain network access control:

- Access list entries are evaluated in the order you enter them, and the first matching entry is used. To improve performance, place the most commonly matched entries near the beginning of the access list.

- An implicit *deny everything* entry is defined at the end of an access list unless you include an explicit *permit everything* entry at the end of the list.

- All new entries to an existing list are placed at the end of the list. You cannot add an entry to the middle of a list. This means that if you have previously included an explicit *permit everything* entry, new entries will never be scanned. The solution is to delete the access list and retype it with the new entries.

To create an access list, perform the following task in global configuration mode:

| Task | Command |
|------|---------|
| Create an Apollo Domain access list. | **apollo access-list** *access-list-name* {**deny** \| **permit**} [*firstnet-*]*lastnet.host* [*wildcard-mask*] |

To apply an access list to an interface and activate it on that interface, perform the following task in interface configuration mode:

| Task | Command |
| --- | --- |
| Apply an access list name to an interface. | **apollo access-group** *access-list-name* |

For an example of creating and applying an access list, see the "Access List Example" section at the end of this chapter.

---

**NOTES**

To display the filters defined on an interface, use the **show apollo interface** command.

---

## TUNING APOLLO DOMAIN NETWORK PERFORMANCE

To tune Apollo Domain network performance, perform one or more of the following tasks:

- Configuring Static Routes
- Setting Routing Table Update Timers
- Setting the Maximum Paths

### Configuring Static Routes

The Cisco IOS software uses metrics to determine the best path over which packets should be transmitted. You may, however, want to add static routes to the routing table to explicitly specify paths to certain destinations. Static routes always override any paths determined by metrics.

Be careful when assigning static routes. When links associated with static routes are lost, traffic may stop being forwarded, or traffic may be forwarded to a nonexistent destination, even though an alternative path might be available.

To add a static route to the Cisco IOS software's routing table, perform the following task in global configuration mode:

| Task | Command |
| --- | --- |
| Add a static route to the routing table. | **apollo route** *destination-network network.host* |

### Setting Routing Table Update Timers

You can set the number of times the entries in the routing table are updated. Note, however, that you should set this interval only in a configuration in which all routers are Cisco routers.

To set how often the entries in the routing table are updated, perform the following task in interface configuration mode:

| Task | Command |
|------|---------|
| Set the interval after which the routing table should be updated. | **apollo update-time** *interval* |

For an example of setting routing table update timers, see the "Routing Table Update Timer Example" section at the end of this chapter.

## Setting the Maximum Paths

You can set the maximum number of equal-cost, parallel paths to a destination. (Note that when paths have differing costs, the Cisco IOS software chooses lower-cost routes in preference to higher-cost routes.) The software distributes output on a packet-by-packet basis in round-robin fashion. That is, the first packet is sent along the first path, the second packet along the second path, and so on. If the final path is reached before all packets are sent, the next packet is sent to the first path, the next to the second path, and so on. This round-robin scheme is used regardless of whether fast switching is enabled.

Limiting the number of equal-cost paths can save memory on routers with limited memory or very large configurations. Additionally, in networks with a large number of multiple paths and systems with limited ability to cache out-of-sequence packets, performance might suffer when traffic is split between many paths.

To set the maximum number of paths, perform the following task in global configuration mode:

| Task | Command |
|------|---------|
| Set the maximum number of equal-cost paths to a destination. | **apollo maximum-paths** *paths* |

For an example of setting the maximum number of equal-cost, parallel paths to a destination, see the section "Apollo Domain Routing Example" later in this chapter.

## MONITORING THE APOLLO DOMAIN NETWORK

To monitor an Apollo Domain network, perform one or more of the following tasks at the EXEC prompt:

| Task | Command |
|------|---------|
| List the entries in the Apollo Domain ARP table. | **show apollo arp** |

| Task | Command |
| --- | --- |
| Display the status of the Apollo Domain interfaces configured in the Cisco IOS software and the parameters configured on each interface. | **show apollo interface** [*type number*] |
| List the entries in the Apollo Domain routing table. | **show apollo route** [*network*] |
| Display information about the Apollo Domain packets transmitted and received. | **show apollo traffic** |

## APOLLO DOMAIN CONFIGURATION EXAMPLES

Use the configuration examples in the following sections to help in configuring Apollo Domain routing:

- Apollo Domain Routing Example
- Access List Example
- Routing Table Update Timer Example

## Apollo Domain Routing Example

The following is an example of configuring Apollo Domain routing on a router with two Ethernet interfaces. The first set of commands enables the Apollo Domain routing protocol, assigns an Apollo Domain network address, and assigns network numbers to two Ethernet interfaces.

The second set of commands peforms the following:

- Assigns the router whose host number is 23d5a to handle all traffic routed over network 35.
- Allows traffic to be routed over a maximum of four paths.
- Sets the timer to update the routing table for Ethernet interface 0 every 40 seconds.
- Creates an access list called doc that denies access to networks 2a through 2f, and applies this access list to Ethernet interface 1. This means that packets destined for these networks that are sent out Ethernet interface 1 will be blocked.

```
apollo routing 23d5a
interface ethernet 0
 apollo network 5f
interface ethernet 1
 apollo network 4e
 !
apollo route 35 23d5a
apollo maximum-paths 4
interface ethernet 0
```

```
 apollo update-time 40
 apollo access-list doc deny 2a-2f
interface ethernet 1
 apollo access-group doc
```

## Access List Example

The following example creates an Apollo Domain access list and applies it to Ethernet interface 0. In this example, the first line denies access to networks 3a through 3f, the second line denies access to the host 5fe.1293.c, and the third line permits access to all other networks and hosts. The access list conditions will be applied to all routed packets going out Ethernet interface 0.

```
apollo access-list eng deny 3a-3f.0 ffff
apollo access-list eng deny 5fe.1293c
apollo access-list eng permit -1.0 ffff
!
interface ethernet 0
 apollo access-group eng
```

## Routing Table Update Timer Example

The following example sets the update times on two interfaces in the router. The update timer granularity would be 20 seconds, because this is the lowest value specified.

```
interface serial 0
 apollo update-time 40
interface ethernet 0
 apollo update-time 20
interface ethernet 1
 apollo update-time 25
```

# CHAPTER 8

# Apollo Domain Commands

The Apollo Domain routing protocol is the native-mode networking protocol for Apollo workstations. This chapter describes how to configure Apollo Domain routing. It also describes how to control access to the Apollo Domain network, optimize Apollo Domain network performance, and monitor the Apollo Domain network.

---

**NOTES**

Not all Cisco access servers support the Apollo Domain protocol. For more information, refer to the release notes for the current Cisco IOS release.

---

## APOLLO ACCESS-GROUP

To apply an access list to an interface, use the **apollo access-group** interface configuration command. To remove the access list, use the **no** form of this command.

> **apollo access-group** *access-list-name*
> **no apollo access-group**

*Syntax* | *Description*
--- | ---
*access-list-name* | Name of an access list to apply to the interface.

*Default*

No access list is applied by default.

*Command Mode*

Interface configuration

## Usage Guidelines

This command first appeared in Cisco IOS Release 10.3.

The **apollo access-group** command applies an access list to an interface. You use the **apollo access-list** command to specify the filtering conditions.

You can apply only one access list to an interface.

## Example

In the following example, the access list named eng is assigned to the first Ethernet interface:

```
interface ethernet 0
  apollo access-group eng
```

## Related Commands

Search online for documentation for related commands.

**apollo access-list**
**show apollo interface**

## APOLLO ACCESS-LIST

To define an Apollo Domain access list, use the **apollo access-list** global configuration command. To remove an access list, use the **no** form of this command.

> **apollo access-list** *access-list-name* {**deny** | **permit**} [*firstnet-*]*lastnet.host*
> [*wildcard-mask*]
> **no apollo access-list** *access-list-name*

| Syntax | Description |
| --- | --- |
| *access-list-name* | Name of the access list. |
| **deny** | Denies access if the conditions are matched. |
| **permit** | Permits access if the conditions are matched. |
| *firstnet* | (Optional) Number that specifies the lower limit of a selected Apollo network range. |
| *lastnet.host* | Number that specifies the upper limit of a selected Apollo network range. This is a 32-bit Apollo address consisting of a network number and a host number separated by a period. To specify all networks, use a value of -1. |
| *wildcard-mask* | (Optional) A wildcard mask that uses the one bits to ignore the host part of the network address. Host bits corresponding to wildcard mask bits set to zero are used in comparisons. |

### Default

No Apollo Domain access lists are defined.

### Command Mode

Global configuration

### Usage Guidelines

This command first appeared in Cisco IOS Release 10.3.

Use this command in conjunction with the **apollo access-group** command to restrict access to the Apollo network. Apollo Domain access lists are collections of permit and deny conditions that apply to defined Apollo network and host numbers. The Cisco IOS software sequentially tests the network and host numbers against conditions set in the access lists. The first match determines whether the software accepts or rejects the network and host number. Because the software stops testing conditions after the first match, the order of the conditions is critical. If no conditions match, the software rejects the network and host number.

Apollo Domain access lists are identified by a name, not by a number.

You can define Apollo access lists for a single network or for a range of Apollo networks. An access list can contain an indefinite number of actual and wildcard addresses. A wildcard address has a nonzero mask and thus potentially matches more than one actual address. The software examines the actual addresses, then the wildcard addresses. The order of the wildcard addresses is important because the software stops examining access list entries once it finds a match.

After creating an access list, apply the list restrictions to specific interfaces with the **apollo access-group** command.

### Example

In the following example, the first line denies access to networks 3a to 3f, the second line denies access to a specific host, and the third line permits everyone else:

```
apollo access-list eng deny 3a-3f.0 fffff
apollo access-list eng deny 5fe.1293c
apollo access-list eng permit -1.0 ffff
```

### Related Commands

You can use the master indexes or search online for documentation of related commands.

**apollo access-group**
**show apollo interface**

## APOLLO MAXIMUM-PATHS

To set the maximum number of paths the Cisco IOS software uses when sending packets, use the **apollo maximum-paths** global configuration command. To restore the default value, use the **no** form of this command.

> **apollo maximum-paths** *paths*
> **no apollo maximum-paths**

| Syntax | Description |
|--------|-------------|
| *paths* | Maximum number of equal-cost paths from which the software chooses. The argument *paths* can be a value from 1 to 512. The default is 1. |

### Default

1 path

### Command Mode

Global configuration

### Usage Guidelines

This command first appeared in Cisco IOS Release 10.3.

A router can use multiple paths to reach an Apollo Domain destination in order to increase throughput in the network. By default, the Cisco IOS software chooses one best path and sends all traffic on this path. You can, however, configure it to remember two or more paths that have equal costs and to balance the traffic load across all the available paths. (Note that when paths have differing costs, the software chooses lower-cost routes in preference to higher-cost routes.) Packets are distributed over the multiple paths in round-robin fashion on a packet-by-packet basis. That is, the first packet is sent along the first path, the second packet along the second path, and so on. If the final path is reached before all packets are sent, the next packet is sent to the first path, the next to the second path, and so on.

Limiting the number of equal-cost paths can save memory on routers with limited memory or very large configurations. Additionally, in networks with a large number of multiple paths and systems with limited ability to cache out-of-sequence packets, performance might suffer when traffic is split between many paths.

### Example

The following command sets a maximum of three equal-cost paths:

```
apollo maximum-paths 3
```

### Related Commands

You can use the master indexes or search online for documentation of related commands.

**show apollo route**

## APOLLO NETWORK

To enable Apollo Domain routing on a particular interface, use the **apollo network** interface configuration command. To disable Apollo Domain routing on an interface, use the **no** form of this command.

> **apollo network** *number*
> **no apollo network** *number*

| Syntax | Description |
|--------|-------------|
| *number* | Network number. This is an eight-digit hexadecimal number consisting of the network address followed by the host address. |

### Default

Disabled

### Command Mode

Interface configuration

### Usage Guidelines

This command first appeared in Cisco IOS Release 10.3.

You must enable Apollo Domain routing on the router with the **apollo routing** command before issuing the **apollo network** command.

### Example

The following example enables Apollo Domain routing, specifying that Apollo networks 5f and 4e are connected to two of the router's Ethernet interfaces:

```
apollo routing 23d5a
interface ethernet 0
 apollo network 5f
interface ethernet 1
 apollo network 4e
```

### Related Commands

You can use the master indexes or search online for documentation of related commands.

**apollo routing**
**show apollo interface**

## APOLLO ROUTE

To add a static route to the Apollo Domain routing table, use the **apollo route** global configuration command. To remove a route from the routing table, use the **no** form of this command.

**apollo route** *destination-network network.host*
**no apollo route** *destination-network network.host*

| Syntax | Description |
|---|---|
| *destination-network* | Network to which you want to establish a static route. This is a 12-bit hexadecimal number. You can omit leading zeros. |
| *network.host* | Network address of the router to which to forward packets destined for *destination-network*. |
| | The argument *network* is a 12-bit hexadecimal number. You can omit leading zeros. |
| | The argument *host* is the host number of the target router. This is a 20-bit hexadecimal value. |

### Default

No routes are predefined in the routing table.

### Command Mode

Global configuration

### Usage Guidelines

This command first appeared in Cisco IOS Release 10.3.

Static routes always override any paths determined by metrics.

Be careful when assigning static routes. When links associated with static routes are lost, traffic may stop being forwarded even though alternative paths might be available.

### Example

In the following example, all packets addressed to network 33 are forwarded to a router at the address of 45.91ac6:

```
apollo route 33 45.91ac6
```

### Related Commands

You can use the master indexes or search online for documentation of related commands.

**show apollo route**

### APOLLO ROUTING

To enable Apollo Domain routing, use the **apollo routing** global configuration command. To disable Apollo Domain routing, use the **no** form of this command.

**apollo routing** *host*
**no apollo routing** *host*

*Syntax*          *Description*

*host*            Host number of the router. This is a five-digit hexadecimal host address
                  that is unique across the Apollo Domain internetwork.

*Default*

Disabled

*Command Mode*

Global configuration

*Usage Guidelines*

This command first appeared in Cisco IOS Release 10.3.

This command must be used in conjunction with the **apollo network** command.

*Example*

In the following example, Apollo Domain routing is enabled on the router whose host address
is 23d5a:

```
apollo routing 23d5a
```

*Related Commands*

You can use the master indexes or search online for documentation of related commands.

**apollo network**
**show apollo interface**

## APOLLO UPDATE-TIME

To set the interval between Apollo Domain routing updates, use the **apollo update-time** interface
configuration command. To restore the default value, use the **no** form of this command.

**apollo update-time** *interval*
**no apollo update-time**

*Syntax*          *Description*

*interval*        Interval, in seconds, at which Apollo Domain routing updates are sent.
                  The minimum interval is 10 seconds, and the maximum is 2493644 sec-
                  onds. The default is 30 seconds.

*Default*

30 seconds

*Command Mode*

Interface configuration

*Usage Guidelines*

This command first appeared in Cisco IOS Release 10.3.

The **apollo update-time** command sets the routing update timer on a per-interface basis. To display the current value, use the **show apollo route** command.

Routers exchange information about routes by sending broadcast messages when they are brought up and shut down, and periodically while they are running. The **apollo update-time** command enables you to modify the periodic update interval.

You can set Routing Information Protocol (RIP) timers only in a configuration in which all routers are Cisco routers. The timers should be the same for all devices connected to the network.

The update interval you choose affects the internal Apollo Domain timers as follows:

- Apollo Domain routes are marked invalid if no routing updates for those routes are heard within six times the value of the update interval (6 × *interval*).

- Apollo Domain routes are removed from the routing table if no routing updates are heard within eight times the value of the update interval (8 × *interval*).

- If you define an update timer for more than one interface in a router, the granularity of the update timer is determined by the lowest value defined for one of the interfaces in the router. The Cisco IOS software "wakes up" at this granularity interval and sends out updates.

  The concept of granularity is best explained by an example. (This is illustrated in the following "Example" section.) If you have two interfaces in the router and you set the update timer on one to 20 seconds and the other to 30 seconds, the Cisco IOS software wakes up every 20 seconds to try to send routing updates. So at time 0:00:20, the software sends an update out the first interface only, and at time 0:00:40 it sends updates out the first and second interfaces. The software does not wake up at 0:00:30 to see if it needs to send an update out the second interface. This means that routing updates are sent out the second interface at N:NN:40 and N:NN:00. That is, the interval alternates between 40 seconds and 20 seconds; it is never 30 seconds. The interval on the first interface is always 20 seconds.

Ensure that all timers are the same for all routers attached to the same network segment.

Do not use the **apollo update-time** command in a multivendor router environment.

### Example

The following example sets the update timers on three interfaces in the router. The update timer granularity would be 20 seconds because this is the lowest value specified.

```
interface serial 0
 apollo update-time 40
interface ethernet 0
 apollo update-time 20
interface ethernet 1
 apollo update-time 25
```

### Related Commands

You can use the master indexes or search online for documentation of related commands.

**show apollo interface**

## SHOW APOLLO ARP

To list the entries in the Apollo Domain Address Resolution Protocol (ARP) table, use the **show apollo arp** EXEC command.

> **show apollo arp**

### Syntax      Description

This command has no arguments or keywords.

### Command Mode

EXEC

### Usage Guidelines

This command first appeared in Cisco IOS Release 10.3.

### Sample Display

The following is sample output from the **show apollo arp** command:

```
Router# show apollo arp

Protocol  Address        Age (min)   Hardware Addr    Type    Interface
Apollo    123A.CAFE          -        0000.0c00.62e6  ARPA    Ethernet0
```

Table 8–1 describes the fields shown in the display.

**Table 8–1**   *Show Apollo ARP Field Descriptions*

| Field | Description |
|---|---|
| Protocol | Protocol for which the interface has been configured. This should be Apollo. |
| Address | Apollo address of the interface. |
| Age (min) | Time, in minutes, that this entry has been in the ARP table. A hyphen indicates that this is a new entry. |
| Hardware Addr | MAC address of this interface. |
| Type | Encapsulation type. |
| Interface | Type and number of the interface. |

## SHOW APOLLO INTERFACE

To display the status of the Apollo Domain interfaces configured in the router and the parameters configured on each interface, use the **show apollo interface** EXEC command.

    **show apollo interface** [*type number*]

| Syntax | Description |
|---|---|
| *type* | (Optional) Interface type. It can be one of the following types: asynchronous, dialer, Ethernet (IEEE 802.3), loopback, null, serial, or tunnel. |
| *number* | (Optional) Interface number. |

### Command Mode
EXEC

### Usage Guidelines
This command first appeared in Cisco IOS Release 10.3.

### Sample Display
The following is sample output from the **show apollo interface** command:

```
Router# show apollo interface ethernet 0

Ethernet 0 is up, line protocol is up
    Apollo address is 123A.CAFE
    Update time is 30 seconds
    Outgoing access list is not set
```

Table 8–2 describes the fields shown in the display.

**Table 8–2** *Show Apollo Interface Field Descriptions*

| Field | Description |
|---|---|
| Ethernet 0 is... | The interface is currently active and inserted into the network (up) or is inactive and not inserted (down). |
| line protocol is... | Indicates whether the software processes that handle the line protocol believe that the interface is usable (that is, whether keepalives are successful). |
| Apollo address is 123A.CAFE | Address of the Apollo Domain interface, followed by its subnet mask, if any. |
| Update time is 30 seconds | How often the Cisco IOS software sends RIP updates, as configured with the **apollo update-time** command. |
| Outgoing access list is not set | Indicates whether an access list has been enabled with the **apollo access-list** command. |

### Related Commands

You can use the master indexes or search online for documentation of related commands.

**apollo access-group**
**apollo access-list**
**apollo update-time**

## SHOW APOLLO ROUTE

To display the contents of the Apollo Domain routing table, use the **show apollo route** EXEC command.

> **show apollo route** [*network*]

### Syntax

*network*

### Description

(Optional) Number of the network to which the route is directed. This is a 12-bit hexadecimal number.

### Command Mode

EXEC

### Usage Guidelines

This command first appeared in Cisco IOS Release 10.3.

*Sample Display*

The following is sample output from the **show apollo route** command:

```
Router# show apollo route

Codes: R - RIP derived, C - connected, S - static, 1 learned routes

Maximum allowed path(s) are/is 1
C Net 123A is directly connected, 0 uses, Ethernet0
C Net 123B is directly connected, 0 uses, Ethernet1
R Net 123C [1/0] via 123A.CAFB, 4 sec, 0 uses, Ethernet0
```

Table 8–3 describes the fields shown in the display.

**Table 8–3**    *Show Apollo Route Field Descriptions*

| Field | Description |
|---|---|
| Codes: | Codes defining source of route. |
| R | Route learned from a RIP update. |
| C | Directly connected network. |
| S | Statically defined route via the **apollo route** command. |
| 1 learned routes | Number of routes learned from RIP updates. |
| Maximum allowed path(s) are/is 1 | Maximum number of paths for which the Cisco IOS software has been configured with the **apollo maximum-paths** command. |
| Net 123A | Apollo network number. |
| Is directly connected | Indicates that this network is directly connected to the router. |
| Uses | Fair estimate of the number of times a route gets used. It indicates the number of times the route has been selected for use prior to operations such as access list filtering. |
| Ethernet 0 | Possible interface through which you can reach the remote network via the specified router. |
| [1/0] | Delay/Metric. The delay is the delay between sending routing updates. The metric is the Apollo Domain metric used in making routing decisions. |
| Via | Address of a router that is the next hop to the remote network. |
| Sec | Number of seconds since information about this network was last heard. |

*Related Commands*

You can use the master indexes or search online for documentation of related commands.

**apollo maximum-paths**
**apollo route**

## SHOW APOLLO TRAFFIC

To display information about the number and type of Apollo Domain packets transmitted and received by the Cisco IOS software, use the **show apollo traffic** EXEC command.

**show apollo traffic**

*Syntax      Description*

This command has no arguments or keywords.

*Command Mode*

EXEC

*Usage Guidelines*

This command first appeared in Cisco IOS Release 10.3.

*Sample Display*

The following is sample output from the **show apollo traffic** command:

```
Router# show apollo traffic

Rcvd:  8 total, 0 format errors, 0 checksum errors, 0 bad hop count,
       8 local destination, 0 multicast
Bcast: 8 received, 0 sent
Sent:  16 generated, 0 forwarded
       0 encapsulation failed, 0 no route
       0 unknown
```

Table 8–4 describes the fields shown in the display.

**Table 8–4**   *Show Apollo Traffic Field Descriptions*

| Field | Description |
|-------|-------------|
| Rcvd: | Description of the Apollo Domain packets received. |
| 8 total | Total number of packets received. |
| 0 format errors | Number of bad packets discarded (for example, packets with a corrupted header). |

**Table 8–4** *Show Apollo Traffic Field Descriptions, Continued*

| Field | Description · |
|---|---|
| 0 checksum errors | Number of packets discarded because they contained checksum errors. This field should always have a value of 0, because Apollo Domain does not use a checksum. |
| 0 bad hop count | Number of packets discarded because their hop count exceeded 16 (that is, the packets timed out). |
| 8 local destination | Number of packets sent to the local broadcast address or specifically to the router. |
| 0 multicast | Number of packets received that were addressed to multiple destinations. |
| Bcast: | Number of broadcast packets received and sent. |
| Sent: | Description of the Apollo Domain packets sent. |
| 16 generated | Number of packets the router transmitted that it generated itself. |
| 0 forwarded | Number of packets the router transmitted that it forwarded from other sources. |
| 0 encapsulation failed | Number of packets the router was unable to encapsulate. |
| 0 no route | Number of times the router could not locate in the routing table a route to the destination. |
| Unknown: | Number of packets the router was unable to forward, for example, because of a misconfigured helper address or because no route was available. |

# CHAPTER 9

# Configuring Banyan VINES

This chapter describes how to configure VINES and provides configuration examples.

Not all Cisco access servers support Banyan VINES. For more information, refer to the release notes for the current Cisco IOS release.

## VINES ADDRESSES

VINES network-layer addresses are 48-bit addresses that consist of a network number (better described as a server number) and a subnetwork number (better described as a host number). In this manual, VINES addresses are expressed in the format *network:host*.

The network number identifies a VINES logical network, which consists of a single server and a group of client nodes. The network number is 33 bytes long, and is the serial number of the service node. Figure 9–1 shows two logical networks: network 1 and network 2.

The subnetwork number is 16 bits (2 bytes) long. For service nodes, the subnetwork number is always 1. For client nodes, it can have a value from 0x8001 through 0xFFFE.

The following is an example of a VINES network address:

```
3000577A:0001
```

In this address, the server number (or more specifically, the serial number of the service node) is 3000577A and the host number is 0001, indicating that this is a service node. Both portions of the address are expressed in hexadecimal.

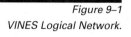

*Figure 9–1*
*VINES Logical Network.*

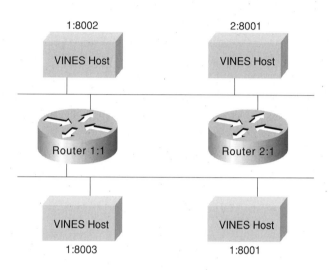

## VINES CONFIGURATION TASK LIST

To configure VINES routing, complete the tasks in the following sections. Only the first task is required; the remaining tasks are optional.

- Configuring VINES Routing
- Controlling Access to the VINES Network
- Configuring VINES Network Parameters
- Configuring VINES over WANs
- Configuring VINES Routing between Virtual LANs
- Monitoring and Maintaining the VINES Network

**NOTES**

For configuration examples, see the "VINES Configuration Examples" section at the end of this chapter.

## CONFIGURING VINES ROUTING

To configure VINES routing, first enable it on the router, then enable it on each interface. These are the only two tasks you must perform.

If you are configuring a VINES serverless network, you must also configure the Cisco IOS software to respond to ARP requests. You probably also will want to configure it for serverless support.

## Enabling VINES Routing on the Router

To enable VINES routing on the router, perform the following task in global configuration mode:

| Task | Command |
|------|---------|
| Enable VINES RTP routing on the router. | **vines routing** [*address*] |

Enabling VINES routing on the router or access server starts the VINES Routing Table Protocol (RTP) by default.

To enable Sequenced Routing Update Protocol (SRTP), you must perform the following tasks in global configuration mode:

| Task | Command |
|------|---------|
| **Step 1**  Enable VINES RTP routing on the router. | **vines routing** [*address*] |
| **Step 2**  Enable VINES SRTP routing on the router. | **vines srtp-enabled** |

---

> **NOTES**
>
> For an example of how to enable VINES routing, see the "Typical VINES Network Configuration Example" section at the end of this chapter.

---

## Enabling VINES Routing on an Interface

After you enable VINES on the router, enable it on each interface that will handle VINES traffic. When you enable VINES processing on a specified interface, you can optionally set the metric for that interface. The metric sets the distance to another router or client accessible through that interface. The routing table uses metrics to determine which interface provides the best routing path. If you do not specify a metric, the system automatically chooses a reasonable value that is based on the interface type. The metrics are chosen to match as closely as possible the numbers that a Banyan server would choose for the same type and speed of interface.

To enable VINES routing on an interface other than a serial interface, perform the following task starting in EXEC mode:

| Task | Command |
|------|---------|
| Enable VINES routing on an interface. | **vines metric** [*whole* [*fractional*]] |

To enable VINES routing on a serial interface, perform the following tasks in interface configuration mode:

| Task | Command |
|------|---------|
| **Step 1** Determine the bandwidth of the interface. | **show interfaces** |
| **Step 2** Enable VINES routing, explicitly setting the metric. | **vines metric** [*whole* [*fractional*]] |

## Enabling Concurrent Routing and Bridging

You can route VINES on some interfaces and transparently bridge it on other interfaces simultaneously. To do this, you must enable concurrent routing and bridging. To enable concurrent routing and bridging for the router, perform the following task in global configuration mode:

| Task | Command |
|------|---------|
| Enable concurrent routing and bridging for the router. | **bridge crb** |

## Enabling VINES on Serverless Networks

No special configuration is necessary for serverless Banyan VINES networks, such as separate networks of clients and servers connected by routers. On serverless networks, the Cisco IOS software provides special processing for certain broadcast packets and certain packets directed at the router. This allows clients on the serverless network to find the services that are provided by a server on another network. This special processing is especially important when two networks, one with a server and one without a server, are connected to the same router.

Client systems on VINES networks are assigned network addresses dynamically. When a VINES client boots, it has no knowledge of its address or preferred server. Immediately after it initializes its hardware interface, the client sends a broadcast request asking a server to provide it with a network-layer address. One of our routers will respond to this broadcast request if there are no VINES servers on the physical network segment. The Cisco IOS software then assigns an address to the network client. (In previous releases, the software would not respond by default.) The software generates a unique network number for the client based on its own VINES address. If the software assigns an address to a client, the router or access server then acts as a network communication service provider for that client. A VINES file server must still be present somewhere on the network in order for the client to connect to all other network services.

For an example of how to configure VINES routing for various network topologies that include serverless networks, see the "Serverless Network Configuration Examples" section at the end of this chapter.

## CONTROLLING ACCESS TO THE VINES NETWORK

To control access to VINES networks, you create access lists and then apply them to filters on individual interfaces. An *access list* is a list of VINES network numbers that is maintained by the router. The list controls access to or from a particular interface. Access lists are useful for providing network security.

You can use the following two types of VINES access lists to filter routed traffic:

- Standard access list—Restricts traffic based on the protocol, source address and mask, and destination address and mask. You can further restrict traffic by specifying a source and a destination port. Standard VINES access lists have numbers from 1 to 100.

- Extended access list—Restricts traffic in the same way as the standard access list, except that you can also specify masks for the source and destination ports. Extended VINES access lists have numbers from 101 to 200.

VINES has a third type of access list, called a *simple access list*, that restricts traffic based on source address and source address mask. This type of access list is used to decide from which stations to accept time updates, not to filter traffic. Simple access lists have numbers from 201 to 300.

You can define the following two types of filters on VINES networks:

- Filters on a packet's protocol, source and destination addresses, address masks, and explicit port numbers

- Filters on a packet's protocol, source and destination addresses, address masks, port numbers, and port masks

Keep these points in mind when configuring VINES network access control:

- You can assign only one access list to an interface.

- The conditions in the access list are applied to all outgoing packets not sourced by the router.

- Access list entries are scanned in the order you enter them. The first matching entry is used.

- An implicit *deny everything* entry is defined at the end of an access list unless you include an explicit *permit everything* entry at the end of the list.

- All new entries to an existing list are placed at the end of the list. You cannot add an entry to the middle of a list. This means that if you have previously included an explicit *permit everything* entry, new entries will never be scanned. The solution is to delete the access list and retype it with the new entries.

To control access to VINES network, perform the following tasks:

| | |
|---|---|
| **Step 1** | Create an access list. |
| **Step 2** | Apply an access list to an interface. |

To create a VINES access list, perform one or more of the following tasks in global configuration mode:

| Task | Command |
| --- | --- |
| Create a standard access list. | **vines access-list** *access-list-number* {**deny** \| **permit**} *protocol source-address source-mask* [*source-port*] *destination-address destination-mask* [*destination-port*] |
| Create an extended access list. | **vines access-list** *access-list-number* {**deny** \| **permit**} *protocol source-address source-mask* [*source-port source-port-mask*] *destination-address destination-mask* [*destination-port destination-port-mask*] |
| Create a simple access list. | **vines access-list** *access-list-number* {**deny** \| **permit**} *source-address source-mask* |

To apply an access list to an interface, perform the following task in interface configuration mode. Remember that you can apply only one access list to each interface.

| Task | Command |
| --- | --- |
| Apply a VINES access list to an interface. | **vines access-group** *access-list-number* |

For an example of how to create a VINES access list, see the "Access List Example" section at the end of this chapter.

## CONFIGURING VINES NETWORK PARAMETERS

To configure VINES network parameters, perform one or more of the tasks in the following sections:

- Selecting an Encapsulation Type
- Controlling the Display of Host Addresses
- Controlling the Base of Host Addresses
- Controlling RTP Routing Updates
- Controlling RTP and SRTP Routing Updates
- Disabling Fast Switching
- Setting the Time
- Configuring Static Routes
- Configuring Static Paths
- Controlling the Forwarding of Broadcast Packets

## Selecting an Encapsulation Type

You can choose a MAC-level encapsulation type for each Ethernet, Token Ring, and IEEE 802.2 interface. This controls the type of encapsulation used by the Cisco IOS software when sending broadcast packets.

To select an encapsulation type, perform the following task in interface configuration mode:

| Task | Command |
|------|---------|
| Set the MAC-level encapsulation type. | **vines encapsulation [arpa | snap | vines-tr]** |

---

**NOTES**

You should not use the **vines encapsulation** command with the current versions of VINES software. This command is provided for future interoperability when Banyan begins using encapsulation types other than the current default ones.

---

## Controlling the Display of Host Addresses

By default, you enter VINES addresses as numerical values. In addition, addresses are displayed numerically in the output of the **show, ping,** and **trace** commands. You can assign a host name to each VINES address. Names are easier to remember and type. Assigning a host name enables you to enter the name instead of the address. It also means that the name rather than the numeric address is displayed in output.

To assign a host name to a VINES network address, perform the following task in global configuration mode:

| Task | Command |
|------|---------|
| Assign a host name to an address. | **vines host** *name address* |

## Controlling the Base of Host Addresses

By default, VINES addresses are represented as hexadecimal numbers. This applies to both the input of addresses and the representation of addresses in output from the router. You can configure the Cisco IOS software to display addresses in decimal for consistency with Banyan network management displays.

Names are always preferred when printing addresses. If a name is not available, the address will be printed as a number in the base specified.

To display VINES addresses as decimal numbers, perform the following task in global configuration mode:

| Task | Command |
| --- | --- |
| Interpret VINES addresses in decimal. | **vines decimal** |

## Controlling RTP Routing Updates

You can control the routing updates sent by the Cisco IOS software in the following ways:

- Control the interval at which the software sends RTP routing updates. The default interval is 90 seconds. The routing update interval should be the same on all VINES-speaking entities on the same physical network.

 **NOTES**

The **vines update interval** command does not apply to the SRTP routing protocol.

- Modify the way that routing information is propagated across the network. On LAN media, using this command causes the software to stop transmitting and to stop expecting periodic full-routing updates. Instead, the software transmits and expects a periodic empty routing update, also known as a hello message. On WAN media, using this command causes the software to transmit three normally spaced full-routing updates, and then cease transmission. The software does *not* send periodic hello messages.

- Disable split horizon. Normally, the software sends RTP updates that list only routes that it learned via other interfaces. This eliminates information that is normally redundant and will be ignored by all routers receiving the update. When split horizon is disabled, routing updates sent out on a given interface will include all routers known by the router. This is useful on X.25 and Frame Relay networks on which there is not a full-mesh topology.

To control routing-update frequency and propagation, perform one or both of the following tasks in interface configuration mode:

| Task | Command |
| --- | --- |
| Change the frequency of sending routing updates. | **vines update interval** *seconds* |
| Change how routing information is propagated. | **vines update deltas** |

**NOTES**

The **vines update deltas** command does not apply to the SRTP routing protocol.

To control the content of transmitted or received routing updates, or to control the source address of received routing updates, perform one or more of the following tasks in interface configuration mode:

| Task | Command |
|------|---------|
| Control the source address of received routing information. | **vines input-router-filter** *access-list-number* |
| Filter the content of received routing information. | **vines input-network-filter** *access-list-number* |
| Filter the content of transmitted routing information. | **vines output-network-filter** *access-list-number* |

To disable split horizon, perform the following task in interface configuration mode:

| Task | Command |
|------|---------|
| Disable split horizon when sending routing updates. | **no vines split-horizon** |

**NOTES**

SRTP updates do not use split horizon.

## Controlling RTP and SRTP Routing Updates

The VINES RTP sends several types of messages, including *redirect* messages. If the Cisco IOS software detects that a suboptimal path between two nodes is being used, it sends redirect messages to the nodes to indicate the better path.

To control the frequency of redirect messages on a specified interface, perform the following task in interface configuration mode:

| Task | Command |
|------|---------|
| Set the frequency of RTP and SRTP redirect messages. | **vines redirect** [*seconds*] |

## Disabling Fast Switching

Fast switching allows higher throughput by switching packets using a cache created by previous packets. Fast switching also provides load sharing on a per-packet basis. Fast switching is enabled by default on all interfaces on which it is supported. Fast switching is not supported on serial interfaces using encapsulations other than HDLC.

Packet transfer performance is generally better when fast switching is enabled. However, you might want to disable fast switching in order to save memory space on interface cards and to help avoid congestion when high-bandwidth interfaces are writing large amounts of information to low-bandwidth interfaces.

To disable fast switching on an interface, perform the following task in interface configuration mode:

| Task | Command |
| --- | --- |
| Disable fast switching. | **no vines route-cache** |

## Setting the Time

Banyan VINES servers synchronize time across the entire network by sending zero-hop and two-hop broadcast messages. The Cisco IOS software can process and generate time-synchronization messages. It can also retrieve the local time and place it into the VINES time system (which is most useful when running NTP locally) and can use the VINES time system to set a local clock. It is also possible to provide the software with a list of up to 20 destinations for time messages.

To set the VINES network time, perform one or more of the following tasks in global configuration mode:

| Task | Command |
| --- | --- |
| Enable the sending of time messages by the local router. | **vines time participate** |
| Periodically synchronize the router's time with the VINES network time. | **vines time set-system** |
| Periodically synchronize the VINES network time with the router's time. | **vines time use-system** |
| Accept time updates from the stations permitted by the specified simple access list. | **vines time access-group** *access-list-number* |
| Send time updates only to the specified station. | **vines time destination** *address* |

For an example of how to set VINES time, see the "Time-of-Day Service Example" section at the end of this chapter.

## Configuring Static Routes

VINES uses the RTP to determine the best path when several paths to a destination exist. RTP then dynamically updates the routing table. However, you might want to add static routes to the routing table to explicitly specify paths to certain destinations.

The decision to use a static route or a dynamic route is always determined by the relative metric numbers. Be careful when assigning static routes. If a static route is assigned with a better metric than the dynamic routes, and the links associated with the static routes are lost, traffic may stop being forwarded, even though an alternative route might be available.

To add a static route to the routing table, perform the following task in global configuration mode:

| Task | Command |
|------|---------|
| Add a static route to the routing table. | **vines route** *number address* [*whole* [*fractional*]] |

You can configure static routes that can be overridden by dynamically learned routes. These are referred to as *floating static routes*. You can use a floating static route to create a path of last resort that is used only when no dynamic routing information is available.

To avoid the possibility of a routing loop occurring, by default, floating static routes are not redistributed into other dynamic protocols. Floating static routes must not be advertised on interfaces that are paths to the destination. To configure a floating static route, assign a metric to the static route that is worse (higher) than all dynamic routes.

To add a floating static route to the routing table, perform the following task in global configuration mode:

| Task | Command |
|------|---------|
| Add a floating static route to the routing table. | **vines route** *number address* [*whole* [*fractional*]] |

## Configuring Static Paths

You can specify static paths to neighbor stations on the network. This is useful for testing VINES networks with test equipment that does not generate hello packets.

To add a static path to a neighbor station, perform the following task in interface configuration mode:

| Task | Command |
| --- | --- |
| Add a static path to the neighbor station. | **vines neighbor** *address mac-address encapsulation* [*whole* [*fractional*]] |

### Controlling the Forwarding of Broadcast Packets

Normally, the Cisco IOS software decides whether to forward a broadcast packet on an interface based on the presence of local servers and on the settings of both the "hop count" and "class" fields of the VINES IP header. If there are any local servers present, the software follows the normal rules of VINES IP and forwards the broadcast after examining both the "hop count" and "class" fields. If no local servers are present, then the "class" field is ignored when making the forwarding decision. You can override this default behavior in either of two ways. The first override is to have the software always ignore the "class" field and make the broadcast forwarding decision solely based on hop count. The second override is to have the software never ignore the "class" field and always make the broadcast forwarding decision based upon both the "class" and "hop count" fields.

To have the software modify the way in which it forwards broadcast packets, perform the following tasks in interface configuration mode:

| Task | | Command |
| --- | --- | --- |
| Step 1 | Ensure that the software never ignores the "class" field when forwarding broadcast packets. | **no vines propagate** |
| Step 2 | Ensure that the software always ignores the "class" field when forwarding broadcast packets. | **vines propagate** |

## Configuring VINES over WANs

You can configure VINES over X.25, Frame Relay, and SMDS networks. You can also configure VINES over HDLC and PPP; address maps are not necessary for these two protocols. You can fast switch VINES over serial interfaces configured for HDLC, Frame Relay, PPP, SMDS, and ATM.

## Configuring VINES Routing between Virtual LANs

Banyan VINES can be routed over virtual LAN (VLAN) subinterfaces using the Inter-Switch Link (ISL) encapsulation protocol. Full-feature Cisco IOS software is supported on a per-VLAN basis, allowing standard Banyan VINES capabilities to be configured on VLANs.

## MONITORING AND MAINTAINING THE VINES NETWORK

To monitor and maintain a VINES network, perform one or more of the following tasks at the EXEC prompt:

| Task | Command |
|---|---|
| Delete entries from the VINES fast-switching cache table. | **clear vines cache** [**interface** *interface* \| **neighbor** *address* \| **server** *network*] |
| Delete VINES IPC connection blocks from the router. | **clear vines ipc** *number* |
| Delete entries from the neighbor table. | **clear vines neighbor** {*network* ¦ *\**} |
| Delete network addresses from the routing table. | **clear vines route** {*network* \| *\**} |
| Zero the VINES-related traffic statistics displayed by the **show vines traffic** command. | **clear vines traffic** |
| Send datagrams to a host to determine network connectivity. | **ping vines** [*address*] |
| Display the VINES access lists currently defined. | **show vines access** [*access-list-number*] |
| Display the contents of the VINES fast-switching cache table. | **show vines cache** [*address* \| **interface** *type number* \| **neighbor** *address* \| **server** *network*] |
| Display the entries in the VINES host name table. | **show vines host** [*name*] |
| Display VINES-related interface settings. | **show vines interface** [*type number*] |
| Display information about any currently active IPC connections. | **show vines ipc** |
| Display the contents of the VINES neighbor table. | **show vines neighbor** [*address* \| **interface** *type number* \| **server** *number*] |
| Display the contents of the VINES routing table. | **show vines route** [*number* \| **neighbor** *address*] |
| Display information about the router's application layer support. | **show vines service** [**fs** \| **nsm** \| **ss** \| **vs**] |

| Task | Command |
|------|---------|
| Display the statistics about VINES protocol traffic. | **show vines traffic** [*type number*] |
| Determine the path a packet takes when traversing a VINES network. | **trace** [**vines** \| **oldvines**] [*address*] |

If you find that two routers have the same VINES network address, you can have the routers dynamically recompute their addresses. To do this, perform the following task in global configuration mode on each of the two routers:

| Task | Command |
|------|---------|
| Dynamically redetermine the router's address. | **vines routing recompute** |

## VINES CONFIGURATION EXAMPLES

Use the configuration examples in the following sections to help in configuring VINES routing on your network:

- Typical VINES Network Configuration Example
- Serverless Network Configuration Examples
- Access List Example
- Time-of-Day Service Example

## Typical VINES Network Configuration Example

Figure 9–2 illustrates how to configure a simple VINES network.

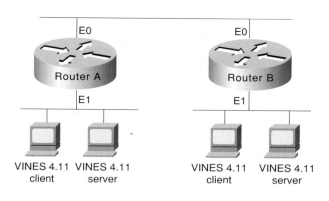

*Figure 9–2*
*VINES Simple Configuration.*

The following is a sample configuration for Routers A and B:

```
vines routing
!
interface ethernet 0
 vines metric 2
!
interface ethernet 1
 vines metric 2
```

## Serverless Network Configuration Examples

The following examples illustrate how to configure VINES routing for various network topologies that include serverless networks. The first example illustrates how to configure a simple serverless network (see Figure 9–3). Note that this is no longer any different from the configuration of a network that has servers.

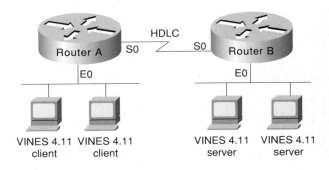

*Figure 9–3*
*VINES Serverless*
*Configuration.*

### Configuration for Router A

```
vines routing
!
interface ethernet 0
 vines metric 2
!
interface serial 0
 vines metric 45
```

### Configuration for Router B

```
vines routing
!
interface ethernet 0
 vines metric 2
!
interface serial 0
 vines metric 45
```

The configuration in Figure 9–4 has an X.25 interface instead of an HDLC serial line, and it also has multiple versions of VINES software running simultaneously. Again, note that this configuration is no longer any different from the configuration of a network that has servers.

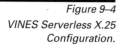

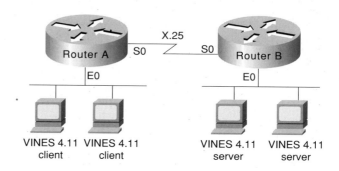

*Figure 9–4*
*VINES Serverless X.25 Configuration.*

### Configuration for Router A

```
vines routing
!
interface ethernet 0
 vines metric 2
!
interface serial 0
 vines metric 55
```

### Configuration for Router B

```
vines routing
!
interface ethernet 0
 vines metric 2
!
interface serial 0
 vines metric 55
```

The configuration in Figure 9–5 has an FDDI interface instead of a serial line. It also has the servers for the different VINES versions on different physical networks and has a requirement that the clients be able to run any VINES version.

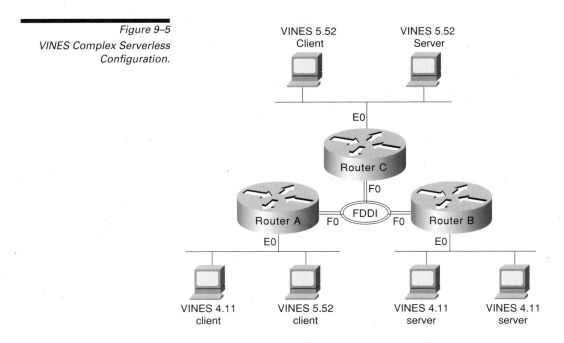

*Figure 9–5*
*VINES Complex Serverless Configuration.*

The best way to configure this topology would be one of the following configurations.

## Configuration for Router A

```
vines routing
!
interface ethernet 0
 vines metric 2
 vines serverless broadcast
!
interface fddi 0
 vines metric 1
```

## Configuration for Routers B and C

```
vines routing
!
interface ethernet 0
 vines metric 2
!
interface fddi 0
 vines metric 1
```

The **broadcast** keyword on the **vines serverless** command on server A causes it to forward packets onto the FDDI ring as broadcasts, instead of sending them to either Router B or Router C. This allows the **default serverless processing** on both routers to forward the frame from the FDDI ring to the Ethernet network.

## Access List Example

Figure 9–6 illustrates how to configure an access list that filters all packets between two VINES servers. For this example, the servers in the upper-left and lower-right corners are configured.

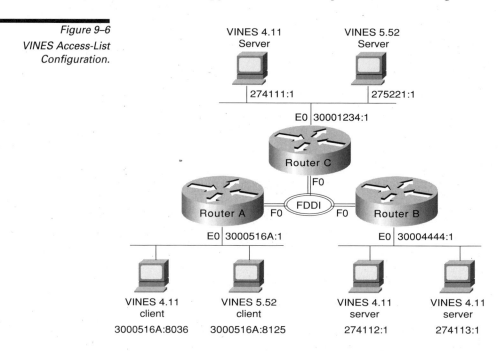

**Figure 9–6**
*VINES Access-List Configuration.*

On Router B, you would set up the following configuration:

```
vines routing
vines access-list 1 deny IP 274113:1 0:0 274111:1 0:0
vines access-list 1 permit IP 0:0 FFFFFFFF:FFFF 0:0 FFFFFFFF:FFFF
!
interface ethernet 0
 vines metric 2
 vines access-group 1
!
interface fddi 0
 vines metric 1
```

The first line in the access list prohibits any communication between the two servers, while the second line allows all other communication to pass through the router.

If you wanted to allow only mail traffic between these two servers, you would need the following configuration. Port 4 is the VINES Mail port.

```
vines routing
vines access-list 101 permit IPC 274113:1 0:0 0 FFFF 274111:1 0:0 4 0
vines access-list 101 permit IPC 274111:1 0:0 4 0 274113:1 0:0 0 FFFF
```

```
vines access-list 101 deny IP 274111:1 0:0 274113:1 0:0
vines access-list 101 permit IP 0:0 FFFFFFFF:FFFF 0:0 FFFFFFFF:FFFF
!
interface ethernet 0
 vines metric 2
 vines access-group 101
!
interface fddi 0
 vines metric 1
```

The first line in the access list allows mail messages being sent from the server in the lower-right to the server in the upper-left. The second line allows mail messages in the other direction. The third line prohibits all other communication between these two servers. The last line allows all other communication to pass through the router.

## Time-of-Day Service Example

The following example, using the configuration shown in , illustrates how to configure the "time of day" support in a VINES network. Router C also is configured as a NTP server and will provide time to the VINES network.

### Configuration for Routers A and B

```
vines routing
!
interface ethernet 0
 vines metric 2
!
interface fddi 0
 vines metric 1
!
vines access-list 201 permit 30001234:1 0:0
vines access-list 201 deny 0:0 FFFFFFFF:FFFF
vines time access-group 201
vines time participate
vines time set-system
```

### Configuration for Router C

```
vines routing
!
interface ethernet 0
 vines metric 2
!
interface fddi 0
 vines metric 1
!
ntp peer 128.9.2.129
vines time participate
vines time use-system
```

The access list on Routers A and B is not absolutely necessary. It prevents the routers from learning the time from anyone other than Router C. The reason this is not very important is that each time message from Router C will override any time that has been previously learned (because of the **vines time use-system** command).

# CHAPTER 10

# Banyan VINES Commands

The Banyan Virtual Network System (VINES) protocol is a networking system for personal computers. This proprietary protocol was developed by Banyan and is derived from the Xerox Network Systems (XNS) protocol. Cisco's implementation of VINES was designed in conjunction with Banyan.

Cisco's implementation of Banyan VINES provides routing of VINES packets on all media. Although the software automatically determines a metric value that it uses to route updates based on the delay set for the interface, Cisco's software implementation allows you to customize the metric. Cisco's implementation also offers address resolution to respond to address requests. Media Access Control (MAC)-level echo support is also available for Ethernet, IEEE 802.2, Token Ring, and Fiber Distributed Data Interface (FDDI) media. Name-to-address mapping for VINES host names is also supported, as are access lists to filter outgoing packets.

---
**NOTES**
---

Not all Cisco access servers support Banyan VINES. For more information, refer to the release notes for the release you are running.

---

Use the commands in this chapter to configure and monitor VINES networks.

## CLEAR VINES CACHE

To delete entries from the VINES fast-switching cache, use the **clear vines cache** EXEC command.

> **clear vines cache** [**interface** *interface* | **neighbor** *address* | **server** *network*]

| Syntax | Description |
|---|---|
| interface *interface* | (Optional) Deletes from the fast-switching cache table any entry that has one or more paths that go through the specified interface. |
| neighbor *address* | (Optional) Deletes from the fast-switching cache table any entry that has one or more paths via the specified neighbor router. |
| server *network* | (Optional) Deletes from the fast-switching cache table any entry whose network number part of the destination address matches the specified network address. The argument *network* can be either a 4-byte hexadecimal number or a 4-byte decimal number (if you have issued a **vines decimal** command). |

## Command Mode
EXEC

## Usage Guidelines
This command first appeared in Cisco IOS Release 10.0.

The fast-switching cache is a table of routes used when fast switching is enabled.

If you do not specify any keywords or arguments, all entries in the fast-switching cache are deleted.

## Examples
The following example deletes all entries from the VINES fast-switching cache table:

```
clear vines cache
```

The following example deletes all entries whose destination server has the address 30002E6D:

```
clear vines cache server 30002E6D
```

## Related Commands
You can use the master indexes or search online for documentation of related commands.

show vines cache
vines decimal
vines route-cache

## CLEAR VINES IPC
To delete VINES Interprocess Communications Protocol (IPC) connection blocks, use the **clear vines ipc** EXEC command.

```
clear vines ipc number
```

| Syntax | Description |
|--------|-------------|
| *number* | Hexadecimal number of the IPC connection to delete. |

### Command Mode
EXEC

### Usage Guidelines
This command first appeared in Cisco IOS Release 10.0.

An IPC connection entry is built each time the Cisco IOS software initiates or receives an IPC DATA message from a router that is not already in this table.

### Examples
The following example deletes IPC connection 0x1D from the table of VINES IPC connections:

```
clear vines ipc 1D
```

### Related Commands
You can use the master indexes or search online for documentation of related commands.

**show vines ipc**

## CLEAR VINES NEIGHBOR

To delete entries from the neighbor table, use the **clear vines neighbor** EXEC command.

**clear vines neighbor** {*network* | *\**}

| Syntax | Description |
|--------|-------------|
| *network* | Network number of the neighbor whose entry should be deleted from the neighbor table. The argument *network* can be either a 4-byte hexadecimal number or a 4-byte decimal number (if you have issued a **vines decimal** command). |
| * | Deletes all entries from the neighbor path table except the entry for the local router. |

### Command Mode
EXEC

### Usage Guidelines
This command first appeared in Cisco IOS Release 10.0.

The neighbor table contains an entry for each of the router's neighbor nodes.

Deleting an entry from the neighbor table also deletes any routes in the routing table that have that neighbor as the first hop and all fast-switching cache entries that have that neighbor as the first hop in any of their paths.

## Example

The following example deletes all entries from the neighbor table:

```
clear vines neighbor *
```

## Related Commands

You can use the master indexes or search online for documentation of related commands.

**clear vines route**
**show vines neighbor**
**show vines route**
**vines decimal**
**vines neighbor**
**vines route**

## CLEAR VINES ROUTE

To delete network addresses from the routing table, use the **clear vines route** EXEC command.

    **clear vines route** {*network* | *\**}

| Syntax | Description |
|---|---|
| *network* | Network number of the entry to delete from the routing table. The argument *network* can be either a 4-byte hexadecimal number, a 4-byte decimal number (if you have issued a **vines decimal** command), or a host name (if you have issued a **vines host** command). |
| * | Deletes all entries from the routing table. |

## Command Mode

EXEC

## Usage Guidelines

This command first appeared in Cisco IOS Release 10.0.

Deleting an entry from the routing table with the **clear vines route** command also deletes any entries in the fast-switching table that are a part of that logical network.

## Example

The following example deletes all entries from the VINES routing table:

```
clear vines route *
```

*Related Commands*

You can use the master indexes or search online for documentation of related commands.

**clear vines route**
**show vines neighbor**
**show vines route**
**vines decimal**
**vines host**
**vines route**

## CLEAR VINES TRAFFIC

To clear all VINES-related statistics that are displayed by the **show vines traffic** command, use the **clear vines traffic** EXEC command.

    **clear vines traffic**

*Syntax      Description*

This command has no arguments or keywords.

*Command Mode*

EXEC

*Usage Guidelines*

This command first appeared in Cisco IOS Release 10.0.

The **clear vines traffic** command clears only the statistics displayed by the **show vines traffic** command. It has no effect on the value of the VINES counters retrieved by Simple Network Management Protocol (SNMP).

*Example*

The following example zeros all VINES-related traffic statistics:

    clear vines traffic

*Related Commands*

You can use the master indexes or search online for documentation of related commands.

**show vines traffic**

## PING

To determine basic network connectivity, use the **ping** EXEC command.

    **ping** [**vines**] [*address*]

*Command Reference*

| Syntax | Description |
| --- | --- |
| **vines** | (Optional) Specifies the VINES protocol. If you omit this keyword, the Cisco IOS software prompts for it. |
| *address* | (Optional) Address of system to ping. If you omit the address, the software prompts for it. |

## Command Mode

EXEC

## Usage Guidelines

This command first appeared in Cisco IOS Release 10.0.

The **ping** command determines network connectivity by sending datagrams to another host on the network.

## Sample Display

The following is sample output from the **ping** command:

```
Router# ping vines 27AF92:1

Type escape sequence to abort.
Sending 5, 100-byte VINES Echos to 27AF92:1,
timeout is 2 seconds:
!!!!!
Success rate is 100 percent, round-trip min/avg/max = 4/7/8 ms

Router# ping

Protocol [ip]: vines
Target VINES address: 27AF92:1
Repeat count [5]: 10
Datagram size [100]: 500
Timeout in seconds [2]:
Verbose [n]:
Type escape sequence to abort.
Sending 10, 500-byte VINES Echos to 27AF92:1,
timeout is 2 seconds:
!!!!!!!!!!
Success rate is 100 percent, round-trip min/avg/max = 4/7/8 ms
```

## SHOW VINES ACCESS

To display the VINES access lists currently defined, use the **show vines access** EXEC command.

    **show vines access** [*access-list-number*]

| Syntax | Description |
| --- | --- |
| *access-list-number* | (Optional) Number of the access list to display. |

## Command Mode

EXEC

## Usage Guidelines

This command first appeared in Cisco IOS Release 10.0.

If no access list number is specified, all access lists are displayed.

## Sample Display

The following is sample output from the **show vines access** command:

```
Router# show vines access

Vines access list 1
  deny   SPP 30015800:0001 00000000:00000000 202 00123456:8005 00000000:0000 249
  permit IP 00000000:0000 FFFFFFFF:FFFF 00000000:0000 FFFFFFFF:FFFF
Vines access list 101
  deny   SPP 00112233:0001 00000000:0000 0006 0000
             00123456:8005 00000000:00000000 0000 FFFF
  permit IP 00000000:0000 FFFFFFFF:FFFF 00000000:0000 FFFFFFFF:FFFF
```

Table 10–1 describes the fields shown in the display.

**Table 10–1** *Show VINES Access Field Descriptions*

| Field | Description |
| --- | --- |
| Vines access list... | Number of the VINES access list. |
| deny | Networks to which access is denied. |
| permit | Networks to which access is permitted. |

## Related Commands

You can use the master indexes or search online for documentation of related commands.

**vines access-list (extended)**
**vines access-list (simple)**
**vines access-list (standard)**

## SHOW VINES CACHE

To display the contents of the VINES fast-switching cache, use the **show vines cache** EXEC command.

> **show vines cache** [*address* | **interface** *type number* | **neighbor** *address* | **server** *network*]

| Syntax | Description |
|---|---|
| *address* | (Optional) Displays the entry in the fast-switching cache for the specified station. |
| **interface** *type number* | (Optional) Displays all neighbors in the fast-switching cache that are accessible via the specified interface type and number. |
| **neighbor** *address* | (Optional) Displays all routes in the VINES fast-switching cache that have the specified neighbor as their first hop. The argument *address* is a 6-byte hexadecimal number in the format *network:host*, where *network* is 4 bytes and *host* is 2 bytes, a 4-byte decimal number in the same format (if you have issued a **vines decimal** command), or a host name (if you have issued a **vines host** command). |
| **server** *network* | (Optional) Displays all entries in the VINES fast-switching cache that are in the specified logical network. The argument *network* can be either a 4-byte hexadecimal number or a 4-byte decimal number (if you have issued a **vines decimal** command). |

## Command Mode

EXEC

## Usage Guidelines

This command first appeared in Cisco IOS Release 10.0.

If no keywords or arguments are specified, all entries in the fast-switching cache are displayed.

## Sample Display

The following is sample output from **show vines cache** command. This sample shows all entries in the VINES fast-switching cache.

```
Router# show vines cache

VINES fast switching cache information:
  Current: 0 entries, 0 paths
  History:
      Added:       0 server,        0 router,        0 client
      Updated:     0 server,        0 router,        0 client
      Expired:     0 server,        0 router,        0 client
      Removed:     0 server,        0 router,        0 client
      Flushes:     4 by neighbor,        1 by server
                   8 by interface,        1 entire table

  Hash  Destination    Int    Age  Length  Type  MAC Header
  13/00 Router1        *T0     46   16/18   1     10005A746A3600003080FB06BCBC03BA
```

```
  27/00 Router2            E1      11    14/14  1    00000C01D87C00000C0158010BAD
                          *T0      11    16/18  1    00003000435500003080FB06BCBC03BA
  3E/00 Router3           *T0      42    16/18  1    10005A6FBC15000003080FB06BCBC03BA
  72/00 30002E6D:0001      E1      32    14/14  1    00000C01D87C00000C0158010BAD
                          *T0      32    16/18  1    00003000435500003080FB07BCBC03BA
                           T0      32    16/18  1    10005A6FBC1500003080FB06BCBC03BA
                           T0      32    16/18  1    10005A6FBC1500003080FB06BCBC03BA
  FE/00 Router4           *E2     264    14/14  1    00000C0124EA00000C0151AF0BAD
```

Table 10–2 describes fields shown in the display.

**Table 10–2**   *Show VINES Cache Field Descriptions*

| Field | Description |
| --- | --- |
| Current: | Number of entries and paths currently in the cache. |
| History: | Number of events since the last time the counters were cleared. |
| Added: | Number of server, router, and client entries added to the cache. |
| Updated: | Number of server, router, and client entry updates. |
| Expired: | Number of server, router, and client entries that timed out. |
| Removed: | Number of server, router, and client entries removed from the cache. |
| Flushes: | Number of neighbor, server, interface, and entire table flushes. |
| Hash | Position of this entry in the neighbor table. |
| Destination | Name or address of the destination station. |
| Int | Interface out of which the packet is sent. An asterisk preceding the interface name indicates that this is the next entry that will be used for the destination. |
| Age | Age of the entry, in seconds. |
| Length | Stored length of the packet's MAC header, followed by a slash and the actual length of the MAC header. Both lengths do not include the length of the Type field. These two lengths may differ because the initial bytes of Token Ring and FDDI frames are not stored. |
| Type | Local encapsulation type. |
| MAC Header | MAC header used to reach the destination. |

Note that neighbor information is not explicitly displayed by the **show vines cache** command. However, you can determine it by looking at the neighbor and routing tables (using the **show vines neighbor** and **show vines route** commands, respectively).

*Related Commands*

You can use the master indexes or search online for documentation of related commands.

**clear vines route**
**show vines neighbor**
**show vines route**
**vines decimal**
**vines route-cache**

## SHOW VINES HOST

To display the entries in the VINES host name table, use the **show vines host** EXEC command.

> **show vines host** [*name*]

| *Syntax* | *Description* |
|---|---|
| *name* | (Optional) Displays the entry in the VINES name table that has the specified name. |

*Command Mode*

EXEC

*Usage Guidelines*

This command first appeared in Cisco IOS Release 10.0.

If no name is specified, all entries in the host name table are displayed.

*Sample Display*

The following is sample output from the **show vines host** command:

```
Router# show vines host

Name       Address
Router1    0027AF9A:0001
Router2    0027D0E4:0001
Router3    002ABFAA:0001
Router4    30015800:0001
```

Table 10–3 describes the fields shown in the display.

**Table 10–3**   *Show VINES Host Field Descriptions*

| Field | Description |
|---|---|
| Name | Name of the VINES host. |
| Address | Address of the VINES host. |

## Related Commands

You can use the master indexes or search online for documentation of related commands.

**vines host**

## SHOW VINES INTERFACE

To display status of the VINES interfaces configured in the Cisco IOS software and the parameters configured on each interface, use the **show vines interface** EXEC command.

> **show vines interface** [*type number*]

| Syntax | Description |
|--------|-------------|
| *type* | (Optional) Interface type. |
| *number* | (Optional) Interface number. |

## Command Mode

EXEC

## Usage Guidelines

This command first appeared in Cisco IOS Release 10.0.

If you omit all keywords, this command displays values for all interfaces and displays all VINES global parameters.

## Sample Display

The following is sample output from the **show vines interface** command:

```
Router# show vines interface

VINES address is 3000902D:0001
  Next client will be 3000902D:8001
  Addresses are displayed in hexadecimal format.
  Slowest update interval is 90 seconds
  Roll Call timer queue:
   Neighbor Router3-Et2-0000.0c01.24ea in 180 seconds
  Sequence: 01029DD7, Packet ID: 00000003
  Reassembly timer queue:  (empty)
  Retry timer queue:  (empty)
  Participating in vines time of day synchronization
Hssi0 is down, line protocol is down
  VINES protocol processing disabled
Fddi0 is up, line protocol is up
  VINES broadcast encapsulation is ARPA
  Interface metric is 0008 [0 5000] (0.1000 seconds)
  Split horizon is enabled
  ARP processing is dynamic, state is learning (for another 18 seconds)
```

```
Special serverless net processing enabled
Outgoing access list is not set
Fast switching is enabled
Routing updates every 90 seconds. Next in 50 seconds.
Next synchronization update in 11:58:17.
Nodes present:  0 5.5x servers, 0 5.5x routers, 0 5.5x clients
                0 4.11 servers, 0 4.11 routers, 0 4.11 clients
Neighbors: none.
```

Table 10–4 describes the fields that may be shown in the display.

**Table 10–4**   *Show VINES Interface Field Descriptions*

| Field | Description |
|---|---|
| VINES address | Address of the router. |
| Next client will be | Address the router assigns to the next client that requests an address. This line is important only if the router has been configured via the **vines arp-enable** command to respond to address assignment requests. |
| Addresses | Indicates whether addresses are displayed as decimal or hexadecimal numbers. |
| Slowest update interval | Indicates the longest time interval (in seconds) between routing updates on any of the router's interfaces. |
| Roll Call timer Neighbor | Displays a list of all neighbor paths for which a Routing Table Protocol (RTP) request is sent on a regular basis, and the interval until that timer expires. |
| Sequence | Current Sequenced Routing Update Protocol (SRTP) sequence number for this router. |
| Packet ID | Identifier number that is used on the last SRTP update message sent by this router. |
| Reassembly timer | Displays a list of all neighbor paths for which an SRTP update is currently being reassembled, and the interval until that timer expires. |
| Retry timer | Displays a list of all neighbor paths for which an SRTP request is currently being retried, and the interval until that timer expires. |
| Participating in vines time of day synchronization | Indicates whether the router is participating in VINES time-of-day synchronization. This is controlled by the **vines time participate** global configuration command. |

**Table 10–4** *Show VINES Interface Field Descriptions, Continued*

| Field | Description |
|---|---|
| Hssi0/Ethernet 0/Ethernet 1/ Fddi0 is up/down | Type and number of interface, and whether it is currently active and inserted into network (up) or inactive and not inserted (down). |
| Line protocol is | Indicates whether the software processes that handle the line protocol believe the interface is usable (that is, whether keepalives are successful). This field can report the values "up," "down," and "administratively down." |
| VINES protocol processing disabled | Indicates that VINES processing is not enabled on the interface (that is, you have not issued a **vines metric** command on the interface). |
| VINES broadcast encapsulation | Type of encapsulation used for VINES broadcast packets, as defined with the **vines encapsulation** command. This field can report the values "arpa," "vines-tr," and "snap." |
| Interface metric | Metric that has been configured for the interface with the **vines metric** command. The metric is shown in internal form, configuration form, and in seconds. |
| Split horizon | Indicates whether split horizon has been enabled or disabled (via the **vines split-horizon** command). |
| ARP processing | Indicates whether this interface will process ARP packets, as specified by the **vines arp-enable** command. |
| Special serverless net processing | Indicates whether this interface is defined via the **vines serverless** command as being connected to a serverless network. |
| Outgoing access list | Indicates whether an access list is set. |
| Fast switching | Indicates whether fast switching has been enabled via the **vines route-cache** command. The value reported in this field can be "enabled," "disabled," or "not supported." |
| Routing updates every<br>  Next in | Frequency of routing updates, in seconds. This also indicates when the next routing update will be transmitted on the interface. You set the update interval with the **vines update interval** command. |

**Table 10–4**    *Show VINES Interface Field Descriptions, Continued*

| Field | Description |
|---|---|
| Routing updates | Indicates whether routing updates contain all entries in the routing table or just changes to the table since the last update was sent. You set the method used with the **vines update deltas** command. |
| Next synchronization | Indicates when the next SRTP synchronization update will be sent. |
| Nodes present | Indicates the number and type of all VINES-speaking devices present on the given physical network segment. |
| Neighbors: none | List of all VINES neighbors on that interface and what version of the RTP protocol they are running (0 means RTP, and 1 means SRTP). |

## Related Commands

You can use the master indexes or search online for documentation of related commands.

**vines arp-enable**
**vines encapsulation**
**vines metric**
**vines route-cache**

## SHOW VINES IPC

To display information about any currently active IPC connections, use the **show vines ipc** EXEC command.

> **show vines ipc**

## Syntax    Description

This command has no arguments or keywords.

## Command Mode

EXEC

## Usage Guidelines

This command first appeared in Cisco IOS Release 10.0.

Information about the IPC protocol formats, data sequences, and state machines can be found in Banyan documentation.

*Sample Display*

The following is sample output from the **show vines ipc** command:

```
Router# show vines ipc

Vines IPC Status:

Next Port: 513
Next Connection: 3
Next check in: 27 sec

Connection 2, state: connected
  Local address: Router1, id 0002, last port: 0200
  Remote address: Router2, id 0002, last port: 0001
  Last send seq: 0005, Last rcvd seq: 0005
  Next send ack: 0005, Last sent ack: 0005
  Server metric 4, last hop 0, bias 0, total 800 (ms)
  Send ACK in 0 ms, Retransmit in 0 ms
  Idle check in 0 sec
  Retransmit queue contains 0 packets
  No packet in reassembly
```

Table 10–5 describes the fields shown in the display.

**Table 10–5**  *Show VINES IPC Field Descriptions*

| Field | Description |
| --- | --- |
| Next Port: | IPC port number that the router uses when a new, unique IPC port number is needed. |
| Next Connection: | IPC connection number that the Cisco IOS software uses when a new, unique IPC connection number is needed. |
| Next check in: | When the software makes the next pass of the IPC connection table to examine each of the connection-specific timers. |
| Connection 2, state: | State of a particular connection. Possible states are connecting, connected, idle, and dead. |
| Local address: | VINES IP address of the local side of the connection. |
| last port: | Last port number used on this particular connection by the local host. |
| Remote address: | VINES IP address of the remote side of the connection. |
| last port: | Last port number used on this particular connection by the remote host. |
| Last send seq: | Last sequence number sent on this particular connection used by the local host. |
| Last rcvd seq: | Last sequence number received on this particular connection used by the local host. |

*Command Reference*

**Table 10–5**  *Show VINES IPC Field Descriptions, Continued*

| Field | Description |
|---|---|
| Next send ack: | Next acknowledgment number that is sent on this particular connection by the local host. |
| Last sent ack: | Last acknowledgment number that has been sent on this particular connection by the local host. |
| Server metric | Metric value from this host to the remote host's server or router. |
| last hop | Metric value from the remote host's server or router to the remote host itself. If the remote host is a server or router, this value should be zero. |
| bias | Bias added to the metric to account for variance in the round-trip delay of a message going to the remote host. |
| total | Total metric value used to reach the remote host. It is the sum of the three previous numbers. |
| Send ACK | Time, in seconds, until the next acknowledgment message is sent by the local host. |
| Retransmit | Time, in seconds, until a message is retransmitted by the local host. |
| Idle check in | Time, in seconds, until this connection is checked to see if it has been idle for 30 seconds. |
| Retransmit queue contains... packets | Number of messages that have been sent but not acknowledged. |
| No packet in reassembly | Number of packets that have been received and are being reassembled into a larger message. |

## SHOW VINES NEIGHBOR

To display the entries in the VINES neighbor table, use the **show vines neighbor** EXEC command.

> **show vines neighbor** [*address* | **interface** *type number* | **server** *number*]

| Syntax | Description |
|---|---|
| *address* | (Optional) Displays the entry for the specified neighbor. |
| **interface** *type number* | (Optional) Displays all neighbor paths in the neighbor table that use the specified interface. |
| **server** *number* | (Optional) Displays all entries in the neighbor table that have the specified network number. |

## Command Mode

EXEC

## Usage Guidelines

This command first appeared in Cisco IOS Release 10.0.

If no keywords or arguments are specified, all entries in the neighbor table are displayed.

## Sample Displays

The following is sample output from the **show vines neighbor** command. This sample shows all entries in the VINES neighbor table.

```
Router# show vines neighbor

6 neighbors, 7 paths, version 14, next update 34 seconds

Address         Hardware Address   Type  Int   Flag Age  Metric  Uses

Router1         -                  HDLC  Se0   R0*  n/a  0230    7
Router2         -                  -     -     C1   -    -       -
Router3         0000.0c01.24ea     ARPA  Et2   R0*  42   0020    9
Router4         -                  PPP   Se1   R1   n/a  0230    0
Router4         0000.0c01.0506     ARPA  Et0   R1.  n/a  0020    0
Router4         0000.0c01.9ac9     VINES To0   R1*  n/a  0020    0
```

The following is sample output from the **show vines neighbor** command for a specific server. This sample shows all entries in the VINES neighbor table for *router3*.

```
Router# show vines neighbor router3

3 neighbors, 4 paths, version 7, next update 24 seconds

Address         Hardware Address   Type  Int    Flag Age  Metric  Uses

Router3         0000.0c01.24ea     ARPA  Et2    R0*  42   0020    9

  RTP Counters:

    Interface Ethernet2, address Router3-Et2-0000.0c01.24ea
      Timers:
        Roll Call:  00:03:00
      Received counters:
        Requests:   00000000
        Responses:  00000000
        Updates:    00000000
        Redirects:  00000000
        Unknown:    00000000
```

Table 10–6 describes the fields shown in the display.

**Table 10–6**  *Show VINES Neighbor Field Descriptions*

| Field | Description |
|---|---|
| neighbors | Number of neighbors in the neighbor table. |
| paths | Number of paths to the neighbor. |
| version | Version number of the VINES neighbor table. The number is incremented each time a route or path is added to or deleted from this table. |
| next update | Time, in seconds, until the next routing update is sent. |
| Address | Address of the neighbor station. The neighbor's name is displayed if you have issued a **vines host** command. |
| Hardware Address | MAC address of the router interface through which the VINES neighbor in this entry can be reached. |
| Type | Type of MAC-level encapsulation used to communicate with this neighbor. |
| Int | Type and number of interface through which the VINES neighbor can be reached. |
| Flag | This field is a three-column field. |
| | The first column indicates how the path was learned. It can be one of the following values: |
| | • C—Connected (that is, this is the entry for this router). |
| | • D—Learned via an RTP redirect message. |
| | • P—Placeholder. This neighbor is currently used as the next hop for a static route. |
| | • R—Learned via an RTP update message. |
| | • S—Static path entry (entered with the **vines neighbor** command). |
| | The second column indicates what version of the RTP protocol this neighbor is running. It can be one of the following values: |
| | • 0—Version 0 of the RTP protocol. This is the version used by VINES servers prior to VINES version 5.50. |
| | • 1—Version 1 of the RTP protocol, commonly called SRTP. This is the version used by VINES servers in VINES version 5.50 and later. |

**Table 10–6**  *Show VINES Neighbor Field Descriptions, Continued*

| Field | Description |
|---|---|
| Flag (*Continued*) | The third column indicates how this path is used. It can be one of the following values:<br><br>• *—An asterisk means that this is the next path used when forwarding a frame to that neighbor.<br><br>• .—A dot means that this is the alternate path used in round-robin fashion.<br><br>• Blank—No value means this is a backup path that is not used.<br><br>In the sample output, there are two paths to Router4 with the same metric. These two paths will be used in a round-robin fashion, and the Token Ring path will be the next one of the two used. There is a third path to Router4 via the serial line, but this will not be used unless both of the other paths are lost. |
| Age | Age of this VINES neighbor table entry, in seconds. This entry shows an age of "n/a" for RTP Version 0 neighbors on WAN interfaces, when the interface has been configured for delta-only updates. In all other cases, this entry contains a number. |
| Metric | Distance to this neighbor. This normally is the same as the interface metric, but may be different because of network topology or router configuration. |
| Uses | For all entries except placeholders, indicates the number of times that path was used to forward a packet. For placeholder entries, indicates the number of static routes that use the neighbor as the first hop. |
| RTP Counters: | This section shows counters that are specific to a neighbor port that is running the RTP protocol only. If the neighbor has multiple interfaces, multiple sections show up in this part of the display. |
| Interface... | Identifies the network interface and full identifier for a neighbor port. |
| Timers:<br>    Roll Call | Identifies whether the roll call timer is active for this neighbor, and if so, when it will expire. |
| Received Counters | Indicates the number and type of RTP packets received from this neighbor port. |
| SRTP Counter: | This section shows counters that are specific to a neighbor port that is running the SRTP protocol. If the neighbor has multiple interfaces, multiple sections show up in this part of the display. |
| Interface | Identifies the network interface and full identifier for a neighbor port. |

**Table 10–6**  *Show VINES Neighbor Field Descriptions, Continued*

| Field | Description |
|---|---|
| Timers: Reassembly | Identifies whether the reassembly timer is active for this neighbor, and if so, when it will expire. |
| Timers: Retry | Identifies whether the retry timer is active for this neighbor, and if so, when it will expire. |
| Received Counters | Indicates the number, type, and sequence number of matching SRTP packets received from this neighbor port. |
| Transmitted Counters | Indicated the number and type of SRTP packets transmitted explicitly to this neighbor port. |

## Related Commands

You can use the master indexes or search online for documentation of related commands.

**clear vines neighbor**
**clear vines route**
**show vines cache**
**vines host**
**vines neighbor**
**vines update deltas**
**vines update interval**

## SHOW VINES ROUTE

To display the contents of the VINES routing table, use the **show vines route** EXEC command.

> **show vines route** [*number* | **neighbor** *address*]

| Syntax | Description |
|---|---|
| *number* | (Optional) Displays the routing table entry for the specified network. |
| **neighbor** *address* | (Optional) Displays all routes in the VINES routing table that have the specified neighbor as their first hop. |

## Command Mode

EXEC

## Usage Guidelines

This command first appeared in Cisco IOS Release 10.0.

If no keywords or arguments are specified, all entries in the routing table are displayed.

## Sample Display

The following is sample output from the **show vines route** command. This sample shows all entries in the VINES routing table.

```
Router# show vines route

Worf            Worf            R0*     2       2       0
Succubus        Succubus        R1*     2       2       0
Aloe            -               C1      -       -       -
Vera            Vera            R0*     2       2       0
Falcon          Falcon          R0*     2       2       0
Zangbutt        Worf            R0*     2       4       0
Zangbutt        Vera            R0      .2      4       0
```

The following is sample output from the **show vines route** command for a specific neighbor. This sample shows all entries in the VINES routing table for *router1*.

```
Router# show vines route router1

8 servers, 10 routes, version 58, next update 32 seconds

Network     Neighbor    Flags   Age     Metric  Uses    Origin      Local       Flags

Router1     Router2     R0*     n/a     0250    0       001AFE7B    00010FCA    0009
```

Table 10–7 describes the fields shown in the display.

**Table 10–7**  *Show VINES Route Field Descriptions*

| Field | Description |
|---|---|
| servers | Number of servers in the routing table. |
| routes | Number of routes in the routing table. |
| version | Version number of the VINES routing table. This number is incremented each time a server or route is added to or deleted from this table. |
| next update | Time, in seconds, until the next routing update is sent. |
| Hash | Position of this entry in the routing table. |
| Network | Name or number of the remote network. Networks take the name of the server that defines the network. |
| Neighbor | Next hop to the destination network. |

**Table 10–7**   *Show VINES Route Field Descriptions, Continued*

| Field | Description |
|-------|-------------|
| Flags | This field is a series of single-column fields. |
|       | The first column indicates how the route was learned. It can be one of the following values: |
|       | • C—Connected (that is, this is the entry for this router). |
|       | • D—Learned via an RTP redirect message. |
|       | • R—Learned via an RTP update message. |
|       | • S—Static entry (entered with the **vines route** command). |
|       | The second column indicates what version of the RTP protocol this router is running. It can be one of the following values: |
|       | • 0—Version 0 of the RTP protocol. This is the version used by VINES servers prior to VINES version 5.50. This version number is also shown if the route was learned via a pre-5.50 server, and thus the version information was lost. |
|       | • 1—Version 1 of the RTP protocol, commonly called SRTP. This is the version used by VINES servers in VINES version 5.50 and later. |
|       | An asterisk in the third column indicates that this route is used next when forwarding a frame to that server. |
|       | The fourth column indicates whether that route is used to forward a broadcast from a serverless network. It can be one of the following values: |
|       | • N—This server is considered to be the nearest server and is on a directly connected network. |
|       | • n—This server is considered to be the nearest server but is not on a directly connected network. |
|       | The fifth column contains the letter "S" if the route is in a suppression state. |
|       | The sixth column contains the letter "h" if this path has a metric that is higher than the best metric for this neighbor. This indicates that the path is not eligible for use in load sharing. |
| Age | Age of this VINES routing table entry, in seconds. An age of n/a indicates the destination is accessible via a neighbor that is sending delta-only updates. Note that even though the neighbor entry for Pica has an age, there is no age available for its routing table entry or other routing entries reachable via Pica. This is because the periodic hello messages from Pica contain no routing information, only neighbor reachability information. |
| Metric | Distance to this server. This normally is the distance to the neighbor router plus the distance advertised by that neighbor. This does not hold for static routes. |

**Table 10–7** *Show VINES Route Field Descriptions, Continued*

| Field | Description |
|-------|-------------|
| Uses | Number of times this route has been used to forward a packet. |
| Origin | Last known timestamp that originated from this server. If this field is not valid, as indicated by the following set of flags, it will be zero. |
| Local | Local timestamp when this route entry was learned or last changed. |
| Flags | This field is a series of bit flags presented as a hexadecimal number. The following are the defined values:<br>• 0001—The neighbor of this server reaches it through a LAN interface.<br>• 0002—The neighbor of this server reaches it through a WAN interface.<br>• 0004—The neighbor of this server reaches it through a non-VINES interface.<br>• 0008—The origin timestamp for this entry is not valid. The entry is either for a pre-5.50 server, or the entry was learned via a pre-5.50 server. |

## Related Commands

You can use the master indexes or search online for documentation of related commands.

clear vines neighbor
clear vines route
show vines cache
vines route
vines neighbor
vines update deltas
vines update interval

## SHOW VINES SERVICE

To display information about the application layer support, use the **show vines service** EXEC command.

show vines service [fs | nsm | ss | vs]

| Syntax | Description |
|--------|-------------|
| fs | (Optional) Displays file service information. |
| nsm | (Optional) Displays network and system management service information. |
| ss | (Optional) Displays server service information. |
| vs | (Optional) Displays security service information. |

*Command Mode*

EXEC

*Usage Guidelines*

This command first appeared in Cisco IOS Release 10.0.

*Sample Displays*

The following is sample output from the **show vines service** command:

```
Router# show vines service

Vines Files Service:
    Name:    FS@Doc-ags+1@Servers (FS)
    Ports:   Well Known 6, Transient 0
    Timer:   not running

Network & System Management Service:
    Name:    NSM@Doc-ags+1@Servers (NSM)
    Ports:   Well Known 25, Transient 0
    Timer:   not running

Server Service:
    Name:    SS@Doc-ags+1@Servers (SS)
    Ports:   Well Known 7, Transient 0
    Emulates: 5.50(0), Supports: 3.22(49) - 6.99(49)
    Timer:   not running

VINES Security Service:
    Name:    VS@Doc-ags+1@Servers (VS)
    Ports:   Well Known 19, Transient 0
    Timer:   not running
```

Table 10–8 describes the fields shown in the display.

**Table 10–8**  *Show VINES Service Field Descriptions*

| Field | Description |
|---|---|
| Name: | Name of the service. |
| Ports: | Ports on which the service is running. |
| Timer: | Time at which this service will wake up and perform some periodic functions. |

The following is sample output from the **show vines service** command using the **fs, nsm, ss,** and **vs** keywords:

```
Router# show vines service fs

Vines Files Service:
   Periodic timer not running.

Router# show vines service nsm

Network & System Management Service:
   Next wakeup in 00:00:29.

Router# show vines service ss

Server Service:
   Next wakeup in 00:01:51.
   Time is 17:12:55 PDT Jun 23 1994
   Time last set by Doc-ags, 0:28:09 ago.
   Time epoch is SS@Doc-ags@Servers-9, started 00:28:09 ago.
     Participating in vines time of day synchronization.
     Sending time messages to the broadcast address.
     Synchronizing vines time with system time.

Router# show vines service vs

VINES Security Service:
   Periodic timer not running.
```

Table 10–9 describes the fields shown in the displays.

**Table 10–9**  *Show VINES Service (fs, nsm, ss, and vs) Field Descriptions*

| Field | Description |
|---|---|
| Periodic timer not running | Indicates that this service has no periodic functions to perform. |
| Next wakeup in... | Time, in seconds, until the service performs its periodic actions. For the Server service, this is to send a time synchronization message. For the Network System and Management (NSM) service, this is to send any requested trace packets. The periodic interval for the NSM service is 30 seconds when no trace messages are pending. |
| Time is... | Current time (in the format *hours:minutes:seconds*) and date. |
| Time last set... | Server that last adjusted the time, how much it adjusted the time, and how long ago it was adjusted. For times within the last 24 hours, the time format is *hours:minutes:seconds*. For times longer than 24 hours, the time format is *weeks*w*days*d. |
| Time epoch is... | Name of the current time epoch (in the format *name-number*), and when it was established. |

*Command Reference*

*Related Commands*

You can use the master indexes or search online for documentation of related commands.

**vines time access-group**
**vines time participate**
**vines time set-system**
**vines time use-system**

## SHOW VINES TRAFFIC

To display the statistics maintained about VINES protocol traffic, use the **show vines traffic** EXEC command.

      **show vines traffic** [*type number*]

| Syntax | Description |
|--------|-------------|
| *type* | (Optional) Interface type. |
| *number* | (Optional) Interface number. |

*Command Mode*

EXEC

*Usage Guidelines*

This command first appeared in Cisco IOS Release 10.0.

If no interface is specified, values for all interfaces are displayed.

*Sample Display*

The following is sample output from the **show vines traffic** command:

```
Router# show vines traffic

SYSTEM TRAFFIC:
  Rcvd: 204 total, 12708 bytes, 0 format errors, 0 not enabled,
        15 local dst, 189 bcast, 0 forwarded
        0 no route, 0 zero hops
        0 checksum errors, 3 IP unknown, 0 IPC unknown
        3 bcast forwarded, 1 bcast helpered, 0 dup bcast
  Sent: 21 packets, 1278 bytes
        0 unicast, 21 bcast, 0 forwarded
        0 encap failed, 0 access failed, 0 down
        0 bcast fwd, 3 not fwd (toward source)
        0 notlan, 0 not gt4800, 0 no pp charge
 ARPv0: Rcvd 0/0/0/0/0, Sent 0/0/0/0
 ARPv1: Rcvd 0/0/0/0/0, Sent 0/0/0/0
   ICP: Rcvd 0/0/0, Send 0/0
   IPC: Rcvd 17, Sent 8
```

```
     RTPv0: Rcvd 2/10/0/0/170/0/0/5, Sent 0/6/00/0/91/10/0
     RTPv1: Rcvd 0/0/0/0/0/0, Sent 0/3/60/0
       SPP: Rcvd 0, Sent 0
      Echo: Rcvd 5, Sent 5
     Proxy: Rcvd 0, Sent 0
IPC TRAFFIC BY PORT NUMBER:
Broadcast: Other:00000000, 01:00000000, 02:00000000, 03:00000000, 04:00000000
           05:00000000, 06:00000000, 07:00000000, 08:00000000, 09:00000000
           0A:00000000, 0B:00000000, 0C:00000000, 0D:00000000, 0E:00000000
           0F:00000000, 10:00000000, 11:00000000, 12:00000000, 13:00000000
           14:00000000, 15:00000000, 16:00000000, 17:00000000, 18:00000000
           19:00000000
 Helpered: Other:00000000, 01:00000000, 02:00000000, 03:00000000, 04:00000000
           05:00000000, 06:00000000, 07:00000000, 08:00000000, 09:00000000
           0A:00000000, 0B:00000000, 0C:00000000, 0D:00000000, 0E:00000000
           0F:00000000, 10:00000000, 11:00000000, 12:00000000, 13:00000000
           14:00000000, 15:00000000, 16:00000000, 17:00000000, 18:00000000
           19:00000000
  Unicast: Other:00000000, 01:00000000, 02:00000000, 03:00000000, 04:00000000
           05:00000000, 06:00000000, 07:00000000, 08:00000000, 09:00000000
           0A:00000000, 0B:00000000, 0C:00000000, 0D:00000000, 0E:00000000
           0F:00000000, 10:00000000, 11:00000000, 12:00000000, 13:00000000
           14:00000000, 15:00000000, 16:00000000, 17:00000000, 18:00000000
           19:00000000
  Proxied: Other:00000000, 01:00000000, 02:00000000, 03:00000000, 04:00000000
           05:00000000, 06:00000000, 07:00000000, 08:00000000, 09:00000000
           0A:00000000, 0B:00000000, 0C:00000000, 0D:00000000, 0E:00000000
           0F:00000000, 10:00000000, 11:00000000, 12:00000000, 13:00000000
           14:00000000, 15:00000000, 16:00000000, 17:00000000, 18:00000000
           19:00000000
P_Replies: Other:00000000, 01:00000000, 02:00000000, 03:00000000, 04:00000000
           05:00000000, 06:00000000, 07:00000000, 08:00000000, 09:00000000
           0A:00000000, 0B:00000000, 0C:00000000, 0D:00000000, 0E:00000000
           0F:00000000, 10:00000000, 11:00000000, 12:00000000, 13:00000000
           14:00000000, 15:00000000, 16:00000000, 17:00000000, 18:00000000
           19:00000000

Interface Hssi0:
  Rcvd: 0 packets, 0 bytes, 0 format errors, 0 not enabled,
        0 local dst, 0 bcast, 0 forwarded,
        0 no route, 0 zero hops
        0 checksum errors, 0 IP unknown, 0 IPX unknown
        0 bcast forwarded, 0 bcast helpered, 0 dup bcast
  Sent: 0 packets, 0 bytes
        0 unicast, 0 bcast, 0 forwarded
        0 encap failed, 0 access failed, 0 down
        0 bcast fwd, 0 not fwd (toward source)
        0 notlan, 0 not gt4800, 0 no pp charge
  ARPv0: Rcvd 0/0/0/0/0, Sent 0/0/0/0
  ARPv1: Rcvd 0/0/0/0/0, Sent 0/0/0/0
    ICP: Rcvd 0/0/0, Send 0/0
```

```
  IPC: Rcvd 0, Sent 8
RTPv0: Rcvd 0/10/0/0/0/0/0/0, Sent 0/0/00/0/0/0/0/0
RTPv1: Rcvd 0/0/0/0/0/0/0, Sent 0/3/60/0
  SPP: Rcvd 0, Sent 0
 Echo: Rcvd 0, Sent 0
Proxy: Rcvd 0, Sent 0
```

Table 10–10 describes the fields shown in the display.

**Table 10–10**  *Show VINES Traffic Field Descriptions*

| Field | Description |
|---|---|
| SYSTEM TRAFFIC: | This section displays statistics about all VINES packets handled by the Cisco IOS software. |
| Rcvd: | This section displays statistics about VINES packets received by the software. |
| packets | Total number of VINES packets received. |
| bytes | Total bytes in all the VINES packets received. |
| format errors | Number of VINES packets that had errors in the format of the VINES IP header. Currently, the only thing checked is the length field in the header. The number of packets with format errors is included in the count of total packets received (in the Rcvd: field). |
| not enabled | Number of VINES packets received on an interface on which VINES was not enabled. These packets are not included when counting the total packets received (in the Rcvd: field). |
| local dst | Number of packets accepted for further processing because they were addressed to the router's unicast address. |
| bcast | Number of packets accepted for further processing because they were addressed to the router's broadcast address. |
| forwarded | Number of packets·not accepted for further processing but simply forwarded out another interface. |
| no route | Number of packets discarded because the Cisco IOS software did not know how to reach the destination. |
| zero hops | Number of packets discarded because the hop count field in the VINES IP header was zero. |
| checksum errors | Number of packets accepted for further processing (the sum of the "local dest" and "bcast" fields) that were discarded because the checksum was bad. |

**Table 10–10** *Show VINES Traffic Field Descriptions, Continued*

| Field | Description |
|---|---|
| IP unknown | Number of packets accepted (the sum of the "local dest" and "bcast" fields) that were discarded because the IP protocol type was unknown. |
| IPC unknown | Number of packets accepted for further processing (the sum of the "local dest" and "bcast" fields) that were discarded because the IPC port number was unknown. |
| bcast forwarded | Number of broadcast packets accepted for further processing (as shown in the "bcast" field) that were forwarded because they had a nonzero hop count. (Note that the sum of the "bcast forwarded," "bcast helpered," and "dup bcast" fields will not equal the total number of broadcast packets received.) |
| bcast helpered | Number of broadcast packets accepted (as shown in the "bcast" field) that were "helpered" to a Banyan server. (Note that the sum of the "bcast forwarded," "bcast helpered," and "dup bcast" fields will not equal the total number of broadcast packets received.) |
| dup bcast | Number of broadcast packets accepted (as shown in the "bcast" field) that were classified as duplicates and discarded. (Note that the sum of the "bcast forwarded," "bcast helpered," and "dup bcast" fields will not equal the total number of broadcast packets received.) |
| Sent: | This section displays statistics about VINES packets sent by the router. |
| packets | Total number of VINES packets sent. |
| bytes | Total bytes in all the VINES packets sent. |
| unicast | Number of unicast packets originating at the router. |
| bcast | Number of broadcast packets originating at the router. |
| forwarded | Number of unicast packets that were forwarded from another interface. |
| encap failed | Number of packets not sent because of an encapsulation failure. This usually happens when entries in a map for a public data network, such as X.25 or Frame Relay, are missing. |
| access failed | Number of packets not sent because the destination was denied by an access list. |
| down | Number of packets not sent because the interface was down. |

**Table 10–10**  *Show VINES Traffic Field Descriptions, Continued*

| Field | Description |
|---|---|
| bcast fwd | Number of broadcast packets that were forwarded from another interface. |
| not fwd (toward source) | Number of broadcast packets that were not forwarded because this interface is the interface on which the broadcast was received. |
| not lan | Number of broadcast packets that were not forwarded because they were marked for LANs only and this interface is not a LAN (for example, it might be a serial interface.) |
| not gt | Number of broadcast packets that were not forwarded because they were marked for high-speed interfaces only and this interface is a low-speed interface (line speed of 4800 baud or less). |
| no pp charge | Number of broadcast packets that were not forwarded because they were marked to send only to networks that do not have per-packet charging and this interface is to a network that has per-packet charging. |
| ARPv0: | This section displays statistics about VINES ARP packets sent and received. |
| Rcvd *x/x/x/x/x* | Number of ARP packets received of type 0, 1, 2, 3, and other. |
| Sent *x/x/x/x* | Number of ARP packets sent of type 0, 1, 2, and 3. |
| ARPv1: | This section displays statistics about VINES SARP packets sent and received. |
| Rcvd *x/x/x/x/x* | Number of SARP packets received of type 0, 1, 2, 3, and other. |
| Sent *x/x/x/x* | Number of SARP packets sent of type 0, 1, 2, and 3. |
| ICP: | This section displays statistics about VINES ICP packets sent and received. |
| Rcvd *x/x/x* | Number of ICP packets received of type 0, 1, and other. |
| Sent *x/x* | Number of ICP packets sent of type 0 and 1. |
| IPC: | This section displays statistics about VINES IPC packets sent and received. |
| Rcvd | Number of IPC packets received. |

**Table 10–10** *Show VINES Traffic Field Descriptions, Continued*

| Field | Description |
|---|---|
| Sent | Number of IPC packets sent. |
| RTPv0: | This section displays statistics about VINES RTP packets sent and received. |
| Rcvd *x/x/x/x/x/x/x/x* | Number of RTP packets received of type 0, 1, 2, 3, 4, 5, 6, and other. The counts of type 0, type 2, type 3, and other RTP packets should always be zero. |
| Sent *x/x/x/x/x/x/x* | Number of RTP packets sent of type 0, 1, 2, 3, 4, 5, and 6. |
| RTPv1: | This section displays statistics about VINES SRTP packets sent and received. |
| Rcvd *x/x/x/x/x* | Number of SRTP packets received of type 0, 1, 2, 3, and other. The count of other SRTP packets should always be zero. |
| Sent *x/x/x/x/x* | Number of SRTP packets sent of type 0, 1, 2, 3. |
| SPP: | This section displays statistics about VINES Sequence Packet Protocol (SPP) packets sent and received. |
| Rcvd | Number of SPP packets received |
| Sent | Number of SPP packets sent. |
| Echo: | This section displays statistics about VINES echo packets sent and received. |
| Rcvd | Number of MAC-level echo packets received. |
| Sent | Number of MAC-level echo packets sent. |
| Proxy: | This section displays statistics about VINES proxies sent and received. A proxy is when a client sends a query directly to the router for which the router does not have the intelligence to respond. The Cisco IOS software then sends these queries to a Banyan server, and when it receives the response from the server, the software relays it back to the client. |
| Rcvd | Number of proxy queries received. |
| Sent | Number of proxy queries sent. |

*Command Reference*

**Table 10–10**   *Show VINES Traffic Field Descriptions, Continued*

| Field | Description |
|---|---|
| IPC TRAFFIC BY PORT NUMBER: | This section displays statistics about VINES IPC packets. The information displayed in this section is particularly useful when a serverless network is connected to the router. |
| Broadcast: | Number of VINES IPC messages, by destination port number, received by the router because they were addressed to the VINES IP broadcast address. |
| Helpered: | Number of broadcast messages that were sent toward a Banyan server because they were received on an interface for a serverless network. |
| Unicast: | Number of VINES IPC messages, by destination port number, received by the router because they were specifically addressed to the VINES IP address of the router. |
| Proxied: | Number of unicast messages received that were sent to a Banyan server because they were received on a serverless interface and because the router did not know how to respond to the message. |
| P_Replies: | Number of responses to a proxy query that were received from a Banyan server. |
| Interface | This section displays statistics about the individual interfaces in the router. The fields in this section have the same meanings as the fields of the same name in the "SYSTEM TRAFFIC" section, except that the statistics are for the particular interface, not for the entire router. |

## Related Commands

You can use the master indexes or search online for documentation of related commands.

**clear vines traffic**
**vines serverless**

## TRACE

To determine the path that a packet takes when traversing a VINES network, use the **trace** EXEC command.

> **trace** [**vines** | **oldvines**] [*address*]

| Syntax | Description |
|---|---|
| **vines** | (Optional) Specifies the VINES protocol. This trace is compatible with the Banyan VINES traceroute function. |
| **oldvines** | (Optional) Specifies the VINES protocol. This trace is compatible with our **trace** function prior to Cisco IOS Release 10.2. |
| *address* | (Optional) Address of a node. This is a 6-byte hexadecimal number in the format *network:host*, where *network* is 4 bytes and *host* is 2 bytes. |

## Command Mode

EXEC

## Usage Guidelines

This command first appeared in Cisco IOS Release 10.0. The **oldvines** keyword first appeared in Cisco IOS Release 10.3.

The **trace** EXEC command supports the Banyan traceroute function. This enables trace requests on a VINES network to reach all servers on the network.

This command does not produce the names of any VINES servers that are traversed.

## Sample Displays

The following is sample output from the VINES **trace** command when you specify the **vines** keyword:

```
Router# trace vines

Target Vines address: wayfinder
Source Vines address: coinspinner
From: 0002801578 Coinspinner      To: 0002609380 Wayfinder

Server                  Gate                    metric media address
0002801578 Coinspinner  0805371606 Router          4     40 000030C0FEB6
0805371606 Router       0002609380 Wayfinder        2   2560 10005A746A36
```

The following is sample output from the VINES **trace** command when you specify the **oldvines** keyword:

```
Router# trace oldvines

Target vines address: 27AF92:1
Numeric display [n]:
Timeout in seconds [3]:
Probe count [3]:
Minimum Time to Live [0]:
Maximum Time to Live [15]:
Type escape sequence to abort.
```

```
Tracing the route to COINSPINNER (27AF92:1)
 0 Farslayer (30002A2D:1) 0 msec 4 msec 4 msec
 1 Coinspinner (27AF92:1) 4 msec 4 msec 8 msec
```

The value *nn* msec indicates the round-trip time for each probe in milliseconds, for each node.

## VINES ACCESS-GROUP

To apply an access list to an interface, use the **vines access-group** interface configuration command. To remove the access list, use the **no** form of this command.

> **vines access-group** *access-list-number*
> **no vines access-group** *access-list-number*

*Syntax*

*access-list-number*

*Description*

Number of the access list. All outgoing packets defined with either standard or extended access lists and forwarded through the interface are filtered by the entries in this access list. For standard access lists, *access-list-number* is a decimal number from 1 to 100. For extended access lists, *access-list-number* is a decimal number from 101 to 200.

*Default*

No access list is applied.

*Command Mode*

Interface configuration

*Usage Guidelines*

This command first appeared in Cisco IOS Release 10.0.

The **vines access-group** command applies an access list created with the **vines access-list** (**extended**) command to an interface.

You can apply only one access list to an interface.

*Example*

In the following example, access list 1 is applied to Ethernet interface 0:

```
interface ethernet 0
 vines access-group 1
```

*Related Commands*

You can use the master indexes or search online for documentation of related commands.

**vines access-list** (**extended**)

## VINES ACCESS-LIST (EXTENDED)

To create an extended VINES access list, use this version of the **vines access-list** global configuration command. To remove an extended access list, use the **no** form of this command.

> **vines access-list** *access-list-number* {**deny** | **permit**} *protocol source-address*
> *source-mask* [*source-port source-port-mask*] *destination-address*
> *destination-mask* [*destination-port destination-port-mask*]
> **no vines access-list** *access-list-number*

| Syntax | Description |
|---|---|
| *access-list-number* | Number of the access list. This is a decimal number from 101 to 200. |
| **deny** | Denies access if the conditions are matched. |
| **permit** | Allows access if the conditions are matched. |
| *protocol* | VINES protocol ID number or name. The number can be a value from 1 to 255, or one of the following protocol keywords: |

- **arp**—Address Resolution Protocol (ARP)
- **icp**—Internet Control Protocol (ICP)
- **ip**—VINES Internet Protocol
- **ipc**—Interprocess Communications (IPC)
- **rtp**—Routing Table Protocol (RTP)
- **spp**—Sequence Packet Protocol (SPP)

| | |
|---|---|
| *source-address* | Address of the network from which the packet is being sent. This is a 6-byte hexadecimal number in the format *network:host*, where *network* is 4 bytes and *host* is 2 bytes. |
| *source-mask* | Mask to be applied to *source-address*. This is a 6-byte hexadecimal value. Place ones in the bit positions you want to mask. These bits correspond to the bits in the address that should be ignored. |
| *source-port* | (Optional) Number of the local port from which the packet is being sent. This argument is required when the protocol specified is IPC or SPP, and is not accepted when any other protocol is specified. It can be a number from 0x0000 to 0xFFFF. Well-known local port numbers have values from 0x0001 to 0x01FF. Transient local port numbers have values from 0x0200 to 0xFFFE. Table 10–11 in the "Usage Guidelines" section lists some IPC port numbers. |
| *source-port-mask* | (Optional) Mask to be applied to *source-port*. This argument is required when the protocol specified is IPC or SPP, and is not accepted when any other protocol is specified. It can be a number from 0x0000 to 0xFFFF. These bits correspond to the bits in the port that should be ignored. |

*Command Reference*

| Syntax | Description |
|--------|-------------|
| *destination-address* | VINES address of the network to which the packet is being sent. This is a 6-byte hexadecimal number in the format *network:host*, where *network* is 4 bytes and *host* is 2 bytes. |
| *destination-mask* | Mask to be applied to *destination-address*. This is a 6-byte hexadecimal value. Place ones in the bit positions you want to mask. These bits correspond to the bits in the address that should be ignored. |
| *destination-port* | (Optional) Number of the local port to which the packet is being sent. This argument is required when the protocol specified is IPC or SPP, and is not accepted when any other protocol is specified. It can be a number from 0x0000 to 0xFFFF. Well-known local port numbers have values from 0x0001 to 0x01FF. Transient local port numbers have values from 0x0200 to 0xFFFE. Table 10–11 in the "Usage Guidelines" section lists some IPC port numbers. |
| *destination-port-mask* | (Optional) Mask to be applied to *destination-port*. This argument is required when the protocol specified is IPC or SPP, and is not accepted when any other protocol is specified. It can be a number from 0x0000 to 0xFFFF. These bits correspond to the bits in the port that should be ignored. |

### Default
No extended VINES access list is specified.

### Command Mode
Global configuration

### Usage Guidelines
This command first appeared in Cisco IOS Release 10.0.

An extended VINES access list filters packets based on their protocol, source and destination addresses, and source and destination address masks, and optionally on their source and destination ports, and source and destination port masks. This differs from the standard access list filters in that you can specify port masks.

Use the **vines access-group** command to assign an access list to an interface.

Keep the following in mind when configuring VINES network access control:

- You can apply only one access list to an interface.
- The conditions in the access list are applied to all outgoing packets that are forwarded by the Cisco IOS software. Packets generated by the software are not subject to the access list.
- Access list entries are scanned in the order you enter them. The first matching entry is used.

- An implicit *deny everything* entry is defined at the end of an access list unless you include an explicit *permit everything* entry at the end of the list.
- All new entries to an existing list are placed at the end of the list. You cannot add an entry to the middle of a list. This means that if you have previously included an explicit *permit everything* entry, new entries will never be scanned. The solution is to delete the access list and retype it with the new entries.

If you specify a protocol type of IPC, the port (either *source-port* or *destination-port*) can be one of the values shown in Table 10–11.

**Table 10–11** *Some VINES IPC Port Numbers*

| IPC Port Number (Hexadecimal) | Service |
|---|---|
| 0x0003 | Back End (only on PCs; it is the 25th line notification) |
| 0x0004 | Mail Service |
| 0x0006 | "VINES Files" File Service |
| 0x0007 | Server Service |
| 0x000F | StreetTalk Service |
| 0x0012 | Network Management |
| 0x0013 | VINES Security |
| 0x0016 | StreetTalk Directory Assistance |
| 0x0017 | StreetTalk Directory Assistance Service Listening Port |
| 0x0019 | Systems and Network Management |

### Example

In the following example, the first line prohibits communication from any client process to the service on IPC port 0x14; the second line permits all other communication.

```
vines access-list 101 deny   IPC 0:0 ffffffff:ffff 0x14 0 0:0 ffffffff:ffff 0 0xFFFF
vines access-list 101 permit IP 0:0 ffffffff:ffff     0:0 ffffffff:ffff
```

### Related Commands

You can use the master indexes or search online for documentation of related commands.

**priority-list protocol**
**show vines access**
**vines access-group**
**vines access-list (simple)**

## VINES ACCESS-LIST (SIMPLE)

To create a simple VINES access list, use this version of the **vines access-list** global configuration command. To remove a simple access list, use the **no** form of this command.

> **vines access-list** *access-list-number* {**deny** | **permit**} *source-address source-mask*
> **no vines access-list** *access-list-number*

| Syntax | Description |
|---|---|
| *access-list-number* | Access list number. It is a number from 201 to 300. |
| **deny** | Denies access if the conditions are matched. |
| **permit** | Allows access if the conditions are matched. |
| *source-address* | Address of the network from which the packet is being sent. This is a 6-byte hexadecimal number in the format *network:host*, where *network* is 4 bytes and *host* is 2 bytes. |
| *source-mask* | Mask to be applied to *source-address*. This is a 6-byte hexadecimal value. Place ones in the bit positions you want to mask. These bits correspond to the bits in the address that should be ignored. |

### Default

No simple VINES access list is specified.

### Command Mode

Global configuration

### Usage Guidelines

This command first appeared in Cisco IOS Release 10.0.

A simple VINES access list filters packets based on their source address and source address mask. These access lists are used to decide from which stations to accept time updates.

Use the **vines access-group** command to assign an access list to an interface.

Keep the following in mind when configuring VINES network access control:

- You can assign only one access list to an interface.
- The conditions in the access list are applied to all outgoing packets that are forwarded by the Cisco IOS software. Packets generated by the software are not subject to the access list.
- Access list entries are scanned in the order you enter them. The first matching entry is used.
- An implicit *deny everything* entry is defined at the end of an access list unless you include an explicit *permit everything* entry at the end of the list.
- All new entries to an existing list are placed at the end of the list. You cannot add an entry to the middle of a list. This means that if you have previously included an explicit *permit*

*everything* entry, new entries will never be scanned. The solution is to delete the access list and retype it with the new entries.

## Example

The following example defines an access list that accepts time updates only from the servers on networks 30015800 and 30004355; it denies time updates from all other sources.

```
vines access-list 201 permit 30015800:0001 00000000:0000
vines access-list 201 permit 30004355:0001 00000000:0000
vines access-list 201 deny 00000000:0000 FFFFFFFF:FFFF
interface ethernet 0
 vines time access-group 201
```

## Related Commands

You can use the master indexes or search online for documentation of related commands.

**show vines access**
**vines access-group**
**vines access-list (extended)**
**vines time access-group**
**vines time participate**
**vines time set-system**
**vines time use-system**

## VINES ACCESS-LIST (STANDARD)

To specify a standard VINES access list, use this version of the **vines access-list** global configuration command. To remove the access list, use the **no** form of this command.

> **vines access-list** *access-list-number* {**deny** | **permit**} *protocol source-address*
> *source-mask* [*source-port*] *destination-address destination-mask*
> [*destination-port*]
> **no vines access-list** *access-list-number*

| Syntax | Description |
| --- | --- |
| *access-list-number* | Number of the access list. This is a decimal number from 1 to 100. |
| **deny** | Denies access if the conditions are matched. |
| **permit** | Allows access if the conditions are matched. |

| Syntax | Description |
|--------|-------------|
| *protocol* | VINES protocol ID number or name. It can be a value from 1 to 255 or one of the following protocol keywords: |

- **arp**—Address Resolution Protocol (ARP)
- **icp**—Internet Control Protocol (ICP)
- **ip**—VINES Internet Protocol
- **ipc**—Interprocess Communications (IPC)
- **rtp**—Routing Table Protocol (RTP)
- **spp**—Sequence Packet Protocol (SPP)

| Syntax | Description |
|--------|-------------|
| *source-address* | Address of the network from which the packet is being sent. This is a 6-byte hexadecimal number in the format *network:host*, where *network* is 4 bytes and *host* is 2 bytes. |
| *source-mask* | Mask to be applied to *source-address*. This is a 6-byte hexadecimal value. Place ones in the bit positions you want to mask. These bits correspond to the bit in the address that should be ignored. |
| *source-port* | (Optional) Number of the local port from which the packet is being sent. This argument is required when the protocol specified is IPC or SPP, and is not accepted when any other protocol is specified. It can be a number from 0x0000 to 0xFFFF. Well-known local port numbers have values from 0x0001 to 0x01FF. Transient local port numbers have values from 0x0200 to 0xFFFE. Table 10–12 lists some IPC port numbers. |
| *destination-address* | Address of the network to which the packet is being sent. This is a 6-byte hexadecimal number in the format *network:host*, where *network* is 4 bytes and *host* is 2 bytes. |
| *destination-mask* | Mask to be applied to *destination-address*. This is a 6-byte hexadecimal value. Place ones in the bit positions you want to mask. These bits correspond to the bits in the address that should be ignored. |
| *destination-port* | (Optional) Number of the local port to which the packet is being sent. This argument is required when the protocol specified is IPC or SPP, and is not accepted when any other protocol is specified. It can be a number from 0x0000 to 0xFFFF. Well-known local port numbers have values from 0x0001 to 0x01FF. Transient local port numbers have values from 0x0200 to 0xFFFE. Table 10–12 in the "Usage Guidelines" section lists some IPC port numbers. |

## Default

No standard VINES access list is specified.

### Command Mode

Global configuration

### Usage Guidelines

This command first appeared in Cisco IOS Release 10.3.

A standard VINES access list filters packets based on their protocol, source and destination addresses, and source and destination address masks, and optionally on their source and destination ports.

Use the **vines access-group** command to apply an access list to an interface.

Keep the following in mind when configuring VINES network access control:

- You can apply only one access list to an interface.
- The conditions in the access list are applied to all outgoing packets that are forwarded by the Cisco IOS software. Packets generated by the software are not subject to the access list.
- Access list entries are scanned in the order you enter them. The first matching entry is used.
- An implicit *deny everything* entry is defined at the end of an access list unless you include an explicit *permit everything* entry at the end of the list.
- All new entries to an existing list are placed at the end of the list. You cannot add an entry to the middle of a list. This means that if you have previously included an explicit *permit everything* entry, new entries will never be scanned. The solution is to delete the access list and retype it with the new entries.

If you specify a protocol type of IPC, the port (either *source-port* or *destination-port*) can be one of the values shown in Table 10–12.

**Table 10–12** *Some IPC Port Numbers for a Standard VINES Access List*

| IPC Port Number (Hexadecimal) | Service |
|---|---|
| 0x0003 | Back End (only on PCs; it is the 25th line notification) |
| 0x0004 | Mail Service |
| 0x0006 | "VINES Files" File Service |
| 0x0007 | Server Service |
| 0x000F | StreetTalk Service |
| 0x0012 | Network Management |
| 0x0013 | VINES Security |

*Command Reference*

**Table 10–12**  *Some IPC Port Numbers for a Standard VINES Access List, Continued*

| IPC Port Number (Hexadecimal) | Service |
|---|---|
| 0x0016 | StreetTalk Directory Assistance |
| 0x0017 | StreetTalk Directory Assistance Service Listening Port |
| 0x0019 | Systems and Network Management |

## Examples

In the following example, the first line prohibits any communication on StreetTalk port (port number 0xF); the second line permits all other communication.

```
vines access-list 1 deny   IPC 0:0 ffffffff:ffff 0xf 0:0 ffffffff:ffff 0xf
vines access-list 1 permit IP 0:0 ffffffff:ffff     0:0 ffffffff:ffff
```

The following example filters all mail service on Ethernet interface 0 and permits all other traffic:

```
interface Ethernet 0
 vines access-group 101
!
vines access-list 101 deny ipc 0:0 FFFFFFFF:FFFF 4 0 0:0 FFFFFFFF:FFFF 0 0xF FFF
```

## Related Commands

You can use the master indexes or search online for documentation of related commands.

**priority-list protocol**
**show vines access**
**vines access-group**
**vines access-list** (extended)
**vines access-list** (simple)

## VINES ARP-ENABLE

To enable the processing of ARP packets, use the **vines arp-enable** interface configuration command. To disable the processing of ARP packets, use the **no** form of this command.

> **vines arp-enable** [**dynamic**]
> **no vines arp-enable** [**dynamic**]

| Syntax | Description |
|---|---|
| **dynamic** | (Optional) Responds to ARP and SARP requests on this interface only if there are no other VINES servers present. |

## Default

The interface always responds to ARP and SARP requests.

## Command Mode

Interface configuration

## Usage Guidelines

This command first appeared in Cisco IOS Release 10.0.

Client systems on VINES networks are assigned network addresses dynamically. When a VINES client boots, it has no knowledge of their addresses and preferred servers. Immediately after it initializes its hardware interface, the client sends broadcast requests asking a server to provide it with a network-layer address. In a network that has a server, Cisco routers do not normally respond to these broadcast requests. However, on a network that has only clients and no servers (called a *serverless network*), the Cisco IOS software does need to respond to the broadcast requests so that all the clients on that serverless network can acquire network addresses. By default, the software responds to ARP requests and assigns addresses to network clients only if there is no VINES server present on that network segment. When it does, the software then acts as a network communication service provider for the client. You may configure the software to respond to these requests even if a VINES server is present, or never to respond to these requests. If the software assigns an address, it generates a unique network number based on its own VINES address.

A VINES file server must still be present somewhere on the network in order for the client to continue the booting process.

## Examples

The following example configures a router when Ethernet interface 1 is a network that does not contain any VINES servers:

```
interface ethernet 0
 vines metric 2
!
interface ethernet 1
 vines metric 2
```

The following example configures a router to always provide ARP service on Ethernet interface 1, even when VINES servers are present on that network:

```
interface ethernet 0
 vines metric 2
!
interface ethernet 1
 vines metric 2
 vines arp-enable
```

## Related Commands

You can use the master indexes or search online for documentation of related commands.

**vines propagate**
**vines serverless**

## VINES DECIMAL

To display VINES addresses in decimal notation, use the **vines decimal** global configuration command. To return to displaying the addresses in hexadecimal, use the **no** form of this command.

> **vines decimal**
> **no vines decimal**

*Syntax          Description*

This command has no arguments or keywords.

*Default*

Addresses are displayed in hexadecimal.

*Command Mode*

Global configuration

*Usage Guidelines*

This command first appeared in Cisco IOS Release 10.0.

When displaying addresses, the Cisco IOS software always uses a name if one has been configured via the **vines host** command. The **vines decimal** command affects the radix in which the address is presented when a name is not available.

*Example*

The following example displays VINES addresses in decimal:

```
vines decimal
```

*Related Commands*

You can use the master indexes or search online for documentation of related commands.

clear vines cache
clear vines neighbor
clear vines route
show vines cache
vines host

## VINES ENCAPSULATION

To set the MAC-level encapsulation used for VINES broadcast packets, use the **vines encapsulation** interface configuration command. To disable encapsulation, use the **no** form of this command.

> **vines encapsulation** [**arpa** | **snap** | **vines-tr**]
> **no vines encapsulation**

| Syntax | Description |
|---|---|
| arpa | (Optional) Advanced Research Projects Agency (ARPA) encapsulation. This is the default encapsulation for Ethernet interfaces. |
| snap | (Optional) Subnetwork Access Protocol (SNAP) encapsulation. This encapsulation uses an IEEE 802.2 SNAP header. It is the default encapsulation for all media except Ethernet and Token Ring. |
| vines-tr | (Optional) Our VINES Token Ring encapsulation. This is the default encapsulation for Token Ring interfaces. |

## Defaults

ARPA encapsulation for Ethernet
VINES-TR Token Ring encapsulation for Token Ring
SNAP encapsulation for all other media

## Command Mode

Interface configuration

## Usage Guidelines

This command first appeared in Cisco IOS Release 10.0.

You can choose a MAC-level encapsulation type for each Ethernet, Token Ring, or IEEE 802.2 interface.

Setting the MAC-level encapsulation type with the **vines encapsulation** command affects broadcast packets sent by the Cisco IOS software. The software keeps track of which encapsulation is used by each of its neighbors and uses the same style of encapsulation when talking directly to a neighbor.

You should not use this command with the current versions of VINES software that are available. This command is present for future interoperability when Banyan begins using encapsulations other than the current default ones.

## Example

The following example configures IEEE 802.2 SNAP encapsulation on Ethernet interface 0:

```
vines routing
!
interface ethernet 0
 vines metric 2
 vines encapsulation snap
```

## VINES HOST

To associate a host name with a VINES address, use the **vines host** global configuration command. To delete the association, use the **no** form of this command.

**vines host** *name address*
**no vines host** *name*

| Syntax | Description |
|--------|-------------|
| *name* | VINES host name. It can be any length and sequence of characters separated by white space. |
| *address* | Number of a VINES network. You enter it in the current VINES radix, in the format *network:host*, where *network* is 4 bytes and *host* is 2 bytes. |

### Default

Hosts are displayed by address.

### Command Mode

Global configuration

### Usage Guidelines

This command first appeared in Cisco IOS Release 10.0.

The Cisco IOS software maintains a table of the mappings between host names and addresses.

When displaying addresses, the software uses the name instead of the numerical address if you have configured one with the **vines host** command.

Cisco IOS software provides only static name-to-address bindings for the VINES protocol. This is completely separate from Banyan's distributed naming system, StreetTalk. The software does not learn names from StreetTalk, nor does the software provide names to StreetTalk.

### Example

The following example assigns names to four VINES servers:

```
! Cisco names
vines host FARSLAYER 30002A2D:0001
vines host DOOMGIVER 30000A83:0001
! VINES PS/2 server
vines host COINSPINNER 0027AF92:0001
! PC clone client
vines host STUFF 0027AF92:8001
```

### Related Commands

You can use the master indexes or search online for documentation of related commands.

**clear vines neighbor**
**clear vines route**
**show vines host**
**vines decimal**

## VINES INPUT-NETWORK-FILTER

To filter the information contained in routing messages received from other stations, use the **vines input-network-filter** interface configuration command. To disable this filtering, use the **no** form of this command.

> **vines input-network-filter** *access-list-number*
> **no vines input-network-filter**

| Syntax | Description |
|--------|-------------|
| *access-list-number* | Number of the access list. It is a decimal number from 201 to 300. |

### Default

No filtering

### Command Mode

Interface configuration

### Usage Guidelines

This command first appeared in Cisco IOS Release 10.0.

VINES routing messages contain topological entries that allow service and client nodes to select the best paths to destinations. This command provides filtering capability to administrators so that they may selectively determine which routing entries should be accepted from other routers and which routing entries should be dropped. This command may be useful in enforcing administrative policies of local server usage.

### Example

The following example prevents a route to one specific server from ever being learned via Ethernet interface 0:

```
vines routing
!
vines access-list 201 deny 27AF9A:1 0:0
vines access-list 201 permit 0:0 FFFFFFFF:FFFF
!
interface ethernet 0
 vines metric 2
 vines input-network-filter 201
```

## VINES INPUT-ROUTER-FILTER

To filter received routing messages based upon the address of the sending station, use the **vines input-router-filter** interface configuration command. To disable this filtering, use the **no** form of this command.

vines input-router-filter *access-list-number*
no vines input-router-filter

*Syntax*                    *Description*

*access-list-number*        Number of the access list. It is a decimal number from 201 to 300.

*Default*

No filtering

*Command Mode*

Interface configuration

*Usage Guidelines*

This command first appeared in Cisco IOS Release 10.0.

VINES routing messages contain topological entries that allow service and client nodes to select the best paths to destinations. This command provides filtering ability to administrators so that they may selectively determine the routers from which routing entries are accepted.

*Example*

The following example prevents the Cisco IOS software from ever learning routing information from a specific server on Ethernet interface 0:

```
vines routing  .
!
vines access-list 201 deny 27AF9A:1 0:0
vines access-list 201 permit 0:0 FFFFFFFF:FFFF
!
interface ethernet 0
 vines metric 2
 vines input-router-filter 201
```

## VINES METRIC

To enable VINES routing on an interface, use the **vines metric** interface configuration command. To disable VINES routing, use the **no** form of this command.

vines metric [*whole* [*fractional*]]
no vines metric

| Syntax | Description |
|--------|-------------|
| *whole* | (Optional) Integer cost value associated with the interface. It is optional for all interface types. If you omit *whole*, the Cisco IOS software automatically chooses a reasonable value. These values are listed in Table 10–13 in the "Usage Guidelines" section. If whole is zero, then a fractional portion must be supplied. |
| *fractional* | (Optional) Fractional cost value associated with the interface expressed in 10,000ths. It is optional for all interface types, but may only be present if a whole number portion is specified. This number is rounded to the nearest 1/16. If you omit both whole and fractional numbers, the software automatically chooses a reasonable value. These values are listed in Table 10–13. For additional information, refer to the discussion in the "Usage Guidelines" section. |

### Default

Disabled

### Command Mode

Interface configuration

### Usage Guidelines

This command first appeared in Cisco IOS Release 10.0.

The metric is the cost value associated with the interface media type. It is generally inversely proportional to the speed of the interface. The lower the delay metric, the more likely it is that the software will use that interface.

The Cisco IOS software automatically chooses a reasonable metric. These numbers match as closely as possible the numbers a Banyan server would choose for an interface of the same type and speed.

When enabling VINES for a serial interface, you should keep in mind that the VINES metric is based upon the configured bandwidth for the interface. To ensure that the software selects the correct VINES metric, you must make sure that the correct bandwidth is configured. To do this, first issue the **show interface** command to determine the speed of the interface. Then issue the **bandwidth** command to set the bandwidth rate that is appropriate for that interface type and speed. After that, issue the **vines metric** command, and the software will choose a metric appropriate to that speed. If you do not issue the **bandwidth** command first, you must either reissue the **vines metric** command or issue it with a metric number to get an appropriate metric.

Banyan servers use these metrics to compute timeouts when communicating with other hosts. If you do specify a metric, be careful that you do not set this number too high or too low. Doing so could disrupt the normal function of the Banyan servers.

Table 10–13 lists some example delay metric values.

**Table 10–13**  *Example Delay Metric Values*

| Interface Type | Old Format | New Internal Format | New Configuration File Format | Seconds |
|---|---|---|---|---|
| FDDI | 1 | 0010 | 1 0000 | 0.2000 |
| Ethernet | 2 | 0020 | 2 0000 | 0.4000 |
| 16-Mb Token Ring | 2 | 0020 | 2 0000 | 0.4000 |
| 4-Mb Token Ring | 4 | 0040 | 4 0000 | 0.8000 |
| T1 High-Level Data Link Control (HDLC) | 35 | 0230 | 35 0000 | 7.0000 |
| 56-kb HDLC | 45 | 02D0 | 45 0000 | 9.0000 |
| 9600-baud HDLC | 90 | 05A0 | 90 0000 | 18.0000 |
| 4800-baud HDLC | 150 | 0960 | 150 0000 | 30.0000 |
| 2400-baud HDLC | 250 | 0F00 | 250 0000 | 50.0000 |
| 1200-baud HDLC | 450 | 1C20 | 450 0000 | 90.0000 |
| T1 X.25 | 45 | 02D0 | 45 0000 | 9.0000 |
| 56-kb X.25 | 55 | 0370 | 55 0000 | 11.0000 |
| 9600-baud X.25 | 100 | 0640 | 100 0000 | 20.0000 |
| 4800-baud X.25 | 160 | 0A00 | 160 0000 | 32.0000 |
| 2400-baud X.25 | 260 | 1040 | 260 0000 | 52.0000 |
| 1200-baud X.25 | 460 | 1CC0 | 460 0000 | 92.0000 |

*Examples*

The following example enables VINES routing on Ethernet interface 0 and sets the metric to 2:

```
vines routing
!
interface ethernet 0
 vines metric 2
```

The following example enables VINES routing on FDDI interface 0 and sets the metric to 0.25:

```
vines routing
!
interface fddi 0
 vines metric 0 2500
```

*Related Commands*

You can use the master indexes or search online for documentation of related commands.

**bandwidth**
**vines routing**
**vines update deltas**
**vines update interval**

## VINES NEIGHBOR

To specify a static path to a neighbor station, use the **vines neighbor** interface configuration command. To remove a static path from the neighbor table, use the **no** form of this command.

> **vines neighbor** *address mac-address encapsulation* [*whole* [*fractional*]]
> **no vines neighbor** *address mac-address*

| *Syntax* | *Description* |
|---|---|
| *address* | VINES IP address of the station to which to add or remove a static path. |
| *mac-address* | MAC-level address used to reach the neighbor station. |
| *encapsulation* | Encapsulation type to use on the media. It can be one of the following values: |
| | • **arpa**—Use ARPA encapsulation. This is recommended for Ethernet interfaces. |
| | • **snap**—Use an IEEE 802.2 SNAP header. This is recommended for FDDI interfaces. |
| | • **vines-tr**—Use our VINES Token Ring encapsulation. This is recommended for Token Ring interfaces. |

*Command Reference*

| Syntax | Description |
|---|---|
| *whole* | (Optional) Delay metric to use on the neighbor. If you omit this argument, the metric used is that specified with the **vines metric** command for the selected interface. |
| *fractional* | (Optional) Fractional metric value associated with this neighbor. This number is rounded to the nearest 1/16. If you omit both whole and fractional numbers, the interface metric is used. |

### Default

No static paths are specified.

### Command Mode

Interface configuration

### Usage Guidelines

This command first appeared in Cisco IOS Release 10.0.

You can configure static neighbor entries only on Ethernet, FDDI, and Token Ring interfaces.

The decision to use a static path or a dynamic path is always determined by the relative metric numbers.

Be careful when assigning static paths. If a static path is assigned with a better metric than the dynamic paths and the link associated with the static path is lost, traffic may stop being forwarded, even though an alternative path might be available.

The metric is the cost value associated with the interface media type. It is generally inversely proportional to the speed of the interface. The lower the delay metric, the more likely it is that the software will use that interface.

This command is useful for testing VINES networks with test equipment that does not generate hello packets.

Table 10–14 lists some example delay metric values.

**Table 10–14**    *Example Delay Metric Values to Specify a Static Path*

| Interface Type | Old Format | New Internal Format | New Configuration File Format | Seconds |
|---|---|---|---|---|
| FDDI | 1 | 0010 | 1  0000 | 0.2000 |
| Ethernet | 2 | 0020 | 2  0000 | 0.4000 |
| 16-Mb Token Ring | 2 | 0020 | 2  0000 | 0.4000 |

**Table 10–14**   *Example Delay Metric Values to Specify a Static Path, Continued*

| Interface Type | Old Format | New Internal Format | New Configuration File Format | Seconds |
|---|---|---|---|---|
| 4-Mb Token Ring | 4 | 0040 | 4  0000 | 0.8000 |
| T1 HDLC | 35 | 0230 | 35  0000 | 7.0000 |
| 56-kb HDLC | 45 | 02D0 | 45  0000 | 9.0000 |
| 9600-baud HDLC | 90 | 05A0 | 90  0000 | 18.0000 |
| 4800-baud HDLC | 150 | 0960 | 150  0000 | 30.0000 |
| 2400-baud HDLC | 250 | 0F00 | 250  0000 | 50.0000 |
| 1200-baud HDLC | 450 | 1C20 | 450  0000 | 90.0000 |
| T1 X.25 | 45 | 02D0 | 45  0000 | 9.0000 |
| 56-kb X.25 | 55 | 0370 | 55  0000 | 11.0000 |
| 9600-baud X.25 | 100 | 0640 | 100  0000 | 20.0000 |
| 4800-baud X.25 | 160 | 0A00 | 160  0000 | 32.0000 |
| 2400-baud X.25 | 260 | 1040 | 260  0000 | 52.0000 |
| 1200-baud X.25 | 460 | 1CC0 | 460  0000 | 92.0000 |

## Example

The following example defines a static path to the neighbor station at address 12345678:0001 using ARPA encapsulation:

```
interface ethernet 0
  vines neighbor 12345678:0001 0001.0002.0003 arpa 20
```

## Related Commands

You can use the master indexes or search online for documentation of related commands.

**clear vines neighbor**
**show vines neighbor**
**show vines route**
**vines route**

## VINES OUTPUT-NETWORK-FILTER

To filter the information contained in routing updates transmitted to other stations, use the **vines output-network-filter** interface configuration command. To disable this filtering, use the **no** form of this command.

> **vines output-network-filter** *access-list-number*
> **no vines output-network-filter**

| Syntax | Description |
|--------|-------------|
| *access-list-number* | Number of the access list. It is a decimal number from 201 to 300. |

### Default

No filtering

### Command Mode

Interface configuration

### Usage Guidelines

This command first appeared in Cisco IOS Release 10.0.

VINES routing messages contain topological entries that allow service and client nodes to select the best paths to destinations. This command provides filtering ability to administrators so that they may selectively determine which routing entries should be passed on to other routers. This command may be useful in enforcing administrative policies of local server usage.

### Example

The following example prevents all routes from being advertised to Ethernet interface 0 except the route to a single server:

```
vines routing
!
vines access-list 201 permit 27AF9A:1 0:0
vines access-list 201 deny 0:0 FFFFFFFF:FFFF
!
interface ethernet 0
 vines metric 2
 vines output-network-filter 201
```

## VINES PROPAGATE

To modify how the Cisco IOS software forwards a broadcast packet, use the **vines propagate** interface configuration command. To return to the default forwarding scheme, use the **dynamic** form of this command.

vines propagate [dynamic]
no vines propagate [dynamic]

| Syntax | Description |
|---|---|
| dynamic | (Optional) Propagate broadcasts on this interface only if there are no servers on any local network. |

### Default

Dynamic forwarding

### Command Mode

Interface configuration

### Usage Guidelines

This command first appeared in Cisco IOS Release 10.0.

If you specify the **vines propagate** command with no keywords, broadcast messages are always propagated on the interface.

The **vines propagate** command affects how the software decides whether to forward a broadcast packet out an interface. The normal decision is based on the settings of both the "hop count" and "class" fields of the VINES IP header, and also whether any servers are present on any of the local network segments. In the default configuration, the software first looks to see if there are any local servers, and if so, follows the normal rules of VINES IP and forwards the broadcast out this interface based upon the "hop count" and the "class" field. If there are no local servers, then the software looks only at the "hop count" field before forwarding the broadcast out this interface. Enabling this command with no argument tells the software to always ignore the "class" field and make the forwarding decision based solely upon the "hop count" field. The **no** form of this command tells the software to always examine both the "hop count" and "class" fields.

### Example

The following example always ignores the "class" field of the VINES IP header when deciding whether to forward a broadcast packet on serial interface 0:

```
interface serial 0
  vines propagate
```

### Related Commands

You can use the master indexes or search online for documentation of related commands.

**vines arp-enable**
**vines serverless**

**VINES REDIRECT**

To determine how frequently the Cisco IOS software sends an RTP redirect message on an interface, use the **vines redirect** interface configuration command. To restore the default, use the **no** form of this command.

> **vines redirect** [*seconds*]
> **no vines redirect**

| Syntax | Description |
|--------|-------------|
| *seconds* | (Optional) Interval, in seconds, that the software waits after sending a redirect message on an interface before it sends another redirect message on that same interface. If you specify a value of 0, the software never sends redirect messages on that interface. |

*Default*

1 second

*Command Mode*

Interface configuration

*Usage Guidelines*

This command first appeared in Cisco IOS Release 10.0.

VINES routing redirect packets contain topological entries that allow service and client nodes to select the best paths to destinations. When a service node determines that it should not be forwarding packets between two nodes, it sends a redirect packet to the sending node informing it of the better path.

*Example*

The following example prevents redirect messages from ever being sent on Ethernet interface 0:

```
vines routing
!
interface ethernet 0
 vines metric 2
 vines redirect 0
```

**VINES ROUTE**

To specify a static route to a server, use the **vines route** global configuration command. To remove a static route from the routing table, use the **no** form of this command.

> **vines route** *number address* [*whole* [*fractional*]]
> **no vines route** *number address* [*whole* [*fractional*]]

| Syntax | Description |
|--------|-------------|
| *number* | Number of the server to which to add or remove the static route. |
| *address* | VINES IP address of the neighbor station to use to reach the server. |
| *whole* | (Optional) Metric value assigned to this route. |
| *fractional* | (Optional) Fractional cost value associated with this route. |

### Default

No static routes are specified.

### Command Mode

Global configuration

### Usage Guidelines

This command first appeared in Cisco IOS Release 10.0.

The decision to use a static route or a dynamic route is always determined by the relative metric numbers.

Be careful when assigning static routes. If a static route is assigned with a better metric than the dynamic routes and the links associated with the static routes are lost, traffic may stop being forwarded, even though an alternative route might be available.

Floating static routes are static routes that can be overridden by dynamically learned routes. Floating static routes allow you to switch to another path whenever routing information for a destination is lost. One application of floating static routes is to provide back-up routes in topologies where dial-on-demand routing (DDR) is used.

To configure a floating static route, assign a metric to the static route that is worse (higher) than all dynamic routes. If you configure a floating static route, the Cisco IOS software checks to see if an entry for the route already exists in its routing table. If a dynamic route already exists, the floating static route is placed in reserve as part of a floating static route table. When the software detects that the dynamic route is no longer available, it replaces the dynamic route with the floating static route for that destination. If the route is later relearned dynamically, the dynamic route replaces the floating static route and the floating static route is again placed in reserve.

**NOTES**

By default, floating static routes are not redistributed into other dynamic protocols.

### Examples

The following example establishes a static route to the server at ABCD1234:

```
vines route ABCD1234 12345678:1 35
```

The following example establishes a floating static route to the server at 3000000:

```
vines route 3000000 3001000:1
```

## Related Commands

You can use the master indexes or search online for documentation of related commands.

**clear vines neighbor**
**clear vines route**
**show vines neighbor**
**show vines route**
**vines neighbor**
**vines output-network-filter**

## VINES ROUTE-CACHE

To enable fast switching, use the **vines route-cache** interface configuration command. To disable fast switching, use the **no** form of this command.

> **vines route-cache**
> **no vines route-cache**

## Syntax    Description

This command has no arguments or keywords.

## Default

Enabled

## Command Mode

Interface configuration

## Usage Guidelines

This command first appeared in Cisco IOS Release 10.0.

The **vines route-cache** command enables the fast switching of VINES packets being transmitted out of the interface. However, forwarding of broadcast packets and responding to packets destined for the local router still occur at the process level. When fast switching is disabled, all packets are forwarded at the process level.

Fast switching allows higher throughput by switching a packet using a cache created by previous packets. Fast switching provides load sharing on a per-packet basis just as slow switching does. Fast switching is enabled by default on all interfaces where it is supported. It is not supported on very old Ethernet, serial, and Token Ring interfaces, nor is it supported on serial interfaces using an encapsulation other than HDLC.

Packet transfer performance is generally better when fast switching is enabled. However, you may want to disable fast switching in order to save memory space on interface cards and help avoid congestion when high-bandwidth interfaces are writing large amounts of information to low-bandwidth interfaces.

When fast switching is enabled, the Cisco IOS software maintains a fast-switching cache table. When transmitting a packet that is eligible to be fast switched, the software first checks the fast-switching cache table. If it finds an entry for the destination, the software uses that path. Otherwise, it searches the standard routing table and places the route it finds into the fast-switching cache table. The next time the software receives a packet for that destination, it uses the route in the fast-switching cache table.

### Example

The following example disables fast switching on serial interface 0:

```
interface serial 0
  bandwidth 19200
  vines metric
  no vines route-cache
```

### Related Commands

You can use the master indexes or search online for documentation of related commands.

**clear vines cache**
**show vines cache**
**show vines route**

## VINES ROUTING

To enable VINES routing, use the **vines routing** global configuration command. To disable VINES routing, use the **no** form of this command.

> **vines routing** [*address* | **recompute**]
> **no vines routing**

| Syntax | Description |
| --- | --- |
| *address* | (Optional) Network address of the router. You should specify an address on a router that does not have any Ethernet or FDDI interfaces. You also can specify an address in the unlikely event that two routers map themselves to the same address. |
| **recompute** | (Optional) Dynamically redetermine the router's network address. |

### Default

Disabled

## Command Mode

Global configuration

## Usage Guidelines

This command first appeared in Cisco IOS Release 10.0.

Enabling VINES routing with the **vines routing** command starts both the VINES RTP and SRTP protocols. The Cisco IOS software dynamically determines which version of the VINES routing protocol stations on the network is being used and then uses one or the other, or both protocols, as appropriate.

If a router contains Ethernet or FDDI interfaces, you do not need to specify an address because the Cisco IOS software automatically maps itself into the VINES address space that is reserved for Cisco routers. If you do specify an address, the software will use the specified address.

If a router contains only Token Ring interfaces (or Token Ring and serial interfaces), either the Token Ring interface must be fully initialized before you issue the **vines routing** command or you must specify an address in the **vines routing** command. This is because Token Ring interfaces have MAC addresses of 0000.0000.0000 until they are fully initialized.

Banyan has assigned Cisco a portion of the overall VINES network number space. This portion is the set of all numbers that begin with the first 11 bits (of the 32) of 0011 0000 000. This number set appears in all Cisco IOS software displays as a hexadecimal number beginning with 0x300 or 0x301. Devices attempt to automatically map themselves into our number space based upon the first nonzero Ethernet, Token Ring, or FDDI address found.

In theory, address conflicts are impossible, because VINES servers use their Banyan-assigned, unique key serial numbers as their network numbers and use a subnetwork number of one. Because the keys are unique, the server addresses are unique. VINES clients do not have addresses, per se. The clients use a modified version of the address of the first file server found on the physical network: they assume the server's network number and are assigned a subnetwork number by that server. This address-assignment scheme means that it is likely that two clients on the same physical LAN will have different addresses. It requires that the Cisco IOS software keep a cache of local neighbors as well as a cache of routing entries.

If you do not specify a network address and the software cannot compute one from a MAC address, the software selects a random address. There is no guarantee that this will be a unique address.

If you find that two routers have the same VINES network address, you should issue the **vines routing recompute** command on both routers. When recomputing its address, the software uses the same method used when originally determining its network address. If you issue this command on a router on which you have enabled the processing of ARP packets (with the **vines arp-enable** command) and if the device's address changes when it is recomputed, any clients that received their VINES network addresses from the router will lose all network connectivity, and you will have to reboot them.

Older implementations of our software mapped themselves to numbers beginning with 0xF80. This was done before Banyan made the address assignment.

### Example

The following example enables VINES routing on Ethernet interface 0:

```
vines routing
!
interface ethernet 0
 vines metric 2
```

### Related Commands

You can use the master indexes or search online for documentation of related commands.

**vines arp-enable**
**vines metric**

## VINES SERVERLESS

To configure a Banyan VINES network that does not have a server, use the **vines serverless** interface configuration command. To disable this feature, use the **no** form of this command.

> **vines serverless [dynamic | broadcast]**
> **no vines serverless [dynamic | broadcast]**

| Syntax | Description |
|---|---|
| **dynamic** | (Optional) Forward broadcasts toward one server only if there are no servers present on this interface. |
| **broadcast** | (Optional) Always flood broadcasts out all other router interfaces to reach all servers. |

### Default

Dynamic forwarding

### Command Mode

Interface configuration

### Usage Guidelines

This command first appeared in Cisco IOS Release 10.0.

If all keywords are omitted, broadcasts are always forwarded toward one server.

The **vines serverless** command provides special processing for certain broadcast packets and certain packets directed at the router.

When you have a Banyan VINES network that has no server, by default the Cisco IOS software provides special processing for certain broadcast packets and certain packets directed at the router. This is necessary for proper functioning of the clients on a network without a server. This special processing allows a client to find the services that are provided by a server on another network. The dynamic nature of this processing allows the software to switch over from not providing serverless support to providing serverless support if the last server on a network fails. If you want the router to always provide serverless support, even when there are local servers present, you may override the default processing by issuing the **vines serverless** command with no argument. If you do not want the router to ever provide serverless support, you may also override the default in this way by issuing the **no vines serverless** command.

When the Cisco IOS software receives a zero-hop broadcast on a serverless network, it does not follow the normal processing rules for VINES packets and discards the frames. Instead, it looks in its routing table for the nearest Banyan server. If this server is on a directly connected network, the software resends the broadcast message on that network as a MAC-level broadcast so that server and any others present can respond to it. If the nearest Banyan server is not on a directly connected network, the software resends the broadcast message on that network as a MAC-level unicast message directed at the first hop to that server. The next router will perform these same steps, assuming it is also configured for serverless support. The router can also be configured to always flood these broadcasts on all interfaces by using the command **vines serverless broadcast**. The decision on whether or not to flood is a trade-off between network bandwidth and finding more servers.

If you have configured this interface to forward toward a single destination, you may see which server has been selected as the forwarding target by looking at the output of the **show vines route** command. All servers on the same physical network as the target server receive the broadcast.

### Examples

The following example configures Ethernet interface 1, which is a network with no VINES servers:

```
interface ethernet 0
 vines metric 2
!
interface ethernet 1
 vines metric 2
```

The **vines serverless** command is not necessary because the default setting is what is desired.

The following example configures Ethernet interface 1, which is a network with no VINES servers to always flood broadcasts to all other interfaces in the router:

```
interface ethernet 0
 vines metric 2
!
interface ethernet 1
 vines metric 2
 vines serverless broadcast
```

The **vines serverless** command is necessary here because a nondefault setting is desired.

*Related Commands*

You can use the master indexes or search online for documentation of related commands.

**show vines route**
**vines arp-enable**
**vines propagate**

## VINES SPLIT-HORIZON

To use split horizon when sending routing updates, use the **vines split-horizon** interface configuration command. To disable split horizon, use the **no** form of this command.

  vines split-horizon
  no vines split-horizon

*Syntax        Description*

This command has no arguments or keywords.

*Default*

Enabled

*Command Mode*

Interface configuration

*Usage Guidelines*

This command first appeared in Cisco IOS Release 10.0.

The **vines split-horizon** command also affects whether broadcasts packets received on an interface are resent on the same interface.

The **vines split-horizon** command determines how much information is included in routing updates sent out an interface. It also determines whether received broadcasts are retransmitted on the same interface. When you enable split horizon, routing updates sent out on a given interface will not include any information that was originally learned from that interface, and broadcasts will not be retransmitted on the receiving interface. This is because split horizon is designed for networks that are either broadcast networks or are fully connected mesh networks. In these types of networks, resending this information is a waste of network bandwidth because all other stations on that network have already heard the information. Disabling split horizon causes the Cisco IOS software to include all information in routing updates and to resend broadcast packets on the network from which they were received.

You can use this command on any interface, but generally it makes sense to use it only for X.25 and Frame Relay interfaces. You should disable split horizon on X.25 and Frame Relay networks that are not fully connected mesh topologies.

## Example

The following example disables split horizon on an X.25 network:

```
interface serial 0
 no vines split-horizon
```

## VINES SRTP-ENABLED

To enable SRTP, use the **vines srtp-enabled** global configuration command. To disable SRTP, use the **no** form of this command.

**vines srtp-enabled**
**no vines srtp-enabled**

## Syntax        Description

This command has no arguments or keywords.

## Default

The router runs Banyan's RTP routing protocol only.

## Command Mode

Global configuration

## Usage Guidelines

This command first appeared in Cisco IOS Release 10.3.

When SRTP is enabled, the Cisco IOS software dynamically determines whether it needs to send RTP messages, SRTP messages, or both.

## Example

The following example enables SRTP:

```
interface serial 0
 vines routing
 vines srtp-enabled
```

## Related Commands

You can use the master indexes or search online for documentation of related commands.

**vines routing**

## VINES TIME ACCESS-GROUP

To control the servers from which the router will accept VINES network time, use the **vines time access-group** global configuration command. To accept VINES network time messages from any server, use the **no** form of this command.

> **vines time access-group** *access-list-number*
> **no vines time access-group**

| Syntax | Description |
|---|---|
| *access-list-number* | Number of the access list. It is a decimal number from 201 to 300. |

### Default

Disabled

### Command Mode

Global configuration

### Usage Guidelines

This command first appeared in Cisco IOS Release 10.0.

### Example

The following example applies an access list to incoming time messages:

```
vines access-list 201 permit 27AF9A:1 0:0
vines access-list 201 deny 0:0 FFFFFFFF:FFFF
!
vines time participate
vines time access-group 201
```

### Related Commands

You can use the master indexes or search online for documentation of related commands.

**show vines service**
**vines access-list (simple)**
**vines time destination**
**vines time participate**
**vines time set-system**
**vines time use-system**

## VINES TIME DESTINATION

To control the servers to which the Cisco IOS software sends VINES network time, use the **vines time destination** global configuration command. To send VINES network time messages to all servers, use the **no** form of this command.

> **vines time destination** *address*
> **no vines time destination**

| Syntax | Description |
|--------|-------------|
| *address* | Destination VINES address for the network time messages. |

### Default

Disabled

### Command Mode

Global configuration

### Usage Guidelines

This command first appeared in Cisco IOS Release 10.0.

By default, the software sends VINES network time messages to the broadcast address.

You can enter the **vines time destination** command up to 20 times for 20 destination addresses.

### Example

The following example specifies the servers to receive VINES time messages:

```
vines time participate
vines time destination 0027AF9F:0001
vines time destination 300001239:001
```

### Related Commands

You can use the master indexes or search online for documentation of related commands.

**show vines service**
**vines time access-group**
**vines time participate**
**vines time set-system**
**vines time use-system**

## VINES TIME PARTICIPATE

To enable participation in the synchronization of time across a VINES network, use the **vines time participate** global configuration command. To disable participation in time synchronization, use the **no** form of this command.

> **vines time participate**
> **no vines time participate**

### Syntax     Description

This command has no arguments or keywords.

### Default

Enabled

### Command Mode

Global configuration

### Usage Guidelines

This command first appeared in Cisco IOS Release 10.0.

The Cisco IOS software always listens to the time synchronization messages on the network, and it tracks the network time. This command controls only the sending of time synchronization messages by the software. This arrangement means that you can use the **show vines services** EXEC command to see the network time even if the router is not actively participating in time synchronization.

### Example

The following example disables participation in the sending of VINES time messages:

```
no vines time participate
```

### Related Commands

You can use the master indexes or search online for documentation of related commands.

**show vines service**
**vines access-list (simple)**
**vines access-group**
**vines time destination**
**vines time set-system**
**vines time use-system**

## VINES TIME SET-SYSTEM

To set the internal time based upon the received VINES network time, use the **vines time set-system** global configuration command. To uncouple the time from VINES network time, use the **no** form of this command.

> **vines time set-system**
> **no vines time set-system**

### Syntax · Description

This command has no arguments or keywords.

### Default

Disabled

### Command Mode

Global configuration

### Usage Guidelines

This command first appeared in Cisco IOS Release 10.0.

You should not use the **vines time set-system** command when running NTP on a router, because this command has no effect on these systems. NTP is considered to be a higher-priority clock than VINES, because it is a much more accurate timekeeping system.

### Example

The following example sets the time from received VINES time messages:

```
vines time participate
vines time set-system
```

### Related Commands

You can use the master indexes or search online for documentation of related commands.

**show vines service**
**vines access-list (simple)**
**vines time destination**
**vines time participate**
**vines time use-system**

## VINES TIME USE-SYSTEM

To set VINES network time based upon the internal time, use the **vines time use-system** global configuration command. To uncouple VINES network time from the time, use the **no** form of this command.

**vines time use-system**
**no vines time use-system**

## Syntax    Description

This command has no arguments or keywords.

## Default

Disabled

## Command Mode

Global configuration

## Usage Guidelines

This command first appeared in Cisco IOS Release 10.0.

The **vines time use-system** command causes the Cisco IOS software to import the locally available time source (such as NTP, the calendar system, or DNSIX time) into the VINES time world as an authoritative clock. This is most useful when running NTP on the router. The router appears to the VINES network as a server dialing the NIST clock.

When you specify the **vines time use-system** command, VINES extracts the system time and propagates it into the VINES world only if the system time is valid. If you are running NTP, the system time becomes valid when NTP synchronizes with a master. If you are not running NTP, but you do have an internal calendar system, you can force that time to be valid by specifying the **clock calendar-valid** command. This allows VINES to propagate time based upon the clock chip of the calendar system.

## Example

The following example sets VINES network time from the router's internal time:

```
ntp peer 131.108.13.111 version 2
!
vines time participate
vines time use-system
```

## Related Commands

You can use the master indexes or search online for documentation of related commands.

**clock calendar-valid**
**show vines service**
**vines access-list (simple)**
**vines time access-group**
**vines time destination**
**vines time participate**
**vines time set-system**

## VINES UPDATE DELTAS

To modify the manner in which routing updates are sent, use the **vines update deltas** interface configuration command. To return to the default method, use the **no** form of this command.

> **vines update deltas**
> **no vines update deltas**

*Syntax     Description*

This command has no arguments or keywords.

*Default*

No deltas

*Command Mode*

Interface configuration

*Usage Guidelines*

This command first appeared in Cisco IOS Release 10.0.

The **vines update deltas** command significantly modifies the way that routing information is propagated across the network.

On LAN media, using this command causes the Cisco IOS software to stop transmitting and to stop expecting periodic routing updates. Instead, the software transmits and expects a periodic hello message. The difference between these two messages is whether routing information is included. The software continues to send flash updates to inform its neighbors of any changes to current routing table information. This is the same frequency and type of routing updates used on LANs by VINES version 5.50, but Cisco's packet format differs from the VINES format.

On WAN media, using this command causes the software to transmit three normally spaced routing updates and then cease transmission. The software does *not* send periodic hello messages. The software will, however, continue to send flash updates to inform its neighbors of any changes to current routing table information. This is the same frequency and type of routing updates used on LANs by all versions of VINES, but Cisco's packet format differs from the VINES format.

*Example*

The following example modifies the propagation of routing update information on the WAN interface connected to serial interface 0:

```
interface serial 0
  vines metric
  vines update deltas
```

## Related Commands

You can use the master indexes or search online for documentation of related commands.

**show vines interface**
**show vines neighbor**
**show vines route**
**vines metric**

## VINES UPDATE INTERVAL

To modify the frequency at which routing updates are sent, use the **vines update interval** interface configuration command. To return to the default frequency, use the **no** form of this command.

> **vines update interval** [*seconds*]
> **no vines update interval** [*seconds*]

| Syntax | Description |
|--------|-------------|
| *seconds* | (Optional) Interval, in seconds, between the sending of periodic VINES routing updates. This can be a number in the range 0 to $2^{32}$ and is rounded up to the nearest 5 seconds. The default value is 90 seconds. If you omit *seconds* or specify a value of 0, the default value of 90 seconds is used. |

## Default

90 seconds

## Command Mode

Interface configuration

## Usage Guidelines

This command first appeared in Cisco IOS Release 10.0.

The **vines update interval** command controls the interval at which the Cisco IOS software sends routing updates. The routing update interval should be the same on all VINES-speaking entities on the same physical network.

For networks on which other vendors' entities are present, it is safe to use any setting in the range 30 to 100 seconds on networks. This is the range of update intervals supported by Banyan servers. You should use values outside of this range (with the exception of zero) only on networks that contain only Cisco routers. You can use a value of zero on networks with only Cisco routers or on WAN links connecting Cisco routers and Banyan servers. In this configuration, you must also address application-level security requirements.

For Banyan VINES sites that support "change-only" updates on LAN networks, you can use the **vines update interval** command in LAN networks with both Cisco routers and Banyan servers.

*Example*

The following example sets the update interval on serial interface 0 to a value of 270 seconds:.

```
interface serial 0
  vines metric
  vines update interval 270
```

*Related Commands*

You can use the master indexes or search online for documentation of related commands.

**show vines interface**
**show vines neighbor**
**show vines route**
**vines metric**

# CHAPTER 11

# Configuring DECnet

This chapter describes how to configure your implementation of the DECnet routing protocol.

Not all Cisco access servers support the DECnet protocol. For more information, refer to the release notes for the current Cisco IOS release.

## DECNET CONFIGURATION TASK LIST

To configure DECnet routing, complete the tasks in the following sections. (Only the first task is required; the remaining tasks are optional.)

- Enabling DECnet Routing
- Enabling Concurrent Routing and Bridging
- Configuring DECnet on Token Rings
- Configuring Address Translation
- Specifying Name-to-DECnet Address Mapping
- Enabling Phase IV-to-Phase V Conversion
- Propagating Phase IV Areas through an OSI Backbone
- Establishing the Routing Table Size
- Configuring Level 1 Routers
- Configuring Level 2 Routers
- Specifying Designated Routers
- Configuring Static Routing
- Controlling Access to DECnet Networks
- Configuring DECnet Accounting

- Enhancing DECnet Performance
- Configuring DECnet over DDR
- Configuring DECnet over PPP
- Configuring DECnet over WANs
- Routing DECnet over ISL in Virtual LANs
- Monitoring and Maintaining the DECnet Network

See the "DECnet Configuration Examples" section at the end of this chapter for configuration examples.

## ENABLING DECNET ROUTING

In order to enable DECnet routing, you must complete the tasks in the following sections:

- Either "Enabling DECnet Phase IV Routing" or "Enabling DECnet Phase IV Prime Routing"
- "Assigning a DECnet Cost to Each Interface"
- "Specifying the DECnet Node Type"

## Enabling DECnet Phase IV Routing

To enable DECnet Phase IV routing, perform the following task in global configuration mode:

| Task | Command |
| --- | --- |
| Enable the DECnet Phase IV routing protocol on a global basis. | **decnet** [*network-number*] **routing** *decnet-address* |

A DECnet host exists as a *node* in an *area*. An area spans many routers, and a single interface can have many areas attached to it. Therefore, if a router exists on many cables, it uses the same area and node for itself on all of them. Note how this differs from other routing protocols, where each interface is given a different internetwork address. Figure 11–1 shows the DECnet approach.

Enabling DECnet changes the MAC addresses of the router's interfaces. This is not a problem on routers equipped with nonvolatile memory. On systems that attempt to get their Internet Protocol (IP) network addresses from network servers instead of from nonvolatile memory, there might be a problem with the hardware addresses changing and confusing other IP-speaking hosts. If you are attempting to use DECnet on such a configuration, be sure to set all global DECnet parameters before enabling DECnet routing on the interfaces.

With DECnet Phase IV Prime, the change of MAC addresses is not an issue because you can change the MAC address of the interface.

---

**NOTES**

---

If you plan to use DECnet and Internet Packet Exchange (IPX) routing concurrently on the same interface, you should enable DECnet routing first, then enable IPX routing without specifying the optional MAC address. If you do this in the reverse order (that is, enable IPX, then DECnet), IPX routing will be disrupted.

---

After you enable DECnet routing, you can obtain MAC addresses by using the **show interfaces** EXEC command. To disable DECnet routing, use the **no decnet routing** command.

*Figure 11–1*
*DECnet Nodes and Area.*

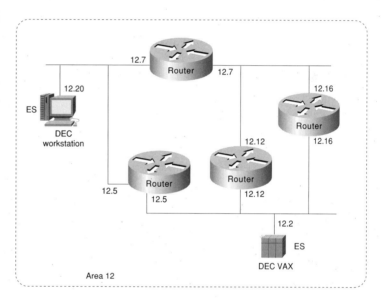

## Enabling DECnet Phase IV Prime Routing

DECnet Phase IV requires that a MAC station address be constructed using DECnet addressing conventions, with a standard high-order byte string (AA-00-04-00) concatenated with the byte-swapped DECnet node address. This can cause problems in configurations in which DECnet nodes must coexist with systems running protocols that have other MAC address restrictions.

DECnet Phase IV Prime allows an arbitrary MAC address on the LAN. An address can be assigned globally (that is, assigned by the IEEE), or it can be assigned locally by a system administrator.

To enable or disable DECnet Phase IV Prime, perform (in global configuration mode) one of the following tasks:

| Task | Command |
| --- | --- |
| **Step 1** Specify Phase IV Prime routing. | **decnet** [*network-number*] **routing iv-prime** *decnet-address* |
| **Step 2** Stop DECnet Phase IV or Phase IV Prime routing. | **no decnet routing** |

Optionally, you can map a DECnet multicast address to a Token Ring functional address other than the default functional address. To do so, perform the following task in interface configuration mode:

| Task | Command |
| --- | --- |
| Specify the type of multicast address and the functional address to which the multicast ID will map. | **decnet multicast-map** *multicast-address-type functional-address* |

## Assigning a DECnet Cost to Each Interface

After you enable DECnet routing, you must assign a cost to each interface over which you want DECnet to run. Assigning a cost to an interface enables DECnet on the interface and, using a standard formula, assigns a different MAC address than that "burned in" by the manufacturer. This section describes how to assign a cost to each interface.

DECnet routing decisions are based on cost, an arbitrary measure used to compare paths on the internetwork. Costs are based on such measures as hop count or media bandwidth. The lower the cost, the better the path. You must assign a cost to each interface.

To assign a cost to each interface for DECnet Phase IV Prime, perform the following task in interface configuration mode:

| Task | Command |
| --- | --- |
| Assign a cost to an interface. | **decnet cost** *cost-value* |

Most DECnet installations have individualized routing strategies for using costs. Therefore, check the routing strategy used at your installation to ensure that the costs you specify are consistent with those set for other hosts on the network.

Figure 11–2 shows four routers (three Ethernets) and the various routes linking them. Each link has a different cost associated with it. The least-expensive route from Router 7 to Router 20 is via Router 12.

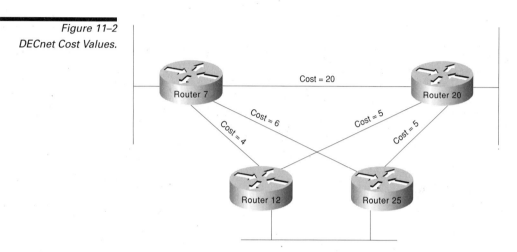

Figure 11–2
DECnet Cost Values.

## Specifying the DECnet Node Type

DECnet routing nodes are referred to as either Level 1 or Level 2 routers. You must specify the router's node type. A Level 1 router exchanges packets with other end nodes and routers in the same area and ignores Level 2 packets; this is called *intra-area routing*. Level 2 routers participate in the DECnet routing protocol with other routers and route packets to and from routers in other areas; this is called *interarea routing*. Level 2 routers also act as Level 1 routers in their own area.

The keyword **area** indicates a Level 2, interarea, router. The keyword **routing-iv** indicates a Level 1, intra-area, router; this is the default. In Level 1 mode, the Cisco IOS software sends packets destined for other areas to a designated interarea router, which forwards them outside the area.

To specify the node types, perform one of the following tasks in global configuration mode:

| Task | Command |
|---|---|
| Specify an interarea node type of the router. | **decnet** [*network-number*] **node-type area** |
| Specify an intra-area node type of the router. | **decnet** [*network-number*] **node-type routing-iv** |

For an example of how to configure DECnet, see the "DECnet Example" section at the end of this chapter.

## ENABLING CONCURRENT ROUTING AND BRIDGING

You can route DECnet on some interfaces and transparently bridge it on other interfaces simultaneously. To do this, you must enable concurrent routing and bridging. To configure an interface for concurrent routing and bridging, you use the **bridge crb** command.

To enable concurrent routing and bridging, perform the following task in global configuration mode:

| Task | Command |
|------|---------|
| Enable concurrent routing and bridging. | **bridge crb** |

## CONFIGURING DECNET ON TOKEN RINGS

If any Cisco routers are running Release 9.0 or earlier, you can use the Token Ring as a backbone or transit network for DECnet routing but you cannot communicate with non-Cisco DECnet nodes on the Token Ring.

If all Cisco routers are running Release 9.1 or later, you can set DECnet encapsulation to allow Cisco interoperation with non-Cisco equipment.

If you have both Releases 9.0 and 9.1 routers in the same network, and you want them to interoperate, you must set the encapsulation type to **pre-dec** on the Release 9.1 routers.

To run DECnet on Token Ring interfaces, perform the following tasks in interface configuration mode:

| Task | | Command |
|------|------|---------|
| **Step 1** | Enable DECnet on the Token Ring interface, and then enter interface configuration mode. | **interface tokenring** *number* |
| **Step 2** | Configure the DECnet encapsulation mode for the specified interface. | **decnet encapsulation** {pre-dec | dec} |

Use the keyword **dec** with routers running Release 9.1 or later. Use the keyword **pre-dec** with routers running Release 9.0 or earlier, or in a network where routers running 9.0 and 9.1 must interoperate.

## CONFIGURING ADDRESS TRANSLATION

If you set up multiple networks, Cisco recommends that you configure address translation in order to avoid problems with duplicate addressing between networks. If you have multiple DECnet networks, you must establish an address translation table for selected nodes between networks. This eliminates any potential problems with duplicate addressing occurring between networks. The ATG allows you to define multiple DECnet networks and map between them.

## Mapping between Networks

Configuring ATG allows the Cisco IOS software to route traffic for multiple independent DECnet networks, and to establish a user-specified address translation for selected nodes between networks. Address translation allows connectivity between DECnet networks that might not otherwise be possible because of address conflicts (duplicate addresses) between them. Configuring ATG can be done over all media types.

When you use ATG, all the DECnet configuration commands implicitly apply to network number 0, unless you specify otherwise.

To translate a virtual DECnet address to a real network address, perform the following task in global configuration mode:

| Task | Command |
|------|---------|
| Establish a translation entry to translate a virtual DECnet address to a real DECnet address for the router. | **decnet** *first-network* **map** *virtual-address second-network real-address* |

To display the address mapping information used by the DECnet ATG, use the **show decnet map** EXEC command.

For a simple example of how to configure address translation, see the "Address Translation Example" section at the end of this chapter.

## Making a "Poor Man's Routing" Connection

As an additional feature and security precaution, DECnet "Poor Man's Routing" can be used between nodes outside of the translation map, provided those nodes have access to nodes that are in the map. For example, as illustrated in in the "Address Translation Example" section at the end of this chapter, a user on node B could issue the following VMS operating system command:

```
$ dir A::D::E::
```

When a Poor Man's Routing connection is made between two networks, only the two adjacent nodes between the networks will have any direct knowledge of the other network. Application-level network access can then be specified to route through the connection.

---

**NOTES**

---

Cisco does not support Poor Man's Routing directly; the intermediate nodes must be VMS systems with Poor Man's Routing enabled in the file-access language.

---

## SPECIFYING NAME-TO-DECNET ADDRESS MAPPING

You can define a name-to-DECnet address mapping, which can be used instead of typing the set of numbers associated with a DECnet address.

To define a name-to-DECnet address mapping, perform the following task in global configuration mode:

| Task | Command |
| --- | --- |
| Define a name-to-DECnet address mapping. | **decnet host** *name decnet-address* |

The assigned DECnet name is displayed, where applicable, in the output of the **decnet route** and **show hosts** EXEC commands.

## ENABLING PHASE IV-TO-PHASE V CONVERSION

Routers that have conversion enabled advertise reachability to both Phase IV and Phase V hosts in both Phase IV and Phase V routing updates. If you have Phase IV hosts in Phase V networks and vice versa, you must enable Phase IV-to-Phase V conversion (and vice versa) in order for all nodes to communicate with each other. To enable DECnet conversion, you must have both DECnet and ISO CLNS configured on your router; then perform the following task in global configuration mode:

| Task | Command |
| --- | --- |
| Enable DECnet Phase IV-to-Phase V (and vice versa) conversion on the router. | **decnet conversion** *nsap-prefix* |

Verify that the area you specify in the **decnet conversion** global configuration command is the same as the area you specified in the ISO CLNS address. You must also enable CLNS on all interfaces, even if the router has only Phase IV hosts on some of the interfaces. This enables information about those routers to be included in link-state packets and, consequently, enables other routers to be informed about the routers connected by that interface.

For an example of how to enable a Phase IV area through an OSI backbone, see the "Phase IV-to-Phase V Conversion Example" section at the end of this chapter.

## PROPAGATING PHASE IV AREAS THROUGH AN OSI BACKBONE

One limitation of the Phase IV-to-Phase V conversion has been the inability to propagate Phase IV area routes through OSI clouds. Using the *advertise* feature, you can explicitly configure any DECnet Phase IV areas that you want to propagate outward. You configure the border routers at the Phase IV/Phase V junction.

When distant routers send a packet destined across the cloud to a border router, the router converts the route and sends it as an OSI packet. In order for the converting router to have the corresponding OSI entry to which to convert the Phase IV packet, the other border router at the Phase IV/V junction must inject *static discard* routes. In this way, the first router converts the packet from Phase IV to Phase V, sending it through the cloud. At the other end, the router advertising the static discard route converts the packet back to Phase IV and discards the Phase V packet. In effect, a fake entry is created in the Phase IV area table to propagate this information to other routers. This entry will not overwrite a native Phase IV entry if one already exists in the table.

To enable Phase IV areas to propagate through an OSI backbone on the router, perform the following task in global configuration mode:

| Task | Command |
| --- | --- |
| Enable DECnet Phase IV areas to propagate through an OSI backbone on the router. | **decnet advertise** *decnet-area hops cost* |

To enable the border router *at the far end* to convert the Phase V packet back to Phase IV, the router must advertise a static discard route. To configure the far-end border router, perform the following task in global configuration mode:

| Task | Command |
| --- | --- |
| Advertise a static discard route on the far-end border router. | **clns route** *nsap-prefix* **discard** |

For an example of how to enable a Phase IV area through an OSI backbone, see the "Phase IV Areas through an OSI Backbone Example" section at the end of this chapter.

## ESTABLISHING THE ROUTING TABLE SIZE

You can configure the maximum number of addresses and areas allowed in the Cisco IOS software routing table. It is best to keep routing updates small. All areas or nodes that cannot be reached must be advertised as unreachable. When configuring the routing table size, indicate the maximum node and area numbers that can exist in the network. In general, all routers on the network should use the same values for maximum addresses and nodes.

To establish the routing table size, perform one or both of the following tasks in global configuration mode:

| Task | Command |
| --- | --- |
| Set the maximum node address that can exist in the network. | **decnet** [*network-number*] **max-address** *value* |
| Set the largest number of areas that the Cisco IOS software can handle in its routing table. | **decnet** [*network-number*] **max-area** *area-number* |

## CONFIGURING LEVEL 1 ROUTERS

Perform any of the tasks in this section for the routers you have configured as Level 1 (intra-area) routers. In Level 1 mode, the router sends packets destined for other areas to a designated interarea router, which forwards them outside the area.

### Setting Areas as Unreachable

You can set the maximum cost that the Cisco IOS software considers usable for intra-area routing. The software ignores routes within its local area that have a cost greater than the value you specify.

### Setting Maximum Number of Hops

You can also set the maximum number of hops (or traversal of different paths) that the Cisco IOS software considers usable for intra-area routing. The software ignores routes within its local area that have a value greater than you specify.

To set certain intra-areas as unreachable based on cost value or hop count, perform one or both of the following tasks in global configuration mode:

| Task | Command |
| --- | --- |
| Set the maximum cost value for intra-area routing. | **decnet** [*network-number*] **max-cost** *cost* |
| Set the maximum hop count value for intra-area routing. | **decnet** [*network-number*] **max-hops** *hop-count* |

## CONFIGURING LEVEL 2 ROUTERS

Perform any of the tasks in the following section for the routers you have configured as Level 2 (interarea) routers. In Level 2 mode, the Cisco IOS software sends packets destined for other areas via the least-cost path to another interarea router.

## Setting Areas as Unreachable

You can set the maximum cost for a usable route to a distant area. The Cisco IOS software treats as unreachable any route with a cost greater than the value you specify.

## Setting Maximum Number of Hops

You can also set the maximum number of hops for a usable route to a distant area. The Cisco IOS software treats as unreachable any route with a hop count greater than the value you specify.

To set certain interareas as unreachable based on cost value or hop count, perform one or both of the following tasks in global configuration mode:

| Task | Command |
|------|---------|
| Set the maximum cost specification value for interarea routing. | decnet [*network-number*] area-max-cost *value* |
| Set the maximum hop count value for interarea routing. | decnet [*network-number*] area-max-hops *value* |

## SPECIFYING DESIGNATED ROUTERS

You can determine the router to which all end nodes on an Ethernet communicate if they do not know where else to send a packet. This router is called the *designated* router and is the router with the highest priority. When two or more routers on a single Ethernet in a single area share the same highest priority, the router with the highest node number is selected. You can reset the priority to help ensure that it is elected designated router in its area. This is specified on a per-interface basis.

To specify designated routers, perform the following task in interface configuration mode:

| Task | Command |
|------|---------|
| Assign or change a priority number to a router on a per-interface basis to receive packets for which no destination is specified. | decnet router-priority *value* |

## CONFIGURING STATIC ROUTING

Static routing is used when it is not possible or desirable to use dynamic routing. The following are some instances of when you would use static routing:

- The routers do not support the same dynamic routing protocol.
- Your network includes WAN links that involve paying for connect time or for per-packet charges.

- You want routers to advertise connectivity to external networks, but you are not running an interdomain routing protocol.
- You must interoperate with another vendor's equipment that does not support any of the dynamic routing protocols that we support.
- The router operates over X.25, Frame Relay, or SMDS networks.

**NOTES**

An interface that is configured for static routing cannot reroute around failed links.

To configure static routing, complete any of the tasks in the following sections:

- Configuring a Static Route
- Configuring a Static Route for an Interface
- Configuring a Default Static Route
- Configuring a Default Static Route for an Interface
- Configuring DECnet Static Route Propagation

## Configuring a Static Route

You can configure a specific static route and apply it globally even when you use dynamic routing.

To apply a specific static route globally, perform the following task in global configuration mode:

| Task | Command |
|------|---------|
| Configure a specific static route. | **decnet route** *decnet-address next-hop-address* [*hops*] [*cost*] |

## Configuring a Static Route for an Interface

You can select a specific interface for a specific static route when you do not know the address of your neighbor.

To apply a specific static route to a specific interface, perform the following task in global configuration mode:

| Task | Command |
|------|---------|
| Configure a specific static route for a specific interface. | **decnet route** *decnet-address next-hop-type number* [*snpa-address*] [*hops* [*cost*]] |

## Configuring a Default Static Route

You can configure a default static route and apply it globally, even when you use dynamic routing.

To apply a default static route globally, perform the following task in global configuration mode:

| Task | Command |
| --- | --- |
| Configure a default route. | **decnet route default** *next-hop-address* [*hops* [*cost*]] |

## Configuring a Default Static Route for an Interface

You can configure a specific interface for a default static route when you do not know the address of your neighbor.

To apply a default static route to a specific interface, perform the following task in global configuration mode:

| Task | Command |
| --- | --- |
| Configure a specific default route for a specific interface. | **decnet route default** *next-hop-type number* [*snpa-address*] [*hops* [*cost*]] |

## Configuring DECnet Static Route Propagation

When you use static routes or default static routes, you can specify whether the static routes are propagated. By default, DECnet static routes will not be propagated to other routers.

To enable or disable static route propagation, perform the following tasks in global configuration mode:

| Task | Command |
| --- | --- |
| **Step 1** Enable static route propagation. | **decnet propagate static** |
| **Step 2** Disable static route propagation. | **no decnet propagate static** |

## CONTROLLING ACCESS TO DECNET NETWORKS

Cisco provides several layers of access control for network security. You can complete any or all of the tasks in the following sections:

- Creating an Access List Based on Source Addresses
- Creating an Access List Based on Source and Destination Addresses
- Adding Filters to Access Lists

- Configuring Access Groups
- Configuring Routing Filters

## Creating an Access List Based on Source Addresses

You can configure lists globally to control access by source addresses. The standard form of the DECnet access list has a source DECnet address followed by a source-mask address, with bits set wherever the corresponding bits in the address should be ignored. DECnet addresses are written in the form *area.node*. For example, 50.4 is area 50, node 4. All addresses and masks are in decimal notation.

To create a standard DECnet access list, perform the following task in global configuration mode:

| Task | Command |
|------|---------|
| Create an access list to restrict access to a single address. | **access-list** *access-list-number* {**permit** \| **deny**} *source source-mask* |

To disable the list, use the **no access-list** command.

## Creating an Access List Based on Source and Destination Addresses

The extended form of the DECnet access list has a source DECnet address and mask pair, followed by a destination DECnet address and mask pair.

To configure an extended DECnet access list, perform the following task in global configuration mode:

| Task | Command |
|------|---------|
| Create an extended access list for several addresses. | **access-list** *access-list-number* {**permit** \| **deny**} *source source-mask* [*destination destination-mask*] |

To disable the extended access list, use the **no access-list** command.

## Adding Filters to Access Lists

DECnet access lists can be used to filter *connect initiate* packets. With these packets, you can filter by DECnet object type, such as MAIL.

To add filters to access lists, perform the following task in global configuration mode:

| Task | Command |
| --- | --- |
| Add filtering (by DECnet object type) to an access list. | access-list *access-list-number* {permit \| deny} *source source-mask* [*destination destination-mask* {eq \| neq} [[*source-object*] [*destination-object*] [*identification*]] any] |

## Configuring Access Groups

You can restrict access to specific interfaces by applying an access list to them. Interfaces that are associated with the same access list are considered to be an access group.

To configure access groups, perform the following task in interface configuration mode:

| Task | Command |
| --- | --- |
| Assign an access list to a specified interface. | decnet access-group *access-list-number* |

## Configuring Routing Filters

You can control access to hello messages or routing information being received or sent out on an interface. Addresses that are not in the access list are shown in the update message as unreachable.

To configure routing filters, perform one or both of the following tasks, as needed, in interface configuration mode:

| Task | Command |
| --- | --- |
| Control access to hello messages or routing information received on a specified interface. | decnet in-routing-filter *access-list-number* |
| Control access to routing information being sent out on a specified interface. | decnet out-routing-filter *access-list-number* |

## Configuring DECnet Accounting

DECnet accounting enables you to collect information about DECnet packets and the number of bytes that are switched through the Cisco IOS software. You collect accounting information based on the source and destination DECnet addresses. DECnet accounting tracks only DECnet traffic that is routed out an interface on which DECnet accounting is configured; it does not track traffic generated by or terminating at the router itself.

DECnet access lists and fast switching support DECnet accounting statistics. Autonomous and SSE switching do not support DECnet accounting statistics.

The Cisco IOS software maintains two accounting databases: an active database and a checkpoint database. The active database contains accounting data tracked until the database is cleared. When the active database is cleared, its contents are copied to the checkpoint database. Using these two databases together enables you to monitor both current traffic and traffic that has previously traversed the router.

To configure DECnet accounting, perform the tasks described in these sections:

- Enabling DECnet Routing on the Router
- Enabling DECnet Accounting
- Customizing DECnet Accounting

## Enabling DECnet Routing on the Router

To enable DECnet routing, perform the following tasks in global configuration mode:

| Task | Command |
| --- | --- |
| Step 1  Enable DECnet routing. | decnet [*network-number*] routing [iv-prime] *decnet-address* |
| Step 2  Specify the node type (interarea or intra-area). | decnet [*network-number*] node-type [area | routing-iv] |

## Enabling DECnet Accounting

To enable DECnet accounting on a specific interface, begin the following tasks in global configuration mode:

| Task | Command |
| --- | --- |
| Step 1  Specify the serial interface. | interface *type slot/port* |
| Step 2  Specify the cost value for the interface. | decnet cost *cost-value* |
| Step 3  Enable DECnet accounting. | decnet accounting |

---

**NOTES**

If DECnet accounting is enabled on an interface but no accounting list is specified, DECnet accounting will track all traffic through the interface, up to the accounting threshold limit.

---

## Customizing DECnet Accounting

To customize DECnet accounting, perform one or more of the following tasks in global configuration mode:

| Task | Command |
|------|---------|
| Specify the maximum number of accounting entries. | **decnet accounting threshold** *threshold* |
| Specify the maximum number of transit entries. | **decnet accounting transits** *count* |
| Specify the source and destination pair addresses for which DECnet accounting information is kept. Enter one command for each source and destination pair. | **decnet accounting list** *src-dec-address dest-dec-address* |

## ENHANCING DECNET PERFORMANCE

To optimize internetwork performance, complete any or all of the tasks in the following sections:

- Setting Maximum Equal-Cost Paths
- Establishing Selection for Paths of Equal Cost
- Setting Maximum Visits
- Adjusting the Hello Timer
- Disabling Fast Switching
- Setting the Congestion Threshold
- Adjusting the Broadcast Routing Timer

## Setting Maximum Equal-Cost Paths

You can set the maximum number of equal-cost paths to a destination on a global basis. Limiting the number of equal-cost paths can save memory on routers with limited memory or with very large configurations. Additionally, in networks with a large number of multiple paths and end systems with limited ability to cache out-of-sequence packets, performance might suffer when traffic is split between many paths.

To set maximum equal-cost paths, perform the following task in global configuration mode:

| Task | Command |
|------|---------|
| Set the maximum number of equal-cost paths to a destination. Paths are set in the routing table. | **decnet** [*network-number*] **max-paths** *value* |

Use the **show decnet route** EXEC command to display the first hop route to a specified address and to show all equal-cost paths to a single destination.

## Establishing Selection for Paths of Equal Cost

You can establish one of two methods for selecting among paths of equal cost on the router: on a round-robin basis, which is the default, or by configuring the Cisco IOS software so that traffic for any higher-layer session is always routed over the same path.

In the round-robin or *normal* mode, the first packet is sent to the first node, the second packet to the second node, and so on. If the final node is reached before all packets are sent, the next packet in line is sent to the first node, then to the second node, and so forth.

The *interim* mode supports older implementations of DECnet (VMS Versions 4.5 and earlier) that do not support out-of-order packet caching. Other sessions might take another path, thus using equal-cost paths that a router might have for a particular destination.

To select normal or interim mode on the router, perform one of the following tasks in global configuration mode:

| Task | Command |
|------|---------|
| Specify that traffic is routed over equal-cost paths on a round-robin basis. | **decnet path-split-mode normal** |
| Specify that traffic is always routed over the same path. | **decnet path-split-mode interim** |

## Setting Maximum Visits

You can determine the number of times that a packet can pass through a router. The Cisco IOS software ignores packets that have a value greater than the amount of visits you specify. Digital recommends that the value be at least twice the number of maximum hops, to allow packets to reach their destinations when routes are changing.

To set the number of times a packet can pass through a router, perform the following task in global configuration mode:

| Task | Command |
| --- | --- |
| Set the number of times a packet can pass through a router. | **decnet** [*network-number*] **max-visits** *value* |

## Adjusting the Hello Timer

Hosts use the hello messages to identify the hosts with which they can communicate directly. The Cisco IOS software sends hello messages every 15 seconds by default. On extremely slow serial lines, you might want to increase this value on a per-interface basis to reduce overhead.

To adjust the interval for sending hello messages, perform the following task in interface configuration mode:

| Task | Command |
| --- | --- |
| Adjust the interval (in seconds) for sending hello messages on interfaces with DECnet enabled. | **decnet hello-timer** *seconds* |

## Disabling Fast Switching

By default, our DECnet routing software implements fast switching of DECnet packets. You might want to disable fast switching to save memory space on interface cards and to help avoid congestion when high-bandwidth interfaces are writing large amounts of information to low-bandwidth interfaces. This is especially important when using rates slower than T1.

To disable fast switching of DECnet packets, perform the following task in interface configuration mode:

| Task | Command |
| --- | --- |
| Disable fast switching of DECnet packets on a per-interface basis. | **no decnet route-cache** |

## Setting the Congestion Threshold

If a router configured for DECnet experiences congestion, it sets the *congestion-experienced* bit. You can define the congestion threshold on a per-interface basis. By setting this threshold, you will cause the system to set the congestion-experienced bit if the output queue has more than the specified number of packets in it.

To set the congestion threshold, perform the following task in interface configuration mode:

| Task | Command |
| --- | --- |
| Set the congestion threshold. | decnet congestion-threshold *number* |

### Adjusting the Broadcast Routing Timer

Other routers use broadcast updates to construct local routing tables. Increasing the time between routing updates on a per-interface basis reduces the amount of unnecessary network traffic. Digital calls this parameter the *broadcast routing timer* because Digital uses a different timer for serial lines. Our DECnet implementation does not make this distinction.

To adjust the broadcast routing timer, perform the following task in interface configuration mode:

| Task | Command |
| --- | --- |
| Adjust how often the Cisco IOS software sends routing updates that list all the hosts that the router can reach on a per-interface basis. | decnet routing-timer *seconds* |

## CONFIGURING DECNET OVER DDR

Dial-on-demand routing (DDR) is now supported for DECnet.

## CONFIGURING DECNET OVER PPP

DECnet packets can now be fast switched over PPP.

## CONFIGURING DECNET OVER WANS

You can configure DECnet over X.25, SMDS, and Frame Relay networks. To do this, configure the appropriate address mappings.

### Enabling Split Horizon

When split horizon is enabled, routing updates sent out on an interface do not include any information that was originally learned from that interface, and broadcasts are not retransmitted on the receiving interface. Disabling split horizon causes the Cisco IOS software to include all information in routing updates, and to resend broadcast packets on the network from which they were received.

To disable split horizon, perform the following task in interface configuration mode:

| Task | Command |
| --- | --- |
| Disable split horizon when sending routing updates. | **no decnet split-horizon** |

## ROUTING DECNET OVER ISL IN VIRTUAL LANS

DECnet can be routed over virtual LAN (VLAN) subinterfaces using Inter-Switch Link (ISL) encapsulation protocol. Full-feature Cisco IOS is supported on a per-VLAN basis, allowing standard DECnet capabilities to be configured on VLANs.

## MONITORING AND MAINTAINING THE DECNET NETWORK

To clear counters, test network node reachability, and display information about DECnet networks, perform the following tasks in EXEC mode:

| Task | | Command |
| --- | --- | --- |
| Step 1 | Clear the DECnet counters. | **clear decnet counters** |
| Step 2 | Test network node reachability. | **ping decnet** {*host* | *address*} |
| Step 3 | Display the global DECnet parameters. | **show decnet** |
| Step 4 | Display the global DECnet status and configuration for all interfaces, or the status and configuration for a specified interface, including address, paths, cost, access lists, and more. | **show decnet interface** [*type number*] |
| Step 5 | List address mapping information used by the DECnet ATG. | **show decnet map** |
| Step 6 | Display all Phase IV and Phase IV Prime neighbors and the MAC address associated with each neighbor. | **show decnet neighbors** |
| Step 7 | Display DECnet routing table. | **show decnet route** [*decnet-address*] |
| Step 8 | Display static DECnet routing table. | **show decnet static** |
| Step 9 | List DECnet traffic statistics, including datagrams sent, received, and forwarded. | **show decnet traffic** |

## Configuring MOP

You can enable Maintenance Operation Protocol (MOP) on an interface by performing the following task in interface configuration mode:

| Task | Command |
|------|---------|
| Enable MOP. | mop enabled |

You can enable an interface to send out periodic MOP system identification messages on an interface by performing the following task in interface configuration mode:

| Task | Command |
|------|---------|
| Enable MOP message support. | mop sysid |

## DECNET CONFIGURATION EXAMPLES

The following sections provide examples that show some common DECnet configuration activities:

- DECnet Phase IV Prime Examples
- DECnet Example
- Address Translation Example
- Phase IV-to-Phase V Conversion Example
- Phase IV Areas through an OSI Backbone Example
- DECnet Accounting Configuration Example

## DECnet Phase IV Prime Examples

This section includes examples of configuring DECnet Phase IV Prime support for inherent MAC addresses. The comments in these examples point out some possible configuration errors, in addition to explaining correct command lines.

In the following example, Ethernet interface 0 is configured for DECnet Phase IV Prime:

```
decnet routing iv-prime 1.1
interface ethernet 0
 decnet cost 10
! Interface Ethernet 0 will have aa-00-04-00 form of MAC address. Router is
! bilingual on interface Ethernet 0.
```

In the following example, Token Ring interface 1 is configured with a MAC address that is not supported by DECnet Phase IV:

```
decnet routing 2.1
interface tokenring 1
 decnet cost 5
```

```
 mac-address 0000.0c00.62e6
 ! Interface Token Ring 1 has MAC address as set
 ! This is an error because the token ring interface has a MAC address that is
 ! not Phase IV-compatible, and the router is not running Phase IV Prime.
```

In the following example, the router is not configured to support DECnet Phase IV Prime until later in the configuration:

```
interface tokenring 1
 decnet cost 5
 mac-address 0000.0c00.62e6
 ! invalid configuration, since router is only Phase IV.
 decnet routing iv-prime 5.5
 ! Become a Phase IV Prime router

interface tokenring 1
 mac-address 0000.0c00.62e6
 ! Valid configuration since the router is now running Phase IV Prime.
```

The following example shows valid and invalid ways of using the **decnet multicast-map** command:

```
decnet routing iv-prime 3.4

interface tokenring 1
 decnet multicast-map phiv-prime-all-bridges c000.2000.0000
 ! Invalid value (phiv-prime-all-bridges) for multicast ID string

interface tokenring 1
 decnet multicast-map iv-prime-all-routers d000.2000.0000
 ! Invalid value (d000.2000.0000) for functional address

interface tokenring 1
 decnet multicast-map iv-prime-all-routers c000.2000.0000
 ! This will work. The command redefines the multicast to functional address
 ! mapping for the "all Phase IV Prime routers" multicast.
```

## DECnet Example

The following example illustrates the commands required for enabling DECnet. DECnet routing is established on a router at address 4.27. The node is configured as a Level 2, or interarea router. A cost of four is set for the Ethernet 0 interface. A cost of ten is set for the serial 1 interface.

```
decnet routing 4.27
decnet node area
interface ethernet 0
 decnet cost 4
interface serial 1
 decnet cost 10
```

## Address Translation Example

In Figure 11–3, the router is connected to two DECnet networks using Ethernet. The following example illustrates how to configure an ATG between Network 0 and Network 1.

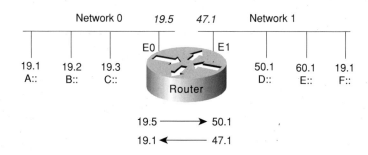

**Figure 11–3**
*ATG Configuration Example.*

In Network 0, the router is configured at address 19.4 and is a Level 1 router. In Network 1, the router is configured at address 50.5 and is an area router. At this point, no routing information is exchanged between the two networks. Each network in the router has a separate routing table.

```
decnet 0 routing 19.4
decnet 0 node routing-iv
interface ethernet 0
 decnet 0 cost 1
!
decnet 1 routing 50.5
decnet 1 node area
interface ethernet 1
 decnet 1 cost 1
```

To establish a translation map, enter the following commands:

```
decnet 0 map 19.5 1 50.1
decnet 1 map 47.1 0 19.1
```

Packets in Network 0 sent to virtual address 19.5 will be routed to Network 1, and the destination address will be translated to 50.1. Packets sent to virtual address 47.1 in Network 1 will be routed to Network 0 as 19.1.

Table 11–1 defines the parameters for the translation map.

**Table 11–1**  *Packet Exchange between Nodes A and D*

| Source | | Destination | |
|---|---|---|---|
| A packet addressed as: | 19.1 | 19.5 | is received on Ethernet 0 as 19.5 |
| Translates to: | 47.1 | 50.1 | and is transmitted out Ethernet 1 as 50.1 |
| A reply packet: | 50.1 | 47.1 | is received on Ethernet 1 |
| Translates to: | 19.5 | 19.1 | and is transmitted on Ethernet 0 |

Network 0 uses a block of addresses from its area to map the remote nodes. In Network 0, the router will advertise nodes 19.5 and 19.6. These nodes must not already exist in Network 0.

Network 1 uses another area for the address translation. Since the Cisco IOS software will be advertising the availability of area 47, that area should not already exist in Network 1, because DECnet area fragmentation could occur.

Only nodes that exist in the maps on both networks will be able to communicate directly. Network 0 node 19.1 will be able to communicate with Network 1 node 50.1 (as 19.5), but will not be able to communicate directly with Network 1 node 60.1.

When naming nodes, use the appropriate address in each network. See the lists that follow for examples.

### Network 0 VMS NCP Command File Sample

```
$MCR NCP
define node 19.1 name A
define node 19.2 name B
define node 19.3 name C
define node 19.4 name GS
define node 19.5 name D
define node 19.6 name F
```

### Network 1 VMS NCP Command File Sample

```
$MCR NCP
define node 50.1 name D
define node 50.5 name GS
define node 60.1 name E
define node 19.1 name F
define node 47.1 name A
define node 47.2 name C
```

## Phase IV-to-Phase V Conversion Example

Figure 11–4 shows that for the DECnet Phase IV-to-Phase V conversion to work properly, CLNS IS-IS must be configured on certain interfaces.

Note that although Router A has only Phase IV hosts connected by its Ethernet 0 interface, the interface must be configured for CLNS IS-IS for Router A to convert the Phase IV adjacency information into Phase V. If the Ethernet interface 0 on Router A is not configured for CLNS IS-IS, Router B will never get information about Router D and endnode 1.

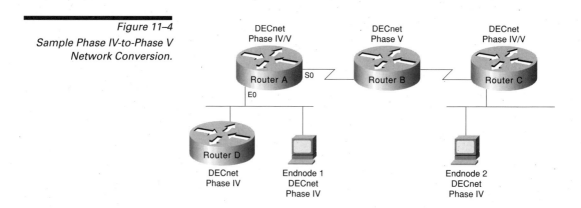

*Figure 11–4*
*Sample Phase IV-to-Phase V Network Conversion.*

## Configuration for Router A

```
decnet routing 1.1
decnet conversion 49
clns routing
router isis
 net 49.0001.aa00.0400.0104.00
interface ethernet 0
 clns router isis
 decnet cost 4
interface s 0
 clns router isis
```

## Sample Configuration for Router D

```
decnet routing 1.10
interface ethernet 0
 decnet cost 4
```

## Phase IV Areas through an OSI Backbone Example

The following example illustrates how to configure border routers to propagate Phase IV areas through an OSI backbone using the advertise feature. In this example, Router X in area 8 wants to communicate with Router Y in area 9. Figure 11–5 illustrates the network, and the configurations that follow illustrate the commands required for enabling the advertise feature.

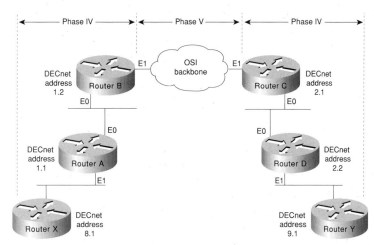

*Figure 11–5*
*Sample Phase IV/Phase V*
*Backbone Network.*

## Configuration for Router B

```
decnet conversion 49
! Propagate Area 9 reachability information
decnet advertise 9 4 2
! Create dummy OSI route to force conversion to Phase IV
clns route 49.0008 discard
```

## Configuration for Router C

```
decnet conversion 49
! Propagate Area 8 reachability information
decnet advertise 8 6 3
! Create dummy OSI route to force conversion to Phase IV
clns route 49.0009 discard
```

The routing table for Router A will then contain the following, as displayed with the **show decnet route** EXEC command:

| Area | Cost | Hops | Next Hop to Node | Expires | Prio | |
|------|------|------|------------------|---------|------|---|
| *1 | 0 | 0 | (Local) -> 1.1 | | | |
| *8 | 4 | 1 | Ethernet1 -> 8.1 | 35 | 64 | A |
| *9 | 5 | 2 | Ethernet0 -> 1.2 | | | |
| Node | Cost | Hops | Next Hop to Node | Expires | Prio | |
| *(Area) | 0 | 0 | (Local) -> 1.1 | | | |
| *1.1 | 0 | 0 | (Local) -> 1.1 | | | |
| *1.2 | 4 | 1 | Ethernet4 -> 1.2 | 38 | 64 | VA |

The routing table for Router B will then contain the following:

| Area | Cost | Hops | Next Hop to Node | | Expires | Prio | |
|------|------|------|------------------|------|---------|------|---|
| *1   | 0    | 0    | (Local)          | -> 1.2 |         |      |   |
| *8   | 8    | 2    | Ethernet0        | -> 1.1 |         |      |   |
| *9   | 4    | 2    | (OSI)            | -> 1.2 |         |      |   |

| Node | Cost | Hops | Next Hop to Node | | Expires | Prio | |
|------|------|------|------------------|------|---------|------|----|
| *(Area) | 0 | 0  | (Local)          | -> 1.2 |         |      |    |
| *1.1 | 4    | 1    | Ethernet0        | -> 1.1 | 37      | 64   | VA |
| *1.2 | 0    | 0    | (Local)          | -> 1.2 |         |      |    |

The routing table for Router C will then contain the following:

| Area | Cost | Hops | Next Hop to Node | | Expires | Prio | |
|------|------|------|------------------|------|---------|------|---|
| *2   | 0    | 0    | (Local)          | -> 2.1 |         |      |   |
| *8   | 6    | 3    | (OSI)            | -> 2.1 |         |      |   |
| *9   | 8    | 2    | Ethernet0        | -> 2.2 |         |      |   |

| Node | Cost | Hops | Next Hop to Node | | Expires | Prio | |
|------|------|------|------------------|------|---------|------|----|
| *(Area) | 0 | 0  | (Local)          | -> 2.1 |         |      |    |
| *2.1 | 0    | 0    | (Local)          | -> 2.1 |         |      |    |
| *2.2 | 4    | 1    | Ethernet0        | -> 2.2 | 33      | 64   | VA |

## DECnet Accounting Configuration Example

Figure 11–6 illustrates DECnet accounting configured on the outbound serial interfaces for Routers A and C. Note that because Routers A and C exist in two different DECnet areas, they must be configured as inter-area, or Level 2, routers.

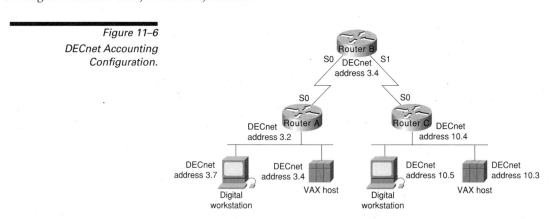

Figure 11–6
DECnet Accounting
Configuration.

On Router A, DECnet accounting is enabled on an interface that is routing DECnet traffic. With no other commands entered for the interface configuration, DECnet accounting on Router A tracks all DECnet traffic outbound on that interface up to the default accounting threshold of 512 source and destination pair addresses.

### Configuration for Router A

```
decnet routing 3.2
decnet node-type area
interface serial 0
 decnet cost 20
 decnet accounting
interface e0
 decnet cost 4
```

Router B is configured to track traffic between all pairs specified in the **decnet accounting list** command. Router B also tracks traffic for pairs not specified in the decnet accounting list command up to the value specified for the **decnet accounting transit** command. If traffic between a source and destination end-point pair not listed traverses the router, that traffic is added to the aggregate value which appears in the display for the **show decnet accounting** command.

### Configuration for Router B

```
decnet routing 12.7
interface serial 0
 decnet cost 20
 decnet accounting
interface serial 1
 decnet cost 20
 decnet accounting
decnet node type area
decnet accounting list 3.4 10.5
decnet accounting list 3.7 10.5
decnet accounting list 3.4 10.3
decnet accounting transits 2
```

Router C is configured to track DECnet traffic according to the values specified with the DECnet commands. The accounting threshold is set to 1000, which means that DECnet accounting will track all traffic passing through the router for up to 1000 source and destination address pairs.

### Configuration for Router C

```
decnet routing 10.4
decnet node-type area
interface serial 0
 decnet cost 20
 decnet accounting
 decnet accounting threshold 1000
interface e0
 decnet cost 4
```

# CHAPTER 12

# DECnet Commands

Digital Equipment Corporation developed the DECnet protocol to provide a way for its computers to communicate with one another. Currently in its fifth major product release, DECnet Phase V is a superset of the Open System Interconnection (OSI) protocol suite, supports all OSI protocols, and is compatible with the previous release (Phase IV). DECnet Phase IV Prime supports inherent MAC addresses, which allow DECnet nodes to coexist with systems running other protocols that have MAC address restrictions. DECnet support on Cisco routers includes local-area and wide-area DECnet Phase IV routing over Ethernet, Token Ring, FDDI, and serial lines such as X.25, Frame Relay, and Switched Multimegabit Data Service (SMDS).

Use the commands in this chapter to configure and monitor DECnet networks.

---

**NOTES**

---

Not all Cisco access servers support DECnet. For more information, refer to the release notes for the current Cisco IOS release.

---

## ACCESS-LIST (EXTENDED)

To create an extended access list, use the **access-list** global configuration command. To delete the entire access list, use the **no** form of this command.

> **access-list** *access-list-number* {**permit** | **deny**} *source source-mask* [*destination destination-mask*]
> **no access-list**

| Syntax | Description |
|--------|-------------|
| *access-list-number* | Integer you choose between 300 and 399 that uniquely identifies the access list. |
| **permit** | Permits access when there is an address match. |
| **deny** | Denies access when there is an address match. |
| *source* | Source address. DECnet addresses are written in the form *area.node*. For example, 50.4 is node 4 in area 50. All addresses are in decimal. |
| *source-mask* | Mask to be applied to the address of the source node. All masks are in decimal. |
| *destination* | (Optional) Destination node's DECnet address in decimal format. DECnet addresses are written in the form *area.node*. For example, 50.4 is node 4 in area 50. |
| *destination-mask* | (Optional) Destination mask. DECnet addresses are written in the form *area.node*. For example, 50.4 is node 4 in area 50. All masks are in decimal. |

### Default

No access list is defined.

### Command Mode

Global configuration

### Usage Guidelines

This command first appeared in Cisco IOS Release 10.0.

### Example

In the following example, access list 301 is configured to allow traffic from any host in networks 1 and 3. It implies no other traffic is permitted. (The end of a list contains an implicit "deny all else" statement.)

```
access-list 301 permit 1.0 0.1023 0.0 63.1023
access-list 301 permit 3.0 0.1023 0.0 63.1023
```

### Related Commands

Search online to find documentation of related commands.

**access-list (filter connect initiate packets)**
**access-list (standard)**
**decnet access-group**

decnet in-routing-filter
decnet out-routing-filter
show decnet interface

## ACCESS-LIST (FILTER CONNECT INITIATE PACKETS)

To create an access list that filters *connect initiate* packets, use this version of the **access-list** global configuration command. To disable the access list, use the **no** form of this command.

> **access-list** *access-list-number* {**permit** | **deny**} *source source-mask*
> [*destination destination-mask* ] {**eq** | **neq**} [[*source-object*] [*destination-object*]
> [*identification*] any]
>
> **no access-list**

The optional argument *source-object* consists of the following string:

> **src** [{**eq** | **neq** | **gt** | **lt**} *object-number*] [**exp** *regular-expression*] [**uic** [*group, user*]]

The optional argument *destination-object* consists of the following string:

> **dst** [{**eq** | **neq** | **gt** | **lt**} *object-number*] [**exp** *regular-expression*] [**uic** [*group, user*]]

The optional argument *identification* consists of the following string:

> [**id** *regular-expression*] [**password** *regular-expression*] [**account** *regular-expression*]

| Syntax | Description |
|---|---|
| *access-list-number* | Integer you choose between 300 and 399 that uniquely identifies the access list. |
| **permit** | Permits access when there is an address match. |
| **deny** | Denies access when there is an address match. |
| *source* | Source address. DECnet addresses are written in the form *area.node*. For example, 50.4 is node 4 in area 50. All addresses are in decimal. |
| *source-mask* | Mask to be applied to the address of the source node. All masks are in decimal. |
| *destination* | (Optional) Destination node's DECnet address in decimal format. DECnet addresses are written in the form *area.node*. For example, 50.4 is node 4 in area 50. All addresses are in decimal. |
| *destination-mask* | (Optional) Destination mask. DECnet addresses are written in the form *area.node*. For example, 50.4 is node 4 in area 50. All masks are in decimal. |
| **eq** \| **neq** | Use either of these keywords: <br><br> • **eq**—Item matches the packet if *all* the specified parts of *source-object*, *destination-object*, and *identification* match data in the packet. <br><br> • **neq**—Item matches the packet if *any* of the specified parts do *not* match the corresponding entry in the packet. |

| Syntax | Description |
|---|---|
| *source-object* | (Optional) Contains the mandatory keyword **src** and one of the following optional keywords: |
| | • **eq** | **neq** | **lt** | **gt**—Equal to, not equal to, less than, or greater than. These keywords must be followed by the argument *object-number*, a numeric DECnet object number. |
| | • **exp**—Stands for expression; followed by a regular expression that matches a string. See the "Regular Expressions" appendix in the *Dial Solutions Command Reference* for a description of regular expressions. |
| | • **uic**—Stands for user identification code; followed by a numeric user ID (UID) expression. The argument [*group, user*] is a numeric UID expression. In this case, the bracket symbols are literal; they must be entered. The group and user parts can either be specified in decimal, in octal by prefixing the number with a 0, or in hex by prefixing the number with 0x. The *uic* expression displays as an octal number. |
| *destination-object* | (Optional) Contains the mandatory keyword **dst** and one of the following optional keywords: |
| | • **eq** | **neq** | **lt** | **gt**—Equal to, not equal to, less than, or greater than. These keywords must be followed by the argument *object-number*, a numeric DECnet object number. |
| | • **exp**—Stands for expression; followed by a regular expression that matches a string. See the "Regular Expressions" appendix in the *Dial Solutions Command Reference* for a description of regular expressions. |
| | • **uic**—Stands for user identification code; followed by a numeric user ID (UID) expression. In this case, the bracket symbols are literal; they must be entered. The group and user parts can either be specified in decimal, in octal by prefixing the number with a 0, or in hex by prefixing the number with 0x. The *uic* expression displays as an octal number. |
| *identification* | (Optional) Uses any of the following three keywords: |
| | • **id**—Regular expression; refers to user ID. |
| | • **password**—Regular expression; the password to the account. |
| | • **account**—Regular expression; the account string. |
| **any** | (Optional) Item matches if *any* of the specified parts *do* match the corresponding entries for *source-object*, *destination-object*, or *identification*. |

## Default

No access list is defined.

## Command Mode

Global configuration

## Usage Guidelines

This command first appeared in Cisco IOS Release 10.0.

Depending upon the arguments you use, you can define access lists in three ways:

- Restrict access based on source addresses

  Use the *source* and *source-mask* arguments only.

- Restrict access based on destination addresses

  Use the *source*, *source-mask*, *destination*, and *destination-mask* arguments.

- Add filters to further narrow access

  Use the *source*, *source-mask*, *destination*, and *destination-mask* arguments, the **eq, neq,** or **any** keywords and any or all of the following arguments: *source-object*, *destination-object*, and *identification*.

Table 12–1 lists the DECnet object numbers.

**Table 12–1** *Common DECnet Object Numbers*

| Name | Number | Description |
|------|--------|-------------|
| FAL | 17 | File Access Listener |
| HLD | 18 | Host Loader |
| NML | 19 | Network Monitor Link/NICE |
| MIRROR | 25 | Loopback mirror |
| EVL | 26 | Event logger |
| MAIL | 27 | Mail |
| PHONE | 29 | Phone |
| NOTES | 33 | VAX Notes |
| CTERM | 42 | Terminal sessions |
| DTR | 63 | DECnet Test Sender/Receiver |

*Examples*

The following example illustrates an access list for matching all connect packets for object number 27:

```
access-list 300 permit 0.0 63.1023 eq dst eq 27
```

The following example illustrates an access list for matching all connect packets *except* for the object number 17:

```
access-list 300 permit 0.0 63.1023 neq dst eq 17
```

The following example illustrates an access list for matching all connect packets where the access identification was *SYSTEM*:

```
access-list 300 permit 0.0 63.1023 eq id ^SYSTEM$
```

The following example illustrates an access list for matching all connect packets from area 1 to object number 27 (27 = VAX/VMS Personal Utility or MAIL) where *SYSTEM* is the originating user:

```
access-list 300 permit 1.0 0.1023 eq src exp ^SYSTEM$ dst eq 27
```

The following example illustrates an access list for matching any connect packet and can be used at the end of a list to permit any packets not already matched:

```
access-list 300 permit 0.0 63.1023 eq any
```

*Related Commands*

Search online to find documentation of related commands.

**access-list (extended)**
**access-list (standard)**
**decnet access-group**
**decnet in-routing-filter**
**decnet out-routing-filter**
**show decnet interface**

## ACCESS-LIST (STANDARD)

To create a standard access list, use the standard version of the **access-list** global configuration command. To delete the entire access list, use the **no** form of this command.

> **access-list** *access-list-number* {**permit** | **deny**} *source source-mask*
> **no access-list**

| Syntax | Description |
|---|---|
| *access-list-number* | Integer you choose between 300 and 399 that uniquely identifies the access list. |
| **permit** | Permits access when there is an address match. |
| **deny** | Denies access when there is an address match. |

| Syntax | Description |
|--------|-------------|
| *source* | Source address. DECnet addresses are written in the form *area.node*. For example, 50.4 is node 4 in area 50. All addresses are in decimal. |
| *source-mask* | Mask to be applied to the address of the source node. Bits are set wherever the corresponding bits in the address should be ignored. All masks are in decimal. |

### Default

No access list is defined.

### Command Mode

Global configuration

### Usage Guidelines

This command first appeared in Cisco IOS Release 10.3.

In contrast with IP masks, a DECnet mask specification of "all ones" is entered as the decimal value 1023. In IP, the equivalent is 255.

### Example

The following example sets up access list 300 to deny packets coming from node 4.51 and permit packets coming from 2.31:

```
access-list 300 deny 4.51 0.0
access-list 300 permit 2.31 0.0
```

### Related Commands

Search online to find documentation of related commands.

**access-list (extended)**
**access-list (filter connect initiate packets)**
**decnet access-group**
**decnet in-routing-filter**
**decnet out-routing-filter**
**show decnet interface**

## CLEAR DECNET ACCOUNTING

Use the **clear decnet accounting** EXEC command to delete all entries in the accounting database when DECnet accounting is enabled.

> **clear decnet accounting** [checkpoint]

| Syntax | Description |
|---|---|
| **checkpoint** | (Optional) Clears the checkpoint database. |

## Command Mode

EXEC

## Usage Guidelines

This command first appeared in Cisco IOS Release 11.2 F.

Specifying the **clear decnet accounting** command without the **checkpoint** keyword copies the active database to the checkpoint database and clears the active database.

The active data set is copied to the checkpoint database; the active database entry values are reset to zero. If there are entries in the database that were found dynamically, they are deleted. If there are entries that were entered statically, such as decnet accounting list 5.3.17.26, they are not removed. Their values are reset to zero.

Any traffic that traverses the router after the **clear decnet accounting** command has been issued is saved in the active database. Accounting information in the checkpoint database at that time reflects traffic prior to the most recent **clear decnet accounting** command.

You can also delete all entries in both the active and the checkpoint databases by issuing the **clear decnet accounting** command twice in succession.

## Example

In the following example, the first display from the **show decnet accounting** command shows the active database before a clear command is issued. The clear decnet accounting command is issued and a second show display shows no accounting information in the active database. The display from the **show decnet accounting checkpoint** command shows the data collected in the active database prior to the **clear decnet accounting** command:

```
Router# show decnet accounting

Source  DestinationBytesPackets
2.32937.41536
5.77.83264
27.10027.1071455
7.85.715212
27.10727.1005005
37.42.329784

Accounting data age is 12.41

Router# clear decnet accounting
Router# show decnet accounting

Source  DestinationBytesPackets
```

```
Accounting data age is 0
Router# show decnet accounting checkpoint

Source   Destination    Bytes       Packets
2.329          37.4        153          6
5.7             7.8        326          4
27.100       27.107        145          5
7.8             5.7        152         12
27.107       27.100        500          5
37.4          2.329         78          4

Accounting data age is 12.41
```

## Related Commands

Search online to find documentation of related commands.

**decnet accounting**
**decnet accounting list**
**decnet accounting threshold**
**decnet accounting transits**
**show decnet accounting**

## CLEAR DECNET COUNTERS

To clear DECnet counters that are shown in the output of the **show decnet traffic** EXEC command, use the **clear decnet counters** EXEC command.

    **clear decnet counters**

## Syntax    Description

This command has no arguments or keywords.

## Command Mode

EXEC

## Usage Guidelines

This command first appeared in Cisco IOS Release 10.0.

## Example

The following example zeros all DECnet counters:

```
clear decnet counters
```

## Related Commands

Search online to find documentation of related commands.

**show decnet traffic**

## DECNET ACCESS-GROUP

To create a DECnet access group, use the **decnet access-group** interface configuration command.

    **decnet access-group** *access-list-number*

| *Syntax* | *Description* |
|---|---|
| *access-list-number* | Either a standard or extended DECnet access list. A standard DECnet access list applies to source addresses. The value (or values in the case of extended lists) can be in the range 300 to 399. |

### Default

No access group is defined.

### Command Mode

Interface configuration

### Usage Guidelines

This command first appeared in Cisco IOS Release 10.0.

### Example

The following example applies access list 389 to Ethernet interface 1:

```
interface ethernet 1
  decnet access-group 389
```

### Related Commands

Search online to find documentation of related commands.

**access-list (standard)**
**show decnet interface**

## DECNET ACCOUNTING

To enable DECnet accounting, use the **decnet accounting** interface configuration command. To disable DECnet accounting, use the **no** form of this command.

    **decnet accounting**
    **no decnet accounting**

*Syntax*     *Description*

This command has no arguments or keywords.

## Default

Disabled

## Command Mode

Interface configuration

## Usage Guidelines

This command first appeared in Cisco IOS Release 11.2 F.

The Cisco IOS software maintains two accounting databases: an active database and a checkpoint database. The active database contains accounting data tracked until the database is cleared. When the active database is cleared, its contents are copied to the checkpoint database. Using these two databases together allows you to monitor both current traffic and traffic which has previously traversed the router.

DECnet accounting statistics will be accurate, even if DECnet fast switching is enabled, or if DECnet access lists are being used.

Enabling DECnet accounting significantly decreases the performance of a fast-switched interface.

DECnet accounting is disabled if autonomous or SSE switching is enabled.

## Example

This example shows DECnet accounting enabled on a serial interface 0:

```
interface serial 0
  decnet accounting
```

## Related Commands

Search online to find documentation of related commands.

**clear decnet accounting**
**decnet accounting list**
**decnet accounting threshold**
**decnet accounting transits**
**show decnet accounting**

## DECNET ACCOUNTING LIST

Use the **decnet accounting list** global configuration command to specify the source and destination address pairs for which DECnet accounting information is kept. DECnet accounting tracks all traffic that traverses the router between the source and destination address pairs specified with this command. To remove the accounting filter, use the **no** form of this command.

**decnet accounting-list** *src-dec-address dest-dec-address*
**no decnet accounting list** {*src-dec-address dest-dec-address* | **all**}

| Syntax | Description |
|---|---|
| *src-dec-address* | DECnet address for the source. The address is in the form *area.node*, for example, 5.3. |
| *dest-dec-address* | DECnet address for the destination. The address is in the form *area.node*, for example, 5.3. |
| **all** | Disables DECnet accounting for all source and destination address pairs specified previously with the **decnet accounting list** command. |

### Default

No filters are predefined.

### Command Mode

Global configuration

### Usage Guidelines

This command first appeared in Cisco IOS Release 11.2 F.

The source and destination addresses of each DECnet packet are paired to create an entry in the database. When DECnet traffic traverses the router and a match is found, accounting information about the DECnet packet is entered into the accounting database. If DECnet accounting is enabled on an interface, but no accounting list is specified, the transit parameter does not come into play. DECnet accounting will track all traffic through the interface, up to the accounting threshold limit. All traffic up to the threshold limit is collected and added to the aggregate value for all DECnet traffic passing through the router.

Use the **no decnet accounting list all** to delete the entire entry list.

### Example

The following example adds DECnet host pair 5.37 and 6.126 to the list of networks for which accounting information is kept:

```
decnet accounting list 5.37 6.126
```

### Related Commands

Search online to find documentation of related commands.

**clear decnet accounting**
**decnet accounting**
**decnet accounting threshold**
**decnet accounting transits**
**show decnet accounting**

## DECNET ACCOUNTING THRESHOLD

To set the maximum number of accounting database entries, use the **decnet accounting threshold** global configuration command. To restore the default, use the **no** form of this command.

> **decnet accounting threshold** *threshold*
> **no decnet accounting threshold** *threshold*

| Syntax | Description |
|--------|-------------|
| *threshold* | Maximum number of entries (source and destination address pairs) that the Cisco IOS software can accumulate. |

### Default

512 entries

### Command Mode

Global configuration

### Usage Guidelines

This command first appeared in Cisco IOS Release 11.2 F.

The accounting threshold defines the maximum number of entries (source and destination address pairs) that the software accumulates. The threshold is designed to prevent DECnet accounting from consuming all available free memory. This level of memory consumption could occur in a router that is switching traffic for many hosts. To determine whether overflows have occurred, use the **show decnet accounting** EXEC command.

### Example

The following example sets the DECnet accounting database threshold to 256 entries:

```
decnet accounting threshold 256
```

### Related Commands

Search online to find documentation of related commands.

**clear decnet accounting**
**decnet accounting**
**decnet accounting list**
**decnet accounting transits**
**show decnet accounting**

## DECNET ACCOUNTING TRANSITS

To set the maximum number of transit entries that will be stored in the DECnet accounting database, use the **decnet accounting transits** global configuration command. To disable this function, use the **no** form of this command.

> **decnet accounting transits** *count*
> **no decnet accounting transits**

| Syntax | Description |
|--------|-------------|
| *count* | Number of transit entries that will be stored in the DECnet accounting database. |

### Default

0 entries

### Command Mode

Global configuration

### Usage Guidelines

This command first appeared in Cisco IOS Release 11.2 F.

Transit entries are those that do not match any of the source and destination address pair filters specified by **decnet accounting list** global configuration commands. If an accounting list is not defined, DECnet accounting will track all traffic through the interface (all transit entries) up to the accounting threshold limit.

To maintain accurate accounting totals, the Cisco IOS software maintains two accounting databases: an active database and a checkpoint database.

### Example

The following example specifies a maximum of 100 transit records to be stored in the DECnet accounting database:

```
decnet accounting transits 100
```

### Related Commands

Search online to find documentation of related commands.

**clear decnet accounting**
**decnet accounting list**
**decnet accounting threshold**
**show decnet accounting**

## DECNET ADVERTISE

To configure border routers to propagate Phase IV areas through an OSI backbone, use the **decnet advertise** global configuration command. To disable this feature, use the **no** form of this command.

> **decnet advertise** *decnet-area hops cost*
> **no decnet advertise** [*decnet-area*]

| Syntax | Description |
|---|---|
| *decnet-area* | Phase IV area that you want propagated. |
| *hops* | Hop count to be associated with the route being advertised. Default is 0. |
| *cost* | Cost to be associated with the route being advertised. Default is 0. |

### Default

Disabled

### Command Mode

Global configuration

### Usage Guidelines

This command first appeared in Cisco IOS Release 10.0.

The output from the **show decnet route** EXEC command shows the cost and hop count for routes.

The **decnet advertise** command is used by border routers for propagating Phase IV areas through an OSI backbone.

The **decnet advertise** command and the **clns route** *nsap-prefix* **discard** command work together. When a router has DECnet Phase IV/V conversion enabled, any packet with the specified Connectionless Network Service (CLNS) Network Service Access Point (NSAP) prefix will cause CLNS to behave as if no route were found. That router then looks up the route to the border router that is advertising the Phase IV route. In turn, the router that is advertising the DECnet Phase IV route converts the packet to Phase V and sends it through the OSI cloud to the border router that is advertising the CLNS discard static route. After the packet gets to the border router, it is converted back to Phase IV.

The CLNS discard routes are created dynamically when the advertised adjacencies are propagated through the CLNS cloud. When a DECnet interface is disabled, the adjacencies are lost and the CLNS discard route is deleted. The DECnet area routing states are displayed in the output from the **show decnet route** EXEC command.

## Example

The following example shows a partial use of the **decnet advertise** command:

```
decnet conversion 49
decnet advertise 4
clns route 49.0001 discard
```

## Related Commands

Search online to find documentation of related commands.

**clns route discard**
**show decnet route**

## DECNET AREA-MAX-COST

To set the maximum cost specification value for *interarea* routing, use the **decnet area-max-cost** global configuration command.

   decnet [*network-number*] **area-max-cost** *value*

| Syntax | Description |
|--------|-------------|
| *network-number* | (Optional) Network number from 0 to 3. Specified when using Address Translation Gateway (ATG). If not specified, the default is network 0. |
| *value* | Maximum cost for a route to a distant area that the Cisco IOS software may consider usable; the software treats as unreachable any route with a cost greater than the value you specify. A valid range for cost is 1 to 1022. This parameter is only valid for area routers. The default is 1022. |

## Defaults

*network-number*: 0
*value*: 1022

## Command Mode

Global configuration

## Usage Guidelines

This command first appeared in Cisco IOS Release 10.0.

Be sure that you have used the **decnet node-type area** global configuration command before using this command.

## Example

In the following example, the node type is specified as area and the maximum cost is set to 500. Any route with a cost exceeding 500 is considered unreachable by this router.

```
decnet node-type area
decnet area-max-cost 500
```

## Related Commands

Search online to find documentation of related commands.

**decnet area-max-hops**
**decnet node-type**
**show decnet interface**

## DECNET AREA-MAX-HOPS

To set the maximum hop count value for *interarea* routing, use the **decnet area-max-hops** global configuration command.

> **decnet** [*network-number*] **area-max-hops** *value*

| Syntax | Description |
|---|---|
| *network-number* | (Optional) Network number in the range 0 to 3. Specified when using ATG. If not specified, the default is network 0. |
| *value* | Maximum number of hops for a usable route to a distant area. The Cisco IOS software treats as unreachable any route with a count greater than the value you specify. A valid range for the hop count is 1 to 30. The default is 30 hops. |

## Default

30 hops

## Command Mode

Global configuration

## Usage Guidelines

This command first appeared in Cisco IOS Release 10.0.

This command is only valid for area routers. Be sure that you have issued the **decnet node-type area** global configuration command before using this command.

*Example*

The following example sets the router to be a Level 2 router, then sets a maximum hop count of 21:

```
decnet node-type area
decnet area-max-hops 21
```

*Related Commands*

Search online to find documentation of related commands.

**decnet area-max-cost**
**decnet node-type**
**show decnet interface**

## DECNET CONGESTION-THRESHOLD

To set the congestion-experienced bit if the output queue has more than the specified number of packets in it, use the **decnet congestion-threshold** interface configuration command. To remove the parameter setting and set it to 0, use the **no** form of this command.

**decnet congestion-threshold** *number*
**no decnet congestion-threshold**

| *Syntax* | *Description* |
|---|---|
| *number* | Number of packets that are allowed in the output queue before the system sets the congestion experience bit. This value is an integer between 0 and 0x7fff. The value zero prevents this bit from being set. Only relatively small integers are reasonable. The default is 1 packet. |

*Default*

1 packet

*Command Mode*

Interface configuration

*Usage Guidelines*

This command first appeared in Cisco IOS Release 10.0.

If a router configured for DECnet experiences congestion, it sets the congestion-experienced bit. A *number* value of zero or the **no** form of the command prevents this bit from being set.

*Example*

The following example sets the congestion threshold to 10:

```
interface ethernet 0
 decnet congestion-threshold 10
```

## DECNET CONVERSION

To allow Phase IV routers (running Cisco Release 9.1 or higher) to run in a Phase V network and vice versa, enable conversion with the **decnet conversion** global configuration command. To disable conversion, use the **no** form of this command.

> **decnet conversion** *nsap-prefix*
> **no decnet conversion** *nsap-prefix*

| Syntax | Description |
|--------|-------------|
| *nsap-prefix* | Value used for the IDP field when constructing NSAPs from a Phase IV address. |

### Default

Disabled

### Command Mode

Global configuration

### Usage Guidelines

This command first appeared in Cisco IOS Release 10.0.

To enable DECnet conversion, you must configure both DECnet and ISO CLNS on your router.

DECnet Phase V is OSI-compatible and conforms to the ISO 8473 (CLNP/CLNS) and ISO 9542 (ES-IS) standards. Digital has defined algorithms for mapping a subset of the Phase V address space onto the Phase IV address space and for converting Phase IV and Phase V packets back and forth. This enables a network administrator to support both Phase IV hosts in Phase V networks and Phase V hosts in Phase IV networks.

Cisco's implementation differs from Digital's in how reachability information is advertised. Cisco's implementation allows you to add Phase V support without modifying your existing Phase IV support. It also delays converting packets from Phase IV to Phase V, while Digital's implementation converts as soon as possible.

It is essential that the area you specify in the **decnet routing** global configuration command is the same as the local area you specified with the **net** router configuration command for the CLNS network.

Be sure that the area you specify in the **decnet conversion** command is the same as the area you specified for the CLNS network. Also note that the DECnet area is specified in decimal, and the CLNS area is specified in hexadecimal.

The **decnet routing** command is specified with a decimal address, while the **net** command address is specified in hexadecimal. In addition, the *nsap-prefix* specified on the **decnet conversion** command must match one of the NETs for this router.

The following guidelines apply:

- Host connectivity across multiple areas is only possible if a Level 2 path exists for which every Level 2 router in the path supports a common protocol: Phase IV or Phase V. If not all routers support both protocols, those routers that do *must* have conversion enabled.

- Host connectivity across a single area is only possible if a Level 1 path exists for which every Level 1 router in the path supports a common protocol: Phase IV or Phase V. If not all routers support both protocols, those routers that do *must* have conversion enabled.

- The Level 2 backbone *must* have conversion enabled in all Level 2 routers that support an area that needs conversion.

### Example

The following example enables DECnet conversion on a router with the area tag *xy* and Phase IV address 20.401 using an ISO IGRP router:

```
clns routing
decnet routing 20.401
decnet max-address 600
!
router iso-igrp xy
 net 47.0004.004d.0014.aa00.0400.9151.00
!
decnet conversion 47.0004.004d
!
interface ethernet 0
 decnet cost 4
 clns router iso-igrp xy
```

### Related Commands

Search online to find documentation of related commands.

**net**
**show decnet interface**
**show decnet route**

### DECNET COST

To set a cost value for an interface, use the **decnet cost** interface configuration command. To disable DECnet routing for an interface, use the **no** form of this command.

> **decnet cost** *cost-value*
> **no decnet cost**

| Syntax | Description |
| --- | --- |
| *cost-value* | Integer from 1 to 63. There is no default cost for an interface, although a suggested cost for FDDI is 1, for Ethernet is 4, and for serial links is greater than 10. |

## Default

Disabled

## Command Mode

Interface configuration

## Usage Guidelines

This command first appeared in Cisco IOS Release 10.0.

The decnet cost command is required for all interfaces on which DECnet routing is configured.

After DECnet routing has been enabled, you must assign a cost to each interface over which you want DECnet to run. Assigning a cost in effect enables DECnet routing for an interface. Most DECnet installations have an individualized routing strategy for using costs. Therefore, check the routing strategy used at your installation to ensure that costs you specify are consistent with those set for other hosts on the network.

## Example

The following example establishes a DECnet routing process for a router and sets the router's DECnet address to 21.456, then sets a cost of 4 for the Ethernet interface 0:

```
decnet routing 21.456
interface ethernet 0
 decnet cost 4
```

## Related Commands

Search online to find documentation of related commands.

decnet encapsulation
decnet node-type
decnet routing
show decnet interface
show decnet route

## DECNET ENCAPSULATION

To provide DECnet encapsulation over Token Ring, use the **decnet encapsulation** interface configuration command.

**decnet encapsulation** {pre-dec | dec}

| *Syntax* | *Description* |
|---|---|
| pre-dec | Configures routers for operation on the same Token Ring with routers running software versions prior to Cisco IOS Release 9.1. In this mode, Cisco routers cannot communicate with non-Cisco equipment. Referred to as Cisco-style encapsulation. |
| dec | Provides encapsulation that is compatible with other Digital equipment. All Cisco routers must be running Cisco IOS Release 9.1 or later. |

### Default

Encapsulation is compatible with other Digital equipment.

### Command Mode

Interface configuration

### Usage Guidelines

This command first appeared in Cisco IOS Release 10.0.

If you have both Release 9.0 and 9.1 routers in the same network, you must use the **pre-dec** encapsulation type on the 9.1 routers.

— **NOTES** ——————————————————————————————————

You must first enable DECnet routing on the selected Token Ring interface before you can configure the DECnet encapsulation mode.

### Example

The following example sets Cisco-style encapsulation for DECnet routing, which means that Cisco and Digital equipment will not interoperate over Token Ring:

```
interface tokenring 0
  decnet encapsulation pre-dec
  decnet cost 4
```

### Related Commands

Search online to find documentation of related commands.

**decnet cost**
**show decnet interface**

## DECNET HELLO-TIMER

To change the interval for sending broadcast hello messages, use the **decnet hello-timer** interface configuration command. To restore the default value, use the **no** form of this command.

> **decnet hello-timer** *seconds*
> **no decnet hello-timer**

*Syntax*          *Description*

*seconds*          Interval at which the Cisco IOS software sends hello messages. It can be a decimal number in the range 1 to 8191 seconds. The default is 15 seconds.

*Default*

15 seconds

*Command Mode*

Interface configuration

*Usage Guidelines*

This command first appeared in Cisco IOS Release 10.0.

The Cisco IOS software broadcasts hello messages on all interfaces with DECnet enabled. Other hosts on the network use the hello messages to identify the hosts with which they can communicate directly. On extremely slow serial lines, you may want to increase the default value to reduce overhead on the line.

*Example*

The following example increases the hello interval to 2 minutes (120 seconds) on serial interface 1:

```
interface serial 1
  decnet hello-timer 120
```

*Related Commands*

Search online to find documentation of related commands.

**show decnet interface**

## DECNET HOST

To associate a name-to-DECnet address mapping, use the **decnet host** global configuration command, which shows up in the output of various commands. To disable name mapping, use the **no** form of this command.

> **decnet host** *name decnet-address*
> **no decnet host** *name*

| Syntax | Description |
|---|---|
| *name* | A name you choose that uniquely identifies this DECnet address. |
| *decnet-address* | Source address. DECnet addresses are written in the form *area.node*. For example, 50.4 is node 4 in area 50. All addresses are in decimal. |

## Default

No name is defined.

## Command Mode

Global configuration

## Usage Guidelines

This command first appeared in Cisco IOS Release 10.3.

The assigned name is displayed, where applicable, in **show decnet route** and **show hosts** EXEC command output.

The name can also be used with the **ping decnet** command.

## Example

The following example defines name-to-DECnet address mapping:

```
decnet host cisco1 3.33
```

## Related Commands

Search online to find documentation of related commands.

**ping (privileged)**
**show decnet route**
**show hosts**

## DECNET IN-ROUTING-FILTER

To provide access control to hello messages or routing information received on an interface, use the **decnet in-routing-filter** interface configuration command. To remove access control, use the **no** form of this command.

> **decnet in-routing-filter** *access-list-number*
> **no decnet in-routing-filter**

| Syntax | Description |
|---|---|
| *access-list-number* | Standard DECnet access list. This list applies to source addresses. The value can be in the range 300 to 399. |

## Default

No access control is defined.

## Command Mode

Interface configuration

## Usage Guidelines

This command first appeared in Cisco IOS Release 10.0.

## Example

In the following example, Ethernet interface 0 is set up with a DECnet in-routing filter of 321, which means that any hello messages sent from addresses that are denied in list 321 are ignored. Additionally, all node addresses listed in received routing messages on this interface are checked against the access list, and only routes passing the filter are considered usable.

```
interface ethernet 0
  decnet in-routing-filter 321
```

## Related Commands

Search online to find documentation of related commands.

**access-list (standard)**
**decnet out-routing-filter**
**show decnet interface**

## DECNET MAP

To establish an address translation for selected nodes, use the **decnet map** global configuration command.

   **decnet** *first-network* **map** *virtual-address second-network real-address*

| Syntax | Description |
| --- | --- |
| *first-network* | DECnet network numbers in the range 0 to 3. |
| *virtual-address* | Numeric DECnet address (10.5, for example). |
| *second-network* | DECnet network number you map to; DECnet numbers range 0 to 3. |
| *real-address* | Numeric DECnet address (10.5, for example). |

## Default

No address translation is defined.

## Command Mode

Global configuration

## Usage Guidelines

This command first appeared in Cisco IOS Release 10.0.

Keep the following limitations in mind when configuring the address translation gateway (ATG):

- Both nodes that want to communicate across the ATG must exist in the translation map. Other nodes outside of the map will see route advertisements for the mapped address, but will be unable to communicate with them. An unmapped node trying to communicate with a mapped node will always get the message, "Node unreachable." This can be confusing if another nearby node can communicate with mapped nodes because it is also a mapped node.

- Third-party DECnet applications could fail if they pass node number information in a data stream (most likely a sign of a poorly designed application).

- Routing information for mapped addresses is static and does not reflect the reachability of the actual node in the destination network.

As an additional feature and security caution, DECnet "Poor Man's Routing" can be used between nodes outside of the translation map as long as those nodes have access to nodes that are in the map, so that a user on node B could issue the following VMS command:

**$ dir A::D::E::**

When a Poor Man's Routing connection is made between two networks, only the two adjacent nodes between the networks will have any direct knowledge about the other network. Application-level network access may then be specified to route through the connection.

---

**NOTES**

Cisco does not support "Poor Man's Routing" directly; the intermediate nodes must be VMS systems with "Poor Man's Routing" enabled in file-access language.

---

## Example

In the following example, packets in Network 0 sent to address 19.5 will be routed to Network 1, and the destination address will be translated to 50.1. Packets sent to address 47.1 in Network 1 will be routed to Network 0 as 19.1.

```
decnet 0 map 19.5 1 50.1
decnet 1 map 47.1 0 19.1
```

## Related Commands

Search online to find documentation of related commands.

**show decnet map**

## DECNET MAX-ADDRESS

To configure the Cisco IOS software with a maximum number of node addresses, use the **decnet max-address** global configuration command.

> **decnet** [*network-number*] **max-address** *value*

| Syntax | Description |
|---|---|
| *network-number* | (Optional) Network number in the range 0 to 3. Specified when using ATG. If not specified, the default is network 0. |
| *value* | A number less than or equal to 1023 that represents the maximum address possible on the network. In general, all routers on the network should use the same value for this argument. The default is 1023. |

### Default

1023 node addresses

### Command Mode

Global configuration

### Usage Guidelines

This command first appeared in Cisco IOS Release 10.0.

DECnet routers do not have the concept of aging out a route. Therefore, all possible areas or nodes must be advertised as unreachable if they cannot be reached. Because it is best to keep routing updates small, you must indicate the default maximum possible node and area numbers that can exist in the network.

### Example

The following example configures a small network to a maximum address value of 300:

```
decnet max-address 300
```

### Related Commands

Search online to find documentation of related commands.

**decnet max-area**

## DECNET MAX-AREA

To set the largest number of areas that the Cisco IOS software can handle in its routing table, use the **decnet max-area** global configuration command.

> **decnet** [*network-number*] **max-area** *area-number*

| Syntax | Description |
|--------|-------------|
| *network-number* | (Optional) Network number in the range 0 to 3. Specified when using ATG. If not specified, the default is network 0. |
| *area-number* | Area number from 1 to 63. Like the **decnet max-address** global configuration command value, this argument controls the sizes of internal routing tables and of messages sent to other nodes. All routers on the network should use the same maximum address value. The default is 63. |

## Default

63 areas

## Command Mode

Global configuration

## Usage Guidelines

This command first appeared in Cisco IOS Release 10.0.

## Example

In the following example, the largest area to be stored in the routing table is 45:

```
decnet max-area 45
```

## Related Commands

Search online to find documentation of related commands.

**decnet max-address**
**show decnet interface**

## DECNET MAX-COST

To set the maximum cost specification for *intra-area* routing, use the **decnet max-cost** global configuration command.

> **decnet** [*network-number*] **max-cost** *cost*

| Syntax | Description |
|--------|-------------|
| *network-number* | (Optional) Network number in the range 0 to 3. Specified when using ATG. If not specified, the default is network 0. |
| *cost* | Cost from 1 to 1022. The default is 1022. |

## Default

1022

## Command Mode

Global configuration

## Usage Guidelines

This command first appeared in Cisco IOS Release 10.0.

The Cisco IOS software ignores routes within its local area that have a cost greater than the value you specify.

## Example

In the following example, the node type is specified as a Level 1 router and the maximum cost is set to 335. Any route whose cost exceeds 335 is considered unreachable by this router.

```
decnet node-type routing-iv
decnet max-cost 335
```

## Related Commands

Search online to find documentation of related commands.

decnet max-hops
decnet max-paths
decnet node-type
decnet path-split-mode
show decnet interface

## DECNET MAX-HOPS

To set the maximum hop count specification value for *intra-area* routing, use the **decnet max-hops** global configuration command.

> **decnet** [*network-number*] **max-hops** *hop-count*

| Syntax | Description |
| --- | --- |
| *network-number* | (Optional) Network number in the range 0 to 3. Specified when using ATG. If not specified, the default is network 0. |
| *hop-count* | Hop count from 1 to 30. The Cisco IOS software ignores routes that have a hop count greater than the corresponding value of this parameter. The default is 30 hops. |

*Default*

30 hops

*Command Mode*

Global configuration

*Usage Guidelines*

This command first appeared in Cisco IOS Release 10.0.

*Example*

The following example sets the router to be a Level 1 router, then sets a maximum hop count of 2:

```
decnet node-type routing-iv
decnet max-hops 2
```

*Related Commands*

Search online to find documentation of related commands.

**decnet max-cost**
**decnet max-paths**
**decnet multicast-map**
**decnet node-type**

## DECNET MAX-PATHS

To define the maximum number of equal-cost paths to a destination that the Cisco IOS software keeps in its routing table, use the **decnet max-paths** global configuration command.

> **decnet** [*network-number*] **max-paths** *value*

| Syntax | Description |
|---|---|
| *network-number* | (Optional) Network number in the range 0 to 3. Specified when using ATG. If not specified, the default is network 0. |
| *value* | Decimal number equal to the maximum number of equal-cost paths the software will save. The valid range is 1 to 31. The default is 1. |

*Default*

1 equal-cost path

*Command Mode*

Global configuration

## Usage Guidelines

This command first appeared in Cisco IOS Release 10.0.

Limiting the number of equal-cost paths can save memory on routers with limited memory or very large configurations. Additionally, in networks with a large number of multiple paths and end-systems with limited ability to cache out-of-sequence packets, performance may suffer when traffic is split between many paths.

Limiting the size of the routing table does not affect your routers's ability to recover from network failures transparently, provided that you do not make the maximum number of paths too small. If more than the specified number of equal-cost paths exist, and one of those paths suddenly becomes unusable, the software will discover an additional path from the paths it has been ignoring.

## Example

In the following example, the software saves no more than three equal-cost paths:

```
decnet max-paths 3
```

## Related Commands

Search online to find documentation of related commands.

decnet max-cost
decnet max-hops
decnet path-split-mode
show decnet interface
show decnet route

## DECNET MAX-VISITS

To set the limit on the number of times a packet can pass through a router, use the **decnet max-visits** global configuration command.

> **decnet** [*network-number*] **max-visits** *value*

| Syntax | Description |
|---|---|
| *network-number* | (Optional) Network number in the range 0 to 3. Specified when using ATG. If not specified, the default is network 0. |
| *value* | Number of times a packet can pass through a router. It can be a decimal number in the range 1 to 63. If a packet exceeds *value*, the Cisco IOS software discards the packet. Digital recommends that the value of the **max-visits** parameter be at least twice that of the **max-hops** parameter, to allow packets to still reach their destinations when routes are changing. The default is 63 times. |

*Default*

63 times

*Command Mode*

Global configuration

*Usage Guidelines*

This command first appeared in Cisco IOS Release 10.0.

*Example*

The following example of intra-area routing configuration specifies Level 1 routing, a maximum hop count of 28, and maximum number of visits of 62 (which is more than twice 28):

```
decnet node-type routing-iv
decnet max-hops 28
decnet max-visits 62
```

*Related Commands*

Search online to find documentation of related commands.

**decnet max-hops**
**show decnet interface**
**show decnet traffic**

## DECNET MULTICAST-MAP

To specify a mapping between DECnet multicast addresses and Token Ring functional addresses, other than the default mapping, use the **decnet multicast-map** interface configuration command. To delete the specified information, use the **no** form of this command.

> **decnet multicast-map** *multicast-address-type functional-address*
> **no decnet multicast-map** *multicast-address-type functional-address*

| Syntax | Description |
|---|---|
| *multicast-address-type* | Type of multicast address that is used. The following are valid values for the argument: |
| | • **iv-all-routers** (All Phase-IV routers) |
| | • **iv-all-endnodes** (All Phase-IV end nodes) |
| | • **iv-prime-all-routers** (All Phase IV Prime routers) |
| *functional-address* | Functional MAC address to which this multicast ID maps; in the form of "c000.xxxx.yyyy." |

*Default*

Enabled, with the default mapping listed in Table 12–2.

*Command Mode*

Interface configuration

*Usage Guidelines*

This command first appeared in Cisco IOS Release 10.0.

This command is valid for Token Ring interfaces only. The command will reject a functional address that does not start with "C000" or "c000."

Routing multicasts and end node multicasts must be on different functional addresses.

**Table 12–2** *Default Mapping of DECnet Multicast Address Types and Token Ring Functional Addresses*

| DECnet Multicast Address Type | Token Ring Functional Address |
|---|---|
| L1 router<br>L2 router | C000.1000.0000 |
| End node | C000.0800.0000 |
| DECnet Phase IV-Prime router | C000.1000.0000 |

*Example*

In the following example, Token Ring interface 1 is configured for multicasts of all Phase IV end nodes and the multicast ID is configured to map to MAC address c000.2222.3333.

```
interface tokenring 1
 decnet multicast-map iv-all-endnodes c000.2222.3333
```

**DECNET NODE-TYPE**

To specify the node type, use the **decnet node-type** global configuration command.

**decnet** [*network-number*] **node-type** {**area** | **routing-iv**}

| Syntax | Description |
|---|---|
| *network-number* | (Optional) Network number in the range 0 to 3. Specified when using ATG. If not specified, the default is network 0. |
| **area** | Router participates in the DECnet routing protocol with other area routers, as described in the Digital documentation, and routes packets from and to routers in other areas. This is sometimes referred to as Level 2 (or *interarea*) routing. An area router does not just handle interarea routing, it also acts as an intra-area or Level 1 router in its own area. |
| **routing-iv** | Router acts as an intra-area (standard DECnet Phase IV, Level 1 router) and ignores Level 2 routing packets. In this mode, it routes packets destined for other areas to a designated interarea router, exchanging packets with other end nodes and routers in the same area. |

### Default

No node type is specified.

### Command Mode

Global configuration

### Usage Guidelines

This command first appeared in Cisco IOS Release 10.0.

### Example

In the following example, the router node type is specified as *area*, or Level 2:

```
decnet node-type area
```

### Related Commands

Search online to find documentation of related commands.

**decnet cost**
**decnet routing**
**show decnet interface**

## DECNET OUT-ROUTING-FILTER

To provide access control to routing information being sent out on an interface, use the **decnet out-routing-filter** interface configuration command. To remove access control, use the **no** form of this command.

> **decnet out-routing-filter** *access-list-number*
> **no decnet out-routing-filter**

| *Syntax* | *Description* |
|---|---|
| *access-list-number* | Standard DECnet access list applying to source addresses. The value can be in the range 300 to 399. |

### Default

No access control to routing information is defined.

### Command Mode

Interface configuration

### Usage Guidelines

This command first appeared in Cisco IOS Release 10.0.

Addresses that fail this test are shown in the update message as unreachable.

### Example

In the following example, Ethernet interface 1 is set up with a DECnet out-routing filter of 351. This filter is applied to addresses in the transmitted routing updates. Transmitted hello messages are not filtered.

```
interface ethernet 1
  decnet out-routing-filter 351
```

### Related Commands

Search online to find documentation of related commands.

**access-list (standard)**
**decnet in-routing-filter**
**show decnet interface**

### DECNET PATH-SPLIT-MODE

To specify how the Cisco IOS software splits the routable packets between equal-cost paths, use the **decnet path-split-mode** global configuration command with the appropriate keyword.

> **decnet path-split-mode {normal | interim}**

| Syntax | Description |
|--------|-------------|
| normal | Normal mode, where equal-cost paths are selected on a round-robin basis. This is the default. |
| interim | Traffic for any particular (higher-layer) session is always routed over the same path. This mode supports older implementations of DECnet (VMS Versions 4.5 and earlier) that do not support out-of-order packet caching. Other sessions may take another path, thus using equal-cost paths that a router may have for a particular destination. |

### Default

Normal mode

### Command Mode

Global configuration

### Usage Guidelines

This command first appeared in Cisco IOS Release 10.0.

### Example

In the following example, a router will split routable packets between equal-cost paths using the round-robin (or first-come, first-served) basis:

```
decnet path-split-mode normal
```

### Related Commands

Search online to find documentation of related commands.

decnet max-cost
decnet max-paths

## DECNET PROPAGATE STATIC

To enable static route propagation, use the **decnet propagate static** global configuration command. To disable propagation, use the **no** form of this command.

> decnet propagate static
> no decnet propagate static

### Syntax     Description

This command has no arguments or keywords.

*Command Reference*

## Default

No default routes are propagated.

## Command Mode

Global configuration

## Usage Guidelines

This command first appeared in Cisco IOS Release 11.0

By default, DECnet static routes are not propagated to other routers. Use the **decnet propagate static** command to enable static route propagation. A default route is used only after DECnet conversion is checked.

## Example

The following example shows how to enable static route propagation for the specified static and default routes:

```
decnet propagate static
!
decnet route 3.0 ethernet 0 aa00.0400.0404
decnet route 5.0 serial 0
decnet route 5.100 serial 2
decnet route default 2.100
decnet route 6.0 2.3 4 5
```

## Related Commands

Search online to find documentation of related commands.

**decnet route (interface static route)**
**decnet route (to enter a static route)**
**show decnet**
**show decnet static**

## DECNET ROUTE (INTERFACE STATIC ROUTE)

To create an interface static route, use this version of the **decnet route** global configuration command. To remove this route, use the **no** form of this command.

**decnet route** *decnet-address next-hop-type number* [*snpa-address*] [*hops* [*cost*]]
**no decnet route** *decnet-address next-hop-type number*

| Syntax | Description |
|--------|-------------|
| *decnet-address* | DECnet address. This value is entered into a static routing table and used to match a destination DECnet address. Use a node address value of 0 to specify an area static route. |
| *next-hop-type* | Interface type. |
| *number* | Interface number. |
| *snpa-address* | (Optional) Optional for serial links; required for multiaccess networks. |
| *hops* | (Optional) Hop count to be associated with the route being advertised. Default is 0. |
| *cost* | (Optional) Cost to be associated with the route being advertised. Default is 0. |

### Default

No interface static routes are created.

### Command Mode

Global configuration

### Usage Guidelines

This command first appeared in Cisco IOS Release 10.3.

If you do not specify a Subnetwork Point of Attachment (SNPA) address when you have a multi-access network, you receive an error message indicating a bad SNPA. By default, DECnet static routes are not propagated to other routers. Use the **decnet propagate static** command to enable propagation.

### Examples

The following example shows how to create a static route for a serial interface. No SNPA need be specified for point-to-point interfaces.

```
decnet route 3.1 serial 1
```

The following example shows how to create a static route for an Ethernet interface. The SNPA must be specified for an interface that is not point-to-point.

```
decnet route 3.2 ethernet 1 aa00.0400.0104
```

### Related Commands

Search online to find documentation of related commands.

**decnet propagate static**
**decnet route (to enter a static route)**

decnet route default (interface default route)
decnet route default (to enter a default route)
show decnet static

## DECNET ROUTE (TO ENTER A STATIC ROUTE)

To enter a specific static route, use this version of the **decnet route** global configuration command. DECnet addresses that match are forwarded to the *next-hop-address*. To remove this route, use the **no** form of this command.

> **decnet route** *decnet-address next-hop-address* [*hops* [*cost*]]
> **no decnet route** *decnet-address next-hop-address*

| Syntax | Description |
|---|---|
| *decnet-address* | DECnet address. This value is entered into a static routing table and used to match a destination DECnet address. Use a node address value of 0 to specify an area static route. |
| *next-hop-address* | This value is used to establish the next hop of the route for forwarding packets. |
| *hops* | (Optional) Hop count to be associated with the route being advertised. Default is 0. |
| *cost* | (Optional) Cost to be associated with the route being advertised. Default is 0. |

### Default

No interface static routes are created.

### Command Mode

Global configuration

### Usage Guidelines

This command first appeared in Cisco IOS Release 10.3.

Area static routes can be configured by specifying a DECnet node address of 0. By default, DECnet static routes are not propagated to other routers. Use the **decnet propagate static** command to enable propagation.

### Examples

The following example shows how to create a static route for 1.1 that points to 1.9 and uses default values of 0 for the *hops* and *cost*:

```
decnet route 1.1 1.9
```

The following example shows how to create a static route for 3.100 that points to 3.4 and specifies values for the *hops* and *cost*:

```
decnet route 3.100 3.4 9 8
```

The following example shows how to create a static route for area 1 that points to 2.999:

```
decnet route 1.0 2.999
```

### Related Commands

Search online to find documentation of related commands.

**decnet propagate static**
**decnet route (interface static route)**
**decnet route default (interface default route)**
**decnet route default (to enter a default route)**
**show decnet static**

## DECNET ROUTE DEFAULT (INTERFACE DEFAULT ROUTE)

To create an interface default route, use this version of the **decnet route default** global configuration command. Use the **no** form of this command to remove this route.

> **decnet route default** *next-hop-type number* [*snpa-address*] [*hops* [*cost*]]
> **no decnet route default** *next-hop-type number*

| Syntax | Description |
|---|---|
| *next-hop-type* | Interface type. |
| *number* | Interface number. |
| *snpa-address* | (Optional) Optional for serial links; required for multiaccess networks. |
| *hops* | (Optional) Hop count to be associated with the route being advertised. Default is 0. |
| *cost* | (Optional) Cost to be associated with the route being advertised. Default is 0. |

### Default

No interface default routes are created.

### Command Mode

Global configuration

### Usage Guidelines

This command first appeared in Cisco IOS Release 11.0

If you do not specify an SNPA address when you have a multiaccess network, you receive an error message indicating a bad SNPA.

A default route is used only after DECnet conversion is checked. DECnet default routes are not propagated to other routers.

### Examples

The following example shows how to create a default route for a serial interface. No SNPA need be specified for point-to-point interfaces.

```
decnet route default serial 1
```

The following example shows how to create a default route for an Ethernet interface. The SNPA must be specified for an interface that is not point-to-point.

```
decnet route default ethernet 1 aa00.0400.0104
```

### Related Commands

Search online to find documentation of related commands.

**decnet propagate static**
**decnet route (interface static route)**
**decnet route default (interface default route)**
**decnet route default (to enter a default route)**
**show decnet static**

## DECNET ROUTE DEFAULT (TO ENTER A DEFAULT ROUTE)

To enter a specific default route, use this version of the **decnet route default** global configuration command. To remove this route, use the **no** form of this command.

> **decnet route default** *next-hop-address* [*hops* [*cost*]]
> **no decnet route default** *next-hop-address*

| Syntax | Description |
| --- | --- |
| *next-hop-address* | This value is used to establish the next hop of the route for forwarding packets. |
| *hops* | (Optional) Hop count to be associated with the route being advertised. Default is 0. |
| *cost* | (Optional) Cost to be associated with the route being advertised. Default is 0. |

### Default

No interface default routes are created.

## Command Mode

Global configuration

## Usage Guidelines

This command first appeared in Cisco IOS Release 10.3.

A default route is used only after DECnet conversion is checked. By default, DECnet static routes are not propagated to other routers. Use the **decnet propagate static** command to enable propagation.

DECnet packets not for the current area are forwarded to the *next-hop-address*.

## Example

The following example shows how to create a default route for 1.3 which uses default values of 0 for hops and cost:

```
decnet route default 1.3
```

## Related Commands

Search online to find documentation of related commands.

**decnet propagate static**
**decnet route (interface static route)**
**decnet route (to enter a static route)**
**decnet route default (interface default route)**
**show decnet static**

## DECNET ROUTE-CACHE

To enable fast switching, use the **decnet route-cache** interface configuration command. To disable fast switching, use the **no** form of this command.

> **decnet route-cache**
> **no decnet route-cache**

## Syntax     Description

This command has no arguments or keywords.

## Default

Enabled

## Command Mode

Interface configuration

## Usage Guidelines

This command first appeared in Cisco IOS Release 10.0.

By default, Cisco's DECnet routing software implements fast switching of DECnet datagrams. There are times when it makes sense to disable fast switching. This is especially important when using rates slower than T1.

Fast switching uses memory space on interface cards. In situations where a high-bandwidth interface is writing large amounts of information to a low-bandwidth interface, additional memory could help avoid congestion on the slow interface.

## Example

In the following example, fast switching is disabled on Ethernet interface 0:

```
interface ethernet 0
  no decnet route-cache
```

## DECNET ROUTER-PRIORITY

To elect a designated router to which packets are sent when no destination is specified, use the **decnet router-priority** interface configuration command.

> **decnet router-priority** *value*

| Syntax | Description |
|--------|-------------|
| *value* | Priority of the router. This can be a number in the range 0 to 127. The larger the number the higher the priority. The default priority is 64. |

## Default

64

## Command Mode

Interface configuration

## Usage Guidelines

This command first appeared in Cisco IOS Release 10.0.

The *designated* router is the router to which all end nodes on an Ethernet communicate if they do not know where else to send a packet. The designated router is chosen through an election process in which the router with the highest priority gets the job. When two or more routers on a single Ethernet in a single area share the same highest priority, the unit with the highest node number is elected. You can reset a router's priority to help ensure that it is elected designated router in its area.

On a LAN with both DECnet IV and DECnet IV Prime hosts, make sure that a bilingual router always becomes the designated router.

DECnet end systems use the designated router only when they have no other information about how to reach a particular system. The end systems maintain a cache of how to reach other systems on the network. The cache contains the following information:

```
<remote system DECnet address>  <next hop DECnet address>
```

When an end system receives a packet, it examines three pieces of information: the intra-LAN bit, the source address, and the previous hop. If the intra-LAN bit is set, indicating that the packet has never left this wire (and, thus, the remote system is reachable without a router), a cache entry is created as follows:

```
<remote system DECnet address> = <source address>
<next hop DECnet address> = <source address>
```

If the intra-LAN bit is not set, indicating that the packet has come from another network, the cache entry is created as follows:

```
<remote system DECnet address> = <source address>
<next hop DECnet address> = <previous hop>
```

If there is no cache entry, then the designated router is used. This means that when starting a session, the designated router is used, but the reverse traffic will populate a cache entry so that the router can later communicate directly.

A DECnet IV Prime end node sends a packet to the Unknown Destination multicast if it has no cache entry for the destination and has no designated router.

### Example

In the following example, DECnet priority for this router is set to 110 on Ethernet interface 1:

```
interface ethernet 1
 decnet router-priority 110
```

## DECNET ROUTING

To enable DECnet routing, use the **decnet routing** global configuration command. To disable DECnet routing, use the **no** form of this command.

> **decnet** [*network-number*] **routing** [**iv-prime**] *decnet-address*
> **no decnet routing**

| Syntax | Description |
| --- | --- |
| *network-number* | (Optional) Network number in the range 0 to 3. Specified when using ATG. If not specified, the default is network 0. |
| **iv-prime** | (Optional) Enables DECnet Phase IV Prime routing. |
| *decnet-address* | Address in DECnet format X.Y, where X is the area number and Y is the node number. |

*Default*

Disabled

*Command Mode*

Global configuration

*Usage Guidelines*

This command first appeared in Cisco IOS Release 10.0.

Enabling DECnet changes the MAC addresses of the router's interfaces. This is not a problem on routers equipped with nonvolatile memory. On systems that attempt to get their IP network addresses from network servers rather than from nonvolatile memory, there may be a problem as with the hardware addresses changing and confusing other IP-speaking hosts. This potential problem can be avoided by configuring and enabling DECnet before enabling other protocols.

---

**NOTES** ─────────────────────────────────────────────────

You can configure up to four DECnet networks (numbered 0 to 3). To set up multiple DECnet networks, use the **decnet** global configuration commands with the appropriate network number and keywords. If the network number is omitted from the commands, network 0 is configured for DECnet routing.

---

DECnet Phase IV Prime eliminates the DEC addressing restrictions so that DECnet nodes can coexist with systems running other protocols that have other MAC address restrictions. If **iv-prime** is not specified, only Phase IV is enabled; configuring the MAC address will then make DECnet inoperable. The standard "AA-00-04-00" form will be set as the address of the interface on which DECnet is enabled. If Phase IV Prime was already running and this command is reissued without the **iv-prime** keyword (that is, going from Phase IV Prime to Phase IV), the command returns an error if any of the interfaces that have DECnet enabled have MAC addresses that are not compliant with DECnet Phase IV, requiring the user to evaluate conflicting interface commands.

The **no** form of this command disables Phase IV and Phase IV Prime routing.

*Example*

In the following example, DECnet routing is enabled for the router in area 21 with node number 456:

```
decnet routing 21.456
```

*Related Commands*

Search online to find documentation of related commands.

**decnet cost**
**decnet node-type**

## DECNET ROUTING-TIMER

To specify how often the Cisco IOS software sends routing updates that list the hosts that the router can reach, use the **decnet routing-timer** interface configuration command. Use the **no** form of this command to disable the routing update timer.

> **decnet routing-timer** *seconds*
> **no decnet routing-timer**

| Syntax | Description |
|--------|-------------|
| *seconds* | Time, in seconds, from 1 to 65535. The default is 40 seconds. |

### Default

40 seconds

### Command Mode

Interface configuration

### Usage Guidelines

This command first appeared in Cisco IOS Release 10.0.

Other routers use this information to construct local routing tables. In a network where changes occur infrequently or do not need to be responded to immediately (it is small and uncomplicated, applications are not particularly sensitive to delays or occasional packet loss, slow serial links, and so on), increasing the time between routing updates reduces the amount of unnecessary network traffic. Digital calls this argument the *broadcast routing timer* because they use a different timer for serial lines; Cisco's DECnet implementation does not make this distinction.

### Example

In the following example, a serial interface is set to broadcast routing updates every 2 minutes (120 seconds):

```
interface serial 0
  decnet routing-timer 120
```

## DECNET SPLIT-HORIZON

To use split horizon when sending routing updates, use the **decnet split-horizon** interface configuration command. To disable split horizon, use the **no** form of this command.

> **decnet split-horizon**
> **no decnet split-horizon**

| Syntax | Description |
|--------|-------------|

This command has no arguments or keywords.

*Default*

Enabled

*Command Mode*

Interface configuration

*Usage Guidelines*

This command first appeared in Cisco IOS Release 10.2.

The **decnet split-horizon** command also affects whether broadcast packets received on an interface are resent on the same interface.

The **decnet split-horizon** command determines how much information is included in routing updates sent out to an interface. It also determines whether received broadcasts are retransmitted on the same interface. When you enable split horizon, routing updates sent out on a given interface will not include any information that was originally learned from that interface, and broadcasts will not be retransmitted on the receiving interface. This is because split horizon is designed for networks that are either broadcast networks, or are fully connected mesh networks. In these types of networks, resending this information is a waste of network bandwidth because all other stations on that network have already heard the information. Disabling split horizon causes the Cisco IOS software to include all information in routing updates, and to resend broadcast packets on the network from which they were received.

You can use this command on any interface, but generally it makes sense to use it only for X.25 and Frame Relay interfaces. You should disable split horizon on X.25 and Frame Relay networks that are not fully connected mesh topologies.

*Example*

The following example disables split horizon on an X.25 network:

```
interface serial 0
  no decnet split-horizon
```

## LAT HOST-DELAY

To set the delayed acknowledgment for incoming LAT slave connections, use the **lat host-delay** global configuration command. To restore the default, use the **no** form of this command.

> **lat host-delay** *number*
> **no lat host-delay**

*Syntax Description*

| | |
|---|---|
| *number* | Delay in milliseconds. |

*Default*

Disabled

### Command Mode

Global configuration

### Usage Guidelines

This command first appeared in Cisco IOS Release 10.3.

### Example

The following example sets the acknowledgment for incoming LAT slave connections to 100 ms:

```
lat host-delay 100
```

## LAT SERVICE AUTOCOMMAND

To associate a command with a service, use the **lat service autocommand** global configuration command. To remove the specified autocommand, use the **no** form of this command.

**lat service** *service-name* **autocommand** *command*
**no lat service** *service-name* **autocommand** *command*

| Syntax | Description |
|---|---|
| *service-name* | Name of the service. |
| *command* | Command to be associated with the service. |

### Default

No commands are automatically associated with a service.

### Command Mode

Global configuration

### Usage Guidelines

This command first appeared in Cisco IOS Release 10.0.

When an inbound connection is received for the specified service, the command associated with the service is automatically executed instead of the user receiving a virtual terminal session.

Authentication is bypassed for these services; only the LAT password is checked.

---

**NOTES**

---

Do not use this option with the **rotary** keyword.

---

## Example

The following example associates the command **telnet readings** to the service *readings*:

```
lat service readings autocommand telnet readings
```

## PING (PRIVILEGED)

To send DECnet echo packets to test the reachability of a remote host over a DECnet network, use the DECnet **ping** privileged EXEC command.

    **ping**

## Syntax    Description

This command has no arguments or keywords.

## Command Mode

Privileged EXEC

## Usage Guidelines

This command first appeared in Cisco IOS Release 10.0.

To terminate a **ping** command session, type the escape sequence (by default, Ctrl-^ X, which is done by simultaneously pressing the Ctrl, Shift, and 6 keys, releasing the keys, and then pressing the X key).

Table 12–3 describes the test characters that the ping facility sends.

**Table 12–3**  *Ping Test Characters (DECnet Privileged)*

| Character | Description |
|-----------|-------------|
| ! | Each exclamation point indicates receipt of a reply. |
| . | Each period indicates the network server timed out while waiting for a reply. |
| U | A destination unreachable error Protocol Data Unit (PDU) was received. |
| C | A congestion-experienced packet was received. |
| I | User interrupted test. |
| ? | Unknown packet type. |
| & | Packet lifetime exceeded. |

*Sample Display*

The following display shows a sample DECnet **ping** session that uses a DECnet address to specify the source:

```
router# ping
Protocol [ip]: decnet
Target DECnet address: 2.16
Repeat count [5]:
Datagram size [100]:
Timeout in seconds [2]:
Type escape sequence to abort.
Sending 5, 100-byte DECnet Echos to 2.16,
timeout is 2 seconds:
!!!!!
Success rate is 100 percent, round-trip min/avg/max = 1/4/8 ms
```

Table 12–4 describes the fields shown in the display.

**Table 12–4**    *Ping Field Descriptions (DECnet)*

| Field | Description |
| --- | --- |
| Protocol [ip]: | Default is IP. |
| Target DECnet address: | Prompts for the DECnet address of the destination node you plan to test with the **ping** command. |
| Repeat count [5]: | Number of **ping** packets that are sent to the destination address. Default is 5. |
| Datagram size [100]: | Size of the **ping** packet (in bytes). Default: 100 bytes. |
| Timeout in seconds [2]: | Timeout interval (in seconds). Default: 2 seconds. |

*Related Commands*

Search online to find documentation of related commands.

**ping decnet (user)**

## PING DECNET (USER)

To send DECnet echo packets to test the reachability of a remote host over a DECnet network, use the **ping decnet** user EXEC command.

     **ping decnet** {*host* | *address*}

| *Syntax* | *Description* |
| --- | --- |
| decnet | DECnet protocol keyword. |

| Syntax | Description |
|--------|-------------|
| *host* | DECnet host of system to **ping**. |
| *address* | DECnet address of system to **ping**. |

### Command Mode

EXEC

### Usage Guidelines

This command first appeared in Cisco IOS Release 10.0.

The **ping** EXEC command provides a basic user **ping** facility for DECnet users who do not have system privileges. This feature allows the Cisco IOS software to perform the simple default **ping** functionality for the DECnet protocol. Only the nonverbose form of the **ping** command is supported for user-level pings.

To terminate a **ping** command session, type the escape sequence (by default, Ctrl-^ X, which is done by simultaneously pressing the Ctrl, Shift, and 6 keys, releasing the keys, and then pressing the X key).

Table 12–5 describes the test characters that the **ping** facility sends.

**Table 12–5** *Ping Test Characters (DECnet User)*

| Character | Description |
|-----------|-------------|
| ! | Each exclamation point indicates receipt of a reply. |
| . | Each period indicates the network server timed out while waiting for a reply. |
| U | A destination unreachable error PDU was received. |
| C | A congestion-experienced packet was received. |
| I | User interrupted test. |
| ? | Unknown packet type. |
| & | Packet lifetime exceeded. |

### Sample Display

The following display shows sample ping output when you ping the DECnet address of 2.16:

```
router> ping decnet 2.16
Sending 5, 100-byte DECnet Echos to 2.16,
timeout is 2 seconds:
!!!!!
Success rate is 100 percent, round-trip min/avg/max = 1/4/8 ms
```

*Related Commands*

Search online to find documentation of related commands.

**ping (privileged)**

## SHOW DECNET

To display the global DECnet parameters, use the **show decnet** privileged EXEC command.

> **show decnet**

*Syntax        Description*

This command has no arguments or keywords.

*Command Mode*

Privileged EXEC

*Usage Guidelines*

This command first appeared in Cisco IOS Release 10.0.

*Sample Display*

The following is sample output from the **show decnet** command:

```
router# show decnet

Global DECnet parameters for network 0:
    Local address is 19.15, node type is area (Phase-IV Prime)
    Level-2 'Attached' flag is FALSE, nearest level-2 router is 19.5
    Maximum node is 350, maximum area is 63, maximum visits is 63
    Maximum paths is 1, path split mode is normal
    Local maximum cost is 1022, maximum hops is 30
    Area maximum cost is 1022, maximum hops is 30
    Static routes *NOT* being sent in routing updates
    Default route configured; next hop address of 2.100
```

Table 12–6 describes significant fields shown in the display.

**Table 12–6**   *Show DECnet Field Descriptions*

| Field | Description |
|---|---|
| Global DECnet parameters for network 0: | Indicates the DECnet network number of the network being described. |
| Local address is 19.15 | DECnet address. |

**Table 12–6** *Show DECnet Field Descriptions, Continued*

| Field | Description |
|---|---|
| node type is area | Indicates the DECnet node type with which the interface has been configured. Possible values include area (area router) or routing-iv (intra-area router). |
| Level-2 'Attached' flag is FALSE | (DECnet Level-2 routers only) Indicates that this Level-2 router is not "attached" (cannot reach other DECnet Phase IV areas). If the '"Attached" flag is TRUE, the router has reachability to other areas. |
| | If the "Attached" flag is FALSE, other displays on this line are the following: |
| | • Nearest Level-2 router is NONE—(DECnet Level-1 routers only) Indicates that this Level-1 router has not heard from any eligible Level-2 router (to send out-of-area packets to) |
| | • Nearest Level-2 router is 1.200—(DECnet Level-1 routers only) Indicates that this router's nearest Level-2 router is 1.200. Any packets received by this router destined for other areas are sent to 1.200. |
| (Phase-IV Prime) | Indicates that the router is running DECnet Phase IV Prime routing. |
| Maximum node is 350 | Highest node number that the router will recognize. |
| maximum area is 63 | Indicates the maximum DECnet area number, which is used to control the size of internal routing tables and messages sent to other routers. Range: 1 to 63. Default: 63. |
| maximum visits is 63 | Indicates the maximum number of times (visits) a packet can pass through a router. Range: 1 to 63. Default: 63. |
| Maximum paths is 1 | Indicates the maximum number of equal-cost paths the router will save. Range: 1 to 31. Default: 1. |
| path split mode is normal | Indicates how the router splits the routable packets among equal-cost paths. Possible values: normal (default) or interim. |
| Local maximum cost is 1022 | For intra-area routes. Router ignores routes in its area that have a cost greater than this value. |
| maximum hops is 30 | Indicates the maximum number of hops for a usable route within the local area. The router ignores routes within the local area that use more than this number of hops. |

Command Reference

**Table 12–6**    *Show DECnet Field Descriptions, Continued*

| Field | Description |
|-------|-------------|
| Area maximum cost is 1022 | Indicates the maximum cost specification for interarea routing. The router ignores routes to other areas that have a cost greater than this value. Range: 1 to 1022: Default: 1022. |
| maximum hops is 30 | Indicates the maximum number of hops for a usable route to other areas. The router ignores routes to other areas that use more than this number of hops. |
| Static routes *NOT* being sent in routing updates | Indicates static routes are not included in routing updates. |
| Default route configured; next hop address of 2.100 | Indicates a default route is configured on this router and shows the next hop address. |

## SHOW DECNET ACCOUNTING

To display the active accounting or checkpointed database, use the **show decnet accounting** EXEC command.

> **show decnet accounting [checkpoint]**

| *Syntax* | *Description* |
|----------|---------------|
| checkpoint | (Optional) Displays entries in the checkpoint database. |

### Command Mode

EXEC

### Usage Guidelines

This command first appeared in Cisco IOS Release 11.2 F.

### Sample Display

This sample output from the **show decnet accounting** command shows accounting data collected for traffic passing between the DECnet address pair 27.100 and 27.107:

```
Router# show decnet accounting

Source     Destination   Bytes    Packets
27.100          27.107    145        5
27.107          27.100    500        5

Accounting data age is 5
```

Table 12–7 describes the fields shown in the display.

**Table 12–7**  *Show DECnet Accounting Field Descriptions*

| Field | Description |
|-------|-------------|
| Source | Source address of the packet. |
| Destination | Destination address of the packet. |
| Bytes | Number of bytes transmitted from the source address to the destination address. |
| Packets | Number of packets transmitted from the source address to the destination address. |
| Accounting data age is ... | Time reported since the accounting database has been cleared. It can be in one of the following formats: $mm$, $hh{:}mm$, $dd{:}hh$, and $ww{:}dd$, where $m$ is minutes, $h$ is hours, $d$ is days, and $w$ is weeks. |

### Related Commands

Search online to find documentation of related commands.

**clear decnet accounting**
**decnet accounting**
**decnet accounting list**
**decnet accounting threshold**
**decnet accounting transits**
**show decnet accounting**

## SHOW DECNET INTERFACE

To display the global DECnet status and configuration for all interfaces, or the status and configuration for a specified interface, use the **show decnet interface** EXEC command.

**show decnet interface** [*type number*]

| Syntax | Description |
|--------|-------------|
| *type* | (Optional) Interface type. |
| *number* | (Optional) Interface number. |

*Command Mode*

EXEC

*Usage Guidelines*

This command first appeared in Cisco IOS Release 10.0.

*Sample Displays*

The following is sample output from the **show decnet interface** command:

```
router# show decnet interface

Global DECnet parameters for network 0:
  Local address is 19.15, node type is area
  Maximum node is 350, maximum area is 63, maximum visits is 63
  Maximum paths is 1, path split mode is normal
  Local maximum cost is 1022, maximum hops is 30
  Area maximum cost is 1022, maximum hops is 30
Ethernet 1 is up, line protocol is up, encapsulation is ARPA
  Interface cost is 4, priority is 64, DECnet network: 0
  The designated router is 1.9
  Sending HELLOs every 15 seconds, routing updates 40 seconds
  Smallest router blocksize seen is 1498 bytes
  Routing input list is not set, output list is not set
  Access list is not set
  DECnet fast switching is enabled
  Number of L1 router adjacencies is: 3
  Number of non-PhaseIV+ router adjacencies is: 3
  Number of PhaseIV+ router adjacencies is: 0
  Router is bilingual
```

Table 12–8 describes significant fields shown in the display.

**Table 12–8**  *Show DECnet Interface Field Descriptions—Interface Not Specified*

| Field | Description |
|-------|-------------|
| Global DECnet parameters for network 0: | Indicates the DECnet network number of the network being described. |
| Local address is 19.15 | DECnet address of the router. |
| node type is area | Indicates the DECnet node type with which the interface has been configured. Possible values include area (area router) or routing-iv (intra-area router). |
| Maximum node is 350 | Highest node number that the router will recognize. |
| maximum area is 63 | Indicates the maximum DECnet area number, which is used to control the size of internal routing tables and messages sent to other routers. Range: 1 to 63. Default: 63. |
| maximum visits is 63 | Indicates the maximum number of times (visits) a packet can pass through a router. Range: 1 to 63. Default: 63. |
| Maximum paths is 1 | Indicates the maximum number of equal-cost paths the router will save. Range: 1 to 31. Default: 1. |
| path split mode is normal | Indicates how the router splits the routable packets among equal-cost paths. Possible values: normal (default) or interim. |
| Local maximum cost is 1022 | For intra-area routes. Router ignores routes in its area that have a cost greater than this value. |
| maximum hops is 30 | Indicates the maximum number of hops for a usable route within the local area. The router ignores routes within the local area that use more than this number of hops. |
| Area maximum cost is 1022 | Indicates the maximum cost specification for interarea routing. The router ignores routes to other areas that have a cost greater than this value. Range: 1 to 1022: Default: 1022. |
| maximum hops is 30 | Indicates the maximum number of hops for a usable route to other areas. The router ignores routes to other areas that use more than this number of hops. |
| Ethernet 0 is up | Indicates whether the interface hardware is currently active and if it has been taken down by an administrator. |

**Table 12–8**    *Show DECnet Interface Field Descriptions—Interface Not Specified, Continued*

| Field | Description |
|-------|-------------|
| line protocol is up | Indicates whether the software processes that handle the line protocol believe the interface is usable (that is, whether keepalives are successful). |
| encapsulation is ARPA | Indicates the encapsulation type. |
| Interface cost is 4 | Indicates the cost that has been assigned to this interface using the **decnet cost** interface configuration command. If there are multiple paths to a destination, the one with the lowest cost is selected. |
| priority is 64 | Indicates the priority that has been assigned to this router on this interface. End systems select the router with the highest priority as their designated router. |
| DECnet network: 0 | Indicates that this interface is on DECnet network 0. This fact is significant only if ATG is turned on. |
| The designated router is 1.3 | Indicates the designated router on this particular LAN. |
| Sending HELLOs every 15 seconds | Indicates the frequency of hello packets. |
| routing updates 40 seconds | Indicates the frequency of routing updates. |
| Smallest router blocksize seen is 1498 bytes | Indicates the largest size of packets being sent on all routers on the LAN. |
| Routing input list is not set, output list is not set | Indicates that no access restrictions on incoming (or outgoing) router update or hello messages have been set for this interface. |
| Access list is not set | Indicates that no access lists have been configured for the interface. |
| DECnet fast switching is enabled | Indicates that fast switching is enabled. |
| Number of L1 router adjacencies is : 3 | Indicates how many Level 1 adjacencies the router has on this interface. |
| Number of non-PhaseIV+ router adjacencies is: 3 | Number of L1 and L2 routers on this interface that are not running Phase IV+. |

**Table 12–8** *Show DECnet Interface Field Descriptions—Interface Not Specified, Continued*

| Field | Description |
|-------|-------------|
| Number of PhaseIV+ router adjacencies is: 0 | Number of L2 routers on this interface that are running Phase IV+. |
| Router is bilingual | The router's MAC address on this interface is Phase IV-compatible (that is, it takes the form AA-00-04-00-xx-yy or 55-00-20-00-aa-bb on interfaces where the address is bit swapped). This means that the router behaves as both a Phase IV and a Phase IV Prime router. |

The following is sample output from the **show decnet interface** command when you specify an interface:

```
router# show decnet interface ethernet 0

Ethernet0 is up, line protocol is up, encapsulation is ARPA
   Interface cost is 4, priority is 64, DECnet network: 0
   The designated router is 1.3
   Sending HELLOs every 15 seconds, routing updates 40 seconds
   Smallest router blocksize seen is 1498 bytes
   Routing input list is not set, output list is not set
   Access list is not set
   DECnet fast switching is enabled
   Number of L1 router adjacencies is: 1
   Number of non-PhaseIV+ router adjacencies is: 3
   Number of PhaseIV+ router adjacencies is: 0
   Router is bilingual
```

Table 12–9 describes significant fields shown in the display.

**Table 12–9** *Show DECnet Interface Field Descriptions—Interface Specified*

| Field | Description |
|-------|-------------|
| Ethernet 0 is up | Indicates whether the interface hardware is currently active and if it has been taken down by an administrator. |
| line protocol is up | Indicates whether the software processes that handle the line protocol believe the interface is usable (that is, whether keepalives are successful). |
| encapsulation is ARPA | Indicates the encapsulation type. |
| Interface cost is 4 | Indicates the cost that has been assigned to this interface using the **decnet cost** interface configuration command. If there are multiple paths to a destination, the one with the lowest cost is selected. |

**Table 12–9** *Show DECnet Interface Field Descriptions—Interface Specified, Continued*

| Field | Description |
|-------|-------------|
| priority is 64 | Indicates the priority that has been assigned to this router on this interface. End systems select the router with the highest priority as their designated router. |
| DECnet network: 0 | Indicates that this interface is on DECnet network 0. This fact is significant only if ATG is turned on. |
| The designated router is 1.3 | Indicates the designated router on this particular LAN. |
| Sending HELLOs every 15 seconds | Indicates the frequency of hello packets. |
| routing updates 40 seconds | Indicates the frequency of routing updates. |
| Smallest router blocksize seen is 1498 bytes | Indicates the largest size of packets being sent on all routers on the LAN. |
| Routing input list is not set, output list is not set | Indicates that no access restrictions on incoming (or outgoing) router update or hello messages have been set for this interface. |
| Access list is not set | Indicates that no access lists have been configured for the interface. |
| DECnet fast switching is enabled | Indicates that fast switching is enabled. |
| Number of L1 router adjacencies is : 1 | Indicates how many Level 1 adjacencies the router has on this interface. |
| Number of non-PhaseIV+ router adjacencies is: 3 | Number of L1 and L2 routers on this interface that are not running Phase IV+. |
| Number of PhaseIV+ router adjacencies is: 0 | Number of L2 routers on this interface that are running Phase IV+. |
| Router is bilingual | The router's MAC address on this interface is Phase IV-compatible (that is, it takes the form AA-00-04-00-xx-yy or 55-00-20-00-aa-bb on interfaces where the address is bit swapped). This means that the router behaves as both a Phase IV and a Phase IV Prime router. |

## SHOW DECNET MAP

To display the address mapping information used by the DECnet Address Translation Gateway, use the **show decnet map** EXEC command.

     **show decnet map**

*Syntax      Description*

This command has no arguments or keywords.

*Command Mode*

EXEC

*Usage Guidelines*

This command first appeared in Cisco IOS Release 10.0.

*Sample Display*

The following is sample output from the **show decnet map** command:

```
router# show decnet map

Net Node   -> Net Node   Uses    Cost Hops
   0 1.100      1 2.100   0
```

Table 12–10 describes significant fields shown in the display.

**Table 12–10**  *Show DECnet Map Field Descriptions*

| Field | Description |
| --- | --- |
| Net Node -> Net Node | Network number and node address. |
| Uses | Number of times this map was used. |
| Cost | Cost associated with the route. |
| Hops | Number of hops to destination mode. |

## SHOW DECNET NEIGHBORS

To display all Phase IV and Phase IV Prime adjacencies and the MAC address associated with each neighbor, use the **show decnet neighbors** privileged EXEC command.

**show decnet neighbors**

*Syntax      Description*

This command has no arguments or keywords.

*Command Mode*

Privileged EXEC

*Command Reference*

## Usage Guidelines

This command first appeared in Cisco IOS Release 10.0.

## Sample Display

The following is sample output from the **show decnet neighbors** command:

```
router# show decnet neighbors

Net Node     Interface    MAC address      Flags
 0   3.11    Ethernet0    aa00.0400.0b0c   A
 0   1.1     Ethernet0    aa00.0400.0104   V
 0   1.3     Ethernet1    aa00.0400.0304   V
 0   1.6     Ethernet1    aa00.0400.0604   V
 0   2.2     TokenRing    5500.2000.4020   V  IV-PRIME
```

Table 12–11 describes the fields shown in the display.

**Table 12–11**  *Show DECnet Neighbors Field Descriptions*

| Field | Description |
|-------|-------------|
| Net | Number of the DECnet network this adjacency is in. |
| Node | DECnet address of the adjacency. |
| Interface | Interface over which this adjacency was heard. |
| MAC address | MAC address that this adjacency is using on this interface. |
| Flags | A: L2 adjacency.<br>V: L1 adjacency.<br>IV-PRIME: DECnet Phase IV Prime adjacency. |

## SHOW DECNET ROUTE

To display the DECnet routing table, use the **show decnet route** EXEC command.

   **show decnet route** [*decnet-address*]

| Syntax | Description |
|--------|-------------|
| *decnet-address* | (Optional) DECnet address and, when specified, the first hop route to that address is displayed. |

## Command Mode

EXEC

## Usage Guidelines

This command first appeared in Cisco IOS Release 10.0.

## Sample Display

The following is sample output from the **show decnet route** command when a DECnet address name was not specified, so the entire routing table is displayed:

```
router# show decnet route

    Area      Cost  Hops   Next Hop to Node      Expires  Prio

     1         4     1     Ethernet1 -> 1.300       26      64    A
    *1         4     1     Ethernet1 -> 1.400       37      64    A
    *2         8     2     Ethernet1 -> 1.400
    *5         0     0        (Local) -> 5.5
   *10         4     1     Ethernet2 -> 10.1        36      64    A
   *13        11     3     Ethernet1 -> 1.400
   *44        22     6     Ethernet1 -> 1.400
   *51        18     4     Ethernet1 -> 1.400
   *61         1     1          (OSI) -> 5.5
   *62         1     1          (OSI) -> 5.5
    *3         0     0       (STATIC)   Ethernet0, snpa aa00.0400.0404
    *4         0     0       (STATIC)   Serial0
    *6         5     4       (STATIC)   forwarding to 2.3

    Node      Cost  Hops   Next Hop to Node      Expires  Prio

  *(Area)      0     0        (Local) -> 5.5
   *5.5        0     0        (Local) -> 5.5          32      64    A+

   *DEFAULT*:   0     0     using next hop address of 2.100
```

As the display shows, the **show decnet route** command can display more than one route for a destination when equal-cost paths have been set with the **decnet max-paths** global configuration command, and when there is more than one equal-cost path to a destination. The display also shows that this node is an area router.

Table 12–12 describes significant fields shown in the display.

**Table 12–12** *Show DECnet Route Field Descriptions*

| Field | Description |
|-------|-------------|
| * | Currently selected route for a particular destination. In interim mode, the selected route will never appear to change. |
| Node | DECnet address of this (reachable) destination. |
| (Area) | All Level 1 routes are displayed in this section except for this the first entry, which points to the nearest Level 2 router. |
| Cost | Assigned cost for the interface, based on a recommended value for the underlying media. Range: 1 to 63. No default. |
| Hops | Number of hops to this node from the router being monitored. |

**Table 12–12**    *Show DECnet Route Field Descriptions, Continued*

| Field | Description |
| --- | --- |
| Next Hop to Node | DECnet address of the next hop a packet will take to get to the final destination as well as the interface. |
| (Local) | The address that the router is configured with. |
| (OSI) | Indicates that this entry was created by the **decnet accounting list** command. |
| (STATIC) | Indicates that this entry was created by the **decnet route** command. |
| Expires | Displays how many seconds from now this entry expires. |
| Prio | Router priority of this node. |
| V | Adjacent Level 1 router. |
| A+ | Adjacent Level 2 (area) router; A indicates that this is an adjacency created from a Phase IV hello, A+ indicates that this is an adjacency created from a Phase IV+ hello. |

## SHOW DECNET STATIC

To display all statically configured DECnet routes, use the **show decnet static** privileged EXEC command.

     **show decnet static**

*Syntax*      *Description*

This command has no arguments or keywords.

*Command Mode*

Privileged EXEC

*Usage Guidelines*

This command first appeared in Cisco IOS Release 11.1.

All static routes are stored in a static route queue, which allows static routes to be reinstated when DECnet routing is turned off then on again.

Not all routes in the static route queue will show up in the routing table. This happens under the following conditions:

- The router is a Level 1 router and any of the following apply. Assume the router DECnet address is 1.1:
  - A Level 2 area static route is configured.
    ```
    decnet route 2.0 1.2
    ```

- A static route is configured not in the same area as the router.

  ```
  decnet route 3.10 1.200
  ```

- A static route is configured for the same address as the router.

  ```
  decnet route 1.1 1.200
  ```

- The router is a Level 2 router and any of the following apply. Assume the router DECnet address is 2.1:

  - A Level 1 static router is not in the same area as the router.

    ```
    decnet route 4.1 10.200
    ```

    A static route appears because a Level 2 route is installed to area 4.

    ```
    decnet route 4.0 10.200
    ```

  - A Level 2 static route is configured for the router's own area.

    ```
    decnet route 2.0 10.200
    ```

  - A static route is configured for the same address as the router.

    ```
    decnet route 2.1 5.4 s 1
    ```

## Sample Display

The following is sample output from the **show decnet static** command:

```
router# show decnet static

Address     Cost    Hops    Next hop        SNPA

3           0       0       Ethernet0   aa00.0400.0404
5           0       0       Serial0
5.100       0       0       Serial2
DEFAULT     0       0         2.100
6           5       4         2.3
```

Note that this router is a Level 2 router with a DECnet address of 1.2, so a static route configured for 5.100 is not relevant here. This route appears in the **show decnet static** display, but not in the routing table.

## SHOW DECNET TRAFFIC

To show the DECnet traffic statistics (including datagrams sent, received, and forwarded), use the **show decnet traffic** EXEC command.

> **show decnet traffic**

## *Syntax    Description*

This command has no arguments or keywords.

*Command Mode*

EXEC

*Usage Guidelines*

This command first appeared in Cisco IOS Release 10.0.

*Sample Display*

The following is sample output from the **show decnet traffic** command:

```
router# show decnet traffic

Total: 42 received, 0 format errors, 0 unimplemented
0 not a gateway, 0 no memory, 0 no routing vector
0 congestion encountered
Hellos: 21 received, 0 bad, 0 other area, 16 sent
Level 1 routing: 14 received, 0 bad, 0 other area, 16 sent
Level 2 routing: 7 received, 0 not primary router, 8 sent
Data: 0 received, 0 not long format, 0 too many visits
0 forwarded, 0 returned, 0 converted, 0 local destination
0 access control failed, 0 no route, 0 encapsulation failed
0 inactive network, 0 incomplete map
```

Table 12–13 describes the fields shown in the display.

**Table 12–13**   *Show DECnet Traffic Field Descriptions*

| Field | Description |
| --- | --- |
| Total: | Displays the totals of packet types received. |
| received | Total of all types of DECnet packets received. |
| format errors | Lists the number of packets that appeared to be DECnet, but were formatted incorrectly. The number in the received field includes these packets. |
| 0 unimplemented | Reports the number of incoming packets that are DECnet control packets, and how many specify a service that the router does not implement. This includes services implemented to forward Level 1 and Level 2 routing information, and router and end-system hello packets. |
| 0 not a gateway | Reports the total number of packets received while not routing DECnet. |
| 0 no memory | Records transaction attempts when the system has run out of memory. |

**Table 12–13** *Show DECnet Traffic Field Descriptions, Continued*

| Field | Description |
|---|---|
| 0 no routing vector | Indicates that either a routing update came in from another router when the router did not have an adjacency for it, or it had no routing vector for the type of routing update. Use the **debug decnet-routing** EXEC command for more information. |
| 0 congestion encountered | Number of times the DECnet output process encounters a non-empty interface output queue. |
| HELLOs: | Displays the number of hello messages received and sent. |
| received | Displays the total number of hello messages received. All protocol types are included. |
| bad | Displays the total number of "bad" hello messages received. Invoke the EXEC command **debug decnet** to display more information about why the hello message was judged as bad. |
| other area | Displays the total number of hello messages received from nodes on other areas when the router is a Level 1 router only. |
| sent | Displays the total number of hello messages sent. |
| Level 1 routing: | Displays the Level 1 routing updates received and sent. |
| received | Displays the total number of Level 1 routing updates received. |
| bad | Displays the total number of Level 1 updates received that were judged to be bad. |
| other area | Displays the total number of Level 1 updates from nodes in other areas. |
| sent | Displays the total number of Level 1 updates sent. |
| Level 2 routing: | Displays the Level 2 routing updates received and sent. |
| received | Displays the total number of Level 2 updates received. |
| not primary router | Should always be zero. |
| sent | Displays the total number of Level 2 updates sent. |
| Data: | Displays the number of data packets received and sent. |
| received | Displays the total number of noncontrol (data) packets received. |
| not long format | Displays the number of packets received which are not in the long DECnet format. This number should always be zero. If it is not, investigate the source of the improperly formatted packets. |

**Table 12–13**   *Show DECnet Traffic Field Descriptions, Continued*

| Field | Description |
|-------|-------------|
| too many visits | Lists the number of packets received which have visited too many routers and have been flushed. |
| forwarded | Lists the total number of packets forwarded. |
| returned | Lists the total number of packets returned to the sender at the senders' request. |
| converted | Displays the number of Phase IV packets converted to Phase V packets. |
| local destination | Packets received that are destined for this router. |
| access control failed | Lists the packets dropped because access control required it. |
| no route | Lists the total packets dropped because the router did not know where to forward them. |
| encapsulation failed | Lists the number of packets that could not be encapsulated. This usually happens where there are entries missing in a map for a public data network, such as X.25 or Frame Relay. This can also occur if an interface is set for an encapsulation for which there is no defined DECnet encapsulation, such as Point-to-Point Protocol (PPP) on serial interfaces. |
| inactive network | Displays the number of packets that appear to come from a known interface, or that ATG returned because they did not make sense. |
| incomplete map | Counts the number of packets that failed address translation. This usually means a node that is not in the ATG map is trying to access a node in another network advertised by the ATG. |

# CHAPTER 13

# Configuring ISO CLNS

The ISO CLNS protocol is a standard for the network layer of the OSI model. This chapter describes how to configure ISO CLNS. Cisco access servers currently support only ES-IS, but not IS-IS.

## ISO CLNS CONFIGURATION TASK LIST

To configure ISO CLNS, you must configure the routing processes, associate addresses with the routing processes, and customize the routing processes for your particular network.

You must perform some combination of the tasks in the following sections to configure the ISO CLNS protocol:

- Understanding Addresses
- Understanding Routing Processes
- Configuring ISO IGRP Dynamic Routing
- Configuring IS-IS Dynamic Routing
- Configuring CLNS Static Routing
- Configuring Miscellaneous Features
- Configuring CLNS over WANs
- Enhancing ISO CLNS Performance
- Monitoring and Maintaining the ISO CLNS Network
- Configuring TARP on ISO CLNS

See the "ISO CLNS Configuration Examples" section at the end of this chapter for configuration examples.

## UNDERSTANDING ADDRESSES

Addresses in the ISO network architecture are referred to as *NSAP addresses* and *network entity titles* (NETs). Each node in an OSI network has one or more NETs. In addition, each node has many NSAP addresses. Each NSAP address differs from one of the NETs for that node in only the last byte. This byte is called the *N-selector*. Its function is similar to the port number in other protocol suites.

Cisco's implementation supports all NSAP address formats that are defined by ISO 8348/Ad2; however, they provide ISO IGRP or IS-IS dynamic routing only for NSAP addresses that conform to the address constraints defined in the ISO standard for IS-IS (ISO 10589).

An NSAP address consists of the following two major fields, as shown in Figure 13–1:

- The initial domain part (IDP) is made up of 1-byte authority and format identifier (AFI), and a variable-length initial domain identifier (IDI). The length of the IDI and the encoding format for the domain specific part (DSP) are based on the value of the AFI.

- The DSP is made up of a high-order DSP, an area identifier, a system identifier, and a 1-byte N-selector (labeled S).

*Figure 13–1*
*NSAP Address Fields.*

| IDP | DSP |
|-----|-----|

| AFI | IDI | HODSP | Area | System ID | S |
|-----|-----|-------|------|-----------|---|

Assign addresses or NETs for your domains and areas. The domain address uniquely identifies the routing domain. All routers within a given domain are given the same domain address. Within each routing domain, you can set up one or more areas, as shown in Figure 13–2. Determine the routers that are to be assigned to the designated areas. The area address uniquely identifies the routing area, and the system ID identifies each node.

*Figure 13–2*
*Sample Domain and Area Addresses.*

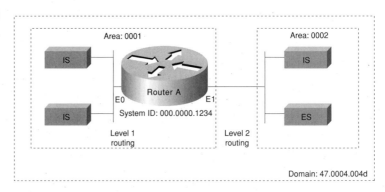

The key difference between the ISO IGRP and IS-IS NSAP addressing schemes is in the definition of area addresses. Both use the system ID for Level 1 routing (routing within an area); however, they differ in the way addresses are specified for area routing. An ISO IGRP NSAP address includes three separate fields for routing: the *domain*, *area*, and *system ID*. An IS-IS address includes two fields: a single continuous *area* field (comprising the domain and area fields) and the *system ID*.

## ISO IGRP NSAP Address

The ISO IGRP NSAP address is divided into three parts: a domain part, an area address, and a system ID. Domain routing is performed on the domain part of the address. Area routing for a given domain uses the area address. System routing for a given area uses the system ID part. The NSAP address is laid out as follows:

- The domain part is of variable length and comes before the area address.
- The area address is the 2 bytes before the system ID.
- The system ID is the 6 bytes before the N-selector.
- The N-selector (S) is the last byte of the NSAP address.

Cisco's ISO IGRP routing implementation interprets the bytes from the AFI up to (but not including) the area field in the DSP as a *domain identifier*. The area field specifies the *area*, and the system ID specifies the *system*.

Figure 13–3 illustrates the ISO IGRP NSAP addressing structure. The maximum address size is 20 bytes.

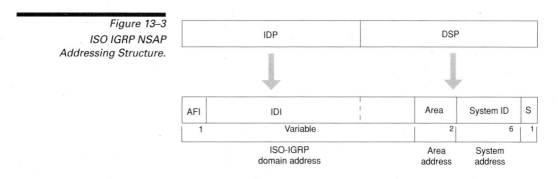

*Figure 13–3*
*ISO IGRP NSAP*
*Addressing Structure.*

## IS-IS NSAP Address

An IS-IS NSAP address is divided into two parts: an area address and a system ID. Level 2 routing (routing between areas) uses the area address. Level 1 routing (routing within an area) uses the system ID address. The NSAP address is laid out as follows:

- The area address is the NSAP address, not including the system ID and N-selector.
- The system ID is found between the area address and the N-selector byte.
- The N-selector (S) is the last byte of the NSAP address.

The IS-IS routing protocol interprets the bytes from the AFI up to (but not including) the system ID field in the DSP as an *area identifier*. The system ID specifies the *system*.

Figure 13–4 illustrates the IS-IS NSAP addressing structure. The maximum address size is 20 bytes.

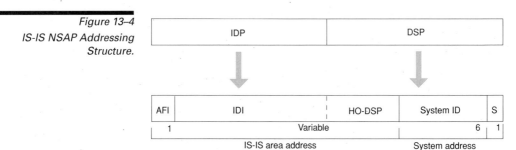

**Figure 13–4**
*IS-IS NSAP Addressing Structure.*

## Addressing Rules

All NSAP addresses must obey the following constraints:

- No two nodes can have addresses with the same NET; that is, addresses that match all but the N-selector (S) field in the DSP.

- No two nodes residing within the same area can have addresses in which the system ID fields are the same.

- ISO IGRP requires at least 10 bytes of length: 1 byte for domain, 2 bytes for area, 6 bytes for system ID, and 1 byte for N-selector.

- ISO IGRP and IS-IS should not be configured for the same area. Do *not* specify an NSAP address where all bytes up to (but not including) the system ID are the same when enabling both ISO IGRP and IS-IS routing.

- A router can have one or more area addresses. The concept of multiple area addresses is described in the "Assigning Multiple Area Addresses to IS-IS Areas" section later in this chapter.

- Cisco's implementation of IS-IS requires at least 8 bytes: one byte for area, 6 bytes for system ID, and 1 byte for N-selector.

## Addressing Examples

The following are examples of OSI network and GOSIP NSAP addresses using the ISO IGRP implementation.

The following is the OSI network NSAP address format:

```
|     Domain|Area|     System ID| S|
 47.0004.004D.0003.0000.0C00.62E6.00
```

The following is an example of the GOSIP NSAP address structure. This structure is mandatory for addresses allocated from the International Code Designator (ICD) 0005 addressing domain.

```
|                      Domain|      Area|System ID| S|
47.0005.80.ffff00.0000.ffff.0004.0000.0c00.62e6.00
   |    |  . |    |      |     |
  AFI  IDI  DFI  AAI   Resv   RD
```

## Sample Routing Table

You enter static routes by specifying NSAP prefix and next-hop NET pairs (by using the **clns route** command). The NSAP prefix can be any portion of the NSAP address. NETs are similar in function to NSAP addresses.

If an incoming packet has a destination NSAP address that does not match any existing NSAP addresses in the routing table, the Cisco IOS software will try to match the NSAP address with an NSAP prefix to route the packet. In the routing table, the best match means the longest NSAP prefix entry that matches the beginning of the destination NSAP address.

Table 13–1 shows a sample static routing table in which the next-hop NETs are listed for completeness, but are not necessary to understand the routing algorithm. Table 13–2 offers examples of how the longest matching NSAP prefix can be matched with routing table entries in Table 13–1.

**Table 13–1**   *Sample Routing Table Entries*

| Entry | NSAP Address Prefix | Next-Hop NET |
|-------|---------------------|--------------|
| 1 | 47.0005.000c.0001 | 47.0005.000c.0001.0000.1234.00 |
| 2 | 47.0004 | 47.0005.000c.0002.0000.0231.00 |
| 3 | 47.0005.0003 | 47.0005.000c.0001.0000.1234.00 |
| 4 | 47.0005.000c | 47.0005.000c.0004.0000.0011.00 |
| 5 | 47.0005 | 47.0005.000c.0002.0000.0231.00 |

**Table 13–2**   *Hierarchical Routing Examples*

| Datagram Destination NSAP Address | Table Entry Number Used |
|-----------------------------------|-------------------------|
| 47.0005.000c.0001.0000.3456.01 | 1 |
| 47.0005.000c.0001.6789.2345.01 | 1 |
| 47.0004.1234.1234.1234.1234.01 | 2 |
| 47.0005.0003.4321.4321.4321.01 | 3 |
| 47.0005.000c.0004.5678.5678.01 | 4 |
| 47.0005.0001.0005.3456.3456.01 | 5 |

---

**NOTES**

Octet boundaries must be used for the internal boundaries of NSAP addresses and NETs.

---

## UNDERSTANDING ROUTING PROCESSES

The basic function of a router is to forward packets: receive a packet in one interface and send it out another (or the same) interface to the proper destination. All routers do this by looking up the destination address in a table. The tables can be built either dynamically or statically. If you are configuring all the entries in the table yourself, you are using *static* routing. If you use a routing process to build the tables, you are using *dynamic* routing. It is possible, and sometimes necessary, to use both static and dynamic routing simultaneously.

When you configure only ISO CLNS and not routing protocols, the Cisco IOS software only makes forwarding decisions. It does not perform other routing-related functions. In such a configuration, the software compiles a table of adjacency data, but does not advertise this information. The only information that is inserted into the routing table is the NSAP and NET addresses of this router, static routes, and adjacency information.

You can route ISO CLNS on some interfaces and transparently bridge it on other interfaces simultaneously. To do this, you must enable concurrent routing and bridging by using the **bridge crb** command.

### Dynamic Routing

Cisco supports the following two dynamic routing protocols for ISO CLNP networks:

- ISO IGRP
- IS-IS

When dynamically routing, you can choose either ISO IGRP or IS-IS, or you can enable both routing protocols at the same time. Both routing protocols support the concept of *areas*. Within an area, all routers know how to reach all the system IDs. Between areas, routers know how to reach the proper area.

ISO IGRP supports three levels of routing: *system routing*, *area routing*, and *interdomain routing*. Routing across domains (interdomain routing) can be done either statically or dynamically with ISO IGRP. IS-IS supports two levels of routing: *station routing* (within an area) and *area routing* (between areas).

### Intermediate Systems (IS) and End Systems (ES)

Some ISs keep track of how to communicate with all the ESs in their areas and thereby function as Level 1 routers (also referred to as *local routers*). Other ISs keep track of how to communicate with other areas in the domain, functioning as Level 2 routers (sometimes referred to as *area routers*). Cisco routers are always Level 1 and Level 2 routers when routing ISO IGRP; they can be configured to be Level 1 only, Level 2 only, or both Level 1 and Level 2 routers when routing IS-IS.

ESs communicate with ISs using the ES-IS protocol. Level 1 and Level 2 ISs communicate with each other using either ISO IS-IS or Cisco's ISO IGRP protocol.

## Static Routing

Static routing is used when it is not possible or desirable to use dynamic routing. The following are some instances of when you would use static routing:

- If your network includes WAN links that involve paying for connect time or for per-packet charges, you would use static routing, rather than paying to run a routing protocol and all its routing update packets over that link.

- If you want routers to advertise connectivity to external networks, but you are not running an interdomain routing protocol, you *must* use static routes.

- If you must interoperate with another vendor's equipment that does not support any of the dynamic routing protocols that Cisco supports, you must use static routing.

- For operation over X.25, Frame Relay, or SMDS networks, static routing is generally preferable.

---

**NOTES**

---

An interface that is configured for static routing cannot reroute *around* failed links.

---

## Routing Decisions

A CLNP packet sent to any of the defined NSAP addresses or NETs will be received by the router. The Cisco IOS software uses the following algorithm to select which NET to use when it sends a packet:

- If no dynamic routing protocol is running, use the NET defined for the outgoing interface, if it exists; otherwise, use the NET defined for the router.

- If ISO IGRP is running, use the NET of the ISO IGRP routing process that is running on the interface.

- If IS-IS is running, use the NET of the IS-IS routing process that is running on the interface.

## CONFIGURING ISO IGRP DYNAMIC ROUTING

The ISO IGRP is a dynamic distance-vector routing protocol designed by Cisco for routing an autonomous system that contains large, arbitrarily complex networks with diverse bandwidth and delay characteristics.

To configure ISO IGRP, complete the tasks in the following sections. Only enabling ISO IGRP is required; the remaining task is optional, although you might be required to perform it, depending upon your specific application:

- Enable ISO IGRP
- Configure ISO IGRP Parameters

In addition, you can also configure the following miscellaneous features, described later in this chapter:

- Filter routing information (see the "Creating Packet-Forwarding Filters and Establishing Adjacencies" section).
- Redistribute routing information from one routing process to another (see the "Redistributing Routing Information" section).
- Configure administrative distances (see the "Specifying Preferred Routes" section).

## Enabling ISO IGRP

To configure ISO IGRP dynamic routing, you must enable the ISO IGRP routing process, identify the address for the router, and specify the interfaces that are to route ISO IGRP. Optionally, you can set a level for your routing updates when you configure the interfaces. CLNS routing is enabled by default on routers when you configure ISO IGRP. You can specify up to ten ISO IGRP routing processes.

To configure ISO IGRP dynamic routing on the router, perform the following tasks in global configuration mode:

| Task | | Command |
|------|---|---------|
| Step 1 | Enable the ISO IGRP routing process and enter router configuration mode. | **router iso-igrp** [*tag*] |
| Step 2 | Configure the NET or address for the routing process. | **net** *network-entity-title* |

Although IS-IS allows you to configure multiple NETs, ISO IGRP allows only one NET per routing process.

You can assign a meaningful name for the routing process by using the *tag* option. You can also specify a name for a NET in addition to an address. For information on how to assign a name, see the "Specifying Shortcut NSAP Addresses" section, later in this chapter.

You can configure an interface to advertise Level 2 information only. This option reduces the amount of router-to-router traffic by telling the Cisco IOS software to send out only Level 2 routing updates on certain interfaces. Level 1 information is not passed on the interfaces for which the Level 2 option is set.

To configure ISO IGRP dynamic routing on the interface, perform the following task in interface configuration mode:

| Task | Command |
|------|---------|
| Enable ISO IGRP on specified interfaces; also set the level type for routing updates. | **clns router iso-igrp** *tag* [**level 2**] |

See the "Dynamic Routing in Overlapping Areas Example," "Dynamic Interdomain Routing Example," and "ISO CLNS over X.25 Example" sections at the end of this chapter for examples of configuring dynamic routing.

## Configuring ISO IGRP Parameters

Cisco's ISO IGRP implementation allows you to customize certain ISO IGRP parameters. You can perform the optional tasks discussed in the following sections:

- Adjusting ISO IGRP Metrics
- Adjusting ISO IGRP Timers
- Enabling or Disabling Split Horizon

### Adjusting ISO IGRP Metrics

You have the option of altering the default behavior of ISO IGRP routing and metric computations. This, for example, enables the tuning of system behavior to allow for transmissions via satellite. Although ISO IGRP metric defaults were carefully selected to provide excellent operation in most networks, you can adjust the metric.

---
**NOTES**
---

Adjusting the ISO IGRP metric can dramatically affect network performance, so ensure that all metric adjustments are made carefully. Because of the complexity of this task, it is not recommended unless it is done with guidance from an experienced system designer.

---

You can use different metrics for the ISO IGRP routing protocol on CLNS. To configure the metric constants used in the ISO IGRP composite metric calculation of reliability and load, perform the following task in router configuration mode:

| Task | Command |
|------|---------|
| Adjust the ISO IGRP metric. | **metric weights** *qos k1 k2 k3 k4 k5* |

Two additional ISO IGRP metrics can be configured: the bandwidth and delay associated with an interface.

---
**NOTES**
---

Using the **bandwidth** and **delay** commands to change the values of the ISO IGRP metrics also changes the values of IP IGRP metrics.

---

### Adjusting ISO IGRP Timers

The basic timing parameters for ISO IGRP are adjustable. Because the ISO IGRP routing protocol executes a distributed, asynchronous routing algorithm, it is important that these timers be the same for all routers in the network.

To adjust ISO IGRP timing parameters, perform the following task in router configuration mode:

| Task | Command |
| --- | --- |
| Adjust the ISO IGRP timers (in seconds). | **timers basic** *update-interval holddown-interval invalid-interval* |

### Enabling or Disabling Split Horizon

Split horizon blocks information about routes from being advertised out the interface from which that information originated. This feature usually optimizes communication among multiple routers, particularly when links are broken.

To either enable or disable split horizon for ISO IGRP updates, perform the following tasks in interface configuration mode:

| Task | Command |
| --- | --- |
| **Step 1**  Enable split horizon for ISO IGRP updates. | **clns split-horizon** |
| **Step 2**  Disable split horizon for ISO IGRP updates. | **no clns split-horizon** |

The default for all LAN interfaces is for split horizon to be enabled; the default for WAN interfaces on X.25, Frame Relay, or SMDS networks is for split horizon to be disabled.

## CONFIGURING IS-IS DYNAMIC ROUTING

IS-IS is a dynamic routing specification described in ISO 10589. Cisco's implementation of IS-IS allows you to configure IS-IS as an ISO CLNS routing protocol.

To configure IS-IS, complete the tasks in the following sections. Only enabling IS-IS is required; the remainder of the tasks are optional, although you might be required to perform them depending upon your specific application.

- Enabling IS-IS
- Assigning Multiple Area Addresses to IS-IS Areas
- Configuring IS-IS Parameters
- Configuring IS-IS Interface Parameters

In addition, you can also configure the following miscellaneous features described later in this chapter:

- Filter routing information (see the "Creating Packet-Forwarding Filters and Establishing Adjacencies" section).

- Redistribute routing information from one routing process to another (see the "Redistributing Routing Information" section).

- Configure administrative distances (see the "Specifying Preferred Routes" section).

## Enabling IS-IS

To configure IS-IS dynamic routing, you must enable the IS-IS routing process, identify the address for the router, and specify the interfaces that are to route IS-IS. CLNS routing is enabled by default when you configure IS-IS dynamic routing. You can specify *only one* IS-IS process per router.

To configure IS-IS dynamic routing on the router, perform the following tasks in global configuration mode:

| Task | Command |
|---|---|
| **Step 1** Enable IS-IS routing and enter router configuration mode. | **router isis** [*tag*] |
| **Step 2** Configure the NET for the routing process. | **net** *network-entity-title* |

You can assign a meaningful name for the routing process by using the *tag* option. You can also specify a name for a NET in addition to an address. For information on how to assign a name, see the "Specifying Shortcut NSAP Addresses" section later in this chapter.

To configure IS-IS dynamic routing on an interface, perform the following task in interface configuration mode:

| Task | Command |
|---|---|
| Specify the interfaces that should be actively routing IS-IS. | **clns router isis** [*tag*] |

— **NOTES**

For IS-IS, multiple NETs per router are allowed, with a maximum of three. However, only one IS-IS process is allowed, whether you run it in integrated mode, ISO CLNS only, or IP only.

For examples of configuring IS-IS routing, see the "IS-IS Routing Configuration Examples" section at the end of this chapter.

## Assigning Multiple Area Addresses to IS-IS Areas

IS-IS routing supports the assignment of multiple area addresses on the same router. This concept is referred to as *multihoming*. Multihoming provides a mechanism for smoothly migrating network addresses, as follows:

- Splitting up an area—Nodes within a given area can accumulate to a point that they are difficult to manage, cause excessive traffic, or threaten to exceed the usable address space for an area. Multiple area addresses can be assigned so that you can smoothly partition a network into separate areas without disrupting service.

- Merging areas—Use transitional area addresses to merge as many as three separate areas into a single area that shares a common area address.

- Transition to a different address—You may need to change an area address for a particular group of nodes. Use multiple area addresses to allow incoming traffic intended for an old area address to continue being routed to associated nodes.

You must statically assign the multiple area addresses on the router. Cisco currently supports assignment of up to three area addresses on a router. The number of areas allowed in a domain is unlimited.

All the addresses must have the same system ID. For example, you can assign one address (*area1* plus system ID), and two additional addresses in different areas (*area2* plus system ID and *area3* plus system ID) where the system ID is the same.

A router can dynamically learn about any adjacent router. As part of this process, the routers inform each other of their area addresses. If two routers share at least one area address, the set of area addresses of the two routers are merged. The merged set cannot contain more than three addresses. If there are more than three, the three addresses with the lowest numerical values are kept, and all others are dropped.

To configure multiple area addresses in IS-IS areas, perform the following tasks beginning in global configuration mode:

| Task | Command |
|------|---------|
| **Step 1** Enable IS-IS routing and enter router configuration mode. | **router isis** [*tag*] |
| **Step 2** Configure NETs for the routing process. The router can have up to three NETs. Enter each command separately. | **net** *network-entity-title* |

See the "NETs Configuration Examples" section at the end of this chapter for examples of configuring NETs and multiple area addresses.

## Configuring IS-IS Parameters

Cisco's IS-IS implementation enables you to customize certain IS-IS parameters. You can perform the optional tasks discussed in the following sections:

- Specifying Router-Level Support
- Configuring IS-IS Authentication Passwords
- Ignoring IS-IS Link-State Packet (LSP) Errors
- Log Adjacency State Changes
- Changing IS-IS LSP MTU Size

### *Specifying Router-Level Support*

It seldom is necessary to configure the IS type because the IS-IS protocol will automatically establish this. You can, however, configure the router to act as a Level 1 (intra-area) router, as both a Level 1 router and a Level 2 (interarea) router, or as an interarea router only.

To configure the IS-IS level, perform the following task in router configuration mode:

| Task | Command |
|------|---------|
| Configure the IS-IS level at which the router is to operate. | **is-type {level-1 | level-1-2 | level-2-only}** |

### *Configuring IS-IS Authentication Passwords*

You can assign authentication passwords to areas and domains. An area password is inserted in Level 1 (station router) link-state PDUs (LSPs), complete sequence number PDUs (CSNPs), and partial sequence number PDUs (PSNPs). A routing domain authentication password is inserted in Level 2 (area router) LSP, CSNP, and PSNP.

To configure area or domain passwords, perform the following tasks in router configuration mode:

| Task | Command |
|------|---------|
| **Step 1** Configure the area authentication password. | **area-password** *password* |
| **Step 2** Configure the routing domain authentication password. | **domain-password** *password* |

### *Ignoring IS-IS Link-State Packet (LSP) Errors*

You can configure the router to ignore IS-IS LSPs that are received with internal checksum errors, rather than purging the LSPs. LSPs are used by the receiving routers to maintain their routing tables.

The IS-IS protocol definition requires that a received LSP with an incorrect data-link checksum be purged by the receiver, which causes the initiator of the LSP to regenerate it. However, if a network has a link that causes data corruption while still delivering LSPs with correct data-link checksums, a continuous cycle of purging and regenerating large numbers of LSPs can occur, rendering the network nonfunctional.

To allow the router to ignore LSPs with an internal checksum error, perform the following task in router configuration mode:

| Task | Command |
|---|---|
| Ignore LSPs with internal checksum errors rather than purging the LSPs. | ignore-lsp-errors |

### Log Adjacency State Changes

You can configure IS-IS to generate a log message when an IS-IS adjacency changes state (up or down). This may be useful when monitoring large networks. Messages are logged using the system error message facility. Messages are of the following form:

```
%CLNS-5-ADJCHANGE: ISIS: Adjacency to 0000.0000.0034 (Serial0) Up, new adjacency
%CLNS-5-ADJCHANGE: ISIS: Adjacency to 0000.0000.0034 (Serial0) Down, hold time expired
```

To generate log messages when an IS-IS adjacency changes state, perform the following task in router configuration mode:

| Task | Command |
|---|---|
| Log IS-IS adjacency state changes. | log-adjacency-changes |

### Changing IS-IS LSP MTU Size

Under normal conditions, the default maximum transmission unit (MTU) size should be sufficient. If the MTU of a link is lowered to less than 1500 bytes, however, the LSP MTU must be lowered accordingly on each router in the network. If this is not done, routing will become unpredictable.

The MTU size must be less than or equal to the smallest MTU of any link in the network. The default size is 1497 bytes.

─── CAUTION ──────────────────────────────────────────────

The CLNS MTU of a link (which is the applicable value for IS-IS, even if it is being used to route IP) may differ from the IP MTU. To be certain about a link MTU as it pertains to IS-IS, use the **show clns interface** command to display the value.

To change the MTU size of IS-IS link state packets, perform the following task in router configuration mode:

| Task | Command |
|------|---------|
| Specify the maximum LSP packet size, in bytes. | **lsp-mtu** *size* |

---

**NOTES**

The preceding rule applies for all routers in a network. If any link in the network has a reduced MTU, all routers must be changed, not just the routers directly connected to the link.

---

## Configuring IS-IS Interface Parameters

Cisco's IS-IS implementation enables you to customize certain interface-specific IS-IS parameters. You can perform the optional tasks discussed in the following sections:

- Adjusting IS-IS Link-State Metrics
- Setting the Advertised Hello Interval and Hello Multiplier
- Setting the Advertised CSNP Interval
- Setting the Retransmission Interval
- Specifying Designated Router Election
- Specifying the Interface Circuit Type
- Configuring IS-IS Password Authentication

You are not required to alter any of these parameters; however, some interface parameters must be consistent across all routers in the network. Therefore, be sure that if you do configure any of these parameters, the configurations for all routers on the network have compatible values.

### Adjusting IS-IS Link-State Metrics

You can configure a cost for a specified interface. The default metric is used as a value for the IS-IS metric. This is the value assigned when there is no quality of service (QoS) routing performed. The only metric that is supported by the Cisco IOS software that you can configure is the *default-metric*, which you can configure for Level 1 or Level 2 routing or both.

To configure the link state metric, perform the following task in interface configuration mode:

| Task | Command |
|------|---------|
| Configure the metric (or cost) for the specified interface. | **isis metric** *default-metric* {**level-1** \| **level-2**} |

### Setting the Advertised Hello Interval and Hello Multiplier

You can specify the length of time (in seconds) between hello packets that the Cisco IOS software sends on the interface. You can also change the default hello packet multiplier used on the interface to determine the hold time transmitted in IS-IS hello packets (the default is 3).

The hold time determines how long a neighbor waits for another hello packet before declaring the neighbor down. This time determines how quickly a failed link or neighbor is detected so that routes can be recalculated.

To set the advertised hello interval and multiplier, perform the following tasks in interface configuration mode:

| Task | Command |
|------|---------|
| **Step 1** Specify the length of time, in seconds, between hello packets the software sends on the specified interface. | **isis hello-interval** *seconds* {**level-1** \| **level-2**} |
| **Step 2** Specify the number used to multiply the hello interval seconds by to determine the total holding time transmitted in the IS-IS hello packet. If not specified, a multiplier of 3 is used. | **isis hello-multiplier** *multiplier* [{**level-1** \| **level-2**}] |

The hello interval can be configured independently for Level 1 and Level 2, except on serial point-to-point interfaces. (Because there is only a single type of hello packet sent on serial links, the hello packet is independent of Level 1 or Level 2.) Specify an optional level for X.25, SMDS, and Frame Relay multiaccess networks.

Use the **isis hello-multiplier** command in circumstances where hello packets are lost frequently and IS-IS adjacencies are failing unnecessarily. You can raise the hello multiplier and lower the hello interval (**isis hello-interval** command) correspondingly to make the hello protocol more reliable without increasing the time required to detect a link failure.

### Setting the Advertised CSNP Interval

CSNPs are sent by the designated router to maintain database synchronization.

You can configure the IS-IS CSNP interval for the interface by performing the following task in interface configuration mode:

| Task | Command |
|------|---------|
| Configure the IS-IS CSNP interval for the specified interface. | **isis csnp-interval** *seconds* {**level-1** \| **level-2**} |

This feature does not apply to serial point-to-point interfaces. It does apply to WAN connections if the WAN is viewed as a multiaccess meshed network.

### Setting the Retransmission Interval

You can configure the number of seconds between retransmission of LSPs for point-to-point links.

To set the retransmission level, perform the following task in interface configuration mode:

| Task | Command |
| --- | --- |
| Configure the number of seconds between retransmission of IS-IS LSPs for point-to-point links. | **isis retransmit-interval** *seconds* |

The value you specify should be an integer greater than the expected round-trip delay between any two routers on the network. The setting of this parameter should be conservative, or needless retransmission will result. The value you determine should be larger for serial lines and virtual links.

### Specifying Designated Router Election

You can configure the priority to use for designated router election. Priorities can be configured for Level 1 and Level 2 individually. The designated router enables a reduction in the number of adjacencies required on a multiaccess network, which in turn reduces the amount of routing protocol traffic and the size of the topology database.

To configure the priority to use for designated router election, perform the following task in interface configuration mode:

| Task | Command |
| --- | --- |
| Configure the priority to use for designated router election. | **isis priority** *value* {level-1 \| level-2} |

### Specifying the Interface Circuit Type

It normally is not necessary to configure the interface circuit type, because the IS-IS protocol automatically determines area boundaries and keeps Level 1 and Level 2 routing separate. You can, however, specify the adjacency levels on a specified interface.

To configure the adjacency for neighbors on the specified interface, perform the following task in interface configuration mode:

| Task | Command |
| --- | --- |
| Configure the type of adjacency desired for neighbors on the specified interface (specify the interface circuit type). | isis circuit-type {level-1 | level-1-2 | level-2-only} |

If you specify Level 1, a Level 1 adjacency is established if there is at least one area address common to both this node and its neighbors. If you specify both Level 1 and Level 2 (the default value), a Level 1 and 2 adjacency is established if the neighbor is also configured as both Level 1 and Level 2 and there is at least one area in common. If there is no area in common, a Level 2 adjacency is established. If you specify Level 2 only, a Level 2 adjacency is established. If the neighbor router is a Level 1 router, no adjacency is established.

### Configuring IS-IS Password Authentication

You can assign different authentication passwords for different routing levels. By default, authentication is disabled. Specifying Level 1 or Level 2 enables the password only for Level 1 or Level 2 routing, respectively. If you do not specify a level, the default is Level 1.

To configure an authentication password for an interface, perform the following task in interface configuration mode:

| Task | Command |
| --- | --- |
| Configure the authentication password for an interface. | isis password password {level-1 | level-2} |

## CONFIGURING CLNS STATIC ROUTING

You do not need to explicitly specify a routing process to use static routing facilities. You can enter a specific static route and apply it globally, even if you have configured the router for ISO IGRP or IS-IS dynamic routing.

To configure a static route, complete the tasks in the following sections. Only enabling CLNS is required; the remaining tasks are optional, although you might be required to perform them depending upon your specific application.

- Enabling Static Routes
- Configuring Variations of the Static Route
- Mapping NSAP Addresses to Media Addresses

## Enabling Static Routes

To configure static routing, you must enable CLNS on the router and on the interface. CLNS routing is enabled on the router by default when you configure ISO IGRP or IS-IS routing protocols. NSAP addresses that start with the NSAP prefix you specify are forwarded to the next-hop node.

To configure CLNS on the router, perform the following tasks in global configuration mode:

| Task | Command |
| --- | --- |
| **Step 1** Configure CLNS. | **clns routing** |
| **Step 2** Assign an NSAP address to the router if the router has not been configured to route CLNS packets dynamically using ISO IGRP or IS-IS. | **clns net** {*net-address* \| *name*} |
| **Step 3** Enter a specific static route. | **clns route** *nsap-prefix* {*next-hop-net* \| *name*} |

— **NOTES** —————————————————————————————————————

If you have not configured the router to route CLNS packets dynamically using ISO IGRP or IS-IS, you must assign an address to the router.

You also must enable ISO CLNS for each interface you want to pass ISO CLNS packet traffic to end systems, but for which you do not want to perform any dynamic routing on the interface. This is done automatically when you configure IS-IS or ISO IGRP routing on an interface; however, if you do not intend to perform any dynamic routing on an interface, you must manually enable CLNS. You can assign an NSAP address for a specific interface. This enables the Cisco IOS software to advertise different addresses on each interface. This is useful if you are doing static routing and need to control the source NET used by the router on each interface.

To configure CLNS on an interface, perform the following tasks in interface configuration mode:

| Task | Command |
| --- | --- |
| **Step 1** Enable ISO CLNS for each interface. | **clns enable** |
| **Step 2** Optionally, assign an NSAP address to a specific interface. | **clns net** {*nsap-address* \| *name*} |

For examples of configuring static routes, see the "Basic Static Routing Examples," "Static Intradomain Routing Example," and "Static Interdomain Routing Example" sections at the end of this chapter.

## Configuring Variations of the Static Route

You can perform the following tasks that use variations of the **clns route** global configuration command:

- Bind the next hop to a specified interface and media address when you do not know the NSAP address of your neighbor. Note that this version of the **clns route** command is not literally *applied* to a specific interface.
- Tell the Cisco IOS software to discard packets with the specified NSAP prefix.
- Specify a default prefix.

To enter a specific static route, discard packets, or configure a default prefix, perform the following tasks in global configuration mode:

| Task | Command |
|------|---------|
| **Step 1** Enter a specific static route for a specific interface. | **clns route** *nsap-prefix type number* [*snpa-address*] |
| **Step 2** Explicitly tell the software to discard packets with the specified NSAP prefix. | **clns route** *nsap-prefix* **discard** |
| **Step 3** Configure a default prefix rather than specify an NSAP prefix. | **clns route default** *nsap-prefix type number* |

## Mapping NSAP Addresses to Media Addresses

Conceptually, each ES lives in one area. It discovers the nearest IS by listening to ES-IS packets. Each ES must be able to communicate directly with an IS in its area.

When an ES wants to communicate with another ES, it sends the packet to any IS on the same medium. The IS looks up the destination NSAP address and forwards the packet along the best route. If the destination NSAP address is for an ES in another area, the Level 1 IS sends the packet to the nearest Level 2 IS. The Level 2 IS forwards the packet along the best path for the destination area until it gets to a Level 2 IS that is in the destination area. This IS then forwards the packet along the best path inside the area until it is delivered to the destination ES.

ESs need to know how to get to a Level 1 IS for their area, and Level 1 ISs need to know all of the ESs that are directly reachable through each of their interfaces. To provide this information, the routers support the ES-IS protocol. The router dynamically discovers all ESs running the ES-IS protocol. ESs that are not running the ES-IS protocol must be configured statically.

It is sometimes desirable for a router to have a neighbor configured statically rather than learned through ES-IS, ISO IGRP, or IS-IS.

---

> **NOTES**

It is necessary to use static mapping only for ESs that do *not* support ES-IS. The Cisco IOS software continues to dynamically discover ESs that *do* support ES-IS.

---

> **NOTES**

If you have configured interfaces for ISO IGRP or IS-IS, the ES-IS routing software automatically turns on ES-IS for those interfaces.

---

To enter static mapping information between the NSAP protocol addresses and the subnetwork point of attachment (SNPA) addresses (media) for ESs or ISs, perform the following tasks (as needed) in interface configuration mode:

| Task | Command |
|------|---------|
| **Step 1** Configure all end systems that will be used when you manually specify the NSAP-to-SNPA mapping. | **clns es-neighbor** *nsap snpa* |
| **Step 2** Configure all intermediate systems that will be used when you manually specify the NSAP-to-SNPA mapping. | **clns is-neighbor** *nsap snpa* |

For more information, see the "Configuring CLNS over WANs" section, later in this chapter.

---

> **NOTES**

The SNPA is a data link layer address (such as an Ethernet address, X.25 address, or Frame Relay DLCI address) used to configure a CLNS route for an interface.

---

## CONFIGURING MISCELLANEOUS FEATURES

Perform the optional tasks in the following sections to configure miscellaneous features of an ISO CLNS network:

- Specifying Shortcut NSAP Addresses
- Using the IP Domain Name System to Discover ISO CLNS Addresses
- Creating Packet-Forwarding Filters and Establishing Adjacencies
- Redistributing Routing Information
- Specifying Preferred Routes
- Configuring ES-IS Hello Packet Parameters
- Configuring DECnet OSI or Phase V Cluster Aliases

- Configuring Digital-Compatible Mode
- Allowing Security Option Packets to Pass

## Specifying Shortcut NSAP Addresses

You can define a name-to-NSAP address mapping. This name can then be used in place of typing the long set of numbers associated with an NSAP address.

To define a name-to-NSAP address mapping, perform the following task in global configuration mode:

| Task | Command |
|------|---------|
| Define a name-to-NSAP address mapping. | **clns host** *name nsap* |

The assigned NSAP name is displayed, where applicable, in **show** and **debug** EXEC commands. However, some effects and requirements are associated with using names to represent NETs and NSAP addresses.

The **clns host** global configuration command is generated after all other CLNS commands when the configuration file is parsed. As a result, you cannot edit the nonvolatile random access memory (NVRAM) version of the configuration to specifically change the address defined in the original **clns host** command. You must specifically change any commands that refer to the original address. This affects all commands that accept names.

The commands that are affected by these requirements include the following:

- **net** (router configuration command)
- **clns is-neighbor** (interface configuration command)
- **clns es-neighbor** (interface configuration command)
- **clns route** (global configuration command)

## Using the IP Domain Name System to Discover ISO CLNS Addresses

If your router has both ISO CLNS and IP enabled, you can use the Domain Naming System (DNS) to query ISO CLNS addresses by using the NSAP address type, as documented in RFC 1348. This feature is useful for the ISO CLNS **ping** EXEC command and when making Telnet connections. This feature is enabled by default.

To enable or disable DNS queries for ISO CLNS addresses, perform the following tasks in global configuration mode:

| Task | Command |
|------|---------|
| **Step 1** Enable DNS queries for CLNS addresses. | **ip domain-lookup nsap** |
| **Step 2** Disable DNS queries for CLNS addresses. | **no ip domain-lookup nsap** |

## Creating Packet-Forwarding Filters and Establishing Adjacencies

You can build powerful CLNS filter expressions, or access lists. These can be used to control either the forwarding of frames through router interfaces, or the establishment of adjacencies with, or the application of filters to, any combination of ES or IS neighbors, ISO IGRP neighbors, or IS-IS neighbors.

CLNS filter expressions are complex logical combinations of CLNS filter sets. CLNS filter sets are lists of address templates against which CLNS addresses are matched. Address templates are CLNS address *patterns* that are either simple CLNS addresses that match just one address, or match multiple CLNS addresses through the use of wildcard characters, prefixes, and suffixes. Frequently used address templates can be given *aliases* for easier reference.

To establish CLNS filters, perform the following tasks in global configuration mode:

| Task | | Command |
|------|--|---------|
| Step 1 | Create aliases for frequently used address templates. | **clns template-alias** *name template* |
| Step 2 | Build filter sets of multiple address template permit and deny conditions. | **clns filter-set** *sname* [**permit** \| **deny**] *template* |
| Step 3 | Build filter expressions, using one or more filter sets. | **clns filter-expr** *ename term* |

To apply filter expressions to an interface, perform the following tasks in interface configuration mode:

| Task | | Command |
|------|--|---------|
| Step 1 | Apply a filter expression to frames forwarded in or out of an interface. | **clns access-group** *name* [**in** \| **out**] |
| Step 2 | Apply a filter expression to IS-IS adjacencies. | **isis adjacency-filter** *name* [**match-all**] |
| Step 3 | Apply a filter expression to ISO IGRP adjacencies. | **iso-igrp adjacency-filter** *name* |
| Step 4 | Apply a filter expression to ES or IS adjacencies. | **clns adjacency-filter** {**es** \| **is**} *name* |

See the "CLNS Filter Example" section at the end of this chapter for examples of configuring CLNS filters.

## Redistributing Routing Information

In addition to running multiple routing protocols simultaneously, the Cisco IOS software can redistribute information from one routing process to another.

You can also configure the Cisco IOS software to do interdomain dynamic routing by configuring two routing processes and two NETs (thereby putting the router into two domains) and redistributing the routing information between the domains. Routers configured this way are referred to as *border* routers. If you have a router that is in two routing domains, you might want to redistribute routing information between the two domains.

---

**NOTES**

It is not necessary to use redistribution between areas. Redistribution only occurs for Level 2 routing.

---

To configure the router to redistribute routing information into the ISO IGRP domain, perform the following tasks beginning in global configuration mode:

| Task | | Command |
| --- | --- | --- |
| Step 1 | Specify the routing protocol and tag (if applicable) into which you want to distribute routing information. | **router iso-igrp** [*tag*] |
| Step 2 | Specify one or more ISO IGRP routing protocol and tag (if applicable) you want to redistribute. | **redistribute iso-igrp** [*tag*] [**route-map** *map-tag*] |
| Step 3 | Specify the IS-IS routing protocol and tag (if applicable) you want to redistribute. | **redistribute isis** [*tag*] [**route-map** *map-tag*] |
| Step 4 | Specify the static routes you want to redistribute. | **redistribute static** [**clns** | **ip**] |

To configure the router to redistribute routing information into the IS-IS domains, perform the following tasks beginning in global configuration mode:

| Task | | Command |
| --- | --- | --- |
| Step 1 | Specify the routing protocol and tag (if applicable) into which you want to distribute routing information. | **router isis** [*tag*] |
| Step 2 | Specify the IS-IS routing protocol and tag (if applicable) you want to redistribute. | **redistribute isis** [*tag*] [**route-map** *map-tag*] |

---

**NOTES**

By default, static routes are redistributed into IS-IS.

---

You can conditionally control the redistribution of routes between routing domains by defining *route maps* between the two domains. Route maps allow you to use tags in routes to influence route redistribution.

To conditionally control the redistribution of routes between domains, perform the following task in global configuration mode:

| Task | Command |
|------|---------|
| Define any route maps needed to control redistribution. | **route-map** *map-tag* {**permit** \| **deny**} *sequence-number* |

One or more **match** commands and one or more **set** commands typically follow a **route-map** command to define the conditions for redistributing routes from one routing protocol into another. If there are no **match** commands, everything matches. If there are no **set** commands, nothing is done (other than the match).

Each **route-map** command has a list of **match** and **set** commands associated with it. The **match** commands specify the *match criteria*—the conditions under which redistribution is allowed for the current **route-map command**. The **set** commands specify the redistribution *set actions*—the particular redistribution actions to perform if the criteria enforced by the **match** commands are met. When all **match** criteria are met, all **set** actions are performed.

The **match route-map** configuration command has multiple formats. The **match** commands may be given in any order, and *all* defined match criteria must be satisfied to cause the route to be redistributed according to the *set actions* given with the **set** commands.

To define the match criteria for redistribution of routes from one routing protocol into another, perform at least one of the following tasks in route-map configuration mode:

| Task | Command |
|------|---------|
| Match routes that have a network address matching one or more of the specified names (the names can be a standard access list, filter set, or expression). | **match clns address** *name* [*name...name*] |
| Match routes that have a next hop address matching one or more of the specified names (the names can be a standard access list, filter set, or expression). | **match clns next-hop** *name* [*name...name*] |

| Task | Command |
|------|---------|
| Match routes that have been advertised by routers matching one or more of the specified names (the names can be a standard access list, filter set, or expression). | **match clns route-source** *name* [*name...name*] |
| Match routes that have the next hop out matching one or more of the specified interfaces. | **match clns interface** *type number* [*type number...type number*] |
| Match routes that have the specified metric. | **match metric** *metric-value* |
| Match routes that have the specified route type. | **match route-type** {level-1 I level-2} |

To define set actions for redistribution of routes from one routing protocol into another, perform at least one of the following set tasks in route-map configuration mode:

| Task | Command |
|------|---------|
| Set the routing level of the routes to be advertised into a specified area of the routing domain. | **set level** {level-1 I level-2 I level-1-2} |
| Set the metric value to give the redistributed routes. | **set metric** *metric-value* |
| Set the metric type to give the redistributed routes. | **set metric-type** {internal I external} |
| Set the tag value to associate with the redistributed routes. | **set tag** *tag-value* |

See the "Dynamic Interdomain Routing Example" and "TARP Configuration Examples" sections at the end of this chapter for examples of configuring route maps.

## Specifying Preferred Routes

When multiple routing processes are running in the same router for CLNS, it is possible for the same route to be advertised by more than one routing process. The Cisco IOS software always chooses the route whose routing protocol has the lowest administrative distance. The lower the value of the distance, the more preferred the route.

By default, the following administrative distances are assigned:

- Static routes—10
- ISO IGRP routes—100
- IS-IS routes—110

If you must change an administrative distance for a route, however, perform the following task in router configuration mode:

| Task | Command |
|------|---------|
| Specify preferred routes by setting the lowest administrative distance. | distance *value* [**clns**] |

---

**NOTES**

If you want an ISO IGRP prefix route to override a static route, you must set the distance for the routing process to be lower than 10.

---

## Configuring ES-IS Hello Packet Parameters

You can configure ES-IS parameters for communication between end systems and routers. In general, you should leave these parameters at their default values.

When configuring an ES-IS router, be aware of the following:

- ES-IS does not run over X.25 links unless the *broadcast* facility is enabled.
- ES hello packets and IS hello packets are sent without options. Options in received packets are ignored.

ISs and ESs periodically send out hello packets to advertise their availability. The frequency of these hello packets can be configured.

The recipient of a hello packet creates an adjacency entry for the system that sent it. If the next hello packet is not received within the interval specified, the adjacency times out and the adjacent node is considered unreachable.

A default rate has been set for hello packets and packet validity; however, you can change the defaults by performing the following tasks in global configuration mode:

| Task | Command |
|------|---------|
| Step 1 Specify the rate at which ES hello and IS hello packets are sent. | **clns configuration-time** *seconds* |
| Step 2 Allow the sender of an ES hello or IS hello packet to specify the length of time you consider the information in these packets to be valid. | **clns holding-time** *seconds* |

A default rate has been set for the ES Configuration Timer (ESCT) option; however, you can change the default by performing the following task in interface configuration mode:

| Task | Command |
|------|---------|
| Specify how often the end system should transmit ES hello packet PDUs. | clns esct-time *seconds* |

## Configuring DECnet OSI or Phase V Cluster Aliases

DECnet Phase V *cluster aliasing* allows multiple systems to advertise the same system ID in end-system hello packets. The Cisco IOS software does this by caching multiple ES adjacencies with the same NSAP address, but different SNPA addresses. When a packet is destined to the common NSAP address, the software splits the packet loads among the different SNPA addresses. A router that supports this capability forwards traffic to each system. You can do this on a per-interface basis.

To configure cluster aliases, perform the following task in interface configuration mode:

| Task | Command |
|------|---------|
| Allow multiple systems to advertise the same system ID in end-system hello packets. | clns cluster-alias |

If DECnet Phase V cluster aliases are disabled on an interface, ES hello packet information is used to replace any existing adjacency information for the NSAP address. Otherwise, an additional adjacency (with a different SNPA) is created for the same NSAP address.

See the "TARP Configuration Examples" section at the end of this chapter for an example of configuring DECnet OSI cluster aliases.

## Configuring Digital-Compatible Mode

If you have an old DECnet implementation of ES-IS in which the NSAP address advertised in an IS hello packet does not have the N-selector byte present, you may want to configure the Cisco IOS software to allow IS hello packets sent and received to ignore the N-selector byte. The N-selector byte is the last byte of the NSAP address.

To enable Digital-compatible mode, perform the following task in interface configuration mode:

| Task | Command |
|------|---------|
| Allow IS hello packets sent and received to ignore the N-selector byte. | clns dec-compatible |

## Allowing Security Option Packets to Pass

By default, the Cisco IOS software discards any packets with security options set. You can disable this behavior. To allow such packets to pass through, perform the following task in global configuration mode:

| Task | Command |
|------|---------|
| Allow the software to accept any packets it sees as set with security options. | **clns security pass-through** |

**NOTES**

The ISO CLNS routing software ignores the Record Route option, the Source Route option, and the QoS option other than congestion experienced. The Security option causes a packet to be rejected with a bad option indication.

## CONFIGURING CLNS OVER WANS

This section provides general information about running ISO CLNS over WANs.

You can use CLNS routing on serial interfaces with HDLC, PPP, LAPB, X.25, Frame Relay, DDR, or SMDS encapsulation. Both incoming and outgoing CLNS packets can be fast switched over PPP.

To use HDLC encapsulation, you must have a router at both ends of the link. If you use X.25 encapsulation, and if IS-IS or ISO IGRP is not used on an interface, you must manually enter the NSAP-to-X.121 address mapping. The LAPB, SMDS, Frame Relay, and X.25 encapsulations interoperate with other vendors.

Both ISO IGRP and IS-IS can be configured over WANs.

X.25 is not a broadcast medium and, therefore, does not broadcast protocols (such as ES-IS) that automatically advertise and record mappings between NSAP/NET (protocol addresses) and SNPA (media addresses). (With X.25, the SNPAs are the X.25 network addresses, or the X.121 addresses. These are usually assigned by the X.25 network provider.) If you use static routing, you must configure the NSAP-to-X.121 address mapping with the **x25 map** command.

Configuring a serial line to use CLNS over X.25 requires configuring the general X.25 information and the CLNS-specific information. First, configure the general X.25 information, and then enter the CLNS static mapping information.

See the "ISO CLNS over X.25 Example" section at the end of this chapter for an example of configuring CLNS over X.25.

## ENHANCING ISO CLNS PERFORMANCE

You generally do not need to change the router's default settings for CLNS packet switching, but there are some modifications you can make when you decide to make changes in your network's performance. The following sections describe ISO CLNS parameters that you can change:

- Specifying the MTU Size
- Disabling Checksums
- Disabling Fast Switching through the Cache
- Setting the Congestion Threshold
- Transmitting Error Protocol Data Units (ERPDUs)
- Controlling Redirect Protocol Data Units (RDPDUs)
- Configuring Parameters for Locally Sourced Packets

---

**NOTES**

See the "Performance Parameters Example" section at the end of this chapter for examples of configuring various performance parameters.

---

### Specifying the MTU Size

All interfaces have a default maximum packet size. To reduce fragmentation, however, you can set the MTU size of the packets sent on the interface. The minimum value is 512; the default and maximum packet size depends on the interface type.

Changing the MTU value with the **mtu** interface configuration command can affect the CLNS MTU value. If the CLNS MTU is at its maximum given the interface MTU, the CLNS MTU will change with the interface MTU. The reverse, however, is not true; changing the CLNS MTU value has no effect on the value for the **mtu** interface configuration command.

To set the CLNS MTU packet size for a specified interface, perform the following task in interface configuration mode:

| Task | Command |
|------|---------|
| Set the MTU size of the packets sent on the interface. | **clns mtu** *size* |

---

**NOTES**

The CTR card does not support the switching of frames larger than 4472 bytes. Interoperability problems might occur if CTR cards are intermixed with other Token Ring cards on the same network. These problems can be minimized by lowering the CLNS MTU sizes to be the same on all routers on the network.

---

## Disabling Checksums

When the ISO CLNS routing software originates a CLNS packet, it generates checksums by default. To disable this function, perform the following task in interface configuration mode:

| Task | Command |
|------|---------|
| Disable checksum generation. | no clns checksum |

**— NOTES**

Enabling checksum generation has no effect on routing packets (ES-IS, ISO IGRP, and IS-IS) originated by the router; it applies to pings and traceroute packets.

## Disabling Fast Switching through the Cache

Fast switching through the cache is enabled by default for all supported interfaces. To disable fast switching, perform the following task in interface configuration mode:

| Task | Command |
|------|---------|
| Disable fast switching. | no clns route-cache |

**— NOTES**

The cache still exists and is used after the **no clns route-cache** interface configuration command is used; the software just does not do fast switching through the cache.

## Setting the Congestion Threshold

If a router configured for CLNS experiences congestion, it sets the congestion-experienced bit. You can set the congestion threshold on a per-interface basis. By setting this threshold, you cause the system to set the congestion-experienced bit if the output queue has more than the specified number of packets in it.

To set the congestion threshold, perform the following task in interface configuration mode:

| Task | Command |
|------|---------|
| Set the congestion threshold. | clns congestion-threshold *number* |

## Transmitting Error Protocol Data Units (ERPDUs)

When a CLNS packet is received, the routing software looks in the routing table for the next hop. If it does not find one, the packet is discarded and an error protocol data unit (ERPDU) is sent.

You can set an interval between ERPDUs. Doing so reduces bandwidth if this feature is disabled. When you set the minimum interval between ERPDUs, the Cisco IOS software does not send ERPDUs more frequently than one per interface per ten milliseconds.

To transmit ERPDUs, perform the following tasks in interface configuration mode:

| Task | Command |
|---|---|
| **Step 1** Send an ERPDU when the routing software detects an error in a data PDU; this is enabled by default. | **clns send-erpdu** |
| **Step 2** Set the minimum interval, in milliseconds, between ERPDUs. | **clns erpdu-interval** *milliseconds* |

## Controlling Redirect Protocol Data Units (RDPDUs)

If a packet is sent out the same interface it came in on, a redirect protocol data unit (RDPDU) also can be sent to the sender of the packet. You can control RDPDUs in the following ways:

- By default, CLNS sends RDPDUs when a better route for a given host is known. You can disable this feature. Disabling this feature reduces bandwidth, because packets may continue to go unnecessarily through the router.

- You can set the interval times between RDPDUs.

— **NOTES**

SNPA masks are never sent, and RDPDUs are ignored by the Cisco IOS software when the router is acting as an IS.

To control RDPDUs, perform either of the following tasks in interface configuration mode:

| Task | Command |
|---|---|
| Send redirect PDUs when a better route for a given host is known. | **clns send-rdpdu** |
| Set the minimum interval time, in milliseconds, between RDPDUs. | **clns rdpdu-interval** *milliseconds* |

## Configuring Parameters for Locally Sourced Packets

To configure parameters for packets originated by a specified router, perform either of the following tasks in global configuration mode:

| Task | Command |
|------|---------|
| Specify in seconds the initial lifetime for locally generated packets. | clns packet-lifetime *seconds* |
| Specify whether to request ERPDUs on packets originated by the router. | clns want-erpdu |

You should set the packet lifetime low in an internetwork that has frequent loops.

> **NOTES**
>
> The **clns want-erpdu** global configuration command has no effect on routing packets (ES-IS, ISO IGRP, and IS-IS) originated by the router; it applies to pings and traceroute packets.

## MONITORING AND MAINTAINING THE ISO CLNS NETWORK

The following EXEC commands monitor and maintain the ISO CLNS caches, tables, and databases:

| Task | Command |
|------|---------|
| Clears and reinitializes the CLNS routing cache. | clear clns cache |
| Removes ES neighbor information from the adjacency database. | clear clns es-neighbors |
| Removes IS neighbor information from the adjacency database. | clear clns is-neighbors |
| Removes CLNS neighbor information from the adjacency database. | clear clns neighbors |
| Removes dynamically derived CLNS routing information. | clear clns route |
| Invokes a diagnostic tool for testing connectivity | ping clns {*host* \| *address*} |
| Displays information about the CLNS network. | show clns |
| Displays the entries in the CLNS routing cache. | show clns cache |
| Displays ES neighbor entries, including the associated areas. | show clns es-neighbors [*type number*] [**detail**] |

| Task | Command |
|------|---------|
| Displays filter expressions. | **show clns filter-expr** [*name*] [**detail**] |
| Displays filter sets. | **show clns filter-set** [*name*] |
| Lists the CLNS-specific or ES-IS information about each interface. | **show clns interface** [*type number*] |
| Displays IS neighbor entries, according to the area in which they are located. | **show clns is-neighbors** [*type number*] [**detail**] |
| Displays both ES and IS neighbors. | **show clns neighbors** [*type number*] [**detail**] |
| Lists the protocol-specific information for each IS-IS or ISO IGRP routing process in this router. | **show clns protocol** [*domain* \| *area-tag*] |
| Displays all the destinations to which this router knows how to route packets. | **show clns route** [*nsap*] |
| Displays information about the CLNS packets this router has seen. | **show clns traffic** |
| Displays the IS-IS link state database. | **show isis database** [**level-1**] [**level-2**] [**l1**] [**l2**] [**detail**] [*lspid*] |
| Displays the IS-IS Level 1 routing table. | **show isis routes** |
| Displays a history of the SPF calculations for IS-IS. | **show isis spf-log** |
| Displays all route maps configured or only the one specified. | **show route-map** [*map-name*] |
| Discovers the paths taken to a specified destination by packets in the network. | **trace clns** *destination* |
| Displays the routing table in which the specified CLNS destination is found. | **which-route** {*nsap-address* \| *clns-name*} |

## CONFIGURING TARP ON ISO CLNS

Some applications (typically used by telephone companies) running on Synchronous Optical Network (SONET) devices identify these devices by a target identifier (TID). Therefore, it is necessary for the router to cache TID-to-network address mappings. Because these applications usually run over OSI, the network addresses involved in the mapping are OSI NSAPs.

When a device must send a packet to another device it does not know about (that is, it does not have information about the NSAP address corresponding to the remote device's TID), the device needs a way to request this information directly from the device or from an intermediate device in the network. This functionality is provided by an address resolution protocol called Target Identifier Address Resolution Protocol (TARP).

Requests for information and associated responses are sent as TARP protocol data units (PDUs), which are sent as CLNP data packets. TARP PDUs are distinguished by a unique N-selector in the NSAP address. Following are the five types of TARP PDUs:

- Type 1—Sent when a device has a TID for which it has no matching NSAP. Type 1 PDUs are sent to all Level 1 (IS-IS and ES-IS) neighbors. If no response is received within the specified time limit, a Type 2 PDU is sent. To prevent packet looping, a loop detection buffer is maintained on the router. A Type 1 PDU is sent when you use the **tarp resolve** command.

- Type 2—Sent when a device has a TID for which it has no matching NSAP and no response was received from a Type 1 PDU. Type 2 PDUs are sent to all Level 1 and Level 2 neighbors. A time limit for Type 2 PDUs can also be specified. A Type 2 PDU is sent when you use the **tarp resolve** command and specify the option 2.

- Type 3—Sent as a response to a Type 1, Type 2, or Type 5 PDU. Type 3 PDUs are sent directly to the originator of the request.

- Type 4—Sent as a notification when a change occurs locally (for example, a TID or NSAP change). A Type 4 PDU is sent when you use the **tarp query** command.

- Type 5—Sent when a device needs a TID that corresponds to a specific NSAP. Unlike Type 1 and Type 2 PDUs that are sent to all Level 1 and Level 2 neighbors, a Type 5 PDU is sent only to a particular router.

In addition to the type, TARP PDUs contain the sender's NSAP, the sender's TID, and the target's TID (if the PDU is a Type 1 or Type 2).

## TARP Configuration Task List

To configure TARP on the router, complete the tasks in the following sections (only the first task is required, all other tasks are optional):

- Enabling TARP and Configure a TARP TID
- Disabling TARP Caching
- Disabling TARP PDU Origination and Propagation
- Configuring Multiple NSAP Addresses
- Configuring Static TARP Adjacency and Blacklist Adjacency
- Determining TIDs and NSAPs
- Configuring TARP Timers
- Configuring Miscellaneous TARP PDU Information
- Monitoring and Maintaining the TARP Protocol

For several examples of configuring TARP, see the "TARP Configuration Examples" section at the end of this chapter.

### Enabling TARP and Configure a TARP TID

TARP must be explicitly enabled before the TARP functionality becomes available and the router must have a TID assigned. Also, before TARP packets can be sent out on an interface, each interface must have TARP enabled and the interface must be able to propagate TARP PDUs.

The router will use the CLNS capability to send and receive TARP PDUs. If the router is configured as an IS, the router must be running IS-IS. If the router is configured as an ES, the router must be running ES-IS.

To turn on the TARP functionality, perform the following tasks in global configuration mode:

| Task | Command |
|------|---------|
| **Step 1** Turn on the TARP functionality. | **tarp run** |
| **Step 2** Assign a TID to the router. | **tarp tid** *tid* |

To enable TARP on one or more interfaces, perform the following task in interface configuration mode:

| Task | Command |
|------|---------|
| Enable TARP on the interface. | **tarp enable** |

### Disabling TARP Caching

By default, TID-to-NSAP address mappings are stored in the TID cache. Disabling this capability clears the TID cache. Re-enabling this capability restores any previously cleared local entry and all static entries.

To disable TID-to-NSAP address mapping in the TID cache, perform the following task in global configuration mode:

| Task | Command |
|------|---------|
| Disable TARP TID-to-NSAP address mapping. | **no tarp allow-caching** |

### Disabling TARP PDU Origination and Propagation

By default, the router originates TARP PDUs and propagates TARP PDUs to its neighbors, and the interface propagates TARP PDUs to its neighbor. Disabling these capabilities means that the router no longer originates TARP PDUs, and the router and the specific interface no longer propagate TARP PDUs received from other routers.

To disable origination and propagation of TARP PDUs, perform the following tasks in global configuration mode:

| Task | Command |
|------|---------|
| **Step 1**  Disable TARP PDU origination. | **no tarp originate** |
| **Step 2**  Disable global propagation of TARP PDUs. | **no tarp global-propagate** |

To disable propagation of TARP PDUs on a specific interface, perform the following task in interface configuration mode:

| Task | Command |
|------|---------|
| Disable propagation of TARP PDUs on the interface. | **no tarp propagate** |

## Configuring Multiple NSAP Addresses

A router may have more than one NSAP address. When a request for an NSAP is sent (Type 1 or Type 2 PDU), the first NSAP address is returned. To receive all NSAP addresses associated with the router, enter a TID-to-NSAP static route in the TID cache for each NSAP address.

To create a TID-to-NSAP static route, perform the following task in global configuration mode:

| Task | Command |
|------|---------|
| Enter a TID-to-NSAP static route. | **tarp map** *tid nsap* |

## Configuring Static TARP Adjacency and Blacklist Adjacency

In addition to all its IS-IS/ES-IS adjacencies, a TARP router propagates PDUs to all its static TARP adjacencies. If a router is not running TARP, the router discards TARP PDUs rather than propagating the PDUs to all its adjacencies. To allow TARP to bypass routers enroute that may not have TARP running, TARP provides a static TARP adjacency capability. Static adjacencies are maintained in a special queue.

To create a static TARP adjacency, perform the following task in global configuration mode:

| Task | Command |
|------|---------|
| Enter a static TARP adjacency. | **tarp route-static** *nsap* |

To stop TARP from propagating PDUs to an IS-IS/ES-IS adjacency that may not have TARP running, TARP provides a blacklist adjacency capability. The router will not propagate TARP PDUs to blacklisted routers.

To blacklist a router, perform the following task in global configuration mode:

| Task | Command |
| --- | --- |
| Bypass a router not running TARP. | **tarp blacklist-adjacency** *nsap* |

## Determining TIDs and NSAPs

To determine an NSAP address for a TID or a TID for an NSAP address, perform the following tasks in EXEC mode:

| Task | | Command |
| --- | --- | --- |
| **Step 1** | Get the TID associated with a specific NSAP. | **tarp query** *nsap* |
| **Step 2** | Get the NSAP associated with a specific TID. | **tarp resolve** *tid* [1 | 2] |

To determine the TID, the router first checks the local TID cache. If there is a TID entry in the local TID cache, the requested information is displayed. If there is no TID entry in the local TID cache, a TARP Type 5 PDU is sent out to the specified NSAP address.

To determine the NSAP address, the router first checks the local TID cache. If there is an NSAP entry in the local TID cache, the requested information is displayed. If there is no NSAP entry in the local TID cache, a TARP Type 1 or Type 2 PDU is sent out. By default, a Type 1 PDU is sent to all Level 1 (IS-IS and ES-IS) neighbors. If a response is received, the requested information is displayed. If a response is not received within the response time, a Type 2 PDU is sent to all Level 1 and Level 2 neighbors. Specifying the EXEC command **tarp resolve** *tid* **2** causes only a Type 2 PDU to be sent.

You can configure the length of time that the router will wait for a response (in the form of a Type 3 PDU).

## Configuring TARP Timers

TARP timers provide default values and typically do not need to be changed.

You can configure the amount of time that the router waits to receive a response from a Type 1 PDU, a Type 2 PDU, and a Type 5 PDU. In addition, you can also configure the PDU's lifetime based on the number of hops.

You can also set timers that control how long dynamically created TARP entries remain in the TID cache, and how long the system ID-to-sequence number mapping entry remains in the loop detection buffer table. The loop detection buffer table prevents TARP PDUs from looping.

To configure TARP PDU timers, control PDU lifetime, and set how long entries remain in cache, perform the following tasks in global configuration mode:

| Task | Command |
|------|---------|
| **Step 1** Configure the number of seconds that the router will wait for a response from a TARP Type 1 PDU. | **tarp t1-response-timer** *seconds* |
| **Step 2** Configure the number of seconds that the router will wait for a response from a TARP Type 2 PDU. | **tarp t2-response-timer** *seconds* |
| **Step 3** Configure the number of seconds that the router will wait for a response from a TARP Type 2 PDU after the default timer has expired. | **tarp post-t2-response-timer** *seconds* |
| **Step 4** Configure the number of seconds that the router will wait for a response from a TARP Type 5 PDU. | **tarp arp-request-timer** *seconds* |
| **Step 5** Configure the number of routers that a TARP PDU can traverse before it is discarded. | **tarp lifetime** *hops* |
| **Step 6** Configure the number of seconds a dynamically-created TARP entry remains in the TID cache. | **tarp cache-timer** *seconds* |
| **Step 7** Configure the number of seconds that a system ID-to-sequence number mapping entry remains in the loop detection buffer table. | **tarp ldb-timer** *seconds* |

## Configuring Miscellaneous TARP PDU Information

TARP default PDU values typically do not need to be changed.

You can configure the sequence number of the TARP PDU, set the update remote cache bit used to control whether the remote router updates its cache, specify the N-selector used in the PDU to indicate a TARP PDU, and specify the network protocol type used in outgoing PDUs.

To configure miscellaneous PDU information, perform the following tasks in global configuration mode:

| Task | | Command |
|---|---|---|
| **Step 1** | Change the sequence number in the next outgoing TARP PDU. | **tarp sequence-number** *number* |
| **Step 2** | Set the update remote cache bit in all subsequent outgoing TARP PDUs so that the remote router does or does not update the cache. | **tarp urc** [0 \| 1] |
| **Step 3** | Specify the N-selector used to identify TARP PDUs. | **tarp** *selector hex-digit* |
| **Step 4** | Specify the protocol type used in outgoing TARP PDUs. Only FE (to indicate CLNP) is supported. | **tarp** *protocol hex-digit* |

## Monitoring and Maintaining the TARP Protocol

Use the following EXEC commands to monitor and maintain the TARP caches, tables, and databases:

| Task | | Command |
|---|---|---|
| **Step 1** | Reset the TARP counters that are shown with the **show tarp traffic** command. | **clear tarp counters** |
| **Step 2** | Remove all system ID-to-sequence number mapping entries in the TARP loop detection buffer table. | **clear tarp ldb-table** |
| **Step 3** | Remove all dynamically created TARP TID-to-NSAP address mapping entries in the TID cache. | **clear tarp tid-table** |
| **Step 4** | Display all global TARP parameters. | **show tarp** |
| **Step 5** | List all adjacencies that are blacklisted (that is, adjacencies that will not receive propagated TARP PDUs). | **show tarp blacklisted-adjacencies** |
| **Step 6** | Display information about a specific TARP router stored in the local TID cache. | **show tarp host** *tid* |
| **Step 7** | List all interfaces on the router that are TARP enabled. | **show tarp interface** [*type number*] |

| Task | Command |
|------|---------|
| **Step 8** Display the contents of the loop detection buffer table. | show tarp ldb |
| **Step 9** List all the static entries in the TID cache. | show tarp map |
| **Step 10** List all static TARP adjacencies. | show tarp static-adjacencies |
| **Step 11** Display information about the entries in the TID cache. | show tarp tid-cache |
| **Step 12** Display statistics about TARP PDUs. | show tarp traffic |

## ISO CLNS CONFIGURATION EXAMPLES

The following sections provide configuration examples of both intra- and interdomain static and dynamic routing using static, ISO IGRP, and IS-IS routing techniques:

- NETs Configuration Examples
- Dynamic Routing within the Same Area Example
- Dynamic Routing in More Than One Area Example
- Dynamic Routing in Overlapping Areas Example
- Dynamic Interdomain Routing Example
- IS-IS Routing Configuration Examples
- Router in Two Areas Example
- Basic Static Routing Examples
- Static Intradomain Routing Example
- Static Interdomain Routing Example
- CLNS Filter Example
- Route Map Examples
- DECnet Cluster Aliases Example
- ISO CLNS over X.25 Example
- Performance Parameters Example
- TARP Configuration Examples

### NETs Configuration Examples

The following are simple examples of configuring NETs for both ISO IGRP and IS-IS.

## ISO IGRP

The following example illustrates specifying an NET:

```
router iso-igrp Finance
  net 47.0004.004d.0001.0000.0c11.1111.00
```

The following example illustrates using a name for an NET:

```
clns host NAME 39.0001.0000.0c00.1111.00
router iso-igrp Marketing
  net NAME
```

The use of this **net** router configuration command configures the system ID, area address, and domain address. Only a single NET per routing process is allowed.

```
router iso-igrp local
  net 49.0001.0000.0c00.1111.00
```

## IS-IS

The following example illustrates specifying a single NET:

```
router isis Pieinthesky
  net 47.0004.004d.0001.0000.0c11.1111.00
```

The following example illustrates using a name for an NET:

```
clns host NAME 39.0001.0000.0c00.1111.00
router isis
  net NAME
```

### IS-IS Multihoming Example

The following example illustrates the assignment of three separate area addresses for a single router using **net** commands. Traffic received that includes an area address of 47.0004.004d.0001, 47.0004.004d.0002, or 47.0004.004d.0003 and that has the same system ID is forwarded to this router.

```
router isis eng-area1
!  ¦       IS-IS Area¦    System ID¦ S¦
  net 47.0004.004d.0001.0000.0C00.1111.00
  net 47.0004.004d.0002.0000.0C00.1111.00
  net 47.0004.004d.0003.0000.0C00.1111.00
```

## Dynamic Routing within the Same Area Example

Figure 13–5 and the example configuration that follows illustrate how to configure dynamic routing within a routing domain. The router can exist in one or more areas within the domain. The router named Router A exists in a single area.

*Figure 13–5*
*CLNS Dynamic Routing*
*within a Single Area.*

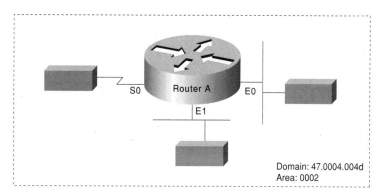

Domain: 47.0004.004d
Area: 0002

```
! define a tag castor for the routing process
router iso-igrp castor
! configure the net for the process in area 2, domain 47.0004.004d
 net 47.0004.004d.0002.0000.0C00.0506.00
! specify iso-igrp routing using the previously specified tag castor
interface ethernet 0
 clns router iso-igrp castor
 ! specify iso-igrp routing using the previously specified tag castor
interface ethernet 1
 clns router iso-igrp castor
! specify iso-igrp routing using the previously specified tag castor
interface serial 0
 clns router iso-igrp castor
```

## Dynamic Routing in More Than One Area Example

Figure 13–6 and the example configuration that follows illustrate how to configure a router named Router A that exists in two areas.

*Figure 13–6*
*CLNS Dynamic Routing*
*within Two Areas.*

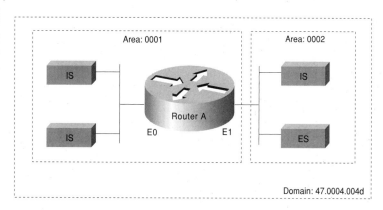

Domain: 47.0004.004d

```
! define a tag orion for the routing process
router iso-igrp orion
! configure the net for the process in area 1, domain 47.0004.004d
 net 47.0004.004d.0001.212223242526.00
! specify iso-igrp routing using the previously specified tag orion
interface ethernet 0
 clns router iso-igrp orion
! specify iso-igrp routing using the previously specified tag orion
interface ethernet 1
 clns router iso-igrp orion
```

## Dynamic Routing in Overlapping Areas Example

The example that follows illustrates how to configure a router with overlapping areas:

```
! define a tag capricorn for the routing process
router iso-igrp capricorn
! configure the NET for the process in area 3, domain 47.0004.004d
 net 47.0004.004d.0003.0000.0C00.0508.00
! define a tag cancer for the routing process
router iso-igrp cancer
! configure the NET for the process in area 4, domain 47.0004.004d
 net 47.0004.004d.0004.0000.0C00.0506.00
! specify iso-igrp routing on interface ethernet 0 using the tag capricorn
interface ethernet 0
 clns router iso-igrp capricorn
! specify iso-igrp routing on interface ethernet 1 using the tags capricorn and cancer
interface ethernet 1
 clns router iso-igrp capricorn
 clns router iso-igrp cancer
! specify iso-igrp routing on interface ethernet 2 using the tag cancer
interface ethernet 2
 clns router iso-igrp cancer
```

## Dynamic Interdomain Routing Example

Figure 13–7 and the configurations that follow illustrate how to configure three domains that are to be transparently connected.

*Figure 13–7*
*CLNS Dynamic*
*Interdomain Routing.*

### Router Chicago

The following configuration shows how to configure Router Chicago for dynamic interdomain routing:

```
! define a tag A for the routing process
router iso-igrp A
! configure the NET for the process in area 2, domain 47.0007.0200
 net 47.0007.0200.0002.0102.0104.0506.00
! redistribute iso-igrp routing information throughout domain A
redistribute iso-igrp B
! define a tag B for the routing process
router iso-igrp B
! configure the NET for the process in area 3, domain 47.0006.0200
 net 47.0006.0200.0003.0102.0104.0506.00
! redistribute iso-igrp routing information throughout domain B
redistribute iso-igrp A
! specify iso-igrp routing with the tag A
interface ethernet 0
clns router iso-igrp A
! specify iso-igrp routing with the tag B
interface serial 0
clns router iso-igrp B
```

### Router Detroit

The following configuration shows how to configure Router Detroit for dynamic interdomain routing. Comment lines have been eliminated from this example to avoid redundancy.

```
router iso-igrp B
 net 47.0006.0200.0004.0102.0104.0506.00
 redistribute iso-igrp C
router iso-igrp C
 net 47.0008.0200.0005.0102.01040.506.00
 redistribute iso-igrp B
interface serial 0
 clns router iso-igrp B
interface serial 1
 clns router iso-igrp C
```

Chicago injects a prefix route for domain A into domain B. Domain B injects this prefix route and a prefix route for domain B into domain C.

You also can configure a border router between domain A and domain C.

## IS-IS Routing Configuration Examples

The examples that follow illustrate the basic syntax and configuration command sequence for IS-IS routing.

### Level 1 and Level 2 Routing

The following example illustrates using the IS-IS protocol to configure a single area address for Level 1 and Level 2 routing:

```
! route dynamically using the is-is protocol
router isis
! configure the NET for the process in area 47.0004.004d.0001
 net 47.0004.004d.0001.0000.0c00.1111.00
! enable is-is routing on ethernet 0
interface ethernet 0
 clns router isis
! enable is-is routing on ethernet 1
interface ethernet 1
 clns router isis
! enable is-is routing on serial 0
interface serial 0
 clns router isis
```

### Level 2 Routing Only

The following example illustrates a similar configuration, featuring a single area address being used for specification of Level 1 and Level 2 routing. In this case, however, interface serial interface 0 is configured for Level 2 routing only. Most comment lines have been eliminated from this example to avoid redundancy.

```
router isis
 net 47.0004.004d.0001.0000.0c00.1111.00
interface ethernet 0
 clns router isis
interface ethernet 1
 clns router isis
interface serial 0
 clns router isis
! configure a level 2 adjacency only for interface serial 0
 isis circuit-type level-2-only
```

### OSI Configuration

The following example illustrates an OSI configuration example. In this example, IS-IS runs with two area addresses, metrics tailored, and different circuit types specified for each interface. Most comment lines have been eliminated from this example to avoid redundancy.

```
! enable is-is routing in area 1
router isis area1
! Router is in areas 47.0004.004d.0001 and 47.0004.004d.0011
net 47.0004.004d.0001.0000.0c11.1111.00
net 47.0004.004d.0011.0000.0c11.1111.00
! enable the router to operate as a station router and an interarea router
is-type level-1-2
!
interface ethernet 0
 clns router isis area1
! specify a cost of 5 for the level-1 routes
```

```
 isis metric 5 level-1
! establish a level-1 adjacency
 isis circuit-type level-1
!
interface ethernet 1
 clns router isis area1
 isis metric 2 level-2
 isis circuit-type level-2-only
!
interface serial 0
 clns router isis area1
 isis circuit-type level-1-2
! set the priority for serial 0 to 3 for a level-1 adjacency
 isis priority 3 level-1
 isis priority 1 level-2
```

### *ISO CLNS Dynamic Route Redistribution*

The following example illustrates route redistribution between IS-IS and ISO IGRP domains. In this case, the IS-IS domain is on Ethernet interface 0; the ISO IGRP domain is on serial interface 0. The IS-IS routing process is assigned a null tag; the ISO IGRP routing process is assigned a tag of *remote-domain*. Most comment lines have been eliminated from this example to avoid redundancy.

```
router isis
 net 39.0001.0001.0000.0c00.1111.00
! redistribute iso-igrp routing information throughout remote-domain
redistribute iso-igrp remote-domain
!
router iso-igrp remote-domain
 net 39.0002.0001.0000.0c00.1111.00
! redistribute is-is routing information
redistribute isis
!
interface ethernet 0
 clns router isis
!
interface serial 0
 clns router iso-igrp remote
```

## Router in Two Areas Example

The following two examples show how to configure a router in two areas. The first example configures ISO IGRP; the second configures IS-IS.

## *ISO IGRP*

In the following example, the router is in domain 49.0001 and has a system ID of aaaa.aaaa.aaaa. The router is in two areas: 31 and 40 (decimal). Figure 13–8 illustrates this configuration.

*Figure 13–8*

*ISO IGRP Configuration.*

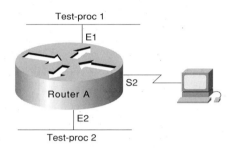

```
router iso-igrp test-proc1
! 001F in the following net is the hex value for area 31
 net 49.0001.001F.aaaa.aaaa.aaaa.00
router iso-igrp test-proc2
! 0028 in the following net is the hex value for area 40
 net 49.0001.0028.aaaa.aaaa.aaaa.00
!
interface ethernet 1
 clns router iso-igrp test-proc1
!
interface serial 2
 clns router iso-igrp test-proc1
!
interface ethernet 2
 clns router iso-igrp test-proc2
```

## *IS-IS*

To run IS-IS instead of ISO IGRP, use this configuration. The illustration in Figure 13–8 still applies. Ethernet interface 2 is configured for IS-IS routing and is assigned the tag of test-proc2.

```
router iso-igrp test-proc1
 net 49.0002.0002.bbbb.bbbb.bbbb.00
router isis test-proc2
 net 49.0001.0002.aaaa.aaaa.aaaa.00
!
interface ethernet 1
 clns router iso-igrp test-proc1
!
interface serial 2
clns router iso-igrp test-proc1
!
interface ethernet 2
 clns router is-is test-proc2
```

To allow CLNS packets only to blindly pass through an interface without routing updates, you could use a simple configuration, such as the following:

```
clns routing
interface serial 2
! permits serial 2 to pass CLNS packets without having CLNS routing turned on
 clns enable
```

## Basic Static Routing Examples

Configuring FDDI, Ethernets, Token Rings, and serial lines for CLNS can be as simple as enabling CLNS on the interfaces. This is all that is ever required on serial lines using HDLC encapsulation. If all systems on an Ethernet or Token Ring support ISO 9542 ES-IS, then nothing else is required.

### Example 1

In the following example, an Ethernet and a serial line can be configured as follows:

```
! enable clns packets to be routed
 clns routing
! configure the following network entity title for the routing process
 clns net 47.0004.004d.0055.0000.0C00.BF3B.00
! pass ISO CLNS traffic on ethernet 0 to end systems without routing
interface ethernet 0
 clns enable
! pass ISO CLNS traffic on serial 0 to end systems without routing
interface serial 0
 clns enable
! create a static route for the interface
 clns route 47.0004.004d.0099 serial 0
 clns route 47.0005 serial 0
```

### Example 2

The following is a more complete example of CLNS static routing on a system with two Ethernet interfaces. After configuring routing, you define a NET and enable CLNS on the Ethernet 0 and Ethernet 1 interfaces. You must then define an ES neighbor and define a static route with the **clns route** global configuration command, as shown. In this situation, there is an ES on Ethernet 1 that does not support ES-IS. Figure 13–9 illustrates this network.

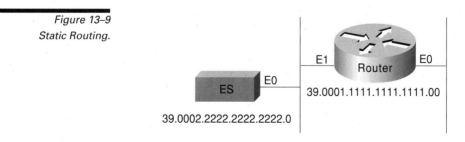

Figure 13–9
Static Routing.

ES E0
39.0002.2222.2222.2222.0

E1 Router E0
39.0001.1111.1111.1111.00

```
clns host sid 39.0001.1111.1111.1111.00
clns host bar 39.0002.2222.2222.2222.00
! assign a static address for the router
clns net sid
! enable CLNS packets to be routed
clns routing
! pass ISO CLNS packet traffic to end systems without routing them
interface ethernet 0
 clns enable
! pass ISO CLNS packet traffic to end systems without routing them
interface ethernet 1
 clns enable
! specify end system for static routing
clns es-neighbor bar 0000.0C00.62e7
! create an interface-static route to bar for packets with the following NSAP address
clns route 47.0004.000c bar
```

## Static Intradomain Routing Example

Figure 13–10 and the configurations that follow demonstrate how to use static routing inside of a domain. Imagine a company with branch offices in Detroit and Chicago, connected with an X.25 link. These offices are both in the domain named Sales.

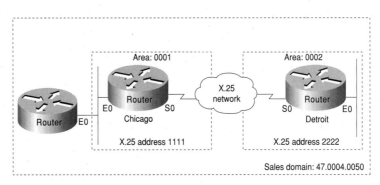

*Figure 13–10*
*CLNS X.25*
*Intradomain Routing.*

The following example shows one way to configure the router in Chicago:

```
! define the name chicago to be used in place of the following NSAP
clns host chicago 47.0004.0050.0001.0000.0c00.243b.00
! define the name detroit to be used in place of the following NSAP
clns host detroit 47.0004.0050.0002.0000.0c00.1e12.00
! enable ISO IGRP routing of CLNS packets
router iso-igrp sales
! configure net chicago, as defined above
 net chicago
! specify iso-igrp routing using the previously specified tag sales
interface ethernet 0
 clns router iso-igrp sales
! set the interface up as a DTE with X.25 encapsulation
```

```
interface serial 0
 encapsulation x25
 x25 address 1111
 x25 nvc 4
 ! specify iso-igrp routing using the previously specified tag sales
 clns router iso-igrp sales
 ! define a static mapping between Detroit's nsap and its X.121 address
 x25 map clns 2222 broadcast
```

This configuration brings up an X.25 virtual circuit between the router in Chicago and the router in Detroit. Routing updates will be sent across this link. This implies that the virtual circuit could be up continuously.

If the Chicago office should grow to contain multiple routers, it would be appropriate for each of those routers to know how to get to Detroit. Add the following command to redistribute information between routers in Chicago:

```
router iso-igrp sales
 redistribute static
```

## Static Interdomain Routing Example

Figure 13–11 and the example configurations that follow illustrate how to configure two routers that distribute information across domains. In this example, Router A (in domain Orion) and Router B (in domain Pleiades) communicate across a serial link.

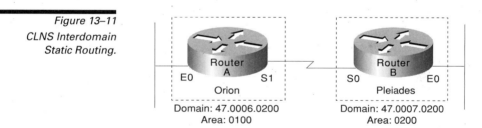

Figure 13–11
CLNS Interdomain
Static Routing.

Domain: 47.0006.0200          Domain: 47.0007.0200
Area: 0100                    Area: 0200

*Router A*

The following configuration shows how to configure Router A for static interdomain routing:

```
 ! define tag orion for net 47.0006.0200.0100.0102.0304.0506.00
router iso-igrp orion
 ! configure the following network entity title for the routing process
 net 47.0006.0200.0100.0102.0304.0506.00
 ! define the tag bar to be used in place of Router B's NSAP
clns host bar 47.0007.0200.0200.1112.1314.1516.00
 ! specify iso-igrp routing using the previously specified tag orion
interface ethernet 0
 clns router iso-igrp orion
 ! pass ISO CLNS traffic to end systems without routing
interface serial 1
```

```
 clns enable
! configure a static route to Router B
 clns route 39.0001 bar
```

*Router B*

The following configuration shows how to configure Router B for static interdomain routing:

```
router iso-igrp pleiades
! configure the network entity title for the routing process
 net 47.0007.0200.0200.1112.1314.1516.00
! define the name sid to be used in place of Router A's NSAP
 clns host sid 47.0006.0200.0100.0001.0102.0304.0506.00
! specify iso-igrp routing using the previously specified tag pleiades
interface ethernet 0
 clns router iso-igrp pleiades
! pass ISO CLNS traffic to end systems without routing
interface serial 0
 clns enable
! pass packets bound for sid in domain 47.0006.0200 through serial 0
 clns route 47.0006.0200 sid
```

CLNS routing updates will not be sent on the serial link; however, CLNS packets will be sent and received over the serial link.

## CLNS Filter Example

The following example allows packets if the address starts with either 47.0005 or 47.0023. It implicitly denies any other address.

```
clns filter-set US-OR-NORDUNET permit 47.0005...
clns filter-set US-OR-NORDUNET permit 47.0023...
```

## Route Map Examples

The following example redistributes two types of routes into the integrated IS-IS routing table (supporting both IP and CLNS). The first routes are OSPF external IP routes with tag 5, and these are inserted into level-2 IS-IS LSPs with a metric of 5. The second routes are ISO IGRP derived CLNS prefix routes that match CLNS filter expression "osifilter." These are redistributed into IS-IS as level-2 LSPs with a metric of 30.

```
router isis
 redistribute ospf 109 route-map ipmap
 redistribute iso-igrp nsfnet route-map osimap
 !
 route-map ipmap permit
 match route-type external
 match tag 5
 set metric 5
 set level level-2
 !
 route-map osimap permit
```

```
match clns address osifilter
set metric 30
clns filter-set osifilter permit 47.0005.80FF.FF00
```

Given the following configuration, a RIP learned route for network 160.89.0.0 and an ISO IGRP learned route with prefix 49.0001.0002 will be redistributed into an IS-IS level-2 LSP with a metric of 5:

```
router isis
 redistribute rip route-map ourmap
 redistribute iso-igrp remote route-map ourmap
 !
 route-map ourmap permit
 match ip address 1
 match clns address ourprefix
 set metric 5
 set level level-2
 !
 access-list 1 permit 160.89.0.0 0.0.255.255
 clns filter-set ourprefix permit 49.0001.0002...
```

## DECnet Cluster Aliases Example

The following example enables cluster aliasing for CLNS:

```
clns routing
clns nsap 47.0004.004d.0001.0000.0C00.1111.00
router iso-igrp pleiades
! enable cluster aliasing on interface ethernet 0
interface ethernet 0
 clns cluster-alias
! enable cluster aliasing on interface ethernet 1
interface ethernet 1
 clns cluster-alias
```

The following example denies packets with an address that starts with 39.840F, but allows any other address:

```
clns filter-set NO-ANSI deny 38.840F...
clns filter-set NO-ANSI permit default
```

The following example builds a filter that accepts end system adjacencies with only two systems, based only on their system IDs:

```
clns filter-set ourfriends...0000.0c00.1234.**
clns filter-set ourfriends...0000.0c00.125a.**

interface ethernet 0
 clns adjacency-filter es ourfriends
```

## ISO CLNS over X.25 Example

In the following example, serial interface 1 on Router A acts as a DTE for X.25. It permits broadcasts to pass through. Router B is an IS, which has a CLNS address of 49.0001.bbbb.bbbb.bbbb.00

and an X.121 address of 31102. Router A has a CLNS address of 49.0001.aaaa.aaaa.aaaa.00 and an address of 31101. Figure 13–12 illustrates this configuration.

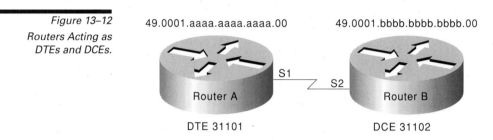

*Figure 13–12*
*Routers Acting as DTEs and DCEs.*

49.0001.aaaa.aaaa.aaaa.00          49.0001.bbbb.bbbb.bbbb.00

S1
S2

Router A          Router B

DTE 31101          DCE 31102

### Router A

```
router iso-igrp test-proc
net 49.0001.aaaa.aaaa.aaaa.00
!
interface serial 1
 clns router iso-igrp test-proc
! assume the host is a DTE and encapsulates x.25
 encapsulation x25
! define the X.121 address of 31101 for serial 1
 X25 address 31101
! set up an entry for the other side of the X.25 link (Router B)
 x25 map clns 31101 broadcast
```

### Router B

```
router iso-igrp test-proc
 net 49.0001.bbbb.bbbb.bbbb.00
!
interface serial 2
 clns router iso-igrp test-proc
! configure this side as a DCE
 encapsulation x25-dce
! define the X.121 address of 31102 for serial 2
 X25 address 31102
! configure the NSAP of Router A and accept reverse charges
 x25 map clns 31101 broadcast accept-reverse
```

## Performance Parameters Example

The following example shows how to set ES hello packet and IS hello packet parameters in a simple ISO IGRP configuration, as well as the MTU for a serial interface:

```
router iso-igrp xavier
 net 49.0001.004d.0002.0000.0C00.0506.00
! send IS/ES hellos every 45 seconds
clns configuration-time 45
```

```
! recipients of the hello packets keep info. in the hellos for 2 minutes
clns holding-time 120
! specify an mtu of 978 bytes; generally, do not alter the default mtu value
interface serial 2
 clns mtu 978
```

## TARP Configuration Examples

The following two sections provide basic and complex examples of TARP configuration.

### Basic TARP Configuration Example

The following example enables TARP on the router and interface Ethernet 0. The router is assigned the TID *myname*.

```
clns routing
tarp run
tarp tid myname

interface ethernet 0
 tarp enable
```

### Complex TARP Configuration Example

Figure 13–13 and the following example show how to enable TARP on Router A and on interface Ethernet 0, and assign the TID *myname*. A static route is created from Router A (49.0001.1111.1111.1111.00) to Router D (49.0004.1234.1234.1234.00), so that Router D can receive TARP PDUs, because Router C is not TARP capable. A blacklist adjacency is also created on Router A for Router B (49.001.7777.7777.7777.00), so that Router A does not send any TARP PDUs to Router B.

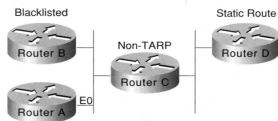

*Figure 13–13*
*Sample TARP Configuration.*

```
clns routing
tarp run
tarp cache-timer 300
tarp route-static 49.0004.1234.1234.1234.00
tarp blacklist-adjacency 49.0001.7777.7777.7777.00
tarp tid myname

interface ethernet 0
 tarp enable
```

# CHAPTER 14

# ISO CLNS Commands

The International Organization for Standardization (ISO) Connectionless Network Service (CLNS) protocol is a standard for the network layer of the OSI model.

Use the commands in this chapter to configure and monitor ISO CLNS networks.

---

**NOTES**

Cisco access servers currently support End System-to-Intermediate System (ES-IS), but not Intermediate System-to-Intermediate System (IS-IS).

---

### AREA-PASSWORD

Use the **area-password** router configuration command to configure the area authentication password. Use the **no area-password** command to disable the password.

> **area-password** *password*
> **no area-password** [*password*]

| Syntax | Description |
|--------|-------------|
| *password* | Password you assign. |

*Default*

No area authentication password is defined.

*Command Mode*

Router configuration

*Usage Guidelines*

This command first appeared in Cisco IOS Release 10.0.

This password is inserted in Level 1 (station router level) link-state PDUs, complete sequence number PDUs (CSNPs), and partial sequence number PDUs (PSNPs).

*Example*

The following example assigns an area authentication password:

```
router isis
  area-password angel
```

*Related Commands*

Search online for documentation for related commands.

**domain-password**


## CLEAR CLNS CACHE

Use the **clear clns cache** EXEC command to clear and reinitialize the CLNS routing cache.

> **clear clns cache**

*Syntax        Description*

This command has no arguments or keywords.


*Command Mode*

EXEC


*Usage Guidelines*

This command first appeared in Cisco IOS Release 10.0.


*Example*

The following example clears the CLNS routing cache:

```
clear clns cache
```

*Related Commands*

**show clns cache**


## CLEAR CLNS ES-NEIGHBORS

Use the **clear clns es-neighbors** EXEC command to remove end system (ES) neighbor information from the adjacency database.

> **clear clns es-neighbors**

*Syntax    Description*

This command has no arguments or keywords.

*Command Mode*

EXEC

*Usage Guidelines*

This command first appeared in Cisco IOS Release 10.0.

*Example*

The following example removes the ES neighbor information from the adjacency database:

```
clear clns es-neighbors
```

*Related Commands*

Search online for documentation for related commands.

**clear clns neighbors**
**show clns es-neighbors**

## CLEAR CLNS IS-NEIGHBORS

Use the **clear clns is-neighbors** EXEC command to remove intermediate system (IS) neighbor information from the adjacency database.

**clear clns is-neighbors**

*Syntax    Description*

This command has no arguments or keywords.

*Command Mode*

EXEC

*Usage Guidelines*

This command first appeared in Cisco IOS Release 10.0.

*Example*

The following example removes the IS neighbor information from the adjacency database:

```
clear clns is-neighbors
```

*Command Reference*

*Related Commands*

Search online for documentation for related commands.

**clear clns neighbors**
**show clns is-neighbors**

## CLEAR CLNS NEIGHBORS

Use the **clear clns neighbors** EXEC command to remove CLNS neighbor information from the adjacency database.

   **clear clns neighbors**

*Syntax     Description*

This command has no arguments or keywords.

*Command Mode*

EXEC

*Usage Guidelines*

This command first appeared in Cisco IOS Release 10.0.

*Example*

The following example removes the CLNS neighbor information from the adjacency database:

```
clear clns neighbors
```

*Related Commands*

Search online for documentation for related commands.

**clear clns es-neighbors**
**clear clns is-neighbors**
**show clns neighbors**

## CLEAR CLNS ROUTE

Use the **clear clns route** EXEC command to remove all of the dynamically derived CLNS routing information.

   **clear clns route**

*Syntax     Description*

This command has no arguments or keywords.

## Command Mode

EXEC

## Usage Guidelines

This command first appeared in Cisco IOS Release 10.0.

## Example

The following example removes all of the dynamically derived CLNS routing information:

```
clear clns route
```

## Related Commands

Search online for documentation for related commands.

**show clns route**

## CLEAR TARP COUNTERS

Use the **clear tarp counters** EXEC command to clear all Target Identifier Address Resolution Protocol (TARP) counters that are shown with the **show tarp traffic** command.

**clear tarp counters**

## Syntax       Description

This command has no arguments or keywords.

## Command Mode

EXEC

## Usage Guidelines

This command first appeared in Cisco IOS Release 11.1.

Clearing the counters can assist you with troubleshooting. For example, you may want to clear the counter and then check to see how many PDUs the router is originating.

## Example

The following example clears the TARP counters:

```
clear tarp counters
```

## Related Commands

Search online for documentation for related commands.

**show tarp traffic**

Command Reference

## CLEAR TARP LDB-TABLE

Use the **clear tarp ldb-table** EXEC command to clear the system ID-to-sequence number mapping entries stored in the TARP loop-detection buffer table.

    **clear tarp ldb-table**

*Syntax     Description*

This command has no arguments or keywords.

*Command Mode*

EXEC

*Usage Guidelines*

This command first appeared in Cisco IOS Release 11.1.

The loop-detection buffer table prevents TARP packets from looping.

Clearing the counters assists you with troubleshooting. For example, clear the loop-detection buffer table and assign a new sequence number (using the **tarp sequence-number** command) to ensure that other hosts update their entries.

*Example*

The following example clears the TARP loop-detection buffer table:

```
clear tarp ldb-table
```

*Related Commands*

Search online for documentation for related commands.

**show tarp ldb**
**tarp ldb-timer**

## CLEAR TARP TID-TABLE

Use the **clear tarp tid-table** EXEC command to clear the dynamically created TARP target identifier (TID)-to-NSAP address mapping entries stored in the TID cache.

    **clear tarp tid-table**

*Syntax     Description*

This command has no arguments or keywords.

*Command Mode*

EXEC

## Usage Guidelines

This command first appeared in Cisco IOS Release 11.1.

Clearing the TID cache is one method to remove old entries. Another method is to set the length of time a dynamically created TARP entry remains in the TID cache using the **tarp-cache-timer** command.

The **clear tarp tid-table** command does not delete the cache entry for its own TID or the cache entries explicitly configured with the **tarp map** command.

## Example

The following example clears the TARP TID table:

```
clear tarp tid-table
```

## Related Commands

Search online for documentation for related commands.

**show tarp map**
**show tarp tid-cache**
**tarp allow-caching**
**tarp cache-timer**
**tarp map**

## CLNS ACCESS-GROUP

Use the **clns access-group** interface configuration command to filter transit CLNS traffic going either into or out of the router or both on a per-interface basis. Use the **no** form of this command to disable filtering of transit CLNS packets.

> **clns access-group** *name* [**in** | **out**]
> **no clns access-group** *name* [**in** | **out**]

| Syntax | Description |
| --- | --- |
| *name* | Name of the filter set or expression to apply. |
| **in** | (Optional) Filter should be applied to CLNS packets entering the router. |
| **out** | (Optional) Filter should be applied to CLNS packets leaving the router. If you do not specify an **in** or **out** keyword, **out** is assumed. |

## Default

Disabled

## Command Mode

Interface configuration

## Usage Guidelines

This command first appeared in Cisco IOS Release 10.0.

This command has no effect on any CLNS packets sourced by the Cisco IOS software. It applies only to packets forwarded by the software. Fast switching is still supported with access groups in place, but its performance will be impacted based on the complexity of the filters.

For descriptions of filter sets and expressions, refer to the **clns filter-expr**, **clns filter-set**, and **clns template-alias** global configuration commands in this chapter.

## Example

The following example shows how to enable forwarding of frames received on Ethernet 0 that had a source address of anything other than 38.840F, and a destination address that started with 47.0005 or 47.0023, but nothing else:

```
clns filter-set US-OR-NORDUNET permit 47.0005...
clns filter-set US-OR-NORDUNET permit 47.0023...
clns filter-set NO-ANSI deny 38.840F...
clns filter-set NO-ANSI permit default
clns filter-expr STRANGE source NO-ANSI and destination US-OR-NORDUNET

interface ethernet 0
 clns access-group STRANGE in
```

## Related Commands

Search online for documentation for related commands.

**clns filter-expr**
**clns filter-set**
**clns template-alias**

## CLNS ADJACENCY-FILTER

Use the **clns adjacency-filter** interface configuration command to filter the establishment of CLNS ES and IS adjacencies. Use the **no** form of this command to disable this filtering.

```
clns adjacency-filter {es | is} name
no clns adjacency-filter {es | is} name
```

| Syntax | Description |
| --- | --- |
| es | ES adjacencies are to be filtered. |
| is | IS adjacencies are to be filtered. |
| name | Name of the filter set or expression to apply. |

## Default

Disabled

## Command Mode

Interface configuration

## Usage Guidelines

This command first appeared in Cisco IOS Release 10.0.

Filtering is performed on full NSAP addresses. If filtering should only be performed on system IDs or any other substring of the full NSAP address, the wildcard-matching capabilities of filter sets should be used to ignore the insignificant portions of the NSAP addresses.

For descriptions of filter sets and expressions, refer to the **clns filter-expr**, **clns filter-set**, and **clns template-alias** global configuration commands in this chapter.

## Example

The following example builds a filter that accepts end system adjacencies with only two systems, based only on their system IDs:

```
clns filter-set ourfriends...0000.0c00.1234.**
clns filter-set ourfriends...0000.0c00.125a.**

interface ethernet 0
 clns adjacency-filter es ourfriends
```

## Related Commands

Search online for documentation for related commands.

**clns filter-expr**
**clns filter-set**
**clns template-alias**

## CLNS CHECKSUM

Use the **clns checksum** interface configuration command to enable checksum generation when ISO CLNS routing software sources a CLNS packet. Use the **no** form of this command to disable checksum generation.

> **clns checksum**
> **no clns checksum**

## Syntax Description

This command has no arguments or keywords.

## Default

Enabled

## Command Mode

Interface configuration

## Usage Guidelines

This command first appeared in Cisco IOS Release 10.0.

This command has no effect on routing packets, such as ES-IS, ISO-Interior Gateway Routing Protocol (IGRP) and IS-IS, sourced by the system. It applies to pings and trace route packets.

## Example

The following example shows how to enable checksum generation:

```
interface ethernet 0
 clns checksum
```

## CLNS CLUSTER-ALIAS

Use the **clns cluster-alias** interface configuration command to allow multiple systems to advertise the same system ID as other systems in ES hello messages. Use the **no** form of this command to disable cluster aliasing.

> **clns cluster-alias**
> **no clns cluster-alias**

## Syntax     Description

This command has no arguments or keywords.

## Default

Disabled

## Command Mode

Interface configuration

## Usage Guidelines

This command first appeared in Cisco IOS Release 10.0.

This feature caches multiple ES adjacencies with the same NSAP, but with different SNPA addresses. When a packet is destined to the common NSAP address, the Cisco IOS software load-splits the packets among the different SNPA addresses. A router that supports this capability forwards traffic to each system.

If DECnet Phase V cluster aliases are disabled on an interface, ES hello packet information is used to replace any existing adjacency information for the NSAP. Otherwise, an additional adjacency (with a different SNPA) is created for the same NSAP.

*Example*

The following example shows how cluster aliasing is enabled on specified interfaces:

```
clns nsap 47.0004.004d.0001.0000.0c00.1111.00
clns routing

interface ethernet 0
 clns cluster-alias

interface ethernet 1
 clns cluster-alias
```

## CLNS CONFIGURATION-TIME

Use the **clns configuration-time** global configuration command to specify the rate at which ES hellos and IS hellos are sent. Use the **no** form of this command to restore the default value.

**clns configuration-time** *seconds*
**no clns configuration-time**

| *Syntax* | *Description* |
| --- | --- |
| *seconds* | Rate in seconds at which ES and IS hello packets are sent. |

*Default*

60 seconds

*Command Mode*

Global configuration

*Usage Guidelines*

This command first appeared in Cisco IOS Release 10.0.

*Example*

The following example specifies that ES hellos and IS hellos are to be sent every 100 seconds:

```
clns configuration-time 100
```

*Related Commands*

Search online for documentation for related commands.

**clns esct-time**
**clns holding-time**

*Command Reference*

## CLNS CONGESTION-THRESHOLD

Use the **clns congestion-threshold** interface configuration command to set the congestion experienced bit if the output queue has more than the specified number of packets in it. A *number* value of zero or the **no** form of this command prevents this bit from being set. Use the **no** form of this command to remove the parameter setting and set it to 0.

     **clns congestion-threshold** *number*
     **no clns congestion-threshold**

| *Syntax* | *Description* |
|---|---|
| *number* | Number of packets that are allowed in the output queue before the system sets the congestion-experienced bit. The value zero (0) prevents this bit from being set. |

### *Default*

4 packets

### *Command Mode*

Interface configuration

### *Usage Guidelines*

This command first appeared in Cisco IOS Release 10.0.

If a router configured for CLNS experiences congestion, it sets the congestion experienced bit. The congestion threshold is a per-interface parameter set by this interface configuration command. An error PDU (ERPDU) is sent to the sending router and the packet is dropped if the number of packets exceeds the threshold.

### *Example*

The following example sets the congestion threshold to 10:

```
interface ethernet 0
 clns congestion-threshold 10
```

## CLNS DEC-COMPATIBLE

Use the **clns dec-compatible** interface configuration command to allow IS hellos sent and received to ignore the N-selector byte. Use the **no** form of this command to disable this feature.

     **clns dec-compatible**
     **no clns dec-compatible**

### *Syntax     Description*

This command has no arguments or keywords.

*Default*

Disabled

*Command Mode*

Interface configuration

*Usage Guidelines*

This command first appeared in Cisco IOS Release 10.0.

*Example*

The following example enables DEC-compatible mode:

```
interface ethernet 0
 clns dec-compatible
```

## CLNS ENABLE

Use the **clns enable** interface configuration command if you do not intend to perform any static or dynamic routing on an interface, but intend to pass ISO CLNS packet traffic to end systems. Use the **no** form of this command to disable ISO CLNS on a particular interface.

    **clns enable**
    **no clns enable**

*Syntax     Description*

This command has no arguments or keywords.

*Default*

Disabled

*Command Mode*

Interface configuration

*Usage Guidelines*

This command first appeared in Cisco IOS Release 10.0.

*Example*

The following example enables ISO CLNS on Ethernet interface 0:

```
interface ethernet 0
 clns enable
```

## CLNS ERPDU-INTERVAL

Use the **clns erpdu-interval** interface configuration command to determine the minimum interval time, in milliseconds, between error ERPDUs. A *milliseconds* value of zero or the **no** form of this command turns off the interval and effectively sets no limit between ERPDUs.

> **clns erpdu-interval** *milliseconds*
> **no clns erpdu-interval** *milliseconds*

| Syntax | Description |
| --- | --- |
| *milliseconds* | Minimum interval time (in milliseconds) between ERPDUs. |

### Default

10 ms

### Command Mode

Interface configuration

### Usage Guidelines

This command first appeared in Cisco IOS Release 10.0.

This command does not send ERPDUs more frequently than 1 per interface per 10 ms. It is wise not to send an ERPDU frequently if bandwidth is precious (such as over slow serial lines).

### Example

The following example sets the ERPDU interval to 30 ms:

```
interface ethernet 0
  clns erpdu-interval 30
```

### Related Commands

Search online for documentation for related commands.

**clns send-erpdu**

## CLNS ESCT-TIME

Use the **clns esct-time** interface configuration command to supply an ES configuration timer option in a transmitted IS hello packet that tells the ES how often it should transmit ES hello packet PDUs. Use the **no** form of this command to restore the default value and disable this feature.

> **clns esct-time** *seconds*
> **no clns esct-time** *seconds*

| Syntax | Description |
| --- | --- |
| *seconds* | Time, in seconds, between ES hello PDUs. Range is 0 to 65535. |

*Default*

0 seconds (disabled)

*Command Mode*

Interface configuration

*Usage Guidelines*

This command first appeared in Cisco IOS Release 10.0.

*Example*

The following example sets the ES configuration time to 10 seconds:

```
interface ethernet 0
  clns esct-time 10
```

*Related Commands*

Search online for documentation for related commands.

**clns configuration-time**
**clns holding-time**

## CLNS ES-NEIGHBOR

Use the **clns es-neighbor** interface configuration command to list all systems that will be used when you manually specify the NSAP-to-SNPA mapping. The SNPAs are the MAC addresses. Use the **no** form of this command to delete the ES neighbor.

**clns es-neighbor** *nsap snpa*
**no clns es-neighbor** *nsap*

| Syntax | Description |
|--------|-------------|
| *nsap* | Specific NSAP to map to a specific MAC address. |
| *snpa* | Data link (MAC) address. |

*Default*

No end systems are listed.

*Command Mode*

Interface configuration

*Usage Guidelines*

This command first appeared in Cisco IOS Release 10.0.

If you have configured either the **clns router iso-igrp** or **clns router isis** interface configuration commands for a particular interface, the ES-IS routing software automatically turns ES-IS on for that interface.

It is only necessary to use static mapping for those end systems that do *not* support ES-IS. The Cisco IOS software will continue to discover dynamically those end systems that *do* support ES-IS.

### Example

The following example defines an ES neighbor on Ethernet interface 0:

```
interface ethernet 0
  clns es-neighbor 47.0004.004D.0055.0000.0C00.A45B.00 0000.0C00.A45B
```

In this case, the end systems with the following NSAP, or network entity title (NET), are configured with an Ethernet MAC address of 0000.0C00.A45B:

```
47.0004.004D.0055.0000.0C00.A45B.00
```

### Related Commands

Search online for documentation for related commands.

**clns host**
**clns is-neighbor**

### CLNS FILTER-EXPR

Use one or more **clns filter-expr** global configuration commands to combine CLNS filter sets and CLNS address templates to create complex logical NSAP pattern-matching expressions. Use the **no** form of this command to delete the expression.

> **clns filter-expr** *ename term*
> **clns filter-expr** *ename* **not** *term*
> **clns filter-expr** *ename term* **or** *term*
> **clns filter-expr** *ename term* **and** *term*
> **clns filter-expr** *ename term* **xor** *term*
> **no clns filter-expr** *ename*

| Syntax | Description |
| --- | --- |
| *ename* | Alphanumeric name to apply to this filter expression. |
| *term* | Filter expression term. A term can be any of the following: |
| | *ename*—Another, previously defined, filter expression. |
| | *sname* (or **destination** *sname*)—A previously defined filter set name, with the filter set applied to the destination NSAP address. |
| | **source** *sname*—A previously defined filter set name, with the filter set applied to the source NSAP address. |

### Default

No filter expression is defined.

### Command Mode

Global configuration

### Usage Guidelines

This command first appeared in Cisco IOS Release 10.0.

Filter expressions can reference previously defined filter expressions, so you can build arbitrarily complex expressions.

The first form listed defines a simple filter expression that is pattern matched only if the pattern given by *term* is matched.

The second form defines a filter expression that is pattern matched only if the pattern given by *term* is *not* matched.

The third form defines a filter expression that is pattern matched if *either* of the patterns given by the two terms is matched.

The fourth form defines a filter expression that is pattern matched only if *both* of the patterns given by the two terms are matched.

The fifth form defines a filter expression that is pattern matched only if *one* of the patterns, but *not both*, given by the two terms is matched.

The sixth and final form of the command deletes the definition of an existing filter expression.

Use this command to define complex filter expressions. See the description of the **clns filter-set** global configuration command to learn how to define filter sets.

### Example

The following example shows how to define a filter expression that matches addresses with a source address of anything besides 39.840F, and a destination address that starts with 47.0005 or 47.0023, but nothing else:

```
clns filter-set US-OR-NORDUNET permit 47.0005...
clns filter-set US-OR-NORDUNET permit 47.0023
clns filter-set NO-ANSI deny 38.840F...
clns filter-set NO-ANSI permit default
!
clns filter-expr STRANGE source NO-ANSI and destination US-OR-NORDUNET
```

### Related Commands

Search online for documentation for related commands.

clns filter-set
clns template-alias
show clns filter-expr

## CLNS FILTER-SET

Use one or more **clns filter-set** global configuration commands to build a list of CLNS address templates with associated permit and deny conditions for use in CLNS filter expressions. CLNS filter expressions are used in the creation and use of CLNS access lists. Use the **no** form of this command to delete the entire filter set.

> clns filter-set *name* [**permit** | **deny**] *template*
> no clns filter-set *name*

| Syntax | Description |
|---|---|
| *name* | Alphanumeric name to apply to this filter set. |
| **permit** \| **deny** | (Optional) Addresses matching the pattern specified by *template* are to be permitted or denied. If neither **permit** nor **deny** is specified, **permit** is assumed. |
| *template* | Address template, template alias name, or the keyword **default**. Address templates and alias names are described under the description of the **clns template-alias** global configuration command. The **default** keyword denotes a zero-length prefix and matches any address. |

### Default

No address templates are defined.

### Command Mode

Global configuration

### Usage Guidelines

This command first appeared in Cisco IOS Release 10.0.

Use this command to define a list of pattern matches and permit/deny conditions for use in CLNS filter expressions. Filter expressions are used in the creation and use of CLNS access lists. See the description of the **clns filter-expr** global configuration command to learn how to define filter expressions and the **clns template-alias** global configuration command to learn how to define address templates and address template aliases.

Each address that must be matched against a filter set is first compared against all the entries in the filter set, in order, for an exact match with the address. If the exact match search fails to find a match, then the entries in the filter set containing wildcard matches are scanned for a match, again, in order. The first template that matches is used. If an address does not match any of the filter set entries, an implicit "deny" is returned as the permit/deny action of the filter set.

### Examples

The following example returns a permit action if an address starts with either 47.0005 or 47.0023. It returns an implicit deny action on any other address.

```
clns filter-set US-OR-NORDUNET permit 47.0005...
clns filter-set US-OR-NORDUNET permit 47.0023...
```

The following example returns a deny action if an address starts with 39.840F, but returns a permit action for any other address:

```
clns filter-set NO-ANSI deny 38.840F...
clns filter-set NO-ANSI permit default
```

### Related Commands

Search online for documentation for related commands.

**clns filter-expr**
**clns template-alias**
**show clns filter-set**

### CLNS HOLDING-TIME

Use the **clns holding-time** global configuration command to allow the sender of an ES hello or IS hello to specify the length of time you consider the information in the hello packets to be valid. Use the **no** form of this command to restore the default value (300 seconds, or 5 minutes).

> **clns holding-time** *seconds*
> **no clns holding-time**

| Syntax | Description |
|---|---|
| *seconds* | Length of time in seconds during which the information in the hello packets is considered valid. |

### Default

300 seconds (5 minutes)

### Command Mode

Global configuration

### Usage Guidelines

This command first appeared in Cisco IOS Release 10.0.

*Command Reference*

Setting this value too high puts extra traffic on a line and adds time to process hellos. However, you want to avoid setting it too low if your topology changes more often than the Cisco IOS software sends updates.

### Example

The following example sets the holding time at 150 seconds:

```
clns holding-time 150
```

### Related Commands

Search online for documentation for related commands.

clns configuration-time
clns esct-time

## CLNS HOST

Use the **clns host** global configuration command to define a name-to-NSAP mapping that can then be used with commands requiring NSAPs.

clns host *name nsap*

| Syntax | Description |
|--------|-------------|
| *name* | Desired name for the NSAP. The first character can be either a letter or a number, but if you use a number, the operations you can perform are limited. |
| *nsap* | NSAP to which that the name maps. |

### Default

No mapping is defined.

### Command Mode

Global configuration

### Usage Guidelines

This command first appeared in Cisco IOS Release 10.0.

The assigned NSAP name is displayed, where applicable, in **show** and **debug** EXEC commands. There are some effects and requirements associated with using names to represent network entity titles (NETs) and NSAPs, however. Although using names as proxies for addresses is allowed with CLNS commands, they are never written out to nonvolatile random-access memory (NVRAM).

The first character can be either a letter or a number, but if you use a number, the operations you can perform (such as **ping**) are limited.

The **clns host** command is generated after all other CLNS commands when the configuration file is parsed. As a result, the NVRAM version of the configuration cannot be edited to specifically change the address defined in the original **clns host** command. You must specifically change any commands that refer to the original address. This affects all commands that accept names.

The commands that are affected by these requirements include the following:

- **net** (router configuration command)
- **clns is-neighbor** (interface configuration command)
- **clns es-neighbor** (interface configuration command)
- **clns route** (global configuration command)

### Example

The following example defines names to NSAPs:

```
clns host cisco1 39.0001.0000.0c00.1111.00
clns host cisco2 39.0002.0000.0c00.1111.00
router iso-igrp
 net cisco1
 !
interface ethernet 0
 clns net cisco2
```

### Related Commands

Search online for documentation for related commands.

clns es-neighbor
clns is-neighbor

## CLNS IS-NEIGHBOR

Use the **clns is-neighbor** interface configuration command to list all intermediate systems that will be used when you manually specify the NSAP-to-SNPA mapping. The SNPAs are the MAC addresses. Use the **no** form of this command to delete the specified IS neighbor.

**clns is-neighbor** *nsap snpa*
**no clns is-neighbor** *nsap*

| Syntax | Description |
| --- | --- |
| *nsap* | NSAP of a specific intermediate system to enter as neighbor to a specific MAC address. |
| *snpa* | Data link (MAC) address. |

### Default

No intermediate systems are listed.

## Command Mode

Interface configuration

## Usage Guidelines

This command first appeared in Cisco IOS Release 10.0.

It is sometimes preferable for a router to have a neighbor entry statically configured rather than learned through ES-IS, ISO IGRP, or IS-IS. This interface configuration command enters an IS neighbor.

## Example

The following example defines an IS neighbor on Ethernet interface 0:

```
interface ethernet 0
  clns is-neighbor 47.0004.004D.0055.0000.0C00.A45B.00 0000.0C00.A45B
```

## Related Commands

Search online for documentation for related commands.

**clns es-neighbor**
**clns host**

## CLNS MTU

Use the **clns mtu** interface configuration command to set the maximum transmission unit (MTU) packet size for the interface. Use the **no** form of this command to restore the default and maximum packet size.

**clns mtu** *bytes*
**no clns mtu**

| Syntax | Description |
|---|---|
| *bytes* | Maximum packet size in bytes. The minimum value is 512; the default and maximum packet size depend on the interface type. |

## Default

Depends on interface type.

## Command Mode

Interface configuration

## Usage Guidelines

This command first appeared in Cisco IOS Release 10.0.

All interfaces have a default maximum packet size. You can set the MTU size of the packets sent on the interface with the **mut** interface configuration command.

All routers on a physical medium must have the same protocol MTU in order to operate.

The CTR card does not support the switching of frames larger than 4472 bytes. Interoperability problems can occur if CTR cards are intermixed with other Token Ring cards on the same network. These problems can be minimized by lowering the CLNS MTUs to be the same on all routers on the network with the **clns mtu** command.

---

**NOTES** ────────────────────────────────────────────

Changing the MTU value with the **mtu** interface configuration command can affect the CLNS MTU value. If the CLNS MTU is at its maximum given the interface MTU, the CLNS MTU will change with the interface MTU. However, the reverse is not true; changing the CLNS MTU value has no effect on the value for the **mtu** interface configuration command.

---

*Command Reference*

### Example

The following example sets the MTU packet size to 1000 bytes:

```
interface ethernet 0
  clns mtu 1000
```

### Related Commands

Search online for documentation for related commands.

**mtu**

## CLNS NET (GLOBAL CONFIGURATION COMMAND)

Use the **clns net** global configuration command to assign a static address for a router. If the Cisco IOS software is configured to support ISO CLNS, but is not configured to dynamically route CLNS packets using ISO IGRP or IS-IS, use this command to assign an address to the router. Use the **no** form of this command to remove any previously configured NET or NSAP address.

> **clns net** {*net-address* | *name*}
> **no clns net** {*net-address* | *name*}

| Syntax | Description |
| --- | --- |
| *net-address* | NET address. Refer to the "Usage Guidelines" section. |
| *name* | CLNS host name to be associated with this interface. |

### Default

No static address is assigned.

## Command Mode

Global configuration

## Usage Guidelines

This command first appeared in Cisco IOS Release 10.0.

A CLNS packet sent to any of the defined NSAPs or NETs will be received by the router. The Cisco IOS software chooses the NET to use when it sends a packet with the following algorithm:

- If no dynamic routing protocol is running, use the NET defined for the outgoing interface if it exists; otherwise, use the NET defined for the router.
- If ISO IGRP is running, use the NET of the routing process that is running on this interface.
- If IS-IS is running, use the NET of the IS-IS routing process that is running on this interface.

## Example

The following example assigns a static address:

```
clns net 49.0001.aa00.0400.9105.00
```

## CLNS NET (INTERFACE CONFIGURATION COMMAND)

Use the **clns net** interface configuration command to assign an NSAP address or name to a router interface. If the Cisco IOS software is configured to support ISO CLNS, but is not configured to dynamically route CLNS packets using an ISO IGRP or IS-IS, use this command to assign an address to the router. Use the **no** form of this command to remove any previously configured NSAP address.

> **clns net** {*nsap-address* | *name*}
> **no clns net** {*nsap-address* | *name*}

| Syntax | Description |
|---|---|
| *nsap-address* | Specific NSAP address. |
| *name* | Name to be associated with this interface. |

## Default

No address or name is assigned.

## Command Mode

Interface configuration

## Usage Guidelines

This command first appeared in Cisco IOS Release 10.0.

This command is useful if you are doing static routing and need to control the source NET used by the router on each interface.

## Examples

The following example assigns an NSAP address to a router interface:

```
interface ethernet 0
  clns net 49.0001.0000.0c00.1111.00
```

The following example assigns a name to a router interface:

```
interface ethernet 0
  clns net cisco
```

## CLNS PACKET-LIFETIME

Use the **clns packet-lifetime** global configuration command to specify the initial lifetime for locally generated packets. Use the **no** form of this command to remove the parameter's settings.

**clns packet-lifetime** *seconds*
**no clns packet-lifetime**

| Syntax | Description |
|--------|-------------|
| *seconds* | Packet lifetime in seconds. |

### Default

32 seconds

### Command Mode

Global configuration

### Usage Guidelines

This command first appeared in Cisco IOS Release 10.0.

### Example

The following example sets a packet lifetime of 120 seconds:

```
clns packet-lifetime 120
```

### Related Commands

Search online for documentation for related commands.

**clns want-erpdu**

## CLNS RDPDU-INTERVAL

Use the **clns rdpdu-interval** interface configuration command to determine the minimum interval time (in milliseconds) between redirect PDUs (RDPDUs). A *milliseconds* value of zero or the **no** form of this command turns off the interval rate and effectively sets no limit between RDPDUs.

> **clns rdpdu-interval** *milliseconds*
> **no clns rdpdu-interval** *milliseconds*

| Syntax | Description |
|--------|-------------|
| *milliseconds* | Minimum interval time (in milliseconds) between RDPDUs. |

### Default

100 ms

### Command Mode

Interface configuration

### Usage Guidelines

This command first appeared in Cisco IOS Release 10.0.

An RDPDU is rate-limited and is not sent more frequently than one per interface per 100 ms. There is no need to change the default. This setting will work fine for most networks.

### Example

The following example sets an interval of 50 ms:

```
interface ethernet 0
  clns rdpdu-interval 50
```

### Related Commands

Search online for documentation for related commands.

**clns send-rdpdu**

## CLNS ROUTE (INTERFACE STATIC ROUTE)

Use this form of the **clns route** global configuration command to create an interface static route. Use the **no** form of this command to remove this route.

> **clns route** *nsap-prefix type number* [*snpa-address*]
> **no clns route** *nsap-prefix*

| Syntax | Description |
|--------|-------------|
| *nsap-prefix* | Network service access point prefix. This value is entered into a static routing table and used to match the beginning of a destination NSAP. The longest NSAP-prefix entry that matches is used. |
| *type* | Interface type. |
| *number* | Interface number. |
| *snpa-address* | (Optional) Specific SNPA address. Optional for serial links; required for multiaccess networks. |

### Default

No interface static routes are created.

### Command Mode

Global configuration

### Usage Guidelines

This command first appeared in Cisco IOS Release 10.0.

If you do not specify an SNPA address when you have a multiaccess network, you will receive an error message indicating a bad SNPA.

### Examples

The following example shows how to create a static route for an Ethernet interface:

```
clns route 39.0002 ethernet 3 aa00.0400.1111
```

The following example shows how to create a static route for a serial interface:

```
clns route 39.0002 serial 0
```

### Related Commands

Search online for documentation for related commands.

**clns route (to enter a static route)**
**clns route default**
**clns route discard**

## CLNS ROUTE (TO ENTER A STATIC ROUTE)

Use this form of the **clns route** global configuration command to enter a specific static route. NSAPs that start with *nsap-prefix* are forwarded to *next-hop-net* or the *name* of the next hop. Use the **no** form of this command to remove this route.

clns route *nsap-prefix* {*next-hop-net* | *name*}
no clns route *nsap-prefix*

| Syntax | Description |
|---|---|
| nsap-prefix | Network service access point prefix. This value is entered into a static routing table and used to match the beginning of a destination NSAP. The longest NSAP-prefix entry that matches is used. |
| next-hop-net | Next-hop NET. This value is used to establish the next hop of the route for forwarding packets. |
| name | Name of the next hop node. This value can be used instead of the next-hop NET to establish the next hop of the route for forwarding packets. |

## Default

No static route is entered.

## Command Mode

Global configuration

## Usage Guidelines

This command first appeared in Cisco IOS Release 10.0.

## Example

The following example forwards all packets toward the specified route:

```
clns route 39.840F 47.0005.80FF.FF00.0123.4567.89AB.00
```

## Related Commands

Search online for documentation of related commands.

clns route (to enter a static route)
clns route default
clns route discard

## CLNS ROUTE-CACHE

Use the **clns route-cache** interface configuration command to allow fast switching through the cache. Use the **no** form of this command to disable fast switching.

clns route-cache
no clns route-cache

*Syntax        Description*

This command has no arguments or keywords.

*Default*

Enabled

*Command Mode*

Interface configuration

*Usage Guidelines*

This command first appeared in Cisco IOS Release 10.0.

The cache still exists and is used after the **no clns route-cache** command is used; the software just does not do fast switching through the cache.

*Example*

The following example shows how to allow fast switching through the cache:

```
interface ethernet 0
  clns route-cache
```

## CLNS ROUTE DEFAULT

Use the **clns route** global configuration command to configure a default zero-length prefix rather than type an NSAP prefix. Use the **no** form of this command to remove this route.

> **clns route default** *nsap-prefix type number*
> **no clns route default**

| Syntax | Description |
|---|---|
| *nsap-prefix* | Network service access point prefix that is a default zero-length prefix. |
| *type* | Interface type. Specify the interface type immediately followed by the interface number; there is no space between the two. |
| *number* | Interface number. |

*Default*

No default prefix is configured.

*Command Mode*

Global configuration

## Usage Guidelines

This command first appeared in Cisco IOS Release 10.0.

## Example

The following example configures a default zero-length prefix:

```
clns route default 39.840F ethernet0
```

## Related Commands

Search online for documentation for related commands.

**clns route (interface static route)**
**clns route (to enter a static route)**
**clns route discard**

## CLNS ROUTE DISCARD

Use the **clns route discard** global configuration command to explicitly tell a router to discard packets with NSAP addresses that match the specified *nsap-prefix*. Use the **no** form of this command to remove this route.

> **clns route** *nsap-prefix* **discard**
> **no clns route** *nsap-prefix*

| Syntax | Description |
|---|---|
| *nsap-prefix* | Network service access point prefix. This value is entered into a static routing table and used to match the beginning of a destination NSAP. The longest NSAP-prefix entry that matches is used. |
| discard | Explicitly tells a router to discard packets with NSAPs that match the specified *nsap-prefix*. |

## Default

No NSAP addresses are identified.

## Command Mode

Global configuration

## Usage Guidelines

This command first appeared in Cisco IOS Release 10.0.

The **decnet advertise** command and the **clns route discard** command work together when DECnet Phase IV/V conversion is enabled. Any packet with the specified CLNS NSAP prefix causes CLNS to behave as if no route were found. Because DECnet Phase IV/V conversion is enabled, the route is then looked up in the Phase IV routing table. The router that is advertising the DECnet Phase IV route converts the packet to OSI and sends it to the router that is advertising the CLNS discard static route. Once it gets there, the packet is converted back to Phase IV.

### Example

The following example discards packets with a destination NSAP address that matches the prefix 47.0005:

```
clns route 47.0005 discard
```

### Related Commands

Search online for documentation of related commands.

clns route (interface static route)
clns route (to enter a static route)
clns route default

## CLNS ROUTER ISIS

Use the **clns router isis** interface configuration command to enable IS-IS routing for OSI on a specified interface. Use the **no** form of this command with the appropriate area tag to disable IS-IS routing for the system.

clns router isis [*tag*]
no clns router isis [*tag*]

| Syntax | Description |
| --- | --- |
| *tag* | (Optional) Meaningful name for a routing process. If not specified, a null tag is assumed. It must be unique among all CLNS router processes for a given router. Use the same text for the argument *tag* as specified in the **router isis** global configuration command. |

### Default

IS-IS routing is not specified for any interface.

### Command Mode

Interface configuration

### Usage Guidelines

This command first appeared in Cisco IOS Release 10.0.

Creating a name for a routing process means that you use names when configuring routing. You can specify *only one* IS-IS process per router.

## Example

The following example enables IS-IS routing for OSI on Ethernet interface 0:

```
router isis cisco
 net 39.0001.0000.0c00.1111.00
interface ethernet 0
 clns router isis cisco
```

## Related Commands

Search online for documentation of related commands.

**router isis**


## CLNS ROUTER ISO-IGRP

Use the **clns router iso-igrp** interface configuration command to specify ISO IGRP routing on a specified interface. Use the **no** form of the global configuration command with the appropriate tag to disable ISO IGRP routing for the system.

**lns router iso-igrp** *tag* **[level 2]**
**no clns router iso-igrp** *tag*

| Syntax | Description |
|--------|-------------|
| *tag* | Meaningful name for routing process. It must be unique among all CLNS router processes for a given router. This tag should be the same as defined for the routing process in the **router iso-igrp** global configuration command. |
| level 2 | (Optional) Allows the interface to advertise Level 2 information. |

## Default

ISO IGRP routing is not specified on any interface.

## Command Mode

Interface configuration
Global configuration

## Usage Guidelines

This command first appeared in Cisco IOS Release 10.0.

If you want this interface to advertise Level 2 information only, use the **level 2** keyword. This option reduces the amount of router-to-router traffic by telling the Cisco IOS software to send out only Level 2 routing updates on certain interfaces. Level 1 information is not passed on the interfaces for which the Level 2 option is set.

## Example

In the following example, the interface advertises Level 2 information only on serial interface 0:

```
router iso-igrp marketing
 net 49.0001.0000.0c00.1111.00
interface serial 0
 clns router iso-igrp marketing level 2
```

## Related Commands

Search online for documentation of related commands.

**router iso-igrp**

## CLNS ROUTING

Use the **clns routing** global configuration command to enable routing of CLNS packets. Use the **no** form of this command to disable CLNS routing.

**clns routing**
**no clns routing**

## Syntax    Description

This command has no arguments or keywords.

## Default

Disabled

## Command Mode

Global configuration

## Usage Guidelines

This command first appeared in Cisco IOS Release 10.0.

## Example

The following example enables routing of CLNS packets:

```
clns routing
```

## Related Commands

Search online for documentation of related commands.

**clns security pass-through**

## CLNS SECURITY PASS-THROUGH

Use the **clns security pass-through** global configuration command to allow the Cisco IOS software to pass packets that have security options set. Use the **no** form of this command to disable this function.

> **clns security pass-through**
> **no clns security pass-through**

### Syntax          Description

This command has no arguments or keywords.

### Default

The software discards any packets it sees as set with security options.

### Command Mode

Global configuration

### Usage Guidelines

This command first appeared in Cisco IOS Release 10.0.

### Example

The following example allows the Cisco IOS software to pass packets that have security options set:

```
clns routing
router iso-igrp
 net 47.0004.004d.0001.0000.0c11.1111.00
clns security pass-through
```

### Related Commands

Search online for documentation of related commands.

**clns routing**

## CLNS SEND-ERPDU

Use the **clns send-erpdu** interface configuration command to allow CLNS to send an error PDU when the routing software detects an error in a data PU. Use the **no** form of this command to disable this function.

> **clns send-erpdu**
> **no clns send-erpdu**

### Syntax          Description

This command has no arguments or keywords.

*Default*

Enabled

*Command Mode*

Interface configuration

*Usage Guidelines*

This command first appeared in Cisco IOS Release 10.0.

When a CLNS packet comes in, the routing software looks in the routing table for the next hop. If it does not find the next hop, the packet is discarded and an ERPDU can be sent.

*Example*

The following example shows how to allow CLNS to send an error PDU when it detects an error in a data PDU:

```
interface ethernet 0
 clns send-erpdu
```

*Related Commands*

Search online for documentation of related commands.

**clns erpdu-interval**

### CLNS SEND-RDPDU

Use the **clns send-rdpdu** interface configuration command to allow CLNS to send redirect PDUs (RPDUs) when a better route for a given host is known. Use the **no** form of this command to disable this function.

> **clns send-rdpdu**
> **no clns send-rdpdu**

*Syntax      Description*

This command has no arguments or keywords.

*Default*

Enabled

*Command Mode*

Interface configuration

### Usage Guidelines

This command first appeared in Cisco IOS Release 10.0.

If a packet is sent out the same interface it came in on, an RDPDU can also be sent to the sender of the packet.

### Example

The following example shows how to allow CLNS to send RPDUs:

```
interface ethernet 0
  clns send-rdpdu
```

### Related Commands

Search online for documentation of related commands.

**clns rdpdu-interval**

## CLNS SPLIT-HORIZON

Use the **clns split-horizon** interface configuration command to implement split horizon for ISO-IGRP updates. Use the **no** form of this command to disable this feature.

>**clns split-horizon**
>**no clns split-horizon**

### Syntax        Description

This command has no arguments or keywords.

### Defaults

Enabled for all LAN interfaces.

Disabled for WAN interfaces on X.25, Frame Relay, or SMDS networks.

### Command Mode

Interface configuration

### Usage Guidelines

This command first appeared in Cisco IOS Release 10.0.

Normally, routers that are connected to broadcast-type OSI networks and that use distance vector routing protocols employ the split-horizon mechanism to prevent routing loops. Split-horizon blocks information about routes from being advertised by a router out any interface from which that information originated. This behavior usually optimizes communications among multiple routers, particularly when links are broken. With nonbroadcast networks, however, such as Frame Relay and SMDS, situations can arise for which this behavior is less than ideal. For all interfaces except those for which either Frame Relay or SMDS encapsulation is enabled, the default condition for this command is for split horizon to be enabled.

If your configuration includes either the **encapsulation frame-relay** or **encapsulation smds** interface configuration commands, the default is for split horizon to be disabled. Split horizon is not disabled by default for interfaces using any of the X.25 encapsulations.

For networks that include links over X.25 PSNs, the **neighbor** interface configuration command can be used to defeat the split horizon feature. As an alternative, you can explicitly specify the **no clns split-horizon** command in your configuration. If you do so, however, you must similarly disable split horizon for all routers in any relevant multicast groups on that network.

Split horizon for ISO IGRP defaults to off for X.25, SMDS, and Frame Relay. Thereby, destinations are advertised out the interface for which the router has a destination.

In general, changing the state of the default for this interface configuration command is not recommended, unless you are certain that your application requires making a change in order to properly advertise routes. Remember that if split horizon is disabled on a serial interface (and that interface is attached to a packet-switched network), you must disable split horizon for all routers in any relevant multicast groups on that network.

### Example

In the following example, split horizon is disabled on a serial link connected to an X.25 network:

```
interface serial 0
  encapsulation x25
  no clns split-horizon
```

## CLNS TEMPLATE-ALIAS

Use one or more **clns template-alias** global configuration commands to build a list of alphanumeric aliases of CLNS address templates for use in the definition of CLNS filter sets. Use the **no** form of this command to delete the alias.

> **clns template-alias** *name template*
> **no clns template-alias** *name*

| Syntax | Description |
| --- | --- |
| *name* | Alphanumeric name to apply as an alias for the template. |
| *template* | Address template, as defined in the "Usage Guidelines" section. |

### Default

No alias list is defined.

### Command Mode

Global configuration

## Usage Guidelines

This command first appeared in Cisco IOS Release 10.0.

Address templates are "pattern forms" that match one or more CLNS addresses. They can be simple single CLNS addresses, which match just themselves, or contain *wildcards*, *prefixes*, and *suffixes*, allowing a single template to match many addresses.

The simplest address template matches just a single address, as shown in this example:

```
47.0005.1234.5678.9abc.def0.00
```

*Wildcard digits*, which can match any value, are indicated with asterisks (*). The following template matches the above address and any other 12-byte long address that starts with 47.0005.1234.5678:

```
47.0005.1234.5678.****.****.**
```

Because OSI addresses are variable in length, it is often useful to build templates that match addresses which share a common prefix. The following template matches any address of any length that begins with the prefix 47.0005.1234.5678:

```
47.0005.1234.5678...
```

In other instances, matching a suffix of the address is also important, such as when matching system IDs. The following template matches any address that ends with the suffix 0000.0c01.2345.00:

```
...0000.0c01.2345.00
```

In other cases, you might want to match addresses on a single-bit granularity, rather than half-byte (four-bit or *nibble*) granularity. This pattern matching is supported by allowing the hex digits that represent four bits to be replaced by groups of four binary bits, represented by 0s and 1s. These four binary digits are enclosed within parentheses. The following template matches any address that starts with 47.0005 followed by the binary bits 10. The final two binary bits in the nibble can be either 0 or 1 and are represented with asterisks.

```
47.0005.(10**)...
```

Use this command to define aliases for commonly referenced address templates. The use of these aliases reduces the chances for typographical error in the creation of CLNS filter sets.

## Example

The following command defines a filter set called COMPLEX-PREFIX for the last example given in the "Usage Guidelines" section:

```
clns template-alias COMPLEX-PREFIX 47.0005.(10**)...
```

## Related Commands

Search online for documentation of related commands.

**clns filter-expr**
**clns filter-set**

## CLNS WANT-ERPDU

Use the **clns want-erpdu** global configuration command to specify whether to request ERPDUs on packets sourced by the router. Use the **no** form of this command to remove the parameter's settings.

**clns want-erpdu**
**no clns want-erpdu**

*Syntax        Description*

This command has no arguments or keywords.

*Default*

To request ERPDUs.

*Command Mode*

Global configuration

*Usage Guidelines*

This command first appeared in Cisco IOS Release 10.0.

This command has no effect on routing packets (ES-IS, ISO IGRP, and IS-IS) sourced by the system. It applies to pings and trace route packets.

*Example*

The following example requests ERPDUs on packets sourced by the router:

```
clns want-erpdu
```

*Related Commands*

Search online for documentation of related commands.

**clns packet-lifetime**

## DISTANCE

Use the **distance** router configuration command to configure the administrative distance for CLNS routes learned. Use the **no** form of this command to restore the administrative distance to the default.

**distance** *value* [**clns**]
**no distance** *value* [**clns**]

| Syntax | Description |
| --- | --- |
| *value* | Administrative distance, indicating the trustworthiness of a routing information source. This argument has a numerical value between 0 and 255. A higher relative value indicates a lower trustworthiness rating. Preference is given to routes with smaller values. The default, if unspecified, is 110. |
| **clns** | (Optional) CLNS-derived routes for IS-IS. |

### Defaults

Static routes—10
ISO IGRP routes—100
IS-IS routes—110

### Command Mode

Router configuration

### Usage Guidelines

This command first appeared in Cisco IOS Release 10.0.

When multiple routing processes are running in the same router for CLNS, it is possible for the same route to be advertised by more than one routing process. The Cisco IOS software always picks the route that has the routing protocol with the lowest administrative distance.

The **show clns protocol** EXEC command displays the default administrative distance for a specified routing process.

### Example

In the following example, the distance value for CLNS routes learned is 90. Preference is given to these CLNS routes rather than routes with the default administrative distance value of 110.

```
router isis
 distance 90 clns
```

## DOMAIN-PASSWORD

Use the **domain-password** router configuration command to configure the routing domain authentication password. Use the **no** form of this command to disable the password.

**domain-password** *password*
**no domain-password** [*password*]

| Syntax | Description |
| --- | --- |
| *password* | Password you assign. |

## Default

No routing domain authentication password is set.

## Command Mode

Router configuration

## Usage Guidelines

This command first appeared in Cisco IOS Release 10.0.

This password is inserted in Level 2 (area router level) link-state PDUs, CSNPs, and PSNPs.

## Example

The following example assigns an authentication password to the routing domain:

```
router isis
  domain-password flower
```

## Related Commands

Search online for documentation of related commands.

**area-password**

## IGNORE-LSP-ERRORS

Use the **ignore-lsp-errors** router configuration command to allow the router to ignore IS-IS link-state packets that are received with internal checksum errors rather than purging the link-state packets. Use the **no** form of this command to disable this function.

**ignore-lsp-errors**
**no ignore-lsp-errors**

## Syntax     Description

This command has no arguments or keywords.

## Default

Purge corrupt link-state packets causing initiator to regenerate link-state packet.

## Command Mode

Router configuration

## Usage Guidelines

This command first appeared in Cisco IOS Release 11.1.

The IS-IS protocol definition requires that a received link-state packet with an incorrect data-link checksum be purged by the receiver, which causes the initiator of the packet to regenerate it. However, if a network has a link that causes data corruption while still delivering link-state packets with correct data link checksums, a continuous cycle of purging and regenerating large numbers of packets can occur. Because this could render the network nonfunctional, use the **ignore-lsp-errors** to ignore these link-state packets rather than purge the packets.

Link-state packets are used by the receiving routers to maintain their routing tables.

### Example

The following example instructs the router to ignore link-state packets that have internal checksum errors:

```
router isis
 ignore-lsp-errors
```

## IP DOMAIN-LOOKUP NSAP

Use the **ip domain-lookup nsap** global configuration command to allow Domain Naming System (DNS) queries for CLNS addresses. Use the **no** form of this command to disable this feature.

**ip domain-lookup nsap**
**no ip domain-lookup nsap**

### Syntax        Description

This command has no arguments or keywords.

### Default

Enabled

### Command Mode

Global configuration

### Usage Guidelines

This command first appeared in Cisco IOS Release 10.0.

With both IP and ISO CLNS enabled on a router, this feature allows you to discover a CLNS address without having to specify a full CLNS address. This feature is useful for the ISO CLNS **ping** EXEC command and when making Telnet connections.

### Example

The following example disables DNS queries of CLNS addresses:

```
no ip domain-lookup nsap
```

### Related Commands

Search online for documentation of related commands.

**ip domain-lookup**
**ping (privileged)**
**ping (user)**

## ISIS ADJACENCY-FILTER

Use the **isis adjacency-filter** interface configuration command to filter the establishment of IS-IS adjacencies. Use the **no** form of this command to disable filtering of the establishment of IS-IS adjacencies.

> **isis adjacency-filter** *name* [**match-all**]
> **no isis adjacency-filter** *name* [**match-all**]

| Syntax | Description |
|---|---|
| *name* | Name of the filter set or expression to apply. |
| **match-all** | (Optional) All NSAP addresses must match the filter in order to accept the adjacency. If not specified (the default), only one address needs to match the filter in order for the adjacency to be accepted. |

### Default

Disabled

### Command Mode

Interface configuration

### Usage Guidelines

This command first appeared in Cisco IOS Release 10.0.

Filtering is performed by building NSAP addresses out of incoming IS-IS hello packets by combining each area address in the hello with the system ID. Each of these NSAP addresses is then passed through the filter. If any one NSAP matches, the filter is considered "passed," unless **match-all** was specified, in which case all addresses must pass. The functionality of the **match-all** keyword is useful in performing "negative tests," such as accepting an adjacency only if a particular address is *not* present.

Filtering is performed on full NSAP addresses. If filtering should only be performed on system IDs, or any other substring of the full NSAP address, the wildcard matching capabilities of filter sets should be used to ignore the insignificant portions of the NSAP addresses.

Filter sets and expressions are described in this manual in the descriptions for the **clns filter-expr, clns filter-set,** and **clns template-alias** global configuration commands.

*Command Reference*

## Example

The following example builds a filter that accepts adjacencies with only two systems, based only on their system IDs:

```
clns filter-set ourfriends...0000.0c00.1234.**
clns filter-set ourfriends...0000.0c00.125a.**
!
interface ethernet 0
 isis adjacency-filter ourfriends
```

## Related Commands

Search online for documentation of related commands.

**clns filter-expr**
**clns filter-set**
**clns template-alias**

## ISIS CIRCUIT-TYPE

Use the **isis circuit-type** interface configuration command to configure the type of adjacency desired for the specified interface. Use the **no** form of this command to reset the circuit type to Level 1 and Level 2.

> **isis circuit-type** {level-1 | level-1-2 | level-2-only}
> **no isis circuit-type**

| Syntax | Description |
|--------|-------------|
| level-1 | Level 1 adjacency is established if there is at least one area address in common between this system and its neighbors. |
| level-1-2 | Level 1 and 2 adjacency is established if the neighbor is also configured as **level-1-2** and there is at least one area in common. If there is no area in common, a Level 2 adjacency is established. This is the default. |
| level-2-only | Level 2 adjacency is established on the circuit. If the neighboring router is a Level 1 only router, no adjacency is established. |

## Default

Level 1 and 2 adjacency is established.

## Command Mode

Interface configuration

## Usage Guidelines

This command first appeared in Cisco IOS Release 10.0.

It is normally not necessary to configure this feature because the IS-IS protocol automatically determines area boundaries and keeps Level 1 and Level 2 routing separate. Indiscriminate use of this feature may cause incorrect operation, such as routing loops brought on by an accidental partitioning of a Level 1 area.

### Example

In the following example, a router is configured to allow only a Level 1 adjacency. If there are no area addresses in common between this system and its neighbors, no adjacency will be formed.

```
clns router isis
interface serial 0
 isis circuit-type level-1
```

### ISIS CSNP-INTERVAL

Use the **isis csnp-interval** interface configuration command to configure the IS-IS CSNP interval for the specified interface. Use the **no** form of this command to restore the default value.

**isis csnp-interval** *seconds* {**level-1** | **level-2**}
**no isis csnp-interval** *seconds* {**level-1** | **level-2**}

| Syntax | Description |
|---|---|
| *seconds* | Interval of time in seconds between transmission of CSNPs on multiaccess networks (only applies for the designated router). The default is 10 seconds. |
| level-1 | Interval of time between transmission of CSNPs for Level 1 independently. |
| level-2 | Interval of time between transmission of CSNPs for Level 2 independently. |

### Default

10 seconds

### Command Mode

Interface configuration

### Usage Guidelines

This command first appeared in Cisco IOS Release 10.0.

This command only applies to the designated router for a specified interface. Only designated routers send CSNP packets in order to maintain database synchronization. The CSNP interval can be configured independently for Level 1 and Level 2. This feature does not apply to serial point-to-point interfaces. It does apply to WAN connections if the WAN is viewed as a multiaccess meshed network.

*Example*

In the following example, serial interface 0 is configured for transmitting CSNPs every 5 seconds. The router is configured to act as a station router.

```
interface serial 0
  isis csnp-interval 5 level-1
```

## ISIS HELLO-INTERVAL

Use the **isis hello-interval** interface configuration command to specify the length of time in seconds between hello packets that the Cisco IOS software sends on the specified interface. Use the **no** form of this command to restore the default value.

> **isis hello-interval** *seconds* {**level-1** | **level-2**}
> **no isis hello-interval** *seconds* {**level-1** | **level-2**}

| Syntax | Description |
|--------|-------------|
| *seconds* | Unsigned integer value. A value three times the hello interval *seconds* is advertised as the *holdtime* in the hello packets transmitted. It must be the same for all routers attached to a common network. With smaller hello intervals, topological changes are detected faster, but there is more routing traffic. The default is 10 seconds. |
| level-1 | Configure the hello interval for Level 1 independently. Use this on X.25, SMDS, and Frame Relay multiaccess networks. |
| level-2 | Configure the hello interval for Level 2 independently. Use with X.25, SMDS, and Frame Relay multiaccess networks. |

*Default*

10 seconds

*Command Mode*

Interface configuration

*Usage Guidelines*

This command first appeared in Cisco IOS Release 10.0.

The hello interval can be configured independently for Level 1 and Level 2, except on serial point-to-point interfaces. (Because there is only a single type of hello packet sent on serial links, it is independent of Level 1 or Level 2.) The **level-1** and **level-2** keywords are used on X.25, SMDS, and Frame Relay multiaccess networks.

## Example

In the following example, serial interface 0 is configured to advertise hello packets every 5 seconds. The router is configured to act as a station router. This causes more traffic than configuring a longer interval, but topological changes will be detected faster.

```
interface serial 0
 isis Hello-interval 5 level-1
```

## Related Commands

Search online for documentation of related commands.

isis hello-multiplier

### ISIS HELLO-MULTIPLIER

Use the **isis hello-multiplier** interface configuration command to specify the hello packet multiplier used on the interface to determine the hold time transmitted in IS-IS hello packets. Use the **no** form of this command to disable this function.

> **isis hello-multiplier** *multiplier* [{level-1 | level-2}]
> **no isis hello-multiplier** [{level-1 | level-2}]

| Syntax | Description |
|---|---|
| *multiplier* | Number from 3 to 1000. The seconds specified by the **isis hello-interval** command are multiplied by the number specified for the **isis hello-multiplier** command to determine the holding time transmitted in the IS-IS hello packet. If this command is not used, the default multiplier is 3. |
| level-1 | (Optional) Configure the multiplier for Level 1 independently. The default is Level 1. |
| level-2 | (Optional) Configure the multiplier for Level 2 independently. |

## Default

The default hello multiplier is 3 for Level 1 and Level 2.

## Command Mode

Interface configuration

## Usage Guidelines

This command first appeared in Cisco IOS Release 11.1

The "holding time" carried in an IS-IS hello packet determines how long a neighbor waits for another hello packet before declaring the neighbor to be down. This time determines how quickly a failed link or neighbor is detected so that routes can be recalculated.

Use the **isis hello-multiplier** command in circumstances where hello packets are lost frequently and IS-IS adjacencies are failing unnecessarily. You can raise the hello multiplier and lower the hello interval (**isis hello-interval** command) correspondingly to make the hello protocol more reliable without increasing the time required to detect a link failure.

### Example

In the following example, serial interface 0 is configured to advertise hello packets every 15 seconds and the multiplier is 5. This causes the hello packet holding time to be 75 seconds.

```
interface serial 0
  isis hello-interval 15 level-2
  isis hello-multiplier 5 level-2
```

### Related Commands

isis hello-interval

## ISIS METRIC

Use the **isis metric** interface configuration command to configure the metric (or cost) for the specified interface. Use the **no** form of this command to restore the default metric value.

> **isis metric** *default-metric* {**level-1** | **level-2**}
> **no isis metric** {**level-1** | **level-2**}

| Syntax | Description |
| --- | --- |
| *default-metric* | Metric used for the redistributed route. The range is 0 to 63. The default value is 10. |
| level-1 | The router acts as a station router (Level 1) only. |
| level-2 | The router acts as an area router (Level 2) only. |

### Default

Default metric = 10

### Command Mode

Interface configuration

### Usage Guidelines

This command first appeared in Cisco IOS Release 10.0.

The *default-metric* is used as a value for the IS-IS metric. This is the value assigned when there is no quality-of-service (QOS) routing performed. Only this metric is supported by Cisco routers. You can configure this metric for Level 1 or Level 2 routing.

Specifying the **level-1** or **level-2** keywords resets the metric only for Level 1 or Level 2 routing, respectively.

## Example

In the following example, serial interface 0 is configured for a default link-state metric cost of 15 for Level 1:

```
interface serial 0
  isis metric 15 level-1
```

## ISIS PASSWORD

Use the **isis password** interface configuration command to configure the authentication password for a specified interface. Use the **no** form of this command to disable authentication for IS-IS.

**isis password** *password* {**level-1** | **level-2**}
**no isis password** {**level-1** | **level-2**}

| Syntax | Description |
|--------|-------------|
| *password* | Authentication password you assign for an interface. |
| **level-1** | Configure the authentication password for Level 1 independently. For Level 1 routing, the router acts as a station router only. |
| **level-2** | Configure the authentication password for Level 2 independently. For Level 2 routing, the router acts as an area router only. |

## Default

Disabled

## Command Mode

Interface configuration

## Usage Guidelines

This command first appeared in Cisco IOS Release 10.0.

Different passwords can be assigned for different routing levels by using the **level-1** and **level-2** keywords.

Specifying the **level-1** or **level-2** keywords disables the password only for Level 1 or Level 2 routing, respectively. If no keyword is specified, the default is **level-1**.

## Example

The following example configures a password for serial interface 0 at Level 1:

```
interface serial 0
  isis password frank level-1
```

## ISIS PRIORITY

Use the **isis priority** interface configuration command to configure the priority of this system for designated router election. Use the **no** form of this command to reset priority to 64.

> **isis priority** *value* {level-1 | level-2}
> **no isis priority** {level-1 | level-2}

| Syntax | Description |
|--------|-------------|
| *value* | Priority of a router; a number from 0 to 127. The default is 64. |
| level-1 | Set priority for Level 1 independently. |
| level-2 | Set priority for Level 2 independently. |

### Default

Priority of 64

### Command Mode

Interface configuration

### Usage Guidelines

This command first appeared in Cisco IOS Release 10.0.

Priorities can be configured for Level 1 and Level 2 independently. Specifying the **level-1** or **level-2** keywords resets priority only for Level 1 or Level 2 routing, respectively.

### Example

The following example sets the Level 1 priority level to 50:

```
interface serial 0
  isis priority 50 level-1
```

## ISIS RETRANSMIT-INTERVAL

Use the **isis retransmit-interval** interface configuration command to configure the number of seconds between retransmission of IS-IS link-state PDU retransmission for point-to-point links. Use the **no** form of this command to restore the default value.

> **isis retransmit-interval** *seconds*
> **no isis retransmit-interval** *seconds*

| Syntax | Description |
|---|---|
| *seconds* | Integer that should be greater than the expected round-trip delay between any two routers on the attached network. The setting of this parameter should be conservative, or needless retransmission will result. The value should be larger for serial lines and virtual links. The default value is 5 seconds. |

### Default

5 seconds

### Command Mode

Interface configuration

### Usage Guidelines

This command first appeared in Cisco IOS Release 10.0.

### Example

The following example configures serial interface 0 for retransmission of IS-IS link-state PDU every 10 seconds for a large serial line:

```
interface serial 0
  isis retransmit-interval 10
```

## ISO-IGRP ADJACENCY-FILTER

Use the **iso-igrp adjacency-filter** interface configuration command to filter the establishment of ISO IGRP adjacencies. Use the **no** form of this command to disable filtering of the establishment of ISO IGRP adjacencies.

> **iso-igrp adjacency-filter** *name*
> **no iso-igrp adjacency-filter** *name*

| Syntax | Description |
|---|---|
| *name* | Name of the filter set or expression to apply. |

### Default

Disabled

### Command Mode

Interface configuration

Command Reference

## Usage Guidelines

This command first appeared in Cisco IOS Release 10.0.

Filtering is performed on full NSAP addresses. If filtering should only be performed on system IDs, or any other substring of the full NSAP address, the wildcard matching capabilities of filter sets should be used to ignore the insignificant portions of the NSAP addresses.

For descriptions of filter sets and expressions, refer to the **clns filter-expr**, **clns filter-set**, and **clns template-alias** global configuration commands in this chapter.

## Example

The following example builds a filter that accepts adjacencies with only two systems, based only on their system IDs:

```
clns filter-set ourfriends...0000.0c00.1234.**
clns filter-set ourfriends...0000.0c00.125a.**
!
interface ethernet 0
 iso-igrp adjacency-filter ourfriends
```

## Related Commands

Search online for documentation of related commands.

**clns filter-expr**
**clns filter-set**
**clns template-alias**

## IS-TYPE

Use the **is-type** router configuration command to configure the IS-IS level at which the Cisco IOS software is to operate. Use the **no** form of this command to reset the parameter to the default.

> **is-type** {level-1 | level-1-2 | level-2-only}
> **no is-type** {level-1 | level-1-2 | level-2-only}

| Syntax | Description |
|---|---|
| level-1 | Causes the router to act as a station router. |
| level-1-2 | Causes the router to act as both a station router and an area router. |
| level-2-only | Causes the router to act as an area router only. |

## Default

The router acts as both a station router and an area router.

## Command Mode

Router configuration

## Usage Guidelines

This command first appeared in Cisco IOS Release 10.3.

It is normally not necessary to configure this feature because the IS-IS protocol automatically determines area boundaries and keeps Level 1 and Level 2 routing separate. Indiscriminate use of this feature may cause incorrect operation, such as routing loops brought on by an accidental partitioning of a Level 1 area.

## Example

The following example specifies a router as capable of being used as an area router only:

```
clns routing
router isis area1
 net 47.0004.004d.0001.0000.0c11.1111.00
 is-type level-2-only
```

## LOG-ADJACENCY-CHANGES

Use the **log-adjacency-changes** router configuration command to cause IS-IS to generate a log message when an IS-IS adjacency changes state (up or down). Use the **no** form of this command to disable this function.

```
log-adjacency-changes
no log-adjacency-changes
```

## Syntax       Description

This command has no arguments or keywords.

## Default

Does not log adjacency changes.

## Command Mode

Router configuration

## Usage Guidelines

This command first appeared in Cisco IOS Release 11.1.

This command allows the monitoring of IS-IS adjacency state changes. This may be very useful when monitoring large networks. Messages are logged using the system error message facility. Messages are of the form:

```
%CLNS-5-ADJCHANGE: ISIS: Adjacency to 0000.0000.0034 (Serial0) Up, new adjacency
%CLNS-5-ADJCHANGE: ISIS: Adjacency to 0000.0000.0034 (Serial0) Down, hold time expired
```

## Example

The following example instructs the router to log adjacency changes:

```
router isis
 log-adjacency-changes
```

## Related Commands

Search online for documentation of related commands.

**logging**

## LSP-MTU

Use the **lsp-mtu** router configuration command to set the MTU size of IS-IS link-state packets. Use the **no** form of this command to disable this function.

**lsp-mtu** *size*
**no lsp-mtu**

| Syntax | Description |
|--------|-------------|
| *size* | Maximum packet size in bytes. The size must be less than or equal to the smallest MTU of any link in the network. The default size is 1497 bytes. |

## Default

1497 bytes

## Command Mode

Router configuration

## Usage Guidelines

This command first appeared in Cisco IOS Release 10.3.

Under normal conditions, the default MTU size should be sufficient. However, if the MTU of a link is below 1500 bytes, the link-state packet MTU must be lowered accordingly on each router in the network. If this is not done, routing becomes unpredictable.

**NOTES**

This rule applies for all routers in a network. If any link in the network has a reduced MTU, all routers must be changed, not just the routers directly connected to the link.

---

**CAUTION**

---

The CLNS MTU of a link (which is the applicable value for IS-IS, even if it is being used to route IP) may differ from the IP MTU. To be certain about a link MTU as it pertains to IS-IS, use the **show clns interface** command to display the value.

---

### Example

The following example sets the MTU size to 1300 bytes:

```
router isis
  lsp-mtu 1300
```

### Related Commands

Search online for documentation of related commands.

**mtu**
**clns mtu**

## MATCH CLNS ADDRESS

Use the **match clns address** route-map configuration command to define the match criterion; routes that have a network address matching one or more of the names—and that satisfy all other defined match criteria—will be redistributed. Use the **no** form of this command to remove the match criterion.

> **match clns address** *name* [*name...name*]
> **no match clns address** *name* [*name...name*]

### Syntax

### Description

*name*  Name of a standard access list, filter set, or expression.

### Default

Disabled

### Command Mode

Route-map configuration

### Usage Guidelines

This command first appeared in Cisco IOS Release 10.0.

Use the **route-map** global configuration command, and the route-map configuration commands **match** and **set**, to define the conditions for redistributing routes from one routing protocol into another. Each **route-map** command has a list of **match** and **set** commands associated with it. The **match** commands specify the *match criteria*—the conditions under which redistribution is allowed for the current **route-map command**. The **set** commands specify the *set actions*—the particular redistribution actions to perform if the criteria enforced by the **match** commands are met. The **no route-map** command deletes the route map.

The **match** route-map configuration command has multiple formats. The **match** commands may be given in any order, and *all* defined **match** criteria must be satisfied to cause the route to be redistributed according to the *set actions* given with the **set** commands. The **no** forms of the **match** commands remove the specified match criteria.

### Related Commands

Search online for documentation of related commands.

**redistribute**
**route-map**
**set level**

### MATCH CLNS NEXT-HOP

Use the **match clns next-hop** route-map configuration command to define the next-hop match criterion; routes that have a next-hop router address matching one of the names—and that satisfy all other defined match criteria—will be redistributed. Use the **no** form of this command to remove the match criterion.

> **match clns next-hop** *name* [*name...name*]
> **no match clns next-hop** *name* [*name...name*]

| Syntax | Description |
|--------|-------------|
| *name* | Name of an access list, filter set, or expression. |

### Default

Disabled

### Command Mode

Route-map configuration

### Usage Guidelines

This command first appeared in Cisco IOS Release 10.0.

Use the **route-map** global configuration command, and the route-map configuration commands **match** and **set**, to define the conditions for redistributing routes from one routing protocol into another. Each **route-map** command has a list of **match** and **set** commands associated with it. The **match** commands specify the *match criteria*—the conditions under which redistribution is allowed for the current **route-map** command. The **set** commands specify the *set actions*—the particular redistribution actions to perform if the criteria enforced by the **match** commands are met. The **no route-map** command deletes the route map.

The **match** route-map configuration command has multiple formats. The **match** commands may be given in any order, and *all* defined **match** criteria must be satisfied to cause the route to be redistributed according to the *set actions* given with the **set** commands. The **no** forms of the **match** commands remove the specified match criteria.

## Related Commands

Search online for documentation of related commands.

redistribute
route-map
set level

## MATCH CLNS ROUTE-SOURCE

Use the **match clns route-source** route-map configuration command to define the route-source match criterion; routes that have been advertised by routers at the address specified by the name—and that satisfy all other defined match criteria—will be redistributed. Use the **no** form of this command to remove the specified match criterion.

> **match clns route-source** *name* [*name...name*]
> **no match clns route-source** *name* [*name...name*]

| Syntax | Description |
|--------|-------------|
| *name* | Name of access list, filter set, or expression. |

## Default

Disabled

## Command Mode

Route-map configuration

## Usage Guidelines

This command first appeared in Cisco IOS Release 10.0.

Use the **route-map** global configuration command, and the route-map configuration commands **match** and **set**, to define the conditions for redistributing routes from one routing protocol into another. Each **route-map** command has a list of **match** and **set** commands associated with it. The **match** commands specify the *match criteria*—the conditions under which redistribution is allowed for the current **route-map command**. The **set** commands specify the *set actions*—the particular redistribution actions to perform if the criteria enforced by the **match** commands are met. The **no** **route-map** command deletes the route map.

The **match** route-map configuration command has multiple formats. The **match** commands may be given in any order, and *all* defined **match** criteria must be satisfied to cause the route to be redistributed according to the *set actions* given with the **set** commands. The **no** forms of the **match** commands remove the specified match criteria.

### Related Commands

Search online for documentation of related commands.

**redistribute**
**route-map**
**set level**

## MATCH INTERFACE

Use the **match interface** route-map configuration command to define the interface match criteria; routes that have the next hop out one of the interfaces specified—and that satisfy all other defined match criteria—will be redistributed. Use the **no** form of this command to remove the specified match criterion.

> **match interface** *type number* [*type number...type number*]
> **no match interface** *type number* [*type number...type number*]

| Syntax | Description |
|--------|-------------|
| *type* | Interface type. |
| *number* | Interface number. |

### Default

Disabled

### Command Mode

Route-map configuration

### Usage Guidelines

This command first appeared in Cisco IOS Release 10.0.

Use the **route-map** global configuration command, and the route-map configuration commands **match** and **set**, to define the conditions for redistributing routes from one routing protocol into another. Each **route-map** command has a list of **match** and **set** commands associated with it. The **match** commands specify the *match criteria*—the conditions under which redistribution is allowed for the current **route-map command**. The **set** commands specify the *set actions*—the particular redistribution actions to perform if the criteria enforced by the **match** commands are met. The **no route-map** command deletes the route map.

The **match** route-map configuration command has multiple formats. The **match** commands may be given in any order, and *all* defined **match** criteria must be satisfied to cause the route to be redistributed according to the *set actions* given with the **set** commands. The **no** forms of the **match** commands remove the specified match criteria.

### Related Commands

Search online for documentation of related commands.

**redistribute**
**route-map**
**set level**

## MATCH METRIC

Use the **match metric** route-map configuration command to define the metric match criteria; routes that have the specified metric—and satisfy all other defined match criteria—will be redistributed. Use the **no** form of this command to remove the specified match criteria.

> **match metric** *metric-value*
> **no match metric** *metric-value*

| Syntax | Description |
|---|---|
| *metric-value* | Route metric. This can be an Interior Gateway Routing Protocol (IGRP) five-part metric. |

### Default

Disabled

### Command Mode

Route-map configuration

### Usage Guidelines

This command first appeared in Cisco IOS Release 10.0.

Use the **route-map** global configuration command, and the route-map configuration commands **match** and **set**, to define the conditions for redistributing routes from one routing protocol into another. Each **route-map** command has a list of **match** and **set** commands associated with it. The **match** commands specify the *match criteria*—the conditions under which redistribution is allowed for the current **route-map command**. The **set** commands specify the *set actions*—the particular redistribution actions to perform if the criteria enforced by the **match** commands are met. The **no route-map** command deletes the route map.

The **match** route-map configuration command has multiple formats. The **match** commands may be given in any order, and *all* defined **match** criteria must be satisfied to cause the route to be redistributed according to the *set actions* given with the **set** commands. The **no** forms of the **match** commands remove the specified match criteria.

*Related Commands*

Search online for documentation of related commands.

**redistribute**
**route-map**
**set level**

## MATCH ROUTE-TYPE

Use the **match route-type** route-map configuration command to define the route-type match criteria; routes that have the specified route type—and satisfy all other defined match criteria—will be redistributed. Use the **no** form of this command to remove the specified match criteria.

> **match route-type** {level-1 | level-2}
> **no match route-type** {level-1 | level-2}

| Syntax | Description |
|--------|-------------|
| level-1 | IS-IS Level 1 routes. |
| level-2 | IS-IS Level 2 routes. |

*Default*

Disabled

*Command Mode*

Route-map configuration

*Usage Guidelines*

This command first appeared in Cisco IOS Release 10.0.

Use the **route-map** global configuration command, and the route-map configuration commands **match** and **set**, to define the conditions for redistributing routes from one routing protocol into another. Each **route-map** command has a list of **match** and **set** commands associated with it. The **match** commands specify the *match criteria*—the conditions under which redistribution is allowed for the current **route-map command**. The **set** commands specify the *set actions*—the particular redistribution actions to perform if the criteria enforced by the **match** commands are met. The **no** **route-map** command deletes the route map.

The **match** route-map configuration command has multiple formats. The **match** commands may be given in any order, and *all* defined **match** criteria must be satisfied to cause the route to be redistributed according to the *set actions* given with the **set** commands. The **no** forms of the **match** commands remove the specified match criteria.

*Related Commands*

Search online for documentation of related commands.

**redistribute**
**route-map**
**set level**

## METRIC WEIGHTS

Use the **metric weights** router configuration command to specify different metrics for the ISO IGRP routing protocol on CLNS. This command allows you to configure the metric constants used in the ISO IGRP composite metric calculation of reliability and load. Use the **no** form of this command to return the five $k$ constants to their default values.

  **metric weights** *qos k1 k2 k3 k4 k5*
  **no metric weights**

| *Syntax* | *Description* |
|---|---|
| *qos* | QOS defines transmission quality and availability of service. The argument must be 0, the *default metric*. |
| *k1, k2, k3, k4, k5* | Values that apply to ISO IGRP for the default metric QOS. The $k$ values are metric constants used in the ISO IGRP equation that converts an IGRP metric vector into a scalar quantity. They are numbers from 0 to 127; higher numbers mean a greater multiplier effect. |

*Defaults*

$qos = 0$
$k1 = 1$
$k2 = 0$
$k3 = 1$
$k4 = 0$
$k5 = 0$

*Command Mode*

Router configuration

*Usage Guidelines*

This command first appeared in Cisco IOS Release 10.0.

Two additional ISO IGRP metrics can be configured. These are the bandwidth and delay associated with an interface.

*Command Reference*

---

---

By default, the IGRP composite metric is a 24-bit quantity that is a sum of the segment delays and the lowest segment bandwidth (scaled and inverted) for a given route. For a network of homogeneous media, this metric reduces to a hop count. For a network of mixed media (FDDI, Ethernet, and serial lines running from 9,600 bps to T1 rates), the route with the lowest metric reflects the most desirable path to a destination.

Use this command to alter the default behavior of IGRP routing and metric computation and allow the tuning of the IGRP metric calculation for QOS.

If k5 equals 0, the composite IGRP metric is computed according to the following formula:

```
metric = [K1 * bandwidth + (K2 * bandwidth) / (256 - load) + K3 * delay]
```

If k5 does not equal zero, the following additional operation is done:

```
metric = metric * [K5 / (reliability + K4)]
```

The default version of IGRP has both k1 and k3 equal to 1, and k2, k4, and k5 equal to 0.

Delay is in units of 10 microseconds. This gives a range of 10 microseconds to 168 seconds. A delay of all ones indicates that the network is unreachable.

Bandwidth is inverse minimum bandwidth of the path in bits per second scaled by a factor of $10^e10$. The range is 1200 bps to 10 Gbps.

Table 14–1 lists the default values used for several common media.

**Table 14–1**  *Bandwidth Values by Media Type*

| Media Type | Delay | Bandwidth |
|---|---|---|
| Satellite | 200,000 (2 sec) | 20 (500 Mbit) |
| Ethernet | 100 (1 ms) | 1,000 |
| 1.544 Mbps | 2000 (20 ms) | 6,476 |
| 64 Kbps | 2000 | 156,250 |
| 56 Kbps | 2000 | 178,571 |
| 10 Kbps | 2000 | 1,000,000 |
| 1 Kbps | 2000 | 10,000,000 |

Reliability is given as a fraction of 255. That is, 255 is 100 percent reliability or a perfectly stable link. Load is given as a fraction of 255. A load of 255 indicates a completely saturated link.

## Example

In the following example, all five metric constants are set:

```
router iso-igrp
  metric weights 0 2 0 1 0 0
```

## Related Commands

Search online for documentation of related commands.

**bandwidth**
**delay**

## NET

Use the **net** router configuration command to configure a NET for the specified routing process. The **no** form of this command removes the specified NET.

> **net** *network-entity-title*
> **no net** *network-entity-title*

| Syntax | Description |
| --- | --- |
| *network-entity-title* | Area addresses for the ISO IGRP or IS-IS area. |

## Default

No NET is specified for any specific routing process.

## Command Mode

Router configuration

## Usage Guidelines

This command first appeared in Cisco IOS Release 10.0.

For IS-IS, multiple NETs per router are allowed, with a maximum of three. There is no default value for this command.

Although IS-IS allows you to configure multiple NETs, ISO IGRP allows only one NET per routing process.

The **net** router configuration command allows you to specify a name for an NET, as well as an address.

## Examples

The following example specifies an NET for ISO IGRP:

```
router iso-igrp Finance
  net 47.0004.004d.0001.0000.0c11.1111.00
```

The following example specifies a single NET for IS-IS:

```
router isis Pieinthesky
  net 47.0004.004d.0001.0000.0c11.1111.00
```

## PING (PRIVILEGED)

Use the ISO CLNS **ping** privileged EXEC command to send ISO CLNS echo packets to test the reachability of a remote router over a connectionless OSI network. The ping command sends an echo request packet to an address, then awaits a reply. Ping output can help you evaluate path-to-host reliability, delays over the path, and whether the host can be reached or is functioning.

**ping clns** {*host* | *address*}

| Syntax | Description |
|---|---|
| **clns** | CLNS protocol. |
| *host* | Host name of system to ping. |
| *address* | Address of system to ping. |

### Command Mode

Privileged EXEC

### Usage Guidelines

This command first appeared in Cisco IOS Release 10.0.

The OSI Connectionless Network Protocol (ISO 8473) does not specify a network-level echo protocol. The Internet Engineering Task Force (IETF) has specified and proposed such a protocol in RFC 1139. Cisco has implemented this specification using the proposed new PDU types Echo Request (1E) and Echo Reply (1F). Non-Cisco routers may or may not forward these packets, depending on whether they are specific about the packet types they will forward. End systems may not recognize these packets, but will typically generate an error packet (ERPDU) as a response. This ERPDU is useful, as it confirms the reachability of the end system.

To abort a ping session, type the escape sequence (by default, Ctrl-^ X, which is done by simultaneously pressing the Ctrl, Shift, and 6 keys, letting go, then pressing the X key).

Table 14–2 describes the test characters that the ping facility sends.

**Table 14–2**   *Ping Test Characters (ISO CLNS Privileged)*

| Character | Description |
|---|---|
| ! | Each exclamation point indicates receipt of a reply. |
| . | Each period indicates the network server timed out while waiting for a reply. |
| U | A destination unreachable error PDU was received. |

**Table 14–2** *Ping Test Characters (ISO CLNS Privileged), Continued*

| Character | Description |
|-----------|-------------|
| C | A congestion experienced packet was received. |
| I | User interrupted test. |
| ? | Unknown packet type. |
| & | Packet lifetime exceeded. |

### Sample ISO CLNS Display Using a Named Source

The following display shows a sample ISO CLNS **ping** session that uses a name to specify the source:

```
router# ping
Protocol [ip]: clns
Target CLNS address: thoth
Repeat count [5]:
Datagram size [100]:
Timeout in seconds [2]:
Source CLNS address [39.000f.aa00.0400.013c.00]:
Type escape sequence to abort.
Sending 5, 100-byte CLNS Echos to
55.0006.0100.0000.0000.0001.8888.1112.1314.151
6.00, timeout is 2 seconds:
!!!!!
Success rate is 100 percent, round-trip min/avg/max = 112/113/116 ms
```

### Sample ISO CLNS Display Using a NET Address

The following display shows a sample ISO CLNS **ping** session that uses a NET address to specify the source:

```
router# ping
Protocol [ip]: clns
Target CLNS address: 47.0004.0050.0002.0000.0c00.243b.00
Repeat count [5]:
Datagram size [100]:
Timeout in seconds [2]:
Source CLNS address [39.000f.aa00.0400.013c.00]:
Type escape sequence to abort.
Sending 5, 100-byte CLNS Echos to 47.0004.0050.0002.0000.0C00.243B.00,
timeout is 2 seconds:
!!!!!
Success rate is 100 percent, round-trip min/avg/max = 1/4/8 ms
```

Table 14–3 describes the fields shown in the display.

**Table 14-3**   *Ping Field Descriptions (ISO CLNS)*

| Field | Description |
| --- | --- |
| Protocol [ip]: | Default is IP. Enter **clns**. |
| Target CLNS address: | Prompts for the CLNS address or host name of the destination node you plan to ping. |
| Repeat count [5]: | Number of ping packets that will be sent to the destination address. Default: 5. |
| Datagram size [100]: | Size of the ping packet (in bytes). Default: 100 bytes. |
| Timeout in seconds [2]: | Timeout interval. Default: 2 (seconds). |
| Source address: | Address that appears in the ping packet as the source address. |

## Sample ISO CLNS Display Using the IP Domain Name System (DNS)

If you have both ISO CLNS and IP enabled, you can use the DNS to query ISO CLNS addresses through use of the "NSAP" type.

For example, suppose your DNS entries look something like the following:

```
finance.cisco.comIN A 1.2.3.4
marketing.cisco.comIN NSAP
47.0005.80.FEFF00.0000.0001.0001.1b2a.0000.0c1a.1bff.00
baz.cisco.comIN A 1.2.3.5
IN NSAP
47.0005.80.FEFF00.0000.0001.0001.1b2a.0000.0c1a.1b2c.00
```

Based on the these entries, the following examples will produce the results as indicated:

```
router# ping finance.cisco.com
! this will do an IP style ping

router# ping marketing.cisco.com
! this will do a CLNS style ping (since only a NSAP entry appears)

Router# ping baz.cisco.com
! this will do an IP style ping (prefers IP if it can get it)

Router# ping
Protocol [ip]: clns
Target CLNS address: baz.cisco.com
! this will do a CLNS ping the NSAP for baz.cisco.com
```

## Related Commands

Search online for documentation of related commands.

**ping (user)**

## PING (USER)

Use the ISO CLNS **ping** user EXEC command to send ISO CLNS echo packets to test the reachability of a remote router over a connectionless OSI network.

    **ping clns** {*host* | *address*}

| Syntax | Description |
|---|---|
| **clns** | CLNS protocol. |
| *host* | Host name of system to ping. |
| *address* | Address of system to ping. |

### Command Mode

User EXEC

### Usage Guidelines

This command first appeared in Cisco IOS Release 10.0.

The OSI Connectionless Network Protocol (ISO 8473) does not specify a network-level echo protocol. The Internet Engineering Task Force (IETF) has specified and proposed such a protocol in RFC 1139. Cisco has implemented this specification using the proposed new PDU types Echo Request (1E) and Echo Reply (1F). Non-Cisco routers may or may not forward these packets, depending on whether they are specific about the packet types they will forward. End systems may not recognize these packets, but will typically generate an error packet (ERPDU) as a response. This ERPDU is useful, as it confirms the reachability of the end system.

The user **ping** feature provides a basic ping facility for CLNS users who do not have system privileges. This feature allows the Cisco IOS software to perform the simple default ping functionality for the CLNS protocol. Only the nonverbose form of the **ping** command is supported for user pings.

If the system cannot map an address for a host name, it returns an "%Unrecognized host or address" error message. To abort a **ping** session, type the escape sequence (by default, Ctrl-^ X, which is done by simultaneously pressing the Ctrl, Shift, and 6 keys, letting go, and then pressing the X key).

Table 14–4 describes the test characters that the ping facility sends.

**Table 14–4**  *Ping Test Characters (ISO CLNS User)*

| Character | Description |
|---|---|
| ! | Each exclamation point indicates receipt of a reply. |
| . | Each period indicates the network server timed out while waiting for a reply. |
| U | A destination unreachable error PDU was received. |
| C | A congestion experienced packet was received. |

*Command Reference*

**Table 14–4**   *Ping Test Characters (ISO CLNS User), Continued*

| Character | Description |
|-----------|-------------|
| I | User interrupted test. |
| ? | Unknown packet type. |
| & | Packet lifetime exceeded. |

### Sample Display

The following display shows sample ping output when you ping the CLNS address 47.0004.0050.0002.0000.0c00.243b.00:

```
router> ping clns 47.0004.0050.0002.0000.0c00.243b.00
Sending 5, 100-byte CLNS Echos to 47.0004.0050.0002.0000.0C00.243B.00,
timeout is 2 seconds:
!!!!!
Success rate is 100 percent, round-trip min/avg/max = 1/4/8 ms
```

### Related Commands

Search online for documentation of related commands.

**ping (privileged)**

## REDISTRIBUTE

Use the **redistribute** router configuration command to redistribute routing information from one domain into another routing domain. Use the **no** form of this command to disable redistribution, or to disable any of the specified keywords.

> **redistribute** *protocol* [*tag*] [**route-map** *map-tag*]
> **no redistribute** *protocol* [*tag*] [**route-map** *map-tag*]
> **redistribute static** [**clns** | **ip**]

| Syntax | Description |
|--------|-------------|
| *protocol* | Type of other routing protocol that is to be redistributed as a source of routes into the current routing protocol being configured. The keywords supported are **iso-igrp, isis,** and **static.** |
| *tag* | (Optional) Meaningful name for a routing process. |
| **route-map** *map-tag* | (Optional) Route map should be interrogated to filter the importation of routes from this source routing protocol to the current routing protocol. If not specified, all routes are redistributed. If this keyword is specified, but no route map tags are listed, no routes will be imported. The argument *map-tag* is the identifier of a configured route map. |

| Syntax | Description |
|---|---|
| static | Keyword **static** is used to redistribute static routes. When used without the optional keywords, this causes the Cisco IOS software to inject any OSI static routes into an OSI domain. |
| clns | (Optional) Keyword **clns** is used when redistributing OSI static routes into an IS-IS domain. |
| ip | (Optional) Keyword **ip** is used when redistributing IP into an IS-IS domain. |

### Default

Disabled, except for static routes, which by default are redistributed into IS-IS routing domains but are not redistributed into ISO IGRP domains. The keyword **clns** is the default with the keyword **static**.

### Command Mode

Router configuration

### Usage Guidelines

This command first appeared in Cisco IOS Release 10.0.

When used with IS-IS, the **redistribute** command causes the routes learned by the routing process tag to be advertised in the IS-IS routing process. Static routes are always redistributed into IS-IS unless a **no redistribute static** is performed. Redistribution only occurs for Level 2 routing.

You can specify only one IS-IS process per router. Creating a name for a routing process means that you use names when configuring routing. If the *tag* argument is not specified, a null tag is assumed. It must be unique among all CLNS router processes for a given router.

When used with ISO IGRP, if you have a router that is in two routing domains, you might want to redistribute routing information between the two domains. The **redistribute** router configuration command configures which routes are redistributed into the ISO IGRP domain. It is not necessary to use redistribution between areas.

The *tag* argument must be unique among all CLNS router processes for a given router. This tag should be the same as defined for the routing process in the **router iso-igrp** global configuration command.

Static routes are only redistributed into ISO IGRP when a **redistribute static** command is entered. The default is to not redistribute static routes into ISO IGRP. Only the router that injects the static route needs to have a **redistribute static** command defined. This command is needed only when you run ISO IGRP.

## Examples

The following example illustrates redistribution of ISO IGRP routes of Michigan and ISO IGRP routes of Ohio into the IS-IS area tagged USA:

```
router isis USA
 redistribute iso-igrp Michigan
 redistribute iso-igrp Ohio
```

The following example illustrates redistribution of IS-IS routes of France and ISO IGRP routes of Germany into the ISO IGRP area tagged Backbone:

```
router iso-igrp Backbone
 redistribute isis France
 redistribute iso-igrp Germany
```

In the following example, the router advertises any static routes it knows about in the Chicago domain:

```
router iso-igrp Chicago
 redistribute static
```

## Related Commands

Search online for documentation of related commands.

**route-map**


## ROUTE-MAP

Use the **route-map** global configuration command to define the conditions for redistributing routes from one routing protocol into another. Use the **no** form of this command to delete the route map.

**route-map** *map-tag* {**permit** | **deny**} *sequence-number*
**no route-map** *map-tag* {**permit** | **deny**} *sequence-number*

| Syntax | Description |
|---|---|
| *map-tag* | Meaningful name for the route map that can either be an expression or a filter set. The **redistribute** command uses this name to reference this route map. Multiple route-maps can share the same map tag name. |
| **permit** | If the match criteria are met for this route map, and **permit** is specified, the route is redistributed as controlled by the set actions. If the match criteria are not met, and **permit** is specified, the next route map with the same map-tag is tested. If a route passes none of the match criteria for the set of route maps sharing the same name, it is not redistributed by that set. |

| Syntax | Description |
|--------|-------------|
| deny | If the match criteria are met for the route map, and **deny** is specified, the route is not redistributed, and no further route maps sharing the same map tag name will be examined. |
| *sequence-number* | Number that indicates the position a new route map is to have in the list of route maps already configured with the same name. If given with the **no** form of this command, it specifies the position of the route map that should be deleted. |

### Command Mode

Global configuration

### Usage Guidelines

This command first appeared in Cisco IOS Release 10.0.

Use the **route-map** global configuration command, and the route-map configuration commands **match** and **set**, to define the conditions for redistributing routes from one routing protocol into another. Each **route-map** command has a list of **match** and **set** commands associated with it. The **match** commands specify the *match criteria*—the conditions under which redistribution is allowed for the current **route-map** command. The **set** commands specify the *set actions*—the particular redistribution actions to perform if the criteria enforced by the **match** commands are met.

### Related Commands

Search online for documentation of related commands.

**match clns address**
**redistribute**
**set level**

### ROUTER ISIS

Use the **router isis** global configuration command to enable the IS-IS routing protocol on your router and to configure the IS-IS routing process. This command identifies the area the router will work in and lets the router know that it will be routing dynamically rather than statically. Use the **no** form of this command with the appropriate tag to disable IS-IS routing for the system.

> **router isis** [*tag*]
> **no router isis** [*tag*]

| Syntax | Description |
|--------|-------------|
| *tag* | (Optional) Meaningful name for a routing process. If it is not specified, a null tag is assumed. The argument *tag* must be unique among all CLNS router processes for a given router. The *tag* argument is used later as a reference to this process. |

*Default*

Disabled

*Command Mode*

Global configuration

*Usage Guidelines*

This command first appeared in Cisco IOS Release 10.0.

Creating a name for a routing process means that you use names when configuring routing. You can specify only one IS-IS process per router. Only one IS-IS process is allowed, whether you run it in integrated mode, ISO CLNS, or IP only.

---

**NOTES**

IS-IS routing is not supported on Cisco access servers.

---

*Example*

The following example starts IS-IS routing with the optional *tag* argument:

```
router isis Pieinthesky
```

*Related Commands*

Search online for documentation of related commands.

**clns router isis**
**net**

## ROUTER ISO-IGRP

Use the **router iso-igrp** global configuration command to identify the area the router will work in and let it know that it will be routing dynamically using the ISO IGRP protocol. Use the **no** form of this command with the appropriate tag to disable ISO IGRP routing for the system.

    **router iso-igrp** [*tag*]
    **no router iso-igrp** [*tag*]

| *Syntax* | *Description* |
| --- | --- |
| *tag* | (Optional) Meaningful name for a routing process. For example, you could define a routing process named *Finance* for the Finance department and another routing process named *Marketing* for the Marketing department. If not specified, a null tag is assumed. The *tag* argument must be unique among all CLNS router processes for a given router. |

### Default

Disabled

### Command Mode

Global configuration

### Usage Guidelines

This command first appeared in Cisco IOS Release 10.0.

Creating a name for a routing process means that you use names when configuring routing. You can specify up to ten ISO IGRP processes.

### Example

In the following example, a router is specified in *Manufacturing*. The command must be typed on one line.

```
router iso-igrp Manufacturing
```

### Related Commands

Search online for documentation of related commands.

**clns router iso-igrp**
**net**

## SET LEVEL

Use the **set level** route-map configuration command to specify the routing level of routes to be advertised into a specified area of the routing domain. Use the **no** form of this command to disable advertising the specified routing level into a specified area.

```
set level {level-1 | level-2 | level-1-2}
no set level {level-1 | level-2 | level-1-2}
```

| Syntax | Description |
|---|---|
| level | Redistributed routes are advertised into this specified area of the routing domain. For IS-IS destinations, the default value is **level-2**. |
| level-1 | Inserted in IS-IS Level 1 link-state PDUs. |
| level-2 | Inserted in IS-IS Level 2 link-state PDUs. |
| level-1-2 | Inserted into both Level 1 and Level 2 IS-IS link-state PDUs. |

### Default

Disabled

## Command Mode

Route-map configuration

## Usage Guidelines

This command first appeared in Cisco IOS Release 10.0.

Use the **route-map** global configuration command, and the route-map configuration commands **match** and **set,** to define the conditions for redistributing routes from one routing protocol into another. Each **route-map** command has a list of **match** and **set** commands associated with it. The **match** commands specify the *match criteria*—the conditions under which redistribution is allowed for the current **route-map command.** The **set** commands specify the redistribution *set actions*—the particular redistribution actions to perform if the criteria enforced by the **match** commands are met. When all match criteria are met, all set actions are performed. The **no route-map** command deletes the route map.

## Example

Given the following configuration, a RIP-learned route for network 160.89.0.0 and an ISO IGRP-learned route with prefix 49.0001.0002 will be redistributed into an IS-IS Level 2 link-state PDU with metric 5:

```
router isis
 redistribute rip route-map ourmap
 redistribute iso-igrp remote route-map ourmap
route-map ourmap permit
 match ip address 1
 match clns address ourprefix
 set metric 5
 set level level-2
 access-list 1 permit 160.89.0.0 0.0.255.255
 clns filter-set ourprefix permit 49.0001.0002...
```

## Related Commands

Search online for documentation of related commands.

**match clns address**
**redistribute**
**route-map**

## SET METRIC

Use the **set metric** route-map configuration command to set the metric value to give the redistributed routes. Use the **no** form of this command to disable redistributing routes of a specific metric.

```
set metric metric-value
no set metric metric-value
```

| *Syntax* | *Description* |
|---|---|
| *metric-value* | Route metric. This can be an IGRP five-part metric. |

### Default

Disabled

### Command Mode

Route-map configuration

### Usage Guidelines

This command first appeared in Cisco IOS Release 10.0.

Use the **route-map** global configuration command, and the route-map configuration commands **match** and **set**, to define the conditions for redistributing routes from one routing protocol into another. Each **route-map** command has a list of **match** and **set** commands associated with it. The **match** commands specify the *match criteria*—the conditions under which redistribution is allowed for the current **route-map command**. The **set** commands specify the redistribution *set actions*—the particular redistribution actions to perform if the criteria enforced by the **match** commands are met. When all match criteria are met, all set actions are performed. The **no route-map** command deletes the route map.

### Example

Given the following configuration, a RIP-learned route for network 160.89.0.0 and an ISO IGRP-learned route with prefix 49.0001.0002 will be redistributed into an IS-IS Level 2 link-state PDU with metric 5:

```
router isis
 redistribute rip route-map ourmap
 redistribute iso-igrp remote route-map ourmap
!
route-map ourmap permit
 match ip address 1
 match clns address ourprefix
 set metric 5
 set level level-2
!
 access-list 1 permit 160.89.0.0 0.0.255.255
 clns filter-set ourprefix permit 49.0001.0002...
```

### Related Commands

Search online for documentation of related commands.

*Command Reference*

match clns address
redistribute
route-map

## SET METRIC-TYPE

Use the **set metric-type** route-map configuration command to set the metric type to give redistributed routes. Use the **no** form of this command to disable redistributing routes of a specific metric type.

> **set metric-type {internal | external}**
> **no set metric-type {internal | external}**

| Syntax | Description |
|--------|-------------|
| **internal** | IS-IS internal metric. |
| **external** | IS-IS external metric. |

### Default

Disabled

### Command Mode

Route-map configuration

### Usage Guidelines

This command first appeared in Cisco IOS Release 10.0.

Use the **route-map** global configuration command, and the route-map configuration commands **match** and **set,** to define the conditions for redistributing routes from one routing protocol into another. Each **route-map** command has a list of **match** and **set** commands associated with it. The **match** commands specify the *match criteria*—the conditions under which redistribution is allowed for the current **route-map command**. The **set** commands specify the redistribution *set actions*—the particular redistribution actions to perform if the criteria enforced by the **match** commands are met. When all match criteria are met, all set actions are performed. The **no route-map** command deletes the route map.

### Related Commands

Search online for documentation of related commands.

match clns address
redistribute
route-map

## SET TAG

Use the **set tag** route-map configuration command to set a tag value to associate with the redistributed routes. Use the **no** form of this command to disable redistributing routes with the specific tag.

> **set tag** *tag-value*
> **no set tag** *tag-value*

| Syntax | Description |
|--------|-------------|
| *tag-value* | Name for the tag. The tag value to associate with the redistributed route. If not specified, the default action is to *forward* the tag in the source routing protocol onto the new destination protocol. |

### Default

Disabled

### Command Mode

Route-map configuration

### Usage Guidelines

This command first appeared in Cisco IOS Release 10.0.

Use the **route-map** global configuration command, and the route-map configuration commands **match** and **set**, to define the conditions for redistributing routes from one routing protocol into another. Each **route-map** command has a list of **match** and **set** commands associated with it. The **match** commands specify the *match criteria*—the conditions under which redistribution is allowed for the current **route-map command**. The **set** commands specify the redistribution *set actions*—the particular redistribution actions to perform if the criteria enforced by the **match** commands are met. When all match criteria are met, all set actions are performed. The **no route-map** command deletes the route map.

### Related Commands

Search online for documentation of related commands.

**match clns address**
**redistribute**
**route-map**

## SHOW CLNS

Use the **show clns** EXEC command to display information about the CLNS network.

> **show clns**

*Syntax      Description*

This command has no arguments or keywords.

## Command Mode

EXEC

## Usage Guidelines

This command first appeared in Cisco IOS Release 10.0.

## Sample Display

The following is sample output from the **show clns** command:

```
router# show clns

Global CLNS Information:
  2 Interfaces Enabled for CLNS
  NET: 39.0004.0030.0000.0C00.224D.00
  NET: 39.0003.0020.0000.0C00.224D.00
  Configuration Timer: 60, Default Holding Timer: 300, Packet Lifetime 64
  ERPDU's requested on locally generated packets
  Intermediate system operation enabled (forwarding allowed)
  ISO IGRP level-1 Router: remote
     Routing for Domain: 39.0003, Area: 0020
  ISO IGRP level-2 Router: DOMAIN_remote
     Routing for Domain: 39.0003
  IS-IS level-1-2 Router:
     Routing for Area: 39.0004.0030
```

Table 14–5 describes significant fields shown in the display.

**Table 14–5**   *Show CLNS Field Description*

| Field | Description |
|-------|-------------|
| 2 Interfaces Enabled for CLNS | Indicates how many interfaces have the CLNS routing protocol enabled. |
| NET: 39.0004.0030.0000.0C00.224D.00 | First of two NETs for this router. |
| Configuration Timer: 60 | Displays the interval (in seconds) after which the router sends out IS hello packets. |
| Default Holding Timer: 300 | Length of time (in seconds) hello packets are remembered. |
| Packet Lifetime 64 | Default value used in packets sourced by this router. |
| ERPDUs requested on locally generated packets | Indicates whether ERPDUs are requested for packets sourced by the router. |

**Table 14–5** *Show CLNS Field Description, Continued*

| Field | Description |
|---|---|
| Intermediate system operation enabled (forwarding allowed) | Indicates whether this router is configured to be an ES or an IS. |
| ISO IGRP level-1 Router: remote | Specifies what CLNS routing type (ISO IGRP or IS-IS) and what routing level (Level 1, Level 2, or both) is enabled on the router. |
| Routing for Domain: 39.0003, Area: 0020 | Specifies the domain (39.0003) and area (0020) for which this CLNS routing type and routing level is enabled. |
| IS-IS level-1-2 Router: | Specifies that IS-IS is running in this router. Its tag is null. It is running Level 1 and Level 2. |
| Routing for Area: 39.0004.0030 | Specifies the IS-IS area this router is in. |

## SHOW CLNS CACHE

Use the **show clns cache** EXEC command to display the CLNS routing cache. The cache contains an entry for each destination that has packet switching enabled. The output of this command includes entries showing each destination for which the router has switched a packet in the recent past. This includes the router itself.

> **show clns cache**

*Syntax        Description*

This command has no arguments or keywords.

*Command Mode*

EXEC

*Usage Guidelines*

This command first appeared in Cisco IOS Release 10.0.

*Sample Display*

The following is sample output from the **show clns cache** command:

```
Router# show clns cache

CLNS routing cache version 433
Destination -> Next hop @ Interface: SNPA Address
[42] *39.0004.0040.0000.0C00.2D55.00 ISOLATOR
-> 0000.0C00.2D55 @ Serial2: 0000.0c00.6fa5
```

Table 14–6 describes significant fields shown in the display.

**Table 14–6**   *Show CLNS Cache Field Descriptions*

| Field | Description |
|-------|-------------|
| CLNS routing cache version 433 | Number identifying this particular CLNS routing cache. |
| Destination -> | Destination NSAP for the packet. |
| Next hop | Next hop system ID used to reach the destination. |
| @ Interface: | Interface through which the router transmitted the packet. |
| [42] | Cache location for this entry. |
| *39.0004.0040.0000.0C00.2D55.00* | NSAP address. |
| ISOLATOR | NSAP host name. |

* A leading asterisk (*) indicates that the entry is an allowable value.

## Related Commands

Search online for documentation of related commands.

clear clns cache

## SHOW CLNS ES-NEIGHBORS

Use the **show clns es-neighbors** EXEC command to list the ES neighbors that this router knows about.

> **show clns es-neighbors** [*type number*] [**detail**]

| Syntax | Description |
|--------|-------------|
| *type* | (Optional) Interface type. |
| *number* | (Optional) Interface number. |
| detail | (Optional) When specified, the areas associated with the end systems are displayed. Otherwise, a summary display is provided. |

## Command Mode

EXEC

## Usage Guidelines

This command first appeared in Cisco IOS Release 10.0.

## Sample Displays

The following is sample output from the **show clns es-neighbors** command when Ethernet interface 0 is specified:

```
router# show clns es-neighbors

System Id        Interface  State  Type  Format
0800.2B14.060E   Ethernet0  Up     ES    Phase V
0800.2B14.0528   Ethernet0  Up     ES    Phase V
```

Table 14–7 describes the significant fields shown in the display.

**Table 14–7** *Show CLNS ES-Neighbors Field Descriptions*

| Field | Descriptions |
|-------|--------------|
| System Id | Identification value of the system. |
| Interface | Interface on which the router was discovered. |
| State | Adjacency state. Up and Init are the states. See the **show clns neighbors** description. |
| Type | Type of neighbor. Only valid value for the **show clns es-neighbors** EXEC command is ES. |
| Format | Indicates if the neighbor is either a Phase V (OSI) adjacency or Phase IV (DECnet) adjacency. |

The following is sample output from the **show clns es-neighbors detail** command:

```
router# show clns es-neighbors detail

System Id        Interface  State  Type  Format
0800.2B14.060E   Ethernet0  Up     ES    Phase V
Area Address(es): 49.0040
0800.2B14.0528   Ethernet0  Up     ES    Phase V
Area Address(es): 49.0040
```

Notice that the information displayed in **show clns es-neighbors detail** output includes everything shown in **show clns es-neighbors** output, but it also includes the area addresses associated with the ES neighbors.

## Related Commands

Search online for documentation of related commands.

**clear clns es-neighbors**

## SHOW CLNS FILTER-EXPR

Use the **show clns filter-expr** EXEC command to display one or all currently defined CLNS filter expressions.

> **show clns filter-expr** [*name*] [detail]

| Syntax | Description |
|--------|-------------|
| *name* | (Optional) Name of the filter expression to display. If none is specified, all are displayed. |
| **detail** | (Optional) When specified, expressions are evaluated down to their most primitive filter set terms before being displayed. |

## Command Mode

EXEC

## Usage Guidelines

This command first appeared in Cisco IOS Release 10.0.

## Sample Displays

The following displays assume filter expressions have been defined with the following commands. FRED, BARNEY, WILMA, and BETTY are all filter sets.

```
clns filter-expr MEN FRED or BARNEY
clns filter-expr WOMEN WILMA or BETTY
clns filter-expr ADULTS MEN or WOMEN
```

The **show clns filter-expr** command would yield the following output:

```
router# show clns filter-expr

MEN = FRED or BARNEY
WOMEN = WILMA or BETTY
ADULTS = MEN or WOMEN
```

The **show clns filter-expr detail** command would yield the following output:

```
router# show clns filter-expr detail

MEN = FRED or BARNEY
WOMEN = WILMA or BETTY
ADULTS = (FRED or BARNEY) or (WILMA or BETTY)
```

## Related Commands

Search online for documentation of related commands.

**clns filter-expr**

## SHOW CLNS FILTER-SET

Use the **show clns filter-set** EXEC command to display one or all currently defined CLNS filter sets.

   **show clns filter-set** [*name*]

| Syntax | Description |
|--------|-------------|
| *name* | (Optional) Name of the filter set to display. If none is specified, all are displayed. |

## Command Mode

EXEC

## Usage Guidelines

This command first appeared in Cisco IOS Release 10.0.

## Sample Display

The following display assumes filter sets have been defined with the following commands:

```
clns filter-set US-OR-NORDUNET 47.0005...
clns filter-set US-OR-NORDUNET 47.0023...
clns filter-set LOCAL 49.0003...
```

The following is a sample output from the **show clns filter-set** command:

```
router# show clns filter-set

CLNS filter set US-OR-NORDUNET
permit 47.0005...
permit 47.0023...
CLNS filter set LOCAL
permit 49.0003...
```

## Related Commands

Search online for documentation of related commands.

**clns filter-set**

## SHOW CLNS INTERFACE

Use the **show clns interface** EXEC command to list the CLNS-specific information about each interface.

  **show clns interface** [*type number*]

| Syntax | Description |
|--------|-------------|
| *type* | (Optional) Interface type. |
| *number* | (Optional) Interface number. |

## Command Mode

EXEC

## Usage Guidelines

This command first appeared in Cisco IOS Release 10.0.

## Sample Display

The following is sample output from the **show clns interface** command that includes information for Token Ring and serial interfaces:

```
router# show clns interface

TokenRing 0 is administratively down, line protocol is down
  CLNS protocol processing disabled
TokenRing 1 is up, line protocol is up
  Checksums enabled, MTU 4461, Encapsulation SNAP
  ERPDUs enabled, min. interval 10 msec.
  RDPDUs enabled, min. interval 100 msec., Addr Mask enabled
  Congestion Experienced bit set at 4 packets
  CLNS fast switching disabled
  DEC compatibility mode OFF for this interface
  Next ESH/ISH in 18 seconds
  Routing Protocol: ISO IGRP
      Routing Domain/Area: <39.0003> <0020>
  Serial 2 is up, line protocol is up
      Checksums enabled, MTU 1497, Encapsulation HDLC
ERPDUs enabled, min. interval 10 msec.
    RDPDUs enabled, min. interval 100 msec., Addr Mask enabled
    Congestion Experienced bit set at 4 packets
    CLNS fast switching enabled
    DEC compatibility mode OFF for this interface
    CLNS cluster alias enabled on this interface
    Next ESH/ISH in 48 seconds
  Routing Protocol: IS-IS
      Circuit Type: level-1-2
      Level-1 Metric: 10, Priority: 64, Circuit ID: 0000.0C00.2D55.0A
      Number of active level-1 adjacencies: 0
      Level-2 Metric: 10, Priority: 64, Circuit ID: 0000.0000.0000.00
      Number of active level-2 adjacencies: 0
      Next IS-IS LAN Level-1 hello in 3 seconds
      Next IS-IS LAN Level-2 hello in 3 seconds
```

Table 14–8 describes significant fields shown in the display.

**Table 14–8**  *Show CLNS Interface Field Descriptions*

| Field | Description |
|---|---|
| TokenRing 0 is administratively down, line protocol is down | (First interface) Shown to be administratively down with CLNS disabled. |
| TokenRing 1 is up, line protocol is up/ Serial 2 is up, line protocol is up | (Second, third interfaces) Shown to be up, and CLNS is up. |
| Checksums enabled | Can be enabled or disabled. |
| MTU | The number following MTU is the maximum transmission size for a packet on this interface. |
| Encapsulation | Describes the encapsulation used by CLNP packets on this interface. |
| ERPDUs | Displays information about the generation of ERPDUs. They can be either enabled or disabled. If they are enabled, they are sent out no more frequently than the specified interval. |
| RDPDUs | Provides information about the generation of RDPDUs. They can be either enabled or disabled. If they are enabled, they are sent out no more frequently than the specified interval. If the address mask is enabled, redirects are sent out with an address mask. |
| Congestion Experienced | Tells when CLNS will turn on the congestion experienced bit. The default is to turn this bit on when there are more than four packets in a queue. |
| CLNS fast switching | Displays whether fast switching is supported for CLNS on this interface. |
| DEC compatibility mode | Indicates whether DEC compatibility has been enabled. |
| CLNS cluster alias enabled on this interface | Indicates that CLNS cluster aliasing has been enabled on this interface. |
| Next ESH/ISH | Displays when the next ES hello or IS hello is sent on this interface. |
| Routing Protocol | Lists the areas that this interface is in. In most cases, an interface will be in only one area. |

*Command Reference*

**Table 14–8**   *Show CLNS Interface Field Descriptions, Continued*

| Field | Description |
|-------|-------------|
| Circuit type | Indicates whether the interface has been configured for local routing (Level 1), area routing (Level 2), or local and area routing (Level 1-2). |
| Remaining fields | Last series of fields displays information pertaining to the ISO CLNS routing protocols enabled on the interface. For ISO IGRP, the routing domain and area addresses are specified. For IS-IS, the Level 1 and Level 2 metrics, priorities, Circuit IDs, and number of active Level 1 and Level 2 adjacencies are specified. |

## SHOW CLNS IS-NEIGHBORS

Use the **show clns is-neighbors** EXEC command to display IS-IS related information for IS-IS router adjacencies. Neighbor entries are sorted according to the area in which they are located.

show clns is-neighbors [*type number*] [**detail**]

| Syntax | Description |
|--------|-------------|
| *type* | (Optional) Interface type. |
| *number* | (Optional) Interface number. |
| **detail** | (Optional) When specified, the areas associated with the intermediate systems are displayed. Otherwise, a summary display is provided. |

### Command Mode
EXEC

### Usage Guidelines
This command first appeared in Cisco IOS Release 10.0.

### Sample Displays
The following is sample output from the **show clns is-neighbors** command:

```
router# show clns is-neighbors

System Id        Interface   State  Type  Priority  Circuit Id          Format
0000.0C00.0C35   Ethernet1   Up     L1    64        0000.0C00.62E6.03   Phase V
0800.2B16.24EA   Ethernet0   Up     L1L2  64/64     0800.2B16.24EA.01   Phase V
0000.0C00.3E51   Serial1     Up     L2    0         04                  Phase V
0000.0C00.62E6   Ethernet1   Up     L1    64        0000.0C00.62E6.03   Phase V
```

Table 14–9 describes significant fields shown in the display.

**Table 14-9** *Show CLNS IS-Neighbors Field Descriptions*

| Field | Descriptions |
|-------|--------------|
| System Id | Identification value of the system. |
| Interface | Interface on which the router was discovered. |
| State | Adjacency state. Up and Init are the states. See the **show clns neighbors** description. |
| Type | L1, L2, and L1L2 type adjacencies. See the **show clns neighbors** description. |
| Priority | IS-IS priority that the respective neighbor is advertising. The highest priority neighbor is elected the designated IS-IS router for the interface. |
| Circuit Id | Neighbor's idea of what the designated IS-IS router is for the interface. |
| Format | Indicates if the neighbor is either a Phase V (OSI) adjacency or Phase IV (DECnet) adjacency. |

The following is sample output from the **show clns is-neighbors detail** command:

```
router# show clns is-neighbors detail

System Id        Interface   State  Type  Priority  Circuit Id          Format
0000.0C00.0C35  Ethernet1   Up     L1    64        0000.0C00.62E6.03   Phase V
   Area Address(es): 47.0004.004D.0001 39.0001
   Uptime: 0:03:35
0800.2B16.24EA  Ethernet0   Up     L1L2  64/64     0800.2B16.24EA.01   Phase V
   Area Address(es): 47.0004.004D.0001
   Uptime: 0:03:35
0000.0C00.3E51  Serial1     Up     L2    0         04                  Phase V
   Area Address(es): 39.0004
   Uptime: 0:03:35
000.0C00.62E6   Ethernet1   Up     L1    64        0000.0C00.62E6.03   Phase V
   Area Address(es): 47.0004.004D.0001
   Uptime: 0:03:35
```

Notice that the information displayed in **show clns is-neighbors detail** output includes everything shown in **show clns is-neighbors** output, but it also includes the area addresses associated with the IS neighbors (intermediate-system adjacencies) and how long (uptime) the adjacency has existed.

### Related Commands

Search online for documentation of related commands.

**clear clns is-neighbors**

## SHOW CLNS NEIGHBORS

Use the **show clns neighbors** EXEC command to display both ES and IS neighbors.

    **show clns neighbors** [*type number*] [**detail**]

| Syntax | Description |
|--------|-------------|
| *type* | (Optional) Interface type. |
| *number* | (Optional) Interface number. |
| **detail** | (Optional) When specified, the area addresses advertised by the neighbor in the hello messages is displayed. Otherwise, a summary display is provided. |

## Command Mode

EXEC

## Usage Guidelines

This command first appeared in Cisco IOS Release 10.0.

## Sample Displays

The following is sample output from the **show clns neighbors** command. This display is a composite of the **show clns es-neighbor** and **show clns is-neighbor** commands.

```
router# show clns neighbors

System Id         SNPA            Interface   State  Holdtime   Type Protocol
0000.0000.0007    aa00.0400.6408  Ethernet0   Init   277        IS   ES-IS
0000.0C00.0C35    0000.0c00.0c36  Ethernet1   Up     91         L1   IS-IS
0800.2B16.24EA    aa00.0400.2d05  Ethernet0   Up     29         L1L2 IS-IS
0800.2B14.060E    aa00.0400.9205  Ethernet0   Up     1698       ES   ES-IS
0000.0C00.3E51    *HDLC*          Serial1     Up     28         L2   IS-IS
0000.0C00.62E6    0000.0c00.62e7  Ethernet1   Up     22         L1   IS-IS
0A00.0400.2D05    aa00.0400.2d05  Ethernet0   Init   24         IS   ES-IS
```

Table 14–10 describes the fields shown in the display.

**Table 14–10**  *Show CLNS Neighbors Field Descriptions*

| Field | Description |
|-------|-------------|
| System Id | Six-byte value that identifies a system in an area. |
| SNPA | Subnetwork Point of Attachment. This is the data link address. |
| Interface | Interface from which the system was learned. |
| State | State of the ES or IS. |
| Init | System is an IS and is waiting for an IS-IS hello message. IS-IS regards the neighbor as not adjacent. |
| Up | Believes the ES or IS is reachable. |
| Holdtime | Number of seconds before this adjacency entry times out. |

**Table 14–10** *Show CLNS Neighbors Field Descriptions, Continued*

| Field | Description |
|-------|-------------|
| Type | The adjacency type. Possible values are as follows: |
| ES | End-system adjacency either discovered via the ES-IS protocol or statically configured. |
| IS | Router adjacency either discovered via the ES-IS protocol or statically configured. |
| L1 | Router adjacency for Level 1 routing only. |
| L1L2 | Router adjacency for Level 1 and Level 2 routing. |
| L2 | Router adjacency for Level 2 only. |
| Protocol | Protocol through which the adjacency was learned. Valid protocol sources are ES-IS, IS-IS, ISO IGRP, Static, and DECnet. |

The following is sample output from the **show clns neighbors detail** command:

```
router# show clns neighbors detail

System Id       SNPA            Interface   State  Holdtime  Type  Protocol
000.0000.0007   aa00.0400.6408  Ethernet0   Init   291       IS    ES-IS
  Area Address(es): 47.0005.80FF.F500.0000.0003.0020
0000.0C00.0C35  0000.0c00.0c36  Ethernet1   Up     94        L1    IS-IS
  Area Address(es): 47.0004.004D.0001 39.0001
0800.2B16.24EA  aa00.0400.2d05  Ethernet0   Up     9         L1L2  IS-IS
  Area Address(es): 47.0004.004D.0001
0800.2B14.060E  aa00.0400.9205  Ethernet0   Up     1651      ES    ES-IS
  Area Address(es): 49.0040
0000.0C00.3E51  *HDLC*          Serial1     Up     27        L2    IS-IS
  Area Address(es): 39.0004
0000.0C00.62E6  0000.0c00.62e7  Ethernet1   Up     26        L1    IS-IS
  Area Address(es): 47.0004.004D.0001
oA00.0400.2D05  aa00.0400.2d05  Ethernet0   Init   29        IS    ES-IS
    Area Address(es): 47.0004.004D.0001
```

Notice that the information displayed in **show clns neighbors detail** output includes everything shown in **show clns neighbors** output, but it also includes the area addresses associated with the ES and IS neighbors.

## Related Commands

Search online for documentation of related commands.

**clear clns neighbors**

**SHOW CLNS PROTOCOL**

Use the **show clns protocol** EXEC command to list the protocol-specific information for each ISO IGRP routing process in the router. There will always be at least two routing processes, a Level 1 and a Level 2, and there can be more.

   **show clns protocol** [*domain* | *area-tag*]

| Syntax | Description |
|--------|-------------|
| *domain* | (Optional) Particular ISO IGRP routing domain. |
| *area-tag* | (Optional) Particular IS-IS area. |

*Command Mode*

EXEC

*Usage Guidelines*

This command first appeared in Cisco IOS Release 10.0.

*Sample Display*

The following is sample output from the **show clns protocol** command:

```
router# show clns protocol

ISO IGRP Level 1 Router: remote
    Routing for domain: 39.0003 area: 0020
    Sending Updates every 45 seconds. Next due in 11 seconds
    Invalid after 135 seconds,
    Hold down for 145 seconds
    Sending Router Hellos every 17 seconds. Next due in 9 seconds
    Invalid after 51 seconds,
    IGRP metric weight K1=1, K2=0, K3=1, K4=0, K5=0
    Interfaces in domain/area:
        TokenRing1
ISO IGRP Level 2 Router: DOMAIN_remote
    Routing for domain: 39.0003
    Redistribute:
        isis (Null Tag)
    Sending Updates every 45 seconds. Next due in 2 seconds
    Invalid after 135 seconds,
    Hold down for 145 seconds
    Sending Router Hellos every 17 seconds. Next due in 0 seconds
    Invalid after 51 seconds,
    ISO IGRP metric weight K1=1, K2=0, K3=1, K4=0, K5=0
    Interfaces in domain/area:
        TokenRing1
IS-IS Router: <Null Tag>
    System Id: 0000.0C00.224D.00 IS-Type: level-1-2
```

```
Manual area address(es):
    39.0004.0030
Routing for area address(es):
    39.0004.0030
Interfaces supported by IS-IS:
    Serial2
Next global update in 530 seconds
Redistributing:
    static
    iso-igrp (remote)
Distance: 110
```

Table 14–11 describes significant fields shown in the display.

**Table 14–11** *Show CLNS Protocol Field Descriptions*

| Field | Description |
|---|---|
| ISO IGRP Level 1 Router: | Indicates what CLNS routing type is enabled on the router (always ISO IGRP when the fields in this section are displayed). Also indicates what routing level (Level 1, Level 2, or both) is enabled on the router. |
| remote | Process tag that has been configured using the **router iso-igrp** global configuration command. |
| Routing for domain: 39.0003 area: 0020 | Domain address and area number for Level 1 routing processes. For Level 2 routing processes, this command lists the domain address. |
| Sending Updates every 45 seconds. | Displays when the next routing updates are sent. |
| Next due in 11 seconds | Indicates when the next update is sent. |
| Invalid after 135 seconds | Indicates how long routing updates are to be believed. |
| Hold down for 145 seconds | Indicates how long a route is held down before new information is to be believed. |
| Sending Router hellos every 17 seconds. Next due in 9 seconds | Indicates how often the Cisco IOS software sends hello packets to each other and when the next is due. |
| Invalid after 51 seconds | Indicates how long a neighbor entry is remembered. |

*Command Reference*

**Table 14–11**    *Show CLNS Protocol Field Descriptions, Continued*

| Field | Description |
|---|---|
| IGRP metric weight K1=1, K2=0, K3=1, K4=0, K5=0 | Displays list of the weights applied to the various components of the metric. These fields are followed by the list of interfaces in this area. |
| Interfaces in domain/area: | Displays list of interface names for which the router process is configured. |

Table 14–12 describes significant fields shown in the IS-IS portion of the display.

**Table 14–12**    *Show CLNS Protocol with IS-IS Field Descriptions*

| Field | Description |
|---|---|
| IS_IS Router: <Null Tag> | Indicates what CLNS routing type is enabled on the router (always IS-IS when the fields in this section are displayed). |
| System Id: 0000.0C00.224D.00 | Identification value of the system. |
| IS-Type: level-1-2 | Indicates what routing level (Level 1, Level 2, or both) is enabled on the router. |
| Manual area address(es): 39.0004.0030 | Area addresses that have been configured. |
| Routing for area address(es): 39.0004.0030 | List of manually configured and learned area addresses. |
| Interfaces supported by IS-IS: | List of interfaces on the router supporting IS-IS. |
| Next global update in 530 seconds | Next expected IS-IS update (in seconds). |
| Redistributing: | Configuration of route redistribution. |
| Distance: | Configured distance. |

## SHOW CLNS ROUTE

Use the **show clns route** EXEC command to display all of the destinations to which this router knows how to route packets. The **show clns route** command shows the IS-IS Level 2 routing table as well as static and ISO IGRP learned prefix routes. This table stores IS-IS area addresses and prefix routes. Destinations are sorted by category.

     **show clns route** [*nsap*]

| *Syntax* | *Description* |
|---|---|
| *nsap* | (Optional) CLNS NSAP address. |

## Command Mode

EXEC

## Usage Guidelines

This command first appeared in Cisco IOS Release 10.0.

## Sample Display

The following is sample output from the **show clns route** command:

```
router# show clns route

ISO IGRP Routing Table for Domain 39.0003, Area 0020
System Id       Next-Hop        SNPA         Interface   Metric  State
0000.0C00.224D  0000.0000.0000  --           --          0       Up

ISO IGRP Routing Table for Domain 39.0003
Area Id         Next-Hop        SNPA         Interface   Metric  State
0020            0000.0000.0000  --           --          0       Up

CLNS Prefix Routing Table
39.0003 [100/0]
  via 39.0004.0030.0000.0C00.224D.00, ISO IGRP, Up
39.0004.0040 [110/10]
  via 0000.0C00.2D55, IS-IS, Up, Serial2
39.0004.0030 [110/0]
  via 0000.0C00.224D, IS-IS, Up
39.0004.0030.0000.0C00.224D.00, Local NET Entry
39.0003.0020.0000.0C00.224D.00, Local NET Entry
39.0001, DECnet discard Entry, Up
```

As the display shows, neighbors are not included in the **show clns route** output.

Table 14–13 describes significant fields shown in the display.

**Table 14–13** *Show CLNS Route Field Descriptions*

| Field | Descriptions |
|---|---|
| The following are for dynamically learned routes: | |
| Domain 39.0003 | The routing domain for which the routes are being displayed. |
| Area 0020 | The area this portion of the routing table describes. |
| System Id | Identification value of the system listed in Level 1 forwarding table. |
| Area Id | The identification value of the area listed in the area forwarding table. |

**Table 14–13**  *Show CLNS Route Field Descriptions, Continued*

| Field | Descriptions |
|---|---|
| Next-Hop | System ID of best cost next-hop to listed address. |
| SNPA | SNPA of next-hop system. |
| Interface | Interface through which next-hop system is known. |
| Metric | ISO IGRP metric for the route. |
| State | Up (active) or Down (nonoperational). |
| **The following are for prefix routes:** | |
| 39.0003 | Destination prefix. |
| [100/0] | Administrative distance/metric. |
| Next-hop address | Either an NET (if a static route) or System ID, if route obtained via IS-IS or ISO-IGRP. |
| ISO IGRP | Indicates whether the route was learned using ISO IGRP or IS-IS. |
| Up | Link status—Up (active) or Down (nonoperational). |
| Serial 2 Local NET Entry | Interface type—Only appears if the specific interface through which the destination is reachable is unambiguously known; Local NET Entry indicates destination is on a directly connected network. |
| DECnet Discard Entry | Static route entry for DECnet. |

Output for the **show clns route** *nsap* command is the same as that for **show clns route,** but only lists a single entry.

### Related Commands

Search online for documentation of related commands.

**clear clns route**

## SHOW CLNS TRAFFIC

Use the **show clns traffic** EXEC command to list the CLNS packets this router has seen.

    **show clns traffic**

*Syntax*     *Description*

This command has no arguments or keywords.

## Command Mode

EXEC

## Usage Guidelines

This command first appeared in Cisco IOS Release 10.0.

## Sample Display

The following is sample output from the **show clns traffic** command:

```
router# show clns traffic

CLNS & ESIS Output: 139885, Input: 90406
CLNS Local: 0, Forward: 0
CLNS Discards:
  Hdr Syntax: 150, Checksum: 0, Lifetime: 0, Output cngstn: 0
  No Route: 0, Dst Unreachable 0, Encaps. Failed: 0
  NLP Unknown: 0, Not an IS: 0
CLNS Options: Packets 19, total 19, bad 0, GQOS 0, cngstn exprncd 0
CLNS Segments: Segmented: 0, Failed: 0
CLNS Broadcasts: sent: 0, rcvd: 0
Echos: Rcvd 0 requests, 69679 replies
  Sent 69701 requests, 0 replies
ESIS(sent/rcvd): ESHs: 0/34, ISHs: 483/1839, RDs: 0/0, QCF: 0/0
ISO IGRP: Querys (sent/rcvd): 0/0 Updates (sent/rcvd): 1279/1402
ISO IGRP: Router Hellos: (sent/rcvd): 1673/1848
ISO IGRP Syntax Errors: 0
IS-IS:Level-1 Hellos(sent/rcvd):0/0
IS-IS:Level-2 Hellos(sent/rcvd):0/0
IS-IS:PTP Hellos(sent/rcvd):0/0
IS-IS:Level-1 LSPs(sent/rcvd):0/0
IS-IS:Level-2 LSPs(sent/rcvd):0/0
IS-IS:Level-1 CSNPs(sent/rcvd):0/0
IS-IS:Level-2 CSNPs(sent/rcvd):0/0
IS-IS:Level-1 PSNPs(sent/rcvd):0/0
IS-IS:Level-2 PSNPs(sent/rcvd):0/0
IS-IS:Level-1 DR Elections:0
IS-IS:Level-2 DR Elections:0
IS-IS:Level-1 SPF Calculations:0
IS-IS:Level-2 SPF Calculations:0
```

Table 14–14 describes significant fields shown in the display.

**Table 14–14** *Show CLNS Traffic Field Descriptions*

| Field | Description |
|---|---|
| CLNS & ESIS Output | Total number of packets that this router has sent. |
| Input | Total number of packets that this router has received. |

*Command Reference*

**Table 14–14**    *Show CLNS Traffic Field Descriptions, Continued*

| Field | Description |
| --- | --- |
| CLNS Local | Lists the number of packets that were generated by this router. |
| Forward | Lists the number of packets that this router has forwarded. |
| CLNS Discards | Lists the packets that CLNS has discarded, along with the reason for the discard. |
| CLNS Options | Lists the options that have been seen in CLNS packets. |
| CLNS Segments | Lists the number of packets that have been segmented and the number of failures that occurred because a packet could not be segmented. |
| CLNS Broadcasts | Lists the number of CLNS broadcasts that have been sent and received. |
| Echos | Lists the number of echo request packets and echo reply packets that have been received. The line following this field lists the number of echo request packets and echo reply packets that have been sent. |
| ESIS (sent/rcvd) | Lists the number of ESH, ISH, and Redirects sent and received. |
| ISO IGRP | Lists the number of IGRP queries and updates sent and received. |
| Router Hellos | Lists the number of IGRP router hello packets that have been sent and received. |
| IS-IS: Level-1 hellos (sent/rcvd) | Lists the number of Level 1 IS-IS hello packets sent and received. |
| IS-IS: Level-2 hellos (sent/rcvd) | Lists the number of Level 2 IS-IS hello packets sent and received. |
| IS-IS: PTP hellos (sent/rcvd) | Lists the number of point-to-point IS-IS hello packets sent and received over serial links. |
| IS-IS: Level-1 LSPs (sent/rcvd) | Lists the number of Level 1 link-state PDUs sent and received. |
| IS-IS: Level-2 LSPs (sent/rcvd) | Lists the number of Level 2 link-state PDUs sent and received. |
| IS-IS: Level-1 CSNPs (sent/rcvd) | Lists the number of Level 1 CSNPs sent and received. |
| IS-IS: Level-2 CSNPs (sent/rcvd) | Lists the number of Level 2 CSNPs sent and received. |
| IS-IS: Level-1 PSNPs (sent/rcvd) | Lists the number of Level 1 PSNPs sent and received. |

**Table 14–14** *Show CLNS Traffic Field Descriptions, Continued*

| Field | Description |
|---|---|
| IS-IS: Level-2 PSNPs (sent/rcvd) | Lists the number of Level 2 PSNPs sent and received. |
| IS-IS: Level-1 DR Elections | Lists the number of times Level 1 designated router election occurred. |
| IS-IS: Level-2 DR Elections | Lists the number of times Level 2 designated router election occurred. |
| IS-IS: Level-1 SPF Calculations | Lists the number of times Level 1 shortest-path-first (SPF) tree was computed. |
| IS-IS: Level-2 SPF Calculations | Lists the number of times Level 2 SPF tree was computed. |

## SHOW ISIS DATABASE

Use the **show isis database** EXEC command to display the IS-IS link state database. A summary display is provided if no options are specified.

    **show isis database** [**level-1**] [**level-2**] [**detail**] [*lspid*]

| Syntax | Description |
|---|---|
| **level-1** | (Optional) Displays the IS-IS link state database for Level 1. You can use the abbreviation **l1**. |
| **level-2** | (Optional) Displays the IS-IS link state database for Level 2. You can use the abbreviation **l2**. |
| **detail** | (Optional) When specified, the content of each link-state PDU is displayed. Otherwise, a summary display is provided. |
| *lspid* | (Optional) Link-state protocol ID. Displays the contents of the specified link-state packet. The Link-state protocol ID must be in the form of xxxx.xxxx.xxxx.yy-zz or name.yy-zz. For a description of these values, see Table 14–15 in the "Usage Guidelines" section. |

### Command Mode

EXEC

### Usage Guidelines

This command first appeared in Cisco IOS Release 10.0.

Each of the options shown in brackets for this command can be entered in an arbitrary string within the same command entry. For example, the following are both valid command specifications and provided the same display: **show isis database detail l2** and **show isis database l2 detail**.

The values for the argument *lspid* are described in Table 14–15:

**Table 14–15**   *Link-State Protocol ID Values*

| Value | Description |
|---|---|
| xxxx.xxxx.xxxx.yy-zz | xxxx.xxxx.xxxx—System ID.<br>yy—Pseudo ID.<br>zz—Link-state PDU number. |
| name.yy-zz | name—CLNS host name.<br>yy—Pseudo ID.<br>zz—Link-state PDU number. |

*Sample Displays*

The following is sample output from the **show isis database** command when specified with no options or as **show isis data l1 l2**:

```
router# show isis database

IS-IS Level-1 Link State Database
LSPID                   LSP Seq Num    LSP Checksum   LSP Holdtime   ATT/P/OL
0000.0C00.0C35.00-00    0x0000000C     0x5696         792            0/0/0
0000.0C00.40AF.00-00*   0x00000009     0x8452         1077           1/0/0
0000.0C00.62E6.00-00    0x0000000A     0x38E7         383            0/0/0
0000.0C00.62E6.03-00    0x00000006     0x82BC         384            0/0/0
0800.2B16.24EA.00-00    0x00001D9F     0x8864         1188           1/0/0
0800.2B16.24EA.01-00    0x00001E36     0x0935         1198           1/0/0

IS-IS Level-2 Link State Database
LSPID                   LSP Seq Num    LSP Checksum   LSP Holdtime   ATT/P/OL
0000.0C00.0C35.03-00    0x00000005     0x04C8         792            0/0/0
0000.0C00.3E51.00-00    0x00000007     0xAF96         758            0/0/0
0000.0C00.40AF.00-00*   0x0000000A     0x3AA9         1077           0/0/0
```

Table 14–16 describes significant fields shown in the display.

**Table 14–16** *Show IS-IS Database Field Descriptions*

| Field | Description |
|---|---|
| LSPID | The link-state PDU ID. The first six octets form the system ID. The next octet is the pseudo ID. When this value is zero, the link-state PDU ID describes links from the system. When it is not zero, the link-state PDU is a pseudo-node link-state PDU. The designated router for an interface is the only system that originates pseudonode link-state PDUs. The last octet is the link-state PDU number. If there is more data than can fit in a single link-state PDU, additional link-state PDUs are sent with increasing link-state PDU numbers. An asterisk (*) indicates that the link-state PDU was originated by the local system. |
| LSP Seq Num | Sequence number for the link-state PDU that allows other systems to determine if they have received the latest information from the source. |
| LSP Checksum | Checksum of the entire link-state PDU packet. |
| LSP Holdtime | Amount of time the link-state PDU remains valid, in seconds. |
| ATT | The attach bit. This indicates that the router is also a Level 2 router, and it can reach other areas. |
| P | The P bit. Detects if the IS is area partition repair capable. |
| OL | The overload bit. Determines if the IS is congested. |

The following is sample output from the **show isis database detail** command:

```
router# show isis database detail

IS-IS Level-1 Link State Database
LSPID                LSP Seq Num  LSP Checksum  LSP Holdtime  ATT/P/OL
0000.0C00.0C35.00-00  0x0000000C  0x5696          325           0/0/0
  Area Address: 47.0004.004D.0001
  Area Address: 39.0001
  Metric: 10    IS 0000.0C00.62E6.03
  Metric: 0     ES 0000.0C00.0C35
0000.0C00.40AF.00-00* 0x00000009   0x8452          608           1/0/0
  Area Address: 47.0004.004D.0001
  Metric: 10    IS 0800.2B16.24EA.01
  Metric: 10    IS 0000.0C00.62E6.03
  Metric: 0     ES 0000.0C00.40AF

IS-IS Level-2 Link State Database
LSPID                LSP Seq Num  LSP Checksum  LSP Holdtime  ATT/P/OL
0000.0C00.0C35.03-00  0x00000005  0x04C8          317           0/0/0
  Metric: 0     IS 0000.0C00.0C35.00
0000.0C00.3E51.00-00  0x00000009  0xAB98          1182          0/0/0
  Area Address: 39.0004
  Metric: 10    IS 0000.0C00.40AF.00
  Metric: 10    IS 0000.0C00.3E51.05
```

*Command Reference*

As the display shows, in addition to the information displayed in **show isis database,** the **show isis database detail** command displays the contents of each link-state PDU.

Table 14–17 describes significant fields shown in the display.

**Table 14–17**   *Show IS-IS Database Detail Field Descriptions*

| Field | Description |
|---|---|
| LSPID | The link-state PDU ID. The first six octets form the System ID. The next octet is the pseudo ID. When this value is zero, the link-state PDU describes links from the system. When it is not zero, the link-state PDU is a pseudo-node link-state PDU. The designated router for an interface is the only system that originates pseudonode link-state PDUs. The last octet is the link-state PDU number. If there is more data than can fit in a single link-state PDU, additional link-state PDUs are sent with increasing link-state PDU numbers. An asterisk (*) indicates that the link-state PDU was originated by the local system. |
| LSP Seq Num | Sequence number for the link-state PDU that allows other systems to determine if they have received the latest information from the source. |
| LSP Checksum | Checksum of the entire link-state PDU packet. |
| LSP Holdtime | Amount of time the link-state PDU remains valid, in seconds. |
| ATT | The attach bit. This indicates that the router is also a Level 2 router, and it can reach other areas. |
| P | The P bit. Detects if the IS is area partition repair-capable. |
| OL | The overload bit. Determines if the IS is congested. |
| Area Address: | Reachable area addresses from the router. |
| Metric: | IS-IS metric for the route. |

## SHOW ISIS ROUTES

Use the **show isis routes** EXEC command to display the IS-IS Level 1 forwarding table for IS-IS learned routes.

> **show isis routes**

*Syntax        Description*

This command has no arguments or keywords.

*Command Mode*

EXEC

## Usage Guidelines

This command first appeared in Cisco IOS Release 10.0.

## Sample Display

The following is sample output from the **show isis routes** command:

```
router# show isis routes

IS-IS Level-1 Routing Table - Version 34
System Id        Next-Hop        SNPA            Interface   Metric   State
0000.0C00.0C35   0000.0C00.0C35  0000.0c00.0c36  Ethernet1   20       Up
0800.2B16.24EA   0800.2B16.24EA  aa00.0400.2d05  Ethernet0   10       Up
0800.2B14.060E   0800.2B14.060E  aa00.0400.9205  Ethernet0   10       Up
0800.2B14.0528   0800.2B14.0528  aa00.0400.9105  Ethernet0   10       Up
0000.0C00.40AF   0000.0000.0000  --              --          0        Up
0000.0C00.62E6   0000.0C00.62E6  0000.0c00.62e7  Ethernet1   10       Up
AA00.0400.2D05   0800.2B16.24EA  aa00.0400.2d05  Ethernet0   10       Up
```

Table 14–18 describes significant fields shown in the display.

**Table 14–18**  *Show ISIS Route Field Descriptions*

| Field | Description |
|---|---|
| Version 34 | Indicates version number of the Level 1 routing table. All Level 1 routes with a version number that does not match this number are flushed from the routing table. The router's version number increments when the configuration changes from Level 1 or Level 1-2 to Level 2 only. |
| System Id | Identification value of the system listed in Level 1 forwarding table. |
| Next-Hop | System ID of best-cost next-hop to listed address. |
| SNPA | SNPA of next-hop system. |
| Interface | Interface through which next-hop system is known. |
| Metric | IS-IS metric for the route. |
| State | Up (active) or Down (nonoperational). |

## SHOW ISIS SPF-LOG

Use the **show isis spf-log** EXEC command to display a history of the SPF calculations for IS-IS.

    **show isis spf-log**

## Syntax   Description

This command has no arguments or keywords.

## Command Mode

EXEC

## Usage Guidelines

This command first appeared in Cisco IOS Release 11.1.

## Sample Display

The following is sample output from the **show isis spf-log** command:

```
router> show isis spf-log

      Level 1 SPF log
   When   Duration  Nodes  Count   Last trigger LSP    Triggers
  0:30:59    1028     84     1       PADTHAI.00-00     TLVCONTENT
  0:27:09    1016     84     1       PADTHAI.00-00     TLVCONTENT
  0:26:30    1136     84     1       PADTHAI.04-00     TLVCONTENT
  0:23:11    1244     84     1       PADTHAI.00-00     TLVCONTENT
  0:22:39     924     84     2       PADTHAI.00-00     TLVCONTENT
  0:22:08    1036     84     1       PADTHAI.04-00     TLVCONTENT
  0:20:02    1096     84     1       PADTHAI.00-00     TLVCONTENT
  0:19:31    1140     84     1       PADTHAI.04-00     TLVCONTENT
  0:17:25     964     84     2                         PERIODIC
  0:16:54     996     84     1       PADTHAI.00-00     TLVCONTENT
  0:16:23     984     84     1        TOMYUM.03-00     TLVCONTENT
  0:15:52    1052     84     1        TOMYUM.03-00     TLVCONTENT
  0:14:34    1112     84     1        TOMYUM.00-00     TLVCONTENT
  0:13:37     992     84     1        TOMYUM.03-00     TLVCONTENT
  0:13:06    1036     84     1        TOMYUM.00-00     TLVCONTENT
  0:12:35    1008     84     1       PADTHAI.00-00     TLVCONTENT
  0:02:52    1032     84     1       PADTHAI.00-00     TLVCONTENT
  0:02:16    1032     84     1                         IPBACKUP  IPQUERY
  0:01:44    1000     84     3       PADTHAI.00-00     TLVCONTENT

      Level 2 SPF log
   When   Duration  Nodes  Count   Last trigger LSP    Triggers
  3:18:31     712     84     1                         PERIODIC
  3:03:24     708     84     1                         PERIODIC
  2:48:17     660     84     1                         PERIODIC
  2:33:12     784     84     1                         PERIODIC
  2:32:00     644     84     1       PADTHAI.00-00     TLVCONTENT
  2:31:29     544     84    63       PADTHAI.03-00     TLVCONTENT
  2:30:58     544     84    36       PADTHAI.00-00     TLVCONTENT
  2:30:27     528     84    39        TOMYUM.00-00     NEWADJ  NEWLSP
  2:29:57     628     84    57        TOMYUM.00-00     TLVCONTENT
  2:18:07     652     84     1                         PERIODIC
  2:02:59     772     84     1                         PERIODIC
  1:47:55     740     84     1                         PERIODIC
  1:32:47     816     84     1                         PERIODIC
  1:17:43     744     84     1                         PERIODIC
```

```
1:02:37      712      84      1                        PERIODIC
0:47:29      664      84      1                        PERIODIC
0:32:27      732      84      1                        PERIODIC
0:17:22      788      84      1                        PERIODIC
0:02:16      660      84      1                        RTCLEARED
```

Table 14–19 describes the fields shown in the display.

**Table 14–19**  *Show ISIS SPF Log Field Descriptions*

| Field | Description |
|---|---|
| When | Amount of time since the SPF calculation took place. |
| Duration | Amount of time (in milliseconds) that the calculation required. |
| Nodes | Number of link-state packets (LSPs) encountered during the calculation. |
| Count | Number of times that the SPF calculation was triggered before it actually took place. An SPF calculation is normally delayed for a short time after the event that triggers it. |
| Last trigger LSP | LSP id of the last LSP that caused a full SPF calculation. This is done for the triggers NEWLSP, LSPEXPIRED, LSPHEADER, TLVCODE, and TLVCONTENT. When multiple LSPs change, only the last one to arrive at the router appears in the log. |
| Triggers | List of the types of triggers that were recorded before the SPF calculation occurred (more than one type may be displayed): |
| | PERIODIC—Periodic SPF calculation (every 15 minutes). |
| | NEWSYSID—New system ID was assigned. |
| | NEWAREA—New area address was configured. |
| | NEWLEVEL—Level of the IS-IS process was changed. |
| | RTCLEARED—CLNS routing table was manually cleared. |
| | NEWMETRIC—Link metric of an interface was reconfigured. |
| | IPBACKUP—IP backup route is needed (because a route from a protocol with a worse administrative distance has been lost). |
| | IPQUERY—IP routing table was manually cleared. |
| | ATTACHFLAG—Level 2 router has become attached or unattached from the rest of the Level 2 topology. |
| | LSPEXPIRED—LSP has expired. |
| | NEWLSP—New LSP has been received. |
| | LSPHEADER—LSP with changed header fields was received. |

*Command Reference*

**Table 14–19**  *Show ISIS SPF Log Field Descriptions, Continued*

| Field | Description |
|---|---|
| Triggers (*Continued*) | TLVCODE—LSP with a changed TLV code field was received. |
| | TLVCONTENT—LSP with changed TLV contents was received. |
| | ADMINDIST—Administrative distance of the IS-IS process was reconfigured. |
| | AREASET—Calculated area address set has changed. |
| | BACKUPOVFL—All known IP backup routes have been lost. |
| | NEWADJ—New neighbor adjacency came up. |
| | DBCHANGED—IS-IS link-state database was manually cleared. |

## SHOW ROUTE-MAP

Use the **show route-map** EXEC command to display all route-maps configured or only the one specified.

> **show route-map** [*map-name*]

| Syntax | Description |
|---|---|
| *map-name* | (Optional) Name of a specific route map. |

### Command Mode

EXEC

### Usage Guidelines

This command first appeared in Cisco IOS Release 10.0.

### Sample Display

The following is sample output from the **show route-map** command:

```
router# show route-map

route-map sid, permit, sequence 10
 Match clauses:
    tag 1 2
 Set clauses:
    metric 5
route-map sid, permit, sequence 20
 Match clauses:
    tag 3 4
 Set clauses:
    metric 6
```

Table 14–20 describes the fields shown in the display:

**Table 14–20** *Show Route-Map Field Descriptions*

| Field | Description |
|---|---|
| route-map | Name of the route map. |
| permit | Indicates that the route is redistributed as controlled by the set actions. |
| sequence | Number that indicates the position a new route map is to have in the list of route maps already configured with the same name. |
| Match clauses: tag | Match criteria—conditions under which redistribution is allowed for the current route map. |
| Set clauses: metric | Set actions—the particular redistribution actions to perform if the criteria enforced by the **match** commands are met. |

### Related Commands

Search online for documentation of related commands.

**redistribute**
**route-map**

### SHOW TARP

Use the **show tarp** EXEC command to display all global TARP parameters.

   **show tarp**

### Syntax     Description

This command has no arguments or keywords.

### Command Mode

EXEC

### Usage Guidelines

This command first appeared in Cisco IOS Release 11.1.

### Sample Display

The following is sample output from the **show tarp** command:

```
router# show tarp

Global TARP information:
  TID of this station is "cerd"
  Timer T1 (timer for response to TARP Type 1 PDU) is 15 seconds
```

*Command Reference*

```
Timer T2 (timer for response to TARP Type 2 PDU) is 25 seconds
Timer T3 (timer for response to ARP request) is 40 seconds
Timer T4 (timer that starts when T2 expires) is 15 seconds
Loop Detection Buffer entry timeout: 300 seconds
TID cache entry timeout: 300 seconds
This station will propagate TARP PDUs
This station will originate TARP PDUs
TID<->NET cache is enabled
Sequence number that next packet originated by this station will have: 9
Update remote cache (URC) bit is 0
Packet lifetime: 100 hops
Protocol type used in outgoing packets: "FE"
N-Selector used in TARP PDU's: "AF"
```

Table 14–21 describes the fields shown in the display.

**Table 14–21**   *Show TARP Field Descriptions*

| Field | Description |
|---|---|
| TID | Target identifier assigned to this router by the **tarp tid** command. |
| Timer T1 | Number of seconds that the router will wait to receive a response from a Type 1 PDU. The T1 timer is set by the **tarp t1-response-timer** command. |
| Timer T2 | Number of seconds that the router will wait to receive a response from a Type 2 PDU. The T2 timer is set by the **tarp t2-response-timer** command. |
| Timer T3 | Number of seconds that the router will wait for a response from a Type 5 PDU. The T3 timer is set by the **tarp arp-request-timer** command. |
| Timer T4 | Number of seconds that the router will wait for a response from a Type 2 PDU after the T2 timer has expired. The T4 timer is set by the **tarp post-t2-response-timer** command. |
| Loop Detection Buffer entry timeout | Number of seconds that a System ID-to-sequence number mapping entry remains in the loop-detection buffer table. The loop-detection buffer timeout is set by the **tarp ldb-timer** command. |
| TID cache entry timeout | Number of seconds that a dynamically created TARP entry remains in the TID cache. The cache timeout is set by the **tarp cache-timer** command. |
| Propagate TARP PDUs | Indicates whether the router can propagate TARP PDUs to its TARP neighbors. This field is set by the **tarp global-propagate** command. |
| Originate TARP PDUs | Indicates whether the router can originate TARP PDUs. This field is set by the **tarp originate** command. |

**Table 14–21** *Show TARP Field Descriptions, Continued*

| Field | Description |
|-------|-------------|
| TID<->NET cache | Indicates whether the router will store TID-to-network (NSAP) address mapping in cache. This field is set by the **tarp allow-caching** command. |
| Sequence number | Number used by the next packet to indicate if the packet is newer than the last information received. This number can be changed by the **tarp sequence-number** command. |
| Update remote cache | Indicates the setting of the URC bit in outgoing PDUs. When the bit is zero, the receiver of the PDU will update its cache entry. When the bit is one, the receiver of the PDU will not update its cache entry. This URC bit is set by the **tarp urc** command. |
| Packet lifetime | Number of hosts that a PDU can traverse before the PDU is discarded. The packet lifetime is set by the **tarp lifetime** command. |
| Protocol type | Hexadecimal representation of the protocol used in outgoing PDUs. The protocol type is set by the **tarp protocol-type** command. Only CLNP (indicated by FE) is supported. |
| N-selector | Hexadecimal representation of the N-selector used to indicate that the packet is a TARP PDU. The N-selector is set by the **tarp nselector-type** command. The default is "AF." |

*Command Reference*

### SHOW TARP BLACKLISTED-ADJACENCIES

Use the **show tarp blacklisted-adjacencies** EXEC command to list all adjacencies that have been blacklisted (that is, adjacencies that this router will not propagate TARP PDUs to) by the **tarp blacklist-adjacency** command.

> **show tarp blacklisted-adjacencies**

*Syntax    Description*

This command has no arguments or keywords.

*Command Mode*

EXEC

*Usage Guidelines*

This command first appeared in Cisco IOS Release 11.1.

*Sample Display*

The following is sample output from the **show tarp blacklisted-adjacencies** command:

```
router# show tarp blacklisted-adjacencies

Adjacencies that we won't propagate TARP PDU's to:

    49.0001.5555.5555.5555.00
```

Table 14–22 describes the field shown in the display.

**Table 14–22**    *Show TARP Blacklisted Adjacencies Field Descriptions*

| Field | Description |
| --- | --- |
| 49.0001.5555.5555.5555.00 | NSAP address of the blacklisted router. |

*Related Commands*

Search online for documentation of related commands.

**tarp blacklist-adjacency**

## SHOW TARP HOST

Use the **show tarp hosts** EXEC command to display information about a specific TARP router stored in the local TID cache.

     **show tarp host** *tid*

| *Syntax* | *Description* |
| --- | --- |
| *tid* | Target identifier of the router from which you want information. Alphanumeric string up to 255 characters. |

*Command Mode*

EXEC

*Usage Guidelines*

This command first appeared in Cisco IOS Release 11.1.

*Sample Display*

The following is sample output from the **show tarp host** command:

```
router# show tarp host artemis

TID of entry: artemis
NET of entry: 49.0001.1111.1111.1111.00
Entry type: DYNAMIC
Expiration time: 280 seconds
```

Table 14–23 describes the fields shown in the display.

**Table 14–23** *Show TARP Host Field Descriptions*

| Field | Description |
|---|---|
| TID | Target identifier of the router. |
| NET | NSAP address of the router. |
| Entry type | Type of entry in the TID cache. Values are local, dynamic, or static. A static entry is created with the **tarp map** command. |
| Expiration time | Amount of time that a dynamically created entry will remain in the TID cache. The cache timer is set by the **tarp cache-timer** command. |

### Related Commands

Search online for documentation of related commands.

**tarp tid**

### SHOW TARP INTERFACE

Use the **show tarp interface** EXEC command to list all interfaces that have TARP enabled.

    **show tarp interface** [*type number*]

| Syntax | Description |
|---|---|
| type | (Optional) Interface type. |
| number | (Optional) Interface number. |

### Command Mode

EXEC

### Usage Guidelines

This command first appeared in Cisco IOS Release 11.1.

### Sample Display

The following is sample output from the **show tarp interface** command:

```
router# show tarp interface

Ethernet0 is up, line protocol is up, encapsulation is ARPA
TARP propagation is enabled on this interface
```

Table 14–24 describes the fields shown in the display.

**Table 14–24**  *Show TARP Interface Field Descriptions*

| Field | Description |
|---|---|
| Ethernet...is {up \| down} ...is administratively down | Indicates whether the interface hardware is currently active (whether carrier detect is present) or if it has been taken down by an administrator. |
| line protocol is {up \| down \| administratively down} | Indicates whether the software processes that handle the line protocol think the line is usable (that is, whether keepalives are successful). |
| Encapsulation | Indicates the encapsulation method assigned to the interface. |
| TARP propagation | Indicates whether this interface can propagate TARP PDUs. The propagation is set by the **tarp propagate** command. |

## Related Commands

Search online for documentation of related commands.

**tarp enable**
**tarp propagate**

## SHOW TARP LDB

Use the **show tarp ldb** EXEC command to display the contents of the loop-detection buffer table.

    **show tarp ldb**

## Syntax    Description

This command has no arguments or keywords.

## Command Mode

EXEC

## Usage Guidelines

This command first appeared in Cisco IOS Release 11.1.

## Sample Display

The following is sample output from the **show tarp ldb** command:

```
router# show tarp ldb

    System ID        Sequence Number     Expiration (sec)
    1111.1111.1111          4            240
```

Table 14–25 describes the fields shown in the display.

**Table 14–25** *Show TARP LDB Field Descriptions*

| Field | Description |
|---|---|
| System ID | System ID of the router. |
| Sequence Number | Sequence number of the last packet sent by the router specified by the system ID. |
| Expiration (sec) | Time, in seconds, left before this entry in the loop-detection buffer table is cleared. The time is set by the **tarp ldb-timer** command. |

### Related Commands

Search online for documentation of related commands.

**clear tarp ldb-table**
**tarp sequence-number**

### SHOW TARP MAP

Use the **show tarp map** EXEC command to list all static entries in the TID cache that were configured with the **tarp map** command.

> **show tarp map**

### Syntax    Description

This command has no arguments or keywords.

### Command Mode

EXEC .

### Usage Guidelines

This command first appeared in Cisco IOS Release 11.1.

### Sample Display

The following is sample output from the **show tarp map** command:

```
router# show tarp map

      . Static MAP entries:

   shashi                    49.0001.6666.6666.6666.00
   sonali                    49.0001.7777.7777.7777.00
```

Table 14–26 describes the fields shown in the display.

**Table 14–26** *Show TARP Map Field Descriptions*

| Field | Description |
|---|---|
| shashi | TID of the static entry. |
| 49.0001.6666.6666.6666.00 | NSAP address of the static entry. |

## Related Commands

Search online for documentation of related commands.

**clear tarp tid-table**
**tarp map**

## SHOW TARP STATIC-ADJACENCIES

Use the **show tarp static-adjacencies** EXEC command to list all static TARP adjacencies that are configured with the **tarp route-static** command.

    **show tarp static-adjacencies**

## Syntax     Description

This command has no arguments or keywords.

## Command Mode

EXEC

## Usage Guidelines

This command first appeared in Cisco IOS Release 11.1.

## Sample Display

The following is sample output from the **show tarp static-adjacencies** command:

```
router# show tarp static-adjacencies

        Manual (static) TARP adjacencies:

        55.0001.0001.1111.1111.1111.1111.1111.1111.1111.00
```

Table 14–27 describes the field shown in the display.

**Table 14–27** *Show TARP Static Adjacencies Field Descriptions*

| Field | Description |
|---|---|
| 55.0001.0001.1111.1111.1111.1111.1111.1111.1111.00 | NSAP address of the TARP adjacency. |

*Related Commands*

Search online for documentation of related commands.

**tarp route-static**

## SHOW TARP TID-CACHE

Use the **show tarp tid-cache** EXEC command to display information about the entries in the TID cache. Entries are created dynamically, statically, or as a result of assigning a TID to the device by using the **tarp tid** command.

> **show tarp tid-cache** [detail]

| *Syntax* | *Description* |
|---|---|
| detail | (Optional) List additional information in the TID/NET cache (such as the expiration time for dynamic entries). |

*Command Mode*

EXEC

*Usage Guidelines*

This command first appeared in Cisco IOS Release 11.1.

*Sample Display*

The following is sample output from the **show tarp tid-cache** command:

```
router# show tarp tid-cache

TID ('*' : static; & : local)          NSAP
* shashi                     49.0001.6666.6666.6666.00
& router                     49.0001.3333.3333.3333.00
* sonali                     49.0001.7777.7777.7777.00
  artemis                    49.0001.1111.1111.1111.00
```

The following is sample output from the **show tarp tid-cache detail** command:

```
router# show tarp tid-cache detail

TID ('*': static; &: local)          NSAP
& router                     49.0001.3333.3333.3333.00
  Expiration time: NONE
```

Table 14–28 describes the fields shown in the displays.

**Table 14–28**   *Show Tarp Interface Field Descriptions*

| Field | Description |
|---|---|
| TID | Target identifier assigned to the TID cache entry. Static entries are flagged with an asterisk (*). The local entry is flagged with an ampersand (&). |
| NSAP | NSAP address of the TID cache entry. |
| * | An asterisk (*) indicates that the entry in the TID cache is static (that is, you have created an entry in the TID cache with the **tarp map** command. |
| & | An ampersand (&) indicates that the entry in the TID cache is the local entry (that is, the router to which you are connected). |
| Expiration time | Amount of time the entry remains in the TID cache. When this time expires, the entry is removed from the TID cache. Only dynamic entries have an expiration time. The local entry indicated by an ampersand (&) and static entries indicated by an asterisk (*) are not removed from the TID cache. |

## Related Commands

Search online for documentation of related commands.

**clear tarp tid-table**
**tarp cache-timer**
**tarp map**
**tarp tid**

## SHOW TARP TRAFFIC

Use the **show tarp traffic** EXEC command to display statistics about TARP PDUs since the last time the counters were cleared.

    **show tarp traffic**

## Syntax      Description

This command has no arguments or keywords.

## Command Mode

EXEC

## Usage Guidelines

This command first appeared in Cisco IOS Release 11.1.

*Sample Display*

The following is sample output from the **show tarp traffic** command:

```
router# show tarp traffic

TARP counters:
        Packets output: 11, Input: 5
        Hdr syntax: 0
        No memory: 0, Invalid packet: 0
        Lifetime exceeded: 0
```

Table 14–29 describes the fields shown in the display.

**Table 14–29**  *Show TARP Traffic Field Descriptions*

| Field | Description |
|---|---|
| Packets output | Indicates the number of PDUs that this router has originated. |
| Input | Indicates the number of PDUs that this router has received. |
| Hdr syntax | Number of PDUs with bad header information. |
| No memory | Number of times a request for memory failed (because of insufficient memory). |
| Invalid packets | Number of received PDUs that contained invalid information. |
| Lifetime exceeded | Number of received PDUs with zero lifetime. |

*Related Commands*

Search online for documentation of related commands.

**clear tarp counters**

## TARP ALLOW-CACHING

Use the **tarp allow-caching** global configuration command to re-enable the storage of TID-to-NSAP address mapping in the TID cache. Use the **no** form of this command to disable this function and clear the TID cache.

> **tarp allow-caching**
> **no tarp allow-caching**

*Syntax     Description*

This command has no arguments or keywords.

*Default*

Enabled

*Command Mode*

Global configuration

*Usage Guidelines*

This command first appeared in Cisco IOS Release 11.1.

By default, storing TID-to-network (NSAP) address mapping in cache is enabled unless you specifically disable the capability with the **no tarp allow-caching** command. If you disable this capability, you must use the **tarp allow-caching** command to re-enable storage of TID-to-network address mapping in cache. After re-enabling this capability, any previously cleared local entry and all static entries are restored.

*Example*

The following example disables storage of TID-to-NSAP address mapping in cache on the router:

```
no tarp allow-caching
```

*Related Commands*

Search online for documentation of related commands.

**clear tarp tid-table**
**show tarp tid-cache**
**show tarp map**
**tarp cache-timer**
**tarp map**

## TARP ARP-REQUEST-TIMER

Use the **tarp arp-request-timer** global configuration command to set the timeout for TARP Type 5 PDUs. Use the **no** form of this command to set the timeout to the default value.

**tarp arp-request-timer** *seconds*
**no tarp arp-request-timer**

| Syntax | Description |
|--------|-------------|
| *seconds* | Number of seconds that the router will wait for a response from a TARP type 5 PDU. The range is 0 to 3600 seconds. The default is 40 seconds. |

*Default*

40 seconds

*Command Mode*

Global configuration

## Usage Guidelines

This command first appeared in Cisco IOS Release 11.1.

You may want to increase the time if your network has a slow link or there are long delay times on the link.

TARP Type 5 PDUs are sent by the **tarp query** command to determine a TID that corresponds to a particular NSAP.

## Example

The following example sets the timeout for TARP type 5 PDUs to 60 seconds (one minute):

```
tarp arp-request-timer 60
```

## Related Commands

Search online for documentation of related commands.

**tarp lifetime**
**tarp query**

## TARP BLACKLIST-ADJACENCY

Use the **tarp blacklist-adjacency** global configuration command to blacklist the specified router so that the router does not receive TARP PDUs propagated by this router. Use the **no** form of this command to remove the specified router from the blacklist so that the router can once again receive propagated TARP PDUs.

> **tarp blacklist-adjacency** *nsap*
> **no tarp blacklist-adjacency** *nsap*

| Syntax | Description |
|--------|-------------|
| *nsap* | NSAP address that cannot receive TARP PDUs. Use the full NSAP address. |

## Default

All hosts receive propagated TARP PDUs.

## Command Mode

Global configuration

## Usage Guidelines

This command first appeared in Cisco IOS Release 11.1.

A TARP router propagates PDUs to all its TARP adjacencies (both dynamic and static). Use the **tarp blacklist-adjacency** command to bypass hosts that may not have TARP running or to bypass hosts to which you do not want to propagate TARP PDUs.

## Example

The following example specifies that the router 49.0001.0000.0c00.1111.1234.00 will not receive propagated TARP PDUs:

```
tarp blacklist-adjacency 49.0001.0000.0c00.1111.1234.00
```

## Related Commands

Search online for documentation of related commands.

**show tarp blacklisted-adjacencies**


## TARP CACHE-TIMER

Use the **tarp cache-timer** global configuration command to specify the length of time that a dynamically created TARP entry remains in the TID cache. Use the **no** form of this command to set the timer to the default value.

> **tarp cache-timer** *seconds*
> **no tarp cache-timer**

| Syntax | Description |
|---|---|
| *seconds* | Number of seconds an entry remains in the TID cache. The range is 30 to 86,400 seconds. The default is 3,600 seconds (one hour). |

## Default

3,600 seconds

## Command Mode

Global configuration

## Usage Guidelines

This command first appeared in Cisco IOS Release 11.1.

Static entries (those created with the **tarp map** command) remain in the TID cache unless cleared by the **no tarp map** command.

If entries frequently change, you may want to use a shorter time period. If entries are stable, you may want to use a longer time period.

## Example

The following example limits the time an entry remains in the TID cache to 1,800 seconds (30 minutes):

```
tarp cache-timer 1800
```

## Related Commands

Search online for documentation of related commands.

**clear tarp tid-table**
**show tarp tid-cache**

## TARP ENABLE

Use the **tarp enable** interface configuration command to enable the TARP on an interface. Use the **no** form of this command to disable TARP on a particular interface.

> **tarp enable**
> **no tarp enable**

## Syntax    Description

This command has no arguments or keywords.

## Default

Disabled

## Command Mode

Interface configuration

## Usage Guidelines

This command first appeared in Cisco IOS Release 11.1.

Enabling TARP allows the interface to request and respond to TARP PDUs. TARP PDUs are identified by a unique N-selector in the NSAP address. You must also have the TARP process running on the router by using the **tarp run** command.

## Example

The following example enables TARP on Ethernet interface 0:

```
interface ethernet 0
  tarp enable
```

*Related Commands*

Search online for documentation of related commands.

**show tarp interface**
**tarp nselector-type**
**tarp propagate**
**tarp run**

## TARP GLOBAL-PROPAGATE

Use the **tarp global-propagate** global configuration command to re-enable the capability to propagate TARP PDUs globally. Use the **no** form of this command to disable global propagation of TARP PDUs.

> **tarp global-propagate**
> **no tarp global-propagate**

*Syntax     Description*

This command has no arguments or keywords.

*Default*

Enabled

*Command Mode*

Global configuration

*Usage Guidelines*

This command first appeared in Cisco IOS Release 11.1.

TARP PDUs are globally propagated to all TARP neighbors by default unless you specifically disable the capability with the **no tarp global-propagate** command. If you disable this capability, you must use the **tarp global-propagate** command to re-enable global purgation of TARP PDUs.

TARP PDUs are propagated on all interfaces by default unless you specifically disable the capability on a specific interface with the **no tarp propagate** command.

--- **NOTES** ---

The **no tarp global-propagate** command disables propagation of TARP PDUs on the router (and thus on all interfaces).

---

*Example*

The following example disables global propagation of TARP PDUs on this router:

```
no tarp global-propagate
```

*Related Commands*

Search online for documentation of related commands.

**tarp propagate**

## TARP LDB-TIMER

Use the **tarp ldb-timer** global configuration command to specify the length of time that a system ID-to-sequence number mapping entry remains in the loop-detection buffer table. Use the **no** form of this command to set the timer to the default value.

> **tarp ldb-timer** *seconds*
> **no tarp ldb-timer**

| *Syntax* | *Description* |
|---|---|
| *seconds* | Number of seconds that a system ID-to-sequence number mapping entry remains in the loop-detection buffer table. The range is 0 to 86,400 seconds. The default is 300 seconds. |

*Default*

300 seconds

*Command Mode*

Global configuration

*Usage Guidelines*

This command first appeared in Cisco IOS Release 11.1.

The loop-detection buffer table prevents TARP PDUs from looping.

*Example*

The following example limits the time an entry remains in the loop-detection buffer table to 600 seconds (10 minutes):

```
tarp ldb-timer 600
```

*Related Commands*

Search online for documentation of related commands.

**clear tarp ldb-table**
**show tarp ldb**
**tarp lifetime**

*Command Reference*

## TARP LIFETIME

Use the **tarp lifetime** global configuration command to specify the lifetime for locally generated TARP PDUs based on the number of hops. Use the **no** form of this command to set the PDU lifetime to the default value.

> **tarp lifetime** *hops*
> **no tarp lifetime**

*Syntax*

*hops*

*Description*

Number of hosts that a PDU can traverse before it is discarded. Each router represents one hop. The range is 0 to 65535 hops. The default is 100 hops.

*Default*

100 hops

*Command Mode*

Global configuration

*Usage Guidelines*

This command first appeared in Cisco IOS Release 11.1.

The number of hops specified is decremented after every hop. A PDU with a lifetime of zero is discarded.

*Example*

The following example specifies that the TARP PDU can traverse 150 hosts before it is discarded:

```
tarp lifetime 150
```

*Related Commands*

Search online for documentation of related commands.

**tarp arp-request-timer**
**tarp ldb-timer**

## TARP MAP

Use the **tarp map** global configuration command to enter a TID-to-NSAP static route in the TID cache. Use the **no** form of this command to remove a static map entry from the TID cache.

> **tarp map** *tid nsap*
> **no tarp map** *tid nsap*

| Syntax | Description |
|--------|-------------|
| tid | Target identifier to be mapped to the specified NSAP. Alphanumeric string up to 255 characters. |
| nsap | NSAP address to map to the specified TID. Use the full NSAP address. |

## Command Mode

Global configuration

## Usage Guidelines

This command first appeared in Cisco IOS Release 11.1.

Use the **tarp map** command to map multiple NSAP addresses on a router. For example, using the **tarp resolve** to get the NSAP for a known TID will always return the first NSAP address. If the router has multiple NSAP addresses, you can use the **tarp map** command to map the TID to multiple NSAP addresses. If a router has NSAP addresses 1, 2, 3, the **tarp resolve** command will always return NSAP address 1. Use the **tarp map** command to map the router to NSAP addresses 2 and 3 so the **tarp query** command will return the TID corresponding to the other NSAP addresses.

## Example

The following example maps the NSAP address 49.0001.000.1111.1111.1234.00 to TID SJ1:

```
tarp map sj1 49.0001.0000.1111.1111.1234.00
```

## Related Commands

Search online for documentation of related commands.

**clear tarp tid-table**
**show tarp map**
**tarp query**
**tarp resolve**

## TARP NSELECTOR-TYPE

Use the **tarp nselector-type** global configuration command to specify the N-selector to be used in CLNP PDUs to indicate that the packet is a TARP. Use the **no** form of this command to set the N-selector to the default value.

```
tarp nselector-type hex-digit
no tarp nselector-type
```

| Syntax | Description |
|--------|-------------|
| hex-digit | Digit in hexadecimal format to be used to identify TARP PDUs. The default is AF. |

*Command Reference*

*Default*

AF

*Command Mode*

Global configuration

*Usage Guidelines*

This command first appeared in Cisco IOS Release 11.1. This feature provides flexibility in using the N-selector field to indicate TARP PDUs. The N-selector must be the same on all hosts running the TARP process.

*Example*

The following example changes the N-selector used in CLNP PDUs to BC:

```
tarp nselector-type BC
```

*Related Commands*

Search online for documentation of related commands.

**show tarp**

## TARP ORIGINATE

Use the **tarp originate** global configuration command to re-enable the router to originate TARP PDUs. Use the **no** form of this command to disable the capability to originate TARP PDUs.

    **tarp originate**
    **no tarp originate**

*Syntax       Description*

This command has no arguments or keywords.

*Default*

Enabled

*Command Mode*

Global configuration

*Usage Guidelines*

This command first appeared in Cisco IOS Release 11.1.

Origination of TARP PDUs is enabled by default unless you specifically disable the capability with the **no tarp originate** command. If you disable this capability, you must use the **tarp originate** command to re-enable origination of TARP PDUs.

*Example*

The following example disables the origination of TARP PDUs on this router:

```
no tarp originate
```

*Related Commands*

Search online for documentation of related commands.

**show tarp**

### TARP POST-T2-RESPONSE-TIMER

Use the **tarp post-t2-response-timer** global configuration command to specify the length of time that a router waits for a response to a Type 2 PDU after the default timer expires. Use the **no** form of this command to set the timer to the default value.

> **tarp post-t2-response-timer** *seconds*
> **no tarp post-t2-response-timer**

| Syntax | Description |
|--------|-------------|
| *seconds* | Number of seconds that the router will wait for a response for a Type 2 PDU after the default timer has expired. The range is 0 to 3,600 seconds. The default is 15 seconds. |

*Default*

15 seconds

*Command Mode*

Global configuration

*Usage Guidelines*

This command first appeared in Cisco IOS Release 11.1.

A Type 1 PDU is sent to all Level 1 (IS-IS and ES-IS) neighbors when a router has a TID for which it has no matching NSAP information. If no response is received within the specified timeout period, a Type 2 PDU is sent to all Level 1 and Level 2 neighbors. If no response is received within the specified timeout period, additional time is allocated based on the number specified in the **tarp post-t2-response-timer** command.

*Command Reference*

### Example

The following example sets the additional time to wait for a response from a Type 2 PDU to 60 seconds:

```
tarp post-t2-response-timer 60
```

### Related Commands

Search online for documentation of related commands.

**tarp t2-response-timer**

## TARP PROPAGATE

Use the **tarp propagate** interface configuration command to re-enable propagation of TARP PDUs on an interface. Use the **no** form of this command to disable propagation of TARP PDUs on a particular interface.

> **tarp propagate**
> **no tarp propagate**

### Syntax     Description

This command has no arguments or keywords.

### Default

Enabled

### Command Mode

Interface configuration

### Usage Guidelines

This command first appeared in Cisco IOS Release 11.1.

TARP PDUs are propagated on all interfaces by default unless you specifically disable the capability on a specific interface with the **no tarp propagate** command. If you disable this capability, you must use the **tarp propagate** command to re-enable purgation of TARP PDUs. Enabling propagation of TARP PDUs allows the interface to propagate PDUs to all neighbors on this interface. TARP PDUs are identified by a unique N-selector in the NSAP.

---

**NOTES**

The **no tarp global-propagate** command disables propagation of TARP PDUs on the router (and, thus, on all interfaces).

---

## Example

The following example starts the TARP process on the router and enables TARP propagation on Ethernet interface 0:

```
interface ethernet 0
  tarp propagate
```

## Related Commands

Search online for documentation of related commands.

**show tarp interface**
**tarp enable**
**tarp global-propagate**
**tarp nselector-type**
**tarp run**

## TARP PROTOCOL-TYPE

Use the **tarp protocol-type** global configuration command to specify the network protocol type to be used in outgoing TARP PDUs. Use the **no** form of this command to set the protocol type to the default value.

```
tarp protocol-type hex-digit
no tarp protocol-type
```

| Syntax | Description |
|--------|-------------|
| *hex-digit* | Digit in hexadecimal format to be used to identify the protocol used in outgoing TARP PDUs. The default is FE (for CLNP). |

## Default

FE

## Command Mode

Global configuration

## Usage Guidelines

This command first appeared in Cisco IOS Release 11.1.

Only FE is supported.

## Related Commands

Search online for documentation of related commands.

**show tarp**

## TARP QUERY

Use the **tarp query** EXEC command to determine a TID corresponding to a specific NSAP address.

> **tarp query** *nsap*

| *Syntax* | *Description* |
|----------|---------------|
| *nsap* | NSAP address that you want the TID for. Use the full NSAP address. |

### Command Mode

EXEC

### Usage Guidelines

This command first appeared in Cisco IOS Release 11.1.

If there is a TID entry in the local TID cache, the requested information is displayed.

If there is no TID entry in the local TID cache, a TARP Type 5 PDU is sent to the specified NSAP address. Because the NSAP address is specified, the PDU is unicast to the particular NSAP address. If a response is received (in the form of a Type 3 PDU), the local TID cache is updated and the requested information is displayed.

The length of time that the router will wait for a response to a Type 5 PDU is controlled by the **tarp arp-request-timer** command.

### Sample Display

The following is sample output from the **tarp query** command:

```
router# tarp query 49.0001.3333.3333.3333.00

Type escape sequence to abort.
Sending TARP type 5 PDU, timeout 40 seconds...

 TID corresponding to NET 49.0001.3333.3333.3333.00 is cerd
```

Table 14–30 describes the fields shown in the display.

**Table 14–30**   *TARP Query Field Descriptions*

| Field | Description |
|-------|-------------|
| Sending TARP type 5 PDU | PDU requesting the TID of the specified NSAP. |
| Timeout... | Number of seconds the router will wait for a response from the Type 5 PDU. The timeout is set by the **tarp arp-request-timer** command. |
| TID corresponding to... is... | Indicates the TID for the specified NSAP address. |

*Related Commands*

show tarp
tarp arp-request-timer

## TARP RESOLVE

Use the **tarp resolve** EXEC command to determine an NSAP address corresponding to a specified TID.

> **tarp resolve** *tid* [1 | 2]

| Syntax | Description |
|--------|-------------|
| *tid* | Target identifier to be mapped to the specified NSAP. Alphanumeric string up to 255 characters. |
| 1 | (Optional) Send a Type 1 PDU. The default is a Type 1 PDU. If a response is not received before the timeout period, a Type 2 PDU is sent. |
| 2 | (Optional) Send only Type 2 PDU. |

*Command Mode*

EXEC

*Usage Guidelines*

This command first appeared in Cisco IOS Release 11.1.

If there is an NSAP entry in the local TID cache, the requested information is displayed.

If there is no NSAP entry in the local TID cache, a TARP Type 1 or Type 2 PDU is sent out. By default a Type 1 PUD is sent. A Type 1 PDU is sent to all Level 1 (IS-IS and ES-IS) neighbors. If a response is received (in the form of a Type 3 PDU), the local TID cache is updated and the requested information is displayed.

If a response from the Type 1 PDU is not received within the timeout period, a Type 2 PDU is sent to all Level 1 and Level 2 neighbors. If a response is received (in the form of a Type 3 PDU), the local TID cache is updated and the requested information is displayed.

The length of time that the router will wait for a response to a Type 1 PDU is controlled by the **tarp t1-response-timer** command. The length of time that the router waits for a response to a Type 2 PDU is controlled by the **tarp t2-response-timer** command and the **tarp-post-t2-response-timer** command.

*Command Reference*

## Sample Display

The following is sample output from the **tarp resolve** command:

```
router# tarp resolve artemis

Type escape sequence to abort.
Sending TARP type 1 PDU, timeout 15 seconds...

   NET corresponding to TID artemis is 49.0001.1111.1111.1111.00
```

Table 14–31 describes the fields shown in the display.

**Table 14–31**   *TARP Resolve Field Descriptions*

| Field | Description |
|---|---|
| Sending TARP type 1 PDU | PDU requesting the NSAP of the specified TID. |
| timeout... | Number of seconds the router will wait for a response from the Type 1 PDU. The timeout is set by the **tarp t1-response-timer** command. |
| NET corresponding to... is... | Indicates the NSAP address (in this case, 49.0001.1111.1111.1111.00) for the specified TID. |

## Related Commands

Search online for documentation of related commands.

**tarp map**
**tarp post-t2-response-timer**
**tarp t1-response-timer**
**tarp t2-response-timer**

## TARP ROUTE-STATIC

Use the **tarp route-static** global configuration command to configure a static TARP adjacency. Use the **no** form of this command to remove a static TARP adjacency from the TARP queue.

> **tarp route-static** *nsap*
> **no tarp route-static** *nsap*

| Syntax | Description |
|---|---|
| *nsap* | NSAP address to create a static TARP adjacency. Use the full NSAP address. |

## Command Mode

Global configuration

### Usage Guidelines

This command first appeared in Cisco IOS Release 11.1.

A TARP router propagates PDUs to all its adjacencies and static TARP adjacencies.

If a router is not running TARP, the router discards TARP PDUs rather than propagating the PDUs to all its adjacencies. To allow propagation of the PDU to hosts that are "beyond" a non-TARP router, you must use the **tarp route-static** command to ensure that the hosts receive PDUs. The **tarp route-static** command allows TARP PDUs to "tunnel" through hosts that are not running TARP.

The specified router, as identified by the NSAP address, is stored in a TARP static adjacencies queue.

Use the **tarp blacklist-adjacency** command to bypass hosts that may not have TARP running.

### Example

The following example adds 49.0001.0000.0c00.1111.1234.00 as a static TARP adjacency to the TARP queue:

```
tarp route-static 49.0001.0000.0c00.1111.1234.00
```

### Related Commands

Search online for documentation of related commands.

**show tarp static-adjacencies**
**tarp blacklist-adjacency**

### TARP RUN

Use the **tarp run** global configuration command to start the TARP process on the router. Use the **no** form of this command to stop the TARP process.

    **tarp run**
    **no tarp run**

### Syntax    Description

This command has no arguments or keywords.

### Default

No TARP process (unless configured to start in NVRAM).

### Command Mode

Global configuration

### Usage Guidelines

This command first appeared in Cisco IOS Release 11.1.

*Command Reference*

You must also enable TARP on the individual interfaces by using the **tarp enable** command.

## Example

The following example starts the TARP process on the router:

```
tarp run
```

## Related Commands

Search online for documentation of related commands.

**tarp enable**
**tarp propagate**

## TARP SEQUENCE-NUMBER

Use the **tarp sequence-number** global configuration command to specify the sequence number to be used in the next outgoing TARP PDU. Use the **no** form of this command to return to the default value.

> **tarp sequence-number** *number*
> **no tarp sequence-number** *number*

| Syntax | Description |
|--------|-------------|
| *number* | Number from 0 to 65535 that will be used as the sequence number in the next outgoing PDU. The default is zero. |

## Default

Zero

## Command Mode

Global configuration

## Usage Guidelines

This command first appeared in Cisco IOS Release 11.1.

The sequence number lets the router determine if information received in the PDU is newer than the last information received. You may want to increase the sequence number to ensure that other hosts update their entries in TID cache.

## Example

The following example causes a sequence number of 10 to be assigned to the next TARP PDU:

```
tarp sequence-number 10
```

*Related Commands*

Search online for documentation of related commands.

**show tarp**
**show tarp ldb**

### TARP T1-RESPONSE-TIMER

Use the **tarp t1-response-timer** global configuration command to specify the length of time the router will wait for a response from a Type 1 PDU. Use the **no** form of this command to set the timer to the default value.

> **tarp t1-response-timer** *seconds*
> **no tarp t1-response-timer**

| Syntax | Description |
| --- | --- |
| *seconds* | Number of seconds that the router will wait to receive a response from a Type 1 PDU. The range is 0 to 3,600 seconds. The default is 15 seconds. |

*Default*

15 seconds

*Command Mode*

Global configuration

*Usage Guidelines*

This command first appeared in Cisco IOS Release 11.1.

A Type 1 PDU is sent to all Level 1 (IS-IS and ES-IS) neighbors when a router has a TID for which it has no matching NSAP information. If no response is received within the timeout period (specified by the **tarp t1-response-timer** command), a Type 2 PDU is sent to all Level 2 neighbors.

*Example*

The following example sets the timeout period for a Type 1 PDU to 60 seconds:

```
tarp t1-response-timer 60
```

*Related Commands*

Search online for documentation of related commands.

**tarp t2-response-timer**

*Command Reference*

## TARP T2-RESPONSE-TIMER

Use the **tarp t2-response-timer** global configuration command to specify the length of time the router will wait for a response from a Type 2 PDU. Use the **no** form of this command to set the timer to the default value.

> **tarp t2-response-timer** *seconds*
> **no tarp t2-response-timer**

| Syntax | Description |
|--------|-------------|
| *seconds* | Number of seconds that the router will wait to receive a response from a Type 2 PDU. The range is 0 to 3,600 seconds. The default is 25 seconds. |

### Default

25 seconds

### Command Mode

Global configuration

### Usage Guidelines

This command first appeared in Cisco IOS Release 11.1.

A Type 1 PDU is sent to all Level 1 (IS-IS and ES-IS) neighbors when a router has a TID for which it has no matching NSAP information. If no response is received within the timeout period (specified by the **tarp t1-response-timer** command), a Type 2 PDU is sent to all Level 2 neighbors. If no response is received within the timeout period (specified by the **tarp t2-response-timer** command), additional time can be allocated by using the **tarp post-t2-response-timer** command.

### Example

The following example sets the timeout period for a Type 2 PDU to 60 seconds:

```
tarp t2-response-timer 60
```

### Related Commands

Search online for documentation of related commands.

**tarp post-t2-response-timer**
**tarp t1-response-timer**

## TARP TID

Use the **tarp tid** global configuration command to assign a TID to the router. Use the **no** form of this command to remove the TID from the router.

**tarp tid** *tid*
**no tarp tid** *tid*

| Syntax | Description |
|--------|-------------|
| *tid* | Target identifier to be used by this router. Alphanumeric string up to 255 characters. |

### Command Mode

Global configuration

### Usage Guidelines

This command first appeared in Cisco IOS Release 11.1.

All hosts using TARP must have a unique TID assigned.

### Example

The following example assigns the TID SJ3 to the router:

```
tarp tid sj3
```

### Related Commands

Search online for documentation of related commands.

**show tarp**
**show tarp host**
**show tarp tid-cache**

## TARP URC

Use the **tarp urc** global configuration command to set the update remote cache bit in all subsequent outgoing PDUs. Use the **no** form of this command to set the update remote cache bit to the default value.

**tarp urc** [0 | 1]
**no tarp urc**

| Syntax | Description |
|--------|-------------|
| 0 | Set the update remote cache bit to 0, which is the default value. When the bit is zero, the receiver's PDU will update its TID cache entry. |
| 1 | Set the update remote cache bit to 1. When the bit is 1, the receiver's TID cache is not updated. |

### Command Mode

Global configuration

### Usage Guidelines

This command first appeared in Cisco IOS Release 11.1.

### Example

The following example sets the update remote cache bit in the outgoing PDU to 1, so the cache at the receiver's end is not updated:

```
tarp urc 1
```

### Related Commands

Search online for documentation of related commands.

**show tarp**

## TIMERS BASIC

Use the **timers basic** router configuration command to configure ISO IGRP timers. Use the **no** form of this command to restore the default values.

     **timers basic** *update-interval holddown-interval invalid-interval*
     **no timers basic** *update-interval holddown-interval invalid-interval*

| Syntax | Description |
| --- | --- |
| *update-interval* | Time, in seconds, between the sending of routing updates. The default value is 90 seconds. |
| *holddown-interval* | Time, in seconds, a system or area router is kept in holddown state, during which routing information regarding better paths is suppressed. (A router enters into a holddown state when an update packet is received that indicates the route is unreachable. The route is marked inaccessible and advertised as unreachable; however, the route is still used for forwarding packets.) When the holddown interval expires, routes advertised by other sources are accepted and the route is no longer inaccessible. The default value is 145 seconds. |
| *invalid-interval* | Time, in seconds, that a route remains in the routing table after it has been determined that it is not reachable. After that length of time, the route is removed from the routing table. The default value is 135 seconds. |

*Defaults*

*update-interval* = 90 seconds
*holddown-interval* = 145 seconds
*invalid-interval* = 135 seconds

*Command Mode*

Router configuration

*Usage Guidelines*

This command first appeared in Cisco IOS Release 10.0.

Because the ISO IGRP routing protocol executes a distributed, asynchronous routing algorithm, it is important that these timers be the same for all routers in the network.

*Example*

In the following example, updates are broadcast every 60 seconds. When an update packet is received that indicates the router is unreachable, the router will be in holddown state for 100 seconds before once more becoming accessible. If a router is not heard from in 130 seconds, the route is removed from the routing table.

```
router iso-igrp
 timers basic 60 100 130
```

## TRACE (PRIVILEGED)

Use the **trace** privileged EXEC command to trace routes on a router configured with the ISO CLNS protocol.

   **trace**

*Syntax       Description*

This command has no arguments or keywords.

*Command Mode*

Privileged EXEC

*Usage Guidelines*

This command first appeared in Cisco IOS Release 10.0.

The **trace** command terminates when the destination responds, when the maximum time to live (TTL) is exceeded, or when the user interrupts the trace with the escape sequence. The information is encoded as follows:

```
hop-count name(nsap) result-of-probe
```

Command Reference

*Sample Display*

The following display shows an example of ISO CLNS **trace** output:

```
router# trace
Protocol [ip]: clns
Target CLNS address: thoth
Timeout in seconds [3]:
Probe count [3]:
Minimum Time to Live [1]:
Maximum Time to Live [30]:
Type escape sequence to abort.
Tracing the route to THOTH (55.0006.0100.0000.0000.0001.8888.1112.1314.1516)
   HORUS(55.0006.0100.0000.0000.0001.6666.3132.3334.3536) 32 msec ! 28 msec
 28 msec !
  2 ISIS(55.0006.0100.0000.0000.0001.7777.2122.2324.2526) 56 msec ! 80 msec
 56 msec !
  3 THOTH(55.0006.0100.0000.0000.0001.8888.1112.1314.1516) 80 msec ! 80 msec ! 8
```

Table 14–32 describes the parameters that can be specified when using the **trace** dialog for CLNS.

**Table 14–32**   *ISO CLNS Trace (Privileged) Field Descriptions*

| Field | Description |
|---|---|
| Protocol [ip] | The default protocol for **trace** is IP. You must specify CLNS to begin tracing a router on a CLNS router. |
| Target CLNS address | You can specify either an NSAP or host name. |
| Timeout in seconds | You can specify the length of time to wait after sending each probe before giving up on getting a response. |
| Probe count | You can specify the number of probes to be sent at each TTL level. The default is 3. |
| Minimum Time to Live [1] | You can set the TTL value for the first probes. The default is 1. Set to a higher value to suppress the display of known hops. |
| Maximum Time to Live [30] | You can set the largest TTL value that can be used. The default is 30. The **trace** command terminates when the destination is reached or when this value is reached. |

Table 14–33 describes characters that can appear in ISO CLNS output.

**Table 14–33**   *ISO CLNS Trace (Privileged) Text Characters*

| Character | Description |
|---|---|
| & | A time-to-live-exceeded error PDU was received. |
| U | A destination unreachable error PDU was received. |

**Table 14–33** *ISO CLNS Trace (Privileged) Text Characters, Continued*

| Character | Description |
|-----------|-------------|
| I | The user interrupted the test. |
| * | The probe timed out. |
| C | A congestion experienced packet was received. |

### Related Commands

Search online for documentation of related commands.

trace (user)

## TRACE (USER)

Use the **trace** user EXEC command to discover the CLNS routes that packets will actually take when traveling to their destination.

    **trace clns** *destination*

| Syntax | Description |
|--------|-------------|
| *destination* | Destination address or host name on the command line. The default parameters for the appropriate protocol are assumed and the tracing action begins. |
| **clns** | CLNS keyword. |

### Command Mode

User EXEC

### Usage Guidelines

This command first appeared in Cisco IOS Release 10.0.

The **trace** command works by taking advantage of the error messages generated by the Cisco IOS software and when a datagram exceeds its Time-to-Live (TTL) value.

The **trace** command starts by sending probe datagrams with a TTL value of 1. This causes the first software to discard the probe datagram and send back an error message. The **trace** command sends several probes at each TTL level and displays the round-trip time for each.

The **trace** command sends out one probe at a time. Each outgoing packet can result in one or two error messages. A *time exceeded* error message indicates that an intermediate router has seen and discarded the probe. A *destination unreachable* error message indicates that the destination node has received the probe and discarded it because it could not deliver the packet. If the timer goes off before a response comes in, **trace** prints an asterisk (*).

*Command Reference*

The **trace** command terminates when the destination responds, when the maximum TTL is exceeded, or when the user interrupts the trace with the escape sequence. By default, to invoke the escape sequence, press Ctrl-^, X—which is done by simultaneously pressing the Ctrl, Shift, and 6 keys, releasing them, and then pressing the X key.

### Sample Display

The following display shows sample CLNS **trace** output when a destination host name has been specified:

```
router# trace clns ABA.NYC.mil

Type escape sequence to abort.
Tracing the route to ABA.NYC.mil (26.0.0.73)
   1 DEBRIS.CISCO.COM (131.108.1.6) 1000 msec 8 msec 4 msec
   2 BARRNET-GW.CISCO.COM (131.108.16.2) 8 msec 8 msec 8 msec
   3 EXTERNAL-A-GATEWAY.STANFORD.EDU (192.42.110.225) 8 msec 4 msec 4 msec
   4 BB2.SU.BARRNET.NET (131.119.254.6) 8 msec 8 msec 8 msec
   5 SU.ARC.BARRNET.NET (131.119.3.8) 12 msec 12 msec 8 msec
   6 MOFFETT-FLD-MB.in.MIL (192.52.195.1) 216 msec 120 msec 132 msec
   7 ABA.NYC.mil (26.0.0.73) 412 msec 628 msec 664 msec
```

Table 14–34 describes the fields shown in the display.

**Table 14–34**   *ISO CLNS Trace (User) Field Descriptions*

| Field | Description |
| --- | --- |
| 1 | Indicates the sequence number of the router in the path to the router. |
| DEBRIS.CISCO.COM | Host name of this router. |
| 131.108.1.6 | Internetwork address of this router. |
| 1000 msec 8 msec 4 msec | Round-trip time for each of the three probes that are sent. |

Table 14–35 describes the characters that can appear in **trace** output.

**Table 14–35**   *ISO CLNS Trace (User) Text Characters*

| Character | Description |
| --- | --- |
| *nn* msec | For each node, the round-trip time in milliseconds for the specified number of probes. |
| * | The probe timed out. |
| ? | Unknown packet type. |
| Q | Source quench. |

**Table 14–35** *ISO CLNS Trace (User) Text Characters, Continued*

| Character | Description |
|-----------|-------------|
| P | Protocol unreachable. |
| N | Network unreachable. |
| U | Port unreachable. |
| H | Host unreachable. |

### Related Commands

Search online for documentation of related commands.

**trace (privileged)**

### WHICH-ROUTE

Use the **which-route** EXEC command if you want to know which next-hop router will be used or if you have multiple processes running and want to troubleshoot your configuration. This command displays the routing table in which the specified CLNS destination is found.

**which-route** {*nsap-address* | *clns-name*}

| Syntax | Description |
|--------|-------------|
| *nsap-address* | CLNS destination network address. |
| *clns-name* | Destination host name. |

### Command Mode

EXEC

### Usage Guidelines

This command first appeared in Cisco IOS Release 10.0.

Route information can reside in the following tables:

- IS-IS Level 1 routing table
- ISO IGRP system-id or area routing table
- Prefix routing table (IS-IS Level 2 routes, ISO IGRP domain routes, and static routes)
- Adjacency database

### Examples

The following example shows that destination information for router gray is found in the IS-IS Level 1 routing table. The destination is on the local system.

*Command Reference*

```
gray# which-route gray
Route look-up for destination 39.0001.0000.0c00.bda8.00, GRAY
 Found route in IS-IS level-1 routing table - destination is local
```

The following example shows that destination information for NSAP address 49.0001.0000.0c00.bda8.00 is found in the ISO IGRP Level 1 routing table. The destination is on the local system.

```
gray# which-route 49.0001.0000.0c00.bda8.00
Route look-up for destination 49.0001.0000.0c00.bda8.00
 Found route in ISO IGRP routing table - destination is local
```

The following example shows that destination information for router green is found in the IS-IS Level 1 routing table. The destination is not on the local system. Table 14–36 describes the display fields in the adjacency entry used to reach system green.

```
gray# which-route green
Route look-up for destination 39.0001.0000.0c00.7f06.00, GREEN
 Found route in IS-IS level-1 routing table

Adjacency entry used:
System Id      SNPA            Interface  State Holdtime Type Protocol
GREEN          0000.0c00.2d55  Ethernet0  Up    91       L1L2 IS-IS
  Area Address(es): 39.0001
```

**Table 14–36**   *Which-Route Field Descriptions*

| Field | Description |
|---|---|
| System ID | Six-byte value that identifies a system in an area. A name is displayed in this field if one has been assigned with the **clns host** global configuration command. |
| SNPA | SNPA data link address. |
| Interface | Interface from which system information was learned. |
| State | State of the ES or IS. Possible values are as follows: Init—The system is an IS and is waiting for an IS-IS hello message. The neighbor to the IS-IS is not adjacent. Up—The ES or IS is reachable. |
| Holdtime | Number of seconds for which the information is valid. |

**Table 14–36** *Which-Route Field Descriptions, Continued*

| Field | Description |
|-------|-------------|
| Type | Adjacency type. Possible values are as follows: |
| | ES—An end-system adjacency that is either discovered by the ES-IS protocol or statically configured. |
| | IS—A router adjacency that is either discovered by the IS-IS protocol or is statically configured. |
| | L1—A router adjacency for Level 1 routing only. |
| | L1L2—A router adjacency for Level 1 and Level 2 routing. |
| | L2—A router adjacency for Level 2 only. |
| Protocol | Protocol through which the adjacency was learned. Valid protocol sources are ES-IS, IS-IS, ISO IGRP, and Static. |

The following example shows that destination information for NSAP address 49.0001.1111.1111.1111.00 is found in the ISO IGRP routing table. Table 14–36 describes the display fields in the adjacency entry used to reach NSAP address 49.0001.1111.1111.1111.00.

```
gray# which-route 49.0001.1111.1111.1111.00
Route look-up for destination 49.0001.1111.1111.1111.00
 Found route in ISO IGRP routing table

Adjacency entry used:
System Id       SNPA            Interface  State Holdtime Type Protocol
1111.1111.1111 0000.0c01.151d  Ethernet1  Up    38       L1L2 ISO IGRP
  Area Address(es): 49.0001
```

The following example indicates that the specified address is not found in a routing table:

```
gray# which-route 47.0003.0000.0000.0000.00
Route look-up for destination 47.0003.0000.0000.0000.00
 Route not found
```

The following example indicates that the specified NSAP address was found in the CLNS prefix routing table. This information is followed by the route entry used to reach NSAP address 49.0003.0000.0000.0000.00.

```
gray# which-route 49.0003.0000.0000.0000.00
Route look-up for destination 49.0003.0000.0000.0000.00
 Found route in CLNS prefix routing table

Route entry used:
49 [10/0]
   via 1111.1111.1111, Ethernet1, Static
```

## Related Commands

Search online for documentation of related commands.

**clns host**

# CHAPTER 15

# Configuring XNS

This chapter describes how to configure standard Xerox Network System (XNS) routing and Ungermann-Bass Net/One XNS routing. It also provides configuration examples. For a complete description of the XNS commands in this chapter, see Chapter 16, "XNS Commands."

---

**NOTES**

Not all Cisco access servers support XNS. For more information, refer to the release notes for the current Cisco IOS release.

---

## UNGERMANN-BASS NET/ONE ENVIRONMENTS

Some of the tasks described in this chapter explain how to configure Ungermann-Bass Net/One XNS routing. Net/One uses XNS at the network layer. However, Net/One as a whole is not equivalent to standard XNS. When using Cisco routers in Net/One environments, keep in mind the following differences between Net/One and standard XNS environments:

- Net/One routers use a proprietary routing protocol instead of the standard XNS RIP. Although they generate both Ungermann-Bass and standard RIP update packets, Net/One routers listen only to Net/One updates. Cisco supports both the reception and the generation of Net/One routing packets. Also, Cisco routers can interoperate with Ungermann-Bass routers.

- Net/One routers send periodic hello packets, which are used by end nodes in discovering routers to be used when sending packets to destinations that are not on the local cable. Standard XNS end hosts use RIP for this purpose. Cisco routers can be configured to generate Net/One hello packets.

- Net/One equipment uses a non-XNS booting protocol for downloading network software. During the downloading process, XNS network numbers are embedded in this protocol's packets. Ungermann-Bass routers pass the booting protocol from network to network and modify the embedded network numbers. Cisco's equipment does not understand the Net/One booting protocol and does not modify the embedded network numbers. For network booting to work through Cisco routers, Net/One Network Management Consoles must be specially configured. Contact Ungermann-Bass for information about how to do this.

- The Net/One Network Resource Monitor (a network management and monitoring tool) uses XNS packets whose destination host addresses are specific nodes, but whose destination network addresses are the broadcast network (network address of -1). These packets are sent as MAC-layer broadcasts and are expected to be flooded throughout the XNS internetwork. On Cisco routers, you enable the flooding of these packets as described in the "Controlling Broadcast Messages" section later in this chapter.

- Net/One equipment uses proprietary network management protocols. Cisco routers do not participate in these protocols.

Net/One uses a distance-vector routing protocol, similar to standard XNS RIP. The major difference between the two protocols is the metrics. Standard RIP uses hop count to determine the best route to a remote network, while the Net/One protocol uses a path-delay metric. The standard RIP protocol maintains information only about hop counts, while the Net/One protocol maintains information about both hop count and its own metrics.

Ungermann-Bass routers generate standard RIP updates by extracting the hop-count values from the Ungermann-Bass routing protocol. When configured in Ungermann-Bass emulation mode, Cisco routers participate in this protocol and behave (insofar as routing protocols are concerned) like Ungermann-Bass routers.

Cisco routers also can be configured to listen to standard RIP updates when in Ungermann-Bass Net/One emulation mode. When a Cisco router in Ungermann-Bass emulation mode receives a RIP packet, each route in that packet is treated as though it had come from an Ungermann-Bass routing packet. The hop count used is the actual hop count from the RIP packet. The delay metric used is computed by assuming that each hop is the longest-delay link used by Ungermann-Bass, which is a 9.6-Kbps serial link. Information from RIP packets is used in creating outgoing Ungermann-Bass updates, and vice versa.

---

**NOTES**

Older versions of Cisco IOS software implemented a restricted version of the Ungermann-Bass routing protocol. Using that software in certain configurations could create routing instability and forwarding loops. If you are planning to use Releases 8.3 and earlier in Ungermann-Bass environments, consult the Release 8.3 documentation for information about the restrictions.

---

## XNS ADDRESSES

An XNS address consists of a network number and a host number expressed in the format *network.host*.

The network number identifies a physical network. It is a 32-bit quantity that must be unique throughout the entire XNS internetwork. The network number is expressed in decimal. A network number of zero identifies the local network. The XNS network number is expressed in decimal format in Cisco's configuration files and routing tables. However, the router internally converts the network number into hexadecimal. This means, for instance, that a network analyzer will display the network number in hexadecimal.

The host number is a 48-bit quantity that is unique across all hosts ever manufactured. It is represented by dotted triplets of four-digit hexadecimal numbers.

The following is an example of an XNS address:

```
47.0000.0x00.23fe
```

When XNS routing is enabled, the address used is either the IEEE-compliant address specified in the XNS routing configuration command or the first IEEE-compliant address in the system. The address also is used as the node address for non-LAN media, notably serial links.

## CONFIGURATION TASK LIST

To configure XNS routing, complete the tasks in the following sections. At a minimum, you must enable routing.

- Enabling XNS Routing
- Controlling Access to the XNS Network
- Tuning XNS Network Performance
- Configuring XNS over WANs
- Routing XNS between Virtual LANs
- XNS can be routed over virtual LAN (VLAN) subinterfaces using the Inter-Switched Link (ISL) VLAN encapsulation protocol. Full-feature Cisco IOS software is supported on a per-VLAN basis, allowing standard XNS capabilities to be configured on VLANs. Monitor the XNS Network.

See the "XNS Configuration Examples" section at the end of this chapter for configuration examples.

## ENABLING XNS ROUTING

When enabling XNS routing, you can enable either standard XNS routing or Ungermann-Bass Net/One routing. You use standard routing for XNS networks that do not have any Ungermann-Bass systems. You use Net/One routing for networks that do have Ungermann-Bass systems.

Standard XNS routing uses the standard XNS RIP protocol, while Net/One uses an Ungermann-Bass proprietary routing protocol. Net/One routers generate both Ungermann-Bass update packets and standard RIP update packets; however, they listen only to Ungermann-Bass updates. The standard XNS RIP uses a hop count to determine the best route to a distant network, while the Ungermann-Bass protocol uses a path-delay metric. The Cisco IOS software supports both the reception and the generation of Ungermann-Bass routing packets.

## Enabling Standard XNS Routing

To enable standard XNS routing, perform the following tasks starting in global configuration mode:

| Task | Command |
| --- | --- |
| **Step 1** Enable XNS routing on the router. | **xns routing** [*address*] |
| **Step 2** Enter interface configuration mode. | **interface** *type number* |
| **Step 3** Enable XNS routing on an interface. | **xns network** *number* |

For an example of how to enable XNS routing, see the "XNS Routing Configuration Example" section at the end of this chapter.

If you omit the address from the **xns routing** global configuration command, the Cisco IOS software uses the address of the first IEEE-compliant (Token Ring, FDDI, or Ethernet) interface MAC address it finds in its interface list. The software uses the address 0123.4567.abcd for non-IEEE–compliant interfaces.

To forward XNS packets across a Token Ring interface, you must specify an XNS encapsulation type to use on the interface. To do this, perform one of the following tasks in interface configuration mode:

| Task | Command |
| --- | --- |
| Encapsulate XNS packets being forwarded across an IBM Token Ring network. | **xns encapsulation snap** |
| Encapsulate XNS packets being forwarded across an Ungermann-Bass Token Ring network. | **xns encapsulation ub** |
| Encapsulate XNS packets being forwarded across an older 3Com Token Ring network. | **xns encapsulation 3com** |

## Enabling Concurrent Routing and Bridging

You can route XNS on some interfaces and transparently bridge it on other interfaces simultaneously. To do this, you must enable concurrent routing and bridging. To enable concurrent routing and bridging for the router, perform the following task in global configuration mode:

| Task | Command |
| --- | --- |
| Enable concurrent routing and bridging for the router. | bridge crb |

## Enabling Ungermann-Bass Net/One Routing

To enable Ungermann-Bass Net/One routing, start in global configuration mode with Step 1, and, optionally, perform Step 2 and Step 3:

| Task | Command |
| --- | --- |
| Step 1 Enable Ungermann-Bass Net/One routing on the router. | xns ub-emulation |
| Step 2 Enter interface configuration mode. | interface *type number* |
| Step 3 Enable the receipt of RIP updates on the interface. | xns hear-rip [*access-list-number*] |

For an example of how to enable Ungermann-Bass Net/One routing, see the "Net/One Routing Configuration Example" section at the end of this chapter.

## CONTROLLING ACCESS TO THE XNS NETWORK

To control access to XNS networks, you create access lists and then apply them with filters to individual interfaces.

Following are the two types of XNS access lists that you can use to filter routed traffic:

- Standard access list—Restricts traffic based on the source network number. You can further restrict traffic by specifying a destination address, and a source and destination address mask. Standard XNS access lists have numbers from 400 to 499.

- Extended access—Restricts traffic based on the XNS protocol type. You can further restrict traffic by specifying source and destination addresses and address masks, and source and destination socket numbers and masks. Extended XNS access lists have numbers from 500 to 599.

Of the following two types of filters you can define for XNS interfaces, you can apply one of each type to each interface:

- Generic filters—These filters control which packets are sent out an interface based on the packet's source and destination addresses, source and destination socket numbers, and XNS protocol type.

- Routing table filters—These filters control which routing (RIP) updates are accepted and advertised by the Cisco IOS software and from which routers the local router accepts RIP updates.

Table 15–1 summarizes the types of filters and the commands you use to define them. Use the **show xns interface** command to display the filters defined on an interface.

**Table 15–1**   *XNS Filters*

| Filter Type | Command Used to Define Filter |
|---|---|
| **Generic filters** | |
| Filter based on protocol, address and address mask, port and port mask. | **xns access-group** *access-list-number* |
| **Routing table filters** | |
| Filter which networks are added to the routing table. | **xns input-network-filter** *access-list-number* |
| Filter which networks are advertised in routing updates. | **xns output-network-filter** *access-list-number* |
| Control the routers from which updates are accepted. | **xns router-filter** *access-list-number* |

You perform one or more of the tasks in the following sections to control access to XNS networks:

- Creating Access Lists
- Creating Generic Filters
- Creating Filters for Updating the Routing Table

Keep the following in mind when configuring XNS network access control:

- Access list entries are evaluated in the order you enter them, and the first matching entry is used. To improve performance, place the most commonly matched entries near the beginning of the access list.

- An implicit *deny everything* entry is defined at the end of an access list unless you include an explicit *permit everything* entry at the end of the list.

- All new entries to an existing list are placed at the end of the list. You cannot add an entry to the middle of a list. This means that if you have previously included an explicit *permit everything* entry, new entries will never be scanned. The solution is to delete the access list and retype it with the new entries.

## Creating Access Lists

To create access lists, perform one or more of the following tasks in global configuration mode:

| Task | Command |
| --- | --- |
| Create a standard XNS access list. | **access-list** *access-list-number* {**deny** \| **permit**} *source-network*[*.source-address* [*source-address-mask*]][*destination-network* [*.destination-address* [*destination-address-mask*]]] |
| Create an extended XNS access list. | **access-list** *access-list-number* {**deny** \| **permit**} *protocol* [*source-network*[*.source-host* [*source-network-mask.*]*source-host-mask*] *source-socket* [*destination-network* [*.destination-host* [*destination-network-mask.destination-host-mask*] [*destination-socket* [*/pep*]]] |

Once you have created an access list, you apply it to a filter on the appropriate interfaces as described in the sections that follow. This activates the access list.

For an example of how to create an access list to control services between networks in a 3Com network, see the "3Com Access List Example" section at the end of this chapter.

## Creating Generic Filters

Generic filters determine which packets to send out an interface, based on the packet's source and destination addresses, XNS protocol type, and source and destination socket numbers.

To create generic filters, perform the following tasks:

**Step 1**    Create a standard or extended access list.

**Step 2**    Apply a filter to an interface.

To create an access list, perform one of the following tasks in global configuration mode:

| Task | Command |
| --- | --- |
| Create a standard XNS access list. | **access-list** *access-list-number* {**deny** \| **permit**} *source-network*[*.source-address* [*source-address-mask*]][*destination-network* [*.destination-address* [*destination-address-mask*]]] |

| Task | Command |
|------|---------|
| Create an extended XNS access list. | **access-list** *access-list-number* {**deny** \| **permit**} *protocol* [*source-network*[*.source-host*[*source-network-mask.*] *source-host-mask*] *source-socket* [*destination-network* [*.destination-host*[*destination-network-mask.destination-host-mask*] [*destination-socket*[*/pep*]]]] |

To apply a generic filter to an interface, perform the following task in interface configuration mode:

| Task | Command |
|------|---------|
| Apply a generic filter to an interface. | **xns access-group** *access-list-number* |

For an example of creating a generic access list, see the "3Com Access List Example" section at the end of this chapter.

## Creating Filters for Updating the Routing Table

Routing table update filters control the entries that the router or access server accepts for its routing table, and the networks that it advertises in its routing updates.

To create filters to control updating of the routing table, perform the following tasks:

**Step 1**     Create a standard or an extended access list.

**Step 2**     Apply one or more filters to an interface.

To create an access list, perform one of the following tasks in global configuration mode:

| Task | Command |
|------|---------|
| Create a standard XNS access list. | **access-list** *access-list-number* {**deny** \| **permit**} *source-network*[*.source-address* [*source-address-mask*]][*destination-network* [*.destination-address* [*destination-address-mask*]]] |
| Create an extended XNS access list. | **access-list** *access-list-number* {**deny** \| **permit**} *protocol* [*source-network*[*.source-host*[*source-network-mask.*] *source-host-mask*] *source-socket* [*destination-network* [*.destination-host* [*destination-network-mask.destination-host-mask*] [*destination-socket*[*/pep*]]]] |

Standard access list numbers can range from 400 to 499. Extended access list numbers can range from 500 to 599.

For an example of how to create an extended access list entry, see the "Extended Access List with Network Mask Option Example" section at the end of this chapter.

To assign routing table update filters to an interface, perform one of the following tasks in interface configuration mode. You can apply one of each of the following filters to each interface.

| Task | Command |
| --- | --- |
| Control which networks are added to the routing table when XNS routing updates are received. | **xns input-network-filter** *access-list-number* |
| Control which networks are advertised in routing updates sent out by the router. | **xns output-network-filter** *access-list-number* |
| Control the routers from which routing updates are accepted. | **xns router-filter** *access-list-number* |

## TUNING XNS NETWORK PERFORMANCE

To tune XNS network performance, perform the tasks in one or more of the following sections:

- Configuring Static Routes
- Setting Routing Table Update Timers
- Setting Maximum Paths
- Controlling Broadcast Messages
- Disabling XNS Fast Switching

### Configuring Static Routes

XNS uses RIP to determine the best path when several paths to a destination exist. RIP then dynamically updates the routing table. Static routes usually are not used in XNS environments because nearly all XNS routers support dynamic routing with RIP. However, you might want to add static routes to the routing table to explicitly specify paths to certain destinations. Static routes always override any dynamically learned paths.

Be careful when assigning static routes. When links associated with static routes are lost, traffic might stop being forwarded, even though an alternative path might be available.

To add a static route to the router's routing table, perform the following task in global configuration mode:

| Task | Command |
| --- | --- |
| Add a static route to the routing table. | **xns route** *network network.host* |

## Setting Routing Table Update Timers

You can set the delay between XNS RIP updates. Normally, RIP sends routing table updates every 30 seconds.

You can set RIP timers only in a configuration in which all routers are Cisco routers, because the timers for all routers connected to the same network segment should be the same, and because you cannot set the timer for systems running the Ungermann-Bass routing protocol.

The RIP update value you choose affects internal XNS timers as follows:

- XNS routes are marked invalid if no routing updates are heard within three times the value of *the update interval* ($3 \times interval$) and are advertised with a metric of infinity.

- XNS routes are removed from the routing table if no routing updates are heard within six times the value of *the update interval* ($6 \times interval$).

To set the RIP update timers, perform the following task in interface configuration mode:

| Task | Command |
| --- | --- |
| Set the RIP update timer. | **xns update-time** *interval* |

For an example of setting the RIP update timer, see the "Routing Update Timers Example" section at the end of this chapter.

## Setting Maximum Paths

You can set the maximum number of equal-cost, parallel paths to a destination. (Note that when paths have differing costs, the Cisco IOS software chooses lower-cost routes in preference to higher-cost routes.) The software distributes output on a packet-by-packet basis in round-robin fashion: That is, the first packet is sent along the first path, the second packet along the second path, and so on. If the final path is reached before all packets are sent, the next packet is sent to the first path, the next to the second path, and so on. This round-robin scheme is used regardless of whether fast switching is enabled.

Limiting the number of equal-cost paths can save memory on routers with limited memory or with very large configurations. Additionally, in networks with a large number of multiple paths and systems with limited ability to cache out-of-sequence packets, performance might suffer when traffic is split between many paths.

To set the maximum number of paths on the router, perform the following task in global configuration mode:

| Task | Command |
| --- | --- |
| Set the maximum number of equal-cost paths to a destination. | **xns maximum-paths** *number* |

## Controlling Broadcast Messages

Network end nodes often send broadcast messages to discover services; a request is broadcast to many or all nodes in the internetwork, and one or more of the nodes that can offer that service reply. Both end nodes and routers sometimes send broadcast messages to contain data that must be received by many other nodes. An example is RIP routing updates.

Although broadcast messages can be very useful, they are not without costs. Every node on a physical network must receive and process all broadcasts sent on that network, even if the processing consists of ignoring the broadcasts. If many nodes answer the broadcast, network load might increase dramatically for a short period of time. Also, if the broadcast is propagated to more than one physical network, there is extra load on the networks and the intervening routers.

The following are the types of broadcasts and how each is handled:

- A *local* broadcast is one that is intended only for nodes on the physical network (typically one Ethernet or Token Ring LAN) on which the packet is originally sent. XNS networks usually denote local broadcasts with a specific network number in the packet's destination field. If a node does not know the number of the local XNS network (common when booting), it can use a network number of zero to denote a local broadcast.

- An *all-nets* broadcast is one that is intended for all nodes throughout the XNS Internet. XNS networks usually denote all-nets broadcasts with a destination network field of all ones (typically written as -1 or as FFFFFFFF).

- A *directed* broadcast is one that is intended for all nodes on a specific remote network. Directed broadcasts are denoted by the use of a specific remote network number in the destination field.

All these broadcast types use the host address FFFF.FFFF.FFFF in the packet's destination host field. The destination MAC address used in the underlying LAN frame is the broadcast address. Directed broadcasts that are intended for remote networks can be sent directly to the MAC address of a router which provides the path to the broadcast's ultimate destination and can be physically broadcast only when the destination is reached.

Some implementations expect all broadcasts to be treated as local broadcasts. Others expect broadcasts with destination network fields of zero to be treated as all-nets broadcasts. Some do not support directed broadcasts. In addition, some implementations expect packets with destination network fields of all ones, but with destination node fields that correspond to specific hosts, to be flooded throughout the Internet as MAC-layer broadcasts. This way, nodes can be located without knowledge of which physical networks they are connected to. Cisco supports all these models by using helpering and flooding features.

*Helpering*, which is typically used for service discovery broadcasts, sends the broadcasts to user-specified candidate servers on remote networks. When a packet is helpered, the Cisco IOS software changes its destination address to be the configured helper address, and the packet then is routed toward that address. The host at the helper address is expected to process the packet and (usually) to reply to the packet's sender. A helper address can be a directed broadcast address, in which case the helpered packet is forwarded to a remote network and is rebroadcasted there.

*Flooding* sends packets throughout the entire XNS Internet. Flooded packets are not modified, except for the hop count field. Flooding is useful when many nodes throughout the Internet need to receive a packet, or when a service that can be anywhere in the Internet must be discovered. You should avoid flooding in large, slow, or heavily loaded networks because the load on the routers, links, and end nodes by heavy flooded traffic is large.

Many broadcast messages are sent when a host first becomes active on the network. A host generates a broadcast packet when it does not know the current address of the host that is supposed to receive its next packet—the local server, for instance. Generally, it is not a good idea to place a router between users and the servers that carry their primary applications; you should minimize Internet traffic. However, if you need that server configuration for some other reason, you must ensure that users can broadcast between networks without cluttering the internetwork with unnecessary traffic.

Whenever the Cisco IOS software receives an XNS broadcast packet, it processes the packet as follows:

- If the packet is a routing update or requests services that are offered by the router itself, the packet is processed by the Cisco IOS software and is not forwarded any further.

- If a helper address is set on the interface on which the packet arrived, and the packet's protocol type appears in the **xns forward-protocol** list, the packet is forwarded to the helper address. The helper address can be a directed broadcast address.

## Forwarding Broadcast Messages to Specified Hosts

To configure helpering, which forwards broadcast messages to the specified host or hosts, perform the following task in interface configuration mode:

| Task | Command |
| --- | --- |
| Forward broadcast messages to the specified host. | **xns helper-address** *network.host* |

You can specify multiple **xns helper-address** configuration mode commands on a given interface.

For an example of forwarding broadcast messages, see the "Helpering Example" section at the end of this chapter.

### Specifying XNS Protocol Types for Forwarding Broadcast Messages

When considering which packets will be forwarded via helpering, you can forward packets that have been generated by a specific XNS protocol. To do this, perform the following task in global configuration mode:

| Task | Command |
|------|---------|
| Forward packets of a specific XNS protocol to a helper address. | **xns forward-protocol** *protocol* |

### Configuring Flooding

Different XNS implementations require different flooding behavior. By default, Cisco routers do no flooding. You can, however, configure interfaces on the router to apply flooding to the packets *received* on an interface.

Whenever the Cisco IOS software receives an XNS broadcast packet, it processes the packet for flooding. An *all-nets* broadcast is one that is forwarded to all networks. XNS networks usually indicate all-nets broadcasts by setting the destination network address to all ones (typically written as -1 or FFFFFFFF). Packets with -1 destination networks and specific destination hosts are sent as MAC-layer broadcasts so that they can be picked up and further flooded by other routers. Flooding is applied to packets *received* on the interfaces.

The Cisco IOS software chooses the interfaces through which flooded packets are sent using rules designed to avoid packet looping and most packet duplication. The underlying principle of these rules is that packets should be flooded *away* from their sources, never *toward* them. Packets that the software is configured to flood are sent out through all interfaces, except in the following cases:

- Packets that would ordinarily be flooded are ignored unless they are received via the interface that would be used to route a unicast packet to the flooded packet's *source* network. If there are multiple paths to the source network, packets received only on the primary path (the first path the software learned) are flooded. If a packet is received on an interface that fails this rule, the interface that passes it will receive another copy of that packet.

- Packets are never flooded out of the router through any interface that is one of the router's paths back toward the packet's source. A copy of the flooded packet will appear on the network connected to such an interface via some other path.

- If the router has no route to a packet's source network, the packet is not flooded. This is to prevent odd behavior during routing convergence after network topology changes.

- Packets that fail the access lists applied to outgoing interfaces are not flooded through those interfaces.

- Packets with destination networks and specific destination hosts are sent as MAC-layer broadcasts so that they can be picked up and further flooded by other routers.

- For backward compatibility, any attempt to set a helper address of -1.FFFF.FFFF.FFFF on an interface results in that interface's having no helper address set, but having **xns flood broadcast allnets** enabled.

To define an interface's flooding behavior, perform one of the following tasks in interface configuration mode:

| Task | Command |
| --- | --- |
| Flood packets whose destination address is -1.FFFF.FFFF.FFFF. | **xns flood broadcast allnets** |
| Flood packets whose destination address is 0.FFFF.FFFF.FFFF. | **xns flood broadcast net-zero** |
| Flood packets with destinations of -1.*specific-host*. | **xns flood specific allnets** |

It is most closely in accordance with the XNS specification to flood packets with destinations of -1.FFFF.FFFF.FFFF and destinations of -1.*specific-host*, but not to flood packets with destinations of 0.FFFF.FFFF.FFFF. However, 3Com environments often require flooding of a broadcast whose network address is all zeros.

## Disabling XNS Fast Switching

Fast switching allows higher throughput by switching a packet using a cache created by previous packets. Fast switching is enabled by default on all interfaces.

Packet transfer performance is generally better when fast switching is enabled. However, you may want to disable fast switching in order to save memory space on interface cards and to help avoid congestion when high-bandwidth interfaces are writing large amounts of information to low-bandwidth interfaces.

To disable XNS fast switching on an interface, perform the following task in interface configuration mode:

| Task | Command |
| --- | --- |
| Disable XNS fast switching. | **no xns route-cache** |

## CONFIGURING XNS OVER WANS

You can configure XNS over X.25, Frame Relay, and SMDS networks. To do this, configure the appropriate address mappings as described in the "Configuring X.25 and LAPB," "Configuring Frame Relay," and "Configuring SMDS" chapters in the *Wide-Area Networking Configuration Guide*.

## ROUTING XNS BETWEEN VIRTUAL LANs

XNS can be routed over virtual LAN (VLAN) subinterfaces using the Inter-Switched Link (ISL) VLAN encapsulation protocol. Full-feature Cisco IOS software is supported on a per-VLAN basis, allowing standard XNS capabilities to be configured on VLANs.

## MONITORING THE XNS NETWORK

To monitor an XNS network, perform one or more of the following tasks at the EXEC prompt:

| Task | Command |
| --- | --- |
| List the entries in the XNS fast-switching cache. | **show xns cache** |
| Display the status of the XNS interfaces configured in the router and the parameters configured on each interface. | **show xns interface** [*type number*] |
| List the entries in the XNS routing table. | **show xns route** [*network*] |
| Display information about the number and type of XNS packets transmitted and received. | **show xns traffic** |
| Diagnose basic XNS network connectivity (user-level command). | **ping xns** *address* |
| Diagnose basic XNS network connectivity (privileged command). | **ping** |

## XNS CONFIGURATION EXAMPLES

Use the following configuration examples to help in configuring XNS routing on your router:

- XNS Routing Configuration Example
- Net/One Routing Configuration Example
- 3Com Access List Example
- Extended Access List with Network Mask Option Example
- Routing Update Timers Example
- Helpering Example

### XNS Routing Configuration Example

The following example enables XNS routing on a router and then enables XNS on three interfaces. On the Ethernet interfaces, the router uses the preassigned MAC-level addresses as XNS host addresses. On the serial interface, the router uses the MAC address associated with the first IEEE 802 interface found on the router.

```
xns routing
interface ethernet 0
```

```
 xns network 20
interface ethernet 1
 xns network 21
interface serial 1
 xns network 24
```

## Net/One Routing Configuration Example

The following example enables Ungermann-Bass Net/One routing. Serial interface 0 is connected to a non-Net/One portion of the XNS Internet, so the **xns hear-rip** command is issued to allow the learning of routes from the standard RIP updates used by the remote routers. There are Ungermann-Bass nodes connected to interface Token Ring 0, so the encapsulation on that interface is set to Ungermann-Bass. Broadcast flooding is configured to match the expectations of Net/One.

```
xns routing
 xns ub-emulation
interface tokenring 0
 xns network 23
 xns flood broadcast allnets
 xns encapsulation ub
 xns flood specific allnets
!
interface ethernet 0
 xns network 20
 xns flood broadcast allnets
 xns flood specific allnets
!
interface ethernet 1
 xns network 21
 xns flood broadcast allnets
 xns flood specific allnets
!
interface serial 0
 xns network 24
 xns hear-rip
 xns flood broadcast allnets
 xns flood specific allnets
```

## 3Com Access List Example

The following partial example controls specific services between networks 1002 and 1006 in a 3Com network. Echo and error packets, as well as all Sequenced Packet Protocol (SPP) and Packet Exchange Protocol (PEP) (that is, normal data traffic) can go from network 1002 to network 1006. However, all NetBIOS requests are denied. The final three lines are blanket permissions for RIP, SPP, and PEP packets.

```
access-list 524 permit 2 1002 0x0000 1006 0x0000
!  permit Echo from 1002 to 1006
access-list 524 permit 3 1002 0x0000 1006 0x0000
!  permit Error from 1002 to 1006
access-list 524 deny 5 -1 0x0000 -1 0x046B
```

```
!  deny all NetBIOS
access-list 524 permit 4 1002 0x0000 1006 0x0000
!  permit PEP from 1002 to 1006
access-list 524 permit 5 1002 0x0000 1006 0x0000
!  permit SPP from 1002 to 1006
access-list 524 permit 1
!  permit all RIP
!
!These are needed if you want PEP and SPP to be permitted from
!networks other than 1002
access-list 524 permit 4
!  permit all PEP
access-list 524 permit 5
!  permit all SPP
```

## Extended Access List with Network Mask Option Example

The following example allows protocol type 20 on any socket, from a certain make of machine (Cisco Ethernet), on network 10 to access any hosts on networks 1000 through 1015 on any socket:

```
access-list 505 permit 20 10.0000.0C00.0000 0000.0000.FFFF 0
1000.0000.0000.0000 15.FFFF.FFFF.FFFF 0
```

## Routing Update Timers Example

The following example creates a routing process that specifies a specific address for use on serial lines and other non-802.x interfaces. It also sets the RIP routing update timers for the three interfaces.

```
xns routing 0000.0C53.4679
!
interface ethernet 0
 xns network 20
 xns update-time 20
!
interface serial 0
 xns network 24
 xns update-time 20
!
interface ethernet 1
 xns network 21
 xns update-time 20
```

## Helpering Example

The following commands set up helpering for the configuration shown in Figure 15–1. The Cisco IOS software forwards packets of protocol type 1 only. Ethernet interface 0 has a helper address set, with the helper on network 12 available through the Ethernet interface 2.

```
xns routing
xns forward-protocol 1
interface ethernet 0
 xns network 5
 xns helper address 12.FFFF.FFFF.FFFF
interface ethernet 1
 xns network 13
interface ethernet 2
 xns network 12
```

*Figure 15–1*
*Helper addresses.*

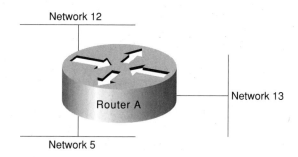

Network 12

Network 13

Router A

Network 5

In this example, the following actions will be taken on broadcast packets:

- Broadcast packets with a network address of 5 are forwarded to the helper address on network 12.

- Broadcast packets addressed to network 0 also are forwarded to the helper address on network 12.

- Broadcast packets addressed to network 13 are directed broadcasts and are sent through the E1 interface directly to network 13. They are not sent to the helper address.

- Broadcast packets of protocol 1, which are destined for network 5, are sent to the helper address.

- Broadcast packets not of protocol 1, which are destined for network 5, are discarded because they do not match the specified protocol.

- Broadcast packets of protocol 1, which are destined for network 0, are sent to the helper address.

- Broadcast packets not of protocol 1, which are destined for network 0, are discarded.

Broadcast packets destined for network 12 are directed broadcasts and are broadcast on Ethernet interface 2 to network 12. This has nothing to do with helpering or protocol forwarding.

# CHAPTER 16

# XNS Commands

Developed by the Xerox Corporation, the XNS protocols are designed to be used across a variety of communication media, processors, and office applications. Ungermann-Bass, Inc. (now a part of Tandem Computers) adopted XNS in developing its Net/One XNS routing protocol. Standard XNS routing uses the RIP update packets and the hop-count metric. Ungermann-Bass Net/One uses hello packets and a path-delay metric.

This chapter describes the commands to configure both standard XNS routing and Ungermann-Bass Net/One XNS routing. You can also configure Cisco routers to interoperate with Ungermann-Bass routers.

---

**NOTES**

Not all Cisco access servers support XNS. For more information, refer to the release notes for the release you are running.

---

### ACCESS-LIST (EXTENDED)

To define an extended XNS access list, use the extended version of the **access-list** global configuration command. To remove an extended access list, use the **no** form of this command.

> **access-list** *access-list-number* {**deny** | **permit**} *protocol* [*source-network*[*.source-host*
> [*source-network-mask.source-host-mask*] *source-socket*
> [*destination-network* [*.destination-host*
> [*destination-network-mask.destination-host-mask*] [*destination-socket*[*/pep*]]]
> **no access-list** *access-list-number* {**deny** | **permit**} *protocol* [*source-network*[*.source-host*
> [*source-network-mask.source-host-mask*]] *source-socket*
> [*destination-network* [*.destination-host*
> [*destination-network-mask.destination-host-mask*] *destination-socket*[*/pep*]]]

**NOTES**

If network masks are used, then all fields are required, except the destination socket and the destination Packet Exchange Protocol (PEP) type.

| Syntax | Description |
|---|---|
| *access-list-number* | Number of the access list. This is a decimal number from 500 to 599. |
| **deny** | Denies access if the conditions are matched. |
| **permit** | Permits access if the conditions are matched. |
| *protocol* | Number of an XNS protocol, in decimal. See the documentation accompanying your host's XNS implementation for a list of protocol numbers. |
| *source-network* | (Optional) Number of the network from which the packet is being sent. This is a 32-bit decimal number. A network number of -1 matches all networks. |
| | You can omit leading zeros from the network number. |
| | Note that you enter the network number in decimal, and this number is expressed in decimal format in Cisco's configuration files and routing tables. However, the Cisco IOS software internally converts the network number into hexadecimal. This means, for instance, that a network analyzer will display the network number in hexadecimal. |
| *source-host* | (Optional) Host on *source-network* from which the packet is being sent. This is a 48-bit hexadecimal value represented as a dotted triplet of 4-digit hexadecimal numbers (*xxxx.xxxx.xxxx*). |
| *source-network-mask* | (Optional) Mask to be applied to *source-network*. The mask is a 32-bit decimal number. The mask must immediately be followed by a period, which must in turn immediately be followed by *source-host-mask*. |
| *source-host-mask* | (Optional) Mask to be applied to *source-host*. This is a 48-bit value represented as a dotted triplet of four-digit hexadecimal numbers (*xxxx.xxxx.xxxx*). Place ones in the bit positions you want to mask. |
| *source-socket* | Number of the socket from which the packet is being sent. This is a 16-bit decimal value. See the documentation accompanying your host's XNS implementation for a list of socket numbers. |

| Syntax | Description |
|---|---|
| *destination-network* | (Optional) Number of the network to which the packet is being sent. This is a 32-bit decimal number. A network number of -1 matches all networks. |
| | You can omit leading zeros from the network number. |
| | Note that you enter the network number in decimal, and this number is expressed in decimal format in Cisco's configuration files and routing tables. However, the Cisco IOS software internally converts the network number into hexadecimal. This means, for instance, that a network analyzer will display the network number in hexadecimal. |
| *destination-host* | (Optional) Host on *destination-network* to which the packet is being sent. This is a 48-bit hexadecimal value represented as a dotted triplet of four-digit hexadecimal numbers (*xxxx.xxxx.xxxx*). |
| *destination-network-mask* | (Optional) Mask to be applied to *destination-network*. The mask is a 32-bit decimal number. The mask must immediately be followed by a period, which must in turn immediately be followed by *destination-host-mask*. |
| *destination-host-mask* | (Optional) Mask to be applied to *destination-host*. This is a 48-bit value represented as a dotted triplet of four-digit hexadecimal numbers (*xxxx.xxxx.xxxx*). Place ones in the bit positions you want to mask. |
| *destination-socket* | (Optional) Number of the socket to which the packet is being sent. This is a 16-bit decimal value. See the documentation accompanying your host's XNS implementation for a list of socket numbers. |
| *pep* | (Optional) Packet Exchange Protocol (PEP) type. PEP is a connectionless-oriented protocol that uses XNS Type 4 initial domain part (IDP) frames. |

## Default

No access lists are defined.

## Command Mode

Global configuration

## Usage Guidelines

This command first appeared in Cisco IOS Release 10.0. The *pep* argument first appeared in Cisco IOS Release 11.0.

Extended XNS access lists filter on protocol type. All other parameters are optional.

Use the **xns access-group** command to assign an access list to an interface. You can apply only one extended or one standard access list to an interface. The access list filters all outgoing packets on the interface.

### Examples

The following example shows two ways to allow protocol type 20 on any socket (from a certain make of machine) on network 10 to access any hosts on networks 1000 to 1015 on any socket. The **access-list** commands were issued without using the network mask option.

```
access-list 505 permit 20 10.0000.0C00.0000 0000.0000.FFFF 0 1000 0
access-list 505 permit 20 10.0000.0C00.0000 0000.0000.FFFF 0 1001 0
access-list 505 permit 20 10.0000.0C00.0000 0000.0000.FFFF 0 1002 0
access-list 505 permit 20 10.0000.0C00.0000 0000.0000.FFFF 0 1003 0
access-list 505 permit 20 10.0000.0C00.0000 0000.0000.FFFF 0 1004 0
access-list 505 permit 20 10.0000.0C00.0000 0000.0000.FFFF 0 1005 0
access-list 505 permit 20 10.0000.0C00.0000 0000.0000.FFFF 0 1006 0
access-list 505 permit 20 10.0000.0C00.0000 0000.0000.FFFF 0 1007 0
access-list 505 permit 20 10.0000.0C00.0000 0000.0000.FFFF 0 1008 0
access-list 505 permit 20 10.0000.0C00.0000 0000.0000.FFFF 0 1009 0
access-list 505 permit 20 10.0000.0C00.0000 0000.0000.FFFF 0 1010 0
access-list 505 permit 20 10.0000.0C00.0000 0000.0000.FFFF 0 1011 0
access-list 505 permit 20 10.0000.0C00.0000 0000.0000.FFFF 0 1012 0
access-list 505 permit 20 10.0000.0C00.0000 0000.0000.FFFF 0 1013 0
access-list 505 permit 20 10.0000.0C00.0000 0000.0000.FFFF 0 1014 0
access-list 505 permit 20 10.0000.0C00.0000 0000.0000.FFFF 0 1015 0
```

In the following example, the **access-list** command performs the same operation, but in a much shorter time, because the *netmask* option is used:

```
access-list 505 permit 20 10.0000.0C00.0000 0000.0000.FFFF 0
1000.0000.0000.0000 15.FFFF.FFFF.FFFF 0
```

### Related Commands

Search online for documentation of related commands.

**access-list** (extended)
**xns access-group**
**xns input-network-filter**

## ACCESS-LIST (STANDARD)

To define a standard XNS access list, use the standard version of the **access-list** global configuration command. To remove a standard access list, use the **no** form of this command.

> **access-list** *access-list-number* {**deny** | **permit**} *source-network[.source-address*
> *[source-address-mask]] [destination-network[.destination-address*
> *[destination-address-mask]]]*
> **no access-list** *access-list-number*

| Syntax | Description |
|---|---|
| *access-list-number* | Number of the access list. This is a decimal number from 400 to 499. |
| **deny** | Denies access if the conditions are matched. |
| **permit** | Permits access if the conditions are matched. |
| *source-network* | Number of the network from which the packet is being sent. This is a 32-bit decimal number. You can omit leading zeros. A network number of -1 matches all networks. |
| | Note that you enter the network number in decimal, and this number is expressed in decimal format in Cisco's configuration files and routing tables; however, the Cisco IOS software internally converts the network number into hexadecimal. This means, for example, that a network analyzer will display the network number in hexadecimal. |
| *source-address* | (Optional) Host on *source-network* from which the packet is being sent. This is a 48-bit hexadecimal value represented as a dotted triplet of four-digit hexadecimal numbers (*xxxx.xxxx.xxxx*). |
| *source-address-mask* | (Optional) Mask to be applied to *source-address*. This is a 48-bit value represented as a dotted triplet of four-digit hexadecimal numbers (*xxxx.xxxx.xxxx*). Place ones in the bit positions you want to mask. |
| *destination-network* | (Optional) Number of the network to which the packet is being sent. This is a 32-bit decimal number. A network number of -1 matches all networks. |
| | You can omit leading zeros from the network number. |
| | Note that you enter the network number in decimal, and this number is expressed in decimal format in Cisco's configuration files and routing tables. However, the Cisco IOS software internally converts the network number into hexadecimal. This means, for instance, that a network analyzer will display the network number in hexadecimal. |
| *destination-address* | (Optional) Host on *destination-network* to which the packet is being sent. This is a 48-bit hexadecimal value represented as a dotted triplet of four-digit hexadecimal numbers (*xxxx.xxxx.xxxx*). |
| *destination-address-mask* | (Optional) Mask to be applied to *destination-address*. This is a 48-bit value represented as a dotted triplet of four-digit hexadecimal numbers (*xxxx.xxxx.xxxx*). Place ones in the bit positions you want to mask. |

### Default

No access lists are defined.

*Command Mode*

Global configuration

*Usage Guidelines*

This command first appeared in Cisco IOS Release 10.0.

Standard XNS access lists filter on the source network only. All other parameters are optional. This means that you cannot use them to prevent traffic from going to or coming from specific hosts.

Use the **xns access-group** command to assign an access list to an interface. You can apply only one extended or one standard access list to an interface. The access list filters all outgoing packets on the interface.

*Examples*

The following example denies access to packets from source network 1 that are destined for network 2. It permits all other traffic.

```
access-list 400 deny 1 2
access-list 400 permit -1 -1
```

The following example adds masks for the source and destination networks:

```
access-list 400 deny 1.0011.1622.0015 0000.0000.0000 2.301D3.020C.0022
    0000.00ff.ffff
access-list 400 permit -1 0000.0000.0000 -1 0000.0000.0000
```

*Related Commands*

Search online for documentation of related commands.

**ping (user)**
**xns access-group**
**xns input-network-filter**

## PING (PRIVILEGED)

To check host reachability and network connectivity, use the **ping** privileged EXEC command.

    **ping**

*Syntax          Description*

This command has no arguments or keywords.

*Command Mode*

Privileged EXEC

*Usage Guidelines*

This command first appeared in Cisco IOS Release 10.0.

The privileged **ping** command provides a complete **ping** facility for users who have system privileges.

If the system cannot map an address for a host name, it returns an "%Unrecognized host or address" error message.

To abort a **ping** session, type the escape sequence. By default, this is Ctrl-^ X. You enter this by simultaneously pressing the Ctrl, Shift, and 6 keys, releasing the keys, and then pressing the X key.

Table 16–1 describes the test characters displayed in **ping** responses.

**Table 16–1** *Ping Test Characters (XNS Privileged)*

| Character | Description |
|-----------|-------------|
| ! | Each exclamation point indicates receipt of a reply. |
| . | Each period indicates the network server timed out while waiting for a reply. |
| U | A destination unreachable error protocol data unit (ERPDU) was received. |
| C | A congestion experienced packet was received. |
| I | User interrupted the test. |
| ? | Unknown packet type. |
| & | Packet lifetime exceeded. |

### Sample Display

The following display shows sample input to and output from the **ping** command:

```
Router# ping
Protocol [ip]: xns
Target XNS address: 2001.aa00.0400.6508
Repeat count [5]:
Datagram size [100]:
Timeout in seconds [2]:
Verbose [n]:n
Type escape sequence to abort.
Sending 5, 100-byte XNS Echos to 2001.aa00.0400.6508, timeout is 2 seconds:
Success rate is 100 percent, round-trip min/avg/max = 4/5/12 ms
```

The following is sample input to and output from the XNS **ping** command in verbose mode. In this mode, the command shows the round-trip time, in milliseconds, for each XNS echo packet sent. In this display, the packets are labeled 0, 1, 2, 3, and 4.

```
Router# ping
Protocol [ip]: xns
Target XNS address: 2001.aa00.0400.6508
Repeat count [5]:
Datagram size [100]:
Timeout in seconds [2]:
Verbose [n]: y
```

```
Type escape sequence to abort.
Sending 5, 100-byte XNS Echos to 2001.aa00.0400.6508, timeout is 2 seconds:
0 in 12 ms
1 in 4 ms
2 in 4 ms
3 in 4 ms
4 in 4 ms
Success rate is 100 percent, round-trip min/avg/max = 4/5/12 ms
```

## PING (USER)

To check host reachability and network connectivity, use the **ping** user EXEC command.

    **ping xns** *address*

| Syntax | Description |
|--------|-------------|
| **xns** | Specifies the XNS protocol. |
| *address* | Address of system to ping. |

### Command Mode

User EXEC

### Usage Guidelines

This command first appeared in Cisco IOS Release 10.0.

The user **ping** (packet internet groper function) command provides a basic ping facility for users who do not have system privileges. This command is equivalent to the nonverbose form of the privileged **ping** command. It sends five 100-byte ping packets.

The **ping** command works only on Cisco's network servers running Release 8.2 or later.

If the system cannot map an address for a host name, it returns an "%Unrecognized host or address" error message.

To abort a **ping** session, type the escape sequence. By default, this is Ctrl-^ X. You enter this by simultaneously pressing the Ctrl, Shift, and 6 keys, releasing the keys, and then pressing the X key.

Table 16–2 describes the test characters displayed in **ping** responses.

**Table 16–2**  *Ping Test Characters (XNS User)*

| Character | Description |
|-----------|-------------|
| ! | Each exclamation point indicates receipt of a reply. |
| . | Each period indicates the network server timed out while waiting for a reply. |
| U | A destination unreachable ERPDU was received. |
| C | A congestion experienced packet was received. |

**Table 16-2**  *Ping Test Characters (XNS User), Continued*

| Character | Description |
|-----------|-------------|
| I | User interrupted the test. |
| ? | Unknown packet type. |
| & | Packet lifetime exceeded. |

### Sample Display

The following display shows sample output from the XNS **ping** command:

```
router> ping xns 1.0000.0c01.f4cf

Type escape sequence to abort.
Sending 5, 100-byte XNS Echoes to 1.0000.0c01.f4cf, timeout is 2 seconds:
!!!!!
Success rate is 100 percent, round-trip min/avg/max = 4/5/12 ms
```

### Related Commands

Search online for documentation of related commands.

**ping (privileged)**

### SHOW XNS CACHE

To display the contents of the XNS fast-switching cache, use the **show xns cache** EXEC command.

> **show xns cache**

### Syntax     Description

This command has no arguments or keywords.

### Command Mode

User EXEC

### Usage Guidelines

This command first appeared in Cisco IOS Release 10.0.

### Sample Display

The following is sample output from the **show xns cache** command:

```
Router# show xns cache

    XNS routing cache version is 23

    Destination          Interface       MAC Header
*   2.0000.00c0.1234     Ethernet1       000000C0123400000C00D8DB0600
```

Table 16–3 describes the fields shown in the display.

**Table 16–3** *Show XNS Cache Field Descriptions*

| Field | Description |
|---|---|
| XNS routing cache version is 23 | Number identifying the fast-switching cache table. It increments each time the table changes. |
| Destination | Destination network for this packet. Valid entries are marked by an asterisk (*). |
| Interface | Router interface through which this packet is transmitted. |
| MAC Header | First bytes of this packet's MAC header. |

### Related Commands

Search online for documentation of related commands.

**xns route-cache**

## SHOW XNS INTERFACE

To display the status of the XNS interfaces configured in the Cisco IOS software and the parameters configured on each interface, use the **show xns interface** EXEC command.

> **show xns interface** [*type number*]

| Syntax | Description |
|---|---|
| *type* | (Optional) Interface type. It can be one of the following types: asynchronous, dialer, Ethernet (IEEE 802.3), loopback, null, serial, or tunnel. |
| *number* | (Optional) Interface number. |

### Command Mode

EXEC

### Usage Guidelines

This command first appeared in Cisco IOS Release 10.0.

### Sample Display

The following is sample output from the **show xns interface** command:

```
Router# show xns interface

Ethernet 0 is up, line protocol is up
XNS address is 60.0000.0c00.1d23
```

```
xns encapsulation is ARPA
Helper address is 912.ffff.ffff.ffff
Outgoing address list is not set
Input filter list is not set
Output filter list is not set
Router filter list is not set
Update timer is not set
XNS fast-switching enabled

Ethernet 1 is administratively down, line protocol is down
XNS protocol processing disabled

Serial 1 is up, line protocol is up
XNS protocol processing disabled
```

Table 16–4 describes the fields shown in the display.

**Table 16–4**  *Show XNS Interface Field Descriptions*

| Field | Description |
|---|---|
| Ethernet 0 is up | Type of interface and whether it is currently active and inserted into the network (up) or inactive and not inserted (down). |
| line protocol is up | Indicates whether the software processes that handle the line protocol believe that the interface is usable (that is, whether keepalives are successful). |
| XNS address | Network and host number of the local router interface. |
| XNS encapsulation | Type of encapsulation configured on the interface. |
| Helper address | Address of a target XNS server or network to which broadcast XNS packets are forwarded, as configured with the **xns helper-address** command. |
| Outgoing address list | Indicates whether an access list has been enabled with the **access-list** command. |
| Input filter list | Number of the input filter applied to the interface with the command. |
| Output filter list | Number of the output filter applied to the interface with the command. |
| Router filter list | Number of the router filter applied to the interface with the command. |
| Update timer | How often the Cisco IOS software sends RIP updates, as configured with the command. |
| XNS fast-switching | Indicates whether XNS fast switching is enabled (default) or disabled for this interface. |
| administratively down | Hardware has been taken down by an administrator. |

*Command Reference*

*Related Commands*

Search online for documentation of related commands.

**access-list (extended)**
**ping (user)**
**xns helper-address**
**xns input-network-filter**
**xns output-network-filter**
**xns router-filter**
**xns update-time**

## SHOW XNS ROUTE

To display the contents of the XNS routing table, use the **show xns route** EXEC command.

    **show xns route** [*network*]

| Syntax | Description |
|--------|-------------|
| *network* | (Optional) Number of the network that the route is to. This is a 32-bit decimal number. You can omit leading zeros. |

*Command Mode*

EXEC

*Usage Guidelines*

This command first appeared in Cisco IOS Release 10.0.

*Sample Display*

The following is sample output from the **show xns route** command:

```
Router# show xns route

Codes: R - RIP derived, C - connected, S - static, 1 learned routes

Maximum allowed path(s) are/is 1
C Net 14 is directly connected, 0 uses, Ethernet0
C Net 15 is directly connected, 0 uses, Ethernet1
R Net 16 [1/0] via 14.0000.0c00.3e3b, 10 sec, 0 uses, Ethernet0
```

Table 16–5 describes the fields shown in the display.

**Table 16–5** *Show XNS Route Field Descriptions*

| Field | Description |
|---|---|
| Codes | Codes defining how the route was learned. |
| R | Route learned from a RIP update. |
| C | Directly connected network. |
| S | Statically defined route via the command. |
| learned routes | Number of routes learned from RIP updates. |
| Maximum allowed paths | Maximum number of paths for which the Cisco IOS software has been configured with the command. |
| Net 14 | XNS network number. |
| is directly connected | Indicates that the network is directly connected to the router. |
| uses | Fair estimate of the number of times a route gets used. It actually indicates the number of times the route has been selected for use prior to operations such as access list filtering. |
| Ethernet0 | Possible interface through which you can reach the remote network via the specified router. |
| [1/0] | Delay/Metric. The delay is the delay between sending routing updates. The metric is the XNS metric used in making routing decisions. |
| via | Address of a router that is the next hop to the remote network. |
| sec | Number of seconds since information about this network was last heard. |

### Related Commands

Search online for documentation of related commands.

**xns maximum-paths**
**xns route**

## SHOW XNS TRAFFIC

To display information about the number and type of XNS packets transmitted and received by the Cisco IOS software, use the **show xns traffic** EXEC command.

    **show xns traffic**

*Syntax     Description*

This command has no arguments or keywords.

## Command Mode

EXEC

## Usage Guidelines

This command first appeared in Cisco IOS Release 10.0.

## Sample Display

The following is sample output from the **show xns traffic** command:

```
Router# show xns traffic

Rec: 3968 total, 0 format errors, 0 checksum errors, 0 bad hop count,
 3968 local destination, 0 multicast
Bcast: 2912 received, 925 sent
Sent: 5923 generated, 500 forwarded, 0 encapsulation failed, 0 not routable
Errors: 10 received, 20 sent
Echo: Recd: 100 requests, 89 replies   Sent: 20 requests, 20 replies
Unknown: 5 packets
```

Table 16–6 describes significant fields shown in the display.

**Table 16–6**   *Show XNS Traffic Statistics Field Descriptions*

| Field | Description |
|---|---|
| Rec: | Description of the XNS packets received. |
| 3968 total | Total number of packets received. |
| 0 format errors | Number of bad packets discarded (for example, packets with a corrupted header). |
| 0 checksum errors | Number of packets discarded because they contained checksum errors. |
| 0 bad hop count | Number of packets discarded because their hop count exceeded 16 (that is, the packets timed out). |
| 3968 local destination | Number of packets sent to the local broadcast address or specifically to the router. |
| 0 multicast | Number of packets received that were addressed to multiple destinations. |
| Bcast: | Number of broadcast packets received and sent. |
| Sent: | Description of the XNS packets the router has sent. |

**Table 16–6** *Show XNS Traffic Statistics Field Descriptions, Continued*

| Field | Description |
|---|---|
| 5923 generated | Number of packets transmitted that it generated itself. |
| 500 forwarded | Number of packets transmitted that it forwarded from other sources. |
| 0 encapsulation failed | Number of packets the router was unable to encapsulate. |
| 0 not routable | Number of times the router could not locate in the routing table a route to the destination. |
| Errors: | Number of packets sent and received that contained errors. |
| Echo: | Number of ping packets received and sent, and the number of replies it received. |
| Unknown: | Number of packets the router was unable to forward, for example, because of a misconfigured helper address or because no route was available. |

## XNS ACCESS-GROUP

To apply a generic filter to an interface, use the **xns access-group** interface configuration command. To remove the access list, use the **no** form of this command.

> **xns access-group** *access-list-number*
> **no xns access-group** *access-list-number*

| *Syntax* | *Description* |
|---|---|
| *access-list-number* | Number of the access list. All outgoing packets defined with either standard or extended access lists and forwarded through the interface are filtered by the entries in this access list. For standard access lists, *access-list-number* is a decimal number from 400 to 499. For extended access lists, *access-list-number* is a decimal number from 500 to 599. |

*Default*

No generic filters are applied by default.

*Command Mode*

Interface configuration

*Usage Guidelines*

This command first appeared in Cisco IOS Release 10.0.

The **xns access-group** command applies a generic filter to an interface. These filters control which packets are sent out an interface based on the packet's source and destination addresses, XNS protocol type, and source and destination socket numbers. You use the **access-list (extended)** and **ping (user)** commands to specify the filtering conditions.

You can apply only one filter to an interface.

### Example

In the following example, the access list 500 is applied to Ethernet interface 0:

```
interface ethernet 0
 xns access-group 500
```

### Related Commands

Search online for documentation of related commands.

**access-list (extended)**
**ping (user)**

## XNS ENCAPSULATION

To select the type of encapsulation used on a Token Ring interface, use the **xns encapsulation** interface configuration command. To disable the encapsulation, use the **no** form of this command.

> **xns encapsulation {snap | ub | 3com}**
> **no xns encapsulation {snap | ub | 3com}**

| Syntax | Description |
|--------|-------------|
| **snap** | 802.2 LLC encapsulation. This is the default encapsulation type. Use this encapsulation type with IBM Token Ring networks. |
| **ub** | Ungermann-Bass encapsulation. |
| **3com** | 3Com encapsulation. Use this encapsulation type when older 3Com Corporation products are present on the network. |

### Default

snap

### Command Mode

Interface configuration

### Usage Guidelines

This command first appeared in Cisco IOS Release 10.0.

You must specify this command on an interface if you want a Token Ring interface to forward XNS packets.

Some 3Com 3+ hosts do not recognize Token Ring packets with the source-route bridging routing information field (RIF) set. You can work around this discrepancy by using the **no multiring xns** interface configuration command on Token Ring interfaces that are used for 3Com XNS routing.

### Example

In the following example, Ungermann-Bass-style encapsulation is used when forwarding Token Ring packets across an interface:

```
interface tokenring 0
 xns network 23
 xns encapsulation ub
```

### Related Commands

Search online for documentation of related commands.

**multiring**
**xns hear-rip**
**xns ub-emulation**

### XNS FLOOD BROADCAST ALLNETS

To flood broadcast packets whose destination address is -1.FFFF.FFFF.FFFF, use the **xns flood broadcast allnets** interface configuration command. To disable this type of flooding, use the **no** form of this command.

> **xns flood broadcast allnets**
> **no xns flood broadcast allnets**

### Syntax    Description

This command has no arguments or keywords.

### Default

Disabled

### Command Mode

Interface configuration

### Usage Guidelines

This command first appeared in Cisco IOS Release 10.0.

The **xns flood broadcast allnets** command configures all-nets flooding. In this type of routing, all broadcast packets are sent to all networks (as indicated by the network address -1) and to all hosts on those networks (as indicated by the host address FFFF.FFFF.FFFF).

You can specify a network address of -1 only with the **xns flood broadcast** commands. In all other commands, it is an invalid address.

Flooding is applied to the packets received on an interface.

It is most closely in accordance with the XNS specification to flood packets with destinations of -1.FFFF.FFFF.FFFF and destinations of -1.*specific-host*, but not to flood packets with destinations of 0.FFFF.FFFF.FFFF.

### Example

The following example configures the interface to flood broadcast packets:

```
interface ethernet 0
 xns network 20
 xns broadcast allnets
```

### Related Commands

Search online for documentation of related commands.

**xns flood broadcast net-zero**
**xns flood specific allnets**
**xns hear-rip**

## XNS FLOOD BROADCAST NET-ZERO

To flood packets whose destinations address is 0.FFFF.FFFF.FFFF, use the **xns flood broadcast net-zero** interface configuration command. To disable this type of flooding, use the **no** form of this command.

> **xns flood broadcast net-zero**
> **no xns flood broadcast net-zero**

### Syntax     Description

This command has no arguments or keywords.

### Default

Disabled

### Command Mode

Interface configuration

## Usage Guidelines

This command first appeared in Cisco IOS Release 10.0.

The **xns flood broadcast net-zero** command sends broadcast packets to all hosts (as indicated by the host address FFFF.FFFF.FFFF) on the local network (as indicated by the network address 0). This broadcast configuration is required in some 3Com environments.

Flooding is applied to the packets received on an interface.

## Example

In the following example, broadcast packets destined for the local network are sent to all hosts on that network:

```
interface ethernet 0
 xns network 20
 xns flood broadcast net-zero
```

## Related Commands

Search online for documentation of related commands.

**xns flood broadcast allnets**
**xns flood specific allnets**
**xns hear-rip**

## XNS FLOOD SPECIFIC ALLNETS

To flood packets whose destination address is -1.*specific-host*, use the **xns flood specific allnets** interface configuration command. To disable this type of flooding, use the **no** form of this command.

> **xns flood specific allnets**
> **no xns flood specific allnets**

## Syntax     Description

This command has no arguments or keywords.

## Default

Disabled

## Command Mode

Interface configuration

## Usage Guidelines

This command first appeared in Cisco IOS Release 10.0.

The **xns flood specific allnets** command forwards broadcast packets as MAC-layer broadcasts so that they can be picked up and further flooded by other routers.

You can specify a network address of -1 only with the **xns flood broadcast** commands. In all other commands, it is an invalid address.

Flooding is applied to the packets received on an interface.

It is most closely in accordance with the XNS specification to flood packets with destinations of -1.FFFF.FFFF.FFFF and destinations of -1.*specific-host*, but not to flood packets with destinations of 0.FFFF.FFFF.FFFF.

### Example

In the following example, packets with destinations of -1.*specific-host* are flooded:

```
interface ethernet 0
 xns network 20
 xns flood broadcast specific allnets
```

### Related Commands

Search online for documentation of related commands.

**xns flood broadcast allnets**
**xns flood specific allnets**
**xns hear-rip**

## XNS FORWARD-PROTOCOL

To forward packets of a specific XNS protocol to a helper address, use the **xns forward-protocol** global configuration command. To disable the forwarding of these packets, use the **no** form of this command.

```
        xns forward-protocol protocol
        no xns forward-protocol protocol
```

| Syntax | Description |
|---|---|
| *protocol* | Number of an XNS protocol, in decimal. See the documentation accompanying your host's XNS implementation for a list of protocol numbers. |

### Default

Disabled

### Command Mode

Global configuration

### Usage Guidelines

This command first appeared in Cisco IOS Release 10.0.

### Example

In the following example, packets of protocol type 2 are forwarded to the specified helper address:

```
xns forward-protocol 2
interface ethernet 0
 xns helper-address 26.FFFF.FFFF.FFFF
```

### Related Commands

Search online for documentation of related commands.

**xns helper-address**

## XNS HEAR-RIP

To receive RIP updates, use the **xns hear-rip** interface configuration command. To disable the receipt of RIP updates, use the **no** form of this command.

> **xns hear-rip** [*access-list-number*]
> **no xns hear-rip**

### Syntax          Description

*access-list-number*   (Optional) Number of the access list. This list defines the routes the Cisco IOS software is to learn through standard RIP. The list is applied to individual routes within the RIP packet, not to the address of the packet's sender. For standard access lists, *access-list-number* is a decimal number from 400 to 499. For extended access lists, *access-list-number* is a decimal number from 500 to 599.

### Default

Disabled

### Command Mode

Interface configuration

### Usage Guidelines

This command first appeared in Cisco IOS Release 10.0.

Delay metrics are computed as if each hop mentioned by the RIP update were a 9.6-kbps serial link. Ordinarily, the result is that the Cisco IOS software prefers an all-Ungermann-Bass path over an all-RIP path. If you want the software to learn only certain routes through standard RIP, specify an access list number as an argument to the **xns hear-rip** command. The software will then learn from

*Command Reference*

RIP packets only routes to networks permitted by the access list. Note that the access list is applied to individual routes within the RIP packet, not to the address of the packet's sender.

In an Ungermann-Bass environment, you should configure all interfaces with the **xns flood broadcast allnets** and **xns flood specific allnets** commands. You should *not* configure them with the **xns flood broadcast net-zero** command. You should configure Token Ring interfaces that are directly connected to Ungermann-Bass nodes with the **xns encapsulation ub** command.

## Example

In the following example, serial interface 0 receives RIP updates:

```
interface serial 0
 xns network 24
 xns hear-rip
```

## Related Commands

Search online for documentation of related commands.

**xns flood broadcast allnets**
**xns flood broadcast net-zero**
**xns flood specific allnets**
**xns ub-emulation**

## XNS HELPER-ADDRESS

To forward broadcast packets to a specified server, use the **xns helper-address** interface configuration command. To disable this function, use the **no** form of this command.

> **xns helper-address** *network.host*
> **no xns helper-address** *network.host*

| Syntax | Description |
| --- | --- |
| *network* | Network on which the target XNS server resides. This is a 32-bit decimal number. |
| *host* | Host number of the target XNS server. This is a 48-bit hexadecimal value represented as a dotted triplet of four-digit hexadecimal numbers (*xxxx.xxxx.xxxx*). The host must be directly connected to one of the router's directly attached networks. A number of FFFF.FFFF.FFFF indicates all hosts on the specified network. |

## Default

Disabled

## Command Mode

Interface configuration

## Usage Guidelines

This command first appeared in Cisco IOS Release 10.0.

Routers normally block all broadcast requests and do not forward them to other network segments. This is done to prevent the degradation of performance over the entire network. The **xns helper-address** command allows broadcasts to be forwarded to other networks. This is useful when a network segment does not have a server capable of handling broadcasts. This command enables you to forward the broadcasts to a server, network, or networks that can process them. Incoming unrecognized broadcast packets that match the access list created with the **xns helper-list** command (if it is present) are forwarded.

When a packet is helpered, the Cisco IOS software changes its destination address to be the configured helper address, and the packet is routed toward that address. The host at the helper address is expected to process the packet and (usually) to reply to the packet's sender. A helper address can be a directed broadcast address, in which case the helpered packet will be forwarded to a remote network and rebroadcast there.

You can specify multiple **xns helper-address** commands on a given interface.

## Example

In the following example, the server at address 0000.0c00.23fe receives all broadcasts on network 51:

```
xns helper-address 51.0000.0c00.23fe
```

## Related Commands

Search online for documentation of related commands.

**xns forward-protocol**

## XNS INPUT-NETWORK-FILTER

To control which networks are added to the routing table, use the **xns input-network-filter** interface configuration command. To remove the filter from the interface, use the **no** form of this command.

**xns input-network-filter** *access-list-number*
**no xns input-network-filter** *access-list-number*

| Syntax | Description |
| --- | --- |
| *access-list-number* | Number of the access list. All incoming packets defined with either standard or extended access lists are filtered by the entries in this access list. For standard access lists, *access-list-number* is a decimal number from 400 to 499. For extended access lists, it is a decimal number from 500 to 599. |

## Default

No networks are added to the routing table.

## Command Mode

Interface configuration

## Usage Guidelines

This command first appeared in Cisco IOS Release 10.0.

The **xns input-network-filter** command controls which networks are added to the routing table based on the networks learned in incoming XNS routing updates (RIP updates) on the interface.

You can issue only one **xns input-network-filter** command on each interface.

## Example

In the following example, access list 476 controls which networks are added to the routing table when RIP packets are received on Ethernet interface 1. Network 16 is the only network whose information will be added to the routing table. Routing updates for all other networks are implicitly denied and are not added to the routing table.

```
access-list 476 permit 16
interface ethernet 1
 xns input-network-filter 476
```

## Related Commands

Search online for documentation of related commands.

**access-list (extended)**
**ping (user)**
**xns output-network-filter**

## XNS MAXIMUM-PATHS

To set the maximum number of paths the Cisco IOS software uses when sending packets, use the **xns maximum-paths** global configuration command. To restore the default value, use the **no** form of this command.

```
xns maximum-paths number
no xns maximum-paths
```

| Syntax | Description |
|--------|-------------|
| *number* | Maximum number of equal-cost paths from which the software chooses. It can be a number from 1 to 512. The default is 1. |

## Default

1 path

## Command Mode

Global configuration

## Usage Guidelines

This command first appeared in Cisco IOS Release 10.0.

A router can use multiple paths to reach an XNS destination to increase throughput in the network. By default, the router picks one best path and sends all traffic on this path, but you can configure it to remember two or more paths that have equal costs (the cost metric is hop count for standard XNS RIP) and to balance the traffic load across all the available paths. (Note that when paths have differing costs, the device chooses lower-cost routes in preference to higher-cost routes.) Packets are distributed over the multiple paths in round-robin fashion on a packet-by-packet basis. That is, the first packet is sent along the first path, the second packet along the second path, and so on. If the final path is reached before all packets are sent, the next packet is sent to the first path, the next to the second path, and so on.

Limiting the number of equal-cost paths can save memory on routers with limited memory or with very large configurations. Additionally, in networks with a large number of multiple paths and systems with limited ability to cache out-of-sequence packets, performance might suffer when traffic is split between many paths.

## Example

In the following example, the router uses up to two alternate paths:

```
xns maximum-paths 2
```

## Related Commands

Search online for documentation of related commands.

**show xns route**

## XNS NETWORK

To enable XNS routing on a particular interface by assigning a network number to the interface, use the **xns network** interface configuration command. To disable XNS routing on an interface, use the **no** form of this command.

> **xns network** *number*
> **no xns network**

| Syntax | Description |
|--------|-------------|
| *number* | Network number. This is a 32-bit decimal number. You can omit leading zeros. |

### Default
XNS routing is disabled.

### Command Mode
Interface configuration

### Usage Guidelines
This command first appeared in Cisco IOS Release 10.0.

Interfaces not enabled to run XNS ignore any XNS packets that they receive.

Every XNS interface must have a unique XNS network number.

### Example
The following example enables XNS routing, specifying that XNS networks 20 and 21 are connected to two of the router's Ethernet interfaces:

```
xns routing
interface ethernet 0
 xns network 20
interface ethernet 1
 xns network 21
```

### Related Commands
Search online for documentation of related commands.

**show xns interface**
**xns routing**

## XNS OUTPUT-NETWORK-FILTER

To control the list of networks included in routing updates sent out an interface, use the **xns output-network-filter** interface configuration command. To remove the filter from the interface, use the **no** form of this command.

> **xns output-network-filter** *access-list-number*
> **no xns output-network-filter** *access-list-number*

| Syntax | Description |
|---|---|
| *access-list-number* | Number of the access list. All outgoing packets defined with either standard or extended access lists are filtered by the entries in this access list. For standard access lists, *access-list-number* is a decimal number from 400 to 499. For extended access lists, it is a decimal number from 500 to 599. |

### Default

No list of networks is included in the routing updates sent out an interface.

### Command Mode

Interface configuration

### Usage Guidelines

This command first appeared in Cisco IOS Release 10.0.

The **xns output-network-filter** command controls which networks the Cisco IOS software advertises in its routing updates (RIP updates).

You can issue only one **xns output-network-filter** command on each interface.

### Example

In the following example, access list 496 controls which networks are specified in routing updates sent out serial interface 1. This configuration causes network 27 to be the only network advertised in routing updates sent on the defined serial interface.

```
access-list 496 permit 27
interface serial 1
 xns output-network-filter 496
```

### Related Commands

Search online for documentation of related commands.

**xns input-network-filter**
**xns router-filter**

## XNS ROUTE

To add a static route to the XNS routing table, use the **xns route** global configuration command. To remove a route from the routing table, use the **no** form of this command.

> **xns route** *network network.host*
> **no xns route** *network network.host*

| Syntax | Description |
|--------|-------------|
| *network* | Network to which you want to establish a static route. This is a 32-bit decimal number. You can omit leading zeros. |
| *network.host* | Router to which to forward packets destined for the specified network. |
| | The argument *network* is a 32-bit decimal number. You can omit leading zeros. |
| | The argument *host* is the host number of the target router. This is a 48-bit value represented by a dotted triplet of four-digit hexadecimal numbers (*xxxx.xxxx.xxxx*). |

## Default

No static routes are added to the XNS routing table.

## Command Mode

Global configuration

## Usage Guidelines

This command first appeared in Cisco IOS Release 10.0.

The **xns route** command forwards packets destined for the specified network (*network*) to the specified router (*network.host*), regardless of whether that Cisco IOS software is sending dynamic routing information.

Static routes usually are not used in XNS environments, because nearly all XNS routers support dynamic routing via RIP. Dynamic routing is enabled by default in Cisco routers.

Be careful when assigning static routes. When links associated with static routes are lost, traffic may stop being forwarded, even though alternative paths might be available.

## Example

In the following example, the router at address 21.0456.acd3.1243 handles all traffic destined for network 25:

```
xns routing
xns route 25 21.0456.acd3.1243
```

## Related Commands

Search online for documentation of related commands.

**show xns route**

## XNS ROUTE-CACHE

To enable XNS fast switching, use the **xns route-cache** interface configuration command. To disable fast switching, use the **no** form of this command.

> **xns route-cache**
> **no xns route-cache**

### Syntax    Description

This command has no arguments or keywords.

### Default

Enabled

### Command Mode

Interface configuration

### Usage Guidelines

This command first appeared in Cisco IOS Release 10.0.

XNS fast switching allows higher throughput by switching packets using a cache created by previous transit packets.

You might want to disable fast switching in two situations. One is if you want to save memory on the interface cards; fast-switching caches require more memory than those used for standard switching. The second situation is to avoid congestion on interface cards when a high-bandwidth interface is writing large amounts of information to a low-bandwidth interface.

### Example

In the following example, XNS fast switching is disabled for serial interface 1:

```
interface serial 1
 no xns route-cache
```

### Related Commands

Search online for documentation of related commands.

**show xns cache**

## XNS ROUTER-FILTER

To control the routers from which packets are accepted, use the **xns router-filter** interface configuration command. To remove the filters from the interface, use the **no** form of this command.

**xns router-filter** *access-list-number*
**no xns router-filter** *access-list-number*

*Syntax*                    *Description*

*access-list-number*        Number of the access list. All incoming packets defined with either
                            standard or extended access lists are filtered by the entries in this access
                            list. For standard access lists, *access-list-number* is a decimal number
                            from 400 to 499. For extended access lists, it is a decimal number from
                            500 to 599.

*Default*

No filters are applied to control the routers from which packets are accepted.

*Command Mode*

Interface configuration

*Usage Guidelines*

This command first appeared in Cisco IOS Release 10.0.

You can issue only one **xns router-filter** command on each interface.

*Example*

In the following example, access list 466 controls the routers from which packets are accepted. For
serial interface 0, only packets from the router at 26.0000.00c0.047d are accepted. All other packets are implicitly denied.

```
access-list 466 permit 26.0000.00c0.047d
interface serial 0
 xns router-filter 466
```

*Related Commands*

Search online for documentation of related commands.

**xns input-network-filter**
**xns output-network-filter**

## XNS ROUTING

To enable XNS routing, use the **xns routing** global configuration command. To disable XNS routing, use the **no** form of this command.

**xns routing** [*address*]
**no xns routing**

| Syntax | Description |
|---|---|
| *address* | (Optional) Host number of the router. This is a 48-bit value represented by a dotted triplet of four-digit hexadecimal numbers (*xxxx.xxxx.xxxx*). It must not be a multicast address. |
| | If you omit *address*, the Cisco IOS software uses the address of the first IEEE-compliant (Token Ring, FDDI, or Ethernet) interface MAC address it finds in its interface list. The software uses the address 0123.4567.abcd for non-IEEE–compliant interfaces. |

### Default

Disabled

### Command Mode

Global configuration

### Usage Guidelines

This command first appeared in Cisco IOS Release 10.0.

The **xns routing** command enables the RIP service on the router.

### Example

The following example enables XNS routing:

```
xns routing
```

### Related Commands

Search online for documentation of related commands.

**xns network**

## XNS UB-EMULATION

To enable Ungermann-Bass Net/One routing, use the **xns ub-emulation** global configuration command. To disable Net/One routing and restore standard routing mode, use the **no** form of this command.

> **xns ub-emulation**
> **no xns ub-emulation**

### Syntax     Description

This command has no arguments or keywords.

Command Reference

*Default*

Disabled

*Command Mode*

Global configuration

*Usage Guidelines*

This command first appeared in Cisco IOS Release 10.0.

The **xns ub-emulation** command enables Ungermann-Bass Net/One routing. This means that hello packets and routing updates on all XNS interfaces are sent out in Ungermann-Bass format.

Net/One is a distance-vector, or Bellman-Ford, protocol and is similar to standard XNS RIP. The major difference between the two protocols is in the metrics used. Standard XNS RIP uses a hop count to determine the best route to distant networks and maintains information only about hop counts. The Ungermann-Bass protocol uses a path-delay metric and maintains information about both hop counts and its own metrics.

Ungermann-Bass routers generate standard RIP updates by extracting the hop-count values from the Ungermann-Bass routing protocol. When configured in Ungermann-Bass emulation mode, routers participate in this protocol and behave (insofar as routing protocols are concerned) like Ungermann-Bass routers.

You can use the **xns hear-rip** command to configure the Cisco IOS software to listen to standard RIP updates when in Ungermann-Bass emulation mode. When Cisco routers in Ungermann-Bass emulation mode receive a RIP packet, each route in that packet is treated as though it had come from an Ungermann-Bass routing packet. The hop count used is the actual hop count from the RIP packet. The delay metric used is computed by assuming that each hop is the longest-delay link used by Ungermann-Bass, which is a 9.6-kbps serial link. Information from RIP packets is used in creating outgoing Ungermann-Bass updates, and vice versa.

This command is never written to nonvolatile configuration memory. Instead, the equivalent individual commands are written. These are an **xns ub-emulation** command for the router, and **xns hear-rip, xns flood broadcast allnets, no xns flood broadcast net-zero,** and **xns flood specific allnets** commands for all interfaces on which XNS is enabled. The **xns ub-routing** command does not modify the encapsulation used on Token Ring interfaces.

Older versions of Cisco IOS software implemented a restricted version of the Ungermann-Bass routing protocol, and in certain configurations could create routing instability and forwarding loops. Before using Releases 8.3 and earlier in Ungermann-Bass environments, consult the 8.3 documentation for information about these restrictions.

*Example*

The following example enables Net/One routing:

```
xns routing
xns ub-emulation
interface tokenring 0
 xns network 23
 xns encapsulation ub
```

*Related Commands*

Search online for documentation of related commands.

**xns hear-rip**

## XNS UPDATE-TIME

To set the XNS routing update timers, use the **xns update-time** interface configuration command. To restore the default value, use the **no** form of this command.

> **xns update-time** *interval*
> **no xns update-time**

| *Syntax* | *Description* |
| --- | --- |
| *interval* | Interval, in seconds, at which XNS routing updates are sent. The minimum interval is 10 seconds, and the maximum is 2493644 seconds, which is about 29 days. The default is 30 seconds. |

*Default*

30 seconds

*Command Mode*

Interface configuration

*Usage Guidelines*

This command first appeared in Cisco IOS Release 10.0.

The **xns update-time** command sets the routing update timer on a per-interface basis. To display the current value, use the **show xns route** command.

Routers exchange information about routes by sending broadcast messages when they are started up and shut down, and periodically while they are running. The **xns update-time** command enables you to modify the periodic update interval.

You can set RIP timers only in a configuration in which all routers are Cisco routers. The timers should be the same for all devices connected to the network.

The update value you choose affects the internal XNS timers as follows:

- XNS routes are marked invalid and placed in holddown if no routing updates for those routes are heard within three times the value of the update interval ($3 \times interval$).
- XNS routes are removed from the routing table if no routing updates are heard within six times the value of the update interval ($6 \times interval$).

This command has no effect on the Ungermann-Bass routing protocol.

## Example

The following example sets the routing update time to 20 seconds:

```
interface ethernet 0
 xns network 20
 xns update-time 20
```

## Related Commands

Search online for documentation of related commands.

**show xns route**

# CISCO CERTIFIED INTERNETWORK EXPERT

Cisco's CCIE certification programs set the professional benchmark for internetworking expertise. CCIEs are recognized throughout the internetworking industry as being the most highly qualified of technical professionals. And, because the CCIE programs certify individuals—not companies—employers are guaranteed any CCIE with whom they work has met the same stringent qualifications as every other CCIE in the industry.

To ensure network performance and reliability in today's dynamic information systems arena, companies need internetworking professionals who have knowledge of both established and newer technologies. Acknowledging this need for specific expertise, Cisco has introduced three CCIE certification programs:

WAN Switching

ISP/Dial

Routing & Switching

CCIE certification requires a solid background in internetworking. The first step in obtaining CCIE certification is to pass a two-hour Qualification exam administered by Sylvan-Prometric. The final step in CCIE certification is a two-day, hands-on lab exam that pits the candidate against difficult build, break, and restore scenarios.

Just as training and instructional programs exist to help individuals prepare for the written exam, Cisco is pleased to announce its first CCIE Preparation Lab. The CCIE Preparation Lab is located at Wichita State University in Wichita Kansas, and is available to help prepare you for the final step toward CCIE status.

Cisco designed the CCIE Preparation Lab to assist CCIE candidates with the lab portion of the actual CCIE lab exam. The Preparation Lab at WSU emulates the conditions under which CCIE candidates are tested for their two-day CCIE Lab Examination. As almost any CCIE will corroborate, the lab exam is the most difficult element to pass for CCIE certification.

Registering for the lab is easy. Simply complete and fax the form located on the reverse side of this letter to WSU. For more information, please visit the WSU Web page at www.engr.twsu.edu/cisco/ or Cisco's Web page at www.cisco.com.

# CISCO CCIE PREPARATION LAB

## REGISTRATION FORM

Please attach a business card or print the following information:

Name/Title: _____

Company: _____

Company Address: _____

City/State/Zip: _____

Country Code (_____) Area Code (_____) Daytime Phone Number _____

Country Code (_____) Area Code (_____) Evening Phone Number _____

Country Code (_____) Area Code (_____) Fax Number _____

E-mail Address: _____

Circle the number of days you want to reserve lab:   1   2   3   4   5

Week and/or date(s) preferred (3 choices):

_____

_____

_____

Have you taken and passed the written CCIE exam?     Yes     No

List any CISCO courses you have attended:


Registration fee: _____ $500 per day × _____ day(s) = Total _____

Check Enclosed (Payable to WSU Conference Office)

Charge to: _____ MasterCard  or  Visa  exp. Date _____

CC# _____

Name on Card_____

Cardholder Signature _____

Refunds/Cancellations: The full registration fee will be refunded if your cancellation is received at least 15 days prior to the first scheduled lab day.

Wichita State University
University Conferences
1845 Fairmount
Wichita, KS  67260
Attn:  Kimberly Moore
Tel:  800-550-1306
Fax:  316-686-6520